MOUNT LAUREL II
CHALLENGE and DELIVERY of LOW-COST HOUSING

MOUNT LAUREL II
CHALLENGE and DELIVERY of LOW-COST HOUSING

Project Leaders

Robert W. Burchell
W. Patrick Beaton
David Listokin

Participating Investigators

George Sternlieb
Robert W. Lake
Richard L. Florida

Routledge
Taylor & Francis Group
NEW YORK AND LONDON

First published 1983 by Rutgers - The State University of New Jersey

Published 2021 by Routledge
605 Third Avenue, New York, NY 10017
2 Park Square, Milton Park, Abingdon, Oxon OX14 4RN

Routledge is an imprint of the Taylor & Francis Group, an informa business

Library of Congress Cataloging in Publication Data

Burchell, Robert W.
Mount Laurel II.

Bibliography: p.
I. Public housing--New Jersey--Mount Laurel (Township) I. Beaton, W. Patrick. II. Listokin, David. III. Title. IV. Title: Mount Laurel 2. V. Title: Mount Laurel Two.
HD7288.78.U52N463 1983 363.5'8 83-25182
ISBN 0-88285-098-9

ISBN 13: 978-0-88285-098-6 (pbk)

TABLE OF CONTENTS

ACKNOWLEDGMENTS

The preparation of this study would have been impossible without the assistance of numerous organizations and individuals.

Financial support was provided jointly by the New Jersey State League of Municipalities and the New Jersey Builders Association. An Advisory Committee, composed of members from both these two organizations gave generously of their time and provided critical insights.

From the League of Municipalities, the Advisory Committee included: Mr. John E. Trafford, its Executive Director; Mr. Charles Guhr, its president; Fred Stickel, III Esq., Co-Chairman, League Legislative Committee; Mr. Arthur R. Kondrup, Executive Board Member, Freehold Township; Mr. Robert F. Rogers, Rogers & Smith, Burlington, N.J.: and A. Lee Talbot, Municipal Engineer, Mount Holly, N.J.

From the New Jersey Builders Association, members of the Advisory Committee included: Mr. Philip J. Cocuzza, CAE, Executive Vice-President; Mr. Stewart M. Hutt, Esq., Hutt Berkow Hollander & Jankowski, Woodbridge, N.J.; Mr. Robert L. Karnell, The Karnell Group, Piscataway, N.J.: and Mr. Robert Washburn, Sherman Silverstein and Kohl, Cherry Hill, N.J.

Additional legal and planning insights came from Mr. Robert S. Greenbaum, Esq., Chairman, Land Use Section, New Jersey Bar Association and partner of: Greenbaum Greenbaum Row Smith Bergstein Yohalem & Bruck; Mr. David J. Frizell, Esq. and Mr. Harry Pozycki, Jr., Esq., Frizell & Pozycki, Metuchen, N.J.; Mr. Henry Hill, Esq., Brener Wallack & Hill, Princeton, N.J.; Mr. Philip B. Caton AICP, Clarke & Caton, Trenton, N.J.; and Mr. Harvey S. Moskowitz AICP of Livingston, N.J.

For information on the cost and technical components of the various bridge mechanisms, support was forthcoming from numerous developers. A selected list includes: Hovnanian Builders, Linpro Co., Eastern Properties, McBride Enterprises, Kaufman and Broad, Paparone Builders, Orleans Builders and Toll Brothers. Special thanks is also extended to the New Jersey

Society of Municipal Engineers and the South Jersey Builders League for their assistance in formulating the bridge mechanisms.

For their technical support in the areas of demographic and housing analyses, we are grateful to Ms. Connie O. Hughes, Staff Director, New Jersey Data Center, and Mr. Arthur F. Young, Chief, Housing Division, Bureau of the Census.

Staff members at the Center for Urban Policy Research were of great assistance. These include: Mr. Edward Duensing, the Center Librarian, Mr. William Dolphin, the Center's Programmer Analyst, and Mr. Felix Barreto, research assistant.

Mrs. Joan Frantz, Mrs. Lydia Lombardi and Mrs. Arlene Pashman, the mainstays of the Center for Urban Policy Research's typing staff, all performed invaluable duties in preparing the manuscript. Their expert production of this challenging document in record time is a testimony to their remarkable skills -- both individually and on a group basis. Ms. Judith Hancock and Mrs. Mary Picarella assisted the manuscript's editing and final publication. Ms. Jean Acker also warrants thanks for her publication efforts.

INTRODUCTION AND ORGANIZATION

INTRODUCTION

This section presents the perspective and organization of the study. The former considers the overall national and specific New Jersey concerns prompting attention to the delivery of lower-income housing. The discussion focuses on the evolution of the courts' scrutiny of local land-use controls, culminating in the landmark 1983 New Jersey decision, Southern Burlington County NAACP v. The Township of Mount Laurel (commonly referred to as Mount Laurel II).[1] The organization of the analysis is then presented. To give the reader a sense of the research charge and direction, the substantive concerns and methodological procedures of each of the ensuing chapters are highlighted.

NATIONAL PERSPECTIVE: LAND-USE REGULATIONS AND LOWER-INCOME HOUSING

For the past two decades there has been growing national attention paid to the issue of how local land-use regulations affect the production and location of housing for low- and moderate-income families. There has been some measure of legislative and executive action in this regard, but more far reaching has been litigation in the courts, typically involving exclusionary zoning suits.[2] This section overviews both the national legislative/executive and judicial activities to foster the production of lower-cost housing. It is followed by a parallel review of initiatives in New Jersey -- a state which judicially has been in the forefront of defining the relationship between local land-use regulations and housing provision.

National Legislative/Executive Action To Foster Lower-Income Housing

Starting in the 1960s, the legislative and executive branches of government have grappled with the relationship of local land use controls and lower-cost housing production. For instance, in 1968, New York State established the Urban Development Corporation (UDC). In addition to its bonding authorization, UDC was empowered to override local restrictions against low- and moderate-income housing.[3] A year later, Massachusetts enacted Chapter 774, more commonly known as the "anti-snob" zoning statute.[4] The latter offered a special appeals process to developers denied the right to build lower-income housing. In 1970, California required all localities to prepare general plans in which adequate provision would be made for the "housing needs of all economic segments of the community."[5] A decade later, California required that local governments "zone lands at appropriate densities to meet all housing needs, prohibit amenity and design requirements that render moderate-cost housing infeasible, and speed up review procedures."[6] Its neighbor to the north, Oregon, has moved with similar intent. In the 1970s, Oregon's Land Conservation and Development Commission established as a mandatory local planning goal the provision of affordable housing.[7] This planning framework was codified into law by a 1981 statute[8] requiring local governments to allow:[9]

> ..."needed housing" (defined as "housing types determined to meet the need shown for housing within an urban growth boundary at particular price ranges and rent levels," and with explicit reference to, inter alia, multiple family units and mobile homes) in one or more zones of sufficient available, suitable, and buildable land inside urban growth boundaries.

The federal government has also intermittently been involved with the issue of local land-use regulations and lower-cost housing. In some cases its influence was indirect. For example, the federal government's A-95 review process, authorized in the late 1960s, fostered the scrutiny of local land-use regulations by regional clearinghouses.[10] It was no mere coincidence that the nation's first fair share plans -- strategies to disperse affordable housing throughout the metropolitan area -- were effected by A-95 clearinghouses such as the Miami Valley Regional Planning Commission and the Metropolitan Washington Council of Governments. In some cases, the federal government more directly broached the issue of local land use regulations and lower-cost housing. For instance, in 1976, HUD enacted an Areawide Housing Opportunity Plan (AHOP).[11] AHOP offered bonus housing subsidy monies to jurisdictions forecasting and responding to the need for lower-income housing. In the late 1970s, HUD's enforcement, albeit limited, of the "expected to reside" projections in the Community Development Block Grant's Housing Assistance Plan (HAP) had a similar goal of inculcating sensitivity to the planning and delivery of affordable housing throughout metropolitan areas.[12]

While numerous examples of legislative and executive activity fostering the construction of lower-cost housing can be isolated, the main arena of activity in this regard has been in the courts, typically involving exclusionary zoning suits. The national legal thrust of litigation involving local land use controls, and the evolution in the courts' attitude on this matter, are considered below.

Land-Use Controls and Lower-Income Housing: Evolution of the Courts' Attitude

In 1926, the United States Supreme Court strongly affirmed local zoning measures in its landmark Euclid v. Ambler decision.[13] This case involved a challenge of Euclid's (Ohio) zoning ordinance, which restricted the use of land, and established minimum lot sizes and maximum building heights in designated zones. The district court ruled that Euclid's zoning statute was unconstitutional because it had the effect of taking property without due process. In language remarkably similar to current decisions condemning exclusionary zoning, the court held that Euclid's zoning ordinance would have the impact of segregating population according to their income or situation in life. The Supreme Court, however, overruled this decision; it declared Euclid's zoning ordinance constitutional, stating that it was justifiable under the state's police power as a necessary measure for the public's general welfare.

For roughly the next four decades following Euclid, most state courts upheld municipal land use controls on the basis that they satisfied the local general welfare -- regional implications were not a dominant concern. Many of the lead decisions in this era were in New Jersey. For instance, in 1952, the New Jersey Supreme Court in Fisher v. Bedminster[14] affirmed a five-acre minimum lot size. In the same year, the State Supreme Court in Lionshead Lake[15] declared that municipal minimum floor-area requirements were constitutional. In 1962, local prohibition aginst mobile homes was upheld in Vickers v. Gloucester.[16] Counterpart decisions were found in other states, such as Senior v. New Canaan[17] (a Connecticut case upholding multi-acre zoning), and Thompson v. Carrollton[18] (a Texas decision upholding minimum floor-area requirements).

Starting in the late 1950s, many courts began to modify their strong defense of restrictive zoning. Inherent in these decisions was a turning from a strictly local to a more regional perspective in examining land use controls. A 1959 Virginia case, Board of County Supervisors of Fairfax County v. Carper,[19] struck down a two-acre minimum lot size as a measure which would exclude the county's low-income people. Six years later, the Pennsylvania Supreme Court, in National Land Investment Co. v. Kohn,[20] decided that a zoning ordinance requiring a large minimum lot size was unconstitutional since it worked to the detriment of the region's welfare:[21]

> The question posed is whether the township can stand in the way of the natural forces which send our growing population into undeveloped areas in search of a comfortable place to live. We have concluded not....

This theme -- that local land-use controls must reflect the regional growth dynamic and the consequent regional need for lower-income housing -- was repeated in the virtual deluge of decisions since 1970 overturning exclusionary zoning. The Pennsylvania Supreme Court, striking down restrictive land-use requirements in a 1971 decision, Appeal of Kit-Mar Builders, reaffirmed its contention that municipalities could not ignore regional low- and moderate-income housing pressures:[22]

> The implication...is that communities must deal with the problems of population growth. They may not refuse to confront the future by adopting zoning regulations that effectively restrict population to near present levels. It is not for any given township to say who may or may not live within its confines, while disregarding the interests of the entire area.

On similar grounds, the Pennsylvania Court in Appeal of Girsh struck down local prohibition of apartment buildings.[23]

In the early 1970s' gestation period of exclusionary zoning litigation, New Jersey often was the judicial pioneer. This will be described in greater depth in the next section. In brief, in 1970, the New Jersey Superior Court in DiSimone v. Greater Englewood Housing Corp.[24] upheld a zoning variance to foster the construction of low- and moderate-income housing. Shortly thereafter, in Oakwood at Madison, Inc. v. Township of Madison,[25] the New Jersey Superior Court declared that local prohibtions against multifamily housing and requirements for large lot zoning were unconstitutional. Repeated in Oakwood v. Madison was the municipal responsibility to "regional housing needs."

This theme was emphasized -- with national reverberations -- in the New Jersey State Supreme Court's two South Burlington County NAACP v. Township of Mount Laurel decisions.[26] The first, commonly referred to as Mount Laurel I, was decided in 1975; the second, Mount Laurel II, in 1983.[27] Mount Laurel I and II, as well as the State Supreme Court's decision in Oakwood at Madison in 1977, are detailed later in the chapter. In summary, these decisions strongly affirmed the local responsibility to the region and enunciated the principle that municipalities provide for their "fair share" of the regional housing need.

These New Jersey cases had a profound influence on the judicial thinking in other states.[28] In 1975, in Berenson v. Town of New Castle,[29] the New York Court of Appeals adopted the spirit of regional responsibility and fair share. A year later, the California Supreme Court in Associated Home Builders v. Livermore,[30] adopted a "regional need approach" to reviewing exclusionary zoning ordinances. In 1977, a Pennsylvania Commonwealth Court in Waynesborough Corp. v. Easttown Zoning Hearing Bd.[31] called for municipal inclusion of multifamily zones in order for a community to meet its "fair share." Specific fair share allocation mechanisms, were examined by the Commonwealth Court. And the Pennsylvania Supreme Court,[32] in Surrick v. Zoning Hearing Board of Township of Upper Providence[32] expressly "adopted a fair share approach to exclusionary zoning."[33]

In summary, over the past two decades, the state courts' attitude toward local land use measures has shifted from near-universal affirmation to close scrutiny, specifically on the issue of the ordinances' impact on lower-income housing. Nowhere has this shift been more pronounced, nor more influential on other jurisdictions, than in New Jersey. As summarized in a recent report:[34]

> In a series of cases spanning almost a decade, the New Jersey Supreme Court has led other state courts in striking down suburban zoning ordinances that severely restrict lower-income housing development. In its pathbreaking 1975 Mt. Laurel I decision...the court opened a new chapter....Now, in its Mt. Laurel II decsion...the court goes further....
>
> The importance of this case extends far beyond New Jersey's boundaries. Several other state courts have held that municipalities have an obligation to consider regional needs in their zoning ordinances....The case also holds lessons for planners in jurisdictions free of such judicial mandates.* Local governments across the country face the problem of how to develop affordable housing given federal subsidy cuts. As New Jersey communities, in cooperation with private developers, respond to their new affirmative responsibilities, experiences useful to cities and suburbs outside of New Jersey will surely emerge.

THE NEW JERSEY PERSPECTIVE: LAND USE REGULATIONS AND LOWER-INCOME HOUSING

New Jersey, as the most urbanized state in the country, has led in the use of land use regulations designed to protect its residential and remaining rural environment. Except for New York, New Jersey has more court deci-

---

*The influence of the Mount Laurel decisions has extended to the legislative arena as well. For example, in 1982, Vermont enacted an amendment to its State Planning and Development Act (VT. REV. STAT. Title 24, Chapter 117) providing an administrative remedy to challenge exclusionary zoning. The remedy operates as follows. The State Attorney General conducts a hearing on whether local zoning is appropriate, where the latter is defined to encompass "equal treatment of housing" and comprehensive housing need -- much in the manner of the Mount Laurel cases (e.g., zoning should consider the existing and projected population and should not have the effect of excluding these groups). See Norman Williams, "The Background/Significance of Mount Laurel II" (unpublished).

sions on land use controls than any other state -- over 1,000 reported cases. Most recently, its Mount Laurel decisions have assumed a national stature as representing the cutting edge of exclusionary zoning litigation and response. But let us start at the beginning.

Zoning in New Jersey, authorized by a 1927 constitutional amendment, is about sixty years old.[35] Even after the passage of this amendment, and the adoption in 1928 of a zoning enabling act, the state courts remained somewhat hostile to local zoning controls.[36] This attitude, however, changed in the post-World War II period, most notably in the lead cases of Fisher v. Bedminster Township (1952), Lionshead Lake, Inc. v. Wayne Township (1952), and Vickers v. Township of Gloucester (1962).[37]

In Fisher v. Bedminster, the New Jersey Supreme Court upheld a zoning ordinance placing most of Bedminster in a residence zone with a minimum lot size of five acres. Such large lot zoning was justified as "necessary to preserve the countryside for its best use."[38] In Lionshead Lake, the Court sustained a zoning ordinance barring the construction of dwellings containing less than roughly 800 square feet of living area on the grounds that this requirement promoted the "general welfare of the community."[39] Finally, in Vickers v. Gloucester Township, a community's prohibition against mobile homes was left undisturbed because the municipal governing body had decided this action was in the community's best interests, and such local judgment was accorded a presumption of validity.[40]

In these lead cases, the New Jersey Supreme Court reflected the principle of local interest hegemony in land use. Yet there were dissenting voices. For example, in Lionshead Lake, Justices Oliphant and Wachenfeld spoke of the implications of restrictive floor-area requirements.[41] Their 1952 dissenting opinion, concerning the implications of upholding Wayne Township's land use controls, foreshadowed the majority opinion of the Mount Laurel decisions almost three decades later. The Justices argued that a severe minimum house size would preclude the entry of the financially-disadvantaged who would then:[42]

> be relegated to living in the large cities...even though it be against what they consider the welfare of their immediate families.

The need for municipal zoning to acknowledge regional and not just local needs was forcefully argued by Justice Hall in his dissent to Vickers v. Gloucester Township -- another example of a minority opinion which ultimately was adopted by the majority. In Hall's words:[43]

> ...legitimate use of the zoning power by such municipalities does not encompass the right to erect barricades on their boundaries through exclusion or too-tight restriction of uses where the real purpose is to prevent feared disruption with a so-called chosen way of life. Nor does it encompass provisions designed to let in as new residents only certain kinds of people

> or those who can afford to live in favored kinds of housing, or to keep down tax bills of present property owners....

A decade after Hall's dissent came the landmark Oakwood at Madison and the two Mount Laurel decisions.

Land Use Regulations and Lower-Income Housing: The New Jersey Lead Decisions

In 1972, the New Jersey Superior Court in Oakwood at Madison, Inc. v. Township of Madison[44] overturned this community's zoning plan. Madison, in an effort to curb population growth and reduce its expenditures, had rezoned its land area to exclude multifamily housing almost completely; it also had stipulated minimum lot sizes of 1 and 2 acres. The Madison decision found this upzoning invalid, declaring that such local action was counter to regional housing needs:[45]

> [I]n pursuing the valid zoning purpose of a balanced community a municipality must not ignore housing needs, that is its fair proportion of the obligation to meet the housing needs of its own population and of the region....Large areas of vacant and developable land should not be zoned as Madison Township has into such minimum lot sizes and with such other restrictions that regional as well as local housing needs are shunted aside.

It was the two Mount Laurel decisions, however, which have embodied the Court's growing scrutiny of restrictive land use controls. Their setting deserves mention. Mount Laurel is a rapidly developing township located approximately twenty miles from the cities of Camden and Philadelphia. Mount Laurel's population roughly doubled from 1950 to 1960 (from 2800 to 5200 residents), doubled again from 1960 to 1970 (from 5200 to 11,300 residents), and grew by roughly another 50 percent from 1970 to 1980 (from 11,300 to 17,600 residents). The community's growth has been spurred by the construction of nearby major highways such as the New Jersey Turnpike and I-295, and the consequent entry of new employment centers to the area.

Like many sister communities, Mount Laurel's zoning ordinance imposed minimum lot size and other restrictions. Starting in the late 1960s, these controls were challenged by a group of plaintiffs who charged that Mount Laurel limited housing construction for low- and moderate-income families. In 1972, the trial court agreed with these charges, declared Mount Laurel's zoning unconstitutional, and ordered the township to meet its obligation for providing low- and moderate-income housing.[46]

In 1975, the State Supreme Court in Mount Laurel I affirmed the lower court's decision.[47] The state's highest court declared that zoning, as an exercise of the police power, had to be directed to satisfying the general welfare -- not only the local general walfare but the regional as well.[48]

Reasoning from this regional interpretation of the general welfare, the State Supreme Court argued that developing communities that stand in the path of growth have a presumptive obligation to ensure a broad housing mix.[49] Such "developing communities" must provide their appropriate or "fair share" of the regional housing need determined by applying the techniques and projections of the fair share approach:[50]

> We conclude that every municipality must, by its land use regulations, presumptively make realistically possible an appropriate variety and choice of housing. More specifically, presumptively it cannot foreclose the opportunity of the classes of people mentioned for low and moderate income housing and in its regulations must affirmatively afford that opportunity, at least to the extent of the municipality's fair share of the present and prospective need therefor.

Mount Laurel I introduced a number of concepts and terms -- "developing community," "region," "affirmatively afford," "fair share," etc. -- which challenged the New Jersey legal and planning community throughout the latter half of the 1970s.[51] Some of these ambiguities were addressed in the State Supreme Court's Oakwood Inc. v. Township of Madison decision of 1977.[52] Oakwood considered a diversity of topics such as: a) the specific local housing responsibility (new units for both low and moderate-income households and provision for future as well as present housing need); b) the exclusionary definition (do local land use controls preclude housing opportunity?); c) fair share (the court recognized the statistical difficulties and expressed its preference for non-rigid "numberless" formula approaches); d) inclusionary zoning (requiring that a set share, say 20 percent, of new housing "be affordable" units); e) "builder's remedy" (direct relief for plaintiff developers); and f) "least cost housing" (least expensive units which can be provided absent public assistance).[53]

Oakwood at Madison resolved some but not all questions and concepts introduced in Mount Laurel I. In its aftermath, frustration grew that few low- and moderate-income units were being delivered. Litigation continued.[54] A group of these cases were joined and heard by the State Supreme Court in 1980. Three years later it handed down its landmark Mount Laurel II decision. Major findings of the Court, in its words follow:[56]

(1) "Every municipality's land use regulations...must provide a realistic opportunity for decent housing for its indigenous poor except where they represent a disproportionately large segment of the population as compared with the rest of the region..."

(2) "The existence of a municipal obligation to provide a realistic opportunity for a fair share of the region's present and prospective low and moderate income housing need will no longer be determined by whether or not a municipality is 'developing.' The obligation extends, instead, to every municipality, any portion of which is designated by the state, through the SDGP (State

Development Guide Plan),* as a 'growth area.'"

(3) "The lower income regional housing need is comprised of both low and moderate income housing." (The former is defined as households whose incomes do not exceed 50 percent of the median income of the area with adjustment for family size; the latter have incomes from 50 to 80 percent of the area median.)*

(4) "Mount Laurel litigation will ordinarily include proof of the municipality's fair share of low and moderate income housing in terms of the number of units needed immediately, as well as the number needed for a reasonable period of time in the future. "Numberless" resolution of the issue based upon a conclusion that the ordinance provides a realistic opportunity for some low and moderate income housing will be insufficient..."

(5) "The Mount Laurel obligation to meet the prospective lower income housing need of the region is, by definition, one that is met year after year in the future throughout the years of the particular projection used in calculating prospective need...."

(6) "The municipal obligation to provide a realistic opportunity for construction of its fair share of low and moderate income housing may require more than the elimination of unnecessary cost-producing requirements and restrictions. Affirmative governmental devices should be used to make that opportunity realistic, including lower-income density bonuses and mandatory set-asides. Furthermore, the municipality should cooperate with the developer's attempts to obtain federal subsidies.... Mobile homes may not be prohibited, unless there is solid proof that sound planning in a particular municipality requires such prohibition."

(7) "Providing a realistic opportunity for the construction of least-cost housing will satisfy a municipality's Mount Laurel obligation if, and only if, it cannot otherwise be satisfied...."

(8) "Builder's remedies (a court order to municipal officials to allow a specific development to be built)* will be afforded to plaintiffs ... on a case by case basis."

(9) "Any future Mount Laurel litigation shall be assigned only to those judges selected by the Chief Justice....The Chief Justice shall define the area of the State for which each of the three judges is responsible."

(10) "The judiciary should manage Mount Laurel litigation to dispose of a case in all of its aspects with one trial and one appeal, unless substantial considerations indicate some other course."

---

*Note added

THE CHALLENGE OF MOUNT LAUREL

The Supreme Court of New Jersey in rendering its decision in Mount Laurel II has presented the State of New Jersey and residential builders within the state, with a challenge that has few parallels. The eight year test of labor which followed Mount Laurel I, had in the subsequent opinion of the Court yielded frustratingly little in the way of result. Thus, the current judicial response is much more structured with definite goals of performance rather than undefined requirements of best efforts. The injunction laid down by the Court is clear in its ultimate requirements: all communities must take measures to provide appropriate housing facilities for their present population occupying deficient housing; communities in growth areas must make provision for their share of housing need generated by future regional growth. And this must be done within a resident shelter cost which is within the resources of two categories of low-income households: those households with incomes below 50 percent and those with the 50-80 percent of regional median household income, respectively.

There is little in the way of prototype to serve as a model as the state comes to grips with these requirements. While much has been made of efforts in California, particularly in Orange County,[57] the unique nature of the real estate market in that locale, together with much more generous income maximums in their program, distinguish it from the post Mount Laurel II requirements for New Jersey communities. Similarly, while a number of municipalities have undertaken pioneering efforts at some measure of fair share allocation, these differ either in demographic or economic strata coverage from those which are currently called for -- and which are the focus of the study which follows.

On the national level, while the late Forties' mandate of a decent housing environment for all Americans was embodied in congressional rhetoric, there has been limited access to programs which would provide such an environment for the needy at prices they could afford. Current estimates suggest that after two generations of legislation less than one-third of nominally qualified households are beneficiaries of any form of federally-aided shelter. Indeed one of the criticisms of federal low-income housing programs is that in order to provide shelter for the poor, deep subsidies are required. And this is so expensive as to limit the range of their coverage. This has been particularly the case in terms of the most sweeping of them, the Section 8 program[58] which has been much reduced in scope in recent years.

Thus, there is a substantial gap between the requirements voiced by the Supreme Court of New Jersey and a level of experience in implementation with which to bring them to fruition. This is most significant as the recent land use legal wars indicate. The history of litigation and debate that followed Mount Laurel I and its progeny was one of confusion as the various players attempted to define such multifaceted terms as housing market, housing demand, least-cost housing, regional responsibility, and a whole host of other elements. The level of semantic and functional ambiguity, furthered the confusion and, in part, was responsible for the limited effectiveness of the results. Communities and developers alike have faced both ruinous legal fees and a lack of reliable views of outcome.

There is no question that the Mount Laurel II decision comes at a unique time in the history of the housing market. In the space of the last decade, housing starts varied enormously on the national level with peaks of two million starts followed by catastrophic one-million year levels. The pattern in New Jersey, as noted elsewhere in this report, has been even more accentuated.

Even the physical parameters of housing units have altered markedly. Where before, attached housing outside of central cities was a rarity, now it is commonplace. The median size of new housing which had escalated just two years ago to well above the 1700 foot mark has been reduced by nearly 20 percent in the most recent year. The condominium form of ownership at the beginning of the Seventies, was just coming into view, confined to a few large cities and resort areas; it is now much more commonplace. Interest rates, after having literally tripled within a score of years from the 6 percent level to a peak of nearly 18 percent, have now subsided -- but to a level (13-14 percent) which a very few years ago would have been thought of as completely inhibitory to housing production. And on a real level, i.e., the gap between current levels of inflation and cost of money, are at close to an all time high.

Even more important to the housing perspective, is the nearly complete retreat of the federal government from significant subsidy programs with which to support shelter provisions for the poor. There have been few times in the more than forty years since the end of World War II in which the housing agenda has been so bereft of federal enabling elements.

New Jersey has shared in all of these parameters, as well as that of job shifts both in kind -- and in location. These latter, in turn, have been complemented by significant rearrangements of population flows. While on the national level the shift to America's Sunbelt has long been a feature of front page stories, its parallel in New Jersey, the absolute losses of the older northern industrial sectors and the relative gains of newer south-central areas, while much less documented, are nonetheless as strong.

Further, in its very nature, housing is the epitome of a long-term capital good. The gap between the concept of development of a particular site, and its fruition in terms of first homes available for occupancy, may easily stretch over a five-year period. Occupancy may often last forty years or more. It is subject to all the vagaries of the market and societal change not only in its gestation period -- but to the final years of the occupied unit. Even when this process is successfully concluded, the sheer costs of housing are made acceptable only by the longevity of the good.

Thus, in generating investment in housing, the perspective must be not only of this year's need or surplus, but rather one that, at minimum, is a generation long. It is a good, which in its placement and configuration, must make economic sense for at least a score of years -- and preferably for several multiples of this time period.

In sum, the realization of the Mount Laurel II mandate would require continuous refinement even in a stable world -- and this latter condition is a luxury which unfortunately is not available. Credit conditions will change, government policy will be altered, real incomes of Americans may well vary over time. The work which is presented here hopefully does provide a series of initial benchmarks, a foundation upon which additional scaffolding and more sophisticated building blocks will be erected.

STUDY ORGANIZATION AND CONTENTS

The following study is divided into seven chapters and a bibliography organized as follows:

Chapter 1: The Definition of a Housing Region

Chapter 2: Definition of the Mount Laurel Population: Present and Prospective Housing Demand

Chapter 3: Socioeconomic and Housing Characteristics of the Present and Prospective Mount Laurel-Eligible Populations

Chapter 4: Present and Prospective Mount Laurel Housing Supply

Chapter 5: Demand Versus Supply -- Unmet Mount Laurel Housing Need

Chapter 6: Bridge Mechanisms to Meet the Mount Laurel Mandate

Chapter 7: An Introduction to the Fair Share Concept

Bibliography

Thus the study defines the basic Mount Laurel areal partition of housing regions; determines the respective regions' housing demand and supply characteristics to define the net Mount Laurel obligation; and finally examines alternative strategies to produce low- and moderate-income housing at the local level.

The research charge and approach for each of the chapters are described in detail below.

The Definition of a Housing Region

One of the most important elements in the State Supreme Court Mount Laurel decisions was the concept that some municipalities have a responsibility not only to appropriately house their own residents, but also one to a broader constituency -- those who are underhoused in the region. The latter term, however, is subject to a variety of interpretations.

The focus of this chapter is on the issue of defining in usable, workable terms, a series of partitions for the state such that each of the several areal subsets becomes a functional, sensible housing region. Key to this purpose is the journey-to-work, i.e., the commuter watershed. But there are other determinants of the housing market which must be considered as well, particularly given the relatively low labor force participation rate which is characteristic of the Mount Laurel II population. Such elements therefore as convenience, the blending of older and more built-up areas with those with much less intense development, of communities which are losing population -- and communities within a reasonable distance which are inheriting population, had to be taken into consideration.

In this effort, as well as in those which follow, compromise was often required in order to maintain continuous availability of consistent data. The definition of region had to be explored not only in terms of current quantitative measures, but also to ensure that periodic updating could be secured with a minimal level of time lag and cost. "Custom built" regions might well optimize the short-run situation but become obsolete and indeed not identifiable, from a statistical point of view, over time.

Recent changes in definitional characteristics of the Standard Metropolitan Statistical Area by the Federal Office of Management and Budget proved most useful in conceptualization of region. The key element remains a living-working-ecological areal definition supported by a firm statistical network -- and which fulfills the conceptual parameters of a housing market within the context of the classic literature on this point.

Definition of the Mount Laurel Population: Present and Prospective Mount Laurel Housing Demand

There are two separate housing groups defined in the Mount Laurel II decision. The first of these consists of persons who currently meet the Mount Laurel income constraints and who live in deficient housing. These are termed present Mount Laurel households. The second group emerges as a function of general population growth, that is, the Mount Laurel income constrained share of future households. These are termed prospective Mount Laurel households. Before the scale of these two groups could be quantified, the issue of the income definition of those households which fell under the Court's mandate, required specification. The Court in its decision referred to two income groups for whom municipalities had shelter responsibilities. These were defined respectively as low income -- those households falling under 50 percent of the regional median income -- and a second group, moderate income -- those who fall between 50-80 percent of regional household income. These threshold data required further adjustment by size of household following the federal Section 8 guidelines. Newly released Census material permitted the definition for each of the several housing regions earlier described -- a median income level by size of household. Using this as a base, the chapter delineated those households who fell within the two Mount Laurel income categories, also adjusted by household size.

Another qualification was required for the definition of present Mount Laurel housing demand -- that the shelter residents currently occupy is deficient. Unfortunately, there is no universally accepted criteria for establishing this condition. Using a variety of computerized probes however, an analog measuring tool was developed which incorporated a number of parameters. Thus, the definition of present Mount Laurel demand encompassed a quantification of income criteria -- adjusted by household size and further partitioned by housing inadequacy. It should be reiterated that the Mount Laurel housing demand data provided here is a first step which can serve as a guideline for individual communities in developing more specific criteria and appraisals. The latter is most important as municipalities review their housing approaches in terms of rehabilitation, enabling ordinances for conversion of extant facilities, as well as for "no frills" new construction.

The prospective demand required a vision of the state's population in the future, with the time horizon for the purpose of this study defined as 1990 and 2000. The basic data source was the population projections of the New Jersey Department of Labor, Office of Economic and Demographic Analysis (ODEA). The transformation of one of ODEA's demographic projections (Demographic Cohort-Model 2) into households, followed by a partitioning of households by income level was then undertaken and presented for each of the state's housing regions.

The focus here and in the material which follows is on the basic consuming unit of dwelling units: the household. For each of the state's counties, individual household headship rates by age cohort were computed and extrapolated into the future utilizing projected headship rates, also by age cohort. This regional differentiation is particularly important in New Jersey, given the existence of great variation in modular sizes of household when viewed by county. This information was summed to the regions of which the counties are a part and future Mount Laurel growth was projected for each region.

Socioeconomic and Housing Characteristics of the Present and Prospective Mount Laurel-Eligible Populations

Grasping the socioeconomic characteristics of the Mount Laurel population as fully as possible is most important in order to ensure an appropriate resolution of their shelter needs. Using the newly available final tabulations of the 1980 U.S. Census of Population and Housing permitted the definition for the present Mount Laurel population such traditional socioeconomic descriptors as age, sex of chief income producer, race, household income, and household size. In addition, labor force participation was examined including what proportion of Mount Laurel households are either employed or recently searched for work, occupation of the chief income producer, journey-to-work in terms of time, means of transportation to work, availability of an automobile to the household, and so on. Using these as a base and adjusting the data for regional growth variation by age cohort, made possible a matrix within which to project the prospective Mount Laurel population in terms of the same detailed characteristics as those cited above.

Again, using the 1980 Census of Population and Housing as a base, the housing characteristics of the shelter presently occupied by the present Mount Laurel population could also be specified. Here, the focus was on such elements as type, age, size, and tenure of unit. For ownership units, the value of the dwelling as well as owner costs and cost-income ratios were tallied. For rental units, both contract rents and present rent-income ratios were secured.

There are differences of consequence between the present and prospective Mount Laurel populations. These are extrapolated in the course of the analysis, further defining the demand characteristics of the Mount Laurel equation. Having these in hand permitted a turning to the issues of supply.

Present and Prospective Mount Laurel Housing Supply

It is essential to develop measures of prospective housing starts by configuration and by consumer cost without the impact of Mount Laurel II, i.e., what would the supply of new housing look like in the future sans this landmark decision? And secondly, once this figure is developed, what share of it, in terms of both of ownership and rental, would be at costs which meet the Court mandate for the Mount Laurel population?

The answer to these questions was framed by first considering both the extant New Jersey housing profile and recent trends in the housing stock. The former is described in terms of gross magnitude, housing type, tenure (own versus rent), and value/rent levels. Recent trends encompass the complex composite reflecting additions to the stock through new construction and conversion of units from single-family to multifamily (or from nonresidential to residential), as well as losses from the housing inventory through demolition, condemnation, and other means.

This analysis provides the basis for projecting the future New Jersey housing supply. Housing supply in the state is projected for all income groups, by region, for 1980 to 1990 and 1990 to 2000 in both the owner and renter sectors. Within tenure catgories, housing supply is further projected by types of unit. The projection relies on historic housing supply in New Jersey dampened slightly by the reduction in the number of households projected over the two time periods.

Using assumed ratios of affordability both for ownership and rental units, the share of new housing available to Mount Laurel households is produced. Share of housing for both Mount Laurel income categories by tenure is tabulated for each projection period.

Demand Versus Supply -- Unmet Mount Laurel Housing Need

In an earlier section of this study, demand for housing by the Mount Laurel-eligible population is tallied by a number of variables. These include location, household size, income category and tenure. Another chapter projects supply according to the same variables, making certain assumptions for value/rent relative to income as well as household size relative to unit size. This was made possible by detailed descriptions of the Mount Laurel populations and a similar scrutinization of the projected housing stock. How well does conventional housing supply meet demand by size, cost, location, and tenure of unit? Once viewed, what is the resulting scale of unmet demand and to which Mount Laurel income sector is this unmet demand related? These are absolutely critical determinations and form the basis of the Mount Laurel housing mandate which must be met.

In order to answer these questions, the Center for Urban Policy Research developed a computer algorithm of the Mount Laurel housing search. The model allows each Mount Laurel household of certain income and size to search for housing within its means, i.e., according to the unit's rent/value, carrying cost, size, and location within the housing market. Mount Laurel households are matched with conventionally supplied new housing and the number and types of Mount Laurel families not housed are then arrayed. This is termed unmet Mount Laurel housing demand.

Unmet demand is presented separately for the present and prospective sectors by region, household size, and income category and is translated to units, unit size and carrying costs, also by region. Here, building on previous chapters, the analysis is able to isolate the component of Mount Laurel demand which must be addressed by zoning solutions.

Further integrated into the basic logic of the analysis is the impact of the filtering and rehabilitation on housing supply. Both of these non-new construction sources of housing supply are difficult to isolate and almost impossible to quantify especially to the level of detail mandated above. Rough orders of magnitude, however, are provided for each of these supply sources.

The basic numbers of the chapter remain, however -- those associated with unmet Mount Laurel housing demand. The next chapter discusses ways in which conventionally delivered housing may be altered to enhance its affordability.

Bridge Mechanisms to Meet the Mount Laurel Mandate

To meet the Mount Laurel mandate, a series of bridge mechanisms are considered. These are techniques to close the gap between what housing currently costs and the shelter budget affordable by low/moderate-income families.

To better comprehend the challenge of and the response to the Mount Laurel mandate, the components of housing costs are presented -- development, construction, delivery, and occupancy expenses. Attention then turns to bridge mechanisms. The State Supreme Court's identification of these strategies is considered first, followed by a more encompassing listing and analysis of such techniques. This discussion is based on national and state studies on affordable housing. The examination of the broad array of bridge approaches is keyed to the components of housing costs. For example, increasing density may lower land and other development expenses, reducing housing size can moderate construction outlays, and providing below-market mortgages would relieve the monthly occupancy charge. Each bridge mechanism is evaluated in terms of its applicability, availability, and effect on reducing housing cost so as to meet the Mount Laurel mandate.

The goal in this section is not to prescribe, but rather to introduce a series of strategies for reducing housing costs. The mix-and-match of these and other subsidy elements, and their optimization must depend upon the specifics of both the private and public sectors -- and their full cooperation.

An Introduction to the Fair Share Concept

The same spirit of presenting alternative approaches, rather than prescribing a specific set response, characterizes the fair share analysis. "Fair share" are plans to distribute the regional housing responsibility to local jurisdictions according to such criteria as placing housing where it will expand housing opportunity, where it is most needed, and where it is most suitable. The chapter details the fair share indices of such nationally noted approaches as the Dayton Housing Opportunity Plan, The Twin Cities Allocation Strategy, The Metropolitan Washington, D.C. Housing Allocation Plan, as well as numerous recent examples in New Jersey. In each case, individual allocation criteria, their weighting, and the resulting formulae are examined in depth.

The thrust of this chapter is to group the fair share variables along common substantive dimensions to derive what might be possible allocation measures to be used in a fair share formula. The grouping categories contained in this section are: (1) measures of local advantage/need (e.g., job growth); (2) measures of local economic capacity (e.g., per capita property value); (3) measures of local development potential (e.g., acres of developable land); and (4) measures of prior subsidized housing production. The most appropriate variable for each measure is presented along with a discussion of importance of this dimension relative to other measures.

This chapter brings together much of the fair share housing literature and develops common substantive indicators which may be used in allocation. No housing is allocated to local communities. It is a substantive base upon which municipalities, developers, and the planning profession at large can view specific allocation proposals.

Bibliography - Housing Lower-Income Households

This section of the report provides a post-1970 summary of the more pertinent literature dealing with each of the substantive areas covered in the previous chapters. The citations were gathered manually from journals and publications of planning as well as the planning-related fields of real estate, economics, sociology, and transportation. To reinforce the manual search, computerized literature searches were undertaken using data bases from housing (HUD USER), economics (ECON), sociology (SOC-SCI), planning (NTIS), transportation (TRIS), government periodicals (GPO-MC) and law (West Law). Only those citations directly related to the study at hand were included.

The citations included here represent the literature most heavily drawn upon to complete this study.

NOTES

1. Southern Burlington County NAACP v. The Township of Mount Laurel, 67 N.J. 151, 336 A. 2d 713, Appeal Dismissed and Cert. Denied, 423 U.S. 808 (1975) (Mount Laurel I); Southern Burlington County NAACP v. The Township of Mount Laurel, 92 N.J. 158, 456 A. 2d 390 (1983) (Mount Laurel II).

2. For some of the "classical" studies see: Norman Williams, Jr., and Edward Wacks, "Segregation of Residential Areas Along Economic Lines: Lionshead Lake Revisited," Wisconsin Law Review, Vol. 1969, pp. 838-839; Richard Babcock and Fred Bosselman, "Suburban Zoning and the Apartment Boom," University of Pennsylvania Law Review, Vol. III, 1963, p. 1060; Mary Brooks, Exclusionary Zoning (ASPO Planning Advisory Service) No. 254,

February 1970; Lawrence Sager, "Tight Little Islands: Exclusionary Zoning, Equal Protection and the Indigent," Stanford Law Review, Vol. 21, No. 4, (April 1970), p. 767; Richard Babcock and Frederick P. Bosselman, Exclusionary Zoning: Land Use Regulation and Housing in the 1970s (New York: Praeger Publishers, 1971); Anthony Downs, Opening up the Suburbs: An Urban Strategy for America (New Haven: Yale University Press, 1973).

3. See William R. Reilly and Sy Schulman, "The New York State Urban Development Corporation: New York Innovation," Urban Lawyer No. 1 (Summer 1969), pp. 129-34.

4. Mass. Gen. Laws Ann. 40B, secs. 30-23 (Supp. 1973), inserted by Statute 1969, ch. 774. See "Massachusetts Zoning Appeals Law," Boston University Law Review, Vol. 54, No. 1 (January 1974) pp. 47-48; Karen Jean Schneider, "Innovations in the State Legislation: The Massachusetts Suburban Zoning Act" (Bachelors honors thesis, Radcliffe College, 1970); MacDonald Barr, "The Massachusetts Zoning Appeals Law: Lessons of the First Three Years" (Paper delivered at conference of the Amerian Institute of Planners, Boston, 1972); Nathaniel Taylor, "Reconsidering the Massachusetts Suburban Housing and Zoning Reform Law: The Need for Change" (Paper delivered at Conference of the American Institute of Planners, Boston, 1972); Metropolitan Area Planning Council, 774 Plus Two: An Interpretive Analysis of Chapter 774 and a Review of Activities (Boston: Metropolitan Area Planning Council, 1972).

5. California Government Code, section 6530(c). This policy mandate language was moved to California Government Code section 65583 by Assembly Bill 2853 (1980), Chapter 1143 of the Statutes of 1980, in a virtually unchanged fashion. Cited in Seymour I. Schwartz and Robert A. Johnston, "Inclusionary Housing Programs," Journal of the American Planning Association, Vol. 49, No. 1 (Winter 1983), p. 20.

6. Assembly Bill 2320 (McCarthy, 1980), Chapter 1152 of the Statutes of 1980. At California Government Code, sections 65800, 65913 and 65913.1 and others. Cited in Schwartz and Johnston, "Inclusionary Housing Programs."

7. John Volkman, "Oregon's LCDC Funded," in Land Use Law and Zoning Digest, Vol. 27, No. 9 (1975).

8. Senate Bill 419, enacted as 1981 New Laws, Ch. 884, p. 1965.

9. Frederic A. Strom (editor), 1983 Zoning and Planning Law Handbook (New York: Bordman, 1983), p. 7.

10. See David Listokin, Fair Share Housing Allocation (New Brunswick: Center for Urban Policy Research, 1976).

11. U.S. Department of Housing and Urban Development, HUD News, No. 76-66 (March 3, 1976).

12. U.S. Department of Housing and Urban Development, Administrative Regulations for Community Development Grant, June 6, 1975, sec. 570.2(a)(6).

13. Euclid v. Ambler, 272 U.S. 365 (1926).

14. Fisher v. Bedminster Township, 11 N.J. 194, 93 A. 2d 378 (1952).

15. Lionshead Lake, Inc. v. Wayne Township, 10 N.J. 165, 89 A. 2d 693 (1952).

16. Vickers v. Township of Gloucester, 37 N.J. 232, 181 A. 2d 129 (1962).

17. Senior v. Zoning Commission of the Town of New Canaan, 146 Conn. 531, A. 2d (415) 1959.

18. Thompson v. Carrollton, 211 S.W. 2d 970 (Tex Civ. App. 1948).

19. Board of County Supervisors of Fairfax County v. Carper, 200 Va. 653, 197. S.E. 2d 390 (1959).

20. National Land and Investment Co. v. Kohn, 419 Pa. 504, 215 A. 2d 597 (1965).

21. Ibid. 215 A. 2d at 597, 215 A. 2d at 610.

22. Appeal of Kit-Mar Builders, 439 Pa. 466, 268 A. 2d 765 (1971).

23. Appeal of Girsh, 437 Pa. 237, 263 A. 2d 395 (1970).

24. DiSimone v. Greater Englewood Housing Corp., 56 N.J. 428, 267 A. 2d 31 (1970).

25. Oakwood at Madison Inc. v. Township of Madison, 117 N.J. Super. 11, 283 A. 2d 353 (1972).

26. See footnote 1 in this chapter.

27. Ibid.

28. See Norman Williams, "Mount Laurel: A Major Transition in American Planning Law," Land Use Law and Zoning Digest, Vol. 27, No. 6 (1975), p. 33; Donald Priest, "A View from the Mount: Laurel and Criticisms for a Major Judicial Advance," Environmental Comment, Vol. 23 (July 1975), p. 1; Frank A. Rubin, "Local Growth Management and Regional Housing Needs," Urban Law Annual (1982), p. 407.

29. Berenson v. Town of New Castle, 38 N.Y. 2d 102, 341 N.E. 2d 236, 378 N.Y.S. 2d 622 (1975).

30. *Associated Home Builders v. Livermore*, 18 Cal. 3d 582, 557, P. 2d 473, 135 Cal. Rptr. 41 (1976).

31. *Waynesborough Corp. v. Easttown Zoning Hearing Bd*. 23 Pa. Common. Ct. 137, 350 A. 2d 895 (1976).

32. *Surrick v. Zoning Hearing Board of Township of Upper Providence* 426 Pa. 182, 382 A. 2d 895 (1976).

33. Rubin, "Local Growth Management and Regional Housing Needs," p. 417.

34. Jerold S. Kayden and Leonard A. Zax, "Mount Laurel II: Landmark Decision in Zoning and Low Income Housing Holds Lessons for Nation," *Zoning and Planning Law Report*, Vol. 6, No. 3, (September 1983).

35. Frederick W. Hall, "An Orientation to Mount Laurel" in Jerome G. Rose and Robert E. Rothman, *After Mount Laurel: The New Suburban Zoning* (New Brunswick: Center for Urban Policy Research, 1977), p. 4.

36. *Ibid*., p. 5.

37. See notes 14 through 16 in this chapter.

38. 93 A. 2d at 383.

39. 89 A. 2d at 697.

40. See note 16 in this chapter.

41. See note 15 in this chapter.

42. *Ibid*.

43. See note 16 in this chapter.

44. See note 25 in this chapter.

45. *Ibid*.

46. See *Southern Burlington County NAACP v. Township of Mount Laurel*, Superior Court of New Jersey Law Division, May 1, 1972.

47. See footnote 1 in this chapter.

48. 67 N.J. at 177.

49. 67 N.J. at 179.

50. 67 N.J. at 174.

51. See, for example, the series of articles authored by Jerome G. Rose: "The Mount Laurel Decision: Is It Based on Wishful Thinking?" Real Estate Law Journal, Vol. 4 (1975); "Is There A Fair Share Housing Allocation Plan That Is Acceptable to Suburban Municipalities?" Urban Law Annual, Vol. 12 (1976); "The Trickle Before the Deluge From Mount Laurel," Real Estate Law Journal, Vol. 5 (1976); "What is a Developing Municipality Within the Meaning of the Mount Laurel Decision?" Real Estate Law Journal, Vol. 4 (1976); "A New Test for Exclusionary Zoning: Does It 'Preclude the Opportunity' for 'Least Cost' Housing?" Real Estate Law Journal, Vol. 6 (1977); "After the Recent New Jersey Supreme Court Decisions: What is the Status of Suburban Zoning?" New Jersey Municipalities (May 1977); "Myths and Conceptions of Exclusionary Zoning Legislation," Real Estate Law Journal, Vol. 9 (1979).

52. Oakwood at Madison, Inc. v. Township of Madison, 72 N.J. 481, 371 A. 2d 1192 (1977).

53. See footnote 51 in this chapter and Robert P. Inman and David L. Rubenfeld, "The Judicial Pursuit of Local Fiscal Equity," Harvard Law Review, Vol. 92, No. 2, June 1979.

54. See the Mount Laurel II decision.

55. Numerous articles have been written discussing the Mount Laurel II decision. Some examples include Jerome G. Rose, "The Mount Laurel II Decision: Is It Based on Wishful Thinking?" Real Estate Law Journal, Vol. 12, No. 2 (Fall 1983); Lewis Goldshore, Esq., "Mount Laurel Revisited - The Environmental Perspective," New Jersey Municipalities, March 1983; Peter A. Buchshaum, "Why Mount Laurel Will Work," New Jersey Law Journal, Thursday, 13 October 1983; Daniel S. Bernstein, "Why Mount Laurel Won't Work...Unless," New Jersey Law Journal, Thursday 13, October 1983; David J. Frizell, "Mount Laurel and Sound Planning," New Jersey Law Annual, Thursday, 13 October, 1983; Alfred L. Ferguson, "Keeping it Green with Mount Laurel II: An Environmental Perspective," New Jersey Law Journal, Thursday, 13 October, 1983; Leonard A. Zax and Jerold S. Kayden, "A Landmark in Land Use," The National Law Journal, Monday, March 14, 1983.

56. As cited in Potomac Institute Metropolitan Housing Program, Metropolitan Housing Memorandum, Memorandum 83-1, February 1983.

57. See Chapter 6 in this study.

58. Section 8 of the United States Housing Act of 1937 (432 U.S.C. 1401 et seq.). See 44 FR 59 408, Oct. 15, 1979, amended 45 FR 18922, Mar. 24, 1980, 48 FR 12702, Mar. 28, 1983.

SUMMARY OF FINDINGS

THE DEFINITION OF A HOUSING REGION

A housing region is a geographic area in which units at the same price are in mutual competition. People choose the location of their housing primarily in relationship to their journey-to-work; housing is usually located somewhere within a reasonable commuting distance/time to work. While most people commute one-way for less than 30 minutes, a worktrip time of more than 45 minutes has been deemed excessive by several sources.

There are at least two ways to approach the definition of a housing region. The first is to establish a point at the core of every major employment center and to draw time/distance rings outward from the employment site. This produces an amoeba-like housing region whose outer boundary is the maximum acceptable commuting time. There may literally be thousands of such housing regions depending upon the number and size of employment centers. Further, each will be part of many other regions.

A second method is to join geographic areas together that are linked by cross-commuting from place of residence to place of work. These common commuting sheds also form housing regions related to journey-to-work. These are separate areas with no overlap which are unique and distinct from one another. Yet, they describe a housing region related to journey-to-work because this is what brings them together. Such regional delineation has been employed by the Center for Urban Policy Research (CUPR) for New Jersey and by the Office of Management and Budget/U.S. Census Bureau also for New Jersey.

Using regions of commuting complementarity as well as other criteria (income, housing costs, vacant land, etc.), six housing regions in New Jersey emerged. These regions, consisting of two-to-four counties each as their basic building blocks, additionally reflect locations of intra-regional differences and inter-regional similarities. Regions contain a mix of rural and urban areas, housing types, and socioeconomic characteristics, yet they are also balanced such that within the statewide parameters one region is not significantly poorer or more urban than another nor are there noticeable differences in either housing types or housing quality.

The U.S. Census independently uses a similar process to designate its Metropolitan Statistical Areas (MSAs). These are locations which demonstrate economic linkages due to commuting patterns and metropolitan characteristics. As of June 30, 1983, a series of new Metropolitan Statistical Areas were designated for New Jersey replacing older SMSA designations. These new designations (MSAs, PMSAs) are important because all subsequent geographic data displays and tabulations for any federal agency will be compiled by these regions. Thus, if for instance, federal funding is dispersed according to an area's socioeconomic characteristics, one versus another area's share is more readily determined if the areas are coterminous with PMSA or MSA designations.

There is basic agreement between the Center for Urban Policy Research (CUPR) and Census designations of regions in New Jersey. The CUPR regions reflect the latest Census information and in addition, take into account the necessary joining of several small counties in New Jersey because data is not presented separately for them by the Public Use Sample. As constructed, eighty-eight percent of the state's low- and moderate-income population live and work in the same region. Their average journey-to-work times are shorter than 20 minutes, which is about the same as the statewide average.* Those who commute out of one region and into another are essentially the same in socioeconomic characteristics as those who do the reverse.

The regions that have been developed for New Jersey offer many benefits such as finite number, data compatibility, socioeconomic balance, vacant land availability, agreement with other areal definitions, etc. These form the basic presentation axes for the information of the report. They are composed by county as follows:

Northeast Region 1	Northwest Region 2	West Central Region 3	East Central Region 4	Southwest Region 5	South-South-West Region 6
Bergen	Essex	Hunterdon	Monmouth	Burlington	Atlantic
Hudson	Morris	Middlesex	Ocean	Camden	Cape May
Passaic	Sussex	Somerset		Gloucester	Cumberland
	Union	Warren		Mercer	Salem

*Does not consider out-of-state worktrips.

DEFINITION OF THE MOUNT LAUREL POPULATION: PRESENT AND PROSPECTIVE HOUSING DEMAND

An accurate measure of the magnitude of the Mount Laurel population is clearly a critical element required for implementing Mount Laurel II. How large is the target population? Developing an accurate count requires a multifaceted procedure.

A definition for Mount Laurel housing need is derived from statements by the Court as to the population to be housed under Mount Laurel II, as well as those who have been designated as underhoused historically. The method used by CUPR in quantifying the Mount Laurel-eligible population differentiates between present and prospective Mount Laurel households. Present Mount Laurel households are defined in terms of two criteria: (1) income; and (2) housing condition. Conceptually, then, present demand reflects households with low or moderate incomes living in deficient housing. Prospective demand refers to projected growth in low- or moderate-income households in the future and is defined solely on the basis of income.

Following the State Supreme Court, the definition of low- and moderate-income households is taken from federal regulations governing implementation of HUD's Section 8 Rent Supplement program. Low-income households are those with incomes below 50 percent of the region's median household income (regions as defined earlier). Moderate-income households are those with incomes more than 50 percent but less than 80 percent of the regional median income. These income levels are further adjusted by household size and controlled for the effects of inflation over time.

In addition to the income eligibility criterion, present Mount Laurel demand is that component of low- and moderate-income households currently living in deficient housing. Housing deficiency has been defined by CUPR on the basis of an index comprising a measure of building age (structure built pre-1940) and/or six additional indicators of housing condition (crowding, non-exclusive use of plumbing, access to unit through another dwelling unit, lack of complete kitchen facilities, lack of central heating, and lack of an elevator in structures over four stories). Identification of housing deficiency followed two selection rules. Units built prior to 1940 were assigned a deficient status if any one of the remaining housing quality surrogates indicated a deficiency. Units built from 1940 on, were defined as deficient if two or more of the deficiency measures were present.

Combining the income and housing deficiency criteria yields a present Mount Laurel housing demand totalling 120,160 households. Two-thirds of these households (81,360) are low-income while the remaining 38,800 are in the moderate-income category. More than half of existing demand (63,880 households, or 53 percent) is occasioned by one- and two-person households. The regional pattern of existing demand shows a sharp north-to-south gradient: fully 43 percent is concentrated in the Northeast Region, declining to a low of 4 percent in the East Central Region.

As distinct from present demand just discussed, prospective demand is measured by projecting the future growth of low- and moderate-income households to 1990 and 2000. These projections are based on total population projections prepared by the New Jersey Department of Labor, adjusted by age cohort, county-specific headship rate projections, and income.

For the state as a whole, growth in the decade of the 1980s will generate an additional demand for Mount Laurel housing (above present demand) at a level of 133,981 households. Two-thirds of this prospective 1980-1990 demand will be generated by small (1-2 person) households, and two-thirds of these will be low-income households. The subsequent decade (1990-2000) is projected to bring with it an additional 79,952 new households in need of lower-cost housing. The regional distribution of prospective demand is virtually the mirror image of present demand. The largest growth in new Mount Laurel need in both decades occurs in the East Central Region, followed in magnitude by that for the Southwest Region. The most populous regions, the Northeast and Northwest, with the highest present demand, generate relatively low prospective demand in the future. In the Northeast Region, outmigration is so strong that an actual net loss of Mount Laurel households occurs in the 1990-2000 decade.

SOCIOECONOMIC AND HOUSING CHARACTERISTICS OF THE PRESENT AND PROSPECTIVE MOUNT LAUREL-ELIGIBLE POPULATIONS

Subsequent to defining the magnitude of the Mount Laurel population is the question: who are these households? Answering this question entails a discussion of socioeconomic and housing characteristics of Mount Laurel households.

As indicated above, present Mount Laurel-eligible households comprise a heterogeneous population with two basic characteristics in common: (1) their incomes are either below 50 percent (low income) or 50 to 80 percent (moderate income) of the median income in their region of residence; and (2) their housing unit is inadequate as defined by the deficiency measure described above. Considerably greater detail is available, however, on the characteristics of present Mount Laurel households beyond that conveyed by those two common elements.

Statewide, close to 60 percent of present Mount Laurel households are white, 30 percent are black, and the remaining 10 percent are in the "other" category of Asians, Pacific Islanders, American Indians, etc. The Spanish population, most of which is in the "white" category above, comprises 25 percent of present Mount Laurel households. In more than half of all Mount Laurel households, the chief income producer is female -- a rate that is double that found in New Jersey's population as a whole. Median household size in the present Mount Laurel population (1.90) is 33 percent smaller than the median New Jersey household.

Considering age structure and household size, the largest single category of present demand is comprised of 1-2 person households with principal earner aged 65 or over and low-income. This group totals 17,560 households. Second highest overall is the 25-44 aged household of 3-4 persons and low-income, with 12,160 households in this category.

Two-thirds of present Mount Laurel households had incomes under $10,000 in 1980. Roughly half have a principal income earner working; of those working, close to 40 percent were employed as laborers or operatives. Approximately 12 percent of those in the labor force were unemployed in 1980.

Turning to housing characteristics, close to 80 percent of present Mount Laurel households are currently living in other than single-family housing units -- roughly double the percentage for the state as a whole. Reflecting these conditions, some 75 percent are in rental units, again close to double the statewide average. For those Mount Laurel households owning their own homes, median value in 1980 was only $28,300, less than one-half the statewide median of $61,200. Median rent in renter-occupied units was $225/month in 1980; fully 37 percent of existing households paid more than 50 percent of their income for rent. Among owners, housing costs exceeded 50 percent of income for 33 percent of households.

Characteristics of prospective Mount Laurel households are projected to be similar to existing households to a certain extent but also to differ in significant ways. Compared to the existing Mount Laurel population, prospective Mount Laurel households (those reflective of growth over the period 1980-2000), are somewhat more likely to be white, to be composed of 1-2 person families and to have household heads over 65 years of age. These shifts reflect projected statewide growth in the elderly and non-family population, much of which falls within Mount Laurel low- and moderate-income categories.

PRESENT AND PROSPECTIVE MOUNT LAUREL HOUSING SUPPLY

Given the measures of need represented by present and prospective Mount Laurel housing demand, how well is that need likely to be met given projected dimensions of New Jersey housing supply? This question considers the capacity of the current housing delivery system in the state to provide housing for Mount Laurel-eligible households within normal market channels, i.e., in the absence of Court-mandated intervention. Stated differently, how much of identified demand will be met under existing production trends, and how large is the resulting gap requiring some form of intervention? Our consideration of these issues encompasses several components: (1) the characteristics of New Jersey's current (1980) housing stock; (2) recent trends in housing supply; (3) housing supply projections through 1990 and 2000; and (4) the proportion of projected growth in housing supply that will be affordable by Mount Laurel-eligible households.

As of 1980, the existing housing stock of the State of New Jersey totalled some 2.7 million units, with the largest concentrations in the Northeast and Northwest Regions. Just over one-half of this statewide inventory consisted of single-family detached units, and 62 percent was owner-occupied. Median housing values for single-family units vary widely by region, ranging from a high of $72,759 in the Northeast Region to a low of $42,857 in the South-Southwest Region, a spread of nearly 60 percent. Comparing these data to the income and housing value/rent characteristics of Mount Laurel households summarized above, it is evident that the current inventory of owner-occupied units is largely priced beyond the reach of most Mount Laurel households.

Recent trends in residential construction in the state reveal a sharp pattern of fluctuation over time. The peak period for recent housing activity in the state was 1971 to 1973, when building permits hovered at the 60,000 level annually. The 1974-75 national recession was clearly felt in the state, as housing starts plummeted to the 25,000 annual mark. A moderate recovery was sustained in 1977-79, but the real crunch came with the 1980s, when annual starts reached the lowest levels in two decades. The first half of 1983 suggests evidence of a slight upswing, indicating the potential for recovery. To summarize, the 1980s have seen a sharp decline in the magnitude of new housing construction in the state, while a growing share of the housing that has been built has been in single-family units. These trends have been deepened with the concentration of housing starts in the growth hubs of the East Central and Southwest Regions, where the lion's share of new construction has been in single-family units.

Net change in the housing stock results not only from new construction but also from net additions and subtractions associated with conversions and demolitions, respectively. Summing all three components of change in the housing inventory, New Jersey's housing stock reflected a net growth of 419,542 units from 1960 to 1970 (a growth rate of 22 percent), and a further net increase of 385,084 between 1970 and 1980 (a rate of 17 percent).

Available data for 1990 and 2000 suggest a continuation of this downward spiral in the rate of growth in net housing supply. Factors expected to influence projected housing starts include the low rate of starts in the first three-and-a-half years of the 1980s, expected continued high interest rates, and projected declines in the rate of new household formation. Based on these factors and available data, CUPR projects a net growth in total housing units of approximately 328,000 units for 1980-1990 (a 12 percent increase) and further growth of 278,000 units between 1990-2000 (for a 9 percent increase).

Given this projected net growth for 1980-2000, what proportion will be within the rent-paying and home-buying ability of Mount Laurel households? The procedure employed in answering this question involves matching the projected net growth in housing units, defined by unit size and cost, against existing and projected Mount Laurel demand, defined in terms of household size and income. Based on this matching procedure, for 1980-1990, 1.3 percent of projected growth in owner-occupied units, and 24.6 percent of growth in renter-occupied units, will be affordable by Mount Laurel households.

DEMAND VERSUS SUPPLY -- UNMET MOUNT LAUREL HOUSING NEED

Aggregate Mount Laurel demand (present plus prospective) is close to 334,000 units through the Year 2000. Net additional (new) housing (new construction plus conversions minus demolitions), as noted previously, will answer some share of this demand.

To obtain a more exact figure on who is/is not housed via conventional supply, a computer matching program is employed which allows Mount Laurel households which are a part of either present or prospective demand to shop for housing within the net new supply of housing in their region. Mount Laurel households of certain income and size are matched with housing of certain rent (carrying costs) and number of rooms in the same regional location. This procedure shows housing available via new construction/conversion and to whom it would be available.

Approximately ten percent of net new housing supply is available to those of Mount Laurel incomes. Most of this housing goes to satisfy some share of moderate-income housing demand. This is primarily new low-end rental housing for small families, some of which may have been built for tax loss purposes. A very small portion of net new housing is available to low-income families. This is housing created mainly from conversion with a small percentage of private subsidized housing (built by unions, church groups, etc.)* included here.

Unanswered Mount Laurel housing demand is approximately 300,000 units including present housing deficient, income-constrained demand, and prospective income-constrained demand for both 1980 to 1990 and 1990 to 2000. Affordable rents required for a family of 3-4 persons of moderate income in the central part of the state range from a high of $540 to a median of $470; affordable rents required for a family of four of low income in the same area range from a high of $315 to a median of $240. Generally speaking, those who can afford more rent are in the central part of the state with lower ranges of affordability in both the North and the South. Unanswered housing need is presented by region, numbers, size of configuration, rental levels and distributions for all six previously-defined regions.

BRIDGE MECHANISMS TO MEET THE MOUNT LAUREL MANDATE

To meet the Mount Laurel mandate of housing production for low/moderate-income households, bridge mechanisms must be employed. Bridge

---

*Publicly-subsidized housing has been removed as a source of future supply due to the future uncertainty and low level of funding of most programs.

mechanisms are techniques to close the gap between what housing currently costs and the shelter budget affordable by low/moderate-income families.

To better understand the need for and workings of bridge mechanisms, the components of housing and their respective costs are considered first. Housing expenses are categorized into the stages of development, construction, delivery, and occupancy.

Following the presentation of the housing cost components, a series of bridge mechanisms, consisting of both regulatory changes (i.e., zoning and subdivision standard modifications), and public subsidies (i.e., Section 8 and Community Development Block Grants), are presented. These are termed individual bridge strategies because they are keyed to reducing the item-by-item expenditures of the housing package.

To illustrate the effects of the individual bridge mechanisms, a modular housing unit example is projected. At today's standards, the dwelling unit is above the range of affordability of the most affluent of the moderate-income Mount Laurel population. With the regulatory bridge mechanisms, the modular unit can house the upper range of moderate-income families. With public subsidy, the model is opened to the middle range of the moderate-incomed.

Additional economies are offered by what are termed encompassing bridge mechanisms -- strategies which influence numerous housing cost components. Two such encompassing mechanisms are examined -- adopting inclusionary zoning and allowing manufactured housing, most notably mobile homes.

Inclusionary provisions either encourage or require the production of affordable housing (i.e. 20 percent of a development's units be available to low- and moderate-income families). To foster compliance, many inclusionary programs offer a density bonus or other inducements. These allowances enable a builder to internally subsidize the delivery price of the affordable units being provided. Depending on its structure, an inclusionary program permits the production of housing affordable by the least affluent of moderate-income Mount Laurel families and in exceptional cases could reach some low-income Mount Laurel families as well. Mobile homes also allow for housing delivery economies. By capitalizing on the efficiencies of factory production, a mobile home can serve as a housing resource for the least affluent of moderate-income Mount Laurel families and some low-income families.

To house the bulk of the Mount Laurel low-income population, subsidies outside the framework of shelter development must be used. These include extensive private market unit subsidy of Mount Laurel units as well as deep public subsidy.

AN INTRODUCTION TO THE FAIR SHARE CONCEPT

Both the first and second Mount Laurel decisions emphasized the importance of fair share. Fair share is a plan or process which determines where housing, especially low- and moderate-income units, should be built within a region. There is no one generally accepted approach. The materials presented here are intended as a summary of the state of the art, not as recommendations prescribing a specific set response.

Such criteria as placing housing where it is most needed, where it will expand housing opportunity, and where it is most suitable are typical fair share parameters. Evident from this definition is fair share's focus on allocation. This in turn entails initial determination of criteria by which to allocate housing, the transformation of these benchmarks into operational indices, and the integration of a range of indices into an actual allocation formula.

While there are variations, in both the national and New Jersey fair share plans there are commonalities in the selection of these three allocation components. Housing is typically distributed according to the criteria of local advantage/need, economic capacity, local development potential, and past subsidized housing production. These categories attempt to allocate housing to suitable areas where suitability is defined as locations benefiting from employment growth, are financially most capable to provide services to new housing development, have suitable developable land to accommodate growth, and which have been slow in meeting their affordable housing responsibility in the past.

Commonalities in allocation indices are also found. Local advantage/need is typically measured by job-related information such as the local share of total regional employment or the municipal share of the region's aggregate job growth. Economic capacity consists of two categories: fiscal and financial. The former measures the resources available to the public sector, usually the property value which can be taxed. Common indicators include valuation per capita or per student. Financial capacity indicates the ability of community residents to absorb the potential costs of new development. The measures employed here include per capita income or household income. Local development potential usually is gauged by the amount of vacant developable land. Finally, past subsidized housing production, a factor applied in inverse proportion in order to foster housing dispersal, is measured by the extant level of local low cost and/or subsidized housing.

Allocation criteria and indices comprise the basic fair share components. Allocation formulae combine and manipulate these components in order to yield concrete numerical allocation quotas. While there are variations, again there are commonalities in both the national and New Jersey fair share state-of-the-art. Most extant fair share plans express the bulk of the allocation criteria/measures in terms of their percentage relationship to the regional profile (e.g. local share of the total regional job growth). These percentages are calculated for each variable and then summed and averaged to derive a composite local ratio. The latter indicates the share of regional prospective housing need to be assigned to each respective community. (Present housing need is primarily the responsibility of local communities characterized by such housing inadequacy.)

Following this detailed methodological analysis, there is a review of the fair share historical legacy, both nationally and in New Jersey. In the latter case this includes both state efforts of the late 1970s as well as more recent attempts to formulate fair share plans in the wake of the Mount Laurel II decision. The historical review sets the stage for the final section which presents a step-by-step procedural framework for developing a fair share strategy. This section considers some alternative approaches for allocation criteria, indicators, and formulae.

CHAPTER 1 — THE DEFINITION OF A HOUSING REGION

INTRODUCTION

The purpose of the following chapter is to trace the concept of housing region/market throughout its developmental history and, on this basis, to develop housing regions in New Jersey. An effort is made to return to basic definition of region, i.e., as a geographical-territorial designation for substantive purposes, and view within it the substantive purpose of housing.

Once housing and region are joined, the concept of housing market is introduced through such fundamental housing technical guides as FHA Techniques of Housing Market Analysis and real estate texts as Fishers' Urban Real Estate.[1] The discussion then turns to an analysis of why people search for housing and the relationship of housing search to the breadth of the housing region. The concepts of journey-to-work and preferred time-distance commuting zones, taken from the transportation and planning fields, are introduced here. Other considerations in the determination of region are also discussed. These include: (1) the necessity of data gathering/maintenance to provide information about the region and its population, and (2) intraregional differences and interregional similarity, to provide necessary variety within and comparability between regions. In the former case, a large section is devoted to recent U.S. Census regional designations for data analysis purposes and the compatability of the new Census Metropolitan Statistical Areas (MSAs) and the regions of this report.

The procedures used in determining housing regions for New Jersey are outlined in the next section of the chapter and the resultant regions, consisting of two-to-four counties each, are derived. Six regions within the State of New Jersey are presented which emphasize the above characteristics relating to journey-to-work, data maintenance and intraregional diversity/interregional similarity. These regions are described in terms of general socioeconomic characteristics of their overall populations as well as the physical characteristics of the land use within their bounds. An appendix to this chapter compares the regions developed here with regional delineations which exist in the state for purposes other than housing. The point made in this final section is that New Jersey is no stranger to regions, and the regions delimited here for housing are not particularly dissimilar to other regions constructed for purposes such as water supply, transportation, labor markets, etc.

THE CONCEPT OF REGION

A region is a broad homogeneous geographic area which takes form according to the substantive nature of its concern.[2] Its outer edges are composed of territorial boundaries which define the uniqueness of whatever is contained within its bounds and its shape varies according to what is being territorially described.[3] Thus, regions vary by purpose -- a water supply region may differ slightly in size and scope from a housing market delineation and both may depart from areas joined by similar transportation dependency.

The definitional choice of region could further depend on the emphasis of the discipline brought to bear upon it. Thus, geographers may prefer physical similarities in defining a region while economists might stress economic interdependence. The wide range of focus and emphasis has been noted, among many others[4], by regional scientist, Walter Isard, who observed that:[5]

> Any selection of a set of regions for specific nongeneral research must be related to the problems to be studied. (emphasis added)

A similar opinion was expressed in naturalist, Vincent Ostrom's observation that:[6]

> The definition of the scope of any particular region will vary with each set of functions being considered. (emphasis added)

Not only is a region reflective of the subject matter necessary to be categorized, it is clear that there may be necessary adjustments to regional delineations reflecting future monitoring of regions with data. The Federal Housing Administration (FHA) in its work on market analysis techniques for housing, outlines this dilemma when it states:[7]

> In conducting any market analysis, a compromise is made between the idealistic and the practical aspects of delineating the housing market area with a view to determining the boundaries which will constitute the most reasonable and useful market area from the standpoint of the availability of data consistent with analytical requirements, having due regard for

adjustments that can be made in available data to serve this objective most satisfactorily. (emphasis added)

Thus, a region reflects the discipline and subject matter that is seeking it, as well as the realities of future data aggregation and presentation.

WHAT IS A HOUSING REGION?

The Federal Housing Administration (FHA) has defined a housing market region or area as "the geographic entity within which non-farm dwelling units are in mutual competition."[8] Ernest and Robert Fisher, who have written several texts on real estate, have an essentially similar definition:[9]

> The extent of a [housing-real estate] market is defined by the area over which units in the standing stock are assumed to be substituted for one another.

Another almost identical definition has been suggested by housing economist Charles Abrams, who referred to a housing market area as:[10]

> The geographic area within which dwelling units are closely substitutable for one another -- that is, which contain all the units that are likely to be considered potential housing accommodations by the resident population.

However, there are no hard and fast rules for determining whether or not housing units are competing with one another. The FHA, for example, has admitted that:[11]

> A technique is not available to determine the exact points at which specific dwelling units are just beyond the range of competition with other units so that the precise limits can be established for delineating the housing market area.

Even the definition of competition could be clearer. Professor William Grigsby, of the University of Pennsylvania, who has conducted multiple studies of the Philadelphia housing market, has pointed out that all housing units within a metropolitan area are linked directly or indirectly in a competition matrix, yet how this is measured eludes exact specification.[12]

Journey-to-Work as a Determinant Of the Housing Region

There is widespread consensus that the length of the journey-to-work has a major influence on the purchase or rental of a dwelling unit and thus the definition of a housing region. Studies have varied from those who contend that residents seek to minimize travel costs to those that argue the goal is to seek an optimum trade-off between travel and housing costs.[13] One study, for example, noted that the most important determinant of the individual's residential choice is the travel or distance from his income earning function, i.e., job or business.[14] Similarly, the FHA has observed that the location of actual and prospective employment centers and the availability of transportation facilities are among the major considerations in the location choice of the working population.[15] The Fishers, as well as Charles Abrams, have also concurred that the most important factor in analyzing a local housing market is journey-to-work.[16] An early planning report was even more emphatic:[17]

> The journey-to-work is a test of the urban layout; excessive costs and hardships of daily traveling can be taken as a symptom that something is wrong with the form of the town or conurbation.

Empirical support for the above contentions can be found in a 1964 survey conducted by University of Michigan's Survey Research Center.[18] Of the sample population studied, 56 percent said that living close to the head of the household's place of work was important; of this group more than one-half felt this to be a very important factor in deciding where to live (see Exhibit 1-1). In terms of specific groups, the accessibility to head of household's workplace was rated as an important consideration by more than 60 percent of both single respondents and childless couples, almost 60 percent of female married respondents, and more than one-half of the male married respondents.

Other surveys have revealed similar findings. A 1967 survey conducted by the Oakland Tribune,[19] for example, indicated that nearness to work was the single most important consideration in selecting housing.

There continues to be occasional small scale studies on desired journey-to-work and journey-to work as it relates to housing.[20] The inclusion of information in the Decennial Census and the Annual Housing Survey on distance/time to work of household heads since 1970 moved much of the discussion of journey-to-work from desired travel times to actual travel times.[21] By this time it was generally accepted that the importance of the work trip in determining household location offered the key element for defining the criterion of mutual competition of housing units, and thus was the prime consideration for delimiting housing regions. By developing planning procedures for calculating time and distances of journeys-to-work, housing regions could be constructed largely on the basis of travel times at peak morning and evening work-trip periods.

EXHIBIT 1-1

IMPORTANCE OF BEING CLOSE TO ONE'S PLACE OF WORK
(Results in Percentages)

At the time of the most recent move, being close to head's (of household) place of work was:

Respondent Group	Very Important (%)	Somewhat Important (%)	Made No Difference; Not Important (%)	Total (%)	Number of Responses
All	32	24	44	100	370
Single, married without children	44	17	39	100	143
Married, with children	24	30	46	100	213
Male married	27	25	48	100	143
Female married	33	26	41	100	150

Source: John Lansing and Eva Mueller, with Nancy Barth, Residential Location and Urban Mobility (Ann Arbor, MI: Survey Research Center, Institute for Social Research, The University of Michigan, 1964), p. 41.

How Far the Journey-to-Work?

The determination of planning standards for work trips is largely judgmental. Two basic ingredients in deriving such a standard are the distances and times people actually travel, and the verbalized preferences of people regarding work-trip length. In the case of the former, in early journey-to-work analyses, the dimension of comparison was always distance. Studies were concerned with road or rail miles from the employment site. It quickly became apparent, however, that to elicit a more clear-cut measure of the real cost (i.e., sacrifice) of the journey-to-work, the dimension of time had to be added. Thus, an individual traveling 30 minutes by automobile sacrifices the same amount of time as another individual opting for a 30-minute trip on a different mode of transit or on foot even though actual distances traveled are considerably different.

New Jersey, for instance, is famous in the journey-to-work literature for post-World War II studies of employment-related, time distance.[22] The purpose of this type of analysis was to view the possibility of extra defense effort which might be gleaned from decreased work-residence commuting time. The philosophy of the New Jersey study as one of several of the period, is cited in an early ASPO Planning Advisory Service Report:[23]

> If we think back to the previous war we can recall instances in which industrial plants were located with little or no reference to the source of labor. This resulted in serious losses of time, which instead of being used for commuting could have been utilized productively in the war effort.

A mid-1960s University of Michigan study revealed that one-half (median) of the families surveyed considered 32 minutes the maximum time they wished to travel.[24] (The exact findings of this study are indicated in Exhibit 1-2.) Similarly, 77 percent of the respondents in the 1967 Oakland newspaper survey cited earlier, expressed their unwillingness to com-

EXHIBIT 1-2

JOURNEY-TO-WORK TIME LIMITS OF RECENT MOVERS
(Results in Percentages)

Travel Time (in minutes)	Limits Given by Those Who Moved Recently Who Had Established Commuting Time Limits (%)	Actual Time Spent Getting to Work by All Those Who Moved Recently (%)
1-4	*	1
5-9	5	12
10-14	7	12
15-19	20	20
20-29	14	17
30-44	42	23
45-59	6	9
60 or more	6	6
TOTAL (%)	100	100
Median	32 min.	23 min.
Number of journeys to work	119	312

*Less than one-half of one percent.

Source: John Lansing, Residential Location and Urban Mobility: The Second Wave of Interviews (University of Michigan, Survey Research Center, 1966).

mute more than 30 minutes to work. More recent literature continues to confirm that most people do not wish to travel more than about one-half hour to their job or that residential satisfaction peaks at the one-half hour commute time.[25]

From 1970 to 1980 Census trends, including specialized reports in the interim Census years, it appears that the average journey-to-work is decreasing slightly for most Americans. Possibly due to the Interstate System-beltways offering improved access, and the movement of employment out of central cities, the time of journey-to-work is also decreasing.

The 1980 Census of Population indicates that the average (mean) distance to work was about 12 miles among householders, while the average travel time was approximately 24 minutes (Exhibit 1-3). The latter is down 7 percent from 1970. The figures for New Jersey are 12 miles and 25 minutes, respectively, and also are below those of 1970.[26]

An interesting paradox exists in the journey-to-work literature. This concerns a "burdensome" journey-to-work versus the travel time of most households. A burdensome commute is defined by FHA Techniques of Housing Market Analysis as greater than one hour.[27] The Journey-to-Work Division of the Bureau of the Census suggests that a "burdensome" commute might be empirically isolated as the point in a commuting distribution where there is a significant break in who does/does not commute that far or for that long.[28] Exhibit 1-3 indicates that the "burdensome" commute might well be at the 30-mile or 45-minute level. Thus, what is believed to be a burdensome commute from both of these sources is approximately double the time/distance experience of most American households. While a one-half hour traveling time "standard" is working its way into the planning literature, its origin reflects the outer range of the time that the majority of Americans actually spend traveling to work. This figure remains significantly smaller than what is deemed burdensome by several sources.

In terms of the mode of trips that contribute to average travel time calculations, it is clear that the automobile dominates. Despite the escalating costs of owning and operating a vehicle, just under two out of every three American workers (16 years old and over) in 1980, drove to work as the sole occupant of an automobile or truck. In addition, another 20 percent carpooled. When these figures are combined, 84 percent of all workers relied totally or in part on an automobile or truck to get to work. Just over 6 percent use public transportation (almost all bus), 5.6 percent walk, 1.6 percent use bicycle/motorcycle or other means, while 2.3 percent work at home.[29]

Metropolitan origins and destinations are also important in the trip time calculation. The majority of workers are now lateral commuters, i.e., they both live and work in the suburbs. With jobs moving to the suburbs and with exurban, non-metropolitan areas serving as prospective residences, the journey-to-work time in non-metropolitan areas has decreased and now is the

EXHIBIT 1-3

DISTANCE AND TRAVEL TIME TO WORK - UNITED STATES SUMMARY, 1975-1979

DISTANCE TO WORK: 1975-79

Distance to work	1975	1976	1977	1978	1979
Total	49,251	50,347	51,699	53,357	54,104
Work at home	1,597	1,324	1,343	1,315	1,261
No fixed place of work	5,099	5,634	5,998	6,098	6,316
Distance not reported	541	782	589	1,024	1,042
Reporting distance to work	42,014	42,607	43,769	44,922	45,485
Percent	100.0	100.0	100.0	100.0	100.0
Less than 1 mile	10.7	9.7	9.9	9.9	9.6
1-4 miles	31.6	31.2	31.5	26.6	26.9
5-9 miles	20.6	20.5	20.1	23.1	23.1
10-29 miles	30.9	32.1	32.0	33.7	33.6
30-49 miles	4.7	4.9	4.9	5.2	5.3
50 miles or more	1.5	1.6	1.6	1.6	1.5
Mean	11.1	12.3	11.4	11.9	11.9

Note: (for the United States: 1979. Reference persons with a job the week prior to interview. Numbers in thousands)

TRAVEL TIME TO WORK: 1975-79

Travel time to work	1975	1976	1977	1978	1979
Total	49,251	50,347	51,699	53,357	54,104
Work at home	1,597	1,324	1,343	1,315	1,261
No fixed place of work	5,099	5,634	5,998	6,098	6,316
Travel time not reported	388	611	366	469	487
Reporting travel time	42,167	42,778	43,992	45,477	46,040
Percent	100.0	100.0	100.0	100.0	100.0
Less than 15 minutes	36.7	36.8	37.0	35.9	36.3
15-29 minutes	35.1	36.2	36.3	36.8	36.5
30-44 minutes	16.8	16.2	15.8	16.1	16.0
45-59 minutes	6.0	5.7	5.7	5.7	5.7
60 minutes or more	5.4	5.2	5.2	5.5	5.4
Mean	24.2	23.9	23.8	24.2	24.1

Source: The Journey-to-Work in the United States: 1979. U.S. Department of Commerce, Bureau of Census, Series P-23, No. 122, 1982.

shortest of all. Beltway and Interstate commuters outside the fringes of metropolitan areas may travel longer distances than their urban counterparts but do so in less time. Those who live outside developed areas have journeys-to-work of 14 miles, yet the trip, on average, takes only 20 minutes.[30]

In sum, the journey-to-work has become a key determinant of the size and shape of the housing market. In terms of dominance, the journey-to-work has become associated with both the automobile and with intra-metropolitan trips. Those in the labor force desire and for the most part achieve work trips of a distance that requires 30 minutes or less of travel time one way.

THE JOURNEY-TO-WORK AND THE HOUSING REGION

Housing sub-regions related to journey-to-work have historically been constructed using travel times on various categories of roads during prime commuting periods. The first formal procedure for the accomplishment of this was published by the American Society of Planning Officials in 1951, following planner-economist, J.D. Carroll's work on journey-to-work analysis and its importance to planning.[31] Points on roads outward from an employment center representing travel times would be connected to each other in the same fashion as if one were to weave together points in the spokes of a wheel (see Exhibit 1-4). These zones of potential residence, emanating outward from the center of an employment zone, would take on an amoeba-like form as various gradations of roadways (collectors, arterials, freeways, etc.) would allow different distances to be traveled for the same travel time. The "isotime zones," as they were called, represented an estimate of all places accessible from the employment center within the time specified on the outer edge of the zone. These were termed local markets or sub-markets.[32]

While this procedure may have gained acceptance for the delineation of a sub-market, clearly for data presentation purposes a more recognizable and permanent market area had to be constructed. The market area, while keyed to journey-to-work, had to take into account the availability of employment data to isolate centers of employment. Historically, this was available only on a county basis in the form of County Business Patterns, an annual tabulation of jobs by category in the United States published by the U.S. Department of Commerce.[33] Recognizing the expanding scope of the market, FHA Techniques of Housing Market Analysis lists the prerequisites for housing market delineation:[34]

> The location of actual and prospective employment centers and the availability of transportation facilities of all types underlie the selection of general locational alternative as places of residence for the working population.

EXHIBIT 1-4

THE USE OF ISO-TIME ZONES IN JOURNEY TO WORK CALCULATIONS TO ESTABLISH HOUSING REGIONS

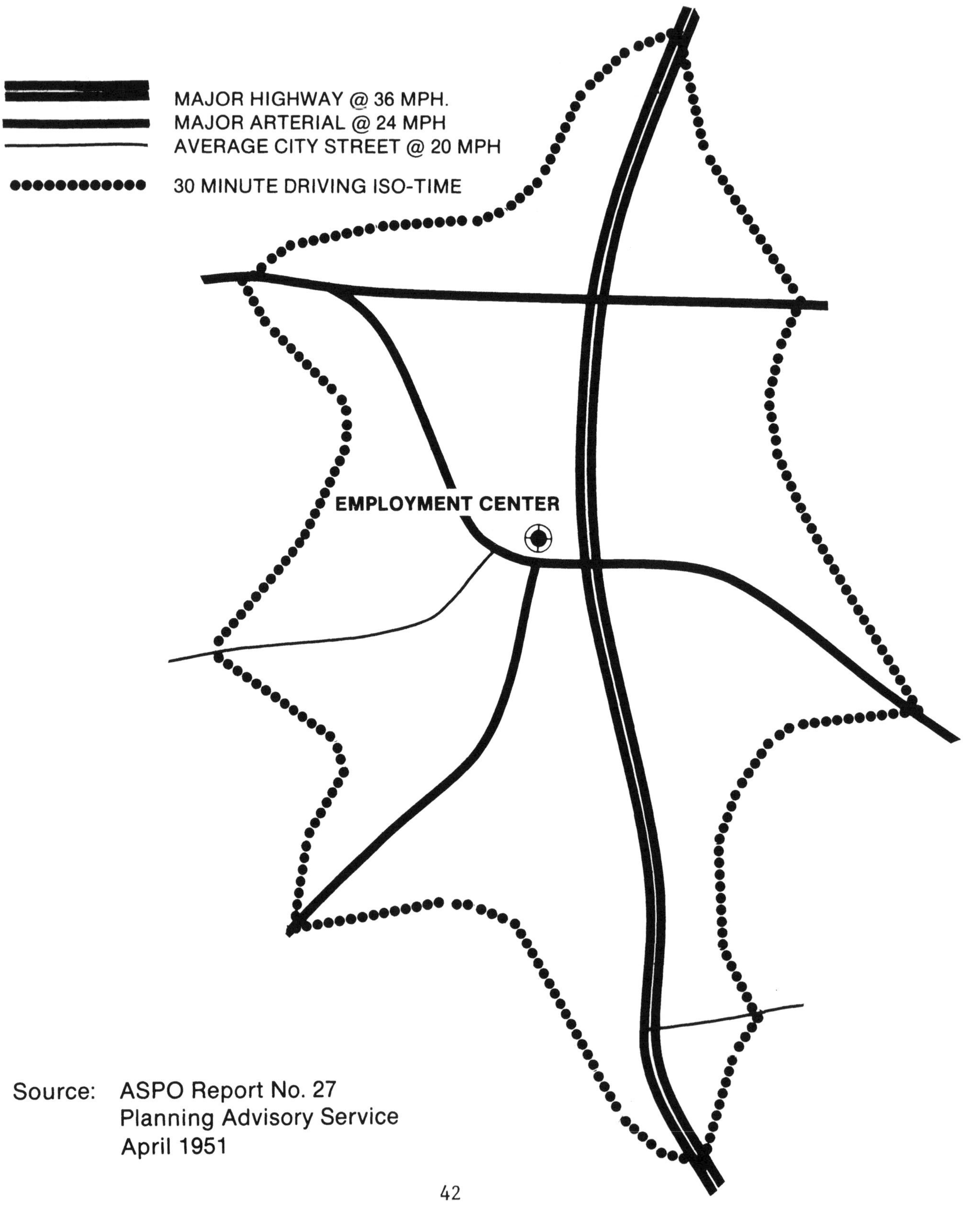

Source: ASPO Report No. 27
Planning Advisory Service
April 1951

The housing market area usually extends beyond city limits regardless of the magnitude of the market under consideration. In the larger markets, the market area may extend into several adjoining counties through the outward growth of the primary metropolitan area.

The actual delineation of a housing market area and submarket areas is determined primarily by Census area definitions.

Another final consideration in delimiting a housing market is the ability to conduct a "top-down" analysis with a finite set of components and with a set of numbers that sum to a total. Thus in Chapter 1, the introduction to FHA Techniques of Housing Market Analysis, one of the purposes stated for deriving the set of techniques contained therein was a need for "comprehensive and integrated market information focused on broad housing market considerations rather than on specific site, property, and neighborhood considerations." In Chapter 2, "Housing Market Area," the FHA describes the overall housing market as generally the Metropolitan Statistical Area which may be adjusted slightly with justification. Chapter 2 also notes that the problem with submarket delineation is that it is less reliable and less preferable. This results not from the delineation process itself, but subsequently in the analytical considerations, because of the greater paucity of data and the greater difficulty of making reliable projections for small areas.[35]

A "top-down" view of housing regions is clearly essential. Only in this way is it possible to view the plausibility of individual attempts at housing production. This is done within the context of a threshold number for demand in the region where production is being attempted, as well as, within demand figures for an even larger area, i.e., possibly for the state as a whole.

A variety of creative attempts may be offered to specify region but whatever the effort at regional delineation, the resultant geographic area must be derived so that this region, together with others, may be summed to a whole.[36] Housing regions must be viewed not only in terms of balance within regions but also balance across regions. An instance of housing production in one locale must allow for the possibility of an equally rational settlement in another, without either interfering with each other or "borrowing from"/"skipping" one-another's region.[37] A region selected, for instance, as one county or ten counties in a state of 21 counties must be fully aware of the market dynamics in the remaining 20 or 11 counties, respectively. If this is not done, the regional delineation falls short. Further, in selecting regions of the type mentioned above, if either a small or large region ignores journey-to-work as the binding force of the area, again the regional delineation is most likely less than adequate.

Thus, major considerations in determining housing regions are journey-to-work, comparability with data available by geographic area and finite integrated areas which may be viewed in terms of an identifiable set of numbers.

HOUSING MARKET SEGMENTATION - FACTORS OTHER THAN GEOGRAPHICAL LOCATION AFFECTING HOUSING SUBMARKETS

It is not sufficient solely to understand the physical or territorial aspects of a housing market as the geographically delineated housing market may itself be segregated into various subgroupings. Housing market segmentation, while it does not alter significantly geographical delineations, impacts on housing choice and thus the shape of the housing market. Housing units are not infinitely interchangeable. They vary in fundamental attributes of price, type, size, tenure, construction and design. In addition, since housing units are situated within political subdivisions, selection of a particular housing unit usually implies selection of a given municipal address. This location, in turn, connotes attributes of neighborhood quality, municipal taxes and services, schools, aesthetics, social status, and lifestyle considerations. Since the selection of residence in proximity to workplace may be only the first in a series of choices for a household, all of the above factors enter into the process whereby a household enters the market and competes for available housing.[38]

This complexity of housing characteristics raises several elements critical to the process of residential selection. First, households often must trade off their preferences for housing unit attributes in selecting a dwelling: few households, if any, are able to realize <u>all</u> of their expectations and preferences regarding the ideal housing unit. Thus, space may be sacrificed for a more favorable tenure option (rent or own), or unit quality or amenities may be sacrificed for a more affordable price. The multiplicity of housing unit attributes forces households to select a smaller number of key features that are particularly important for that household.

Second, the specific housing unit attributes weighted most heavily by a given household are likely to be a function of the household's reason for moving in the first place. A household moving because of a job transfer will select a house based on proximity to the new job. Once this is satisfied, a household may move because the addition of a new family member may make the previous residence inadequate in size. This family, also part of the housing market, will be primarily motivated by the size and interior layout of the new dwelling. Further, a household moving due to dissatisfaction with neighborhood quality or services may seek a new residence that most specifically satisfies these requirements. This family is also part of the market. In short, the reasons influencing selection of a new residence are closely related to the household's reason for moving.

Research evidence from a wide variety of sources reveals the relative importance of housing unit attributes as factors influencing selection of a dwelling unit. According to Peter Rossi's classic study, <u>Why Families Move</u>,[39] once journey-to-work and general affordability considerations have been realized, space attributes of the dwelling unit represent the single most important element in selecting a residence. Thus, the number of rooms and bedrooms, and the overall size of the unit, represent a critical element for many households engaged in the search for housing. This finding may be expected since a change in household size -- an increase or decrease in the number of family members -- represents the most frequent factor causing households to move and seek a new residence.

Following space requirements in frequency as a determinant of housing unit selection, are factors pertaining to the interior design and layout of the dwelling unit and structure. Both structure type (single-family, garden apartment, multifamily high rise, etc.) and interior specifications of the unit ranked high in Rossi's study as determinants of dwelling unit selection, almost equal in frequency to the importance of size of the unit.

The third element cited by homeseekers when selecting a housing unit pertains to particular locational requirements, independent of journey-to-work considerations. That is, homeseekers often have a specific submarket location, i.e. a certain community or neighborhood in mind when they set out to select a new residence within acceptable time-distance relationships to employment. This category of micro-locational attribute subsumes a variety of considerations that, however, are closely associated in space. For instance, location encompasses the quality of municipal services as well as the socioeconomic or lifestyle characteristics of neighbors. As both of these factors often tend to be highly correlated with income and thus clustered spatially, homeseekers can often satisfy a variety of locational requirements simultaneously.

Fourth in importance, according to Rossi's analysis, are the "micro" considerations of housing cost. Thus, once a household has defined its housing needs and preferences in terms primarily of location and general affordability and secondarily, unit size, design, and neighborhood location, the household will try to maximize attainment of those needs within the constraints of housing costs. Put differently, given a household's preferences for location and affordability constraints, the household will attempt to satisfy its housing needs at the lowest possible price level. Given two units identical in regional location, general affordability, size, design, and neighborhood location, the household will tend to select the lowest-priced unit.

Finally, a critical element in housing search is that the overwhelming majority of residential movers, move over a relatively short distance. This suggests that the best predictor of the location of a new residence is the location of the previous residence. The short average distance of residential moves reflects several factors. Perhaps most important is the element of familiarity. Familiarity breeds local ties: friends and relatives tend to be located nearby, and one is knowledgeable about local services, shopping, transportation, and other neighborhood facilities. In addition, familiarity with an area makes it more likely that a household will become aware of residences that come on the market, and therefore will be in a better position to obtain that unit, relative to a household moving over a longer distance. Thirdly, the short distance of most residential moves is explained by the fact that most changes of residence entail lateral moves within the same socioeconomic stratum, rather than upward or downward mobility across socioeconomic levels.

In sum, while indeed the prime rationale of housing market construction relates to a linkage of place of residence and place of employment, housing submarkets are characterized by residential moves that represent an adjustment of housing unit attributes (primarily size and type) to satisfy changing household needs, and most such moves take place within the same social/geographic area. These households come largely from the "natural increase" portion of housing market demand and are an active part of the local housing market.

CONSTRUCTING NEW JERSEY HOUSING REGIONS

The linkage of housing regions and journey to work has been discussed in the previous section. It is now necessary to use this criterion to prescribe housing regions for New Jersey. The procedure employed consists of several steps. Initially, it is necessary to group counties which evidence strong commuting linkages between themselves and other counties. Once grouped according to pre-specified matching criteria, it is then necessary to attempt to maximize within region differences and across region similarities of income and housing characteristics. The following sections detail the statistical procedures used to carry out these objectives.

The Initial Grouping by Journey to Work Linkages

Information on journey-to-work for New Jersey counties may be obtained from the 1980 Census, Public Use Sample (File A) for New Jersey; this is a five percent sample of all New Jersey households.[40] Information is available on times traveled one-way to work (in minutes) for all those employed in households as of April 1980. Also a part of the data set, is origin and destination of the worktrip. The information to be used in the initial grouping procedure concerns worktrip origin and destination. This information is used only at the county level, i.e., for each employed member of the household, worktrip county of origin and county of destination. All modes of travel are included: automobile, bus, rail and miscellaneous (walking, biking, etc.).

Information is available for only nineteen subsets of the state; in two instances (Warren/Hunterdon and Cape May/Salem) the data of two counties has to be joined as they are too small (county populations below 100,000) to be reported individually. In all subsequent analyses any regional grouping of counties always contains these two sets of counties appearing as one.

The program chosen to group counties is the CLUSTER procedure from the Statistical Analysis System (SAS) package.[41] CLUSTER is a grouping procedure designed to help identify groups of observations that have similar attributes. It partitions the data into a smaller number of groups such that data units belonging to one group are "similar" in a certain sense, while data units belonging to different groups are "dissimilar" in the same sense. The procedure is dependent upon "distance" (value separation) between variables. It is unique in that it assumes no conceptual associations or distance values a priori. CLUSTER computes its own distance matrix and standardizes the matrix across the data set.

Certain controls are placed on the grouping mechanism. Counties that could be grouped based on similar commuting ties have to be contiguous. In addition, no less than two nor more than five counties are allowed to cluster as part of any group. The lower threshold is to insure that no single county appeared "leftover"; the upper threshold was chosen to avoid large commuting distances within any one identified region. In the case of the lower threshold, the non-single county criterion also supports the Mount Laurel I definition of what is minimally acceptable to the Court as a region, i.e., more than one county.

The initial grouping of counties produces groups of the following composition:

GROUP 1	GROUP 2	GROUP 3	GROUP 4
Bergen	Essex	Middlesex	Monmouth
Passaic	Morris	Somerset	Ocean
Hudson	Union		

GROUP 5	GROUP 6	GROUP 7
Camden	Atlantic	Hunterdon
Gloucester	Cape May	Warren
Burlington	Cumberland	Sussex
Mercer	Salem	

Group 1 shows particularly strong commuting linkages between Bergen*/Passaic Counties and Hudson/Bergen Counties and less so, between Passaic/Hudson Counties.

Group 2 shows strong commuting linkages between Union/Essex Counties, Morris/Essex Counties, and less so, between Union/Morris Counties.

---

*The county specified before the "slash" is place of work; after the slash is place of residence. This format has meaning only within this section. Only the major commuting linkages are mentioned.

Group 3 shows significant commuting between Middlesex/Somerset Counties.

Group 4 evidences similar heavy commuting between Monmouth/Ocean Counties.

Group 5 shows the heaviest commuting between Burlington/Camden Counties, Camden/Gloucester Counties and Mercer/Burlington Counties. Commuting ties are less in evidence between Gloucester and the two northern counties or between Mercer and the two southern counties.

Group 6 shows strong commuting ties between Atlantic/Cape May-Salem Counties and Cape May-Salem/Cumberland Counties. Less strong commuting ties are in evidence between Atlantic/Cumberland Counties.

Group 7 is joined together as a residual because Warren County unites with Hunterdon County due to data unavailability and as such, prevents Hunterdon County from joining the Somerset County group. Further, since there are some ties between Sussex and Warren Counties, yet almost none between Warren and Morris Counties, Warren County does not allow Sussex to join the Morris County group.

In all cases, the commuting ties between counties of these groups are stronger among each other than between a single county of the group and another group as a whole. There may be selected instances where a single county of one group is related more intensely to a single adjacent county of another group than to members of its own group; yet overall, there are usually weaker commuting ties with the other group as a whole. The above listings provide the first sort of constituent New Jersey counties along commuting lines.

Refining the Grouping by Difference/ Similarity Characteristics

In addition to maximizing the journey-to-work linkage of areas, it is further desired that when the areas are finally joined, they each evidence some socioeconomic variation within them. It is obvious that the State of New Jersey is very different from north to south and also from east to west, and any regional grouping is bound to be characterized by these interregional differences. Yet, to the degree possible, differences within regions (intraregional) are also desired.

In order to achieve this, another grouping program is employed. The procedure chosen here is the Fortran Program H-GROUP.[42] H-GROUP compares a series of score profiles over a series of variables, and progressively associates the profiles into groupings in such a way as to minimize the variation of the profiles within clusters.

The program uses a generalized distance function based on the concept of an error function which it normally attempts to minimize. H-GROUP is a unique program in that it easily may be adjusted to perform exactly the opposite procedure, i.e., associate members into groupings that are dissimilar along a set of variables. This is done by associating members of a group that are characterized by a maximum error function. The variables used to view dissimilarity within regions are:

Income:	% below poverty level Median Income % above $50,000
Housing Costs:	Rent (Median) of Rental Units Value (Median) of Owned Units Owner Costs (Median) of Owned Units
Housing Quality:	% Units built pre-1950 % Units Crowded (>1.01 persons/room)

Controls are also applied to this grouping mechanism. Commuting ties of the new groupings have to equal or exceed those of previous groupings. In addition, grouped counties have to be contiguous, and assembled groups can not be less than two nor exceed five counties.

The dissimilar grouping program allows Hunterdon/Warren Counties to join the Middlesex-Somerset County grouping and Sussex County to join the Essex-Union-Morris County grouping. Thus produced are the following six groupings of counties:

GROUP 1	GROUP 2	GROUP 3	GROUP 4	GROUP 5	GROUP 6
Bergen	Essex	Hunterdon	Monmouth	Burlington	Atlantic
Hudson	Morris	Middlesex	Ocean	Camden	Cape May
Passaic	Sussex	Somerset		Gloucester	Cumberland
	Union	Warren		Mercer	Salem

Maximum similarity across groups is also attempted. Here the H-GROUP Program is used in its unaltered state across the variable set specified previously. Controls emphasized are as follows: maintaining commuting linkages, two county minimum/five county maximum groupings, the contiguousness of grouped counties, and within-group dissimilarity. The program specifies a search of all existing county groups to potentially produce another set of groupings. This set of groupings, in addition to maintaining the above specifications, would allow one county to be traded between groups for another county which might enhance across-group similarity. With the controls specified, the former grouping of the state's counties into six groups of 2-4 counties each, remains intact. More similar groups cannot be found that also meet the control criteria. Thus, the county groups are finalized and given the geographic labels as indicated in Exhibit 1-5. The following section discusses the commuting patterns within these now established housing "regions."

Work Trips and Commuting Times Within Established Mount Laurel Regions

The true regional nature of the geographic areas assembled as regions is apparent from Exhibit 1-6. This exhibit presents the percent of residents living in one of the counties of the region that work within the region as opposed to working elsewhere. It also includes those who work out of state. Clearly, 70 to 80 percent of those who live in one of the region's counties, work within the region. There is an obvious break in the distribution of the data which defines this strong resolution of place of work and place of residence and contains the worktrip within a single region.

In the northern two regions there is some slight worktrip spillover to one another. In the Northeast Region 1 there is also some commuting from Bergen and Hudson Counties out of state, primarily to New York. The West Central Region 3 evidences slight losses to the Northwest Region 2, particularly those residents of Somerset County who travel to jobs in Morris County. The same is true for a small share of Monmouth and Ocean County residents who work in Essex (Newark) and Union (Elizabeth) counties. Residents of the Southwest Region 5 commute significantly within region, except for some share of Camden, Gloucester and Burlington residents that commute out of state to Philadelphia. The South-Southwest Region 6 is characterized by almost total within-region worktrips. Reflecting these patterns of worktrips, the average journey-to-work time in the State of New Jersey, including those who commute out of state, is 24.6 minutes.

In Exhibit 1-7, the analysis is taken one step further. In this exhibit, out-of-state commuters are removed from the sample and the travel patterns of in-state workers are exclusively viewed. There is a further comparison of those households of Mount Laurel income* versus all households (of any income) in the state. As a point of reference, when out-of-state commuters are removed, the average journey-to-work for those who commute anywhere in the State of New Jersey is reduced to approximately 21 minutes. This is true for the whole population as well as for the Mount Laurel component.

Given the regions as specified, over 85 percent of the workers of all households and over 88 percent of workers of Mount Laurel households live

*Households of Mount Laurel income specifications -- 50-80 percent of regional median household income and <50 percent of regional median household income. (See next chapter for actual definition.)

EXHIBIT 1-5
THE MOUNT LAUREL HOUSING REGION COUNTY GROUPS

Region 1 - Northeast

Bergen
Hudson
Passaic

Region 2 - Northwest

Essex
Morris
Sussex
Union

Region 3 - West Central

Hunterdon
Middlesex
Somerset
Warren

Region 4 - East Central

Monmouth
Ocean

Region 5 - Southwest

Burlington
Camden
Gloucester
Mercer

Region 6 - South-Southwest

Atlantic
Cape May
Cumberland
Salem

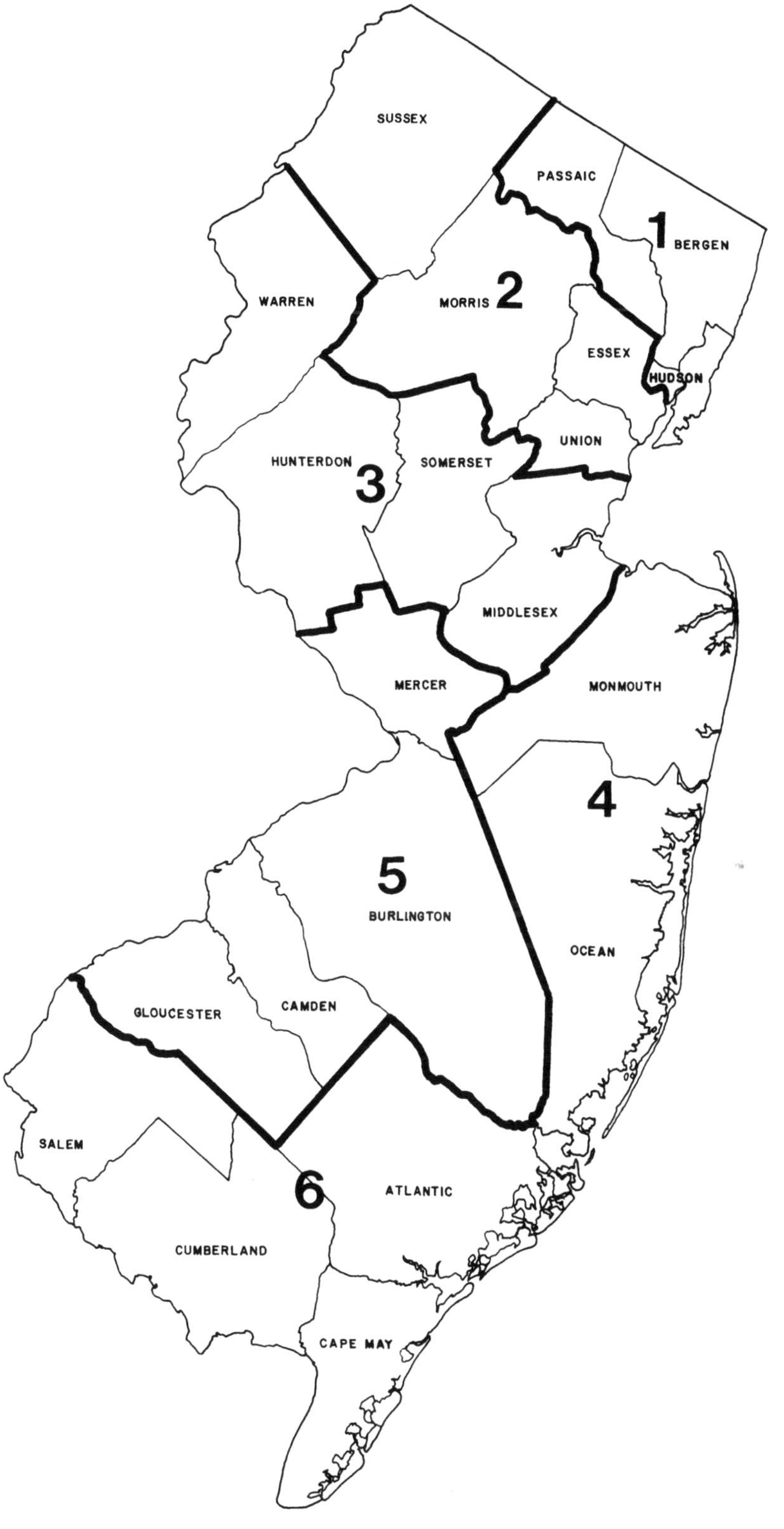

Source: RUTGERS UNIVERSITY Center for Urban Policy Research, Winter, 1983

EXHIBIT 1-6

PERCENTAGES OF RESIDENTS LIVING IN SPECIFIED COUNTIES
WORKING IN SPECIFIED REGIONS

WORK IN REGION:	LIVE IN COUNTY: Bergen	Passaic	Hudson	Essex	Union	Morris	Sussex	Middlesex	Somerset	Hunterdon-Warren	Monmouth	Ocean	Camden	Gloucester	Burlington	Mercer	Atlantic	Cumberland	Cape May-Salem
Northeast Region 1	74	81	72	11	4	11	12	3	2	1	3	2	0	0	0	0	0	0	0
Northwest Region 2	6	13	10	79	78	77	77	15	18	11	7	7	0	0	0	1	0	0	0
West Central Region 3	1	1	1	3	11	5	4	70	72	76	9	6	0	0	1	7	0	0	0
East Central Region 4	0	0	0	0	0	0	0	2	0	0	71	76	0	0	1	1	0	0	0
Southwest Region 5	0	0	0	0	0	0	0	2	4	4	2	5	73	72	81	84	4	4	7
South-Southwest Region 6	0	0	0	0	0	0	0	0	0	0	0	2	2	9	1	0	93	95	86
Out-of-State	20	5	17	7	6	6	7	7	4	7	9	4	24	19	16	7	3	1	7
Total	100	100	100	100	100	100	100	100	100	100	100	100	100	100	100	100	100	100	100

*Numbers may not add to 100 due to rounding.

Source: U.S. Census of Population and Housing, 1980. New Jersey Public Use Sample.

EXHIBIT 1-7

TRAVEL TIMES AND RESIDENCY PERCENTAGES OF NEW JERSEY RESIDENTS

	Northeast Region 1	Northwest Region 2	West Central Region 3	East Central Region 4	Southwest Region 5	South-Southwest Region 6	Total
Percentages of Workers Who Work and Live in the Same Region							
All Households	86.9	81.4	80.6	94.8	93.2	90.6	85.5
Mount Laurel Households	89.6	83.6	81.2	95.2	95.0	90.5	88.2
Average Travel Times of Workers Who Work and Live in New Jersey (Any Region)							
All Households	20.7	23.7	20.9	18.3	19.4	19.3	21.0
Mount Laurel Households	20.2	23.9	20.0	19.4	19.4	20.1	21.0
Average Travel Times of Workers Who Work and Live in the Same Region							
All Households	18.0	20.2	16.6	17.2	18.0	17.0	18.2
Mount Laurel Households	18.2	21.8	16.3	18.5	18.5	17.9	19.0

Source: Bureau of Census, *U.S. Census of Population and Housing*, 1980. New Jersey Public Use Sample.

and work in the same region. For Mount Laurel workers in households, the average worktrip is less than twenty minutes (19.0). The regions thus provide residence sheds for the large bulk of their labor force. They do so at very reasonable commuting times.

THE NEW CENSUS DESIGNATION OF MSAs: COMPARISONS WITH THE MOUNT LAUREL REGIONS

The following section details the new U.S. Census procedure for displaying data areally as it affects geographical regions in New Jersey. Then, Mount Laurel regions, just derived, are placed in the context of the newly-formulated, U.S. Census regions.

It is critical that regional delineation be sensitive not only to the subsequent availability of data but to that which comes from the nation's chief data source: the U.S. Census. In even the most rudimentary type of Mount Laurel analysis, the target population must be identified by income, their housing conditions assessed, and population projections made. This requires the availability of data by geographical area. Thus, FHA's statement about the inevitable parallelism between housing regions and Census regions, earlier cited, is well taken.[43] The several sections which follow detail the interrelationships between the various types of Census regions, as well as the Census regions and Mount Laurel regions.

Background

The nation's Metropolitan Statistical Areas (MSAs), formerly known as SMSAs, have been redefined to reflect the 1980 Census data. The designation of metropolitan areas originally as SMAs and later, as SMSAs has been part of U.S. Census areal data partitions since the 1950s.[44] The revised definitions of MSAs were issued by the Office of Management and Budget and took effect June 30, 1983.[45] The general concept underlying these and previous definitions is that of a geographic area consisting of a large population nucleus (a county)* together with adjacent areas (counties) having a high degree of economic and social integration.

The major purpose of the MSAs is to provide federal agencies with a common areal base in tabulating and publishing data for metropolitan areas. Data are available for individual metropolitan areas on population, housing, industry, trade, employment, payrolls and labor markets.[46] To that end, MSAs are defined in terms of counties, the smallest geographical unit for which a wide range of statistical data can be obtained.

Although MSAs are defined for statistical purposes, federal agencies have often adopted them for nonstatistical programs including some that involve allocation formulas that distribute funds to states and local areas.

---

*Formerly a city rather than county was the basic point of reference.

For example, MSA central cities with populations below 50,000 become entitlement cities for the Community Development Block Grants (CDBG) made by the Department of Housing and Urban Development.[47] Therefore, the identification of MSAs becomes an issue of great interest to local areas which would like to receive CDBG funds. Medicare reimbursement to hospitals administered by the Health Care Financing Administration is also along MSA lines. Besides providing a standard definition for federal and many state agencies, MSAs also have extensive nongovernmental applications. MSAs are used as the basis for national marketing areas; telephone rates, for instance, are often based on the defined boundaries of MSAs.

Basic Definitions

The basis of the Metropolitan Statistical Area is the defined core area. An area qualifies for recognition as an MSA in one of two ways: (1) if there is a city of at least 50,000 population, or (2) an urbanized area of at least 50,000 with a total metropolitan population of at least 100,000. Once the central city and the urbanized area are established and qualify an area as a MSA, certain other definitions come into play which establish the core or central counties as well as the outlying counties (see Exhibit 1-8). This central core must be identified in order to determine the area to which commuting from outlying counties is measured. The Census urbanized area is the basis for determining the central counties. Those counties with at least half their population in the urbanized area, or 2,500 of their population in the central city, qualify for the urban core.

Outlying counties beyond the central core are included if they have at least 15 percent commuting to central counties and they are of metropolitan character. These are counties adjacent to the central counties yet still within the metropolitan area.

The following is the stepped pattern of county inclusion in an MSA -- counties are joined to an MSA core county in terms of journey-to-work and secondarily in terms of density.[48]

Journey-to-Work	Density
1. Over 50% commuting to core county	25 persons/mi.^{2}
2. 40-50% commuting	35 persons/mi.^{2}
3. 25-40% commuting	One of three: 50 persons/mi.^{2} Urban population share 35% Significant population in U/A

EXHIBIT 1-8

COMPONENTS OF THE U.S. CENSUS METROPOLITIAN STATISTICAL AREAS (M.S.A.)

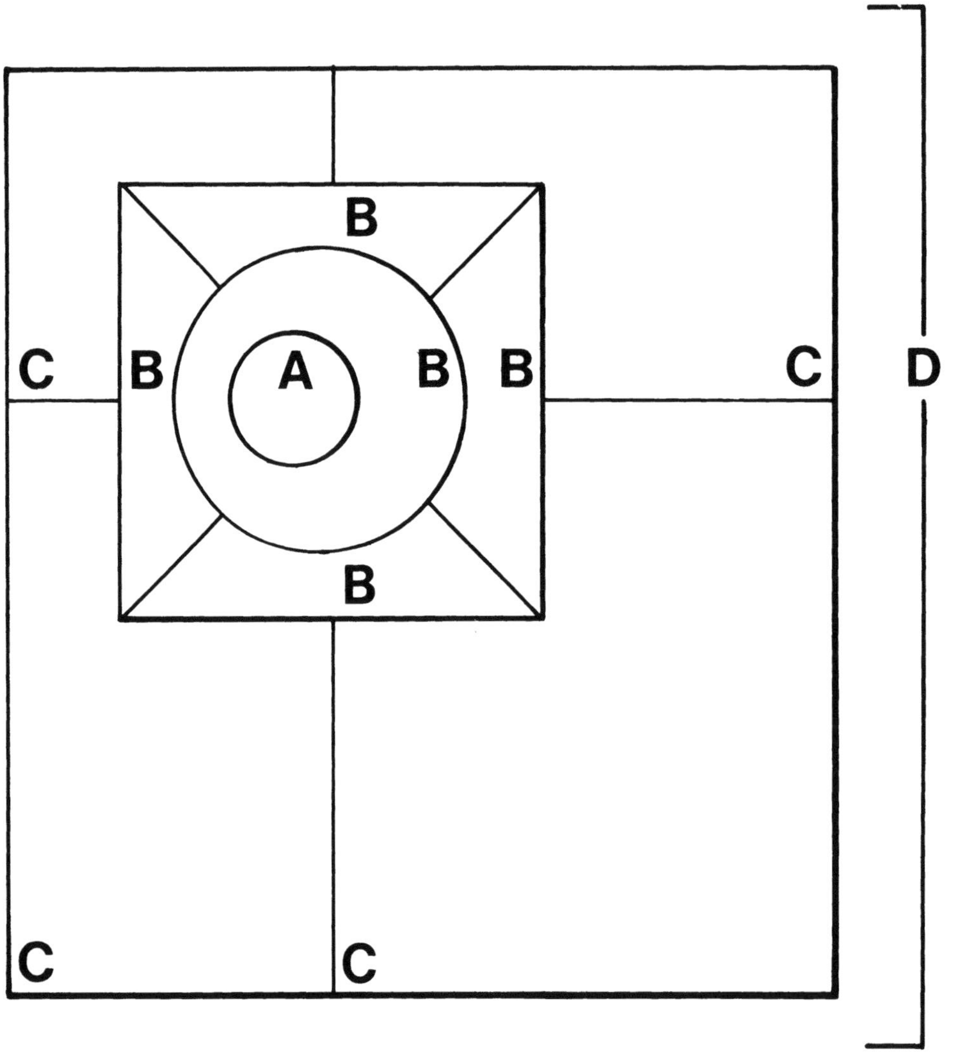

A. CENTRAL CITY
B. CENTRAL COUNTIES
C. OUTLYING COUNTIES
D. METROPOLITIAN STATISTICAL AREA

Source: Rutgers University
Center for Urban Policy Research, 1983

4. 15-25% commuting	Two of four: Above three criteria + large city

To be a central city of an MSA is also related to journey-to-work. Two criteria pertain: (1) 40 percent of the working residents of a city must work within the city; and (2) there must be 75 local jobs per 100 local working residents.

There are four levels or size categories of MSAs:

Level A	1,000,000
Level B	250,000-1,000,000
Level C	100,000-250,000
Level D	Below 100,000

For metropolitan areas greater than one million in population, a two-tier designation exists. The first is recognition of a "greater" area for comparability with other areas around the county; the second is recognition of "component" areas which have recognized local markets and their own commuting centers. A "greater" metropolitan statistical area is identified and termed a Consolidated Metropolitan Statistical Area (CMSA). This consists of one or more "component" Primary Metropolitan Statistical Areas (PMSAs) which meet prior-listed commuting, population and percent-urban criteria.

Adjustment Procedures - Special Exceptions

Local opinion was introduced in several ways. Several previously recognized SMSAs were allowed to maintain separate status as their own PMSA even if commuting patterns tied them to another PMSA. A few components of MSAs where commuting patterns were close were allowed to opt for prior existing relationships of old SMSA ties even though a slight edge in commuting patterns would place them elsewhere. Both of these "grandfathering" mechanisms pertain to the designation of several New Jersey MSAs/PMSAs.

NEW JERSEY PMSA/MSA GROUPINGS

New Jersey MSAs and PMSAs are shown in Exhibits 1-9 and 1-10. These Census designations of region are presented graphically by themselves in Exhibit 1-9 and are compared with the Mount Laurel Regions in Exhibit 1-10.

New Jersey is the first metropolitan state, i.e., the first to have all of its geographic area in one type of metropolitan designation or another.[49] New Jersey is covered for the most part by two large CMSAs:

EXHIBIT 1-9

NEW JERSEY METROPOLITAN STATISTICAL AREAS WITHIN MOUNT LAUREL REGIONS - GRAPHIC SUMMARY

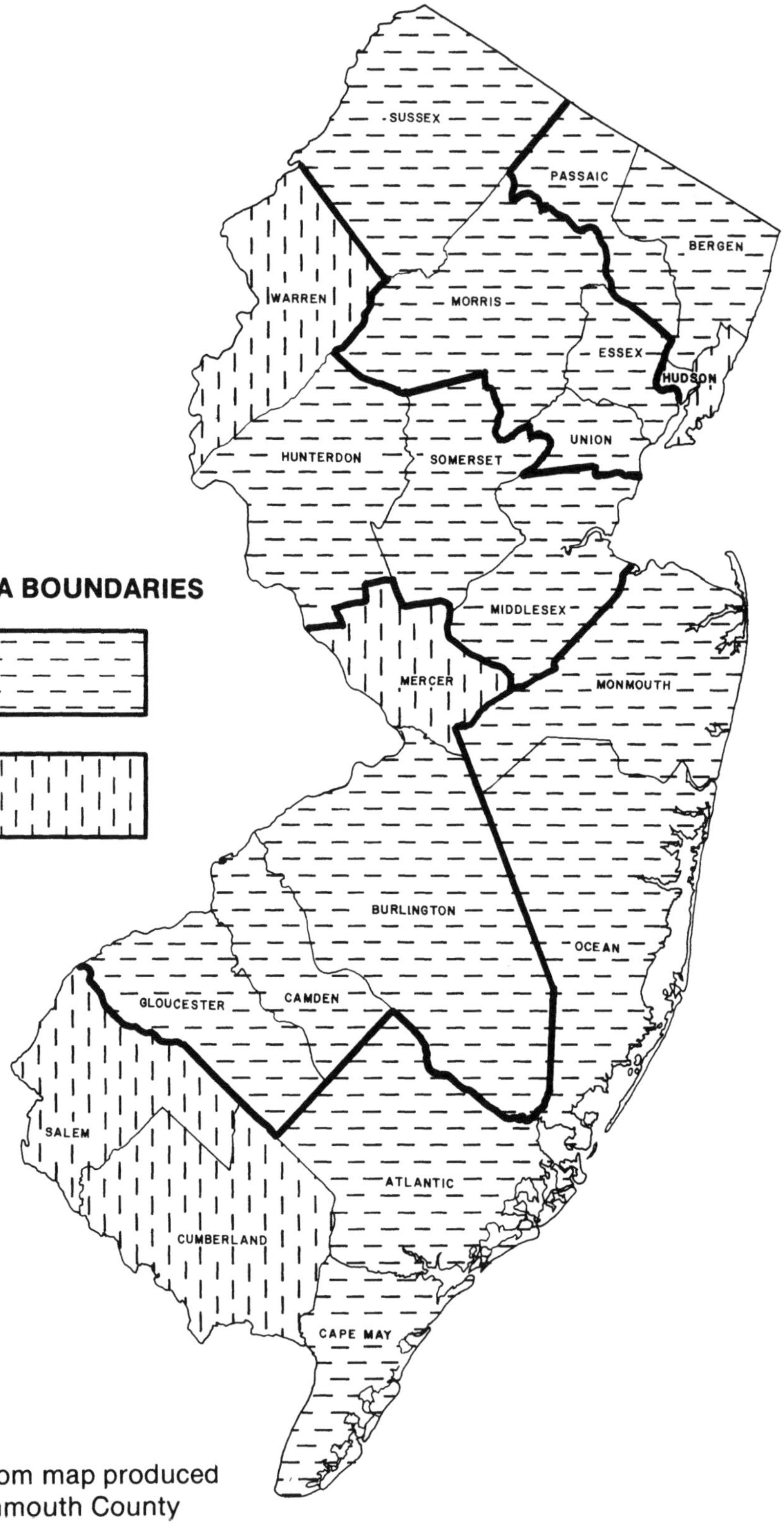

STATISTICAL AREA BOUNDARIES

MAIN AREAS

OTHER AREAS

SOURCE: Adopted from map produced by the Monmouth County Planning Board, July, 1983

(1) New York-Northern New Jersey-Long Island-NY-NJ-CT-CMSA in the northeast part of the state, and (2) the Philadelphia-Wilmington-Trenton-PA-NJ-DE-MD-CMSA in the southwest portion. The remaining area is territorially claimed by two MSAs: (1) Allentown-Bethlehem-PA-NJ-MSA in the Northwest and (2) Atlantic City, NJ-MSA in the southeast part of the state.

Within the two CMSA classifications are contained several PMSAs. There is significant agreement between PMSA designation by the Census and the Mount Laurel regions earlier described. There is exact agreement in two instances. The Newark, NJ-PMSA consisting of Essex, Morris, Sussex and Union Counties is identical to Mount Laurel Northwest Region 2; the Monmouth-Ocean NJ-PMSA is identical to Mount Laurel East Central Region 4.

Three of the remaining four Mount Laurel regions are identical to Census PMSA designations except that they include one more county than does the corresponding PMSA. In each case of the larger Mount Laurel regions, strong commuting linkages exist between the added county and the remaining counties in the Census-designated PMSA. Further, in all cases the county not included in the Census PMSA designation appears as such because it was an existing SMSA or part of an SMSA prior to 1980 and chose to remain as either a separate PMSA or as part of a prior designation in a new PMSA. This is true for Hudson, Mercer and Cumberland Counties which were their own SMSAs prior to 1980 and continue as individual PMSAs currently. It also pertains to Warren County which was originally part of the Allentown-Bethlehem-Easton-SMSA and is now part of the Allentown-Bethlehem-PA-NJ-MSA (Exhibit 1-10).

Thus, Mount Laurel Region 1 -- the Northeast, consisting of Bergen, Passaic and Hudson Counties -- is composed of two PMSAs (Bergen-Passaic-PMSA and Jersey City, NJ-PMSA) which would have been a single PMSA and identical to the Mount Laurel region had it not been Hudson County's choice to remain separate. Mount Laurel Region 5 -- the Southwest, consisting of Burlington, Camden, Gloucester, and Mercer Counties, is also composed of two PMSAs (part of Philadelphia-NJ-PMSA and the Trenton, NJ-PMSA) which would have been a single PMSA and thus one region had not Mercer County also chosen to remain separate.

Mount Laurel Region 3 consisting of Hunterdon, Middlesex, Somerset and Warren Counties is made up of a PMSA (Middlesex-Somerset-Hunterdon-NJ PMSA) as well as a single county (Warren) from the Allentown-Bethlehem MSA. There is additional impetus for keeping Warren and Hunterdon Counties together in that the New Jersey Public Use Sample, the source of much housing and population information on a countywide basis, does not produce information separately for these two counties.

Mount Laurel Region 6 is composed of a PMSA (Vineland-Bridgeton, NJ PMSA -- Cumberland County), an MSA (Atlantic City, NJ-MSA -- Atlantic and Cape May Counties), and a single county (Salem) from the Wilmington-DE-NJ-MD-PMSA. Both Salem and Atlantic/Cape May Counties have strong commuting ties with Cumberland County. Salem chose to remain as part of a prior

EXHIBIT 1-10

NEW JERSEY METROPOLITAN STATISTICAL AREAS WITHIN MOUNT LAUREL REGIONS - DIAGRAMMATIC SUMMARY

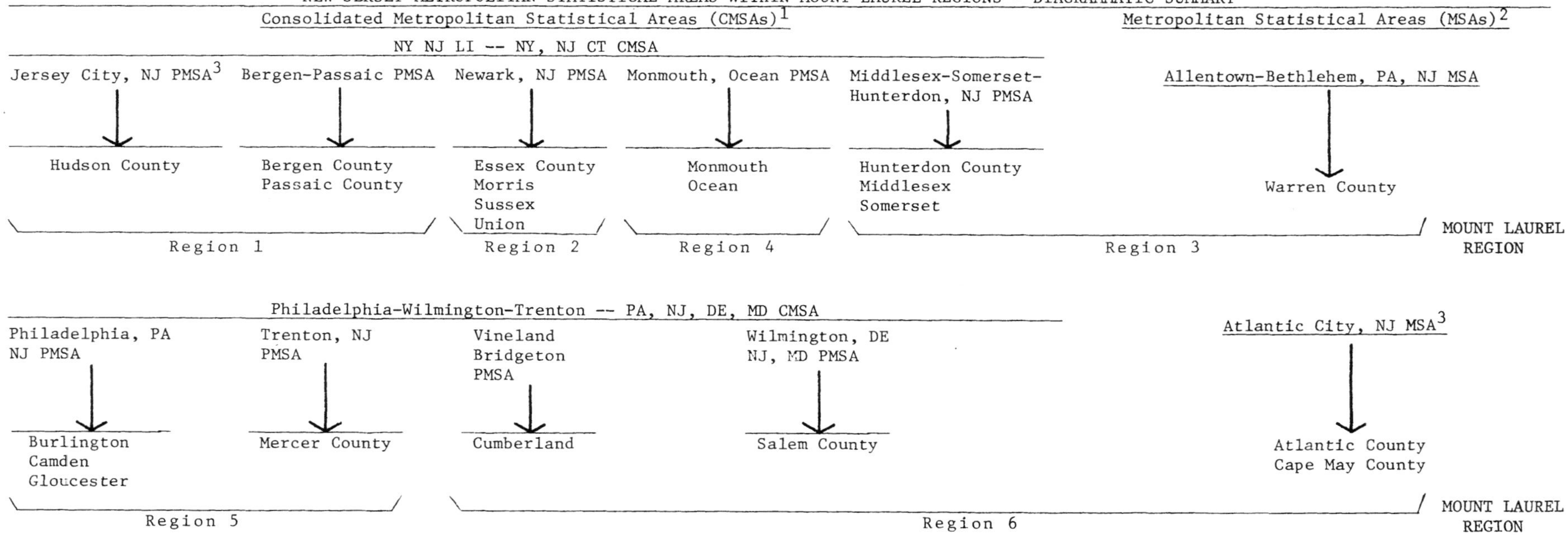

Definition(s):

[1]Consolidated Metropolitan Statistical Area (CMSA) - A cluster of population nuclei and nearby communities which have a high degree of social and economic integration. Each consists of multiple counties that meet specified standards pertaining to population, commuting ties, and metropolitan character.
[2]Metropolitan Statistical Area (MSA) - Identical to CMSA except smaller in scope.
[3]Primary Metropolitan Statistical Area (PMSA) - A major constituent of a CMSA, Multiple PMSAs are found in a CMSA.

Notes:

[1]Two county PMSAs (Hudson County and Mercer County) have not been aggregated with another PMSA due to size and grandfathering clauses; they were large enough to be SMSAs in the 1970s. Substantively, using journey-to-work as the primary criterion, the former may be linked to the Bergen-Passaic PMSA and the latter to the Burlington, Camden, Gloucester PMSA.
[2]The above scenario is also true for Cumberland, Salem and Cape May Counties. Cape May/Salem and Hunterdon/Warren Counties must be joined in the New Jersey Public Use Sample due to smallness of size. Hunterdon and Warren are linked in journey-to-work characteristics.
[3]Cumberland-Cape May/Salem and Atlantic-Cape May/Salem also have strong journey-to-work linkages.

Source: U.S. Department of Commerce, Federal Committee on Standard Metropolitan Statistical Areas, The Metropolitan Statistical Area Classification, December 1979.

established SMSA, and Atlantic County joined with Cape May County in the Atlantic City, NJ MSA (after having been a separate SMSA in 1970) but did not desire its MSA to encompass any additional counties. Further, as is the case for Warren and Hunterdon Counties, Cape May and Salem Counties cannot be separated in data display in the New Jersey Public Use Sample. Thus, their information must appear as part of the same region or not be used.

What Does Similarity Between Mount Laurel Regions and Census MSAs or PMSAs Provide?

What is clear from the above analysis is that, based purely on substantive criteria, absent grandfathering, there is almost exact correspondence between Mount Laurel and U.S. Census regions. The fact that there is not exact correspondence relates not to a violation of substantive linkage but rather to Census adjustments which isolated several counties in the final designation.

The fact that these individual counties for the most part are whole PMSAs means that data are available for them individually and these data may be added to data for another PMSA to sum for a combined region. In delimiting all Mount Laurel regions, sensitivity to U.S. Census areal regions was steadfastly maintained. CMSAs are never violated, for example, by taking Mercer County from Mount Laurel Region 5 and lumping it with Middlesex, Somerset and the other counties of Region 3. Besides having difficulty obtaining data for a geographic area different from the Census, it would violate the commuting and socioeconomic relationships that are inherent in the designation of the New York and Philadelphia CMSAs. This would counter regional journey-to-work linkages.

Thus, the conceptual approach used by the Census in assembling regions in New Jersey related to journey-to-work has been left intact. In addition, the grouping procedure remains sensitive to the limitations of the New Jersey Public Use Sample which has only 19 areal subcuts (Warren/Hunterdon and Cape May/Salem counties are grouped). In both cases, when Mount Laurel regions were developed, those counties which could not be unbundled for data purposes appeared in the same regional grouping.

THE MOUNT LAUREL REGIONS IN PERSPECTIVE

The basis and actual construction of the six Mount Laurel housing regions have been discussed in the initial section of this chapter. These regions have been compared to U.S. Census areal definitions in the section just completed. These two sections have established housing regions in New Jersey and have shown their future durability relative to the most current forms of national data presentation. It now is necessary to briefly examine the social and economic characteristics of the jurisdictions of the state in the context of these established regional partitions. This analysis will be performed in three stages: first, the most relevant elements of the land use and economic sectors of each region will be examined; this will be followed by a description of the socioeconomic characteristics of the region. Finally, the analysis will conclude with an examination of current and past housing trends within the regions.

Land Use and Economic Characteristics

The six regions have been made coterminous with their constituent counties. These counties have been previously identified in Exhibit 1-5. Four of the regions contain four counties (Northwest Region 2, West Central Region 3, Southwest Region 5 and South-Southwest Region 6); the remaining two regions, Northeast Region 1 and East Central Region 4 contain three and two counties, respectively. Each region, except for the South-Southwest Region 6, contains approximately 100 municipalities (see Exhibit 1-11). This is nearly an equal division of the state's 567 municipalities. The region with the most municipalities (114) is the Southwest Region 5; the least is the South-Southwest Region 6 with 68 municipalities.

All regions are characterized by at least some share of both employment and population growth. This takes the form of the presence of counties which evidence either considerably more employment than household growth or more household than employment growth. Each three- or four-county region is essentially in balance with at least one of each type of county; the West Central region has two employment growth and two household growth counties.

In total land area, the regions range from a low of 471 square miles in the Northeast Region 1 to a high of 1,676 square miles in the South-Southwest Region 6. The Northeast Region historically has been characterized by high-density development whereas the southern parts of the State have always been known for low density. The density of the Northeast Region is fifteen times that of the South-Southwest Region. Vacant developable land ranges from a low of 16,000 acres in Northeast Region 1 to a high of 200,000 acres in Southwest Region 5. These developable land estimates from the State of New Jersey's Housing Allocation Report[50] do not include any redevelopable vacant land in the older cities or close-in suburbs. This, as well as land of steep slopes, also not included in the state report, would add additional developable acreage to northern areas.*

The greatest aggregation of taxable property is to be found in the Northwest Region 2, with the least found in the South-Southwest Region 6. On a per capita basis, the older, more developed areas are richer in terms of equalized valuation. This reflects remnant concentrations of commerce and industry in the older cities as well as the ring of shopping centers and industrial parks at the periphery of their close-in suburbs. A somewhat spurious figure exists for the South-Southwest Region 6 which includes

---

*Prime agricultural land is also not included in developable land estimates yet would not relatively impact northern areas significantly.

EXHIBIT 1-11

LAND USE AND ECONOMIC CHARACTERISTICS OF THE MOUNT LAUREL REGIONS

	REGIONS					
	NORTHEAST REGION 1	NORTHWEST REGION 2	WEST CENTRAL REGION 3	EAST CENTRAL REGION 4	SOUTHWEST REGION 5	SOUTH-SOUTHWEST REGION 6
Constituent Counties	a. Bergen b. Hudson c. Passaic	d. Essex e. Morris f. Sussex g. Union	h. Hunterdon i. Middlesex j. Somerset k. Warren	l. Monmouth m. Ocean	n. Burlington o. Camden p. Gloucester q. Mercer	r. Atlantic s. Cape May t. Cumberland u. Salem
Number of municipalities in region[1]	98	106	95	85	114	68
Number of counties where 1970-1980 job growth exceeded household growth[2]	1[a]	2[e,g]	2[i,j]	1[l]	1[q]	1[r]
Number of counties where 1970-1980 household growth exceeded job growth[1]	1[c]	1[f]	2[h,k]	1[m]	1[n]	2[s,u]
State equalized valuation-1980[1] (millions) of region	$39,317	$41,003	$26,092	$19,829	$22,186	$12,872
Per capita 1980 equalized valuation of region	$21,252	$21,833	$16,871	$23,356	$16,532	$27,156
Total land area[1] in region (miles)[2]	471	1,234	1,413	1,088	1,595	1,676
Vacant developable land (acres) in region[3]	15,934	64,738	162,741	143,978	193,831	69,043

Source:
1. 43rd + 33rd Annual Reports of the Division of Local Government Services, State of New Jersey, Department of Community Affairs, Trenton, N.J.
2. Bureau of Census, U.S. Census of Population and Housing, 1970, 1980.
3. State of New Jersey, Department of Community Affairs, A Revised Statewide Housing Allocation Report for New New Jersey (Trenton, 1968).

extensive property valuation in casino development, benefitting only the City of Atlantic City, and is not indicative of the region as a whole.

Socioeconomic Characteristics

As has been shown, the six regions span the entire State of New Jersey. Given the historical growth patterns within New Jersey, each region has necessarily taken on the character of the era in which its major economic development occurred.

The two Northern Regions (1 and 2) as well as the Southwest Region 5 have been marked with the greatest degree of pre-World War II development and, all are shown to have had over a million inhabitants as of 1960. The years following 1960 have, of course, been ones of great change for all regions. The rates of population change shown in Exhibit 1-12 indicate that the northern regions have slowly grown during the decade of the 1960s, yet have declined in absolute numbers during the 1970s. In contrast, the strongest growth rates over both decades have occurred within the two shore counties, identified collectively as the East Central Region 4. The patterns of change clearly suggest a model of interregional population shifts. The highly dense Regions 1 and 2 have been losing population while the three areas of lowest density, Regions 3, 4 and 6, have been growing at a rapid rate.

The regions also pair off in several other interesting ways. The two regions with the highest median age are at opposite extremes of the growth spectrum. The Northeast Region 1, home of several older central cities, is rapidly losing population; the East Central Region 4, site of several retirement communities, is currently growing most rapidly. Both of these areas exhibit median age of householder in excess of 33 years. By far, the youngest region is the Southwest Region 5. This is a portion of the Philadelphia metropolitan area which is home to young, growing families. This factor also shows up in the household size variable wherein the Southwest Region has the largest household size. The Northwest Region 1 and East Central Region 4 vie for the extremes in per capita income distribution across the state. The Northeast Region is highest in per capita income; the East Central Region has one of the lowest per capita incomes.

To a certain extent, the effect of life cycle can also be detected by viewing household size variation across regions. Both Northeast Region 1 and East Central Region 4 have relatively low median size households, indicating the presence of older individuals and the absence of children in the average household (Exhibit 1-12). However, the South-Southwest Region 6 shows the lowest household size and a high median age of the population, thus indicating an even more extreme position in life cycle. This is a region characterized not only by an elderly population but one composed of many of those who live alone.

Separate from life cycle is the role of race and ethnicity in describing regional variation. The regions containing the older central cities of

EXHIBIT 1-12

SOCIOECONOMIC CHARACTERISTICS OF THE MOUNT LAUREL REGIONS

	REGIONS					
	NORTHEAST REGION 1	NORTHWEST REGION 2	WEST CENTRAL REGION 3	EAST CENTRAL REGION 4	SOUTHWEST REGION 5	SOUTH-SOUTHWEST REGION 6
Constituent Counties	a. Bergen b. Hudson c. Passaic	d. Essex e. Morris f. Sussex g. Union	h. Hunterdon i. Middlesex j. Somerset k. Warren	l. Monmouth m. Ocean	n. Burlington o. Camden p. Gloucester q. Mercer	r. Atlantic s. Cape May t. Cumberland u. Salem
Population x (1000)						
1960	1,798	1,739	695	443	1,017	375
1970	1,968	1,934	926	668	1,256	416
1980	1,850	1,878	971	849	1,342	474
Population Change (%)						
1960-1970	9.5	11.2	33.2	50.8	23.4	11.0
1970-1980	-6.0	- 2.9	4.9	27.2	6.8	13.8
Population/mi^2 (1980)	3,928	1,523	687	780	841	282
Persons/Household (1980)	2.8	2.9	3.0	2.9	3.0	2.7
Percent Black (1980)	9.3	22.7	5.1	6.2	14.2	15.1
Median Age (1980)	33.6	32.3	31.3	33.6	30.2	32.2
Median Income (1980)	$11,966	$11,346	$11,592	$10,022	$9,639	$9,299

Source: Bureau of Census, U.S. Census of Population and Housing, 1970, 1980.

Newark and Camden show high concentrations of black population. This also holds true for the South-Southwest Region 6 where a noticeable share of black families are found in the Atlantic City and Vineland areas.

Housing and Property Characteristics

The analysis of property characteristics within the Mount Laurel regions is completed through an examination of parcels as defined for property tax purposes. The parcel identifies a type of land use, not necessarily the level or intensity of use on a unit of land. Thus, there are limits to the possible interpretation of this information. However, the levels and changes taking place in vacant, residential and apartment parcels are certainly valid and quite revealing.

The distribution of parcels by land use type is displayed in Exhibit 1-13. Vacant parcels are clearly highest in the two shore-based regions: the East Central Region 4 and the South-Southwest Region 6. Residential parcels dominate all land use categories with the Northeast, Northwest and Southwest regions forming the top tier in residential use, while the South-Southwest has the lowest number of residential properties relative to the rest of the state. The industrial heartland continues to be found in the Northeastern part of the state (Region 1) whereas commercial development concentrations parallel established population centers (Regions 1, 2 and 5).

Interestingly, the depletion of vacant land is occurring most rapidly in the two northern regions reflecting some continued economic activity there combined with low levels of available land. The West Central Region 3 and East Central Region 4 also show significant withdrawal of land from the vacant category. Growth in residential properties is positive in all regions; however, the two northern regions evidence a rate of growth which is one-fourth to one-sixth the rate of growth of the remaining regions. Again, the central portions of the state, West Central and East Central Regions 3 and 4 show the highest growth rates. Apartment parcels show an absolute decline in the two northern regions; the greatest growth in apartments occurs in the East Central Region 4 and Southwest Region 5. In several instances these have come as a by-product of larger-scale planned developments unique to this part of the state.

The overview of Mount Laurel housing regions is completed by examining several characteristics of the current housing stock. Again, there are significant variations in housing type, tenure and price, and also across regions. The value of residential property is found to be highest in the Northern regions, decreasing as one progresses southward in the state. The range of median housing values in 1980 was over fifty percent, with a high of $69,000 in the Northwest Region and a low of $43,000 in the South-Southwest Region. Median rental values vary by about one-half the percentage of variation in ownership housing; the highest median rent is found in

West Central Region 3 at $268 per month; the lowest is again the South-Southwest Region at approximately $200 monthly (1980).

The structure of the housing stock can also be examined in terms of age, tenure, and physical type. Exhibit 1-13 shows that the popular single-family detached mode of housing is most strongly concentrated in the more suburban East Central Region 4 (71% of all dwelling units) and the West Central Region 3 (65%). The lowest level of single-family detached housing is in the more densely populated northern areas, particularly the Northeast Region 1 (38%). Not surprisingly, multifamily parcels of 5-or-more units are highly concentrated in the Northeast Region (27%) and lowest in the East Central Region (13%). The pattern of statewide single-family/multifamily distribution is also reproduced in the index of age of the housing stock. The region with the largest concentration of dwelling units built prior to 1960 is the Northeast; the East Central Region 4 shows the lowest concentration of units built prior to this time.

Summary

Tied by social and economic linkages, the regions constructed in this section nonetheless cast a diversity of social and economic conditions within a set of six areas which have reasonably similar overall commuting times. Similarities in time/distance of journey-to-work are useful in approximating what may be geographically-based housing markets. Areal similarities and geographic scope should not be allowed to mask the unique social and economic conditions found within each region. The existence of such conditions is why people may choose to live and work in one area versus another. This section concludes with a characterization of each region emphasizing the various summary indicators that portray the land use and demographic characteristics of each of the designated regions.

The Northeast Region 1 is the most populous region of those delimited here. Its residents are both older than average, with fewer children than households in most other regions. Its housing stock is the oldest in the state and contains a large component of multifamily units. Per capita incomes are relatively high; however, homeownership is the lowest of all regions, indicating a large prevalence of both high and medium quality rental units and a resident population that either chooses or is forced to rent.

The Northwest Region 2 is in many respects a mirror image of the Northeast in its size, age of economic development, and wealth of citizens. However, with its urban focus being Newark, it is unique in its high concentration of black population.

The West Central Region 3 is characterized by significant post-World War II suburban single-family housing and an associated high level of home ownership. Its families are relatively young, second highest in per capita income, and for the most part white.

EXHIBIT 1-13

HOUSING AND PROPERTY CHARACTERISTICS OF THE MOUNT LAUREL REGIONS

	REGIONS					
	NORTHEAST REGION 1	NORTHWEST REGION 2	WEST CENTRAL REGION 3	EAST CENTRAL REGION 4	SOUTHWEST REGION 5	SOUTH-SOUTHWEST REGION 6
As of 1980 (Number)	a. Bergen b. Hudson c. Passaic	d. Essex e. Morris f. Sussex g. Union	h. Hunterdon i. Middlesex j. Somerset k. Warren	l. Monmouth m. Ocean	n. Burlington o. Camden p. Gloucester o. Mercer	r. Atlantic s. Cape May T. Cumberland U. Salem
Vacant parcels	27,907	51,234	37,819	92,401	63,468	84,547
Residential parcel	361,787	396,181	235,453	273,603	343,584	161,559
Farm parcels	566	6,682	16,393	5,849	14,471	13,051
Commercial parcels	27,863	25,140	12,720	11,932	19,577	11,889
Industrial parcels	14,405	5,117	2,518	621	1,778	615
Apartment parcels	6,554	5,107	989	2,058	1,423	1,835
Change 1970-80 (Percent)						
Vacant parcels	-21.8%	-24.5%	-15.6%	-7.7%	1.8%	0.8%
Residential parcels	6.5	7.1	47.0	36.9	20.1	24.8
Apartment parcels	-18.0	-20.1	7.0	45.7	30.6	1.4
Average 1980						
Housing value	$64,356	$69,947	$66,350	$58,448	$45,880	$43,793
Gross Rent	236	241	268	245	223	199
Rooms per housing unit	5.1	5.3	5.6	5.5	5.6	5.2
% of households owning home	52.2	56.9	70.1	75.4	71.0	67.5
% of units						
Single-family detached	38.0	49.4	65.0	71.5	59.3	60.5
+ 5 persons per family	26.9	24.6	15.9	13.0	16.5	15.1
Built prior to 1960	77.1	72.7	57.7	46.3	57.3	60.1

Source: 43rd + 33rd Annual Reports of the Division of Local Government Services, State of New Jersey, Department of Community Affairs, Trenton, NJ; U.S. Bureau of Census, U.S. Census of Population and Housing, 1970, 1980.

The East Central Region 4 is characterized by its rapid growth over the past two decades. It has made extensive use of single-family attached and detached housing with the highest rate of homeownership compared to that of the other regions. Its households are somewhat older than average and have fewer children leading one to suggest that retirement may characterize the life cycle of many of its residents.

The Southwest Region 5 is comparable to the Northwest Region 2 in its position as an inner suburb to a major central city (Philadelphia). Similar to Region 2, the Southwest Region has a large black population; however, the region is distinctively different in that it is less densely populated, has a newer housing stock, and a more youthful population. On the other hand, it has the next lowest level of per capita income/housing values and the lowest level of per capita taxable property when compared to all remaining regions.

The South-Southwest Region 6 is largest in area, yet smallest in population. Its population is older than average, living in smaller households and having the lowest incomes, housing values, and rent levels compared to all other regions. With its economic focus being Atlantic City and the shore, this region is characterized by a higher property valuation per capita than is really reflected in residents' properties, yet also with a unique recreational economy, with agriculture and retirement contributing strongly to its regional image.

CONCLUSION

Returning to the basic definitions of region and housing market, six housing regions have been defined for New Jersey. These regions, of two-to-four counties each, have been constructed on the basis of journey-to-work relationships between the counties, a prime criterion of employment and residence linkage. The regions, as constructed, allow 85-90 percent of the employed in-state Mount Laurel population to work and reside in the same region. They do so with journeys-to-work of less than twenty minutes. This is lower than the statewide average of all income classes and only one-half the commuting time that is deemed burdensome by several sources.

The designated Mount Laurel regions blanket the entire State of New Jersey and are in conceptual agreement with U.S. Census designations for the state. As such, they offer the capability of having data produced for and about them.

In addition, the regions are wholly contained within the State of New Jersey and are greater than a single county -- two points that the New Jersey Courts have deemed desirable in regional delineation. The regions thus offer the possibility of making housing need projections within subunits of the State of New Jersey where people live and work. This, in turn, may foster a more equal chance for all residents to achieve maximum employment at minimum distances from residences.

The Mount Laurel regions designated in this chapter form the geographical subcut for the data of all subsequent chapters. An Appendix which follows compares Mount Laurel regions to other informal regional designations which exist in New Jersey primarily for program administration purposes.

NOTES

1. U.S. Department of Housing and Urban Development, Federal Housing Administration (FHA), Economic and Market Analysis Division, FHA Techniques of Housing Market Analysis (Washington, D.C.: Government Printing Office, August 1970); Ernest Fisher and Robert Fisher, Urban Real Estate (New York: Henry Holt, 1954).

2. David Blank and Louis Winnick, "The Structure of the Housing Market," Quarterly Journal of Economics (March 1953), p. 187; Chester Rapkin, Louis Winnick and David Blank in Housing Market Analysis: A Study of Theory and Methods (Washington, D.C.: Housing and Home Finance Agency 1953); Louis Winnick, "Housing Market Analysis-Process Described in Theory and Practice," Journal of Housing (December 1955), p. 432; Charles Abrams, The Language of Cities (New York: Viking Press, 1971).

3. See Brian Berry, Peter Goheen, and Harold Goldstein, Metropolitan Area Definition: A Re-evaluation of Concept and Statistical Products (Washington, D.C.: Government Printing Office, U.S. Bureau of the Census Working Paper, 1960).

4. Howard Odum and Harry Moore, American Regionalism (Gloucester, MA: Peter Smith, 1966).

5. Walter Isard, "Regional Science, The Concept of Region and Regional Structure in Regional Science Association," Papers and Proceedings, Vol. II, 1956, p. 26.

6. Vincent Ostrom, "The Political Dimension of Regional Analysis," in Regional Science Association, Papers and Proceedings (1956), p. 86.

7. Federal Housing Administration, FHA Techniques, p. 13.

8. Ibid., p. 11.

9. Fisher and Fisher, Urban Real Estate, p. 223.

10. Abrams, The Language of Cities.

11. Federal Housing Administration, FHA Techniques, p. 11.

12. William Grigsby, Housing Markets and Market Policy (Philadelphia: University of Pennsylvania Press, 1963). See also Hammer, Greene, Siler Associates, Regional Housing Planning: A Technical Guide (Washington, D.C.: American Institute of Planners, 1972).

13. See Michael Goldberg and George Gau, North American Housing Markets in the Twenty-First Century (Cambridge: Ballinger, 1983); Urban Land Institute, Residential Development Handbook (Washington, D.C.: ULI, 1970).

14. J.P. Nelson, "Accessibility and the Value of Time in Commuting," Southern Economic Journal, Vol. 43 (1975), p. 1321; John L. Goodman, Jr. and Mark Berkman, "Racial Differences in Commuting Behavior: New Evidence From the Panel Study of Income Dynamics," Public Data Use, Vol. 5, No. 4 (July 1977), p. 29; W. D. Fisher, and M. G. Fisher, "The Spatial Allocation of Employment and Residence Within a Metropolitan Area," Journal of Regional Science, Vol. 15 (1975), p. 361; Peter Halvorson, "The Income Factor in the Journey to Work: Attitudes and Behavior," The Professional Geographer, Vol. 25, No. 4, (November 1973), p. 357; J.B. Lansing and G. Hendricks, "How People Perceive the Cost of the Journey to Work," Highway Research Record, No. 197 (1967), p. 44; Arthur Getis, "Residential Location and the Journey from Work," Proceedings, Association of American Geographers, Vol. 1 (1969), p. 55; J. Douglas Carroll, Jr., "The Relation of Homes to Work Places and the Spatial Pattern of Cities," Social Forces, Vol. 30 (1952), p. 271.

15. Federal Housing Administration, FHA Techniques.

16. Fisher and Fisher, Urban Real Estate; Abrams, The Language of Cities.

17. American Society of Planning Officials (ASPO), Relationships of the Journey to Work (Planning Advisory Service Report #15) (Chicago, IL, ASPO, April 1951).

18. John B. Lansing and Eva Mueller (with Nancy Berth), Residential Location and Urban Mobility (Ann Arbor: Survey Research Center, The University of Michigan, 1964), p. 41.

19. The Sunday Tribune, May 28, 1967, Cited in Association of Bay Area Governments, Regional Housing Study, Supplemental Report RA-4, October 1969, p. 26.

20. Irwin P. Levin, et al., "A Survey of the Relationship Between Home Satisfaction, Changes in Travel Behavior, and Commuting Distance," in The University of Ohio, The Institute of Urban and Regional Research, Technical Reports, 197D (January 1981).

21. U.S. Department of Commerce, Bureau of the Census, The 1980 Census of Population and Housing: Public Use Sample (Washington, D.C.: Government Printing Office, 1982).

22. New Jersey War Transportation Committee, Arnold H. Vey, Chairman, Procedures for Mailing, Mapping and Coding (mimeo) 1942.

23. American Society of Planning Officials, Relationships of the Journey to Work.

24. John Lansing, Residential Location and Urban Mobility: The Second Wave of Interviews (Ann Arbor: Survey Research Center, The University of Michigan, January 1966).

25. See footnote 14 in this chapter.

26. U.S. Department of Commerce, Bureau of Census, The Journey-to-Work in the United States: 1979 (Washington, D.C.: Government Printing Office, 1982), Series P-23, No. 122.

27. Federal Housing Administration, FHA Techniques.

28. Bureau of the Census, The Journey-to-Work in the United States.

29. Philip N. Fulton, "Public Transportation: Solving the Commuting Problem." Paper presented at the Annual Meeting of the Transportation Research Board, Washington, D.C., January 18, 1983.

30. Ibid.

31. American Society of Planning Officials, Relationship of the Journey-to-Work.

32. Ibid. See also John S. Adams, "The Definition of Areal Submarkets for Housing in the Minneapolis and Suburban Areas," Hubert S. Humphrey Institute of Public Affairs, University of Minnesota (August 1977) (mimeo).

33. U.S. Department of Commerce, Bureau of the Census and U.S. Department of Labor, County Business Patterns (Washington, D.C.: Government Printing Office, series).

34. Federal Housing Administration, FHA Techniques.

35. Ibid.

36. See Southern Burlington County NAACP v. The Township of Mount Laurel, 67 N.J. 151, 336 A. 2d 713.

37. See footnote 1 in this chapter.

38. See P. Rossi, Why Families Move (Glencoe: Free Press, 1955); W. A. V. Clark, "Modeling Housing Market Search" (New York: St. Martins, 1982); Richard Butler, "Cross-Sectional Variation in the Hedonic Relationship for Urban Housing Markets," Journal of Regional Science, Vol. 20, No. 4 (1980),

p. 439; John F. Kain and William C. Apgar, Jr., "Simulation of Housing Market Dynamics," AREUEA Journal, Vol. 7, 1979, p. 505.

39. Rossi, Why Families Move.

40. Bureau of the Census, The 1980 Census of Population and Housing: Public Use Sample.

41. SPSS Inc., SPSS Users Guide (New York: McGraw Hill, 1983); SAS Institute, Inc., SAS Users Guide (Raleigh: SAS Institute, 1979); Donald J. Veldman, Fortran Programming for the Behavioral Sciences (New York: Holt Rinehart, 1967).

42. Ibid.

43. Federal Housing Administration, FHA Techniques.

44. The Federal Committee on Standard Metropolitan Statistical Areas, The Metropolitan Statistical Area Classification (Washington, D.C.: Government Printing Office, December 1979).

45. See Richard L. Forstall and Donald E. Starsinic, "New Definitions of Metropolitan Statistical Areas," September 6, 1983 (mimeo).

46. Ibid.

47. Ibid.

48. Ibid.

49. "New Jersey: The First Metropolitan State," Population and Census, Issue 31, October 1983 (Trenton, New Jersey).

50. State of New Jersey, Department of Community Affairs, Division of State and Regional Planning, A Revised Statewide Housing Allocation Report for New Jersey (Trenton: 1978).

APPENDIX I

OTHER REGIONAL DESIGNATIONS IN THE STATE OF NEW JERSEY

The purpose of the following Appendix is to describe several regional designations which have been demarcated for planning purposes in the State of New Jersey. These include state water supply and transportation regions as well as federal labor market and housing cost areas. These designations have been made by agencies of the state and federal governments and most show strong linkages to the previously delineated Mount Laurel regions. They have administrative as opposed to regulatory status and are used primarily in the day-to-day operations of state or federal programs.

The intent of this section is not to provide an exhaustive discussion of regional territorial designations in New Jersey. Rather, a few examples of regional delineations will be selected and viewed for their similarities and differences with Mount Laurel regions.

WATER SUPPLY REGIONS AND THE MOUNT LAUREL REGIONS

The State of New Jersey, Department of Environmental Protection (DEP) has designated six water supply regions in New Jersey[1]. These regions are generally defined by major river watershed boundaries. The six regions are shown in Exhibit 1A-1.

Region 1 - Northeastern New Jersey - (Bergen, Hudson, Union, Essex, Middlesex, Somerset, and parts of Passaic, Morris, Sussex, Hunterdon, Mercer, and Monmouth Counties). The above areas are drawn together by three major watersheds with an interrelated yet separate water supply network. These are the Hackensack, Passaic, and Raritan River Basins. Individually, basins could pertain respectively to the Mount Laurel Regions 1, 2 and 3.

Region 2 - Monmouth and Ocean Counties - This is an area joined together by groundwater dependence on resources of the southern coastal plain. Mount Laurel and water supply regions in this area are coterminous.

Region 3 and Region 4 - Atlantic, Cape May, Cumberland and Salem Counties - These two regions are composed of Atlantic, Cape May, Cumberland and Salem Counties. Most counties in this area are also groundwater dependent. DEP groups them in terms of specifying future actions. Grouped, they are identical to Mount Laurel South-Southwest Region 6.

Region 5 - Burlington, Camden and Gloucester Counties - This region is linked to the Delaware River Basin, a primary water resource shared by New York, New Jersey and Pennsylvania. Region 5 is entirely dependent upon groundwater for potable water supplies. It basically parallels Mount Laurel

EXHIBIT 1A-1

WATER SUPPLY REGIONS IN NEW JERSEY

NEW JERSEY WATER SUPPLY PLANNING REGIONS

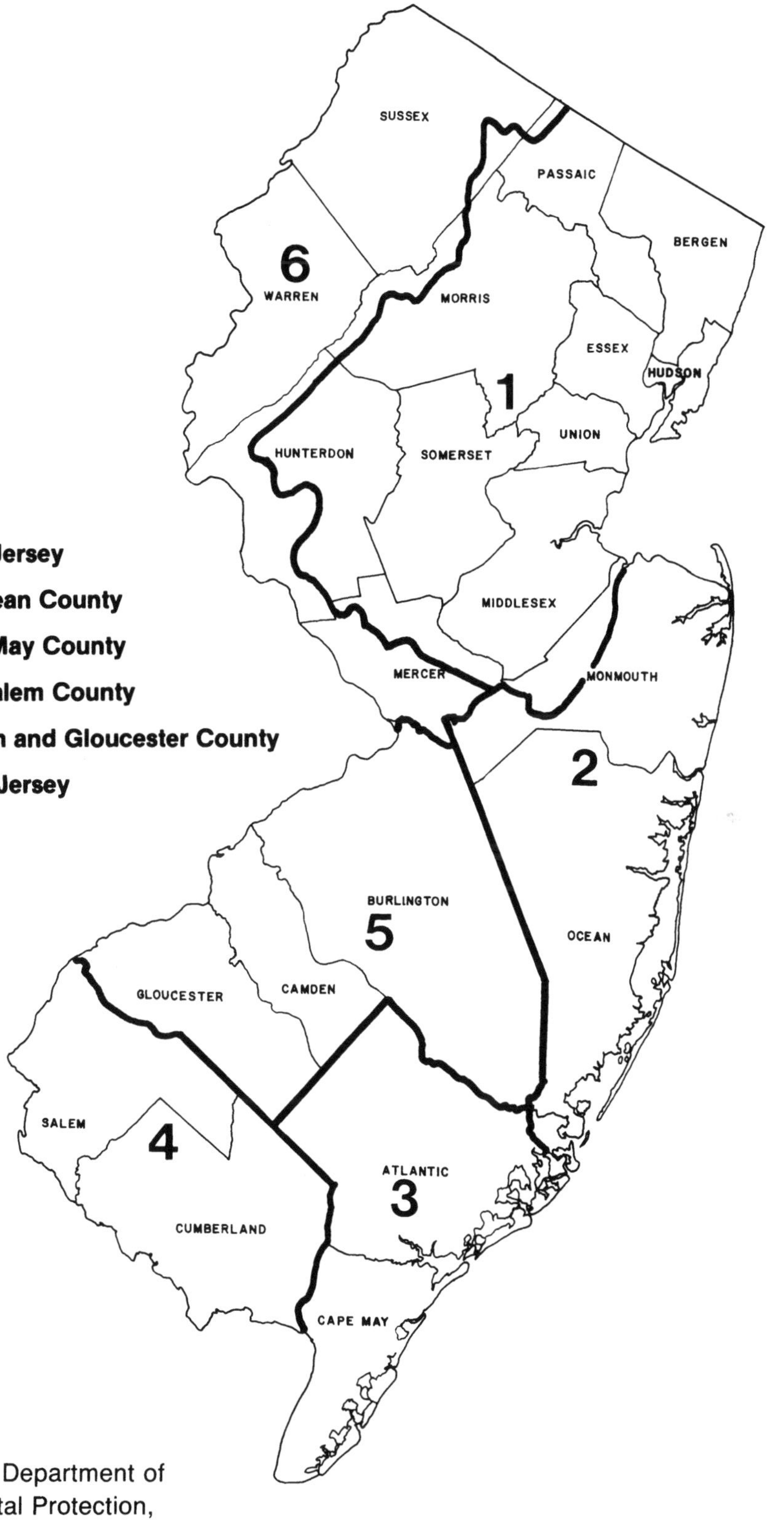

1. **Northeastern New Jersey**
2. **Monmouth and Ocean County**
3. **Atlantic and Cape May County**
4. **Cumberland and Salem County**
5. **Burlington, Camden and Gloucester County**
6. **Northwestern New Jersey**

Source: New Jersey Department of Environmental Protection, New Jersey Statewide Water Supply Master Plan, April 1982

Southwest Region 5 consisting of the same three counties as well as Mercer County.

Region 6 - Mercer, Hunterdon, Warren and Sussex Counties - Region 6, Mercer, Hunterdon, Warren and Sussex Counties, are a part of the Upper Delaware and Walkill River Basins in New Jersey. Most supplies, both current and future, are capable of being answered from surface water from these rivers. The region, which is composed of mostly rural counties from the three north and central Mount Laurel regions, has the least coincidence with any of the Mount Laurel regions.

In sum, the State of New Jersey Department of Environmental Protection has assembled six water supply regions based on river basin influence or dependence on groundwater. If the northern region is divided into its constituent river basins and if the southernmost two regions are joined (the way DEP joins them for planning needs), then, with one exception, there is a great deal of parallelism between Mount Laurel and water supply regions.

TRANSPORTATION REGIONS AND MOUNT LAUREL REGIONS

The New Jersey Department of Transportation (NJDOT) has both long- and short-range transportation plans.[2] Within these plans, regions are designated corridors which correspond to major transportation arteries and their influences. Travel patterns reflect all within-state travel (not exclusively journey-to-work trips) as well as through-state travel. Thus, the origin of the term corridors -- i.e., flows of travel to a terminous.

The seven regions demarcated by NJDOT are as follows (see Exhibit 1A-2):

Region 1 - Suburban Northeast Corridor - This region consists of Passaic and Bergen Counties and is joined by Routes I-80, U.S. 46, NJ 3, 4, 17, 20 and 208. It is characterized by homogenous, high-density development patterns and automobile predominance. It most closely parallels Mount Laurel Northeast Region 1.

Region 2 - Northeast Corridor - This region contains the counties between New York and Philadelphia (Essex, Hudson, Middlesex, Union, Burlington, and Mercer) and houses two major travel subcorridors: New York-Philadelphia and Trenton-Camden. Major routes within this corridor are the New Jersey Turnpike, Interstates 95 and 295 and U.S. Routes 1 and 130. This is obviously a through-state regional designation and does not match well with any Mount Laurel region.

Region 3 - Central Corridor - Morris and Somerset Counties, including Interstate Routes 78, 80, and 287, U.S. Routes 22 and 206, and NJ Routes 24, 28, and 10. This area is characterized by significantly lower auto trips than most northern regions and relatively higher rail trips. It is a combination of one developing county from each of two Mount Laurel regions (Northwest Region 2; West Central Region 3).

EXHIBIT 1A-2

TRANSPORTATION REGIONS IN NEW JERSEY
NEW JERSEY TRANSPORTATION STUDY CORRIDORS

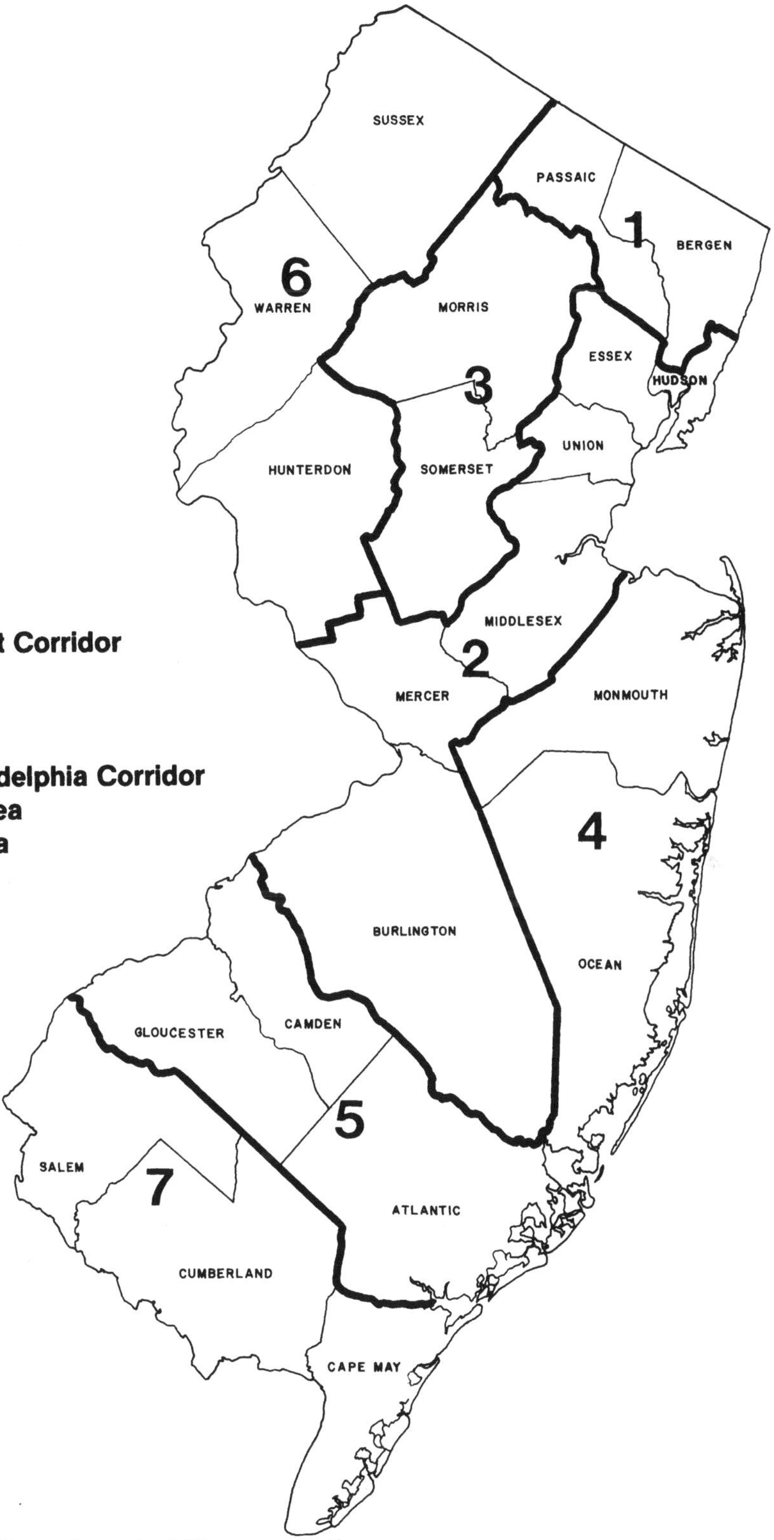

1. **Suburban Northeast Corridor**
2. **Northeast Corridor**
3. **Central Corridor**
4. **Shore Corridor**
5. **Atlantic City - Philadelphia Corridor**
6. **Rural Northwest Area**
7. **Rural Southern Area**

Source: New Jersey Department of Transportation
Long Range Plan
(Surface Passenger Transportation Element)
Trenton, N.J., NJDOT, 1982

Region 4 - The Shore Corridor - Includes Monmouth and Ocean Counties. Within these counties two subareas exist: (1) Monmouth/Northern Ocean County, and (2) Central/Southern Ocean County. Major roads in this area are I-195, the Garden State Parkway, U.S. Route 9 and NJ Routes 33, 34, 35, 36, and 70. This region is identical to Mount Laurel Region 4 -- the East Central Region.

Region 5 - Atlantic City-Philadelphia Corridor - This region includes the counties of Atlantic, Camden, and Gloucester and contains the travel subcorridors of Atlantic City to Philadelphia and Gloucester County to Philadelphia. Development in the corridor is characterized by central city uses at each end of the corridor with low-density and rural development in-between. Major highway routes include the Garden State Parkway, the Atlantic City Expressway, and NJ Routes 30 and 42. The corridor is characterized by average auto trip rates and higher-than-average bus and rail trip generation rates. Oriented to the Philadelphia metropolitan area, it is most similar to Mount Laurel Southwest Region 5.

Regions 6-7 - The Rural Northwest and Rural Southern Areas - The Rural Northwest Area contains Hunterdon, Sussex, and Warren Counties. This area is characterized by rural land use. Major highways include Interstate Routes 78 and 80, U.S. Route 46, and NJ Routes 12, 23, 31, 202 and 206. This area has almost one-half the rate of automobile trips of any other area. It contains two of the counties of the Mount Laurel West Central Region 3.

In sum, transportation regions show less conformity to Mount Laurel regions than do water supply regions. These differences emerge from the fact that the transportation regions used here are based on all within-state travel as well as through-state travel. The journey-to-work, the crux of the Mount Laurel regions, is just one component of the former category of travel. The state is again, however, divided into 6-7 parts. These regions reflect different transportation flows as opposed to work-related origins/destinations but nonetheless divide the state into multiple segments for planning purposes.

LABOR - LABOR AREAS
HUD - SECTION 8, AHS AREAS AND MOUNT LAUREL REGIONS

U.S. Department of Labor

A labor area is defined as a geographic area consisting of a central city or cities and the surrounding territory within commuting distance. Conceptually, it is an economically integrated unit within which workers may readily change jobs without changing their place of residence.[3] They blanket an entire state with no overlap and essentially represent counties of formerly-designated SMSA central cities. The labor area of large central cities can be multiple counties. Also, rural areas can have county labor area designations.

Currently, the Journey-to-Work and Migration Statistics Branch of the Population Division of the U.S. Census is preparing commuting tallies by county for the U.S. Department of Labor. Labor areas will be made to exactly parallel the new MSA and PMSA designations of the Census. New labor areas and employment counts within them should be released by 1985. Once labor areas are brought into agreement with MSAs and PMSAs, they will be in the same agreement with Mount Laurel regions that PMSAs and MSAs currently are.

As of November 1983, sixteen labor areas still existed in New Jersey under former SMSA notations. These areas range from a more affluent white-collar labor market in the northern part of the state to a less-affluent, more blue-collar labor market in the southern part. They are shown in Exhibit 1A-3. Even now, BLS Labor Areas (LAs) show strong correlation to Mount Laurel regions.

Joining the Hackensack, Jersey City and Paterson-Clifton-Passaic Labor Areas (LA) makes them equivalent in geographic scope to Mount Laurel Northeast Region 1. The Newark Labor Area is almost identical to the Northwest Region 2. Joining the Flemington, New Brunswick-Perth Amboy-Sayreville, and Phillipsburg Labor Areas approximates the Mount Laurel West Central Region 3. The Long Branch and Lakewood Labor Areas are equivalent to the East Central Region 4. The Camden/Trenton LA is coterminous with the Southwest Region 5 and adding the LAs of Atlantic City, Vineland-Millville-Bridgeton, Salem, and Ocean City-Wildwood-Cape May recreates Mount Laurel Region 6. Clearly, there is strong current and future compatibility between Mount Laurel regions and Labor Market areas.

U.S. Department of Housing and Urban Development

The U.S. Department of Housing and Urban Development has two widely known territorial designations. The first is the geographic bounds of its Section 8 Fair Market Rents;[4] the second is its geographic area displays within the Annual Housing Survey.[5] The first currently relates very closely to Mount Laurel regions; the second will be made to exactly parallel the MSA/PMSA designations of the Census and thus will indirectly reflect the Mount Laurel regions.

Section 8 Fair Market Rent Areas

Fair market rent is HUD's determination of the rent that would be required to obtain "privately developed and owned spaces of modest design."[6] HUD economists designate the region on the basis of differing housing cost areas or submarkets.

Exhibit 1A-3 shows the relationship between the Fair Market Rent Areas and Mount Laurel regions. Essentially there are eight Fair Market Rent

EXHIBIT 1-A3

BLS/HUD REGIONS AND MOUNT LAUREL REGIONS

U.S. DEPARTMENT OF HOUSING AND URBAN DEVELOPMENT		MOUNT LAUREL REGIONS	U.S. DEPARTMENT OF LABOR BUREAU OF LABOR STATISTICS
	HUD Section 8 Fair Market Rents	Housing Regions	Labor Areas (LA)
1	North Bergen Area (Bergen, Hudson, Passaic)	Northeast Region 1 (Bergen, Hudson, Passaic)	Hackensack LA (Bergen) Jersey City LA (Hudson) Paterson-Clifton-Passaic LA (Passaic)
2	Newark Area (Essex, Morris, Sussex, Union)	Northwest Region 2 (Essex, Morris, Sussex, Union)	Newark LA (Essex, Morris, Somerset, Union
3(a)	Freehold Area (West) (Hunterdon, Middlesex, Somerset, Warren)	West Central Region 3 (Hunterdon, Middlesex, Somerset, Warren)	Flemington LA (Hunterdon) New Brunswick-Perth Amboy-Sayreville LA (Middlesex) Phillipsburg LA (Warren)
3(b)	Freehold Area (East) [Monmouth]	East Central Region 4 (Monmouth, Ocean)	Long Branch-Asbury Park LA (Monmouth) Lakewood-Toms River LA (Ocean)
4	Asbury Area (Ocean)		
5	Burlington, Camden, Gloucester Areas	Southwest Region 5 (Burlington, Camden, Gloucester, Mercer)	Camden LA (Burlington, Camden, Gloucester)
6	Trenton Area (Mercer)		Trenton LA (Mercer)
7	Atlantic City Area (Atlantic, Cape May)	South-Southwest Region 6 (Atlantic, Cape May, Cumberland, Salem)	Atlantic City LA (Atlantic)
8	Vineland Area (Cumberland, Salem)		Vineland-Millville-Bridgeton LA (Cumberland) Salem LA (Salem) Ocean City-Wildwood-Cape May LA (Cape May

Source: U.S. Department of Labor, Bureau of Labor Statistics, New York Area Office, November 1983; U.S. Department of Housing and Urban Development, Newark Area Office, 1983

Areas in New Jersey which vary from a high of rents in the Freehold (West) and Newark Areas to a low of rents in the Vineland Area. As is visible from Exhibit 1A-3, there is reasonable correspondence between the Section 8 Fair Market Rent Areas and the Mount Laurel regions. The North Bergen and Newark Fair Market Rent Areas are identical to Mount Laurel Regions 1 and 2, respectively. The Freehold (East) Area and the Asbury Area taken together are equivalent to the Mount Laurel East Central Region 4. The Burlington/Camden/Gloucester Area in combination with the Trenton Area is equivalent to Southwest Region 5. Atlantic City Fair Market Rent Area plus the Vineland Area is equal to Mount Laurel South-Southwest Region 6. The only area that is somewhat different is the Freehold (West) Area which contains parts of the same counties as Mount Laurel 3, but in some cases, not all parts of the same county. Thus, again we find significant correspondence between existing Section 8 Fair Market Rent Areas and Mount Laurel regions.

Another aspect of U.S. Department of Housing and Urban Development territorial designation concerns the way information will be presented in the Annual Housing Survey. According to HUD personnel currently in the process of designing the 1985 Annual Housing Survey questionnaire, the latter will present housing information for metropolitan areas in accordance with MSA/PMSA designations.[7] It will follow the format of the county as the basic building block of information, and metropolitan formations will be derived from commuting linkages to the core county. Consequently, intercensal housing information will be presented in accordance with the Census format, and thus indirectly, in agreement with the derived Mount Laurel regions.

NOTES

1. State of New Jersey, Department of Environmental Protection, Division of Water Resources, The New Jersey Statewide Water Supply Master Plan (Trenton: April 1982).

2. State of New Jersey, Department of Transportation, New Jersey Transportation Plan (Trenton, no date), draft.

3. See U.S. Department of Labor, Employment and Training Administration, Directory of Important Labor Areas (Washington, D.C.: Government Printing Office, 1980), p. 1.

4. See FR 12702, March 28, 1983.

5. U.S. Department of Commerce, Bureau of the Census, The 1980 Census of Population and Housing: Public Use Sample (Washington, D.C.: Government Printing Office, 1982).

6. FR 12702, March 28, 1983.

7. See Richard L. Forstall and Donald E. Starsinic, "New Definitions of Metropolitan Statistical Areas," September 6, 1983 (mimeo).

CHAPTER 2—
DEFINITION OF THE MOUNT LAUREL POPULATION: PRESENT AND PROSPECTIVE HOUSING DEMAND

INTRODUCTION

It has been roughly eight years since the original Mount Laurel decision. Mount Laurel I clearly enunciated the principle that the general welfare of individuals includes their right to purchase housing absent the premium created by exclusionary land use controls.[1] According to the State Supreme Court, it failed, however, to ensure effective compliance to achieve its goal. The linkage of land use control as well as other legal instruments to increased housing opportunities for low and moderate income citizens anticipated in Mount Laurel had yet to be achieved. To compensate, the Mount Laurel II decision sets out a series of operational definitions designed to identify and determine a jurisdiction's obligation to improve the housing opportunities of its region's low and moderate income population.[2] It is the view of the Mount Laurel II Court that a clear, unbiased quantification of housing need, including both demand and supply, will provide municipalities and developers alike, with a more visible target requirement to which private market and public policies may be directed.

In this chapter we use as an areal base the research presented in Chapter 1 regarding the conceptual requirements and delineation of housing markets/regions in the State of New Jersey. There follows the need to clearly define the population upon which Mount Laurel II is focused: the low and moderate income household. The term "Mount Laurel population" unaccompanied by any modifier, is used to specify gross low and moderate income housing demand within New Jersey. This is related solely to the specification of low and moderate income and the households which fall within these income limitations. Once Mount Laurel eligible incomes are defined, the Mount Laurel-eligible population will be identified: The extant income-constrained and ill-housed population, and the purely income-constrained population projected for a period of time into the future. This categorization into two temporal segments of the state's lower income population reflects the Justices' decision regarding current (present) and future (prospective) lower income housing need. Present housing need is primarily composed of low and moderate income families that are poorly housed; prospective housing need is primarily composed of low and moderate income families that would shift locations in search of jobs, yet cannot find housing because existing land use controls and other municipal hindrances prohibit this housing from being afforded.

Each of these groups of Mount Laurel-eligible households (existing, deficient housing/income constrained and prospective, income-constrained) is described in the chapter which follows. The respective Mount Laurel populations are defined in detail, including the assumptions inherent to the specification of each; we then determine and discuss the exact number of households within these two population groups and present this information by the various housing regions within the state.

DEFINING THE UNDERHOUSED POPULATION

The purpose of the following section is to trace the perception of the underhoused population in the United States and from this to develop workable definitions of both current and future housing need. The section begins with an explanation of who is underhoused in the United States and from this derives a definition of present and prospective Mount Laurel housing need. Other possible definitions are compared to those chosen here and the shortcomings of those alternatives discussed. Finally, several examples of comparable definition selections are cited from recognized national, regional, and state sources.

The underhoused population has been defined by three housing unit characteristics: physical condition, cost, and location. Of the three, the first -- physical condition -- has been the most compelling, both historically and currently.

Housing Physical Condition

To be "underhoused" in the United States has for the most part been associated with physical deterioration of the housing unit or structure. The federal government's earliest involvement in housing was prompted by physical inadequacy. For example, in 1898, $20,000 was appropriated by Congress to investigate "slum conditions" in large cities.[3] A decade later, Theodore Roosevelt appointed a President's Housing Commission with a similar mandate to consider the physical condition of the housing stock:[4]

> This Commission was appointed to evaluate slum conditions. In its report the Commission recommended government loans to build habitable dwellings, condemnation and purchase of slum properties by the government and improvement or replacement of these so that inexpensive and healthful habitations would be available to the poor. (emphasis added)

So paramount was the concern for housing's physical deterioration and its linkage to unsafe and unsanitary conditions that its mediation was sought in many ways -- conducting national architectural design contests, building massive publicly-operated housing projects, enacting the first U.S. Housing Act, and appointing national study commissions to provide standards for healthful housing.[5] Examples of these efforts include the air shaft design which permitted light and air to interior high-rise housing units (1901), Knickerbocker Homes in New York City built under the Reconstruction Finance Corporation in 1932, the Housing Act of 1937, and the Committee on the Hygiene of Housing (American Public Health Association, 1945) which recommended minimum size dwelling units, direct access to each unit, minimum densities, etc.[6]

The physical orientation of designating an underhoused population has been carried on through many of the subsidized housing programs which exist today. These were spawned by numerous Housing Acts.[7] The first in the post-World War II period was the Housing Act of 1949. This legislation declared a "national housing policy and goal" with an emphasis on the alleviation of physically inadequate housing:[8]

> ...Governmental assistance should be given to the elimination of substandard and inadequate housing through clearance of slums and blight and to the provision of adequate housing for families of low incomes where the need is not being met by private enterprise. (emphasis added)

A similar physical orientation characterized ensuing housing programs including Sections 202(1959), 221(d)(3) (1961), 235 and 236 (1968), and Section 8 and the Community Development Block Grant (1974).[9] Most of these provided a subsidy for new construction to replace housing that would have been lost due to deterioration.[10] In each case for grant application, a sponsor of such housing had to produce an estimate of need based on some local or Census measure of deteriorated housing. Further, most forthcoming subsidies had to be linked with tax forgiveness provisions or eminent domain powers also applicable only in deteriorated or blighted areas.[11]

The culmination of the housing deterioration-underhoused need linkage is the Housing Assistance Plan (HAP). The latter had to be prepared by communities as a prerequisite to Community Development Block Grant (CDBG) funding (Title I - Housing and Community Development Act of 1974).[12] Here current need is determined by using a variety of indices including "number of deteriorated units (overcrowded, lacking plumbing facilities, etc.)"[13] The emphasis on physical condition is evident from the 1983 CDBG regulations on the housing conditions which must be described in the HAP:[14]

> (1) Conditions. The grantee shall describe the condition of the current housing stock in the community by providing a statistical profile which describes housing conditions by the number of occupied

and vacant units in standard and substandard condition. The grantee shall develop its own definition of substandard housing which, at a minimum, shall include units which do not meet the Section 8 Existing Housing Quality Standards.... (emphasis added)

Housing Cost

A second conceptualization of underhoused is related to the price the occupant must pay relative to income. Under this approach, a housing unit could be physically sound yet could still be counted as inadequate if the occupant had to bear a burdensome charge. This sense of underhoused, however, has never been adopted as an independent underhoused measure guiding public housing policy -- when used it has always been linked to the physical deterioration of the unit or structure.

In post-World War II federal housing subsidies, the issue of shelter cost-affordability had only come into play as a cut-off mechanism as to who would be eligible for replacement housing for those structures which were seriously deteriorated or potentially to be lost to blight. Families with incomes below certain levels could qualify for public housing, for instance, but resultant rents, reflecting operating costs, were met by tenants regardless of rent-to-income ratios. In fact, tenants were selected based on their ability to pay. Complete families were selected over broken families, in part, because of their resources -- an important factor as operating costs had to be self-sustaining. The poorest of families were not housed in public housing but rather by filtering in the private market.

It was only from the mid-1960s onward, that some efforts were made to modify the federal housing subsidy mechanisms so as to assist the underhoused as defined by their burdensome shelter costs. For example, in the mid-1960s, the Sections 23 and 101 programs first established the principle of income-related subsidies.[15] In both programs, the federal government would pay the difference between market rent and what lower-income families could afford. In 1969, the Brooke Amendment decreed that public housing tenants should pay only one-quarter of their incomes for rent.[16] In 1974, the Section 236 program was replaced by the Section 8 subsidy. While both programs assisted specific buildings/projects, the latter operated in a manner similar to the Brooke Amendment -- rents paid by tenants would equal 25 percent of their earnings and no more.[17] Four years later, the one-quarter share concept was extended to the Experimental Housing Allowance Program (EHAP) of 1978. An important difference with EHAP, however, was that tenants would be allowed to shop for housing with vouchers which were equivalent to cash. Sound housing would not be grouped in one location in favor of another, but rather be privately available in any location whose owner was willing to take the voucher from a program participant who was willing to live there.

The results of the programs linking the idea that a family is underhoused because it pays too much for housing have been open to question. The Brooke Amendment seriously compromised the finances of public housing. While it limited the rents tenants could pay, it never secured the full increase in federal subsidies needed to cover the ensuing shortfall in public housing operating income. The Section 8 program still exists, but its funding has been drastically cut. EHAP and its equivalents are still to be found, but they remain experimental in nature.[18] The costs of addressing the underhoused, when this group is defined by their limited resources to pay for shelter, are so demanding that even the federal government has backed away.

In sum, the idea that a family is underhoused because it pays too high a proportion of its income for shelter is a relatively recent and experimental concept in American housing policy. Moreover, even when it has been employed, it has retained its relationship to the concept of the underhoused as defined by blight. The outer demand figure for all of these programs has been housing occupied by the poor that was <u>inferior</u> and subsequently would be lost to attrition.* Rather than rebuild, those that occupied poor housing would be given public assistance. The idea that <u>all</u> occupants of sound private housing above a certain rent-to-income ratio were paying too much for housing and should be publicly subsidized by places in public housing, Section 8 commitments, housing vouchers, or the like, has yet to be formally adopted in national housing programs. The following commentary on the inception of the Section 101 program is indicative:[19]

> The administration bill . . . went on to limit eligibility within [indicated] income brackets to four specified groups: the elderly; the physically handicapped; those displaced from their homes by governmental action; and those occupying substandard housing . . . . Clearly there would be little reason to make a subsidy available to a family even of eligible income that through some happy circumstance was already adequately housed (in a sound unit) without such assistance (note added).

<u>Housing Location</u>

A third aspect of potentially being underhoused is living in a unit which is poorly sited in that it is located far from one's place of work. A number of journal articles have been written on this subject, some of which are cited in Chapter 1, others of which appear in the bibliography of this report. According to this literature, jobs in increasing frequency, are concentrated in outlying locations. The residences that normally would be

---

*The <u>effective</u> demand figure was related to what the federal government could afford to subsidize which was much less than total deteriorated housing demand.

accessible to these jobs and affordable by workers are not being built or built cheaply there, because of over-restrictive local land use regulations. A household is thus underhoused if it must endure a burdensome journey-to-work from a residence located afar or is denied employment opportunities because of excessive journey-to-work distances. "Excessive" journey-to-work has usually been defined as greater than 45 minutes to one hour for a one-way trip.

This concept of being underhoused is the most recent of all and relates almost exclusively to the exclusionary zoning literature of the early 1970s and later. While a recognized concern of federal housing policy, only the HAP program of the Community Development Block Grant requires that the poor "expected to reside" as a result of job growth be included in the estimate of local housing need. This is also an estimate of prospective rather than present need.

THE UNDERHOUSED AND MOUNT LAUREL II

With this information as a backdrop, let us now use these historical antecedents within the framework of statements of the New Jersey Supreme Court to define an underhoused population in New Jersey both presently and in the future.[20]

> "Every municipality's land use regulations should provide a realistic opportunity for decent housing for at least some part of its resident poor who now occupy dilapidated housing." (Mount Laurel II - slip op. at 26)
>
> "When gross population projections are used for a region, it is more likely that the total lower income housing need will be included and much more likely that whatever lower income housing need is in fact included will be distributed fairly." (Mount Laurel II - slip op. at 96)
>
> "In order to meet their Mount Laurel obligations, municipalities, at the very least must remove all municipally created barriers to the construction of their fair share of lower income housing. Thus to the extent necessary to meet their prospective fair share and provide for their indigenous poor (and, in some cases, a portion of the region's poor) municipalities must remove zoning and subdivision restrictions and exactions that are not necessary to protect health and safety." (Mount Laurel II - slip op. at 97)

To define the underhoused, the three criteria of housing quality, location, and cost, must be considered.

Housing Deterioration

An underhoused family is clearly one that occupies housing which is deteriorated. Although approximately five percent of the general population of New Jersey occupies housing that, via multiple criteria, may be judged deteriorated, only those who fall within Mount Laurel income specifications will be considered as such. This relates to the concern of the Court for public remedy and involves their definition of the income groups which require a Mount Laurel remedy: low-and moderate-income families at less than 50 percent and 50-80 percent of regional median household income, respectively. This follows HUD Section 8 income eligibility standards and will be developed in a later section of this chapter. The concern of the Court clearly relates to those who are underhoused within certain income groups and, by extension, underhoused not by choice. The not by choice concept is a very important one which cuts across many of the components of the underhoused population calculation.

As will be pointed out in a later section, housing deterioration is difficult to define yet clearly is more than pure physical deterioration. A complete kitchen, not being crowded, a family's own bathroom, central heating, and an ability to enter without entry through another dwelling unit, or without having to climb more than four stories all add to a threshold quality of the dwelling unit. In a subsequent section, it will be shown how each of these aspects of housing relate to "housing sufficiency" and an absence of one or more to "housing deficiency."

By signaling the proportion of the population living in a housing deficient state according to characteristics of the unit that will indicate such deficiencies, one can begin to specify a deficiency-related underhoused population as of 1980. Multiple variables of the type listed above are chosen to indicate housing deficiency. The population living in deficient housing as of 1980, is isolated by selecting, from all housing at that time, units with multiple deficiencies. These units are chosen only from those families within Mount Laurel incomes following the direction of the Court in terms of the target population. This is a liberal definition of housing demand as all housing quality indicators which are available to signal deficient housing are employed and no standard of "tolerable deficiency" reflecting housing deficiency in the larger, non-Mount Laurel population is used to reduce the numbers derived here.

Further, there are measures of deficiency which include either crowding or excessive climbing without elevators which are counted in aggregate. In the first case, the addition of several large units to the housing stock for large families currently occupying small units could occasion a chain of moves which would render many more smaller units standard by reducing the number of occupants living in them. In the second case, all units in a four-story or more structure without an elevator are considered deficient even if every one of the units on the first three floors is sound. These somewhat inflate estimates of need related to these particular measures of housing deficiency.

To provide for housing deficiency in the future, any household of Mount Laurel income that would be generated afer 1980 will have a housing unit provided for it. Thus, the share of future Mount Laurel income-specified households likely to live in deficient housing in the future is accounted for by a projection of need which includes all Mount Laurel income-specified households for twenty years into the future, only a share of which might, sans the Court's requirement, have lived in deficient housing.

The Mount Laurel income households living in standard housing in 1980 (and not subject to a household change over the next twenty years) are assumed to remain in standard housing over this period of time. Since currently, close to 90 percent of those with Mount Laurel incomes live in standard housing, and this percentage has increased since 1970 due to formidable 1970 to 1980 housing supply at one end and a high scrappage rate of old housing at the other, this is not an overly severe assumption.

Commuting Distances

A second component of the underhoused population is those families which live at a distance from their jobs whose employment is believed to be limited due to this inaccessibility.

Within Mount Laurel income categories, this has been handled for present need, i.e., to 1980, in the definition of region. Post 1980, it is handled in the projections of housing for all new Mount Laurel households. Any Mount Laurel household which is formed in any locale (natural increase), or any that comes in search of a job (migration), are both accounted for in the projection technique. On the whole, job and population growth in New Jersey is relatively slow growing. Thus, the projections of gains in Mount Laurel households reflect interregional change (in-state shifts) more so than they do net statewide growth.

Prior to 1980, the job-residence linkage has been asssumed to be acceptable if the job and the residence are in the same region. Statewide, eighty-eight percent of those of Mount Laurel incomes live and work in the same region. For those who commute outside their resident region, it is assumed to be by choice, as the percentage levels and rent/income characteristics of those who commute in to but live outside the several regions are similar to those who live inside and commute out.

Finally, when the journey-to-work of the income-qualified Mount Laurel population commuting in-region to the journey-to-work of the New Jersey population at large are compared, they are about the same. Close to six out of seven (82 percent) of those employed with Mount Laurel incomes in 1980 commute less than 30 minutes to work; the average is under 20 minutes (19.4). When out-of-state commuters are added to the aggregate New Jersey population (almost all affluent residents), only two-thirds of this expanded group commutes less than 30 minutes; the average is approximately 25 minutes (24.9). Fully, one-fourth of these New Jersey residents commute from 30 to 60 minutes, almost double the rate of the income constained Mount Laurel population.

Excessive Housing Costs

Another concern, in terms of an underhoused population, are those whose housing costs exceed acceptable limits, i.e., those households, for instance, whose rent-to-income ratios as specified in New Jersey's Supreme Court, are in excess of 25 percent.

For the future population, Mount Laurel income constrained demand is projected for two time periods. Required rental levels by family size and location are estimated. Bridge mechanisms and filtering/rehabilitation are viewed as means which may enable: (1) new construction to reach moderate income affordable limits in the first case, or (2) older housing to reach lower-income affordable limits, in the second. Thus, within defined Mount Laurel income categories, future need by ability to afford (using the 25 percent rule) is accounted for in the projections of need and affordability. Qualitatively-reduced new housing in terms of space, amenities and infrastructure is one of the ways that bridge mechanisms attempt to make the new housing available to moderate-income families. Another vehicle is through the <u>net</u> supply of used standard housing that filters down to lower-income families.

Income-constrained Mount Laurel households in 1980 living in sound (non-deteriorated) housing with rent-to-income ratios in excess of 25 percent, should they be part of households forming over the next two decades (from any age cohort, including sub-families), will be picked up as part of future demand. Income-constrained Mount Laurel households in 1980 living in deficient housing with rent-to-income ratios in excess of 25 percent, will be accounted for as a portion of existing housing-deficient demand.

Finally, those income-constrained Mount Laurel households living in 1980 in sound housing, but whose rent-to-income ratios are in excess of 25 percent, are assumed to continue to occupy this housing at these costs. It is difficult to control for the quality of these units. We do know that many of those of Mount Laurel incomes who occupy units costing more than one-fourth of their income are more spaciously housed and own their units. One-third of those who occupy this space have one room <u>more</u> than those equivalent income groups living at less than 25 percent rent-to-income ratio, and one-half of those who paid more than $300 in monthly occupancy costs in 1980, owned their own units. In addition, while costs are somewhat higher in this sound housing compared to those households who occupy deficient housing, it is still <u>inexpensive</u> relative to the costs of new housing.

It is assumed that overbuilding in response to existing, deficient-housing demand quotas, and the location of a share of this housing away from larger cities to outlying areas, will reduce pressure on the market and the rents in these areas will decline. In addition, general housing supply projections which include some oversupply for non-Mount Laurel income groups will further reduce pressure from the market as more luxurious housing is passed down to lower income groups.

Finally, at the other end of the high rent-to-income scale, are very small one and two person families living as subfamilies which are a part of the aggregate Mount Laurel income-constrained population. Their incomes are so low that they make any rent-to-income ratio extremely high. In terms of the future ability to house these families, even filtering and rehabilitation might be beyond their means and they might best remain as subfamilies in private house-sharing relationships. This is a segment of the population whose support would require massive subsidization from general revenues and thus is outside the purview of this study.

THE DEFINITION OF PRESENT AND PROSPECTIVE HOUSING NEED

The foregoing discussion considered the conceptual origins of defining an underhoused population and related this to the statements and concerns of the Court. As such we define present or existing* Mount Laurel housing need as: income-constrained Mount Laurel households occupying deficient housing.

Housing market regions have been defined which minimize existing journey-to-work as over 88 percent of households who work in a region also live there. Current Mount Laurel purely income-constrained households that are in the labor force and commute within the region do so in less time than the New Jersey population at large. Those who commute out of and live inside the region are balanced by those who live outside and commute in. As their income and rental profiles are relatively similar, if those who commute outside chose to live inside, theoretically there is housing space at a price to accommodate them.

Prospective Mount Laurel housing need is defined as income-constrained households of the future. These are households which, since 1980, are formed due to natural increase in or migration to their defined housing region. This need reflects not deteriorated housing as of 1980 but rather low and moderate income households which will require housing due to population shifts and family growth subsequent to 1980. This need is projected for twenty years into the future using aggregate population projections of the New Jersey Department of Labor. They account for both low- and moder-

---

*Indigenous need is a geographic rather than temporal term which reflects housing need created by situations occurring within the specific geographic location. The term "indigenous" literally means "occurring naturally in an area - not introduced." Indigenous need as used by the Court is a term which relates to a municipality and allocation and as such does not appear elsewhere in this report. It is a term which in addition to subregional versus regional applicability, is particularly difficult to isolate due to the nature of both present and prospective need data bases.

ate-income need based on similar shares of the population which existed in 1980.

While there are other definitions which may be proposed for present/prospective housing need we feel that the definitions adopted in the following chapter reflect the best interpretation of historic designation of both housing need and housing need within the capacity of housing supply.

The State of New Jersey Housing Allocation Report sought by the Court as a potentially acceptable method of determining and allocating housing need defines existing need as deficient housing (dilapidated housing, vacancy, and overcrowding) and prospective need as a projection based on purely low- and moderate-income share of the future population. The Housing Allocation Strategy for Mahwah, New Jersey prepared as one of the first determinations of need subsequent to Mount Laurel II employed a similar strategy. Finally, most of the housing allocation formulae which are discussed in Chapter 7 also begin with similar projections of present and future need.

OTHER POSSIBLE DEFINITIONS OF EXISTING MOUNT LAUREL HOUSING NEED AND WHY THEY HAVE NOT BEEN CHOSEN

Purely Income-Constrained Current Population

There are currently approximately 2.6 million households in New Jersey of which slightly over 1.0 million qualify within Mount Laurel income limitations of 50-80 percent or less than 50 percent of regional median household income. In terms of physical housing condition, 900,000 occupy sound housing according to the specification of deficiency used later in this chapter. Further, within previously defined housing markets, close to 850,000 are within acceptable journey-to-work time vis-à-vis their present residence.

If we were to attempt to provide housing for this entire population, one million net new* additional units would have to be provided and one million households would each have a choice of one of two housing units. The aggregate of units not chosen, one million in total, would go vacant. If we build 400,000 new net units per decade in New Jersey in good housing years, and 25 percent of all new units or 100,000 were to be allocated to those of Mount Laurel income, then under this definition of housing demand, it would take ten decades or 100 years to meet existing/present need.

---

*in the most generous sense (no rehabilitation or filtering considered)

The Proportion of the Current Population With Severe Journeys-to-Work

By definition, a housing region reflects housing brought into competition through mutually acceptable journeys-to-work. The regions developed in Chapter 1 emphasize this relationship between housing and transportation costs. The regions, while reflecting numerous advantages, remain journey-to-work based. Journeys-to-work within regions are neither excessive absolutely nor relative to the New Jersey population at large. Further, for the small share of commuters between regions, it is a relatively equal exchange with minor exceptions.

With this overview of the approach to defining the underhoused completed, we can now detail the definitions and specification of the Mount Laurel population.

DEFINITION AND SPECIFICATION OF MOUNT LAUREL INCOME ELIGIBILITY

The basic purpose of the most current Mount Laurel decision is to improve the housing opportunities of low and moderate income households. Given the many chances for misinterpretation, the Court has provided an operational definition of the population to which housing is to be made available.

The definition of low and moderate income households is taken from the regulations governing the implementation of the Section 8 Rent Supplement program administered by the U.S. Department of Housing and Urban Development under the U.S. Housing Act 1937 at 42 U.S.C. 1437.[21] Low income households are those whose incomes fall below fifty percent (50 percent) of the area's median household income. Moderate income households are those whose incomes fall below eighty percent (80 percent) of the areas' median household income yet are above the 50 percent of median income cutoff for low income households.[22]

Adjustment Factors: Family Size

Following the guidelines of the federal statute implementing the Section 8 program, the definitions of low and moderate income are qualified in three ways. First the household income used to qualify a household under the definition of low or moderate income, is adjusted for household size. The way this is done is through a constant percentage share of an areal median household income which is adjusted for household size. Eighty percent or 50 percent of median household income of a housing service area

(SMSA or CMSA, PMSA, MSA)* is assumed to represent the income average of the upper threshold of a four person moderate or low income household. This average income standard is adjusted downward for households of less than four persons to a minimum of 70 percent of the four person standard (moderate and low) and upwards to a maximum of 125% of the same standard for a household of 8 or more persons (See Exhibit 2-1). This is the procedure used by the U.S. Department of Housing and Urban Development to qualify families of different size for various housing subsidies.[23]

Adjustment Factors: Geographic Area

The second qualification placed upon the operational definition of low and moderate income households involves the construction of the median income value. The median is a statistical term representing a point on a distribution of income that is possessed by the family in the exact middle. Expressed in a different way, the median is the value obtained from a rank ordered distribution in which 50 percent of the cases are above this value and 50 percent are below it.

Any measure of central tendency is influenced by the set of values it is designed to represent. This brings us to the important term, area. The Mount Laurel decision has been handed down in order to improve the housing opportunities of lower income families. This implies that an appropriate areal spatial dimension is incorporated in this term. That is, housing for families in East Orange, cannot be constructed in East Orange alone and be expected to meet the mandate of the Decision. The concept of a regional or substate housing market and the regional evaluation of housing cost across these markets are inherent to the Mount Laurel decision. This has been simulated by again relying on the Section 8 regulations. In these regulations, HUD has constructed median incomes for each SMSA or separate county in the state. SMSAs are determined by the Federal Office of Management and Budget (OMB) and represent geographical subareas upon which data are maintained for purposes of federal grant dispersal and other reasons. These have been revised by OMB to the CMSAs, PMSAs and MSAs described in Chapter 1. The U.S. Department of Housing and Urban Development continues to use the SMSA designation for income calculation purposes. When a change to the CMSAs, PMSAs and MSAs is made by HUD, SMSA incomes will be revised; however, these changes being minor in impact have not yet been scheduled.[24] Sixteen SMSAs in areas over the state (12 PMSAs and 4 counties) for use with the Section 8 program have been defined. These sixteen areas have been made coterminous with the six housing regions based on CMSAs, PMSAs and MSAs by collapsing and weighting the income information provided for the SMSAs and separate counties.

---

*Standard Metropolitan Statistical Area (SMSA), Consolidated Metropolitan Statistical Area (CMSA), Primary Metropolitan Statistical Area (PMSA), Metropolitan Statistical Area (MSA). See the previous chapter for definition of terms and origins of areal designations. See the following two pages for discussion of SMSA versus PMSA.

Within each area exist sixteen possible median incomes: 8 for families of 1 to 8 persons in the moderate income category, and 8 for those in the low income categories. The use of the SMSA and in the future MSA as the legal entities identifying an effective housing market, combines the substantive reasons these areas were clustered together (journey-to-work, density, metropolitan character, etc.) with the realities of future available, regular data gathering. The result is a data base that can be used to test future compliance with the decision.

Adjustment Factors: Income Inflation

The third qualification to the use of the median income data of the Census comes from the recognition of income inflation across the state, as well as income change within one area relative to others. In order to make the Mount Laurel decision effective over time, the basic income definition must be founded upon real value or what income allows families to purchase and not on a dollar figure that fluctuates with national or international conditions and policy. This assures, for instance, that the same amount of housing purchased for say 25% of income in 1980 may be purchased for the same share of income in 1983. The USHUD Section 8 "income limits" are again appropriate to the task in that annual updates of "housing consumer income" by area will be available throughout at least the life of the Section 8 program.

Median Family Incomes: By Year and Area

The most recent "income limits" available for the 16 areas in the state have been reproduced for information purposes in Exhibit 2-1. This table has been prepared to reflect conditions as of 1 April 1983. Interested officials should contact the Area Economist of the U.S. Department of Housing and Urban Development in Newark for more up-to-date information.

Methodology for the Definition of Mount Laurel-Eligible Population

The method used by the Rutgers University, Center for Urban Policy Research in quantifying the conceptual content in the Mount Laurel decision differentiates between Mount Laurel-eligible present and prospective populations. For the present Mount Laurel-eligible population, CUPR has employed the 1980 Public Use Sample of the U.S. Census of Population and Housing as its factual base. This provides the most recent definitive data base.

The effective income limits for inclusion in the Mount Laurel decision were determined from the U.S. Department of Housing and Urban Development's Section 8 Rent Subsidy program, adjusting 1979 median family income deter-

EXHIBIT 2-1

MOUNT LAUREL INCOME LIMITS FOR LOW AND MODERATE INCOME FAMILIES BY AREA OF THE STATE, 1 MARCH, 1983

AREA	MEDIAN INCOME	PROGRAM	INCOME LIMITS 1 Per	2 Per	3 Per	4 Per	5 Per	6 Per	7 Per	8+ Per
SMSA	$27,200	Low income	$ 9,500	$10,900	$12,250	$13,600	$14,700	$15,800	$16,850	$17,950
Allentown-Bethlehem-Easton, PA-NJ		moderate income	15,250	17,400	19,600	21,750	23,100	24,500	25,850	27,200
SMSA	26,500	Low income	9,300	10,600	11,900	13,250	14,300	15,350	16,450	17,500
Atlantic City, NJ		moderate income	14,850	16,950	19,100	21,200	22,500	23,850	25,150	26,500
SMSA	22,600	Low income	8,650	9,900	11,100	12,350	13,350 '	14,350	15,300	16,300
Jersey City, NJ		moderate income	13,850	15,800	17,750	19,750	21,000	22,200	23,450	24,700
SMSA	31,600	Low income	11,050	12,650	14,200	15,800	17,050	18,350	19,600	20,850
Long Branch-Asbury Park, NJ		moderate income	17,700	20,200	22,750	25,300	26,850	28,450	30,000	31,600
SMSA	32,700	Low income	11,450	13,100	14,700	16,350	17,650	18,950	20,250	21,600
New Brunswick-Perth Amboy-Sayreville, NJ		moderate income	18,200	20,800	23,400	26,000	27,600	29,250	30,850	32,500
SMSA	24,900	Low income	10,000	11,400	12,800	14,250	15,400	16,550	17,650	18,800
New York City, NY-NJ		moderate income	15,250	17,400	19,550	21,750	23,100	24,450	25,850	27,200
SMSA	31,500	Low income	11,450	13,100	14,700	16,350	17,650	18,950	20,250	21,600
Newark, NJ		moderate income	17,650	20,150	22,700	25,200	26,750	28,350	29,999	31,500
SMSA	26,800	Low income	10,100	11,500	12,950	14,400	15,550	16,700	17,850	19,000
Paterson-Clifton-Passaic, NJ		moderate income	15,250	17,400	19,550	21,750	23,100	24,450	25,850	27,200
SMSA	27,200	Low income	9,850	11,300	12,700	14,100*	15,250	16,350	17,500	18,600
Philadelphia, PA-NJ		moderate income	15,250	17,400	19,600	21,750	23,100	24,500	25,850	27,200
SMSA	29,300	Low income	10,250	11,700	13,200	14,650	15,800	17,000	18,150	19,350
Trenton, NJ		moderate income	16,400	18,750	21,100	23,450	24,900	26,350	27,850	29,300

EXHIBIT 2-1 (continued)

MOUNT LAUREL INCOME LIMITS FOR LOW AND MODERATE INCOME FAMILIES BY AREA OF THE STATE, 1 MARCH, 1983

AREA	MEDIAN INCOME	PROGRAM	INCOME LIMITS 1 Per	2 Per	3 Per	4 Per	5 Per	6 Per	7 Per	8+ Per
SMSA	22,600	Low income	8,550	9,750	11,000	12,000	13,200	14,150	15,150	16,100
Vineland-Millville-Bridgeton, NJ		moderate income	13,650	15,600	17,550	19,500	20,700	21,950	23,150	24,400
SMSA	28,900	Low income	10,100	11,550	13,000	14,450	15,600	16,750	17,900	19,050
Wilmington, DE-NJ-MD		moderate income	16,200	18,500	20,800	23,100	24,550	26,000	27,450	28,900
County	21,800	Low income	7,650	8,700	9,800	10,900	11,750	12,650	13,500	14,400
Cape May		moderate income	12,200	13,950	15,700	17,450	18,550	19,600	20,700	21,800
County	33,100	Low income	11,600	13,250	14,900	16,550	17,850	19,200	20,500	21,850
Hunterdon		moderate income	18,200	20,800	23,400	26,000	27,600	29,250	30,850	32,500
County	24,100	Low income	8,450	9,650	10,850	12,050	13,000	14,000	14,950	15,900
Ocean		moderate income	13,500	15,400	17,350	19,300	20,500	21,700	22,900	24,100
County	29,200	Low income	10,200	11,700	13,150	14,600	15,750	16,950	18,100	19,250
Sussex		moderate income	16,350	18,700	21,000	23,350	24,800	26,300	27,750	29,200

Source: USDHUD, 1983. NB. USDHUD prepared "Income Limit" bulletin will use the term very low income in place of the Mount Laurel court's use of the term low income. Similarly, the HUD term lower income has been replaced in Mount Laurel usage by the term moderate income.

* Would normally be $13,600. Error in 1980 income estimates has been carried over with 1983 income estimates in order to hold-harmless those households accepted into the program based upon the 1980 figures. HUD hopes that inflationary forces will permit them to correct this figure without harming current Section 8 participants.

minations so that they are comparable in time and geographic coverage with county information of the 1980 Census of Population and Housing, New Jersey Public Use Sample.[25] The basic median family income figures by year and area are shown in Exhibit 2-2.[26] The procedure used to delineate the prospective Mount Laurel population will be discussed in a subsequent section.

Methodology for Definition -- Exceptions, Alterations

As shown in the two preceding sections of this Chapter, it is absolutely essential to identify households that fall within the income limits as corrected by household size. The household size corrections can alter the income limitation by as much as 25 percent, either upward for larger families or downward, for smaller families. This degree of specificity is possible only by examining the individual records of those who have completed the Census forms. This can be done on a sample of the total Census for New Jersey residents through the use of the 1980 Public Use Sample.

The component of the 1980 Public Use Sample used to quantify and characterize both the present and the prospective Mount Laurel eligible population is a 2.5 percent sample of all census records that contained questions about possible work trip length and residence.

The study of housing demand requires household, not individual information; therefore, the initial sample had to be adjusted through several refinement procedures such that a workable file of Mount Laurel-eligible households could be examined. Essentially, four classes of individuals were excluded from further consideration; these were:

1) indivduals living in group quarters,
2) individuals living in institutions,
3) individuals living as boarders, and
4) individuals living as lodgers.

This eliminated college students, prisoners, nursing home occupants and boarders, etc. from being counted as part of the Mount Laurel population. Households were constructed from the individuals remaining in the sample. The final set of households consisted of three classes:

1) groups of related individuals,
2) subfamilies, and
3) unrelated individuals living together.

Some socioeconomic characteristics, such as household income, were derived from a summation of all of the relevant characteristics of the members of the household. Other characteristics, such as age or journey-to-work, were made attributes of the chief income earner. This individual's characteristics, therefore, became representative of the household as a

EXHIBIT 2-2

NEW JERSEY MEDIAN FAMILY INCOME OF A FAMILY OF FOUR FOR 1979 AND 1983 BY AREA*

Area	Median Family Income (4 person family) 1979	1983
Cape May	$17,042	$21,800
Hunterdon	26,618	33,100
Ocean	18,800	24,100
Sussex	23,532	29,200
Warren (Allentown-Bethlehem-Easton, PA-NJ)	21,272	27,200
Hudson (Jersey City, NJ)	17,659	22,600
Middlesex (New Brunswick, Perth Amboy-Sayreville,NJ)	25,603	32,700
Essex, Morris, Somerset Union Counties (Newark, NJ)	24,534	31,500
Burlington, Camden, Gloucester Counties (Philadelphia, PA-NJ)	21,248	27,200
Cumberland County (Vineland-Millville-Bridgeton,NJ)	17,556	22,600
Atlantic County (Atlantic City, NJ)	19,216	26,500
Monmouth County (Long Branch-Asbury Park, NJ)	24,526	31,600
Bergen County (New York City, NY-NJ)	19,268	24,900
Passaic County (Paterson-Clifton-Passaic, NJ)	21,010	26,800
Mercer County (Trenton, NJ)	22,972	29,300
Salem County (Wilmington, DE-NJ-MD)	22,041	28,900

*The median family income of each of the areas listed in this exhibit was derived by the Bureau of the Census. Families as opposed to households were arrayed by ascending order of income in order to acquire a representative value for the area. The median family income value was then assigned to a four person family for purposes of the Section 8 program. While, this may appear somewhat arbitrary, it is basically a mechanism that permits HUD to adjust income ceilings by family size in order to certify a family for eligibility to the Section 8 Rent Supplement program. This breakout was displayed previously on Exhibit 2-1.

Source: Memo, U.S. Department of Housing and Urban Development, 6 April 1983.

whole. In most instances he/she is referred to as the designated household head.

In the case of subfamily designation, the cluster of individuals who identified themselves as a separate family living under the roof of another family were treated as a separate household for the purpose of examining their income eligibility for Mount Laurel consideration.

The final element of data preparation was the aggregation of households into regions. The aggregation procedure was accomplished by use of the county of residence code available for each individual. In two cases the rules ensuring confidentiality for the persons filling out the forms required that the Census aggregate two counties. This necessary grouping, due to data limitations, was taken into account when regions were originally specified (see Chapter 1). The cases of multicounty groupings are: (1) Salem and Cape May Counties, and (2) Warren and Hunterdon Counties. In all other cases individual county of residence was available for use in aggregating cases by region.

SPECIFYING MOUNT LAUREL PRESENT HOUSING DEMAND

In the case of the household currently falling within the Mount Laurel eligibility guidelines, the court has defined the obligation in terms of those residing in what it terms "dilapidated" housing.[27] This distinction is of value in that it recognizes the fact that many households eligible for Mount Laurel consideration under the income thresholds are physically well-housed. Throughout the remainder of this study we shall therefore apply the term: present Mount Laurel-eligible households to those households that both are physically ill-housed and meet the low and moderate income guidelines.

Yet what is the magnitude of New Jersey's low and moderate income households whose current living conditions require significant upgrading? How sure can we be of the various estimates of housing with deficiencies sufficient in magnitude to require alteration of the municipal land use regulations vis-à-vis Mount Laurel II? In order to answer these questions a brief history of attempts at evaluating housing quality must be presented.

Problems of Measurement

The first nationwide attempt at measuring the state of repair of the housing stock took place in 1940.[28] The 1940 Census of Housing broke ground in this area by requiring trained enumerators to judge the state of repair of each dwelling unit examined. Two conditions of repair were available to the enumerator: those units (1) not needing major repairs, and (2) needing major repairs.[29] The criterion for classification was based upon the presence or absence of a condition that, if left unattended, would undermine the soundness of the structure.[30]

On the surface such a definition seemed adequate to meet the needs at hand. However, with rising economic expectations fueled by the end of the war and an almost forgotten depression, no longer was simple soundness of structure thought to provide an adequate residence for Americans. The 1950 Census of Housing incorporated this optimism by shifting emphasis from one of process (needing repairs) to a static labeling of structural condition: dilapidated or not dilapidated. This dichotomy required enumerators to make an additional judgement over those made in the 1940 Census. Not only was the enumerator required to evaluate the dwelling unit's state of repair, but he had to judge and define the unit as adequate or inadequate for human occupancy. This conceptual scheme placed the Bureau of the Census in the middle of a conflict between two interest groups: those interested in slum clearance followed by new development, and those committed to rehabilitation of existing structures.[31]

The 1960 Census of Housing sought to bring a compromise solution to the issue of identifying housing quality. In the process of doing this, the complexity of the enumerator's task was again expanded. The decision process resulting in a definition of dilapidated, remained the same; however, the 1950's category "not dilapidated" was divided into the categories: sound and deteriorating.[32] Those favoring the static definition of sound and dilapidated housing still had their categories of Census information intact. Those favoring rehabilitation could now also point to the category "deteriorating" as a means to forestall massive clearance and social upheaval. However, the promised strong empirical basis for new policy statements was not forthcoming.

Evaluations and retests of the 1960 Census of Housing indicated significant inconsistencies in the enumeration of housing quality, especially from one city to another. Significant undercounts in one locale and overcounts in others of both the number and proportion of dilapidated units were asserted to exist with the 1960 Census.[33] Reasons for such problems were not hard to find. An item analysis of the Census form found a lack of definitions for terms indicating the degree of a defect, for methods used to combine defects, and for situations making the dwelling unit a safety hazard. Clearly, the enumerator was presented a document containing poor instructions; in addition, he was given an average of only one minute to rate the structural condition of the dwelling unit.[34]

If these difficulties were not enough, a new housing quality conceptual element was added to the 1960 Census document: standard or substandard.[35] While not affecting the enumerator's work, the standard-substandard dichotomy adds to the empirical content found in the definition of dilapidated housing, a value judgement as to the proper level of facilities to be found within the basic dwelling unit.[36] To be found substandard in the 1960 Census, the dwelling unit must have been found to be dilapidated or to be lacking either hot running water, a flush toilet for private use, or a bath or shower for private use.[37]

By adding an objective type indicator to the subjective evaluation of structural soundness, the verifiable content of this new housing quality index is heightened over that of the purely subjective structural quality index. However, the content validity of the index is just as problematic as was that of the older indices. While, it can be strongly argued that adequate plumbing is essential for health and safety, our ability to define exactly what must be included in the set of adequate plumbing and under what if any conditions it must be absent for a negative evaluation to be observed, is not settled. Furthermore, over time in this one specific area, we have greatly improved the quality of housing. New housing which has replaced old has been equipped with reasonably full plumbing such that, as of 1980, complete plumbing is found in 97 percent of all housing units some share of which exhibit very poor housing quality.[38]

Returning to the descriptive issue, it has been commonplace since the 1970 Census of Population and Housing to use a set of objective structural and facility-based attributes as surrogates of dilapidation. The reason for this is that due to the confusion over subjective housing quality measurement, questions regarding structural soundness of housing were removed from the Census instrument following the 1960 Census. Several attempts have been made over the past 20 years to test the strength of the relationships between objective facility attributes and structural soundness. For the most part, the results have been disappointing.[39] Since 1971 there have been a series of Annual Housing Surveys performed by the Bureau of the Census for the U.S. Department of Housing and Urban Development. Administered by interviewers, both objective and subjective answers have been solicited from householders. In addition to housing quality, the Annual Housing Survey queries residents regarding neighborhood characteristics. Information on such characteristics as environmental pollution, public services and neighborhood structural deterioration are included in the interview document. However, their ability to accurately measure structural soundness has yet to be confirmed.[40]

In summary, this short history of official housing quality measurement efforts has been shown to be one with severe problems regarding what it is that should be measured, how it should be measured and consequently, the validity and accuracy of what is specified as either good or poor housing quality. While we cannot fully resolve these questions in their relevance to the New Jersey Supreme Court Decision in South Burlington vs. Mount Laurel, we can probe some recently generated data from the U.S. Department of Housing and Urban Development (HUD) project known as the Five City Study to provide insight to measures of housing quality and the ultimate state of disrepair of the unit. The study is one of only a few to possess a high degree of internal agreement among research teams in recognizing and quantifying housing quality.[41]

Empirical Analyses of Measurement

First reported in 1975, the Five City Study brought together professionals from government, private building and trade associations, and from the academic community. Its purpose was the collection and examination of enumerator-acquired data on housing quality. The study linked interviewer administered questions regarding housing and neighborhood quality, with the quality of the dwelling unit and the neighborhood as judged by two teams of housing experts.

Blocks within each of the cities* were stratified by average housing value and rent, and sampled such that all strata would be adequately represented. The results of the study found that 4.1 percent of all of the dwelling units forming the population of the study were rated poor or hazardous (Exhibit 2-3).

The great value of this study is that it allows the researcher to compare the overall rating score with the existence of various census type indicators of deficiencies.

EXHIBIT 2-3

DISTRIBUTION OF FIVE CITIES STUDY HOUSING UNITS BY OVERALL RATING SCORE

Rating	Number of Dwelling Units	% of Dwelling Units
Good	421,100	33.1%
Satisfactory	797,900	62.8
Poor	52,600	4.1
Total	1,271,600	100.0%

Source: USHUD, Five City Study, Summer, 1972.

Exhibit 2-4 displays the joint distribution of housing and neighborhood deficiencies with the rater's overall evaluation of the neighborhood and the housing unit. The characteristics recorded by the "housing experts" represent the type of information collected by either the decennial Census of Population and Housing or by the Annual Housing Survey.

An examination of Exhibit 2-4 shows there are justifiable reasons for accepting these characteristics as surrogates of "poor" housing and neighborhood conditions. The data for the facilities available for use within a dwelling unit show this to be the case. Adequate heating is represented

---

*Trenton, NJ, Chicago, IL, Memphis, TN, Brownsville, TX, and Portland, OR.

EXHIBIT 2-4

A COMPARISON OF PROFESSIONAL RATERS' HOUSING DEFICIENCY EVALUATION WITH THE OCCURRENCE IN THE DWELLING UNIT OF AN OBJECTIVE CENSUS-DETERMINED INDEX OF DEFICIENT HOUSING

	Overall Rating Score of Unit and Neighborhood		
	Good	Satisfactory	Poor
Housing or Neighborhood Deficiency	Percentage of units with a given housing or neighborhood characteristic		
1. Room heaters, not vented or no heaters	18%*	27%	53%
2. With walls having peeling paint, crumbling plaster	5%	8%	62%
3. Lacking complete plumbing	6%	2%	28%
4. Light fixtures in common halls, some or none in working order	9%	5%	60%
5. Buildings in the neighborhood with boarded-up windows or doors	1%	12%	87%
6. Signs of rats or mice	1%	17%	61%
7. More than one person per room	4%	13%	53%
8. Income less than $5,000	16%	29%	65%

*Eighteen percent of all units rated good in quality also had a room heater deficiency.

Source: USDHUD, <u>Five City Study</u>, Summer, 1972.

by whole house heating systems using a flue or otherwise being properly vented. Raters found that 53 percent of the housing units ultimately rated poor did not possess such heating. Similarly, in terms of aspect of plumbing, 28 percent of the units rated poor lacked some plumbing facilities considered essential: hot running water, private toilet, or private bath. The pair of socioeconomic characteristics are also strongly associated with poor housing and neighborhood conditions. Taking income level of under $5,000 as an index of poverty (the national median household income at that time was $9,697), 65 percent of the dwelling units rated poor were occupied by families under the poverty level. Several neighborhood conditions have also been reported each showing strong associations with poor quality housing and neighborhoods. The observed presence of mice was found in 61 percent of the cases of poor quality housing; while buildings in the neighborhood with boarded-up windows or doors were found in 87 percent of the cases of poor housing ratings.

A more critical examination of Exhibit 2-4 shows that in each case the surrogate of dilapidation also provides erroneous values within houses and neighborhoods rated good and satisfactory. In the case of the heating index, 27 percent of satisfactory housing is deficient in this characteristic and 18 percent of good to excellent housing likewise has this deficiency. Similarly, the socioeconomic indices also give erroneous reading if they are interpreted to always represent dilapidation. An example is the linkage with people under the poverty level. The study finds 29 percent of the structures and neighborhoods rated satisfactory and 16 percent in good to excellent condition are occupied by such persons.

The point of this is, that not knowing beforehand what the quality analog is often leaves researchers open to a degree of error, when using these indices as surrogates of dilapidated housing. The linkages are far from inexorable. For example, the 53 percent of poor quality structures-neighborhoods that were deficient in terms of heating equipment represents 27,878 dwelling units. However, given that the same deficiency can be found in units and neighborhoods rated satisfactory or better, an additional 215,433 units rated satisfactory and 75,798 units rated good to excellent would also be erroneously identified by the surrogate index as poor in quality. This gives a combined total of 319,109 units identified by the surrogate as poor in quality where expert judgement finds only 27,878; or an overcount of eleven times the actual number.

The problem of estimating the number of dilapidated or deficient dwelling units can be approached through the aid of a series of Venn diagrams. The circular areas in each diagram represent various ways of clustering the housing stock of an area. The outermost boundary represents the set of all housing units: good, satisfactory and poor. Figure 2-5 shows one subset: deficient housing where the size of the circle containing the deficient label is roughly proportioned to the level of poor housing in the Five City Study. Figure 2-6 shows the same total housing stock with subsets that contain heating and plumbing deficiencies as well as those that are occupied by families under the poverty level. By themselves, these

FIGURE 2-5

Diagram of Total Housing Stock Partitioned
By a Team of Professional Housing Quality Raters
Into Satisfactory and Deficient Quality Housing

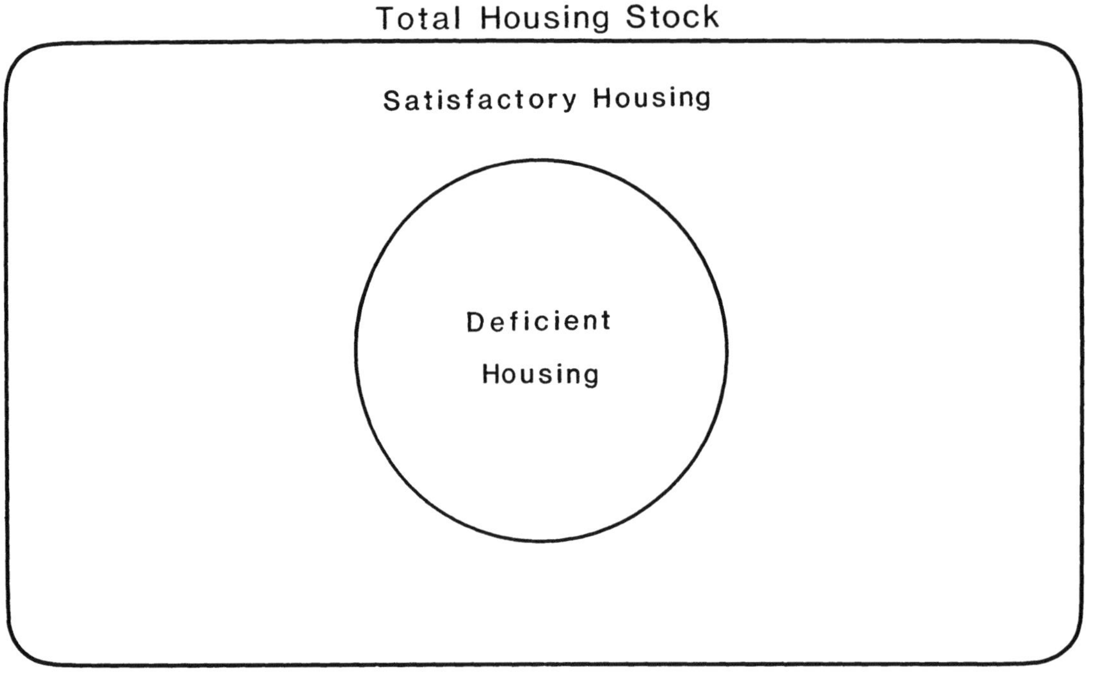

FIGURE 2-6

Diagram of Total Housing Stock
And Subsets of Housing Found Through Census-Type Surveys
To Have Deficient Heating or Plumbing Systems
And/or be Occupied by Low-Income Households

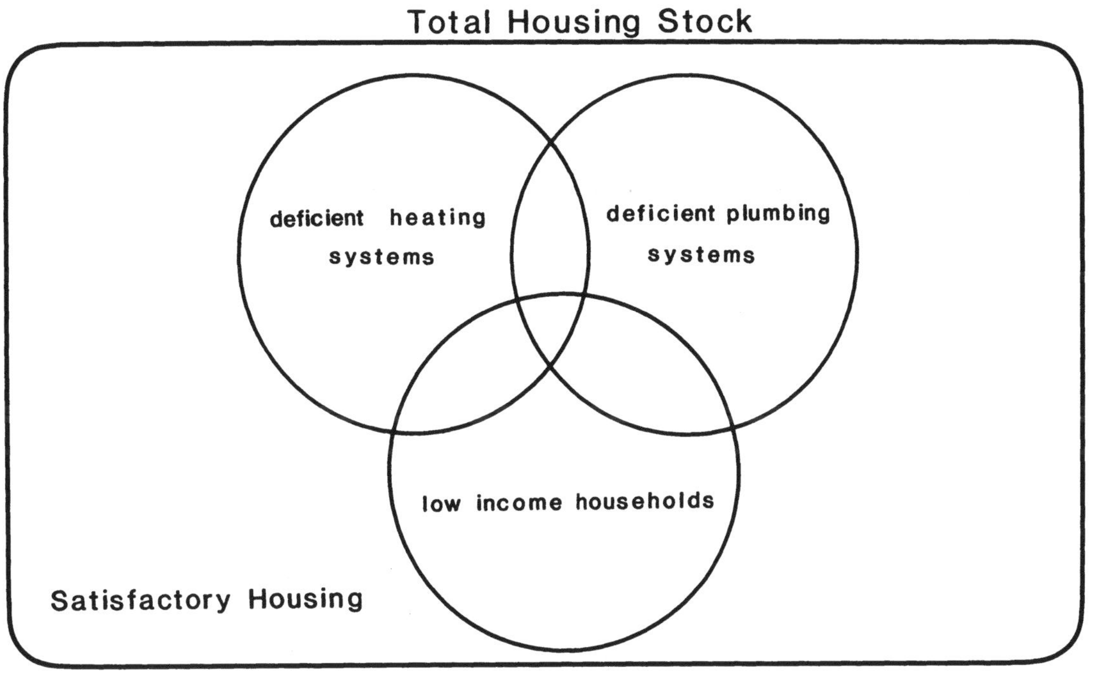

surrogates do not show the existence of dilapidated housing. They show that some low income families live with plumbing and heating deficiencies while others do not. The problem is guessing where the set of truly poor quality housing exists in this attribute space. Figure 2-7 poses two possibilities. Alternative 1 shows that the subset of housing rated poor is totally separate from the overlapping subsets of housing characteristics representing surrogates of poor quality. In such a case the use of these three surrogates would lead to somewhat erroneous estimates of poor quality housing. In the case of Alternative 2, the three overlapping deficiency indicators coincide to a large extent with the subset of housing rated poor in quality. As indicated in Appendix I to this chapter, the variables employed as surrogates of housing deficiency in this study produce the coincidence of deficient housing and deficient components measures indicated in Alternative 2 at least to the degree that they can be checked using the proportion of housing in county and sub-county locations reported by the Annual Housing Survey. Here we find strong parallels between self-rated county and sub-county deficiencies aggregated to the region to those estimated through indices for the region.

METHODOLOGY USED TO DETERMINE PRESENT MOUNT LAUREL HOUSING DEMAND

The preceding section has detailed the problems and existing evidence regarding the use of housing quality surrogates for the purpose of identifying deficient housing. Clearly, the problem is a difficult one; however, one that must be resolved to the best degree that the state of the art can approach.

The problem as exposed above is to count the maximum number of truly deficient units while minimizing the count of satisfactory units flagged for some reason as being deficient. We have seen from the aforementioned discussion that the surrogates chosen to represent deficient housing are relatively independent of one another. We have also seen that the potential exists for a certain degree of error to enter into the estimates of deficient housing due to the erroneous assignment of this status to satisfactory housing. We shall now explore in detail the actual algorithm used by us to identify and quantify the existence of deficient housing in New Jersey in fulfillment of the Court mandate.

The Surrogates of Housing Quality

Seven census-type variables are used as surrogates of housing quality. These represent the full array of variables in the 1980 Census of Population and Housing which describe housing quality.[42] In addition, they represent some of the most often cited indicators of deteriorating housing quality. In combination, the array of variables is felt to offer an excellent and liberal estimate of housing deficiency. The seven variables are:

FIGURE 2-7(a)

ALTERNATIVE 1. Diagram of the Absence of Intersection Between the Set of Housing Judged to be Deficient And the Sets of Housing Found to Have One or More of Three Census-Type Housing Characteristics

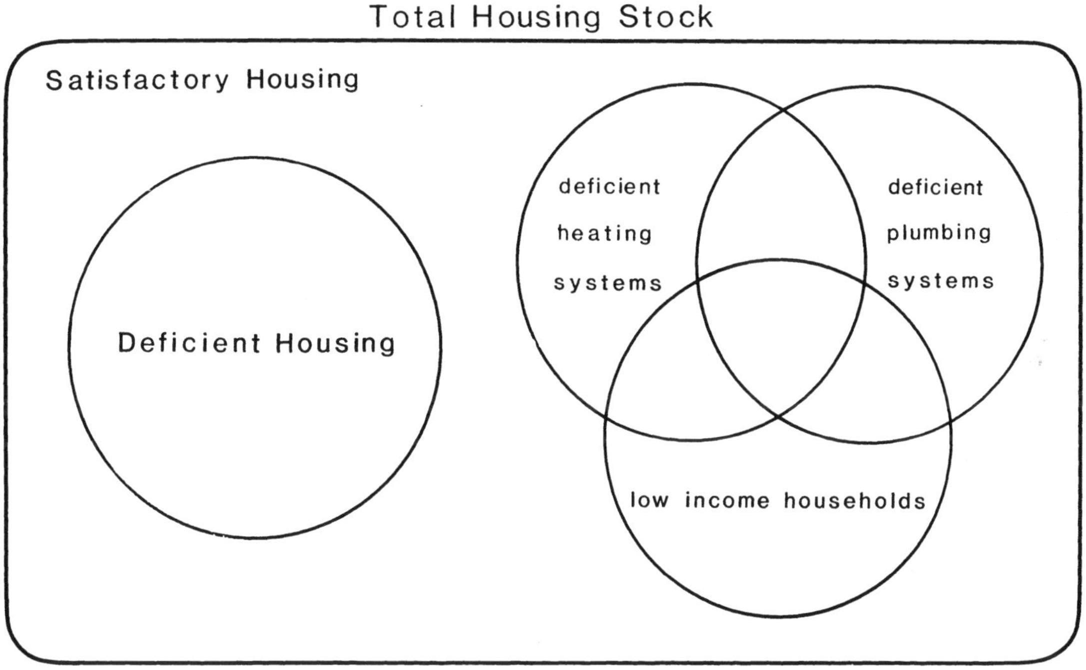

FIGURE 2-7(b)

ALTERNATIVE 2. Diagram of the Intersection Between The Set of Housing Judged to be Deficient and The Sets of Housing Found to Have One or More Of Three Census-Type Housing Characteristics

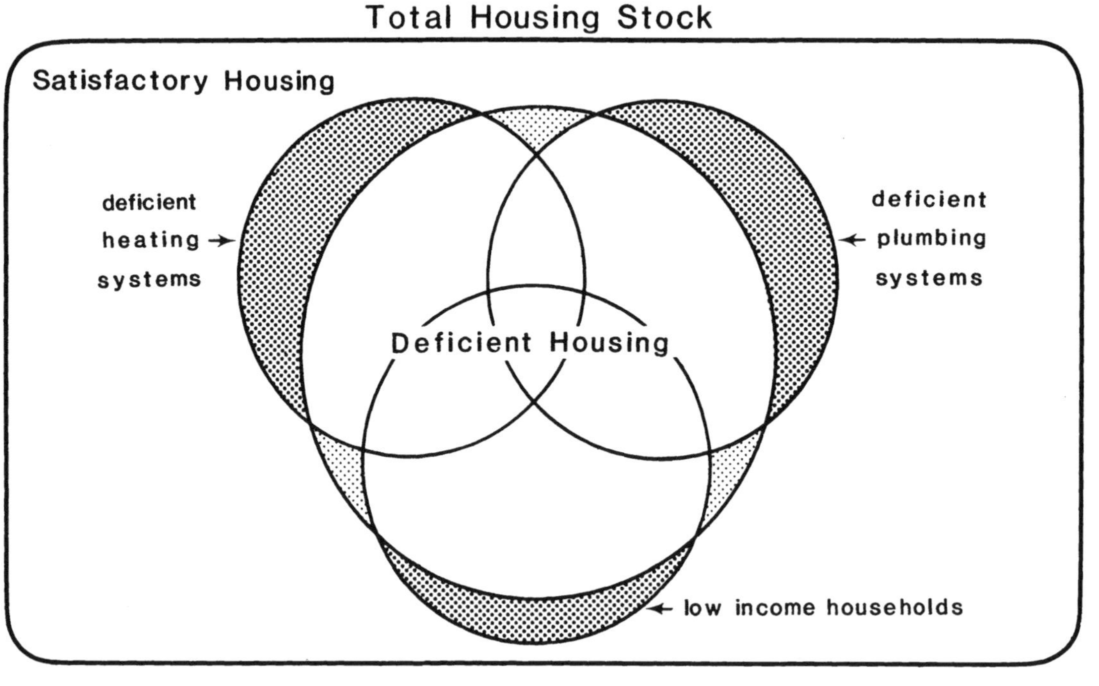

Represents units of the housing stock of poor quality but not counted as such by the surrogate indicator.

Represents units of the housing stock of satisfactory or good quality erroneously counted as poor or dilapidated.

1. Year Built:
   built prior to 1940
   built after 1940
2. Persons per room:
   more than 1.01 persons per room
3. Access to Unit:
   lack of exclusive access
4. Plumbing facilities:
   lack of exclusive plumbing
5. Kitchen facilities:
   lack complete kitchen facilities
6. Heating facilities:
   lacking central heating facilities
7. Elevator:
   lacking elevator in multistory structure of over 4 stories

Conditions Signalling a Deficient Structure

The current condition of the New Jersey housing stock occupied by Mount Laurel households is determined through the use of the 1980 Census of Population and Housing (Public Use Sample). As earlier indicated, Mount Laurel households have been identified through their household income relative to the area median as corrected by household size. Following the identification of this income-related subset of New Jersey households, those housed under deficient conditions were identified. The identification procedure incorporated the use of two selection rules: one for units built prior to 1940, and another for those built during or after 1940. Essentially, a unit built prior to 1940 was assigned a deficient status if any one of the six remaining housing quality surrogates indicated a deficiency. For units built after 1940, a minimum of two housing quality surrogates had to be flagged as inadequate for the unit to be assigned to the subset of deficient units.

There is no unambiguous way of testing the adequacy of this selection rule. The complementarity analysis of Appendix I provides some insight to concurrency of empirical deficiency and enumerated poor quality. Another indicator permitting such a judgement can be derived from the Five City Study. This study found that in the five cities analyzed, 10.3 percent of all dwelling units were occupied by families of low income and were rated to be deficient.* Based upon the Census data, through the selection

---

*In 1972, the year of the Five City Study, the family poverty level was $4,275; as of the 1979 Census, the poverty level was $7,412. This value corresponds to the income category in which 65 percent of the N.J. Mount Laurel population is located. Consequently, the $5,000 family income cutoff used in the Five City Study, is a useful index separating low/moderate income households from the remaining households.

described above, 11.5 percent of New Jersey's low and moderate income households are found to be occupying deficient housing. Thus, while proof on the matter must come from multiple sources, the best evidence to date indicates that the number of units occupied by Mount Laurel households, identified as residing in deficient housing, is within the same order of magnitude as would be predicted based upon the survey of conditions taken by professional housing quality raters.

Year Built

The age of a residential structure is indicative of many housing quality factors. Most immediate, the age of a structure shows the time it has been in the inventory and the duration of time for which abusive treatment can potentially take place. Age is also a factor in the filtering process. As the taste of residential quality changes, once fine, older structures can be passed on to lower income households. As this process continues over time, the income capacity of the receiving group can be insufficient to retain or maintain the structure; at this point it can fall into the deficient category. It can ultimately be eliminated from the stock through demolition or brought back through the gentrification process. The age threshold used in this study to signal a potential deficiency is represented by the year built: 1939 or earlier. Thus housing, at the time of Census survey, was 40 years old with the vast bulk of this stock occupied by Mount Laurel income-equivalent households for at least one-fourth of its structure life. Close to 90 percent of the housing of the housing-deficient Mount Laurel-eligible population (to be specified in detail in the following section)* has been constructed prior to 1940.

Persons Per Room

The degree of crowding within a dwelling unit is directly related to the potential quality of life of the householders as well as the wear and tear sustained by the structure. The American Public Health Association standards support the notion that a degree of privacy is essential for safety and well-being.[43] The actual point at which the number of persons in a dwelling unit becomes a threat to health and safety is uncertain. However, as the rule of thumb the value of more than one person per room (1.01) is commonly used as the threshold for defining living conditions as substandard. Thirty percent of Mount Laurel households live in conditions, which by this definition, are deemed crowded.

---

*This number and all other specifications of housing deficiency refer not to the gross Mount Laurel population, but to the housing-deficient segment of that population.

Access

Access to one's dwelling unit is used as an index of deficient housing to the extent that a household's privacy is violated. Requiring a householder to pass through another's dwelling in order to enter one's own unit is considered to represent a less than adequate condition. While this condition is found relatively seldom in a non-dormitory, non-lodger housing stock, it has also been used to signal inferior housing. Three percent of Mount Laurel households, mostly in central cities, are impacted by this structure condition.

Plumbing Facilities

Exclusive use of plumbing facilities is considered a surrogate of plumbing adequacy.[44] The exercise of good hygienic activities is considered to be aggravated when the essential facilities: hot and cold running water, flush toilet and bathtub or shower are shared with another household. The sharing of such facilities is therefore used as an index of deficient housing conditions. Over 15 percent of the existing Mount Laurel households live in structures wherein plumbing is shared.

Kitchen Facilities

As in the previous case, adequate kitchen facilities are considered essential for food preparation functions. The ingestion of foods prepared under conditions of filth or under such conditions that encourage spoilage is clearly a threat to good health.[45] The basic components considered essential for a complete kitchen are: a sink with piped water, a range or cookstove, and a refrigerator. The absence of any of these facilities is considered to be a signal of deficient housing conditions. Twelve percent of the existing Mount Laurel population have one or more components of the kitchen missing.

Heating Facilities

As with the existence of adequate facilities for handling human waste and preparing food, a key element in the package of services provided by a dwelling unit is shelter from the elements. As discussed in the previous section, adequate shelter as of the 1940 Census was based solely on the state of repair of the unit. This changed by the 1950 Census to consideration by the Census taker of the adequacy of the structures for residential purposes. Difficulties since that time have caused the Census to discontinue the evaluation of the structure. What is left as an index of structure quality is the existence of facilities such as plumbing, kitchen and heating equipment and their completeness or permanency.

The heating equipment index sets as a standard the existence of a central heating plant. The use of room heaters with or without flue is considered an indicator of less than adequate conditions and therefore as a sign of a deficient dwelling unit. One half of the existing, housing-deficient Mount Laurel population relies on primary heat provided from a noncentral heating source.

Elevator

The final surrogate of housing quality is limited to the examination of quality in multistory residential structures. Buildings of four stories or greater are judged to be deficient if they do not possess an elevator. This relates obviously to the necessity to climb to higher floors for those for whom it may be difficult due to age or physical impairment. Twenty-five percent of existing Mount Laurel households are impacted negatively by living in mid-high-rise structures without elevators.

Multiple Housing Deficiencies

The dwelling units of the present Mount Laurel housing deficient population, including age as a problem, have an average of 2.2 deficiencies per unit. Less than 25 percent of existing Mount Laurel units so defined have only one housing deficiency; most have multiple deficiencies. All of the variables used to define housing deficiency have at least a 50 percent conditional probability, and usually significantly more, of being found in the presence of other housing deficiencies. Units which are characterized by access through another's unit, nonexclusive use of plumbing, and incomplete kitchen facilities each have close to a 90 percent probability of having multiple deficiencies. These results are explored in Appendix I.

DETERMINING MOUNT LAUREL PRESENT HOUSING DEMAND

The obligation to improve the housing opportunities of low and moderate income households extends to those households currently living in conditions of insufficient or overcrowded housing. Recognizing the judicial importance placed upon the differentiation of lower-income households into low and moderate income fractions and the need to scale household income by the number of persons in the basic unit, we have assembled a set of summary tables showing the number of households in each Mount Laurel income category currently living in deficient housing -- first in terms of a state total, followed by a disaggregation by region.

Aggregate Mount Laurel Housing Demand Derived From Deficient Housing: The State

Working down the geographic scale, we shall start with state aggregate demand followed by that for each of the six regions. The state aggregate demand for housing derived from households currently residing in what is viewed to be deficient housing is displayed in Exhibit 2-8.

Exhibit 2-8 shows that 120,160 households fall into the deficient housing category; while, at the same time being below the income cutoff designated by the Mount Laurel decision. Two-thirds of these households, are of low income. That is, their household income is less than one-half that of the area median income. Mount Laurel existing housing demand is largest among one- and two-person households, and as will be shown in Chapter 3, many of these households contain an elderly population. Over 50 percent of existing demand (120,160) is occasioned by 1-2 person households (63,880); a figure which is more than double the level of both 3-4 person households (30,640) and 5-or-more person households (25,640).

EXHIBIT 2-8. THE STATE AGGREGATE DEMAND FOR HOUSING BY THE PRESENT MOUNT LAUREL-ELIGIBLE POPULATION -- 1980

Size of Household	Income Level: Low (N)	Moderate (N)	Total (N)
1-2	45,800	18,080	63,880
3-4	20,480	10,160	30,640
5+	15,080	10,560	25,640
Total	81,360	38,800	120,160

Aggregate Mount Laurel Housing Demand Derived from Income Eligible Households Living in Deficient Housing: The Regions

The regional demand for decent housing by these households shows a sharp north-to-south gradient. Exhibit 2-9 shows that 43 percent of this

EXHIBIT 2-9. THE REGIONAL DEMAND FOR HOUSING BY THE PRESENT MOUNT LAUREL ELIGIBLE POPULATION -- 1980

Region	Income Level: Low	Moderate	Total
1.Northeast	35,160	17,000	52,160
2.Northwest	22,440	11,000	33,440
3.West Central	5,280	3,240	8,520
4.East Central	3,880	1,080	4,960
5.Southwest	9,560	3,800	13,360
6.South/Southwest	5,040	2,680	7,720
Total	81,360	38,800	120,160

Source: U.S. Census, Public Use Sample, 1980

demand is derived from the Northeast Region 1, declining to a low of 4 percent in the East Central (Monmouth/Ocean Counties) Region 4.

The regional demand for decent housing for present Mount Laurel-eligible households can be further broken down by income and size of household. This breakdown is important in that building costs are in part a function of floor area, and the predominance of small households suggests that this may be the component of demand met most easily by developers.

Exhibits 2-10 through 2-15 delineate this component of housing demand for the six regions. Clearly evident is a need across all regions for low-income, 1-2 person dwelling units. In all cases, the demand for this configuration is twice the level of either of the other medium or large structural sizes, i.e., the demand for small-sized units by low-income households is approximately the sum of the demand for the two other sizes. Further, the demand occasioned by medium size households is about 20 percent higher than that created by larger households.

EXHIBIT 2-10. THE NORTHEAST REGION 1 - AGGREGATE DEMAND FOR HOUSING BY THE PRESENT MOUNT LAUREL-ELIGIBLE POPULATION -- 1980

Size of Household	Income Level		
	Low	Moderate	Total
1-2	19,960	8,280	28,240
3-4	8,680	4,440	13,120
5+	6,520	4,280	10,800
Total	35,160	17,000	52,160

EXHIBIT 2-11. THE NORTHWEST REGION 2 - AGGREGATE DEMAND FOR HOUSING BY THE PRESENT MOUNT LAUREL-ELIGIBLE POPULATION -- 1980

Size of Household	Income Level		
	Low	Moderate	Total
1-2	12,320	4,920	17,240
3-4	6,120	2,760	8,880
5+	4,000	3,320	7,320
Total	22,440	11,000	33,400

EXHIBIT 2-12. THE WEST CENTRAL REGION 3 - AGGREGATE DEMAND FOR HOUSING BY THE PRESENT MOUNT LAUREL-ELIGIBLE POPULATION -- 1980

Size of Household	Income Level Low	Moderate	Total
1-2	3,120	1,440	4,560
3-4	1,320	920	2,240
5+	840	880	1,720
Total	5,280	3,240	8,520

EXHIBIT 2-13. THE EAST CENTRAL REGION 4 - AGGREGATE DEMAND FOR HOUSING BY THE PRESENT MOUNT LAUREL-ELIGIBLE POPULATION -- 1980

Size of Household	Income Level Low	Moderate	Total
1-2	2,080	560	2,640
3-4	880	360	1,240
5+	920	160	1,080
Total	3,880	1,080	4,960

EXHIBIT 2-14. THE SOUTHWEST REGION 5 - AGGREGATE DEMAND FOR HOUSING BY THE PRESENT MOUNT LAUREL-ELIGIBLE POPULATION -- 1980

Size of Household	Income Level Low	Moderate	Total
1-2	5,000	1,520	6,520
3-4	2,520	960	3,480
5+	2,040	1,320	3,360
Total	9,560	3,800	13,360

EXHIBIT 2-15. THE SOUTH/SOUTHWEST REGION 6 - AGGREGATE DEMAND FOR HOUSING BY THE PRESENT MOUNT LAUREL-ELIGIBLE POPULATION -- 1980

Size of Household	Income Level		
	Low	Moderate	Total
1-2	3,320	1,360	4,680
3-4	960	720	1,680
5+	760	600	1,360
Total	5,040	2,680	7,720

METHODOLOGY TO DETERMINE MOUNT LAUREL PROSPECTIVE HOUSING DEMAND

The procedures and estimating techniques to determine the present or housing deficient/income constrained Mount Laurel-eligible population has been discussed earlier. In this section we describe the procedures used to estimate the prospective or purely income-constrained Mount Laurel-eligible population to the year 2000, a standard for most long-term projections initiated after the 1980 Census.

To determine the future Mount Laurel-eligible population, projection techniques will be employed. The term projection as opposed, for instance, to forecasts or goals, has very specific meaning. It means that the resulting figures are measurements of a future if the rules and assumptions of the method hold as empirically valid.[46] Thus, if the inherent operations of a projection are carried out without error, the projection is correct. While there may be disagreement on rules and/or assumptions, there can be no disagreement on results obtained once there is agreement on assumptions and the model has operated correctly.

Forecasts on the other hand may contain value judgements which are inserted in a model for more accurate prediction. These are often "gut" feelings and usually are not empirically based.[47]

Finally, goals are statements of the future usually of an advocacy nature. For example, populations may be shown to remain constant rather than decrease because psychologically if decrease was shown, it might hasten or contribute to additional decrease. This would go contrary to the goal of growth or sustained viability for the affected area.[48]

The predictions of Mount Laurel future contained here, are projections; they consist of neither intuitive manipulation nor advocacy purpose. For the most part, they draw from an accepted base of population projection developed and promulgated by the New Jersey Department of Labor.[49]

The projections which follow are linked to three empirical components of information which serve as their basis. These are:

1) Population Projections by Age Structure for 1990 and 2000,
2) Headship Rates by County and Projection by Age Structure for 1990 and 2000, and
3) The fraction of the total set of households within low and moderate income categories for each time period.

Each of these building blocks of household projection will now be examined.

Population Projections

The population projections used as the basis for the Mount Laurel eligible household projections are the New Jersey Revised Total, Age and Sex Population Projection (July, 1983) from the New Jersey Department of Labor. The specific series chosen for this purpose is ODEA, The Demographic Cohort Model (2).[50]

The ODEA Demographic Cohort Model is a cohort component method projection. By definition it is concerned with births, deaths and migration. The base population (July 1, 1980) is survived five years in each iteration of the projection cycle and births are projected by applying fertility rates to survived females 15 to 44 years of age to determine the population due to natural increase.[51] The survival rate used for projections is projected in line with the "National Middle Mortality Assumption" projections assuming no inmigration. The county and race specific general fertility rates were calculated and projected in line with the national "Middle Series" projections based on the historical relation of the state and county rates to national rates.[52]

Net migration is computed for both persons under and over 65 based on observed trends in migration pattern by age, sex and race previously in the 1970s. Fifty percent ceilings and floors are set on the ten year change in population due to migration.

The ODEA Demographic Cohort Model is characterized as a narrow increment, historically based model.[53] Its projections of population increase are lower than most other models and reflective of trends that occasioned such population change in the past. Results to the year 2000 are shown by county in Exhibit 2-16 for two of the New Jersey population forecasting models. Projections differ by 0.5 million persons. Reflecting very slow, recession-impacted population growth years 1980 to 1983, we opt for the lower demographic cohort projection. Current thinking is that even this conservative projection might be high. It must also be noted that recently released state population projections by the U.S. Bureau of the Census suggest a relatively flat population profile over the following decade. (See Appendix II to this chapter.)

EXHIBIT 2-16

COMPARISONS OF THE VARIOUS MODEL PROJECTIONS OF NEW JERSEY POPULATION BY COUNTY FOR THE YEAR 2000

County	ODEA Economic/ Demographic Model (1)	ODEA Demographic Cohort Model (2)	Difference in ODEA Models Economic Minus Cohort Model (1) Minus Model (2)
New Jersey	8,396,600	7,851,500	545,100
Atlantic County	277,400	245,800*	31,600*
Bergen County	951,400	707,800	243,600
Burlington County	471,900	487,000	- 15,100
Camden County	555,900	526,400	29,500
Cape May County	91,600	138,300	- 46,700
Cumberland County	142,600	153,700	- 11,100
Essex County	760,700	739,900	20,800
Gloucester County	269,100	265,700	3,400
Hudson County	516,500	506,000	10,500
Hunterdon County	112,800	113,200	- 400
Mercer County	359,400	301,900	57,500
Middlesex County	757,100	603,300	153,800
Monmouth County	588,200	580,800	7,400
Morris County	511,300	423,900	87,400
Ocean County	447,300	605,700	- 158,400
Passaic County	445,100	421,200	23,900
Salem County	69,100	71,400	- 2,300
Somerset County	284,000	199,600	84,400
Sussex County	172,600	198,200	- 25,600
Union County	518,800	454,200	64,600
Warren County	93,800	107,400	- 13,600

* If the ODEA Cohort Model (2) Projection for Atlantic County is adjusted for the impact of the hotel-casino industry from 245,800 to 276,900, then the difference between the two ODEA Model Projections for Atlantic County is reduced from 31,600 to 500.

Note: Projections are rounded in hundreds. Thus, totals may not add.

Source: Office of Demographic and Economic Analysis, Division of Planning and Research, New Jersey Department of Labor.

EXHIBIT 2-17
PROJECTED POPULATION BY AGE AND SEX FOR NEW JERSEY
FOR THE YEARS 1990 AND 2000
ODEA DEMOGRAPHIC COHORT MODEL*

	CENSUSES FOR APRIL 1		PROJECTIONS FOR JULY 1	
Sex and Age Group	1970	1980	1990	2000
Both Sexes, All Ages	7,171,112	7,364,823	7,572,300	7,851,500
Under 5 Years	589,801	463,289	489,600	441,300
5 to 9 Years	693,364	508,447	470,500	478,200
10 to 14 Years	711,132	605,841	472,800	503,400
15 to 19 Years	612,405	670,665	533,600	500,500
20 to 24 Years	509,667	614,828	557,800	448,300
25 to 29 Years	463,624	574,135	566,900	456,600
30 to 34 Years	403,858	563,758	632,000	580,800
35 to 39 Years	414,326	479,749	647,200	645,800
40 to 44 Years	465,907	400,074	584,200	657,800
45 to 49 Years	478,417	394,038	472,500	642,100
50 to 54 Years	439,472	432,520	378,700	562,500
55 to 59 Years	381,013	430,048	359,500	442,500
60 to 64 Years	314,332	367,660	371,400	336,700
65 to 69 Years	245,994	303,670	343,000	299,300
70 to 74 Years	194,302	227,037	269,700	287,700
75 to 79 Years		157,921	199,100	242,800
80 to 84 Years	353,498	98,912	124,000	167,200
85 Years and Over		72,231	99,800	158,100
65 Years and Over	693,794	859,771	1,035,500	1,155,100

Notes: 1) Projections are rounded in hundreds. Thus, totals for Projections may not add.
2) Before using these projections, please read the text for the assumptions behind this model.
3) The total New Jersey population has been revised to 7,365,011 for 1980 as shown in the summary tables. But because the age-sex detail has not been revised for 1980, the total shown here for that year is 7,364,823.

Source: Office of Demographic and Economic Analysis, Division of Planning and Research, New Jersey Department of Labor.

*See Appendix II - A Note On the Population Projections attached to this chapter for a summary of current national Census Bureau forecasts for the state.

ODEA Demographic Cohort Model (2) projects each county's population by 18 age categories. In order to facilitate the integration of population and headship rate projection, the age categories have been aggregated into 8 groups. The results of this aggregation process are shown in Exhibit 2-18.

Headship Rate Projections

The headship rate parameter measures the propensity of society at a given time to group individuals into units that live together for shelter and economic purposes. In post-hoc form, it is the ratio of the number of households to the number of persons within an age cohort.[54]

In its predictive mode the headship rate is an indicator by age of the potential for a segment of the population to form a household. While it is always applied to age groupings, it is the socioeconomic characteristics within the age group such as sex, marital status, education, etc. which determine household formation.[55] Population projections for New Jersey are shown by age in Exhibit 2-17. In this study, headship rate is determined by the ratio of household heads found within an age cohort to the number of persons found in that same cohort.

EXHIBIT 2-18

AGE COHORTS USED BY THE NEW JERSEY DEPARTMENT OF LABOR OF POPULATION PROJECTION PURPOSES AND AGGREGATED COHORTS USED TO INPUT INTO HEADSHIP RATE PROJECTIONS

New Jersey Department of Aggregated Cohorts	Aggregated Age Cohorts
less than 5 years	less than 25 years
5 to 9 years	25 to 29 years
10 to 14	30 to 34 years
15 to 19	35 to 44 years
20 to 24	45 to 54 years
25 to 29	55 to 64 years
30 to 34	65 to 74 years
35 to 39	75 years and over
40 to 44	
45 to 49	
50 to 54	
55 to 59	
60 to 64	
65 to 69	
70 to 74	
75 to 79	
80 to 84	
85 years and over	

Headship rates increased significantly over the Sixties yet have leveled off significantly.[56] Growth in headship rates reflected a reduction in household size which, when the market permits, spawns additional small households. A slowing of growth in headship rates reflects a slowing in decline of household size.[57]

The use of headship rates for the purpose of projecting household change has been documented by MIT's George Masnick.[58] However, for this study the headship rates used to collect the projected population into households have been derived from the 1980 Public Use Sample of the U.S. Census of Population and Housing for New Jersey Counties. The New Jersey-specific headship values differ somewhat from those generated by Masnick for the U.S. as a whole due to a difference in definition (Exhibit 2-19).

EXHIBIT 2-19

HEADSHIP RATES BY AGE COHORT

Age Cohort	MIT Study[a] 1980	MIT Study[a] 1990	New Jersey 1980[b]	New Jersey 1990	New Jersey 2000
less than 25 years	.2020	.2094	.0437*	.0453	.0453
25-29 years	.5113	.5140	.4231	.4253	.4253
30-34 years	.5407	.5391	.4987	.4972	.4972
35-44 years	.5434	.5490	.5353	.5408	.5408
45-54 years	.5460	.5611	.5472	.5623	.5623
55-64 years	.5530	.5645	.5725	.5844	.5844
65-74 years	.5796	.5908	.6185	.6305	.6305
75 years and over	.5652	.6039	.5797	.6194	.6194

a) Masnick, 1983 see Table 8.
b) 1980 New Jersey Public Use Sample, Census of Population and Housing.
* Fraction of persons in an age cohort who are household heads.

Given a somewhat different definitional base, we can see that the MIT study found the U.S. average to have relatively high headship rates during the earlier years of the individual's lifespan; the New Jersey derived figures show somewhat lower headship rates for the less-than-25 year old and 35-to-44 year old cohorts than for the nation as a whole. On the other side, the State of New Jersey has higher than average headship rates for all of its cohorts over 45 years of age. In New Jersey, our college age students reside at home and are counted as part of their parents' household, or, even more frequently, are exported to other states where they may join that state's off-campus students to form independent households. On the other hand, New Jersey has large retirement enclaves where the elderly, at a very late stage in life, form independent households. In other states without these facilities, the elderly often live at home with family, thus reducing this number of late-in-life, independent households.

These differences necessitate the use of the New Jersey specific headship rates by county in preference to national headship rates developed by MIT. However, the MIT demographic projections, reflecting a slackening in the rate of growth in headship rates, contributing to a decrease in the decline of household size, have been used in projecting the 1980 New Jersey county headship rates to 1990.[59] We have assumed that the New Jersey age specific headship rates will change over the decade 1980-1990 in a fashion directly proportional to the national average developed by Masnick. See Exhibit 2-20 for the projected change in headship rates which were applied to New Jersey's 1980 figures to extend them to 1990.

EXHIBIT 2-20

CHANGE IN NATIONAL HEADSHIP RATES USED TO ADJUST NEW JERSEY HEADSHIP RATES FOR YEARS 1990 AND 2000

Age Group	Year		
	1980	1990	Change
15-24	.2020*	.2094	.0074
25-29	.5113	.5140	.0027
30-34	.5407	.5391	(-).0016
35-44	.5434	.5490	.0056
45-54	.5460	.5611	.0151
55-64	.5530	.5645	.0115
65-74	.5796	.5908	.0112
75+	.5652	.6039	.0387

Source: Masnick, George. "The Demographic Factor in Household Growth" (WP-W83-3). (Cambridge, Mass. Joint Center for Urban Studies of MIT and Harvard University, May 1983.)

* This number represents the fraction of all people in the 15 to 24 year age cohort who are either the household head or a spouse.

However, lacking headship projections beyond 1990 for the nation, it was decided to hold the headship rates constant at their 1990 value for the year 2000.

The Mount Laurel Eligible Fraction

The income distribution among a society's population is a function of many past and present conditions. The future size of the lower income or

Mount Laurel eligible population is a function of current savings habits, the extent and depth of funded pension plans, economic conditions such as unemployment, the wage structure of the New Jersey industrial base, and inflationary trends, and lastly, governmental policies toward income maintenance.

Rather than attempting to project these many practically imponderable future conditions, the share of Mount Laurel households as a percent of the regional population base is assumed to remain constant over the time period projected in this study. What this says is that the proportion of those households at 80 percent of median income or less and observed in 1980, will be assumed to remain constant by age cohort into the future. The size of the cohort may change due to the effects of assumptions regarding births, deaths, and migration by age cohort, but the share of Mount Laurel eligibles within each age-cohort will remain the same.

Calculating the Prospective Mount Laurel Population

To summarize, projection of future demand for the Mount Laurel eligible population progresses through three stages. First, the population is projected for each county by age cohort to the years 1990 and 2000. This is done using the New Jersey Department of Labor's Demographic Cohort Model 2 as found in Projections of Age Structure, 1990, 2000, also from the New Jersey Department of Labor. This is basically a conservative projection and primarily reflects aggregate 1970-1980 population trends. The appropriateness of a conservative model is reenforced by observed trends over the most recent period, 1980-1983.

Second, New Jersey county-specific headship rates, adjusted for the predicted change in national headship rates (MIT) are applied to age structure projections for each county. This enables households to be projected using both household information specific to New Jersey counties and national trends of future changes in headship rates. (No change in headship rates are available solely for the State of New Jersey.)

Third, the 1980 gross percentage share of Mount Laurel households within each age cohort by low as well as moderate income partitions, is applied to age cohort household projections. This yields Mount Laurel income constrained households by age cohort and county for each of the time periods. This county information is aggregated to the regional level by summing information by age cohort for each county found within a particular region. The prospective fraction of Mount Laurel-eligible houeholds is determined by subtracting the future number of Mount Laurel households from the estimated number found in 1980.

DETERMINING MOUNT LAUREL PROSPECTIVE HOUSING DEMAND

Our projection of the aggregate demand for housing by low- and moderate-income households provides municipal officials and the courts an indication of the magnitude of the housing problem net of the current Mount Laurel type residents to be faced over the next two decades given rates of change in births/deaths as well as employment shifts over that period as projected by the New Jersey Department of Labor and Industry. The model chosen thus takes into account the two basic components of population change: natural increase and migration.

The prospective Mount Laurel-eligible population is presented by the two basic categories of income, each corrected for the size of household. Finally, the projections are developed for the six multicounty regions as specified in Chapter 1.

Projections: The State

Exhibit 2-21 displays the results of the projection process aggregated to the state level. The categories of income and household size that were presented as the previous chapter have been retained in order to easily examine the several distinct housing markets that exist within this population.

EXHIBIT 2-21. THE GROWTH IN THE STATE AGGREGATE DEMAND FOR HOUSING BY THE PROSPECTIVE MOUNT LAUREL-ELIGIBLE POPULATION 1980-1990 AND 1990-2000

	Prospective Households 1980-1990			Prospective Households 1990-2000		
Size of Household	Income Level: Low	Moderate	Total	Income Level: Low	Moderate	Total
1-2	57,132	33,914	91,046	40,096	21,046	61,142
3-4	15,874	15,058	30,932	10,928	8,991	19,914
5+	5,823	6,180	12,003	3,994	3,617	7,611
Total	78,829	55,152	133,981	55,018	33,654	88,672
Aggregate Loss*				(4,222)	(4,498)	(8,720)
Net Growth				50,796	29,156	79,952

*The Northeast region is projected to have a decline in Mount Laurel-eligible households over the decade 1990-2000.

The cumulative prospective demand for each of two decades -- 1980-1990 and 1990-2000 -- represents in each case the change or net increase in demand for lower and moderate income, Mount Laurel-type housing over and above the base of present housing need created by current, poorly housed, Mount Laurel-eligible households. For the state as a whole, growth during the decade of the 1980s will generate a demand for Mount Laurel housing at a level of 133,981 units. As shown in Exhibit 2-22, two thirds of this demand will be for small households, and two-thirds of this, will be of low income. Large households, those of five persons-and-over, generate the smallest increase in demand statewide; where the 12,003 units projected are split approximately half between low- and moderate-income households.

EXHIBIT 2-22. THE PERCENTAGE DISTRIBUTION OF THE DEMAND FOR HOUSING BY THE PROSPECTIVE MOUNT LAUREL POPULATION 1980-1990 AND 1990-2000

Size of Household	Prospective Households 1980-1990 Income Level Low	Moderate	Total	Prospective Households 1990-2000 Income Level Low	Moderate	Total
1-2	62.8%	37.2%	68.0%	65.6%	34.4%	69.0%
3-4	51.3	48.7	23.1	54.9	45.1	22.5
5+	48.5	51.5	8.9	52.5	47.5	8.6
Total	58.8%	41.2%	100.0%	62.0%	38.0%	100.0%

The subsequent decade is projected to bring with it a continuing decline in the increase of new Mount Laurel-eligible households. Where the decade of the 1980s generates 133,972 units, the 1990s are projected to have 45,000 households less or 88,672 new households in need of lower-cost housing. In one region, the Northeast, it is projected that there will be an absolute drop of close to 10,000 units in the then-present demand for Mount Laurel housing.

For the five regions still supporting a growth in households, the demand by size of household is comparable to that of the preceding decade with a slight shift toward increasing size of low- as opposed to moderate-income households. We shall conclude this section by showing the projected regional demand.

Projections: The Regions

The regional prospective demand for low-cost housing is shown in Exhibit 2-23, the percentage distribution is shown in Exhibit 2-24. The largest growth in housing demand occurs in the East Central Region 4 (Monmouth and Ocean Counties), followed in magnitude by that for the Southwest Region 5. This pattern holds for both decades. Most remarkable is the very low demand projected for the two most populous regions: the Northeast and Northwest. For the Northeast region, the outmigration is so strong that an actual loss of Mount Laurel-eligible households occurs. This can be seen in Exhibit 2-25, where in the decade of the 1980s growth was limited to 6,570 households and in the 1990s a decrease of 8,720 Mount Laurel households.

EXHIBIT 2-23. NUMERICAL DISTRIBUTION OF PROSPECTIVE MOUNT LAUREL HOUSING DEMAND GROWTH BY REGION 1980-1990 AND 1990-2000

	Period					
	1980-1990			1990-2000		
	Income Level			Income Level		
Region	Low	Moderate	Total	Low	Moderate	Total
1.Northeast	4,613	1,957	6,570	-4,222	-4,498	-8,720
2.Northwest	3,629	5,040	8,669	947	566	1,513
3.West Central	13,229	8,773	22,002	8,153	3,802	11,955
4.East Central	25,212	17,874	43,086	21,860	15,008	36,868
5.Southwest	21,415	14,212	35,627	15,568	8,938	24,506
6.South/ Southwest	10,731	7,296	18,027	8,490	5,340	13,830
Total	78,829	55,152	133,981	50,796	29,156	79,952

What remains to be examined is the distribution of Mount Laurel-prospective households by household size. Exhibits 2-26 through 2-30 show that the pattern observed at the state level holds remarkably constant across all regions. In the region receiving the largest number of Mount Laurel households, the East Central, 71 percent of the prospective demand is derived from small families; while, close to two-thirds of this demand come from what is projected to be low income households. This pattern repeats itself across all regions into the final decade of the century.

EXHIBIT 2-24. PERCENTAGE DISTRIBUTION OF PROSPECTIVE MOUNT LAUREL HOUSING DEMAND GROWTH BY REGION 1980-1990 and 1990-2000

	Period					
	1980-1990			1990-2000		
	Income Level			Income Level		
Region	Low	Moderate	Total	Low	Moderate	Total
1.Northeast	70.2%	29.8%	4.9%	48.4%	51.6%	-10.8%
2.Northwest	41.9	58.1	6.5	62.6%	37.4%	1.9%
3.West Central	60.1	39.9	16.4	68.2	31.8	14.9
4.East Central	58.5	41.5	32.2	59.3	40.7	46.1
5.Southwest	60.1	39.9	26.6	63.5	36.5	30.6
6.South/ Southwest	59.5	40.5	13.4	61.4	38.6	17.3
Total	58.8%	41.2%	100.0%	62.0%	38.0%	100.0%

EXHIBIT 2-25. THE NORTHEAST REGION 1 - AGGREGATE DEMAND FOR HOUSING BY THE PROSPECTIVE MOUNT LAUREL-ELIGIBLE POPULATION 1980-1990 AND 1990-2000

	Prospective Households 1980-1990			Prospective Households 1990-2000		
	Income Level			Income Level		
Size of Household	Low	Moderate	Total	Low	Moderate	Total
1-2	3,310 (73.6)	1,176 (26.2)	4,486 (68.3)	-4,886 (73.6)	-1,752 (26.2)	-6,638 (68.3)
3-4	940 (62.9)	554 (37.1)	1,494 (22.7)	-1,388 (62.9)	-818 (37.1)	-2,206 (22.7)
5+	363 (61.5)	227 (38.5)	590 (9.0)	-538 (61.5)	-336 (38.5)	-874 (9.0)
Total	4,613 (70.2)	1,957 (29.8)	6,570 (100.0)	-4,721 (48.6)	-4,998 (51.4)	-9,719 (100.0)

EXHIBIT 2-26. THE NORTHWEST REGION 2 - AGGREGATE DEMAND FOR HOUSING BY THE PROSPECTIVE MOUNT LAUREL-ELIGIBLE POPULATION 1980-1990 AND 1990-2000

	Prospective Households 1980-1990			Prospective Households 1990-2000		
Size of	Income Level			Income Level		
Household	Low	Moderate	Total	Low	Moderate	Total
1-2	2,423	3,040	5,463	632	341	973
	(44.4)	(55.6)	(63.0)	(65.0)	(35.0)	(64.3)
3-4	862	1,413	2,275	225	159	384
	(37.9)	(62.1)	(26.2)	(58.6)	(41.4)	(25.4)
5+	344	587	931	90	66	156
	(36.9)	(63.1)	(10.7)	(57.7)	(42.3)	(10.3)
Total	3,629	5,040	8,669	947	566	1,513
	(41.9)	(58.1)	(100.0)	(62.6)	(37.4)	(100.0)

EXHIBIT 2-27. THE WEST CENTRAL REGION 3 - AGGREGATE DEMAND FOR HOUSING BY THE PROSPECTIVE MOUNT LAUREL ELIGIBLE POPULATION 1980-1990 AND 1990-2000

	Prospective Households 1980-1990			Prospective Households 1990-2000		
Size of	Income Level			Income Level		
Household	Low	Moderate	Total	Low	Moderate	Total
1-2	9,646	4,840	14,486	5,944	2,097	8,041
	(66.6)	(33.4)	(65.8)	(73.9)	(26.1)	(67.3)
3-4	2,729	2,773	5,502	1,682	1,202	2,884
	(49.6)	(50.4)	(25.0)	(58.3)	(41.7)	(24.1)
5+	854	1,160	2,014	527	503	1,030
	(42.4)	(57.6)	(9.2)	(51.2)	(48.8)	(8.6)
Total	13,229	8,773	22,002	8,153	3,802	11,955
	(60.1)	(39.9)	(100.0)	(68.2)	(31.8)	(100.0)

EXHIBIT 2-28. THE EAST CENTRAL REGION 4 - AGGREGATE DEMAND FOR HOUSING BY THE PROSPECTIVE MOUNT LAUREL-ELIGIBLE POPULATION 1980-1990 AND 1990-2000

	Prospective Households 1980-1990			Prospective Households 1990-2000		
	Income Level			Income Level		
Size of Household	Low	Moderate	Total	Low	Moderate	Total
1-2	18,982	11,660	30,642	16,459	9,791	26,250
	(61.9)	(38.1)	(71.1)	(62.7)	(37.3)	(71.2)
3-4	4,607	4,657	9,264	3,994	3,910	7,904
	(49.7)	(50.3)	(21.5)	(50.5)	(49.5)	(21.4)
5+	1,623	1,557	3,180	1,407	1,307	2,714
	(51.0)	(49.0)	(7.4)	(51.8)	(48.2)	(7.4)
Total	25,212	17,874	43,086	21,860	15,008	36,868
	(58.5)	(41.5)	(100.0)	(59.3)	(40.7)	(100.0)

EXHIBIT 2-29. THE SOUTHWEST REGION 5 - AGGREGATE DEMAND FOR HOUSING BY THE PROSPECTIVE MOUNT LAUREL-ELIGIBLE POPULATION 1980-1990 AND 1990-2000

	Prospective Households 1980-1990			Prospective Households 1990-2000		
	Income Level			Income Level		
Size of Household	Low	Moderate	Total	Low	Moderate	Total
1-2	14,898	8,185	23,083	10,831	5,148	15,979
	(64.5)	(35.5)	(64.8)	(67.8)	(32.2)	(65.2)
3-4	4,700	4,107	8,807	3,416	2,583	5,999
	(53.4)	(46.6)	(24.7)	(56.9)	(43.1)	(24.5)
5+	1,817	1,920	3,737	1,321	1,207	2,528
	(48.6)	(51.4)	(10.5)	(52.3)	(47.7)	(10.3)
Total	21,415	14,212	35,627	15,568	8,938	24,506
	(60.1)	(39.9)	(100.0)	(63.5)	(36.5)	(100.0)

EXHIBIT 2-30. THE SOUTH-SOUTHWEST REGION 6 - AGGREGATE DEMAND FOR HOUSING BY THE PROSPECTIVE MOUNT LAUREL-ELIGIBLE POPULATION 1980-1990 AND 1990-2000

	Prospective Households 1980-1990			Prospective Households 1990-2000		
	Income Level			Income Level		
Size of Household	Low	Moderate	Total	Low	Moderate	Total
1-2	7,874 (61.1)	5,012 (38.9)	12,886 (71.5)	6,230 (62.9)	3,669 (37.1)	9,899 (71.6)
3-4	2,036 (56.7)	1,554 (43.3)	3,590 (19.9)	1,611 (58.6)	1,137 (41.4)	2,748 (19.8)
5+	821 (52.9)	730 (47.1)	1,551 (8.6)	649 (54.9)	534 (45.1)	1,183 (8.6)
Total	10,731 (59.5)	7,296 (40.5)	18,027 (100.0)	8,490 (61.4)	5,340 (38.6)	13,830 (100.0)

PRESENT AND PROSPECTIVE MOUNT LAUREL HOUSING DEMAND BY REGION

This chapter has quantified the extent of Mount Laurel housing demand for both those low and moderate households currently ill-housed as well as the future population of low and moderate income households to the Year 2000. What remains is to collect the disparate figures into a single summary statement of housing demand over time.

Exhibit 2-31 initiates this summary by displaying total regional low and moderate income gross housing demand over the three time stages of the study. Total demand through to the year 2000 is shown to approach 350,000 with the major reponsibility being the component of prospective housing demand occurring during the 1980 to 1990 decade.

Total demand over the time period of this study is strongest in the East Central Region 3 (24.7%) and is least in the South-Southwest Region 6 (11.7%). What is most revealing in this Exhibit is the difference in time phasing of demand across regions, reflecting whether demand is: (1) deficient housing based or, (2) purely income constrained. The Northeast and Northwest Regions 1 and 2 dominate the demand for housing for the currently ill-housed Mount Laurel-eligible population. The demand for prospective housing is almost negligible in these two regions while the opposite is the case for the East Central and Southwest Regions 3 and 5 respectively. In the case of the latter two regions, over one-half of the entire state's prospective demand can be attributed to them. Clearly, such a sharp break in the time phasing of demand over space must suggest major policy differences in meeting the disparate housing needs represented by the numerical estimates.

EXHIBIT 2-31

NUMERICAL DISTRIBUTION OF MOUNT LAUREL-ELIGIBLE HOUSING DEMAND TO THE YEAR 2000 BY REGION

Region	Present Mt. Laurel Demand (1980)	Prospective Mt. Laurel Demand (1980-1990)	Prospective Mt. Laurel Demand (1990-2000)	Total Prospective Mt. Laurel Demand to the Year 2000
1. Northeast	52,160	6,570	-8,720	-2,150
2. Northwest	33,440	8,669	1,513	10,182
3. West Central	8,520	22,002	11,955	33,957
4. East Central	4,960	43,086	36,868	79,954
5. Southwest	13,360	35,627	24,506	60,133
6. South-Southwest	7,720	18,027	13,830	31,857
TOTAL	120,160	133,981	79,952	213,933

The next step in this analysis is to disaggregate housing demand by income category. Exhibit 2-32 shows that 129,625 households or 60 percent of the total prospective Mount Laurel-eligible population as of year 2000 will be in the low-income category. For the most part, this category of households parallels the pattern of housing demand over time and region, shown in the aggregate Mount Laurel housing demand exhibit.

Only in the case of the moderate-income category is there a deviation from the pattern, and this, as shown in Exhibit 2-33, is a slight peaking in demand in the East Central Region 3 during the second decade.

EXHIBIT 2-32

NUMERICAL DISTRIBUTION OF LOW-INCOME MOUNT LAUREL-ELIGIBLE HOUSING DEMAND TO THE YEAR 2000 BY REGION

Region	Present Mt. Laurel Demand (1980)	Prospective Mt. Laurel Demand (1980-1990)	Prospective Mt. Laurel Demand (1990-2000)	Total Prospective Mt. Laurel Demand to the Year 2000
1. Northeast	35,160	4,613	-4,222	391
2. Northwest	22,440	3,629	947	4,576
3. West Central	5,280	13,229	8,153	21,382
4. East Central	3,880	25,212	21,860	47,072
5. Southwest	9,560	21,415	15,568	36,983
6. South-Southwest	5,040	10,731	8,490	19,221
TOTAL	81,360	78,829	50,796	129,625

EXHIBIT 2-33

NUMERICAL DISTRIBUTION OF MODERATE-INCOME MOUNT LAUREL-ELIGIBLE HOUSING DEMAND TO THE YEAR 2000 BY REGION

Region	Present Mt. Laurel Demand (1980)	Prospective Mt. Laurel Demand (1980-1990)	Prospective Mt. Laurel Demand (1990-2000)	Total Prospective Mt. Laurel Demand to the Year 2000
1. Northeast	17,000	1,957	-4,498	-2,541
2. Northwest	11,000	5,040	566	5,606
3. West Central	3,240	8,773	3,802	12,575
4. East Central	1,080	17,874	15,008	32,882
5. Southwest	3,800	14,212	8,938	23,150
6. South-Southwest	2,680	7,296	5,340	12,636
TOTAL	38,800	55,152	29,156	84,308

Lastly, it will be useful to examine the household size categories of housing demand to determine if they show any significant spatial or temporal trends. Exhibits 2-34, 2-35 and 2-36 show the regional housing demand for small, medium, and large dwelling units.

Summing over the three exhibits we find that 68 percent of total prospective demand or 145,550 units will be needed for one- to two-person households. Spatially, the pattern of demand and temporal staging is the same as that for the total demand. Present (1980) demand is strongest in the two Northern Regions 1 and 2; while the demand shifts markedly to the East Central Region 3 and Southwest Region 5 for the final decade of the study. While the numbers differ somewhat for the two classes of larger households, the overall pattern remains the same.

There are a number of approaches to meeting the needs projected here. These are detailed in the chapters which follow.

EXHIBIT 2-34

NUMERICAL DISTRIBUTION OF ONE- AND TWO-PERSON HOUSEHOLDS OF MOUNT LAUREL-ELIGIBLE HOUSING DEMAND THROUGH THE YEAR 2000 BY REGION

Region	Present Mt. Laurel Demand (1980)	Prospective Mt. Laurel Demand (1980-1990)	Prospective Mt. Laurel Demand (1990-2000)	Total Prospective Mt. Laurel Demand to the Year 2000
1. Northeast	28,240	4,486	-6,638	-2,152
2. Northwest	17,240	5,463	973	6,436
3. West Central	4,560	14,486	8,041	22,527
4. East Central	2,640	30,642	26,250	56,892
5. Southwest	6,520	23,083	15,979	39,062
6. South-Southwest	4,680	12,886	9,899	22,785
TOTAL	63,880	91,046	54,504	145,550

EXHIBIT 2-35

NUMERICAL DISTRIBUTION OF THREE- AND FOUR-PERSON HOUSEHOLDS OF MOUNT LAUREL-ELIGIBLE HOUSING DEMAND THROUGH THE YEAR 2000 BY REGION

Region	Present Mt. Laurel Demand (1980)	Prospective Mt. Laurel Demand (1980-1990)	Prospective Mt. Laurel Demand (1990-2000)	Total Prospective Mt. Laurel Demand to the Year 2000
1. Northeast	13,120	1,494	-2,206	-712
2. Northwest	8,880	2,275	384	2,659
3. West Central	2,240	5,502	2,884	8,386
4. East Central	1,240	9,264	7,904	17,168
5. Southwest	3,480	8,807	5,999	14,806
6. South-Southwest	1,680	3,590	2,748	6,338
TOTAL	30,640	30,932	17,713	48,645

EXHIBIT 2-36

NUMERICAL DISTRIBUTION OF FIVE-PLUS SIZED HOUSEHOLDS OF MOUNT LAUREL-ELIGIBLE HOUSING DEMAND THROUGH THE YEAR 2000 BY REGION

Region	Present Mt. Laurel Demand (1980)	Prospective Mt. Laurel Demand (1980-1990)	Prospective Mt. Laurel Demand (1990-2000)	Total Prospective Mt. Laurel Demand to the Year 2000
1. Northeast	10,800	590	-874	-284
2. Northwest	7,320	931	156	1,087
3. West Central	1,720	2,014	1,030	3,044
4. East Central	1,080	3,180	2,714	5,894
5. Southwest	3,360	3,737	2,528	6,265
6. South-Southwest	1,360	1,551	1,183	2,734
TOTAL	25,640	12,003	6,737	18,740

NOTES

1. Southern Burlington County NAACP v. Township of Mount Laurel, 67 N.J. 151 336A. 2nd 713 (1975) termed Mt. Laurel I.

2. Southern Burlington County NAACP v. Township of Mount Laurel, 92, N.J. 158, 456 A. nd 390 (1983), hereinafter referred to as Mount Laurel II, Decision.

3. Pub. Res. 52-22, July 20, 1892.

4. President's Housing Commission (1908). See Subcommittee on Banking, Currency and Housing, House of Representatives, Evolution of Role of the Federal Government in Housing and Community Development, 94th Congress, First Session (Washington, D.C.: Government Printing Office, 1975), p. 1.

5. See Laurence Conway Gerckens, "Historical Development of American City Planning" in Frank S. So et al. (editor), The Practice of Local Government Planning (Washington, D.C.: International City Management Associations, 1979), p. 21.

6. See Lawrence Friedman, Government and Slum Housing (Chicago: Rand McNally, 1968).

7. See National Commission on Urban Problems, Report--Building the American City (Washington, D.C.: Government Printing Office, 1968).

8. Housing Act of 1949. National Housing Policy and Goal. See Evolution of Role of the Federal Government, p. 25.

9. See Milton Semer et al., "Evolution of Federal Legislative Policy in Housing: Housing Credits" and "A Review of Federal Subsidized Housing Programs," in U.S. Department of Housing and Urban Development, Housing in the Seventies - Working Papers, Vol. 1 (Washington, D.C.: Government Printing Office, 1975), p. 3.

10. Ibid.

11. See Chapter 6 in this study.

12. See Robert W. Burchell and David Listokin, The Housing Assistance Plan (New Jersey Federation of Planning Officials, Vol. 41, No. 2, Summer 1976.)

13. Ibid.

14. C.F.R. §570.306(e)(1).

15. See Robert Taggart, Low Income Housing: A Critique of Federal Aid (Baltimore: Johns Hopkins Press, 1970).

16. Semer et al., "Evolution of Federal Legislative Policy."

17. David Listokin, Housing Rehabilitation: Economic, Social and Policy Perspectives (New Brunswick: Center for Urban Policy Research, 1983).

18. See W. Eugene Rizor, Phasing Out the Experimental Housing Allowance Program in Connecticut (Santa Monica, Rand, 1983).

19. Semer et al., "Evolution of Federal Legislative Policy," pp. 120-121.

20. See footnote 2 in this chapter.

21. Chapter 42, United States Codes, 1437a (b) (2) 1982 Supplement.

22. Mount Laurel II Decision, p. 36, fn. 8.

23. U.S. Housing Act of 1937, U.S.C. 42, 1437.

24. Phone conversation with the United States Department of Housing and Urban Development, Office of Policy Development and Research.

25. U.S. Department of Commerce, Bureau of the Census, The 1980 Census of Population and Housing, Public Use Sample: New Jersey (Washington, D.C.: Government Printing Office, 1982).

26. United States Department of Housing and Urban Development, Office of the Assistant Secretary for Housing -- Federal Housing Commissioner. Memo, "Approval of revised income limits applicable to the Section 8 Housing Assistance Payments Program," 6 April 1983.

27. Mount Laurel II Decision, p. 72.

28. United States Department of Commerce, Bureau of the Census, Measuring the Quality of Housing: An Appraisal of Census Statistics and Methods (Washington, D.C.: Government Printing Office, 1967), pp. 1-3.

29. Ibid., p. 17.

30. Ibid., p. 23.

31. Ibid., p. 2.

32. Ibid., p. 1.

33. Ibid., pp. 17-19.

34. Ibid., Chap. 4 Passim.

35. Bureau of the Census, Measuring the Quality of Housing, pp. 17-23.

36. Ibid., p. 19.

37. Ibid., p. 21.

38. Bureau of the Census, The 1980 Census of Population and Housing - New Jersey.

39. Grace Horowitz, Housing Quality Data Needs of Users: Needs for Data on Housing Quality (Department of Health Education and Welfare, Office of the Assessment Secretary for Planning and Evaluation, Office of Technical Support and Statistics, Division of Simulation and Modeling, January 10, 1977).

40. Jeanne E. Goedert and John L. Goodman, Jr., Indicators of Housing Quality: An Exploration of the Annual Housing Survey (Washington, D.C.: The Urban Institute Working Paper 249-2, November 1976.)

41. United States Department of Commerce, Bureau of the Census, A Preliminary Look at the Results of the Five City Survey (Washington, D.C.: Government Printing Office, July 9, 1975).

42. Bureau of the Census, The 1980 Census of Population and Housing - New Jersey.

43. American Public Health Association, Inc., Committee on the Hygiene of Housing. Basic Principles of Healthful Housing, (New York, APHA, 1961).

44. Ibid.

45. Ibid.

46. Britton Harris, "Plan or Projection: An Examination of the Uses of Models in Planning." Journal of the American Institute of Planners, Vol. 24, No. 4 (November 1960).

47. Ibid.

48. Ibid.

49. State of New Jersey Department of Labor, New Jersey Revised Total and Age and Sex Population Projections, July 1, 1985 to 2000 (Department of Labor, July 1983).

50. Ibid., p. 13.

51. Ibid.

52. Ibid.

53. Ibid.

54. In its descriptive mode, the headship rate can be interpreted to represent the reciprocal of the average household size indicator; however, in its forecasting mode where only population size is forecasted, three operational definitions must be used in this test.

55. George Sternlieb et al., Demographic Trends and Economic Reality (New Brunswick: Center for Urban Policy Research, 1982).

56. George Sternlieb, James W. Hughes and Connie O. Hughes, Demographic Trends and Economic Reality: Planning and Markets in the '80s (New Brunswick: Center for Urban Policy Research, 1982).

57. George Masnick, The Demographic Factor in Household Growth (Cambridge: Joint Center for Urban Studies of MIT and Harvard University, May 1983), pp. 29-34.

58. Ibid., p. 35.

59. Masnick, The Demographic Factor in Household Growth.

APPENDIX I

THE EMPIRICAL ADEQUACY OF THE HOUSING QUALITY SURROGATE

INTRODUCTION

The use of surrogate variables as housing quality indicators has always posed two problems: 1) how well do they perform their fundamental task: isolating poor quality housing from that of satisfactory quality, and 2) how unique is each surrogate in identifying poor quality housing? That is, can we correctly add the individual estimates of deficient housing derived from the surrogates to produce a reasonable total of such housing, or would this produce some element of overcount requiring a downward adjustment?

At the beginning of Chapter 2, we discussed the problem of quantifying the extent of deficient housing currently being occupied by households qualifying for consideration under Mount Laurel II. Using a series of Venn Diagrams, it was shown that the surrogate indices may or may not signal housing that corresponds to deficient housing. Furthermore, the indices may interact with each other in such a way that combining the number of units targeted by each surrogate as potentially deficient could produce a significant overcount.

The first question deals with the issue of validity; the second question deals with the question of method. Let us start this short appendix with an examination of the appropriateness of the methods used by CUPR to measure deficient housing by comparing its estimates of deficiencies in Mount Laurel households with those estimated to occur in the non-Mount Laurel population.

ASSIGNMENT OF DEFICIENT HOUSING QUALITY STATUS: THE MOUNT LAUREL AND NON-MOUNT LAUREL POPULATION

For the analysis to follow, the ability of non-Mount Laurel households to move into satisfactory units must be assumed. That is, if a unit is truly deficient, then it is the choice of its occupants to reside therein and to use the income savings, relative to this decision for other purposes. In the Northeast Region shown in Exhibit 2A-1, for example, 6.42 percent of the non-Mount Laurel households are labeled by the combinatorial analysis as deficient housing. For the sake of argument, let us accept the assertion that 6.42% represents an erroneous assignment due to the poor quality of information incorporated into the surrogate variables. Assuming that this error is distributed proportionately across both types of households, we can conclude that an overcount of 6.42% exists in our estimate of deficient housing within the Mount Laurel population. After netting out this overcount, the percent deficient within the Mount Laurel population in the Northeast Region is reduced to 11.87% or 34,005 households.

EXHIBIT 2A-1

NUMBER AND PERCENTAGE OF OCCUPIED DWELLING UNITS ASSIGNED SATISFACTORY AND DEFICIENT STATUS BY COMBINATORIAL ANALYSIS OF 7 SURROGATES OF DEFICIENT HOUSING FOR NON-MOUNT LAUREL AND MOUNT LAUREL ELIGIBLE HOUSEHOLDS

	REGION						
	Northeast	Northwest	West Central	East Central	South-west	South-South-west	Total
Non-Mount Laurel Households							
Satisfactory Housing							
Number	375,280	387,386	203,500	227,840	282,440	146,080	1,622,520
% of Regional Total	(93.58)	(95.98)	(98.24)	(97.42)	(97.55)	(92.66)	(95.84)
Deficient Housing							
Number	25,760	16,220	3,640	6,040	7,100	11,580	70,340
% of Regional Total	(6.42)	(4.02)	(1.76)	(2.58)	(2.45)	(7.34)	(4.16)
Mount Laurel Households							
Satisfactory Housing							
Number	234,080	244,640	119,240	121,400	173,200	67,520	960,080
% of Regional Total	(81.71)	(87.91)	(93.3)	(96.01)	(92.80)	(89.6)	(88.81)
Deficient Housing							
Number	52,160	33,440	8,520	4,960	13,360	7,720	120,160
% of Regional Total	(18.29)	(12.09)	(6.70)	(3.91)	(7.2)	(10.4)	(11.19)
Proportion of Housing Erroneously Assigned Deficient	(6.42)	(4.02)	(1.76)	(2.58)	(2.45)	(7.34)	(4.16)
Net Proportion Deficient Housing	(11.87)	(8.07)	(4.94)	(1.39)	(4.75)	(3.06)	(7.03)
Net Number of Housing Units Occupied by Mt. Laurel Households as Deficient	34,005	22,457	6,313	1,158	8,865	2,306	75,104

Using this analysis across the 6 regions of the state, the most conservative estimate of the number of deficient units is 75,104. This represents approximately 7 percent of the total number of Mount Laurel households statewide whereas the original estimate of deficient households within the Mount Laurel population (shown in Exhibit 3-14) was 11 percent or 120,160 dwelling units; a potential overcount of 45,056.

EXAMINATION OF THE COMBINATORIAL METHOD

The preceding analysis suggests an overcount in the number of housing deficiencies occurring within the Mount Laurel population. Can this result be attributed to the combinatorial method devised by CUPR?

The combinatorial method employed by CUPR involves the extensive use of the logical operator: the union. This means that a unit is judged deficient if any surrogate triggers a unit of poor quality by the value appearing in the census, or if any other surrogate so used triggers such a conclusion. Let us examine the type of error created by this method.

The two logical operations that are fruitfully used in this analysis are the union and the intersection. In the logical intersection, each and every attribute must be triggered as poor in quality if the unit is to be assigned the deficient quality status. The union, to the contrary, permits a unit to be assessed deficient if any one of the surrogates is triggered as poor.

A moment's reflection will show that the use of the intersection will minimize the count of units flagged by the surrogates as poor in quality on their respective housing characteristics. If the surrogates largely intersect with deficient housing, this will minimize the count of deficient housing as is represented in Figure 2-7(b), leaving an uncounted residual subset of deficient housing. On the other hand, to the extent that the surrogates do not adequately reflect deficient housing, the level of erroneously labeled housing is minimized.

In the case of the union, the level of success or failure will be in the opposite direction. As discussed in Chapter 2, the CUPR method first employs the logical intersection to discriminate between older and newer units occupied by Mount Laurel eligible households in 1980; this operation is followed by the use of the union of age of structure with one or two of the seven remaining surrogates to flag a deficient unit. Given that many Mount Laurel households can be assumed to live in totally satisfactory units independent of the age of the structure, there is some tendency of the method to overcount the number of deficient units. However, our ability to correct this potential bias is limited by the lack of full knowledge of the interaction between the housing quality surrogates and units rated deficient.

Given the use of this set of logical operations, we must conclude that the CUPR method, if anything, will produce somewhat of an overcount of deficient housing. The comparison of CUPR assessed deficiencies in the set of non-Mount Laurel households with that in Mount Laurel households will probably show a level of deficiencies close to the lower bound of the actual distribution. This conclusion is further borne out by an examination of the contingent probability distribution constructed for the six surrogates, as found within the New Jersey Mount Laurel eligible household population as of 1980, as well as an analysis of self-enumerated housing quality found within the New Jersey segment of the Annual Housing Survey.

THE INTERRELATIONSHIPS AMONG THE SEVEN HOUSING QUALITY SURROGATES

When the accuracy of the surrogates is judged to be problematic, the existence of dependence among the surrogates can provide insights into the way the combinatorial formula should be constructed. In order to judge the effectiveness of the use of the intersection and union in the combinatorial formula, it is of value to know the level of overlap at the dwelling unit level contained in the surrogates used for the Mount Laurel research. Exhibit 2A-2 has been prepared for this purpose. Each row represents the proportion of cases in which a dwelling unit in housing quality condition (i), that is, the row title, will possess each of the other deficiencies (including none of the other deficiencies).

EXHIBIT 2A-2

CONDITIONAL PROBABILITY MATRIX OF HOUSING DEFICIENCY PROBABILITIES GIVEN THE DEFICIENCY NOTED BY THE ROW TITLE

Problem - State of Dwelling Unit	Other Potential Problem - States of the Dwelling Unit						
	Access	Elevator	Kitchen	Crowding	Heating	Plumbing	No Other Problem
Access	1.00	.14[a]	.10	.25	.18	.21	.12
Elevator	0.01	1.00	.06	.18	.21	.07	.47
Kitchen	0.02	.14	1.00	.16	.20	.38	.10
Crowding	0.02	.15	.06	1.00	.29	.09	.39
Heating	0.01	.11	.05	.18	1.00	.08	.49
Plumbing	0.03	.11	.29	.17	.24	1.00	.16

[a]Interpretation: If a Mount Laurel household living in a deficient structure has an access problem the probability is 0.14 that the unit will also have an elevator problem.

The method used to examine the level of interaction among the six housing quality surrogates is through the use of eigenvector analysis.[1] In short, this is done as follows. First a square contingent probability matrix is constructed. Each nondiagonial term represents the relative frequency at which a column head characteristic is present when a given row characteristic is present within the dwelling unit. Every square matrix, such as the 6x6 component of the matrix in Exhibit 2A-2 and represented by [A], possesses a characteristic polynominal equation the roots of which are termed eigenvalues (v). Each eigenvalue can be used to derive a new row vector (V): termed the eigenvector. This vector is a measure of the information held in common (interaction or overlap) by the six housing quality row vectors.

In matrix terms, the relationship showing the common elements of housing quality across the six indices is:

1) $[A]\ [v] = IV$

where A is a 6x6 housing quality matrix
V is a 6x1 eigenvector
I is the identity matrix; and
λ is an eigenvalue derived from the characteristic equation.

The characteristic equation:

2) $|A - \lambda I| = 0$

is the polynominal equation derived from setting the determinants of the adjusted housing quality matrix equal to zero. As indicated in Equation 1, the eigenvector has the quality of remaining unchanged in its direction when multiplied by the original matrix. It is in a sense a fixed point in the six dimensional housing quality space. The value of the eigenvalue shows the level of importance or overlap among the six indicators attributed to the eigenvector.

Given that there are six conditional probability vectors, one for each housing characteristic, if one eigenvalue equals 6 while the remaining 5 are 0, then it could be shown that all six indices measured the same phenomenon. That is, 100% of the trace would be found in one eigenvalue. On the other hand, if the eigenvalues are all equal in value each holding 16.7% of the trace of the matrix, then each index measures a fundamentally different phenomenon and the Venn diagrams are non-overlapping.

Exhibit 2A-3 presents the eigenvalues derived from the 6x6 housing quality matrix shown in Exhibit 2A-2. This exhibit shows that all six eigenvalues are relatively similar in their ability to measure common trends among the original housing quality indicators. The highest eigenvalue contains 27.3% of the trace, while the lowest value contains 11%. The relevance of this to the problem at hand is that the six housing quality indicators appear to be relatively independent of one another since each indicator by itself would hold 16.7% of the trace, given perfect independence.

EXHIBIT 2A-3

THE EIGENVALUES DERIVED FROM THE CONDITIONAL PROBABILITY HOUSING QUALITY MATRIX SHOWN IN EXHIBIT 2A-2

	Eigenvalue		% of Trace
	λ^1	1.64	27.3
	λ^2	1.08	18.0
	λ^3	.99	16.5
	λ^4	.86	14.3
	λ^5	.77	12.8
	λ^6	.66	11.0
Total		6.00	100.0

Source: CUPR Housing Quality Study.

The first two eigenvalues do show a degree of common housing quality measurement capacity; in order to show the elements that combine in these two vectors, the eigenvectors are shown in Exhibit 2A-4.

EXHIBIT 2A-4

EIGENVECTORS DERIVED FROM THE TWO LARGEST EIGENVALUES SHOWN IN EXHIBIT 2A-3

	Access	Elevator	Kitchens	Crowding	Heating	Plumbing
V_1	.21	.12	.23	.13	.11	.21
V_2	.57	-.42	-.30	-.21	-.09	.02

Source: CUPR Housing Quality Study.

The principal eigenvector or collection of housing quality indicators (V1) shows a modest grouping of multiple problems of access and a lack of kitchen and plumbing facilities. This vector may well be picking up reconversions that have not proceeded to completion. The second eigenvector (V2) is perpendicular to the first and shows that access problems can be found in the absence of elevator, kitchen and crowding problems.

What are the consequences of these findings for the methods used to identify deficient housing? The relative lack of common explanatory power by the six housing quality surrogates suggests that a condition somewhat similar to that pictured in Figure 2-7(b) obtains. Such a situation justifies the use of the combinatorial techniques used in this work. That is, to the extent that the indices truly point out deficient housing, the maximum number of deficient units will be identified in the census data. A method using more intersections than that constructed by CUPR would clearly be too restrictive, thus resulting in an undercount. As of the current state of the art, it would appear that the CUPR method is an excellent means to detect deficient housing with the probability of error in isolating such housing falling in favor of the underhoused.

THE CUPR COMBINATORIAL METHOD: A TEST INVOLVING HOUSEHOLDER RATINGS

The ability to consistently and accurately (and we might add inexpensively) identify deficient housing through the analysis of Census-type data depends upon the existence of a truth set. That is, the truth set should permit comparison of all of the surrogates and their logical combinations to effectively identify deficient housing while minimizing overcounting errors.

The Five City Study performed by the Bureau of the Census and USHUD could provide such a truth set if the full data set were made public. Lacking this, the next best alternative appears to be the results from the Annual Housing Survey. There, Census-like attributes are recorded for each unit in the sample as is a housing quality rating score.[2] The housing quality score is given by the occupant of the dwelling unit. Given the known tendency for owners to overestimate the quality of their dwelling unit; while, renters underestimate its quality, its use as a truth set must be performed with caution.[3] With this caveat in mind, the results of the CUPR combinatorial method were compared with those of the Annual Housing Survey.[4]

The results of the comparison of the CUPR method of housing quality assignment and those of the self assignment in the Annual Housing Survey are displayed in Exhibit 2A-5. Here, the householder is given four terms by which to rate the unit: excellent, good, fair, or poor. Exhibit 2A-5 combines excellent and good into one category labeled good, and fair and poor into a category labeled fair. In that these terms are subjectively attributed to the unit by its occupant, the ability to extract useful quality assignments is felt to be improved by collapsing the fourfold system into a two-part good or fair dichotomy.

EXHIBIT 2A-5

CROSS TABULATION OF DWELLING UNITS WHOSE QUALITY IS ASSESSED BASED UPON THE CUPR COMBINATORIAL MODEL VERSUS THE SELF EVALUATION BY OCCUPANTS

A. Non-Mount Laurel Households

CUPR Assessment	Household Evaluation Good	Poor/Fair	
Not Deficient	91.0%[a]	9.0%	100%
Deficient	33.4%	66.6%	100%

a. Table should be read as follows: x % of the units judged "not deficient" by the CUPR assessment system were rated excellent or good by the householder.

B. Mount Laurel Households in 50-80% of Median Income Category

CUPR Assessment		
Non-Deficient	82.1%	17.9%
Deficient	66.5%	33.5%

C. Mount Laurel Households in the Less than 50% of Median Income Category Homeowner Evaluation

CUPR Assessment			
Non-Deficient	76.9%	23.1%	100%
Deficient	42.0%	58.0%	100%

Source: Annual Housing Survey: New Jersey, 1977.

In the case of the non-Mount Laurel household, over 90 percent of the units rated good in the Annual Housing Survey were assigned the non-deficient status by the CUPR combinatorial method; while, 66 percent of the units assigned the deficient status were rated fair to poor by the occupant. The exhibit shows some tendency to overcount deficient housing by the CUPR procedure. However, given the tendency for owners to overestimate their unit's quality, the error rate is probably higher than it should be.

In part B of Exhibit 2A-5, the self-rating by the moderate income category Mount Laurel householder is examined. Here it is shown that a significant overcount of deficient housing exists in the CUPR model in that 66% of the units assigned deficient by CUPR are rated good by the occupant. Finally, in part C of Exhibit 2A-5, the self rating of low income Mount Laurel households is compared with the CUPR procedure. Here, seventy-seven percent of the units labeled non-deficient by the CUPR model were identified as good by the household; while, 58 percent of the units identified as deficient by the CUPR method were rated fair by the occupant.

In summary, the CUPR method appears to be overestimating the number of Mount Laurel households currently living in deficient housing. Fortunately, the level of error appears to be greatest within the moderate income category. This category is relatively small compared with the low income category. What is more, the moderate income category possesses a higher level of homeowners than does the low income category. If homeowners do actually overestimate quality of their dwelling units, then the significance of this level of error is further reduced in terms of the Mount Laurel decision as a whole. In a sense, the results put forth in this chapter represents a worst case situation. Given the uncertainty of measurement, the methods used err in favor of the underhoused population.

LOW-INCOME AS THE SURROGATE OF DEFICIENT HOUSING

One can often come across statements to the effect that: poor housing is where poor people live. However, for such a generalization to have policy consequences, one would have to look beyond a housing maintenance to an income maintenance program. The reason for this is that most low or low and moderate income households reside in satisfactory units (as judged by housing experts). This can be shown from the results of the Five City Study, Exhibit 2A-6.

Exhibit 2A-6 shows that 26.2 percent of the total population of dwelling units in the Five City Study were of low income. This was identified by HUD officials at the time (1972) as a family of four with less than $5,000 of annual income where the median household income was $9,462. Again as with many other housing quality surrogates, there is a great deal of interaction between the income variable and the housing quality rating variable. However, to say that low household income is by itself an adequate surrogate of poor quality housing is to widely overstate its power.

EXHIBIT 2A-6

AGGREGATE DWELLING UNIT AND NEIGHBORHOOD RATING CROSS CLASSIFIED WITH FAMILY INCOME OF THE DWELLING UNIT'S RESIDENTS

	Housing and Neighborhood Quality Satisfactory	Poor	Total
Low Income	298,767	34,190	332,957 (26.2%)
Not Low Income	920,233	18,410	938,643 (73.8%)
Total	1,219,000 (95.9%)	52,600 (4.1%)	1,271,600 (100%)

Source: USDHUD, Five City Study, Summer 1972

It is correct that poor quality housing is disproportionately concentrated within low income households (65%); however, low income households do not live for the most part in poor quality housing. The Five City Study shows that out of the total of 332,957 low income residents included in the study only 34,190 could be concluded to live in poor quality housing, this value represents only 10.3% of the low income population of the five cities referred to in this study.

EXHIBIT 2A-7

COMPARISON OF THE HOUSING QUALITY OF LOWER INCOME HOUSEHOLDS REPORTED IN THE FIVE CITY STUDY AND BY THE CUPR COMBINATORIAL METHOD

	Housing and Neighborhood Quality Satisfactory	Poor	Total
Five City Study (Low Income Households) Only	298,767 89.7%	34,190 10.3%	332,957 (100%)
CUPR Study Low and Moderate Income Households	961,645 88.9%	120,160 11.1%	1.081,805 (73.8%)

The CUPR study while not having the advantage of a set of on-site housing quality ratings has closely reproduced the results found in the Five City Study. Exhibit 2A-7 compared the fraction of low income households living in satisfactory and poor housing with that found by CUPR for the combined low and moderate income households of New Jersey. Where 10.3% low income results are found to live in poor quality housing by HUD, 11.1% of New Jersey's low and moderate income population is found by CUPR to be similarly ill-housed. Such a correspondence between two independent studies lends support to the policy proposals to be based upon the CUPR method.

In conclusion, it is clear that low income places a severe burden upon the acquisition of satisfactory housing. However, more low income residents of the five cities examined in the above referenced report, do live in satisfactory housing. To place an excessive value of the use of income as a surrogate for deficient housing would be to vastly overcount the phenomenon and suggest utilizing scarce resources for the excessive upgrading of the housing stock rather than for other pressing social matters.

APPENDIX II

A NOTE ON THE POPULATION PROJECTIONS

As indicated previously in this chapter, the projections shown here have relied upon those developed by the New Jersey Department of Labor, Demographic and Economic Analysis (ODEA). It should be noted that the specific set utilized was the state "conservative" forecast. Even this projection however, has been seriously challenged in its optimism by those currently promulgated by the U.S. Census Bureau.

In its August, 1983 publication, Provisional Projections of the Population of States, by Age and Sex: 1980 to 2000, the vision of New Jersey's population growth is far more modest. As shown in Exhibit 2A-8, for example, growth from 1980 through 1990 is on the order of 150,000, only 70 percent of the state's forecast. Indeed from 1990 to the year 2000, there is an absolute population decline projected, on the order of 85,000.

As further detailed in Exhibit 2A-8, the pattern of change within age groups, is particularly pertinent to the housing scene. For example, practically the entire increase in the decade of the Eighties in the state's population is equal to the increment in the number of persons, 70 years of age or over. And indeed, the number of such persons expands by nearly 100,000 in the decade of the Nineties despite an aggregate absolute population loss. This pattern within age segments is roughly comparable to the state's projections.

While there are a number of factors at work which underlie the difference between the state and federal projections, one of the more crucial, is that of migration. In the brief five years from 1975 to 1980, New Jersey recorded a net outmigration of some 83,300. The Census forecasts project a continuance of this net decline with a loss of some 58,300 from 1980 to 1990 followed by a nearly equal number -- a decline of 55,000 from 1990 to 2000.

It is noteworthy in this context to examine the pattern of New Jersey's immediate neighbors, New York and Pennsylvania. They have long served as a source of newcomers to our own state. In the five year period to 1980, New York State lost some 648,000 persons to net migration, while Pennsylvania's was a very substantial 177,000. And this at a time when New Jersey, rather than inheriting these migrants in such numbers as to overcome its own occupants leaving the state, suffered a net loss.

This is a pattern which the Census Bureau forecasts as continuing in the decades to come with New York State losing slightly under the 1.6 million mark in net inmigration from 1980 to 1990 -- followed by a decade of loss on the order of 1.5 million. The data on Pennsylvania are similarly less than positive with a decline of nearly 400,000 from 1980 to 1990 and some 351,000 from 1990 to 2000.

EXHIBIT 2A-8

NEW JERSEY PROJECTION OF THE RESIDENT POPULATION BY AGE AND SEX:
1980 TO 2000
(Population rounded to hundreds, as of July 1)

SEX AND AGE	CENSUS, APRIL 1, 1980	PROJECTIONS 1990	2000
TOTAL, ALL AGES	7,364,200	7,513,100	7,427,600
Under 5 Years	463,100	511,300	424,100
5 to 9 Years	508,500	488,600	462,800
10 to 14 Years	605,700	464,700	503,600
15 to 19 Years	670,600	473,900	455,600
20 to 24 Years	614,800	518,000	395,500
25 to 29 Years	574,000	631,600	445,600
30 to 34 Years	563,700	665,700	555,100
35 to 39 Years	479,700	593,500	641,600
40 to 44 Years	400,000	560,200	648,000
45 to 49 Years	394,000	463,000	562,100
50 to 54 Years	432,600	378,000	521,500
55 to 59 Years	430,100	352,100	414,400
60 to 64 Years	367,400	363,800	317,300
65 to 69 Years	303,700	336,400	273,100
70 to 74 Years	226,900	268,900	263,700
75 to 79 Years	157,900	201,600	224,400
80 to 84 Years	98,800	128,400	155,900
85 Years and Over	72,200	113,400	163,400

Source: U.S. Bureau of the Census, Current Population Reports, Series P25, No. 937 Table 4, Provisional Projections of the Population of States, by Age and Sex: 1980 to 2000, Government Printing Office, 1983.

To the degree that New Jersey has served not only as a recipient of migration from these two states, but also has a job base, which at least in part, has risen from service elements (and indeed manufacturing) dedicated to the markets posed in its two neighboring states, these are truly negative forecasts, not only in terms of New Jersey's demography -- but also of employment.

These data are presented here not to provide alternatives to the state forecast, but rather to indicate that the state data used as a basis for our projections in Chapter 2 and 3 may reasonably be seen as fully extending the horizon of the state's demographically-inspired housing needs.

NOTES

1. P.R. Gould, "On the Geographical Interpretation of Eigenvalues," Institute of British Geographers Transactions, No. 42 (December 1967).

2. William T. Bielby, "Measuring Neighborhood Quality in the Annual Housing Survey" (February, 1979). Research conducted for the United States Department of Housing and Urban Development, Contract No. HUD 2513-78.

3. United States Department of Commerce, Bureau of the Census, Measuring the Quality of Housing: An Appraisal of Census Statistics and Methods (Washington, D.C.: Government Printing Office, 1967).

4. United States Department of Commerce, Bureau of the Census, Current Housing Reports, Housing Characteristics for Selected Metropolitan Areas (Washington, D.C.: Government Printing Office, 1980).

CHAPTER 3—
SOCIOECONOMIC AND HOUSING CHARACTERISTICS OF THE PRESENT AND PROSPECTIVE MOUNT LAUREL-ELIGIBLE POPULATIONS

INTRODUCTION

Having defined and specified the magnitude of the Mount Laurel-eligible populations in the previous chapter, we now turn to a discussion of the socioeconomic and housing characteristics of the present Mount Laurel population and the socioeconomic characteristics of the prospective Mount Laurel population.

Sections on current socioeconomic and housing characteristics will begin with a general discussion of conditions in the State of New Jersey to which present Mount Laurel households will be compared. The portion of the chapter concerning characteristics of the future population will be preceded by a discussion of forecasted trends for the general population of the State of New Jersey to which prospective Mount Laurel households will be compared.

Socioeconomic characteristics cover the range of social indicators of the population: race, ethnicity, sex, age, labor force participation, occupation, journey-to-work, etc. and apply to the chief income producer of the household. Other characteristics such as income and automobile availability apply to the aggregate of all household members. Housing characteristics for the existing Mount Laurel population pertain to the unit in which the family resides.

The chapter is organized and will proceed as follows:

I. PRESENT MOUNT LAUREL POPULATION

A. Socioeconomic Characteristics
B. Housing Characteristics

II. PROSPECTIVE MOUNT LAUREL POPULATION

A. Socioeconomic Characteristics

III. PRESENT VERSUS PROSPECTIVE MOUNT LAUREL POPULATION

A. Socioeconomic Characteristics

SOCIOECONOMIC CHARACTERISTICS OF PRESENT MOUNT LAUREL HOUSEHOLDS

The present Mount Laurel eligible population is a heterogeneous population with two basic characteristics in common: (1) their incomes are below 80 percent of the region's median income in the location in which they live; and (2) the house that they occupy is deficient relative to other housing in that region as defined by the measures of deficiency discussed in the previous chapter. In the section to follow, we shall examine several of the characteristics that affect the ability of individuals and families to find adequate housing. Within each of these groups of socioeconomic characteristics, the size of the relevant group statewide and the existence of regional disparities will be discussed. However, prior to moving into this detailed discussion of Mount Laurel households, let us first review the basic socioeconomic characteristics of the entire State of New Jersey.

Selected Socioeconomic Characteristics of New Jersey Households

The total number of households living in New Jersey, as of 1980, is estimated at 2,773,860. Of this number, approximately 85 percent of the householders (chief income producer) are white; 11.5 percent black and the remaining 3.5 percent Asian, Pacific Islander, American Indian, etc. Close to six percent of the householders in the State of New Jersey are of Spanish ethnic origin most of whom classify themselves as white.[1]

The vast majority (75 percent) of householders in the state are male. The median age of the householder is 39.2 with 20 percent of the householders under age 25 and 30 percent over age 65. The median household size in New Jersey is 2.84 persons with 50 percent of the households below 2.0 persons and 15 percent of 5 persons or more.

The median household income in New Jersey, as reported in the 1980, Census* was $19,801; twenty-four percent of the households earned under $10,000 -- 37 percent earned below $15,000. A similar 37 percent of the households had aggregate incomes in excess of $25,000.

In New Jersey, in 1980, just over 70 percent of households were in the

*Income as of May 1979.

labor force, 5 percent* were unemployed (in the labor force but not working) and 24 percent were not members of the labor force. For those who claimed labor force participation, 16 percent worked as professionals or managers, 42 percent were classified as technical, sales or supervisors, 12 percent each were service personnel or craftsmen, and 18 percent worked as operatives or laborers.

The journey-to-work of labor force participating householders in two-thirds of the cases (66%) was less than 30 minutes; in one-fourth of the cases from 30 to 60 minutes, and for slightly less than 8 percent, in excess of one hour. The principal means of journey-to-work in New Jersey is overwhelmingly the automobile (over 80 percent); less than ten percent of the households use either public transportation (9.2%) or "other means" (8.1%).

We now turn to the discussion of the present Mount Laurel-eligible population. As indicated in Chapter 2, this sector of New Jersey's under-housed population is made up of low and moderate income households living in deficient housing. This population of households numbers 120,160 which is 11.1% of the income-eligible Mount Laurel households and approximately 5 percent of all households in New Jersey.

Race and Ethnicity of the Present Mount Laurel Households: The State (Exhibit 3-1)

The majority of the present Mount Laurel-eligible population is white with close to 60 percent of the households statewide (70,960) being so represented; those households claiming black heritage number 34,160 or 30 percent. The remaining 10 percent are in the "others" category of Asian, Pacific Islanders, American Indians, etc. While the Mount Laurel-eligible population is indeed predominantly white, the black representation within this population is over 2.5 times the statewide average of 11.5 percent.

Black families are also overrepresented in the income category of low versus moderate, and household size category of over 5 persons versus smaller family sizes. The white population under consideration is over-represented in household categories of low- and moderate incomes of 1 to 2 persons.[2]

The Spanish population comprises 25 percent of Mount Laurel households, a figure which is four times the statewide average. The Spanish population is more often low income than moderate (60 versus 40 percent) and more often of very large versus very small families (40 versus 20 percent).[3]

---

*For those in the labor force this is a householder unemployment rate of 7-8 percent.

Race and Ethnicity: The Regions (Exhibits 3-3 to 3-13 Odd Numbered)

The six regions of the state differ markedly from one another in both racial and ethnic composition of their present Mount Laurel-eligible population. Three regions reflect a predominantly white population: the Northeast Region 1, West Central Region 3, and East Central Region 4, where the percent white is 66, 81, and 72 percent respectively. The black population is heavily represented in the Northwest Region 2 (Newark) and Southwest Region 5 (Camden) at 46 and 42 percent respectively. Lastly, the Spanish population is overrepresented only in the Northeast Region (Jersey City, Hoboken, West New York, Union City and Paterson) at 37 percent.

The differences in the size of household by race become much sharper at the regional level than they are statewide. In regions where the white population is more pronounced, it is highly concentrated in the 1-to-2 person, low-income household categories; this is especially true of the Northeast Region 1. The households of Spanish origin while similarly concentrated in the Northeast Region are found more often in larger households and are more equally distributed between low- and moderate-income categories. The black population, whose numerical concentration is strongest in the Northwest and Southwest Regions are split evenly between small households (1-to-2 persons) and larger (3-4 and 5+) households.

Sex of Chief Income Producer: The State

Social custom, until recently, has indicated that the senior male within the household will be its principal wage and income earner. Changes in the role of women have increased the independence of the senior female member of the household. Further, the instability of intrafamily relationships has also forced the head of family role upon the adult female in increasing numbers.[4]

The statewide distribution of sex of Mount Laurel householder shows the existence of both patterns. In the aggregate, the role of chief income producer is relatively evenly split between adult male (48.7%) and female (51.3%) members of the household. The representation of the female as the chief income producer (householder) is, however, double than what is found in New Jersey's population at large. Females are only 25 percent of all householders in New Jersey.

When partitioning the existing Mount Laurel-eligible population by income category and size of household, two striking differences emerge. Households within the low income category are in all cases more likely to have a female head than a male head; the opposite, moving closer to statewide figures, is the case for the moderate income category. Second, as the size of family increases, the percentage of male headed households increases across both income categories.

Sex of Chief Income Producer:
The Regions

The Northeast Region 1 has been shown to possess the largest present Mount Laurel-eligible population. As such, it strongly influences the statewide pattern discussed above. The second and third most populous regions for this purpose are the Northwest and Southwest Regions. In both cases we have already seen that a large black population exists; also we now see that the female headed household is somewhat more prominent in these regions than most of the others. While the statewide average found approximately one-half of the households headed by females, these regions exhibit about 10 percent more female-headed households than the average.

Household Size -- The State

The Mount Laurel population has a median household size of 1.90 with its low income component at 1.70 persons and moderate income component, at 3.10 persons. Overall, the median household size of the Mount Laurel population is 20 percent smaller than the median New Jersey household. The Mount Laurel population has about a 10 percent greater share of small (1-2 person) households and 20 percent greater share of large households (over 5 person). It also has a much smaller share of middle-size (3-4 person) households than the population at large.

Household Size -- The Regions

The regions mirror the state averages quite closely. The two regions with the largest Mount Laurel populations, the Northeast and Northwest, have 54 and 52 percent of the ill-housed populations composed of 1 and 2 person households. The lowest level of 1 and 2 person households occurs in the Southwest region where the relative concentration is 49 percent.

Age Structure: The State

Statewide, the modal age category for present Mount Laurel-eligible households is 25 to 44 years. The median age of the Mount Laurel householder is approximately 40 which is about the same as the New Jersey average of 39.2. The Mount Laurel age extremes (less than 25 or over 65) are much more pronounced than the statewide population as a whole, however.[5]

In raw numbers, the 65 and over aged household with 1-2 persons and low income dominates with 17,560 households. Second highest overall is the 25-44 aged household of 3-4 persons and low income; 12,160 households are in this age-size-income category. The households with designated head under 25 years of age are most concentrated in the low income, 1-to-2 person household categories; the second highest concentration of those under 25 are households of moderate income in the 1-2 person category.

Age Structure: The Regions

The distribution of households by age of chief income producer is remarkably uniform across the six regions. The regions with smaller existing Mount Laurel-eligible populations find this population to be slightly more concentrated within the low income, 1-to-2 person household with the chief income producer over 65 years of age, as well as the 5 or more person low income households with the principal income earner between 25 and 44 years of age. This is the case in the West Central, East Central and South-Southwest Regions 3, 4 and 6 respectively.

There is also a slight tendency for the regions with larger present Mount Laurel eligible populations to have a significantly higher concentration of eligible households in the lower income category with the designated head of household either in 1-2 person households and 65 years and older or in the age category of 25 to 44 years across all categories of family size. This is true in the Northeast, Northwest and Southwest Regions.

Household Income: The State

Household income, modified by household size, is the basic criterion for inclusion in the Mount Laurel population. Thus, it should not be surprising to find that the distribution of households by income and household size should be related. Two-thirds of the present Mount Laurel eligible population had incomes under $10,000, as of 1980. The median household income for this population is thus under $10,000. For New Jersey as a whole, the median income was just under $20,000; only 26 percent of the state's households had incomes below $10,000. One-to-two person families under $10,000 income dominate the Mount Laurel low income category. Within the moderate income category, the largest number of households are found in 1-to-2 person households within the income range $10,000 to $14,999. Finally, by definition, as income rises above the 80 percent of median level, the concentration of households shifts exclusively to those of the largest family size (5+ persons).

Household Income: The Regions

The income structure of present Mount Laurel eligible households varies only slightly from region to region; perhaps closest to the state average is the Northeast region. The most significant deviation from the statewide pattern is the concentration of moderate income households of the $10,000 to $14,999 categories into 1 and 2 persons households. Two regions, the Northwest and the West Central have a smaller percentage of households under $10,000 in household income and a larger percentage between $15,000 and $20,000 than the state average; while, the South-Southwest (Region 6), East Central (Region 4), and Southwest (Region 5) are more heavily concentrated in lower income brackets. As would be expected, most of these households have 1 or 2 persons. Thus, while not extremely strong, there is definite evidence of an income gradient across the state with the higher incomes present in the Northern Regions 1 and 2 and lower in Southern Regions 5 and 6.

Labor Force Participation: The State (Exhibit 3-2)

Roughly half of the present Mount Laurel-eligible population are found to have their principal income earner in the labor force category "working." This is about two-thirds of the New Jersey average of 70 percent for its householders.

The break between moderate and low income categories demonstrates the impact of a job on income levels. Within the moderate income category, seventy to eighty percent of the designated heads of household are working, while for low income households, the range is one-half that level, i.e. 30 to 40 percent. The lowest concentration of working heads of household is found in the category of low income, 1-to-2 person households.

Unemployment is increasingly a problem for larger households. The worst problems are in the low income Mount Laurel category wherein close to 10 percent of heads of households with more than 3 persons are unemployed. This is an artificially low number reflecting a significant share of the Mount Laurel population, 40 percent, not in the labor force. The unemployment rate of those in the labor force for the entire Mount Laurel population was approximately 12 percent at a time (April 1980) when, at the end of the Carter years, average unemployment was approximately 9 percent statewide.

Families with designated head of household not in the labor force have two major reasons for this condition: (1) the individual is beyond what is the common retirement age, thus, limiting income for the most part to pensions and social security; or (2) the individual is on one or more of the available welfare programs. This is covered in more detail in an appendix to this chapter.

Labor Force Participation: The Regions (Exhibits 3-4 to 3-14 Even-Numbered)

The degree to which present Mount Laurel-eligible households participate in the labor force varies across the six regions along two principal dimensions: level of participation in labor force, and level of unemployment. Labor force participation is strongest in the Northeast Region 1 and

West Central Region 3, ranging from fifty to sixty percent of the household's designated heads. The remaining four regions have labor force participation rates ranging from 45 percent in the Northwest Region to 39 percent in the East Central Region. The latter undoubtedly reflects the retirement orientation of many households in the shore communities of Monmouth and Ocean Counties.

Given that a person is in the labor force, unemployment can still be a serious problem in terms of income. The state average unemployment level (corrected for labor force participation) for the present Mount Laurel eligible population was 12 percent as of the 1980 Census. The highest regional unemployment level was in the Southwest Region 5 at 18 percent; the lowest rate of unemployment among this group came from the West Central Region 3 at 9 percent. In terms of numbers, the bulk of the existing employed Mount Laurel-eligible population can be found in the Northeast and Northwest regions in moderate income households with 1-to-2 persons.

Occupation: The State

Additional insights into the characteristics of the present Mount Laurel eligible population can be gained by examining the range of occupations held or last held by the designated head (chief income provider) of the household. For the present Mount Laurel population, close to 40 percent of the employed were found to be laborers and/or operatives (machine operators); sales and service occupations were the next most often reported at 22 and 19 percent respectively with professional occupations last in frequency at 7.8 percent. Relative to New Jersey aggregate population figures, the present Mount Laurel population has double the percentage of operatives and laborers and one-half the percentage of service, sales and management employees. Those in the moderate income categories more often have occupations that parallel statewide averages.

Occupation: The Regions

A modest degree of variation in occupational structure exists across the six regions. Given the numerical dominance of the laborer-operative category, we see that it is overrepresented in the East Central Region 4, and to a lesser extent in the West Central and Northeast Regions 3 and 1, respectively. It is underrepresented only in the Southwest and South-Southwest regions. The latter two regions are also characterized by some overrepresentation in service occupations.

Journey to Work: The State

Popularly connected with the study of occupations is the analysis of commuting time. The journey-to-work pattern for the present Mount Laurel eligible householder is consistent across both income classes and household size categories (Exhibit 3-4). Well over 80 percent of the households travel 30 minutes or less to work. Low income householders are somewhat more strongly concentrated in this time category than are moderate income job holders. Statewide New Jersey figures show that Mount Laurel households have travel times approximately 20 percent less* than the average commuter. In fact, commuting time increases with income in both the Mount Laurel and non-Mount Laurel populations.(*including out-of-state commuters)

Journey to Work: The Regions

The Northeast Region 1 is essentially a mirror image of the state's journey-to-work pattern. The five remaining regions vary somewhat from the statewide pattern. The second most populous region from the point of view of this sector of the population is the Northwest Region 2. In this case, the eligible householders have a propensity to travel farther than holds for those in the Northeast Region. A similar phenomenon is observed in the Southwest Region 5 where low income householders are almost twice as likely to be found traveling over 30 minutes in their journey-to-work. Interestingly, a complete reversal occurs in this region with moderate income householders being much more likely to travel under 30 minutes to work than either the state average or their low income neighbors.

Means of Journey to Work: The State

The means of travel for commuters is much less concentrated than the statewide average. Approximately 64 percent of present Mount Laurel households in the labor force use an auto, while 20 percent use public transportation, and 16 percent walk, use bikes or some other means. The non-automobile rate is double the equivalent percentage for all New Jersey households. Automobiles are more likely to be used by moderate income workers in larger Mount Laurel households (over 3 persons); while other means are more often utilized by smaller Mount Laurel households within the low income sector.

Means of Journey to Work: The Regions

The means used for the commute to work by present Mount Laurel households is somewhat dictated by the state's public infrastructure. This can be seen in the cases where public transit is available. The heavily populated Northeast Region 1 has 6 percent less auto use than that of the state average; while, public transit and walking each pick up roughly 3 percent of the non-auto trips. Two disparate regions: the Northwest Region 1 and the South-Southwest Region 6 are approximately the same as the state average in the use of autos; however, the major alternative means of travel diverge. In the Northwest Region, public transit is available and utilized; whereas, in the South-Southwest Region, the rate of participation in public transit is about half that of the state and the gap is picked up by walking, biking or other means.

As mentioned previously, statewide, workers from one and two person households are less likely to use an auto for work-related trips than are workers from larger families. As would be expected, this phenomenon is magnified at the regional level of analysis. In the Northeast region, low income households of 1-and-2 persons are more likely to use public transit than all other groups. This finding, though somewhat diminished, holds true for the Northwest and the Southwest Regions 2 and 5.

Automobiles Available: The State

Just as in the case of the use of public transit hinging on the availability of such facilities, the ownership of an auto is the main factor controlling the use of an auto as the common means to work. A slight exception to this is the existence of car pooling which may swell the use of the auto even though none may be available for individual use.

For the New Jersey population as a whole, 85 percent of householders have access to an automobile. For the Mount Laurel population only slightly over 50 percent of the eligible households have an auto available for personal use. This is a significant difference and reflects the increased share of Mount Laurel households using public transit/other means as well as an increased share that is out of the labor force.

The difference in automobile availability between moderate and low income households is even more remarkable. Depending upon size of household, only 20 to 30 percent of moderate income households lack an auto whereas twice that percentage of low income households are found without vehicles.

Automobiles Available: The Regions

The regions, by and large, mirror the statewide pattern of auto availability. The Northeast and Northwest regions have a higher percentage of persons lacking automobiles and therefore dependent upon the public transit system. The West Central Region has the lowest percentage of persons without autos; while, the two southern regions have roughly 65 percent fewer families without autos than the statewide average.

EXHIBIT 3-1

SOCIOECONOMIC CHARACTERISTICS (RACE, SEX, AGE, INCOME) OF PRESENT MT. LAUREL-ELIGIBLE HOUSEHOLDS - STATEWIDE

	MODERATE INCOME (50-80% of Median)			LOW INCOME (Below 50% of Median)			
	1-2 Person	3-4 Person	5 or more Persons	1-2 Person	3-4 Person	5 or More Persons	TOTAL
Race							
White	13,360 (73.9)	6,480 (63.8)	5,920 (56.1)	29,760 (65.0)	9,680 (47.3)	5,760 (38.2)	70,960 (59.1)
Black	3,440 (19.0)	2,120 (20.9)	2,800 (26.5)	12,200 (26.6)	6,800 (33.6)	6,720 (44.6)	34,160 (28.4)
Other	1,280 (7.1)	1,560 (15.4)	1,840 (17.4)	3,840 (8.4)	3,920 (19.1)	2,600 (17.2)	15,040 (12.5)
Total	18,080 (15.0)	10,160 (8.5)	10,560 (8.8)	45,800 (38.1)	20,480 (17.0)	15,080 (12.5)	120,160 (100.0)
Spanish-Origin							
Not Spanish	15,200 (84.1)	7,240 (71.3)	6,960 (65.9)	38,320 (83.7)	12,400 (60.5)	9,800 (65.0)	89,920 (74.8)
Spanish Origin	2,880 (15.9)	2,920 (28.7)	3,600 (34.1)	7,480 (16.3)	8,080 (39.5)	5,280 (35.0)	30,240 (25.2)
Total	18,080 (15.0)	10,160 (8.5)	10,560 (8.8)	45,800 (38.1)	20,480 (17.1)	15,080 (12.5)	120,160 (100.0)
Sex of Chief Income Producer							
Male	10,280 (56.5)	7,400 (72.8)	8,760 (81.7)	17,880 (38.9)	8,160 (39.5)	6,440 (42.4)	58,920 (48.7)
Female	7,920 (43.5)	2,760 (27.2)	1,960 (18.3)	28,080 (61.1)	12,520 (60.5)	8,760 (57.6)	62,000 (51.3)
Total	18,200 (15.1)	10,160 (8.4)	10,720 (8.9)	45,960 (38.0)	20,680 (17.1)	15,200 (12.6)	120,920 (100.0)
Age of Chief Income Producer							
Under 25	2,400 (13.3)	1,600 (15.7)	800 (7.6)	8,000 (17.5)	4,680 (22.9)	1,680 (11.1)	19,160 (15.9)
25-44	5,160 (28.6)	5,920 (58.3)	7,240 (68.6)	9,360 (20.4)	12,160 (59.4)	10,560 (70.0)	50,400 (41.9)
45-64	6,360 (35.2)	2,280 (22.5)	2,440 (23.1)	10,880 (23.7)	2,920 (14.2)	2,720 (18.0)	27,600 (23.0)
65 and over	4,160 (23.0)	360 (3.6)	80 (0.8)	17,560 (38.3)	720 (3.5)	120 (0.8)	23,000 (19.2)
Total	18,080 (15.0)	10,160 (8.5)	10,560 (8.8)	45,800 (38.1)	20,480 (17.0)	15,080 (12.5)	120,160 (100.0)
Household Income							
Under $10,000	5,920 (32.7)	240 (2.4)	0 (0)	45,440 (99.2)	17,160 (83.8)	12,000 (74.3)	79,960 (66.5)
$10,000-$14,999	11,880 (65.7)	5,800 (57.1)	3,040 (28.8)	320 (0.7)	2,840 (13.9)	3,680 (24.4)	27,560 (22.9)
$15,000-$19,999	280 (1.5)	4,040 (39.8)	6,320 (59.8)	40 (0.1)	320 (1.6)	120 (0.8)	11,120 (9.3)
$20,000-$24,999	0 (0)	40 (0.4)	1,200 (11.4)	0 (0)	80 (0.4)	80 (0.5)	1,400 (1.2)
Total	18,080 (15.0)	10,160 (8.5)	10,560 (8.8)	45,800 (38.1)	20,480 (17.0)	15,080 (12.5)	120,160 (100.0)

Source: Bureau of Census, U.S. Census of Population and Housing: New Jersey Public Use Sample, 1980.

EXHIBIT 3-2

SOCIOECONOMIC CHARACTERISTICS (LABOR FORCE PARTICIPATION, OCCUPATION, JOURNEY-TO-WORK) OF PRESENT MT. LAUREL-ELIGIBLE HOUSEHOLDS - STATEWIDE

	MODERATE INCOME (50-80% of Median)			LOW INCOME (Below 50% of Median)			
	1-2 Person	3-4 Person	5 or more Persons	1-2 Person	3-4 Person	5 or More Persons	TOTAL
Labor Force Participation							
At Work	12,360	8,360	9,040	13,640	8,920	6,400	58,720
	(68.4)	(82.3)	(85.6)	(29.9)	(43.6)	(42.6)	(49.0)
With Job - Not at Work	640	320	360	1,440	440	480	3,680
	(3.5)	(3.1)	(3.4)	(3.2)	(2.1)	(3.2)	(3.1)
Unemployed	800	640	600	3,040	1,960	1,480	8,520
	(4.4)	(6.3)	(5.7)	(6.7)	(9.6)	(9.8)	(7.1)
Not in Labor Force	4,240	840	520	27,480	9,160	6,640	48,880
	(23.5)	(8.3)	(4.9)	(60.3)	(44.7)	(44.1)	(40.8)
Total*	18,080	10,160	10,560	45,600	20,480	15,040	119,920
	(15.1)	(8.5)	(8.8)	(38.0)	(17.1)	(12.5)	(100.0)
*includes armed forces	40	-	40	-	-	40	120
	(0.2)		(0.4)			(0.3)	(0.1)
Occupation							
Manager-Professional	1,600	1,000	1,040	1,680	760	608	6,680
	(10.4)	(10.2)	(10.1)	(6.7)	(5.1)	(6.0)	(7.8)
Technical, Sales, Supervisor	4,240	2,280	1,920	5,400	3,160	1,760	18,760
	(27.6)	(23.4)	(18.7)	(21.6)	(21.1)	(17.5)	(21.9)
Service	2,600	1,160	1,400	6,240	2,600	2,240	16,240
	(16.9)	(11.9)	(13.6)	(25.0)	(17.3)	(22.2)	(19.0)
Farming	160	160	40	520	280	120	1,280
	(1.0)	(1.6)	(0.4)	(2.1)	(1.9)	(1.2)	(1.5)
Precision Craftsman	1,480	1,600	1,920	2,240	1,640	1,200	10,080
	(9.6)	(16.4)	(18.7)	(9.0)	(10.9)	(11.9)	(11.8)
Operatives, Labor	5,280	3,560	3,960	8,920	6,560	4,160	32,440
	(34.4)	(36.5)	(38.5)	(35.7)	(43.7)	(41.3)	(38.0)
Total	15,360	9,760	10,280	25,000	15,000	10,080	85,480
Journey to Work							
Less Than 30 Min.	10,120	6,960	7,520	11,600	7,760	5,480	49,440
	(82.7)	(83.7)	(83.2)	(86.6)	(87.4)	(85.6)	(84.8)
30-60 Min.	1,720	1,080	1,320	1,560	920	840	7,440
	(14.1)	(13.0)	(14.6)	(11.7)	(10.4)	(13.2)	(12.8)
60 Min. and Over	400	280	200	240	200	80	1,400
	(3.3)	(3.4)	(1.9)	(1.8)	(1.1)	(1.2)	(2.4)
Total	12,240	8,320	9,040	13,400	8,880	6,400	58,280
	(21.0)	(14.3)	(15.5)	(23.0)	(15.2)	(11.0)	(100.0)
Means of Journey to Work							
Automobile	7,360	6,320	6,920	7,080	5,600	4,160	37,440
	(59.4)	(75.6)	(76.2)	(51.9)	(62.8)	(64.6)	(63.6)
Public Transit	2,960	760	1,160	3,480	1,720	1,400	11,480
	(23.9)	(9.1)	(12.8)	(25.5)	(19.3)	(21.7)	(19.5)
Other (Walk, Bike)	2,080	1,280	1,000	3,080	1,600	880	9,920
	(16.8)	(15.3)	(11.0)	(22.6)	(17.9)	(13.7)	(16.9)
Total	12,400	8,360	9,080	13,640	8,920	6,440	58,840
	(21.1)	(14.2)	(15.4)	(23.2)	(15.2)	(10.9)	(100.0)
Automobile Available							
None	6,440	2,160	2,040	29,480	10,480	7,720	58,320
	(35.6)	(21.3)	(19.3)	(64.4)	(51.2)	(51.2)	(48.5)
1	9,600	5,640	5,520	14,080	7,760	5,880	48,480
	(53.1)	(55.5)	(52.3)	(30.7)	(37.9)	(39.0)	(40.3)
2 or More	2,040	2,360	3,000	2,240	1,480	2,240	13,360
	(11.3)	(23.2)	(28.4)	(4.9)	(9.8)	(10.9)	(11.1)
Total	18,080	10,160	10,560	45,800	20,480	15,080	120,160
	(15.1)	(8.5)	(8.8)	(38.1)	(17.0)	(12.5)	(100.0)

Source: Bureau of Census, U.S. Census of Population and Housing: New Jersey Public Use Sample, 1980.

EXHIBIT 3-3

SOCIOECONOMIC CHARACTERISTICS (RACE, SEX, AGE, INCOME) OF PRESENT MT. LAUREL-ELIGIBLE HOUSEHOLDS - NORTHEAST

	MODERATE INCOME (50-80% of Median)			LOW INCOME (Below 50% of Median)			
	1-2 Person	3-4 Person	5 or more Persons	1-2 Person	3-4 Person	5 or More Persons	TOTAL
Race							
White	6,520	3,040	2,400	14,720	4,960	3,000	34,640
	(78.7)	(68.5)	(56.1)	(73.7)	(57.1)	(46.0)	(66.4)
Black	760	560	880	2,680	1,600	1,880	8,360
	(9.2)	(12.6)	(20.6)	(13.4)	(18.4)	(28.8)	(16.0)
Other	1,000	840	1,000	2,560	2,120	1,640	9,160
	(12.1)	(18.9)	(23.4)	(12.8)	(24.4)	(25.2)	(17.6)
Total	8,280	4,440	4,280	19,960	8,680	6,520	52,160
	(15.9)	(8.5)	(8.2)	(38.3)	(16.6)	(12.5)	(100.0)
Spanish Origin							
Not Spanish	6,000	2,920	2,560	14,680	3,480	3,000	32,640
	(72.5)	(65.8)	(59.8)	(73.5)	(40.1)	(46.0)	(62.6)
Spanish Origin	2,280	1,520	1,720	5,280	5,200	3,520	19,520
	(27.5)	(34.2)	(40.2)	(26.5)	(59.9)	(54.0)	(37.4)
Total	8,280	4,440	4,280	19,960	8,680	6,520	52,160
	(15.9)	(8.5)	(8.2)	(38.3)	(16.6)	(12.5)	(100.0)
Sex of Chief Income Producer							
Male	4,960	3,160	3,600	7,880	3,640	2,800	26,040
	(59.6)	(71.2)	(83.3)	(39.5)	(41.2)	(42.9)	(49.7)
Female	3,360	1,280	720	12,080	5,200	3,720	26,360
	(40.4)	(28.8)	(16.7)	(60.5)	(58.8)	(57.1)	(50.3)
Total	8,320	4,440	4,320	19,960	8,840	6,520	52,400
	(15.9)	(8.5)	(8.2)	(38.1)	(16.9)	(12.4)	(100.0)
Age of Chief Income Producer							
Under 25	1,080	640	320	3,080	1,760	680	7,560
	(13.0)	(14.4)	(7.5)	(15.4)	(20.3)	(10.4)	(14.5)
25-44	2,600	2,520	2,960	4,720	5,840	4,880	23,520
	(31.3)	(56.7)	(69.2)	(23.6)	(67.3)	(74.8)	(45.1)
45-64	3,040	1,120	960	4,840	1,000	880	11,840
	(36.7)	(25.2)	(15.9)	(24.2)	(11.5)	(13.5)	(22.7)
65 and Over	1,560	160	40	7,320	80	80	9,240
	(18.8)	(3.6)	(0.9)	(22.0)	(0.9)	(1.8)	(17.7)
Total	8,280	4,440	4,280	19,960	8,680	6,520	52,160
	(15.9)	(8.5)	(8.2)	(38.3)	(16.6)	(12.5)	(100.0)
Household Income							
Under $10,000	2,280	0	0	19,880	7,480	4,880	34,520
	(27.5)	(0)	(0)	(99.6)	(86.2)	(74.8)	(66.2)
$10,000-14,999	6,000	2,600	960	80	1,040	1,600	12,280
	(72.5)	(58.6)	(22.4)	(0.4)	(12.0)	(24.5)	(23.5)
$15,000-19,999	0	1,800	2,840	0	120	40	4,800
	(0)	(40.5)	(66.4)	(0)	(1.4)	(0.6)	(9.2)
$20,000-24,999	0	0	480	0	40	0	520
	(0)	(0)	(11.2)	(0)	(0.5)	(0)	(1.0)
Total	8,280	4,440	4,280	19,960	8,680	6,520	52,160
	(15.9)	(8.5)	(8.2)	(38.3)	(16.6)	(12.5)	(100.0)

Source: Bureau of Census, U.S. Census of Population and Housing: New Jersey Public Use Sample, 1980.

EXHIBIT 3-4

SOCIOECONOMIC CHARACTERISTICS (LABOR FORCE PARTICIPATION, OCCUPATION, JOURNEY-TO-WORK) OF PRESENT MT. LAUREL-ELIGIBLE HOUSEHOLDS - NORTHEAST

	MODERATE INCOME (50-80% of Median)			LOW INCOME (Below 50% of Median)			
	1-2 Person	3-4 Person	5 or more Persons	1-2 Person	3-4 Person	5 or More Persons	TOTAL
Labor Force Participation							
At Work	5,880	3,800	3,760	6,400	3,880	3,120	26,840
	(71.0)	(85.6)	(87.9)	(32.2)	(44.7)	(47.9)	(51.5)
With Job	360	40	160	760	200	280	1,800
Not at Work	(4.3)	(0.9)	(3.7)	(3.8)	(2.3)	(4.3)	(3.5)
Unemployed	360	240	280	1,440	960	520	3,800
	(4.3)	(5.4)	(6.5)	(7.2)	(11.1)	(8.0)	(7.3)
Not in Labor Force	1,680	360	80	11,280	3,640	2,600	19,640
	(20.3)	(8.1)	(1.9)	(56.7)	(41.9)	(39.9)	(37.7)
Total	8,280	4,440	4,280	19,880	8,680	6,520	52,080
	(15.9)	(8.5)	(8.2)	(38.2)	(16.7)	(12.5)	(100.0)
Occupation							
Manager	800	280	520	560	200	240	2,600
Professional	(11.1)	(6.6)	(12.1)	(4.8)	(3.1)	(5.2)	(6.8)
Technical, Sales,	2,080	1,120	960	2,800	1,320	1,000	9,280
Supervisor	(28.9)	(26.4)	(22.4)	(24.1)	(20.2)	(21.6)	(24.1)
Service	1,120	480	560	2,560	1,200	640	6,560
	(15.6)	(11.3)	(13.1)	(22.1)	(18.4)	(13.8)	(17.0)
Farming	40	0	0	40	80	40	200
	(0.6)	(0)	(0)	(0.3)	(1.2)	(0.9)	(0.5)
Precision	640	680	680	1,080	880	520	4,480
Craftsman	(8.9)	(16.0)	(15.9)	(9.3)	(13.5)	(11.2)	(11.6)
Operatives, Labor	2,520	1,680	1,560	4,560	2,840	2,200	15,360
	(35.0)	(39.6)	(36.4)	(39.3)	(43.6)	(47.4)	(39.9)
Total	7,200	4,240	4,280	11,600	6,520	4,640	38,480
	(18.7)	(11.0)	(11.1)	(30.1)	(16.9)	(12.1)	(100.0)
Journey-to-work							
Less than 30 min.	4,760	3,160	3,120	5,560	3,400	2,520	22,520
	(81.5)	(84.0)	(83.0)	(86.9)	(87.6)	(81.8)	(84.3)
30-60 min.	920	480	560	760	320	560	3,600
	(15.8)	(12.8)	(14.9)	(11.9)	(8.2)	(18.2)	(13.5)
60 min and Over	160	120	80	80	160	0	600
	(2.7)	(3.2)	(2.1)	(1.3)	(4.1)	(0.0)	(2.2)
Total	5,840	3,760	3,760	6,400	3,880	3,080	26,720
	(21.9)	(14.1)	(14.1)	(24.0)	(14.5)	(11.5)	(100.0)
Means of Journey-to-work							
Automobile	3,240	2,720	2,760	2,920	2,160	1,720	15,520
	(55.1)	(71.6)	(73.4)	(45.6)	(55.7)	(55.1)	(17.8)
Public Transit	1,600	440	520	2,000	760	840	6,160
	(27.2)	(11.6)	(13.8)	(31.3)	(19.6)	(26.9)	(23.0)
Other (walk, bike)	1,040	640	480	1,480	960	560	5,160
	(17.7)	(16.8)	(12.8)	(23.1)	(24.7)	(17.9)	(19.2)
Total	5,880	3,800	3,760	6,400	3,880	3,120	26,840
	(21.9)	(14.2)	(14.0)	(23.8)	(14.5)	(11.6)	(100.0)
Automobile Available							
None	3,160	880	960	14,160	4,840	3,280	27,280
	(38.2)	(19.8)	(22.4)	(70.9)	(55.8)	(50.3)	(52.3)
1	4,400	2,760	2,360	5,280	3,200	2,640	20,640
	(53.1)	(62.2)	(55.1)	(26.5)	(36.9)	(40.5)	(39.6)
2 or More	720	800	960	520	640	600	4,240
	(8.7)	(18.0)	(22.4)	(2.6)	(7.4)	(9.2)	(8.1)
Total	8,280	4,440	4,280	19,960	8,680	6,520	52,160
	(15.9)	(8.5)	(8.2)	(38.3)	(16.6)	(12.5)	(100.0)

Source: Bureau of Census, U.S. Census of Population and Housing: New Jersey Public Use Sample, 1980.

EXHIBIT 3-5

SOCIOECONOMIC CHARACTERISTICS (RACE, SEX, AGE, INCOME) OF PRESENT MT. LAUREL-ELIGIBLE HOUSEHOLDS - NORTHWEST

	MODERATE INCOME (50-80% of Median)			LOW INCOME (Below 50% of Median)			
	1-2 Person	3-4 Person	5 or more Persons	1-2 Person	3-4 Person	5 or More Persons	TOTAL
Race							
White	2,920 (59.3)	1,560 (56.5)	1,760 (53.0)	5,880 (47.7)	1,960 (32.0)	840 (21.0)	14,920 (44.6)
Black	1,840 (37.4)	920 (33.3)	1,040 (31.3)	5,640 (45.8)	3,160 (51.6)	2,720 (68.0)	15,320 (45.8)
Other	160 (3.3)	280 (10.1)	520 (15.7)	800 (6.5)	1,000 (16.3)	440 (11.0)	3,200 (9.6)
Total	4,920 (14.7)	2,760 (8.3)	3,320 (9.9)	12,320 (36.8)	6,120 (18.3)	4,000 (12.0)	33,440 (100.0)
Spanish Origin							
Not Spanish	4,520 (91.9)	1,880 (68.1)	2,000 (60.2)	10,960 (89.0)	4,440 (71.9)	3,120 (78.0)	26,880 (80.4)
Spanish Origin	440 (8.1)	880 (31.9)	1,320 (39.8)	1,360 (11.0)	1,720 (28.1)	880 (22.0)	6,560 (19.6)
Total	4,920 (14.7)	2,760 (8.3)	3,320 (9.9)	12,320 (36.8)	6,120 (18.3)	4,000 (12.0)	33,440 (100.0)
Sex of Chief Income Producer							
Male	2,440 (49.2)	1,920 (69.6)	2,760 (82.1)	4,520 (36.5)	2,080 (34.0)	1,360 (33.7)	15,080 (44.8)
Female	2,520 (50.8)	840 (30.4)	600 (17.9)	7,880 (63.5)	4,040 (66.0)	2,680 (663.)	18,560 (55.2)
Total	4,960 (4.7)	2,760 (8.2)	3,360 (10.0)	12,400 (36.9)	6,120 (18.2)	4,040 (12.0)	33,640 (100.0)
Age of Chief Income Producer							
Under 25	440 (8.9)	200 (7.2)	320 (9.6)	2,640 (21.4)	1,240 (20.3)	480 (12.0)	5,320 (15.9)
25-44	1,640 (33.3)	1,840 (66.6)	2,360 (71.0)	2,320 (18.8)	3,560 (58.2)	2,560 (64.0)	14,280 (42.7)
45-64	1,600 (32.5)	440 (23.1)	640 (19.3)	2,680 (21.7)	1,000 (16.3)	920 (23.0)	7,480 (22.3)
65 and Over	1,240 (25.2)	80 (2.9)	0 (0)	4,680 (38.0)	320 (5.2)	40 (1.0)	6,360 (19.0)
Total	4,920 (14.7)	2,760 (8.3)	3,320 (9.9)	12,320 (36.8)	6,120 (18.3)	4,000 (12.0)	33,440 (100.0)
Household Income							
Under $10,000	1,240 (25.2)	0 (0)	0 (0)	12,160 (98.7)	4,800 (78.4)	2,920 (73.0)	21,120 (63.2)
$10,000-14,999	3,560 (72.4)	1,440 (52.2)	920 (27.7)	120 (1.0)	1,120 (18.3)	1,040 (26.0)	8,200 (24.5)
$15,000-19,999	120 (2.4)	1,320 (47.8)	2,040 (61.4)	40 (0.3)	120 (2.0)	0 (0)	3,640 (10.9)
$20,000-24,999	0 (0)	0 (0)	360 (10.8)	0 (0)	40 (0.7)	40 (1.0)	440 (1.3)
Total	4,920 (14.7)	2,760 (8.3)	3,320 (9.9)	12,320 (36.8)	6,120 (18.3)	4,000 (12.0)	33,440 (100.0)

Source: Bureau of Census, U.S. Census of Population and Housing: New Jersey Public Use Sample, 1980.

EXHIBIT 3-6

SOCIOECONOMIC CHARACTERISTICS (LABOR FORCE PARTICIPATION, OCCUPATION, JOURNEY-TO-WORK) OF PRESENT MT. LAUREL-ELIGIBLE HOUSEHOLDS - NORTHWEST

	MODERATE INCOME (50-80% of Median)			LOW INCOME (Below 50% of Median)			
	1-2 Person	3-4 Person	5 or more Persons	1-2 Person	3-4 Person	5 or More Persons	TOTAL
Labor Force Participation							
At Work	3,400 (69.1)	2,160 (78.3)	2,840 (85.5)	3,000 (24.5)	2,800 (45.8)	1,600 (40.0)	15,800 (47.4)
With Job Not at Work	280 (5.7)	120 (4.3)	160 (4.8)	480 (3.9)	40 (0.7)	40 (1.0)	1,120 (3.4)
Unemployed	120 (2.4)	200 (7.2)	120 (3.6)	680 (5.6)	360 (5.9)	440 (11.0)	1,920 (5.8)
Not in Labor Force	1,120 (22.8)	280 (10.1)	200 (6.0)	8,080 (66.0)	2,920 (47.7)	1,920 (48.0)	14,520 (43.5)
Total	4,920 (14.7)	2,760 (8.3)	3,320 (10.0)	12,230 (36.7)	6,120 (18.3)	4,000 (12.0)	33,360 (100.0)
Occupation							
Manager Professional	320 (7.8)	320 (12.3)	320 (9.9)	760 (12.9)	360 (8.7)	160 (6.6)	2,240 (10.0)
Technical, Sales, Supervisor	1,480 (36.3)	640 (24.6)	560 (17.3)	1,080 (18.4)	1,120 (26.9)	440 (18.0)	5,320 (23.8)
Service	600 (14.7)	240 (9.2)	360 (11.1)	1,680 (28.6)	400 (9.6)	640 (26.2)	3,920 (17.5)
Farming	40 (1.0)	40 (1.5)	40 (1.2)	40 (0.7)	40 (1.0)	40 (1.6)	240 (1.1)
Precision Craftsman	280 (6.9)	400 (15.4)	680 (21.0)	320 (5.4)	360 (8.7)	320 (13.1)	2,360 (10.5)
Operatives, Labor	1,360 (33.3)	960 (36.9)	1,280 (39.5)	2,000 (34.0)	1,880 (45.2)	840 (34.4)	8,320 (37.1)
Total	4,080 (18.2)	2,600 (11.6)	3,240 (14.5)	5,880 (26.3)	4,160 (18.6)	2,440 (10.9)	22,400 (100.0)
Journey-to-work							
Less than 30 min.	2,600 (78.3)	1,720 (79.6)	2,360 (83.1)	2,360 (80.8)	2,440 (87.1)	1,360 (85.0)	12,840 (82.1)
30-60 min.	520 (15.7)	320 (14.8)	360 (12.7)	440 (15.1)	320 (11.4)	200 (12.5)	2,160 (13.8)
60 min. and Over	200 (6.0)	120 (5.6)	120 (4.2)	120 (4.1)	40 (1.4)	40 (2.5)	640 (4.1)
Total	3,320 (21.2)	2,160 (13.0)	2,840 (18.2)	2,920 (18.7)	2,800 (17.9)	1,600 (10.2)	15,640 (100.0)
Means of Journey-to-work							
Automobile	1,920 (56.5)	1,680 (77.8)	2,120 (74.6)	1,400 (46.7)	1,680 (60.0)	1,160 (72.5)	9,960 (63.0)
Public Transit	1,040 (30.6)	240 (11.1)	520 (18.3)	960 (32.0)	840 (30.0)	360 (22.5)	3,960 (25.1)
Other (walk, bike)	440 (12.9)	240 (11.1)	200 (7.0)	640 (21.3)	280 (10.0)	80 (5.0)	1,880 (11.9)
Total	3,400 (21.5)	2,160 (13.7)	2,840 (18.0)	3,000 (19.0)	2,800 (17.7)	1,600 (10.1)	15,800 (100.0)
Automobile Available							
None	2,040 (41.5)	680 (24.6)	760 (22.9)	7,960 (64.6)	3,440 (56.2)	2,360 (59.0)	17,240 (51.6)
1	2,480 (50.4)	1,360 (49.3)	1,640 (49.4)	3,600 (29.2)	2,000 (32.7)	1,400 (35.0)	12,480 (37.3)
2 or More	400 (8.1)	720 (26.1)	920 (27.7)	760 (6.2)	680 (11.1)	240 (6.0)	3,720 (11.1)
Total	4,920 (14.7)	2,760 (8.3)	3,320 (9.9)	12,320 (36.8)	6,120 (18.3)	4,000 (12.0)	33,440 (100.0

Source: Bureau of Census, U.S. Census of Population and Housing: New Jersey Public Use Sample, 1980.

EXHIBIT 3-7

SOCIOECONOMIC CHARACTERISTICS (RACE, SEX, AGE, INCOME) OF PRESENT MT. LAUREL-ELIGIBLE HOUSEHOLDS - WEST CENTRAL

	MODERATE INCOME (50-80% of Median)			LOW INCOME (Below 50% of Median)			
	1-2 Person	3-4 Person	5 or more Persons	1-2 Person	3-4 Person	5 or More Persons	TOTAL
Race							
White	1,360 (94.4)	760 (82.6)	680 (77.3)	2,720 (87.2)	880 (66.7)	520 (61.9)	6,920 (81.2)
Black	80 (5.6)	40 (4.3)	120 (13.6)	200 (6.4)	360 (27.3)	240 (28.6)	1,040 (12.2)
Other	0 (0)	120 (13.0)	80 (9.1)	200 (6.4)	80 (6.1)	80 (9.5)	560 (6.6)
Total	1,440 (16.9)	920 (10.8)	880 (10.3)	3,120 (36.6)	1,320 (15.5)	840 (9.9)	8,520 (100.0)
Spanish Origin							
Not Spanish	1,440 (100.0)	720 (78.3)	640 (72.7)	2,880 (92.3)	960 (72.7)	560 (66.7)	7,200 (84.5)
Spanish Origin	0 (0)	200 (21.7)	240 (27.3)	240 (7.7)	360 (27.3)	280 (33.3)	1,320 (15.5)
Total	1,440 (16.9)	920 (10.8)	880 (10.3)	3,120 (36.6)	1,320 (15.5)	840 (9.9)	8,520 (100.0)
Sex of Chief Income Producer							
Male	960 (66.7)	720 (78.3)	720 (81.8)	1,440 (46.2)	800 (60.6)	560 (63.6)	5,200 (60.7)
Female	480 (33.3)	200 (21.7)	160 (18.2)	1,680 (53.8)	520 (39.4)	320 (36.4)	3,360 (39.3)
Total	1,440 (16.8)	920 (10.7)	880 (10.3)	3,120 (36.4)	1,320 (15.4)	880 (10.3)	8,560 (100.0)
Age of Chief Income Producer							
Under 25	240 (16.7)	200 (21.7)	40 (4.5)	440 (14.1)	360 (27.3)	120 (14.3)	1,400 (16.4)
25-44	320 (22.3)	520 (56.5)	680 (77.3)	520 (16.7)	640 (48.5)	590 (71.4)	3,280 (38.4)
45-64	480 (33.3)	160 (17.3)	160 (18.1)	720 (23.0)	240 (18.2)	120 (14.3)	1,880 (22.0)
65 and Over	400 (27.7)	40 (4.3)	0 (0)	1,440 (46.2)	80 (6.1)	0 (0)	1,960 (23.0)
Total	1,440 (16.9)	920 (10.8)	880 (10.3)	3,120 (36.6)	1,320 (15.5)	840 (9.9)	8,520 (100.0)
Household Income							
Under $10,000	240 (16.7)	0 (0)	0 (0)	3,000 (96.2)	1,000 (75.8)	600 (71.4)	4,840 (56.8)
$10,000-14,999	1,040 (72.2)	240 (26.1)	40 (4.5)	120 (3.8)	280 (21.2)	200 (23.8)	1,920 (22.5)
$15,000-19,999	160 (11.1)	640 (69.6)	640 (72.7)	0 (0)	40 (3.0)	40 (4.8)	1,520 (17.8)
$20,000-24,999	0 (0)	40 (4.3)	200 (22.7)	0 (0)	0 (0)	0 (0)	240 (2.8)
Total	1,440 (16.9)	920 (10.8)	880 (10.3)	3,120 (36.6)	1,320 (15.5)	840 (9.9)	8,520 (100.0)

Source: Bureau of Census, U.S. Census of Population and Housing: New Jersey Public Use Sample, 1980.

EXHIBIT 3-8

SOCIOECONOMIC CHARACTERISTICS (LABOR FORCE PARTICIPATION, OCCUPATION, JOURNEY-TO-WORK) OF PRESENT MT. LAUREL-ELIGIBLE HOUSEHOLDS - WEST CENTRAL

	MODERATE INCOME (50-80% of Median)			LOW INCOME (Below 50% of Median)			
	1-2 Person	3-4 Person	5 or more Persons	1-2 Person	3-4 Person	5 or More Persons	TOTAL
Labor Force Participation							
At Work	1,120 (77.8)	760 (82.6)	840 (95.5)	1,320 (42.9)	560 (42.4)	480 (60.0)	5,080 (60.2)
With Job Not at Work	0 (0)	40 (4.3)	0 (0)	0 (0)	120 (9.1)	40 (5.0)	200 (2.4)
Unemployed	40 (2.8)	40 (4.3)	0 (0)	160 (5.2)	80 (6.1)	80 (10.0)	400 (4.7)
Not in Labor Force	280 (19.4)	80 (8.7)	40 (4.5)	1,600 (51.9)	560 (42.4)	200 (25.0)	2,760 (32.7)
Total	1,440 (17.1)	920 (10.9)	880 (10.4)	3,080 (36.5)	1,320 (15.6)	800 (9.5)	8,440 (100.0)
Occupation							
Manager Professional	200 (15.2)	240 (26.1)	80 (9.5)	40 (2.0)	80 (7.4)	0 (0)	640 (9.5)
Technical, Sales, Supervisor	120 (9.1)	120 (13.0)	160 (19.0)	240 (12.2)	120 (11.1)	160 (25.0)	920 (13.6)
Service	120 (9.1)	120 (13.0)	40 (4.8)	520 (26.5)	320 (29.6)	80 (12.5)	1,200 (17.8)
Farming	40 (3.0)	0 (0)	0 (0)	160 (8.2)	40 (3.7)	0 (0)	240 (3.6)
Precision Craftsman	240 (18.2)	200 (21.7)	40 (4.8)	320 (16.3)	120 (11.1)	160 (25.0)	1,080 (16.0)
Operatives, Labor	600 (45.5)	240 (26.1)	520 (61.9)	680 (34.7)	400 (37.0)	240 (37.5)	2,680 (39.6)
Total	1,320 (19.5)	920 (13.6)	840 (12.4)	1,960 (29.0)	1,080 (16.0)	640 (9.5)	6,760 (100.0)
Journey-to-work							
Less than 30 min.	960 (85.7)	600 (78.9)	720 (90.0)	1,160 (96.7)	520 (92.9)	480 (100.0)	4,440 (90.2)
30-60 min.	160 (14.3)	120 (15.8)	80 (10.0)	40 (3.3)	40 (7.1)	0 (0.0)	440 (8.9)
60 min. and Over	0 (0.0)	40 (5.3)	0 (0.0)	0 (0.0)	0 (0.0)	0 (0.0)	40 (0.8)
Total	1,120 (22.8)	760 (15.4)	800 (16.3)	1,200 (24.4)	560 (11.4)	480 (9.8)	4,440 (100.0)
Means of Journey-to-work							
Automobile	920 (82.1)	600 (78.9)	720 (85.7)	840 (63.6)	480 (85.7)	360 (75.0)	3,920 (77.2)
Public Transit	40 (3.6)	0 (0)	0 (0)	120 (9.1)	0 (0)	40 (8.3)	200 (3.9)
Other (walk, bike)	160 (14.3)	160 (21.1)	120 (14.3)	360 (27.3)	80 (14.3)	80 (16.7)	960 (18.9)
Total	1,120 (22.0)	760 (15.0)	840 (16.5)	1,320 (26.0)	560 (11.0)	480 (9.4)	5,080 (100.0)
Automobile Available							
None	320 (22.0)	160 (17.4)	40 (4.5)	1,560 (50.0)	400 (30.3)	160 (19.0)	2,640 (31.0)
1	800 (55.6)	400 (43.5)	480 (54.5)	1,240 (39.7)	640 (48.5)	440 (52.4)	4,000 (46.9)
2 or More	320 (22.2)	360 (39.1)	360 (40.9)	320 (10.3)	280 (21.2)	240 (28.6)	1,880 (22.1)
Total	1,440 (16.9)	920 (10.8)	880 (10.3)	3,120 (36.6)	1,320 (15.5)	840 (9.9)	8,520 (100.0)

Source: Bureau of Census, U.S. Census of Population and Housing: New Jersey Public Use Sample, 1980.

EXHIBIT 3-9

SOCIOECONOMIC CHARACTERISTICS (RACE, SEX, AGE, INCOME) OF PRESENT MT. LAUREL-ELIGIBLE HOUSEHOLDS - EAST CENTRAL

	MODERATE INCOME (50-80% of Median)			LOW INCOME (Below 50% of Median)			
	1-2 Person	3-4 Person	5 or more Persons	1-2 Person	3-4 Person	5 or More Persons	TOTAL
Race							
White	480	280	120	1,680	560	480	3,600
	(85.7)	(77.8)	(75.0)	(80.8)	(63.6)	(52.2)	(72.6)
Black	80	80	40	360	280	360	1,200
	(14.3)	(22.2)	(25.0)	(17.3)	(31.8)	(39.1)	(24.2)
Other	0	0	0	40	40	80	160
	(0)	(0)	(0)	(1.9)	(4.5)	(8.7)	(3.2)
Total	560	360	160	2,080	880	920	4,960
Spanish Origin							
Not Spanish	560	360	160	2,000	800	720	4,600
	(100.0)	(100.0)	(100.0)	(96.2)	(90.9)	(78.3)	(92.7)
Spanish Origin	0	0	0	80	80	200	360
	(0)	(0)	(0)	(3.8)	(9.1)	(21.7)	(7.3)
Total	560	360	160	2,080	880	920	4,960
	(11.3)	(7.3)	(3.2)	(41.9)	(17.7)	(18.5)	(100.0)
Sex of Chief Income Producer							
Male	440	320	160	840	480	480	2,720
	(78.6)	(88.9)	(80.0)	(40.4)	(54.5)	(50.0)	(54.0)
Female	120	40	40	1,240	400	480	2,320
	(21.4)	(11.1)	(20.0)	(59.6)	(45.5)	(50.0)	(46.0)
Total	560	360	200	2,080	880	960	5,040
	(11.1)	(7.1)	(4.0)	(41.3)	(17.5)	(19.0)	(100.0)
Age of Chief Income Producer							
Under 25	40	80	0	280	160	80	640
	(7.1)	(22.2)	(0)	(13.5)	(18.2)	(8.7)	(12.9)
25-44	40	160	120	320	440	720	1,800
	(7.1)	(44.4)	(75.0)	(11.4)	(50.0)	(78.2)	(36.3)
45-64	280	80	0	560	160	120	1,200
	(50.0)	(22.2)	(0)	(26.9)	(18.1)	(13.0)	(24.2)
65 and Over	200	40	40	920	120	0	1,320
Total	560	360	160	2,080	880	920	4,960
	(11.3)	(7.3)	(3.2)	(41.9)	(17.7)	(18.5)	(100.0)
Household Income							
Under $10,000	280	80	0	2,080	720	680	3,840
	(50.0)	(22.2)	(0)	(100.0)	(81.8)	(73.9)	(77.4)
$10,000-14,999	280	240	120	0	120	200	960
	(50.0)	(66.7)	(75.0)	(0)	(13.6)	(21.7)	(19.4)
$15,000-19,999	0	40	40	0	0	0	80
	(0)	(11.1)	(25.0)	(0)	(0)	(0)	(1.6)
$20,000-24,999	0	0	0	0	0	40	40
	(0)	(0)	(0)	(0)	(0)	(4.3)	(0.8)
Total	560	360	160	2,080	880	920	4,960
	(11.3)	(7.3)	(3.2)	(41.9)	(17.7)	(18.5)	(100.0)

Source: Bureau of Census, U.S. Census of Population and Housing: New Jersey Public Use Sample, 1980.

EXHIBIT 3-10

SOCIOECONOMIC CHARACTERISTICS (LABOR FORCE PARTICIPATION, OCCUPATION, JOURNEY-TO-WORK) OF PRESENT MT. LAUREL-ELIGIBLE HOUSEHOLDS - EAST CENTRAL REGION

	MODERATE INCOME (50-80% of Median)			LOW INCOME (Below 50% of Median)			
	1-2 Person	3-4 Person	5 or more Persons	1-2 Person	3-4 Person	5 or More Persons	TOTAL
Labor Force Participation							
At Work	240	200	80	640	480	320	1,960
	(42.9)	(55.6)	(50.0)	(30.8)	(54.5)	(34.8)	(39.5)
With Job	0	40	0	80	40	40	200
Not at Work	(0)	(11.1)	(0)	(3.8)	(4.5)	(4.3)	(4.0)
Unemployed	40	80	0	40	40	120	320
	(7.1)	(22.2)	(0)	(1.9)	(4.5)	(13.0)	(6.5)
Not in Labor Force	240	40	80	1,320	320	400	2,400
	(42.9)	(11.1)	(50.0)	(63.5)	(36.4)	(43.5)	(48.4)
Total*	560	360	160	2,080	880	920	4,960
	(11.3)	(7.3)	(3.2)	(41.9)	(17.7)	(18.5)	(100.0)
*Includes Armed Forces	40	-	-	-	-	40	80
	(7.1)					(4.3)	(1.6)
Occupation							
Manager	40	0	40	160	40	120	400
Professional	(11.1)	(0)	(50.0)	(13.3)	(6.3)	(25.0)	(13.0)
Technical, Sales,	80	80	0	240	40	0	440
Supervisor	(22.2)	(25.0)	(0)	(20.0)	(5.2)	(0)	(14.3)
Service	40	80	0	280	160	40	600
	(11.1)	(25.0)	(0)	(9.1)	(5.2)	(8.3)	(19.5)
Farming	0	0	0	40	0	0	40
	(0)	(0)	(0)	(3.3)	(0)	(0)	(1.3)
Precision	40	80	40	40	40	120	360
Craftsman	(11.1)	(25.0)	(50.0)	(3.3)	(6.3)	(25.0)	(11.7)
Operatives, Labor	160	80	0	440	360	200	1,240
	(44.4)	(25.0)	(0)	(36.7)	(56.3)	(41.7)	(40.3)
Total	360	320	80	1,200	640	480	3,080
	(11.7)	(10.4)	(2.6)	(39.0)	(20.8)	(15.6)	(100.0)
Journey-to-work							
Less than 30 min.	240	200	80	600	440	320	1,880
	(85.7)	(100.0)	(100.0)	(93.8)	(91.7)	(88.9)	(92.2)
30-60 min.	0	0	0	40	40	0	80
	(0)	(0)	(0)	(6.2)	(8.3)	(0)	(3.9)
60 min. and Over	40	0	0	0	0	40	80
	(14.3)	(0)	(0)	(0)	(0)	(11.1)	(3.9)
Total	280	200	80	640	480	360	2,040
	(13.7)	(9.8)	(3.9)	(31.4)	(23.5)	(17.6)	(100.0)
Means of Journey-to-work							
Automobile	160	120	80	520	400	240	1,520
	(57.1	(60.0)	(100.0)	(81.3)	(83.3)	(66.7)	(74.5)
Public Transit	0	40	0	40	0	40	120
	(0)	(20.0)	(0)	(6.3)	(0)	(11.1)	(5.9)
Other (walk, bike)	120	40	0	80	80	80	400
	(42.9)	(20.0)	(0)	(12.5)	(16.7)	(22.2)	(19.6)
Total	280	200	80	640	480	360	2,040
	(13.7)	(9.8)	(3.9)	(31.4)	(23.5)	(17.6)	(100.0)
Automobile Available							
None	120	80	40	1,120	440	480	2,280
	(21.4)	(22.2)	(25.0)	(53.8)	(50.0)	(52.2)	(46.0)
1	280	200	80	840	280	400	2,080
	(50.0)	(55.6)	(50.0)	(40.4)	(31.8)	(43.5)	(41.9)
2 or More	160	80	40	120	160	40	600
	(28.6)	(22.2)	(25.0)	(5.3)	(18.2)	(4.3)	(12.1)
Total	560	360	160	2,080	880	920	4,960
	(11.3)	(7.3)	(3.2)	(41.9)	(17.7)	(18.5)	(100.0)

Source: Bureau of Census, U.S. Census of Population and Housing: New Jersey Public Use Sample, 1980.

EXHIBIT 3-11

SOCIOECONOMIC CHARACTERISTICS (RACE, SEX, AGE, INCOME) OF PRESENT MT. LAUREL-ELIGIBLE HOUSEHOLDS - SOUTHWEST

	MODERATE INCOME (50-80% of Median)			LOW INCOME (Below 50% of Median)			
	1-2 Person	3-4 Person	5 or more Persons	1-2 Person	3-4 Person	5 or More Persons	TOTAL
Race							
White	960	400	600	2,880	920	800	6,560
	(63.2)	(41.7)	(45.5)	(57.6)	(36.5)	(39.2)	(49.1)
Black	440	400	600	2,040	1,120	1,000	5,600
	(28.9)	(41.7)	(45.5)	(40.8)	(44.4)	(49.0)	(41.9)
Other	120	160	120	80	480	240	1,200
	(7.9)	(16.7)	(9.1)	(1.6)	(19.0)	(11.8)	(9.0)
Total	1,520	960	1,320	5,000	2,520	2,040	13,360
	(11.4)	(7.2)	(9.9)	(37.4)	(18.9)	(15.3)	(100.0)
Spanish Origin							
Not Spanish	1,360	840	1,160	4,840	2,040	1,800	12,040
	(89.5)	(87.5)	(87.9)	(96.8)	(81.0)	(88.2)	(90.1)
Spanish Origin	160	120	160	160	480	240	1,320
	(10.5)	(12.5)	(12.1)	(3.2)	(19.0)	(11.8)	(9.9)
Total	1,520	960	1,320	5,000	2,520	2,040	13,360
	(11.4)	(7.2)	(9.9)	(37.4)	(18.9)	(15.3)	(100.0)
Sex of Chief Income Producer							
Male	640	760	1,080	1,920	920	880	6,200
	(42.1)	(79.2)	(81.8)	(38.1)	(35.9)	(43.1)	(46.1)
Female	880	200	240	3,120	1,640	1,160	7,240
	(57.9)	(20.8)	(18.2)	(61.9)	(64.1)	(56.9)	(53.9)
Total	1,520	960	1,320	5,040	2,560	2,040	13,440
	(11.3)	(7.1)	(9.8)	(37.5)	(19.0)	(15.2)	(100.0)
Age of Chief Income Producer							
Under 25	320	240	40	1,040	800	320	2,760
	(21.1)	(25.0)	(3.0)	(20.8)	(31.7)	(15.7)	(20.7)
25-44	280	560	760	960	1,280	1,160	5,000
	(18.4)	(58.4)	(57.6)	(19.2)	(50.8)	(56.9)	(37.5)
45-64	520	160	520	1,160	360	560	3,280
	(34.2)	(16.7)	(39.4)	(23.2)	(14.3)	(27.5)	(24.6)
65 and Over	400	0	0	1,840	80	0	2,320
	(26.3)	(0)	(0)	(36.8)	(3.2)	(0)	(17.4)
Total	1,520	960	1,320	5,000	2,520	2,040	13,360
	(11.4)	(7.2)	(9.9)	(37.4)	(18.9)	(15.3)	(100.0)
Household Income							
Under $10,000	720	0	0	5,000	2,280	1,440	9,440
	(47.4)	(0)	(0)	(100.0)	(90.5)	(70.6)	(70.7)
$10,000-14,999	800	720	520	0	200	560	2,800
	(52.6)	(75.0)	(39.4)	(0)	(7.9)	(27.5)	(21.0)
$15,000-19,999	0	240	640	0	40	40	960
	(0)	(25.0)	(48.5)	(0)	(1.6)	(2.0)	(7.2)
$20,000-24,999	0	0	160	0	0	0	160
	(0)	(0)	(12.1)	(0)	(0)	(0)	(1.2)
Total	1,520	960	1,320	5,000	2,520	2,040	13,360
	(11.4)	(7.2)	(9.9)	(37.4)	(18.9)	(15.3)	(100.0)

Source: Bureau of Census, U.S. Census of Population and Housing: New Jersey Public Use Sample, 1980.

EXHIBIT 3-12

SOCIOECONOMIC CHARACTERISTICS (LABOR FORCE PARTICIPATION, OCCUPATION, JOURNEY-TO-WORK) OF PRESENT MT. LAUREL-ELIGIBLE HOUSEHOLDS - SOUTHWEST

	MODERATE INCOME (50-80% of Median)			LOW INCOME (Below 50% of Median)			
	1-2 Person	3-4 Person	5 or more Persons	1-2 Person	3-4 Person	5 or More Persons	TOTAL
Labor Force Participation							
At Work	920	760	960	1,400	840	680	5,560
	(60.5)	(79.2)	(72.7)	(28.0)	(33.3)	(33.3)	(41.6)
With Job Not at Work	0	80	40	120	0	80	320
	(0)	(8.3)	(3.0)	(2.4)	(0)	(3.9)	(2.4)
Unemployed	160	40	200	520	400	200	1,520
	(10.5)	(4.2)	(15.2)	(10.4)	(15.9)	(9.8)	(11.4)
Not in Labor Force	440	80	80	2,960	1,280	1,080	5,920
	(28.9)	(8.3)	(6.1)	(59.2)	(50.8)	(52.9)	(44.3)
Total*	1,520	960	1,320	5,000	2,520	2,040	13,360
	(11.4)	(7.2)	(9.9)	(37.4)	(18.9)	(15.3)	(100.0)
*Includes Armed Forces	-	-	40	-	-	-	40
	-	-	(3.0)	-	-	-	(0.3)
Occupation							
Manager Professional	120	120	80	120	40	80	560
	(8.6)	(8.5)	(6.5)	(4.5)	(2.1)	(6.3)	(6.0)
Technical, Sales, Supervisor	360	240	120	720	440	160	2,040
	(25.7)	(25.0)	(9.7)	(27.3)	(23.4)	(12.5)	(21.7)
Service	480	160	280	640	360	520	2,440
	(34.3)	(16.7)	(22.6)	(24.2)	(19.1)	(40.6)	(26.0)
Farming	0	40	0	120	40	0	200
	(0)	(4.2)	(0)	(4.5)	(2.1)	(0)	(2.1)
Precision Craftsman	120	160	360	280	160	80	1,160
	(8.6)	(16.7)	(29.0)	(10.6)	(8.5)	(6.3)	(12.3)
Operatives, Labor	320	240	400	760	840	440	3,000
	(22.9)	(25.0)	(32.3)	(28.8)	(44.7)	(34.4)	(31.9)
Total	1,400	960	1,240	2,640	1,880	1,280	9,400
	(14.9)	(10.2)	(13.2)	(28.1)	(20.0)	(13.6)	(100.0)
Journey-to-work							
Less than 30 min.	840	680	800	1,080	640	600	4,640
	(95.5)	(89.5)	(80.0)	(79.4)	(80.0)	(88.2)	(84.7)
30-60 min.	40	80	200	240	160	80	800
	(4.5)	(10.5)	(20.0)	(17.6)	(20.0)	(11.8)	(14.6)
60 min. and Over	0	0	0	40	0	0	40
	(0.0)	(0.0)	(0.0)	(2.9)	(0.0)	(0.0)	(0.7)
Total	800	760	1,000	1,360	800	680	5,480
	(16.1)	(13.9)	(18.2)	(24.8)	(14.6)	(12.4)	(100.0)
Means of Journey-to-work							
Automobile	600	720	880	760	640	600	4,200
	(65.2)	(94.7)	(88.0)	(54.3)	(76.2)	(88.2)	(75.0)
Public Transit	120	40	40	280	40	80	600
	(13.0)	(5.3)	(4.0)	(20.0)	(4.8)	(11.8)	(10.7)
Other (walk, bike)	200	0	80	360	160	0	800
	(21.7	(0)	(8.0)	(25.7)	(19.0)	0	(14.3)
Total	920	760	1,000	1,400	840	680	5,600
	(16.4)	(13.6)	(17.9)	(25.0)	(15.0)	(12.1)	(100.0)
Automobile Available							
None	400	200	160	2,920	960	1,000	5,640
	(26.3)	(20.8)	(12.1)	(58.4)	(38.1)	(49.0)	(42.2)
1	920	520	640	1,760	1,160	720	5,720
	(60.5)	(54.2)	(48.5)	(35.2)	(46.0)	(35.3)	(42.8)
2 or More	200	240	520	320	400	320	2,000
	(13.2)	(25.0)	(39.4)	(6.4)	(15.9)	(15.7)	(15.0)
Total	1,520	960	1,320	5,000	2,520	2,040	13,360
	(11.4)	(7.2)	(9.9)	(37.4)	(18.9)	(15.3)	(100.0)

Source: Bureau of Census, U.S. Census of Population and Housing: New Jersey Public Use Sample, 1980.

EXHIBIT 3-13

SOCIOECONOMIC CHARACTERISTICS (RACE, SEX, AGE, INCOME) OF PRESENT MT. LAUREL-ELIGIBLE HOUSEHOLDS - SOUTH-SOUTHWEST

	MODERATE INCOME (50-80% of Median)			LOW INCOME (Below 50% of Median)			
	1-2 Person	3-4 Person	5 or more Persons	1-2 Person	3-4 Person	5 or More Persons	TOTAL
Race							
White	1,120	440	360	1,880	400	120	4,320
	(82.4)	(61.1)	(60.0)	(56.6)	(41.7)	(15.8)	(56.0)
Black	240	120	120	1,280	360	520	2,640
	(17.6)	(16.7)	(20.0)	(38.6)	(37.5)	(68.4)	(34.2)
Other	0	160	120	160	200	120	760
	(0)	(22.2)	(20.0)	(4.8)	(20.8)	(15.8)	(9.8)
Total	1,360	720	600	3,320	960	760	7,720
	(17.6)	(9.3)	(7.8)	(43.0)	(12.4)	(9.8)	(100.0)
Spanish Origin							
Not Spanish	1,320	520	440	2,960	720	600	6,560
	(97.1)	(72.2)	(73.3)	(89.2)	(75.0)	(78.9)	(85.0)
Spanish Origin	40	200	160	360	240	160	1,160
	(2.9)	(27.8)	(26.7)	(10.8)	(25.0)	(21.1)	(15.0)
Total	1,360	720	600	3,320	960	760	7,720
	(17.6)	(9.3)	(7.8)	(43.0)	(12.4)	(9.8)	(100.0)
Sex of Chief Income Producer							
Male	840	520	440	1,280	240	360	3,680
	(60.0)	(72.2)	(68.8)	(38.1)	(25.0)	(47.4)	(46.9)
Female	560	200	200	2,080	720	400	4,160
	(40.0)	(27.8)	(31.3)	(61.9)	(75.0)	(52.6)	(53.1)
Total	1,400	720	640	3,360	960	760	7,840
	(17.9)	(9.2)	(8.2)	(42.9)	(12.2)	(9.7)	(100.0)
Age of Chief Income Producer							
Under 25	280	240	80	520	360	0	1,480
	(20.6)	(33.3)	(13.3)	(15.7)	(37.5)	(0)	(19.2)
25-44	280	320	360	520	400	640	2,520
	(20.6)	(44.5)	(60.0)	(15.6)	(41.7)	(84.3)	(32.6)
45-64	440	120	160	920	160	120	1,920
	(32.3	(16.7)	(26.7)	(27.7)	(16.6)	(15.8)	(24.8)
65 and Over	360	40	0	1,360	40	0	1,800
	(26.5)	(5.6)	(0)	(41.0)	(4.2)	(0)	(23.4)
Total	1,360	720	600	3,320	960	760	7,720
	(17.6)	(9.3)	(7.8)	(43.0)	(12.4)	(9.8)	(100.0)
Household Income							
Under $10,000	1,160	160	0	3,320	880	680	6,200
	(85.3)	(22.2)	(0)	(100.0)	(9.7)	(89.5)	(80.3)
$10,000-14,999	200	560	480	0	80	80	1,400
	(14.7)	(77.8)	(80.0)	(0)	(8.3)	(10.5)	(18.1)
$15,000-19,999	0	0	120	0	0	0	120
	(0)	(0)	(20.0)	(0)	(0)	(0)	(1.6)
$20,000-24,999	0	0	0	0	0	0	0
	(0)	(0)	(0)	(0)	(0)	(0)	(0)
Total	1,360	720	600	3,320	960	760	7,720
	(17.6)	(9.3)	(7.8)	(43.0)	(12.4)	(9.8)	(100.0)

Source: Bureau of Census, U.S. Census of Population and Housing: New Jersey Public Use Sample, 1980.

EXHIBIT 3-14

SOCIOECONOMIC CHARACTERISTICS (LABOR FORCE PARTICIPATION, OCCUPATION, JOURNEY TO WORK) OF PRESENT MT. LAUREL-ELIGIBLE HOUSEHOLDS - SOUTH-SOUTHWEST

	MODERATE INCOME (50-80% of Median)			LOW INCOME (Below 50% of Median)			
	1-2 Person	3-4 Person	5 or more Persons	1-2 Person	3-4 Person	5 or More Persons	TOTAL
Labor Force Participation							
At Work	800	680	560	880	360	200	3,480
	(58.8)	(94.4)	(93.3)	(26.5)	(37.5)	(26.3)	(45.1)
With Job	0	0	0	0	40	0	40
Not at Work	(0)	(0)	(0)	(0)	(4.2)	(0)	(0.5)
Unemployed	80	40	0	200	120	120	560
	(5.9)	(5.6)	(0)	(6.0)	(12.5)	(15.8)	(7.3)
Not in Labor Force	480	0	40	2,240	440	440	3,640
	(35.3)	(0)	(6.7)	(67.5)	(45.8)	(57.9)	(47.2)
Total	1,360	720	600	3,320	960	760	7,720
	(17.6)	(9.3)	(7.8)	(43.0)	(12.4)	(9.8)	(100.0)
Occupation							
Manager	120	40	0	40	40	0	240
Professional	(12.0)	(5.6)	(0)	(2.3)	(5.6)	(0)	(4.5)
Technical, Sales,	120	80	120	320	120	0	760
Supervisor	(12.0)	(11.1)	(20.0)	(18.6)	(16.7)	(0)	(14.2)
Service	240	80	160	560	160	320	1,520
	(24.0)	(11.1)	(26.7)	(32.6)	(22.2)	(53.3)	(28.4)
Farming	40	80	0	120	80	40	360
	(4.0)	(11.1)	(0)	(7.0)	(11.1)	(6.7)	(6.7)
Precision	160	80	120	200	80	0	640
Craftsman	(16.0)	(11.1)	(20.0)	(11.6)	(11.1)	(0)	(11.9)
Operatives, Labor	320	360	200	480	240	240	1,840
	(32.0)	(50.0)	(33.3)	(27.9)	(33.3)	(40.0)	(34.3)
Total	1,000	720	600	1,720	720	600	5,360
	(18.7)	(13.4)	(11.2)	(32.1)	(32.1)	(11.2)	(100.0)
Journey-to-work							
Less than 30 min.	720	600	440	840	320	200	3,210
	(90.0)	(88.2)	(78.6)	(95.5)	(88.9)	(100.0)	(89.7)
30-60 min.	80	80	120	40	40	0	360
	(10.0)	(11.8)	(21.4)	(4.5)	(11.1)	(0.0)	(10.3)
60 min and Over	0	0	0	0	0	0	0
	(0.0)	(0.0)	(0.0)	(0.0)	(0.0)	(0.0)	(0.0)
Total	800	680	560	880	360	200	3,480
	(23.0)	(19.5)	(16.1)	(25.3)	(10.3)	(5.7)	(100.0)
Means of Journey-to-work							
Automobile	520	480	360	640	240	80	2,320
	(65.0)	(70.6)	(64.3)	(72.7)	(66.7)	(40.0)	(66.7)
Public Transit	160	0	80	80	80	40	440
	(20.0)	(0)	(14.3)	(9.1)	(22.2)	(20.0)	(12.6)
Other (walk, bike)	120	200	120	160	40	80	720
	(15.0)	(29.4)	(21.4)	(18.2)	(11.1)	(40.0)	(20.7)
Total	800	680	560	880	360	200	3,480
	(23.0)	(19.5)	(16.1)	(25.3)	(10.3)	(5.7)	(100.0)
Automobile Available							
None	400	160	80	1,760	400	440	3,240
	(29.4)	(22.2)	(13.3)	(53.0)	(41.7)	(57.9)	(42.0)
1	720	400	320	1,360	480	280	3,560
	(52.9)	(55.6)	(53.3)	(41.0)	(50.0)	(36.8)	(46.1)
2 or More	240	160	200	200	80	40	920
	(17.6)	(22.2)	(33.3)	(6.0)	(8.3)	(5.3)	(11.9)
Total	1,360	720	600	3,320	960	760	7,720
	(17.6)	(9.3)	(7.8)	(43.0)	(12.4)	(9.8)	(100.0)

Source: Bureau of Census, U.S. Census of Population and Housing: New Jersey Public Use Sample, 1980.

HOUSING CHARACTERISTICS OF THE PRESENT MOUNT LAUREL POPULATION

In the section to follow, the current housing condition of present Mount Laurel eligible households will be examined. As in the case with socioeconomic characteristics, we will begin with a discussion of housing characteristics for the entire State of New Jersey.

Selected Housing Characteristics of New Jersey Householders

For all households in New Jersey, in 1980, just under 60 percent (58.8%) lived in single-family homes. The remaining 40 percent were split relatively evenly between 2-4 family and multifamily (5 or more unit) structures. Less than one percent of New Jersey households occupied mobile homes. The median size of a housing unit in New Jersey in 1980, was 5.0 rooms and 2.0 bedrooms. For owned units, it was 5.5 rooms and 2.5 bedrooms, while for rental units it was 3.6 rooms and 1.1 bedrooms.[6]

Tenure almost exactly parallels structure type occupancy levels. In 1980, 61 percent of New Jersey householders owned their own dwellings, whereas 38 percent rented. Approximately one percent of the state's householders occupied structures which they neither owned nor paid cash rent (no cash rent).

The median age of housing in New Jersey is 30 years. One-third of the state's housing has been built prior to 1939 whereas about one-half this amount (17%) was constructed between 1970 and 1980.

In 1980, the median value of single family homes in New Jersey was $61,800; this translated into median owner costs of $456 monthly for those with a mortgage and $218 for those without a mortgage.

The median monthly gross rent of New Jersey households in 1980 was $270; approximately 23 percent of the state's one million renter households paid less than $200 monthly; roughly one-half that rate (11%) paid in excess of $400. The median rent-income ratio in New Jersey was 25 percent; over one-third (35%) of the state's renter households had rent-income ratios of less than 20 percent; thirty percent had rent-income ratios in excess of 35 percent.

Median owner costs-income ratios were less than 20 percent obviously reflecting significant no and low mortgage payments. Only three percent of residents statewide, in 1980, had owner-costs to income ratios in excess of 35 percent.

This brief synopsis of statewide housing characteristics precedes a detailed discussion of similar characteristics for the present, housing deficient Mount Laurel population.

Housing Type of Present Mount Laurel Households:
The State (Exhibit 3-15)

Close to 80 percent of present Mount Laurel-eligible households are currently living in other than single-family housing accommodations: 45 percent live in multifamily (5 or more units) structures; 35 percent in 2-4 unit structures. This is double the New Jersey percentage (40%) of non-single family structure occupancy. Larger, present Mount Laurel families are more apt to live in single family units with this trend also favoring the moderate income category household. Single family residency percentages in these two categories of occupants are still far below statewide averages.[7]

Housing Type: The Regions
(Exhibit 3-17 to 3-27 Odd-Numbered)

To some degree, the type of structure in which we find the present Mount Laurel-eligible households also parallels the structures most commonly found within a region. Densely developed regions have a predominance of multifamily units and this is where most of our subject population is found. In the Northeast and Northwest Regions 1 and 2 for example, 61 percent and 45 percent of the eligible households are found in multifamily units, trailing off to 6 percent and 12 percent occupancy of single family units repectively. Regions with less dense developmental patterns provide the present Mount Laurel eligible population with somewhat more 2 to 4 and single family units. The highest level of single family use is found in the Southwest Region 5 where 65 percent of the present Mount Laurel-eligible population are so housed. The comparable figure for the general population's single-family occupancy rate in this region is 95 percent. Mobile home utilization as suggested in the state totals are for all practical purposes non-existent. Only in the Southwest Region do the data indicate the use of over 100 of these structures by the Mount Laurel or any population.

Finally, when examining the record for additional regional influences on the current housing configurations of the eligible population, some modest additional insights are secured. Moderate income households favor single and 2-to-4 family units, while low income households are usually found in multifamily structures. Only in the East Central and Southwest Regions 3 and 5 are these trends reversed with greater proportional representation of the low income population in single family structures. In the first case it is the elderly in retirement villages; in the second it is the rowhouse of Camden County.

Housing Size - The State

The size of the median housing unit in New Jersey is five rooms of which two are bedrooms. Approximately one-half of the present Mount Laurel housing-deficient population occupy dwelling units of this size and configuration. Less than 16 percent occupy a six room-or-more structure of 3-4 bedrooms. Close to one-third of this population occupies 1-3 room units of 0 or 1 bedroom.

Housing Size: The Regions

Regional variation again follows characteristics of the existing housing stock. Smaller, multifamily units house the Mount Laurel population in the Northeast Region 1, whereas larger single-family units house this population in the Southwest Region 5. Most of the other regions parallel the statewide average except for the East Central Region 4 which has more of the very small units (1-3 room) and less of the very large units (6 room-or-more).

Housing Tenure: The State

Housing tenure is the term used to identify the householder's legal attachment to the dwelling unit; ownership (including condominiums), rental, or no cash rent being the basic categories. Statewide, the dominant form of tenure is rental -- sustaining over 75 percent of the present Mount Laurel eligible population. This is close to double the statewide average of 40 percent rental tenure.

Owner-occupants comprise the bulk of the 25 percent remaining Mount Laurel population.* Within these major breaks, large households of moderate income are more likely to be owners than are small moderate income households; however, the opposite is the case for low income families wherein the severity of the budget constraint moves even large households into rental tenure.

Housing Tenure: The Regions

All things being equal, housing tenure has traditionally been highly related to structure type. One would therefore expect regions high in multifamily structures to possess a high level of rental occupancy. This is mostly the case for Mount Laurel households. Northeast Region 1 leads in multifamily structures with 61 percent; it correspondingly has 85 percent of its existing Mount Laurel eligible households in rental tenure. The Northwest Region 2, with 45 percent multifamily units, has 79 percent of its eligible population in rental tenure. The Southwest Region 5, with the highest level of single family occupancy (65 percent), also has the highest level of owner occupancy (47 percent).

---

*No cash rent represents less than 2 percent of the Mount Laurel population.

Housing Age: The State

To a certain extent, describing the housing conditions of the present Mount Laurel-eligible population in terms of the age of structure is a circular argument. As was discussed in Chapter 2, the age of structure was used, in part, as a surrogate for housing deficiency. Thus, it is not surprising that a large number of units built prior to 1940 are identified as occupied by Mount Laurel households. Generally speaking, close to 90 percent of the present Mount Laurel-eligible households occupy units built prior to 1940 with only 1.4 percent occupying housing built during the period 1970 to 1980. While almost all Mount Laurel households live in old housing, smaller households have a greater than proportional presence in the oldest structures.

Housing Age: The Regions

It is again not surprising to find a linkage between Mount Laurel eligible households and older housing even in regions commonly thought to have, on average, newer units. The Northeast Region 1, for example, has 90 percent of its eligible population in pre-1940 built units with moderate and low income 1-to-2 person households being overly represented at 95 percent and 93 percent respectively. The West Central Region 3, an area of major suburban growth for two decades, has 97 and 94 percent respectively of the Mount Laurel-eligible low and moderate income population in the oldest age category. The same figures apply to the South-Southwest Region 6, as well. Only in the Southwest Region 5 has there been a significant drop in the concentration of these groups of households into newer units. In the case of the latter, this is especially noticeable among low income households of increasing larger sizes with only 73 percent housed in pre-1940 housing and 22 percent in 1940-to-1969 vintage units. Larger families (over 3 persons per household) are also more likely to be found in newer units in the South-Southwest Region 6, with fully 40 percent of the five person-or-over, moderate income family found in 1940-to-1969 vintage units. These in part, reflect past subsidized housing construction efforts in the Camden, Salem, Vineland and Atlantic City areas.

Housing Value: The State

Housing value reported to the Census is that for owner-occupied, single family units only. Therefore, this data represents the value of housing unit for only a fraction of the Mount Laurel-eligible households assumed to be living in deficient housing. Statewide, a little over 11 percent of the present Mount Laurel-eligible households live in units wherein a value is attached. The most common value category found for these housing units is under $25,000 -- the median value is $28,300. This is slightly less than one-half the 1980 statewide average of $61,200. A rapid drop in frequency of households in the higher value categories occurs as just over 20 percent of Mount Laurel households reside in units valued in excess of $45,000. As would be expected, moderate income households are more highly represented in the higher housing value categories than are those of low income.

Housing Value: The Regions

The popularly-recognized phenomenon that the value of housing is higher in or close to the New York Metropolitan Area than in other metropolitan areas or in rural areas is certainly borne out for the population statewide (see Chapter 5). It is also true for the small share of ownership housing occupied by present Mount Laurel-eligible households. In the Northeast Region 1, for example, the modal housing value category is $45,000 to $59,999; in the Northwest Region 2, the same modal category exists. In the West Central Region 3, the modal category drops to the $35,000-$44,999 range, and in the remaining three regions, the dominant category is that of lowest value and the frequency of occurrence is well over 60 percent in all cases.

Owner occupancy represents a far greater value of structure for Mount Laurel households in the northern part of the state than for those in the southern portion. As will be shown, the same north-south value gradient is not true for rental units. For those families who own their own homes, the unknown category is built-up equity. If the value provided the Census through self-evaluation by the occupant is accurate and no mortgage exists, then a modest to significant nest egg may be held by the household even at the cost of mortgage payments. If the owner occupant has little equity, this may be much less the case.

Rent: The State (Exhibit 3-16)

Statewide, the highest rent reported in 1980 for the existing Mount Laurel-eligible households was in the range of $400 to $500 monthly. The modal category of rent was $200 to $299; the median rent was $225. This is about 20 percent or $50 per month less than the statewide average.

As would be expected, moderate versus low income households pay higher rents. Only in the case of low income households with very large family sizes, is there a concentration of low income households in the higher rent categories.

Rent: The Regions (Exhibit 3-18 to 3-28 Even-Numbered)

We have seen that a predictable value gradient exists from north to south across the state in terms of housing value. A similar pattern of rental levels could easily be presumed to exist. However, judging from the modal rent category and the location of the next most frequent rent payment category, this is not the case. The Northeast and Northwest Regions 1 and 2 have roughly 45 percent of their current rent-paying, Mount Laurel households in the modal category of $200-$299. The next most frequent category is the $100 to $199 rent level. In the West Central Region 3, the bulge toward the lower rates is absent and a normal bell shaped rent distribution is found above and below the modal category $200-$299. In the East Central Region 4, the bulge shifts to the category above the overall modal class. Finally, the Southwest and South-Southwest Regions 5 and 6, return to a similar pattern as that exhibited by the Northeast Region. What appears remarkable in light of the value gradient across the state is the relatively constant rent level grouping for existing Mount Laurel households.

In all regions, save the South-Southwest, moderate- and low-income households support a similar modal rent. When a high concentration of one and two person households exist, the rent category of greatest frequency will drop one step lower to $100 to $199; while, where 3-plus person households dominate, their modal rent category will shift upward to the $300 to $399 level. Only in the case of the South-Southwest Region 6 does income level at all influence the modal rent paying category. Moderate income households are still found in the $200-$299 level whereas the low income household shifts down across all family size categories to the $100 to $199 rental category.

Do income level differences explain these patterns, or is there some other rationale? In the following section we shall analyze the rent-to-income ratio of our Mount Laurel population.

Rent-to-Income Ratio: The State

The rent-to-income ratio provides an index of the role budget constraint plays in the selection of housing. For most New Jersey households this is not a problem. The median rent-to-income ratio in 1980 was 25 percent.

The modal rent-to-income ratio for existing Mount Laurel-eligible households is over 50 percent; 37 percent of the households are above this level. The median rent-to-income ratio is 40 percent. This figure is 60 percent in excess of the statewide average.

Most startling is a comparison of moderate with low income households holding household size constant. For one-to-two person households for example, 56.5 percent of low income households are in the over 50 percent category, whereas only 1.5 percent of moderate income households are at this level.

Rent-to-Income Ratio: The Regions

In two regions of the state, there is evidence of a north to south rent-to-income gradient which works to the disadvantage of those Mount

Laurel households in the southern part of the state. For the Northeast, Northwest and Southwest Regions 1, 2 and 5 respectively, the rent-income ratio, is largely that of the state average. That is, well over 50 percent of the low income households are found to be paying over 50 percent of their income on rent; whereas, most moderate income households pay under 30 percent. However, two regions do support a negative income gradient with constant rent levels thus contributing to higher rent-to-income ratios. The East Central Region 4 finds over 70 percent of its low income households paying over 50 percent of their income for rent; while, their moderate income families have also been ratcheted up to the 20-to-50 percent categories. A similar phenomenon can be seen in the South-Southwest Region 6.

Owner Costs: The State

Owner costs have been taken from the Census as the sum of real estate taxes, homeowners' insurance, utilities, fuel and mortgage payments required on a monthly basis. Statewide, in New Jersey, median owner costs vary from $456 for those owners with a mortgage to $218 for those without.

For the 23 percent of Mount Laurel households who own their own home, these costs are much less. Fully one-third pay less than $200 per month. As owner costs increase, the percentage of Mount Laurel ownership households in each succeeding cost category declines to roughly 10 percent in the over $500 per month category. Finally, while two-thirds of the owners* in the State of New Jersey hold an active mortgage, less than 45 percent of Mount Laurel owner households do. For those that do hold a mortgage the average monthly cost is $230.

When comparing ownership costs across the low and moderate categories, the disparity of vastly higher costs for low income households so obviously apparent in the rental sector is not present in the case of owner-occupied units. Housing currently without a mortgage passed through successions of family ownership acts to cushion the costs of shelter for current low income households. In absolute numbers, as well as relative frequency, low income families exceed moderate income families in the category of owner costs under $200.

Owner Costs: the Regions

Several factors should influence ownership costs within the various regions: proportion of mortgaged properties, tax rate differentials, land values/structure replacement costs, competition from other more exclusive markets, and the like. Excluding proportions of mortgaged properties, it might be presumed that the northern regions would have relatively higher costs for the other factors mentioned above.

---

*Single-family, non-condominium units.

The actual patterns shown in the data show a very consistent pattern in owner costs for Mount Laurel households, across most regions, suggesting that the various factors net out and leave the average present Mount Laurel eligible homeowner with a monthly owner cost somewhere within the $200 to $299 category in most areas. This is certainly the case for small 1-to-2 person households; for larger households, the costs increased in one hundred dollar increments for the two larger household size categories.

Owner Cost-to-Income Ratio: The State

The final housing characteristic under study is the owner cost-to-income ratio. As in the case of the renter rent-to-income ratio this figure provides an indication of the effort required by a homeowner* to remain within this tenure offering. Statewide it is relatively low with owner cost-to-income ratios of under 20 percent. This reflects the high income of owners in New Jersey, as well as early commission to the mortgage obligation by these owners.

Statewide, the aggregate frequency distribution is relatively even with 16 percent of the households having under 20 percent of their income spent on housing, while 33 percent are at over 50 percent. As is the case of the renter, the moderate income homeowner has a median cost-to-income ratio of under 30 percent; while, most low income households exhibit owner cost-to-income ratios in excess of 50 percent. Household size appears to make little difference in the ratios of either low or moderate income households.

Owner Cost-to-Income Ratio: The Regions

For all practical purposes, the pattern of owner costs relative to income are the same for all regions save the most southern. That is for the very small proportions of low income households living in ownership housing, most spend over 50 percent of their income to support it. Moderate income ownership households are commonly spending under the 30 percent level. In the one exception, moderate income households in the South-Southwest Region 6 are found to spend under 20 percent of their income on housing.

---

*Subject to welfare aid.

EXHIBIT 3-15

HOUSING CHARACTERISTICS (HOUSING TYPE, TENURE, AGE, VALUE) OF PRESENT MT. LAUREL-ELIGIBLE HOUSEHOLDS - STATEWIDE

	MODERATE INCOME (50-80% of Median)			LOW INCOME (Below 50% of Median)			
	1-2 Person	3-4 Person	5 or more Persons	1-2 Person	3-4 Person	5 or More Persons	TOTAL
Housing Type							
Single Family	3,120	2,320	3,000	9,360	4,160	3,240	25,200
	(17.3)	(22.8)	(28.4)	(20.4)	(20.3)	(21.5)	(21.0)
2-4 Family	6,200	4,320	4,840	13,200	6,640	5,560	40,760
	(34.3)	(42.5)	(45.8)	(28.8)	(32.4)	(36.9)	(33.9)
Multi-Family	8,720	3,480	2,720	23,240	9,560	6,240	53,960
	(48.2)	(34.3)	(25.8)	(50.7)	(46.7)	(41.4)	(44.9)
Mobile	40	40	0	0	120	40	240
	(0.2)	(0.4)	(0)	(0)	(0.6)	(0.3)	(0.2)
Total	18,080	10,160	10,560	45,800	20,480	15,080	120,160
	(15.0)	(8.5)	(8.8)	(38.1)	(17.0)	(12.5)	(100.0)
Housing Tenure							
Owner Occupied	4,200	3,240	4,160	10,320	3,240	2,520	27,680
	(23.2)	(31.9)	(39.4)	(22.5)	(15.8)	(16.7)	(23.0)
Renter Occupied	13,600	6,680	6,240	34,520	17,040	12,280	90,360
	(75.2)	(65.7)	(59.1)	(75.4)	(83.2)	(81.4)	(75.2)
No Cash Rent	280	240	160	960	200	280	2,120
	(1.5)	(2.4)	(1.5)	(2.1)	(1.0)	(1.9)	(1.8)
Total	18,080	10,160	10,560	45,800	20,480	15,080	120,160
	(15.0)	(8.5)	(8.8)	(38.1)	(17.0)	(12.5)	(100.0)
Housing Age							
Built 1970-1980	120	200	80	520	440	320	1,680
	(0.7)	(2.0)	(0.8)	(1.1)	(2.1)	(2.1)	(1.4)
Built 1940-1969	880	1,160	1,920	3,720	2,840	2,800	13,320
	(4.9)	(11.4)	(18.2)	(8.1)	(13.7)	(18.6)	(11.1)
Built Prior to 1940	17,080	8,800	8,560	41,560	17,200	11,960	105,160
	(94.5)	(86.6)	(81.1)	(90.7)	(84.0)	(79.3)	(87.5)
Total	18,080	10,160	10,560	45,800	20,480	15,080	120,160
	(15.0)	(8.5)	(8.8)	(38.1)	(17.0)	(12.5)	(100.0)
Housing Value							
Less than $25,000	560	400	800	2,720	1,040	560	6,080
	(32.6)	(27.8)	(45.5)	(45.3)	(59.1)	(50.0)	(44.1)
$25,000-34,999	280	120	200	1,440	200	200	2,440
	(16.3)	(8.3)	(11.4)	(24.0)	(11.4)	(17.9)	(17.7)
$35,000-44,999	240	240	280	920	280	280	2,240
	(14.0)	(16.7)	(15.9)	(15.3)	(15.9)	(25.0)	(16.2)
$45,000-59,999	480	520	360	560	200	80	2,200
	(27.9)	(36.1)	(20.5)	(9.3)	(11.4)	(7.1)	(15.9)
$60,000-74,999	160	160	120	360	40	0	840
	(9.3)	(11.1)	(6.8)	(6.0)	(2.3)	(0)	(6.1)
Total	1,720	1,440	1,760	6,000	1,760	1,120	13,800
	(12.5)	(10.4)	(12.8)	(43.5)	(12.8)	(8.1)	(100.0)

Source: Bureau of Census, U.S. Census of Population and Housing: New Jersey Public Use Sample, 1980.

EXHIBIT 3-16

HOUSING CHARACTERISTICS (RENT/OWNER COSTS, INCOME RATIOS) OF PRESENT MT. LAUREL-ELIGIBLE HOUSEHOLDS - STATEWIDE

	MODERATE INCOME (50-80% of Median)			LOW INCOME (Below 50% of Median)			
	1-2 Person	3-4 Person	5 or more Persons	1-2 Person	3-4 Person	5 or More Persons	TOTAL
Rent							
Under $100	360	40	80	2,240	360	480	3,560
	(2.7)	(0.6)	(1.3)	(6.5)	(2.1)	(3.9)	(4.0)
$100-199	6,240	1,560	720	16,480	4,200	2,000	31,200
	(46.0)	(23.6)	(11.7)	(48.0)	(24.8)	(16.4)	(34.7)
$200-299	5,640	3,680	3,280	12,360	8,720	5,960	39,640
	(41.6)	(55.8)	(53.2)	(36.0)	(51.4)	(49.0)	(44.1)
$300-399	1,200	840	1,680	3,000	2,920	2,600	12,240
	(8.8)	(12.7)	(27.3)	(8.7)	(17.2)	(21.4)	(13.6)
$400-599	120	480	400	280	760	1,120	3,160
	13,560	6,600	6,160	34,360	16,960	12,160	89,800
Total	(15.1)	(7.3)	(6.9)	(38.3)	(18.9)	(18.9)	(100.0)
Rent-Income Ratio							
Under 20%	5,360	3,280	3,080	1,360	840	680	14,600
	(39.6)	(49.7)	(50.0)	(4.3)	(5.3)	(5.8)	(17.0)
20 - 30%	5,080	2,440	2,560	3,640	2,120	1.880	17,720
	(37.6)	(37.0)	(41.6)	(11.5)	(13.3)	(15.9)	(20.7)
30 - 50%	2,880	840	520	8,800	4,600	3,720	21,360
	(21.3)	(12.7)	(8.4)	(27.7)	(28.6)	(31.5)	(24.9)
Over 50%	200	40	0	17,920	8,360	5,520	32,040
	(1.5)	(0.6)	(0)	(56.5)	(52.5)	(46.8)	(37.4)
Total	13,520	6,600	6,160	31,720	15,920	11,800	85,720
	(15.8)	(7.7)	(7.2)	(37.2)	(18.6)	(13.8)	(100.0)
Owner Cost							
Under $200	760	320	240	3,120	400	200	5,040
	(45.2)	(22.2)	(13.6)	(52.0)	(22.7)	(17.9)	(36.6)
$200-299	600	320	560	1,560	600	200	3,840
	(35.7)	(22.2)	(31.8)	(26.0)	(34.1)	(17.9)	(27.9)
$300-399	200	440	240	520	440	320	2,160
	(11.9)	(30.6)	(13.6)	(8.7)	(25.0)	(28.6)	(15.7)
$400-499	80	200	320	400	120	200	1,320
	(4.8)	(13.9)	(18.2)	(6.7)	(6.8)	(17.9)	(9.6)
Over $500	40	160	400	400	200	200	1,400
	(2.4)	(11.2)	(22.7)	(22.1)	(11.4)	(17.8)	(10.1)
Total	1,680	1,440	1,760	6,000	1,760	1,120	13,760
	(12.2)	(10.5)	(12.8)	(43.6)	(12.8)	(8.1)	(100.0)
Owner Cost-Income Ratio							
Under 20%	560	480	560	280	120	120	2,120
	(33.3)	(33.3)	(31.8)	(5.1)	(7.3)	(11.5)	(16.3)
20 - 30%	640	520	560	760	360	120	2,960
	(38.1)	(36.1)	(31.8)	(14.0)	(22.0)	(11.5)	(22.8)
30 - 50%	360	400	520	1,560	400	440	3,680
	(21.4)	(27.8)	(29.5)	(28.7)	(24.4)	(42.3)	(28.3)
Over 50%	120	40	120	2,840	760	360	4,240
	(7.1)	(2.8)	(6.8)	(52.2)	(46.3)	(46.3)	(32.6)
Total	1,680	1,440	1,760	5,440	1,640	1,040	13,000
	(12.9)	(11.1)	(13.5)	(41.8)	(12.6)	(8.0)	(100.0)

Source: Bureau of Census, U.S. Census of Population and Housing: New Jersey Public Use Sample, 1980.

EXHIBIT 3-17

HOUSING CHARACTERISTICS (HOUSING TYPE, TENURE, AGE, VALUE)
OF PRESENT MT. LAUREL-ELIGIBLE HOUSEHOLDS - NORTHEAST

	MODERATE INCOME (50-80% of Median)			LOW INCOME (Below 50% of Median)			
	1-2 Person	3-4 Person	5 or more Persons	1-2 Person	3-4 Person	5 or More Persons	TOTAL
Housing Type							
Single Family	480	360	560	920	240	320	2,880
	(5.8)	(8.1)	(13.1)	(4.6)	(2.8)	(4.9)	(5.5)
2-4 Family	2,560	1,800	2,040	5,560	2,800	2,440	17,200
	(30.9)	(40.5)	(47.7)	(27.9)	(32.3)	(37.4)	(33.0)
Multi-Family	5,240	2,280	1,680	13,480	5,460	3,720	32,040
	(63.3)	(51.4)	(39.3)	(67.5)	(65.0)	(57.1)	(61.4)
Mobile	0	0	0	0	0	40	40
	(0.0)	(0.0)	(0.0)	(0.0)	(0.0)	(100.0)	(0.1)
Total	8,280	4,440	4,280	19,960	8,680	6,520	52,160
	(15.9)	(8.5)	(8.2)	(38.3)	(16.6)	(12.5)	(100.0)
Housing Tenure							
Owner Occupied	1,280	800	1,360	2,440	600	760	7,240
	(15.5)	(18.0)	(31.8)	(12.2)	(6.9)	(11.7)	(13.9)
Renter Occupied	6,920	3,480	2,840	17,320	8,000	5,560	44,120
	(83.6)	(78.4)	(66.4)	(86.8)	(92.2)	(85.3)	(84.6)
No Cash Rent	80	160	80	200	80	200	800
	(1.0)	(3.6)	(1.9)	(1.0)	(0.9)	(3.1)	(1.5)
Total	8,280	4,440	4,280	19,960	8,680	6,520	52,160
	(15.9)	(8.5)	(8.2)	(38.3)	(16.6)	(12.5)	(100.0)
Housing Age							
Built 1970-1980	40	40	0	80	40	40	240
	(0.5)	(0.9)	(0)	(0.4)	(0.5)	(0.6)	(0.5)
Built 1940-1969	360	480	640	1,400	1,040	1,000	4,920
	(4.3)	(10.8)	(15.0)	(7.0)	(12.0)	(15.3)	(9.4)
Built Prior to 1940	7,880	3,920	3,640	18,480	7,600	5,480	47,000
	(95.2)	(88.3)	(85.0)	(92.6)	(87.6)	(84.0)	(90.1)
Total	8,280	4,440	4,280	19,960	8,680	6,520	52,160
	(15.9)	(8.5)	(8.2)	(38.3)	(16.6)	(12.5)	(100.0)
Housing Value							
Less than $25,000	40	0	80	160	40	40	360
	(9.1)	(0)	(25.0)	(21.1)	(25.0)	(50.0)	(18.0)
$25,000-34,999	120	0	0	120	0	0	240
	(27.3)	(0)	(0)	(15.8)	(0)	(0)	(12.0)
$35,000-44,999	0	0	40	40	40	40	160
	(0)	(0)	(12.5)	(5.3)	(25.0)	(50.0)	(8.0)
$45,000-59,999	200	160	160	120	40	0	680
	(45.5)	(66.7)	(50.0)	(15.8)	(25.0)	(0)	(34.0)
$60,000-74,999	80	80	40	320	40	0	560
	(18.2)	(33.3)	(12.5)	(42.1)	(25.0)	(0)	(28.0)
Total	440	240	320	760	160	80	2,000
	(22.0)	(12.0)	(16.0)	(38.0)	(8.0)	(4.0)	(100.0)

Source: Bureau of Census, U.S. Census of Population and Housing: New Jersey Public Use Sample, 1980.

EXHIBIT 3-18

HOUSING CHARACTERISTICS (RENT/OWNER COSTS, INCOME RATIOS)
OF PRESENT MT. LAUREL-ELIGIBLE HOUSEHOLDS - NORTHEAST

	MODERATE INCOME (50-80% of Median)			LOW INCOME (Below 50% of Median)			
	1-2 Person	3-4 Person	5 or more Persons	1-2 Person	3-4 Person	5 or More Persons	TOTAL
Rent							
Under $100	40	0	0	720	120	160	1,040
	(0.6)	(0)	(0)	(4.2)	(1.5)	(2.9)	(2.4)
$100-199	3,520	1,000	440	9,560	2,320	960	17,800
	(50.9)	(28.7)	(15.5)	(55.2)	(29.0)	(17.3)	(40.3)
$200-299	2,840	2,040	1,760	5,800	4,240	3,000	19,680
	(41.0)	(58.6)	(62.0)	(33.5)	(53.0)	(54.0)	(44.6)
$300-399	480	280	400	1,120	1,160	1,120	4,560
	(6.9)	(8.0)	(14.1)	(6.5)	(14.5)	(20.1)	(10.3)
$400-599	40	160	240	120	160	320	1,040
	(0.6)	(4.6)	(8.5)	(0.7)	(2.0)	(5.8)	(2.3)
Total	6,920	3,480	2,840	17,320	8,000	5,560	44,120
	(15.7)	(7.9)	(6.4)	(39.3)	(18.1)	(12.6)	(100.0)
Rent-Income Ratio							
Under 20%	2,760	1,960	1,800	600	360	320	7,800
	(39.9)	(56.3)	(63.4)	(3.7)	(4.7)	(4.7)	(18.4)
20 - 30%	2,720	1,320	760	1,640	1,120	800	8,360
	(39.3)	(37.9)	(26.8)	(10.1)	(10.1)	(15.2)	(19.8)
30 - 50%	1,400	200	280	5,320	2,240	1,760	11,200
	(20.2)	(5.7)	(9.9)	(32.9)	(29.3)	(33.3)	(26.5)
Over 50%	40	0	0	8,600	3,920	2,400	14,960
	(0.6)	(0)	(0)	(53.2)	(51.3)	(45.5)	(35.3)
Total	6,920	3,480	2,840	16,160	7,640	5,280	42,320
	(16.4)	(8.2)	(6.7)	(38.2)	(18.1)	(12.5)	(100.0)
Owner Cost							
Under $200	80	0	0	280	40	40	440
	(18.2)	(0)	(0)	(36.8)	(25.0)	(50.0)	(22.0)
$200-299	240	40	40	280	40	0	640
	(54.5)	(16.7)	(12.5)	(36.8)	(25.0)	(0)	(32.0)
$300-399	80	120	80	120	0	40	440
	(18.2)	(50.0)	(25.0)	(15.8)	(0)	(50.0)	(22.0)
$400-499	0	40	120	80	40	0	280
	(0)	(16.7)	(37.5)	(10.5)	(25.0)	(0)	(14.0)
Over $500	40	40	80	0	40	0	200
	(9.1)	(16.7)	(25.0)	(0)	(25.0)	(0)	(10.0)
Total	440	240	320	760	160	80	2,000
	(22.0)	(12.0)	(16.0)	(38.0)	(8.0)	(4.0)	(100.0)
Owner Cost-Income Ratio							
Under 20%	80	0	40	40	0	40	200
	(18.2)	(0)	(12.5)	(5.9)	(0)	(50.0)	(10.4)
20 - 30%	160	160	160	80	80	0	640
	(36.4)	(66.7)	(50.0)	(11.8)	(50.0)	(0)	(33.3)
30 - 50%	160	80	120	240	40	0	640
	(36.4)	(33.3)	(37.5)	(35.3)	(25.0)	(0)	(33.3)
Over 50%	40	0	0	320	40	40	440
	(7.1)	(0)	(0)	(47.1)	(25.0)	(50.0)	(22.9)
Total	440	240	320	680	160	80	1,920
	(22.9)	(12.5)	(16.7)	(35.4)	(8.3)	(4.2)	(100.0)

Source: Bureau of Census, U.S. Census of Population and Housing: New Jersey Public Use Sample, 1980.

EXHIBIT 3-19

HOUSING CHARACTERISTICS (HOUSING TYPE, TENURE, AGE, VALUE) OF PRESENT MT. LAUREL-ELIGIBLE HOUSEHOLDS - NORTHWEST

	MODERATE INCOME (50-80% of Median)			LOW INCOME (Below 50% of Median)			
	1-2 Person	3-4 Person	5 or more Persons	1-2 Person	3-4 Person	5 or More Persons	TOTAL
Housing Type							
Single Family	480	400	520	1,320	680	440	3,840
	(9.8)	(14.5)	(15.7)	(10.7)	(11.1)	(11.0)	(11.5)
2-4 Family	2,120	1,520	2,080	4,440	2,400	1,880	14,440
	(43.1)	(55.1)	(62.7)	(36.0)	(39.2)	(47.0)	(43.2)
Multi-Family	2,320	840	720	6,560	3,040	1,680	15,160
	(47.2)	(30.4)	(21.7)	(53.2)	(49.7)	(42.0)	(45.3)
Mobile	0	0	0	0	0	0	0
	(0.0)	(0.0)	(0.0)	(0.0)	(0.0)	(0.0)	(0.0)
Total	4,920	2,760	3,320	12,320	6,120	4,000	33,440
	(14.7)	(8.3)	(9.9)	(36.8)	(18.3)	(12.0)	(100.0)
Housing Tenure							
Owner Occupied	1,040	1,080	1,240	2,080	720	520	6,680
	(21.1)	(39.1)	(37.3)	(16.9)	(11.8)	(13.0)	(20.0)
Renter Occupied	3,800	1,680	2,040	10,040	5,320	3,480	26,360
	(77.2)	(60.9)	(61.4)	(81.5)	(86.9)	(87.0)	(78.8)
No Cash Rent	80	0	40	200	80	0	400
	(1.6)	(0)	(1.2)	(1.6)	(1.3)	(0)	(1.2)
Total	4,920	2,760	3,320	12,320	6,120	4,000	33,440
	(14.7)	(8.3)	(9.9)	(36.8)	(18.3)	(12.0)	(100.0)
Housing Age							
Built	0	80	80	200	160	40	560
1970-1980	(0)	(2.9)	(2.4)	(1.6)	(2.6)	(1.0)	(1.7)
Built	360	240	520	1,280	960	960	4,320
1940-1969	(7.3)	(8.7)	(15.7)	(10.4)	(15.7)	(24.0)	(12.9)
Built Prior	4,560	2,440	2,720	10,840	5,000	3,000	28,560
to 1940	(92.7)	(88.4)	(81.9)	(88.0)	(81.7)	(75.0)	(85.4)
Total	4,920	2,760	3,320	12,320	6,120	4,000	33,440
	(14.7)	(8.3)	(9.9)	(36.8)	(18.3)	(12.0)	(100.0)
Housing Value							
Less than $25,000	40	0	40	160	40	40	320
	(12.5)	(0)	(14.3)	(18.2)	(14.3)	(25.0)	(14.0)
$25,000-34,999	80	40	80	320	80	0	600
	(25.0)	(11.1)	(28.6)	(36.4)	(28.6)	(0)	(26.3)
$35,000-44,999	40	80	40	200	40	120	520
	(12.5)	(22.2)	(14.3)	(22.7)	(14.3)	(75.0)	(22.8)
$45,000-59,999	120	240	80	160	120	0	720
	(37.5)	(66.7)	(28.6)	(18.2)	(42.9)	(0)	(31.6)
$60,000-74,999	40	0	40	40	0	0	120
	(12.5)	(0)	(14.3)	(4.5)	(0)	(0)	(5.3)
Total	320	360	280	880	280	160	2,280
	(14.0)	(15.8)	(12.3)	(38.6)	(12.3)	(7.0)	(100.0)

Source: Bureau of Census, U.S. Census of Population and Housing: New Jersey Public Use Sample, 1980.

EXHIBIT 3-20

HOUSING CHARACTERISTICS (RENT/OWNER COSTS, INCOME RATIOS) OF PRESENT MT. LAUREL-ELIGIBLE HOUSEHOLDS - NORTHWEST

	MODERATE INCOME (50-80% of Median)			LOW INCOME (Below 50% of Median)			
	1-2 Person	3-4 Person	5 or more Persons	1-2 Person	3-4 Person	5 or More Persons	TOTAL
Rent							
Under $100	80	0	80	760	120	240	1,280
	(2.1)	(0)	(3.9)	(7.6)	(2.3)	(7.0)	(4.9)
$100-199	1,720	240	160	4,280	1,160	440	8,000
	(45.3)	(14.3)	(7.8)	(42.8)	(21.8)	(12.8)	(30.4)
$200-299	1,600	1,000	1,080	3,800	2,960	1,680	12,120
	(42.1)	(59.5)	(38.0)	(38.0)	(55.6)	(48.8)	(46.1)
$300-399	360	400	640	1,040	760	720	3,920
	(9.5)	(23.8)	(31.4)	(10.4)	(14.3)	(20.9)	(14.9)
$400-599	40	40	80	120	320	360	960
	(1.1)	(2.4)	(4.0)	(1.2)	(6.1)	(10.5)	(3.6)
Total	3,800	1,680	2,040	10,000	5,320	3,440	26,280
	(14.5)	(6.4)	(7.8)	(38.1)	(20.2)	(13.1)	(100.0)
Rent-Income Ratio							
Under 20%	1,560	800	920	360	280	240	4,160
	(41.1)	(47.6)	(45.1)	(4.0)	(5.7)	(7.1)	(16.8)
20 - 30%	1,600	640	1,000	1,120	680	560	5,600
	(42.1)	(38.1)	(49.0)	(12.4)	(13.8)	(16.7)	(22.6)
30 - 50%	560	240	120	2,160	1,440	920	5,440
	(14.7)	(14.3)	(5.9)	(24.0)	(29.3)	(27.4)	(21.9)
Over 50%	80	0	0	5,360	2,520	1,640	9,600
	(2.1)	(0)	(0)	(59.6)	(51.2)	(48.8)	(38.7)
Total	3,800	1,680	2,040	9,000	4,920	3,360	24,800
	(15.3)	(6.8)	(8.2)	(36.3)	(19.8)	(13.5)	(100.0)
Owner Cost							
Under $200	120	0	40	400	120	0	680
	(37.5)	(0)	(14.3)	(45.5)	(42.9)	(0)	(29.8)
$200-299	120	40	40	240	0	0	440
	(37.5)	(11.1)	(14.3)	(27.3)	(0)	(0)	(19.3)
$300-399	40	160	0	160	40	80	480
	(12.5)	(44.4)	(0)	(18.2)	(14.3)	(50.0)	(21.1)
$400-499	400	120	80	40	80	40	400
	(12.5)	(33.3)	(28.6)	(4.5)	(28.6)	(25.0)	(17.5)
Over $500	0	40	120	40	40	40	40
	(0)	(11.1)	(42.9)	(4.5)	(14.3)	(25.0)	(1.8)
Total	320	360	280	880	280	160	2,280
	(14.0)	(15.8)	(12.3)	(38.6)	(12.3)	(7.0)	(100.0)
Owner Cost-Income Ratio							
Under 20%	120	40	80	40	40	0	320
	(37.5)	(11.1)	(28.6)	(5.3)	(16.7)	(0)	(15.1)
20 - 30%	160	120	40	240	40	40	640
	(50.0)	(33.3)	(14.3)	(31.6)	(16.7)	(25.0)	(30.2)
30 - 50%	0	200	160	40	80	40	520
	(0)	(55.6)	(57.1)	(5.3)	(33.3)	(25.0)	(24.5)
Over 50%	40	0	0	440	80	80	640
	(12.5)	(0)	(0)	(57.9)	(33.3)	(50.0)	(30.2)
Total	320	360	280	760	240	160	2,120
	(15.1)	(17.1)	(13.2)	(35.8)	(11.3)	(7.5)	(100.0)

Source: Bureau of Census, U.S. Census of Population and Housing: New Jersey Public Use Sample, 1980.

EXHIBIT 3-21

HOUSING CHARACTERISTICS (HOUSING TYPE, TENURE, AGE, VALUE)
OF PRESENT MT. LAUREL-ELIGIBLE HOUSEHOLDS - WEST CENTRAL

	MODERATE INCOME (50-80% of Median)			LOW INCOME (Below 50% of Median)			
	1-2 Person	3-4 Person	5 or more Persons	1-2 Person	3-4 Person	5 or More Persons	TOTAL
Housing Type							
Single Family	320	440	280	1,160	520	280	3,000
	(22.2)	(47.8)	(31.8)	(37.2)	(39.4)	(33.3)	(35.2)
2-4 Family	760	400	480	1,040	480	360	3,520
	(52.8)	(43.5)	(54.5)	(33.3)	(36.4)	(42.9)	(41.3)
Multi-Family	360	80	120	920	320	200	2,000
	(25.0)	(8.7)	(13.6)	(29.5)	(24.2)	(23.8)	(23.5)
Mobile	0	0	0	0	0	0	0
	(0.0)	(0.0)	(0.0)	(0.0)	(0.0)	(0.0)	(0.0)
Total	1,440	920	880	3,120	1,320	840	8,520
	(16.9)	(10.8)	(10.3)	(36.6)	(15.5)	(9.9)	(100.0)
Housing Tenure							
Owner Occupied	480	440	400	1,400	400	240	3,360
	(33.3)	(47.8)	(45.5)	(44.9)	(30.3)	(28.6)	(39.4)
Renter Occupied	960	440	480	1,520	880	600	4,880
	(66.7)	(47.8)	(54.5)	(48.7)	(66.7)	(71.4)	(57.3)
No Cash Rent	0	40	0	200	40	0	280
	(0)	(4.3)	(0)	(6.4)	(3.0)	(0)	(3.3)
Total	1,440	920	880	3,120	1,320	840	8,520
	(16.9)	(10.8)	(10.3)	(36.6)	(15.5)	(9.9)	(100.0)
Housing Age							
Built 1970-1980	40	40	0	0	0	0	80
	(2.8)	(4.3)	(0)	(0)	(0)	(0)	(0.9)
Built 1940-1969	0	40	280	200	200	120	840
	(0)	(4.3)	(31.8)	(6.4)	(15.2)	(14.3)	(9.9)
Built Prior to 1940	1,400	840	600	2,920	1,120	720	7,600
	(97.2)	(91.3)	(68.2)	(93.6)	(84.8)	(85.7)	(89.2)
Total	1,440	920	880	3,120	1,320	840	8,520
	(16.9)	(10.8)	(10.3)	(36.6)	(15.5)	(9.9)	(100.0)
Housing Value							
Less than $25,000	0	40	0	160	40	40	280
	(0)	(14.3)	(0)	(22.2)	(20.0)	(33.3)	(17.9)
$25,000-34,999	0	40	80	240	40	0	400
	(0)	(14.3)	(40.0)	(33.3)	(20.0)	(0)	(25.6)
$35,000-44,999	40	40	80	240	120	40	560
	(100.0)	(14.3)	(40.0)	(33.3)	(60.0)	(33.3)	(35.9)
$45,000-59,999	0	120	0	80	0	40	240
	(0)	(42.9)	(0)	(11.1)	(0)	33.3)	(15.4)
$60,000-74,999	0	40	40	0	0	0	80
	(0)	(14.3)	(20.0)	(0)	(0)	(0)	(5.1)
Total	40	280	200	720	200	120	1,560
	(2.6)	(17.9)	(12.8)	(46.2)	(12.8)	(7.7)	(100.0)

Source: Bureau of Census, U.S. Census of Population and Housing: New Jersey Public Use Sample, 1980.

EXHIBIT 3-22

HOUSING CHARACTERISTICS (RENT/OWNER COSTS, INCOME RATIOS)
OF PRESENT MT. LAUREL-ELIGIBLE HOUSEHOLDS - WEST CENTRAL

	MODERATE INCOME (50-80% of Median)			LOW INCOME (Below 50% of Median)			
	1-2 Person	3-4 Person	5 or more Persons	1-2 Person	3-4 Person	5 or More Persons	TOTAL
Rent							
Under $100	120	0	0	160	0	0	280
	(13.0)	(0)	(0)	(10.8)	(0)	(0)	(5.9)
$100-199	320	0	40	680	0	0	1,040
	(34.8)	(0)	(9.1)	(45.9)	(0)	(0)	(22.0)
$200-299	320	240	200	600	480	280	2,120
	(34.8)	(54.5)	(45.5)	(40.5)	(54.5)	(50.0)	(44.9)
$300-399	120	80	200	40	360	120	920
	(13.0)	(18.2)	(45.5)	(2.7)	(40.9)	(21.4)	(19.5)
$400-599	40	120	0	0	40	160	360
	(4.3)	(27.3)	(0)	(0)	(4.5)	(28.5)	(7.6)
Total	920	440	440	1,480	880	560	4,720
	(19.5)	(9.3)	(9.3)	(31.4)	(18.6)	(11.9)	(100.0)
Rent-Income Ratio							
Under 20%	440	200	200	160	0	0	1,000
	(47.8)	(45.5)	(45.5)	(11.4)	(0)	(0)	(21.9)
20 - 30%	200	120	240	360	80	80	1,080
	(21.7)	(27.3)	(54.5)	(25.7)	(10.0)	(14.3)	(23.7)
30 - 50%	280	120	0	240	400	240	1,280
	(30.4)	(27.3)	(0)	(17.1)	(50.0)	(42.9)	(28.1)
Over 50%	0	0	0	640	320	240	1,200
	(0)	(0)	(0)	(45.7)	(40.0)	(42.9)	(26.3)
Total	920	440	440	1,400	800	560	4,560
	(20.2)	(9.6)	(9.6)	(30.7)	(17.5)	(12.3)	(100.0)
Owner Cost							
Under $200	40	40	40	360	80	0	560
	(100.0)	(14.3)	(20.0)	(50.0)	(40.0)	(0)	(35.9)
$200-299	0	40	40	200	40	0	320
	(0)	(14.3)	(20.0)	(27.8)	(20.0)	(0)	(20.5)
$300-399	0	120	40	80	40	80	360
	(0)	(42.9)	(20.0)	(11.1)	(20.0)	(66.7)	(23.1)
$400-499	0	40	40	40	0	0	120
	(0)	(14.3)	(20.0)	(5.6)	(0)	(0)	(7.7)
Over $500	0	40	40	40	40	40	200
	(0)	(14.3)	(20.0)	(5.6)	(20.0)	(33.3)	(12.8)
Total	40	280	200	720	200	120	1,560
	(2.6)	(17.9)	(12.8)	(46.2)	(12.8)	(7.7)	(100.0)
Owner Cost-Income Ratio							
Under 20%	0	80	80	0	80	0	240
	(0)	(28.6)	(40.0)	(0)	(40.0)	(0)	(15.8)
20 - 30%	40	120	40	160	0	0	360
	(100.0)	(42.9)	(20.0)	(23.5)	(0)	(0)	(23.7)
30 - 50%	0	80	80	240	40	80	520
	(0)	(28.6)	(40.0)	(35.3)	(20.0)	(66.7)	(34.2)
Over 50%	0	0	0	280	80	40	400
	(0)	(0)	(0)	(41.2)	(40.0)	(33.3)	(26.3)
Total	40	280	200	680	200	120	1,520
	(2.6)	(18.4)	(13.2)	(44.7)	(13.2)	(7.9)	(100.0)

Source: Bureau of Census, U.S. Census of Population and Housing: New Jersey Public Use Sample, 1980.

EXHIBIT 3-23

HOUSING CHARACTERISTICS (HOUSING TYPE, TENURE, AGE, VALUE) OF PRESENT MT. LAUREL-ELIGIBLE HOUSEHOLDS - EAST CENTRAL

	MODERATE INCOME (50-80% of Median)			LOW INCOME (Below 50% of Median)			
	1-2 Person	3-4 Person	5 or more Persons	1-2 Person	3-4 Person	5 or More Persons	TOTAL
Housing Type							
Single Family	240	160	40	1,200	440	520	2,600
	(42.9)	(44.4)	(25.0)	(57.7)	(50.0)	(56.5)	(52.4)
2-4 Family	120	160	120	440	240	320	1,400
	(21.4)	(44.4)	(75.0)	(21.2)	(27.3)	(34.8)	(28.2)
Multi-Family	200	40	0	440	200	80	960
	(35.7)	(11.1)	(0)	(21.2)	(22.7)	(8.7)	(19.4)
Mobile	0	0	0	0	0	0	0
	(0)	(0)	(0)	(0)	(0)	(0)	(0)
Total	560	360	160	2,080	880	920	4,960
	(11.3)	(7.3)	(3.2)	(41.9)	(17.7)	(18.5)	(100.0)
Housing Tenure							
Owner Occupied	320	80	40	880	200	200	1,720
	(57.1)	(22.2)	(25.0)	(42.3)	(22.7)	(21.7)	(34.7)
Renter Occupied	240	280	120	1,120	680	680	3,120
	(42.9)	(77.8)	(75.0)	(53.8)	(77.3)	(73.9)	(62.9)
No Cash Rent	0	0	0	80	0	40	120
	(0)	(0)	(0)	(3.8)	(0)	(4.3)	(2.4)
Total	560	360	160	2,080	880	920	4,960
	(11.3)	(7.3)	(3.2)	(41.9)	(17.7)	(18.5)	(100.0)
Housing Age							
Built 1970-1980	NA	NA	NA	NA	NA	NA	NA
Built 1940-1969	40	40	40	160	160	160	600
	(7.1)	(11.1)	(25.0)	(7.7)	(18.2)	(17.4)	(12.1)
Built Prior to 1940	520	320	120	1,920	720	760	4,360
	(92.9)	(88.9)	(75.0)	(92.3)	(81.8)	(82.6)	(87.9)
Total	560	360	160	2,080	880	920	4,960
	(11.3)	(7.3)	(3.2)	(41.9)	(17.7)	(18.5)	(100.0)
Housing Value							
Less than $25,000	80	0	NA	520	120	40	760
	(40.0)	(0)		(68.4)	(75.0)	(50.0)	(61.3)
$25,000-34,999	40	0	NA	80	0	40	160
	(20.0)	(0)		(10.5)	(0)	(50.0)	(12.9)
$35,000-44,999	40	40	NA	120	0	0	200
	(20.0)	(100.0)		(15.8)	(0)	(0)	(16.1)
$45,000-59,999	40	0	NA	40	40	0	120
	(20.0)	(0)		(5.3)	(25.0)	(0)	(9.7)
$60,000-74,999	NA	NA	NA	NA	NA	NA	NA
Total	200	40	NA	760	160	80	1,240
	(16.1)	(3.2)		(61.3)	(12.9)	(6.5)	(100.0)

Source: Bureau of Census, U.S. Census of Population and Housing: New Jersey Public Use Sample, 1980.

EXHIBIT 3-24

HOUSING CHARACTERISTICS (RENT/OWNER COSTS, INCOME RATIOS)
OF PRESENT MT. LAUREL-ELIGIBLE HOUSEHOLDS - EAST CENTRAL

	MODERATE INCOME (50-80% of Median)			LOW INCOME (Below 50% of Median)			
	1-2 Person	3-4 Person	5 or more Persons	1-2 Person	3-4 Person	5 or More Persons	TOTAL
Rent							
Under $100	0 (0)	0 (0)	0 (0)	40 (3.6)	0 (0)	0 (0)	40 (1.3)
$100-199	40 (16.7)	80 (33.3)	0 (0)	280 (25.0)	120 (17.6)	80 (11.8)	600 (19.5)
$200-299	160 (66.7)	160 (66.7)	0 (0)	480 (42.9)	200 (29.4)	120 (17.6)	1,120 (36.4)
$300-399	40 (16.7)	0 (0)	80 (66.7)	320 (28.6)	280 (41.2)	320 (47.1)	1,040 (33.8)
$400-599	0 (0)	0 (0)	40 (33.3)	0 (0)	80 (11.8)	160 (23.5)	360 (9.1)
Total	240 (7.8)	240 (7.8)	120 (3.9)	1,120 (36.4)	680 (22.1)	680 (22.1)	3,080 (100.0)
Rent-Income Ratio							
Under 20%	0 (0)	40 (16.7)	0 (0)	40 (3.6)	40 (6.7)	40 (5.9)	160 (5.3)
20 - 30%	80 (33.3)	160 (66.7)	40 (33.3)	120 (10.7)	40 (6.7)	120 (17.6)	560 (18.7)
30 - 50%	160 (66.7)	40 (16.7)	80 (66.7)	160 (14.3)	80 (13.3)	80 (11.8)	600 (20.0)
Over 50%	0 (0)	0 (0)	0 (0)	800 (71.4)	440 (73.3)	440 (64.7)	1,680 (56.0)
Total	240 (80)	240 (8.0)	120 (4.0)	1,120 (37.3)	600 (20.0)	680 (22.7)	3,000 (100.0)
Owner Cost							
Under $200	80 (50.0)	40 (100.0)	NA	480 (63.2)	40 (25.0)	0 (0)	640 (53.3)
$200-299	40 (25.0)	0 (0)	NA	160 (21.1)	120 (75.0)	40 (50.0)	360 (30.0)
$300-399	40 (25.0)	0 (0)	NA	80 (10.5)	0 (0)	0 (0)	120 (10.0)
$400-499	0 (0)	0 (0)	NA	40 (5.3)	0 (0)	40 (50.0)	80 (6.7)
Over $500	NA	NA	NA	NA	NA	NA	NA
Total	160 (13.3)	40 (3.3)	NA	760 (63.3)	160 (13.3)	80 (6.7)	1,200 (100.0)
Owner Cost-Income Ratio							
Under 20%	40 (25.0)	40 (100.0)	NA	80 (11.1)	0 (0)	0 (0)	160 (14.3)
20 - 30%	80 (50.0)	0 (0)	NA	80 (11.1)	40 (33.3)	0 (0)	200 (17.9)
30 - 50%	40 (25.0)	0 (0)	NA	200 (27.8)	40 (33.3)	40 (50.0)	320 (28.6)
Over 50%	0 (0)	0 (0)	NA	360 (50.0)	40 (33.3)	40 (9.1)	440 (39.3)
Total	160 (14.3)	40 (3.6)	NA	720 (64.3)	120 (10.7)	80 (7.1)	1,120 (100.0)

Source: Bureau of Census, U.S. Census of Population and Housing: New Jersey Public Use Sample, 1980.

EXHIBIT 3-25

HOUSING CHARACTERISTICS (HOUSING TYPE, TENURE, AGE, VALUE)
OF PRESENT MT. LAUREL-ELIGIBLE HOUSEHOLDS - SOUTHWEST

	MODERATE INCOME (50-80% of Median)			LOW INCOME (Below 50% of Median)			
	1-2 Person	3-4 Person	5 or more Persons	1-2 Person	3-4 Person	5 or More Persons	TOTAL
Housing Type							
Single Family	840	680	1,160	2,840	1,760	1,360	8,640
	(55.3)	(70.8)	(87.9)	(56.8)	(69.8)	(66.7)	(64.7)
2-4 Family	360	120	0	1,120	440	440	2,480
	(23.7)	(12.5)	(0.0)	(22.4)	(17.5)	(21.6)	(18.6)
Mobile	0	40	0	0	80	0	120
	(0.0)	(4.2)	(0.0)	(0.0)	(3.2)	(0.0)	(0.9
Multi-Family	320	120	160	1,040	240	240	2,120
	(21.1)	(12.5)	(12.1)	(20.8)	(9.5)	(11.8)	(15.9)
Total	1,520	960	1,320	5,000	2,520	2,040	13,360
	(11.4)	(7.2)	(9.9)	(37.4)	(18.9)	(15.3)	(100.0)
Housing Tenure							
Owner Occupied	720	560	840	2,320	1,080	800	6,320
	(47.4)	(58.3)	(63.6)	(46.4)	(42.9)	(39.2)	(47.3)
Renter Occupied	760	400	440	2,520	1,440	1,240	6,800
	(50.0)	(41.7)	(33.3)	(50.4)	(57.1)	(60.8)	(50.9)
No Cash Rent	40	0	40	160	0	0	240
	(2.6)	(0)	(3.0)	(3.2)	(0.0)	(0)	(1.8)
Total	1,520	960	1,320	5,000	2,520	2,040	13,360
	(11.4)	(7.2)	(9.9)	(37.4)	(18.9)	(15.3)	(100.0)
Housing Age							
Built	0	0	0	200	160	120	480
1970-1980	(0)	(0)	(0)	(4.0)	(6.3)	(5.9)	(3.6)
Built	120	240	200	520	400	440	1,920
1940-1969	(7.9)	(25.0)	(15.2)	(10.4)	(15.7)	(21.6)	(14.4)
Built Prior	1,400	720	1,120	4,280	1,960	1,480	10,960
to 1940	(92.1)	(75.0)	(84.8)	(85.6)	(77.8)	(72.5)	(82.0)
Total	1,520	960	1,320	5,000	2,520	2,040	13,360
	(11.4)	(7.2)	(9.9)	(37.4)	(18.9)	(15.3)	(100.0)
Housing Value							
Less than $25,000	240	240	480	1,080	680	400	3,120
	(50.0)	(66.7)	(66.7)	(56.3)	(89.5)	(58.8)	(63.4)
$25,000-34,999	0	40	40	400	40	160	680
	(0)	(11.1)	(5.6)	(20.8)	(5.3)	(23.5)	(13.8)
$35,000-44,999	120	80	80	280	40	80	680
	(25.0)	(22.2)	(11.1)	(14.6)	(5.3)	(11.8)	(13.8)
$45,000-59,999	80	0	120	160	0	40	400
	(16.7)	(0)	(16.7)	(18.3)	(0.0)	(5.9)	(8.1)
$60,000-74,999	40	0	0	0	0	0	40
	(8.3)	(0)	(0)	(0)	(0)	(0)	(0.8)
Total	480	360	720	1,920	760	680	4,920
	(7.8)	(17.3)	(14.6)	(39.0)	(15.4)	(13.8)	(100.0)

Source: Bureau of Census, U.S. Census of Population and Housing: New Jersey Public Use Sample, 1980.

EXHIBIT 3-26

HOUSING CHARACTERISTICS (RENT/OWNER COSTS, INCOME RATIOS) OF PRESENT MT. LAUREL-ELIGIBLE HOUSEHOLDS - SOUTHWEST

	MODERATE INCOME (50-80% of Median)			LOW INCOME (Below 50% of Median)			
	1-2 Person	3-4 Person	5 or more Persons	1-2 Person	3-4 Person	5 or More Persons	TOTAL
Rent							
Under $100	80	0	0	360	80	80	600
	(10.5)	(0)	(0)	(14.3)	(5.7)	(6.5)	(9.0)
$100-199	280	160	4	880	280	200	1,840
	(36.8)	(44.4)	(10.0)	(34.9)	(20.0)	(16.1)	(27.5)
$200-299	320	40	80	920	640	640	2,640
	(42.1)	(11.1)	(20.0)	(36.5)	(45.7)	(51.6)	(39.5)
$300-399	80	40	240	360	280	200	1,200
	(10.5)	(11.1)	(60.0)	(14.3)	(20.0)	(16.1)	(18.0)
$400-599	0	120	40	0	120	120	400
	(0)	(33.3)	(10.0)	(0)	(8.6)	(9.7)	(6.0)
Total	760	360	400	2,520	1,400	1,240	6,680
	(11.4)	(5.4)	(6.0)	(37.7)	(21.0)	(18.6)	(100.0)
Rent-Income Ratio							
Under 20%	360	160	80	160	120	40	920
	(47.4)	(44.4)	(20.0)	(7.0)	(9.1)	(3.2)	(14.5)
20 - 30%	240	40	320	240	160	120	1,120
	(31.6)	(11.1)	(80.0)	(10.5)	(12.1)	(9.7)	(17.6)
30 - 50%	160	160	0	560	240	520	1,640
	(21.1)	(44.4)	(0)	(24.6)	(18.2)	(41.9)	(25.8)
Over 50%	0	0	0	1,320	800	560	2,680
	(0)	(0)	(0)	(57.9)	(60.6)	(45.2)	(42.1)
Total	760	360	400	2,280	1,320	1,240	6,360
	(11.9)	(5.7)	96.3)	(35.8)	(20.8)	(19.5)	(100.0)
Owner Cost							
Under $200	240	120	120	1,040	120	160	1,800
	(50.0)	(33.3)	(16.7)	(54.2)	(15.8)	(23.5)	(36.6)
$200-299	200	160	360	320	280	160	1,480
	(41.7)	(44.4)	(50.0)	(16.7)	(36.8)	(23.5)	(30.1)
$300-399	0	40	80	80	320	120	640
	(0)	(11.1)	(11.1)	(4.2)	(42.1)	(17.6)	(13.0)
$400-499	40	0	40	200	0	120	400
	(8.3)	(0)	(5.6)	(10.4)	(0)	(17.6)	(8.1)
Over $500	0	40	120	280	40	120	600
	(0)	(11.1)	(16.7)	(14.6)	(5.3)	(17.7)	(12.2)
Total	480	360	720	1,920	760	680	4,920
	(9.8)	(7.3)	(14.6)	(39.0)	(15.4)	(13.8)	(100.0)
Owner Cost-Income Ratio							
Under 20%	160	200	320	80	0	80	840
	(33.3)	(55.6)	(44.4)	(4.8)	(0)	(13.3)	(18.4)
20 - 30%	160	120	240	40	160	80	800
	(33.3)	(33.3)	(33.3)	(2.4)	(32.2)	(13.3)	(17.5)
30 - 50%	120	0	80	560	160	280	1,200
	(25.0)	0	(11.1)	(33.3)	(22.2)	(46.7)	(26.3)
Over 50%	40	40	80	1,000	400	160	1,720
	(8.3)	(11.1)	(11.1)	(59.5)	(55.6)	(26.7)	(37.7)
Total	480	360	720	1,680	720	600	4,560
	(10.5)	(7.9)	(15.8)	(36.8)	(15.8)	(13.2)	(100.0)

Source: Bureau of Census, U.S. Census of Population and Housing: New Jersey Public Use Sample, 1980.

EXHIBIT 3-27

HOUSING CHARACTERISTICS (HOUSING TYPE, TENURE, AGE, VALUE)
OF PRESENT MT LAUREL-ELIGIBLE HOUSEHOLDS - SOUTH-SOUTHWEST

	MODERATE INCOME (50-80% of Median)			LOW INCOME (Below 50% of Median)			
	1-2 Person	3-4 Person	5 or more Persons	1-2 Person	3-4 Person	5 or More Persons	TOTAL
Housing Type							
Single Family	760	280	440	1,920	520	320	4,240
	(55.9)	(38.9)	(73.3)	(57.8)	(54.2)	(42.1)	(54.9)
2-4 Family	280	320	120	600	280	120	1,720
	(20.6)	(44.4)	(20.0)	(18.1)	(29.2)	(15.8)	(22.3)
Multi-Family	280	120	40	800	120	320	1,680
	(20.6)	(16.7)	(6.7)	(24.1)	(12.5)	(42.1)	(21.8)
Mobile	40	0	0	0	40	0	80
	(2.9)	(0.0)	(0.0)	(0.0)	(4.2)	(0.0)	(1.0)
Total	1,360	720	600	3,320	960	760	7,720
	(17.6)	(9.3)	(7.8)	(43.0)	(12.4)	(9.8)	(100.0)
Housing Tenure							
Owner Occupied	360	280	280	1,200	240	0	2,360
	(26.5)	(38.9)	(46.7)	(36.1)	(25.0)	(0)	(30.6)
Renter Occupied	920	400	320	2,000	720	720	5,080
	(67.6)	(55.6)	(53.3)	(60.2)	(75.0)	(94.7)	(65.8)
No Cash Rent	80	40	0	120	0	40	280
	(5.9)	(5.6)	(0)	(3.6)	(0)	(5.3)	(3.6)
Total	1,360	720	600	3,320	960	760	7,720
	(17.6)	(9.3)	(7.8)	(43.0)	(12.4)	(9.8)	(100.0)
Housing Age							
Built 1970-1980	40	40	0	40	80	120	320
	(2.9)	(5.6)	(0)	(1.2)	(8.3)	(15.8)	(4.1)
Built 1940-1969	0	120	240	160	80	120	720
	(0)	(16.7)	(40.0)	(4.8)	(8.3)	(15.8)	(9.3)
Built Prior to 1940	1,320	560	360	3,120	800	520	6,680
	(17.6)	(9.3)	(60.0)	(94.0)	(83.3)	(68.4)	(86.5)
Total	1,360	720	600	3,320	960	760	7,720
	(17.6)	(9.3)	(7.8)	(43.0)	(12.4)	(9.8)	(100.0)
Housing Value							
Less than $25,000	160	120	200	640	120	NA	1,240
	(66.7)	(75.0)	(83.3)	(66.7)	(60.0)	NA	(68.9)
$25,000-34,999	40	0	0	280	40	NA	360
	(16.7)	(0)	(0)	(29.2)	(20.0)	NA	(20.0)
$35,000-44,999	0	0	40	40	40	NA	120
	(0)	(0)	(16.7)	(4.2)	(20.0)	NA	(20.0)
$45,000-59,999	40	0	0	0	0	NA	40
	(16.7)	(0)	(0)	(0)	(0)	NA	(2.2)
$60,000-74,999	0	40	0	0	0	NA	40
	(0)	(25.0)	(0)	(0)	(0)	NA	(2.2)
Total	240	160	240	960	200	NA	1,800
	(13.3)	(8.9)	(13.3)	(53.3)	(11.1)	NA	(100.0)

Source: Bureau of Census, U.S. Census of Population and Housing: New Jersey Public Use Sample, 1980.

NA - No cases found in Public Use Sample.

EXHIBIT 3-28

HOUSING CHARACTERISTICS (RENT/OWNER COSTS, INCOME RATIOS) OF PRESENT MT. LAUREL-ELIGIBLE HOUSEHOLDS - SOUTH-SOUTHWEST

	MODERATE INCOME (50-80% of Median)			LOW INCOME (Below 50% of Median)			
	1-2 Person	3-4 Person	5 or more Persons	1-2 Person	3-4 Person	5 or More Persons	TOTAL
Rent							
Under $100	40	40	0	200	40	0	320
	(4.3)	(10.0)	(0)	(10.4)	(5.9)	(0)	(6.5)
$100-199	360	80	40	800	320	320	1,920
	(39.1)	(20.0)	(12.5)	(41.7)	(47.1)	(47.1)	(39.0)
$200-299	400	200	160	760	200	240	1,960
	(43.5)	(50.0)	(50.0)	(39.6)	(29.4)	(35.3)	(39.8)
$300-399	120	40	120	120	80	120	600
	(13.0)	(10.0)	(37.5)	(6.3)	(11.8)	(17.6)	(12.2)
$400-599	120	80	120	160	120	120	720
	(13.0)	(20.0)	(37.5)	(8.4)	(19.7)	(17.6)	(14.6)
Total	920	400	320	1,920	680	680	4,920
	(18.7)	(8.1)	(6.5)	(39.0)	(13.8)	(13.8)	(100.0)
Rent-Income Ratio							
Under 20%	240	120	80	40	40	40	560
	(27.3)	(30.0)	(25.0)	(2.3)	(6.3)	(5.9)	(12.0)
20 - 30%	240	160	200	160	40	200	1,000
	(27.3)	(40.0)	(62.5)	(9.1)	(6.3)	(29.4)	(21.4)
30 - 50%	320	80	40	360	200	200	1,200
	(36.4)	(20.0)	(12.5)	(20.5)	(31.3)	(29.4)	(25.6)
Over 50%	80	40	0	1,200	360	240	1,920
	(9.1)	(10.0)	(0)	(68.2)	(56.3)	(35.3)	(41.0)
Total	880	400	320	1,760	640	680	4,680
	(18.8)	(8.5)	(6.8)	(37.6)	(13.7)	(14.5)	(100.0)
Owner Cost							
Under $200	200	120	40	560	0	NA	920
	(83.3)	(75.0)	(16.7)	(58.3)	(0)	NA	(51.1)
$200-299	0	40	80	360	120	NA	600
	(0)	(25.0)	(33.3)	(37.5)	(60.0)	NA	(33.3)
$300-399	40	0	40	0	40	NA	120
	(16.7)	(0)	(16.7)	(0)	(20.0)	NA	(6.7)
$400-499	0	0	40	0	0	NA	40
	(0)	(0)	(16.7)	(0)	(0)	NA	(2.2)
Over $500	0	0	40	40	40	NA	120
	(0)	(0)	(16.7)	(4.2)	(20.0)	NA	(6.7)
Total	240	160	240	960	200	NA	1,800
	(13.3)	(8.9)	(13.3)	(53.3)	(11.1)	NA	(100.0)
Owner Cost-Income Ratio							
Under 20%	160	120	40	40	0	NA	360
	(66.7)	(75.0)	(16.7)	(4.3)	(0)	NA	(20.5)
20 - 30%	40	0	80	160	40	NA	320
	(16.7)	(0)	(33.3)	(17.4)	(20.0)	NA	(18.2)
30 - 50%	40	40	80	280	40	NA	320
	(16.7)	(25.0)	(33.3)	(30.4)	(20.0)	NA	(27.3)
Over 50%	0	0	40	440	120	NA	600
	(0)	(0)	(16.7)	(47.8)	(60.0)	NA	(34.1)
Total	240	160	240	920	200	NA	1,760
	(13.6)	(9.1)	(13.6)	(52.3)	(11.4)	NA	(100.0)

Source: Bureau of Census, U.S. Census of Population and Housing: New Jersey Public Use Sample, 1980.

NA - No Cases found in Public Use Sample.

SOCIOECONOMIC CHARACTERISTICS OF THE PROSPECTIVE MOUNT LAUREL POPULATION

As described in Chapter 2, the quantification of the future or prospective Mount Laurel population has employed the New Jersey Department of Labor, Office of Demographic and Economic Analysis's Demographic Cohort (Model 2) projection as the basis for future aggregate population growth to 1990 and 2000. To these projections have been applied New Jersey's headship rates by county, as well as MIT changes in headship rates to provide 1990 and 2000 household counts.

The Mount Laurel share of each age cohort household count, based on 1980 incidence rates, was then tabulated. From these were subtracted 1980 Mount Laurel households to produce the increase in Mount Laurel households by age cohort for the two time periods. As indicated earlier, for 1980 to 1990, expected growth in the Mount Laurel-eligible population (purely income constrained) is approximately 134,000 households; for 1990 to 2000 it is about 80,000 households.[8]

1980 socioeconomic characteristics by age cohort, county of residence, and Mount Laurel income category (50-80% of median income, and <50% of median income) were applied to the net new Mount Laurel population of a particular age/income and in a particular location. These produced estimates of future characteristics of the Mount Laurel population and are discussed for the period 1980 to 1990 in the following sections.

It should be emphasized at this point that the following discussion of socioeconomic characteristics will be of those prospective Mount Laurel households that are purely income-constrained and the difference from the previous discussion is that the prior section concentrated on present Mount Laurel income-constrained households living in deficient housing. The basic data source for socioeconomic characteristics is the 1980 Census of Population and Housing Public Use Sample (New Jersey). The following economic assumptions are implicit to our choice of projection technique and are taken from the state's description.

1. Population change from the components of natural increase will continue the patterns of the 1970s but household size will stabilize and ultimately dampen the increase in households.
2. Change in industrial base of the state will follow the pattern of the 1970s.
3. Net state employment-induced inmigration is zero with New York and Pennsylvania inmigration compensating for losses to those states and the South/Southwest portion of the country.

As a prelude to discussing socioeconomic characteristics of the prospective Mount Laurel population, we will detail expected general statewide growth trends of which the prospective Mount Laurel population will be a part.

New Jersey Towards the End of the Century

The population of New Jersey by the Year 2000 will have undergone continued demographic change similar to what we in the 1980s have experienced since the 1960s. The following paragraphs provide some insight to this expected change.[9]

New Jersey will be older as the baby boom continues to age, longevity increases pass larger shares of the elderly to older age cohorts, and younger college students continue to be exported to other states rather than be educated in-state. Each of these factors contribute to an older median age for the statewide population.[10]

The baby boom generation will cause the age cohort 35-44 to be the fastest growing age sector through the turn of the century. Non-family households (single persons, unrelated individuals, single parent/child households, etc.) and thus smaller households will grow twice as fast as traditional family/larger households. Non-family and smaller households will comprise an increasing share of all households.[11]

Over the next two decades in New Jersey, employment will grow, on average, at twice the rate of population growth. This is due to the tail end of the baby boom entering the labor force and also increasing labor force participation by women. Employment growth in New Jersey will, however, be less than 10 percent from 1980 to 1990; the fifth slowest growth rate in the nation. White collar jobs (18.1 percent growth) will grow faster than blue collar jobs (6.3 percent growth) reflecting faster growth in professional/technical workers and clericals and slower growth in operatives and craft workers.[12]

The largest white collar employment sectors will continue to be clerical workers, at 20 percent of the labor force, followed by professional/technical workers at 17 percent. Blue collar worker growth patterns are dictated by operative and craft workers at 14 and 11 percent of total employment respectively. Service workers, currently representing close to 14 percent of the labor force and not classified as either white or blue collar occupations, will grow the fastest of all employment sectors, exhibiting 23 percent growth from 1980 to 1990.[13]

Households in New Jersey will continue to follow national trends towards increasing outward migration from central cities and even from close-in suburbs. Since New Jersey is the first state to be completely enveloped by metropolitan areas growth will be from the core to the extremes of a single metropolitan area or from more dense to less dense metropolitan areas (see Chapter 1).

As traditional central locations are less sought, so too will public transit drop in use in favor of the automobile. Automobile ownership percentages will rise as will the share of work trips related to the automobile.

Race and Ethnicity: The State (Exhibit 3-29)

As indicated earlier, it is projected that by 1990 an additional 134,000 households (See Chapter 2) will be eligible for consideration under the housing policies growing out of the Mount Laurel II decision. Of these, 82 percent will be white and 14.8 percent black. This is a significant difference from the white percentage of the present population (60 percent) and clearly points to the fact that a housing-deficient, income-constrained population is more likely to be black as opposed to a purely income-constrained population. It also reflects future statewide expectations of growth of the elderly sector in the Southeast and Southwestern areas, most of whom are white and qualify within Mount Laurel income categories.

The pattern in which black households are found to be larger in size than white households in the present Mount Laurel population is also continued here. That is, out of the 14 percent of all new eligible Mount Laurel households that are black, the number in one- and two-person households is roughly equal to those in larger households; whereas, within the white population over twice as many households are in small (one-to-two-person) households.[14]

Statewide, the Mount Laurel-eligible Spanish population is projected to grow by 6,600 households or approximately 5 percent of the total growth. Most of these households will be in the low-income category (67 percent), and most will be in households of over three persons. The Spanish portion of the prospective Mount Laurel population is much smaller than it is in the present Mount Laurel population for exactly the same reasons as the equivalent pattern of black households. International affairs could, of course, drastically alter these conclusions.

Race and Ethnicity: The Regions
(Exhibit 3-31 to 3-41 Odd Numbered)

The dominant pattern regarding the prospective Mount Laurel population and the regions is the shift in numbers from the northern to southern portions of the state. The largest growth in prospective Mount Laurel households is projected to occur in the East Central Region 4, with a growth of 43,086; the smallest increment is projected to occur in the populous Northeast Region, with only 6,571 additional households by 1990.

The racial makeup of the southward-moving Mount Laurel household is predominantly white (90 percent). This is true for the East Central and West Central Regions, while the South-Southwest Regions have a somewhat less skewed distribution of households by race; 75 percent being white and 20 percent black.

While small in number, the fraction of black Mount Laurel-eligible households is projected to be highest in the Northwest Region 2 (Essex County), with the incremental growth in households being 33 percent black.

The regional breakdown of the Mount Laurel income categories sustains the statewide average of 40 percent moderate and 60 percent low-income households; a slight shift to the higher income class from the one-third/two-third moderate/low split found in the existing Mt. Laurel population.

Only in the two northern regions are there significant deviations from this pattern. The Northeast Region 1 is projected to have 70 percent of its new Mount Laurel population in the low-income category: while, the Northwest Region 2 will have only 42 percent in this category. Finally, in terms of household size, the relatively larger-than-average size of the black households contrasted to white is reaffirmed throughout the six regions. In the Northwest Region 2, over 50 percent of the black households will be in household sizes of over three persons; whereas, for the white population, the comparable fraction is less than 30 percent.

From a regional perspective, the Spanish population considered eligible under Mount Laurel is relatively evenly distributed across the six regions with roughly 1,000 new households in each region. This means that in a low-growth region such as the Northeast, the Spanish contribution to growth is larger (18%) whereas in a high-growth area such as in the East Central Region, the incremental proportion drops to 2.6 percent. As with the black population, the majority of Spanish households in the prospective Mount Laurel-eligible category are in large families, a pattern that also does not vary significantly across the six regions.

Sex of Chief Income Producer: The State

Statewide, the sex of the chief income producer of the prospective Mount Laurel household is evenly split between males and females: 67,018 and 66,960 respectively. This is a shift of one percent toward male headed households from percentages noted in the present Mount Laurel population.

Males are more likely to head families of moderate income; while females are more likely to head low income families. Even though one hears much about female headed, large households, this is not the dominant form of household relationship. Large prospective Mount Laurel households (5+ persons) are more apt to be headed by males in both the moderate- and low-income categories. However, it must be noted that female headship is still significant in the low income category. The largest single female headship category is the low income, 1-to-2 person household. This category accounts for 35,905 households. Most are elderly living on pensions or social security.

Sex of Chief Income Producer: The Regions

Where the statewide average shows an essentially even split between male and female-headed households in the prospective Mount Laurel population, the projected changes among the regions show a modest degree of variation in the northern and southern parts of the state. The Northeast and South-Southwest Regions 1 and 6 depart more strongly favoring female headed households by approximately 55 to 45 percent. On the other hand, the region with the largest prospective Mount Laurel population (East Central) favors the male headed household (52 percent) overall, yet the dominant, single category within the East Central Region's population is the female headed low income, small household.

Household Size: The State

The household size composition of prospective Mount Laurel households is quite different from that of the present or currently ill-housed Mount Laurel population.

For the state as a whole, almost 70 percent of the prospective households will be composed of 1 or 2 person families. This represents 15 percent higher level of small households within the future population of low and moderate income families in the state as contrasted to the currently, ill-housed, income constrained Mount Laurel population. Intermediate sized households of 3 to 4 persons contribute approximately 23 percent of the total prospective Mount Laurel population, while large households of 5-or-more persons contribute roughly 9 percent. This latter figure is one-half the equivalent proportional share of large families in the present Mount Laurel population.

Household Size: The Regions

The regions vary but slightly from the trend for prospective Mount Laurel households statewide. The region with the largest prospective Mount Laurel population, the East Central, also has the highest level of 1 and 2 person households (71 percent). This is also true for the other resort/retirement-oriented region, the South-Southwest. The remaining regions, for the most part, reflect the statewide pattern.

Age Structure: The State

Most prospective Mount Laurel-eligible households will have their household head over 65 years of age. The number of such households is projected to be close to 48,000 households or 35.7 percent of the Mount Laurel household growth from 1980 to 1990. This is almost double the proportion of this age group in the present Mount Laurel population. With this concentration in the upper age cohort, it is to be anticipated that small households will dominate. This is found to be the case in the over-65 age category, which is composed of 55 percent of 1-2 person low-income households, and 42 percent of 1-2 person moderate-income households.

Age Structure: The Regions

The regional distribution of the Mount Laurel-eligible population by age category reinforces and heightens the statewide pattern. The highest growth region (East Central) also has the highest concentration of small households headed by persons over 65 years of age: 55 percent for moderate-income and 63 percent for low-income households. In the two low-growth northern regions, there is a slight tendency towards the younger, larger-size household.

Household Income: The State

As we have all learned to expect, household income is subject to many pressures, not the least of which is inflation. The dollar of today will undoubtedly have a different value than it will have ten years hence. The household income data used in this section is based on the 1980 Census record and has not been altered or adjusted to reflect the differential impact of inflation on various types of households. We will thus view future incomes as if they were in 1980 dollars.

The statewide distribution of income within the prospective Mount Laurel population accentuates the importance of the partition between households of different sizes. Most Mount Laurel households, on average, have an income of under $10,000; in turn, most of these households contain one or two persons. The growth of the small household sector in the future and the associated income patterns of this sector influence income distribution in the future. Even though, as seen earlier, there are slightly more moderate income families, overall income is slightly lower. This is due to the income profile of the smaller family having a larger effect on the components of both Mount Laurel income categories. When examining the categorical split between low- and moderate-income households, it is found that 99 percent of low-income one- and two-person households are in this income category: while, in the moderate-income category, 62 percent of the one- and two-person households are in the $10,000 to $14,999 category with only 35 percent in the lowest (below $10,000) income grouping. The general tendency is for larger households to be found in the higher-income categories; however, in the case of low-income families, 70 percent of those with five or more persons remain at the lowest income level.

Household Income: The Regions

The statewide pattern of income distribution is remarkably constant across the six regions.

Labor Force Participation: The State (Exhibit 3-30)

Labor force participation by Mount Laurel-eligible households is a function of both the individual and current labor market conditions. The insights derived from this examination of the prospective Mount Laurel population must be limited by the attributes of the individual. It is felt that the clearest statement regarding our subject population is to be derived from the number and fraction not in the labor force. This too we realize is a function of market conditions, but it is also related to those whom we believe to be in the majority who have been forced due to age or sustained ill-health to be out of the labor force.

Statewide, 47.9 percent of the prospective Mount Laurel-eligible population will not be in the labor force; an increase of 8 percent absolute over the 40 percent non labor-force participants of the present Mount Laurel population. Dominating this category are small, low- and moderate-income households (one to two persons). Obviously, this is significantly influenced by a large retiree contingent.

Labor Force Participation: The Regions (Exhibit 3-32 to 3-42 Even-Numbered)

If 1980 is a reasonable guide to future labor force participation in our six regions, the East Central and South-Southwest regions will be faced with a greater-than-average number of their Mount Laurel-eligible population removed from the labor force with incomes consisting of pensions, transfer payments, social security and the like. The remaining regions are relatively comparable and affect the former two to create the state average. As in the case of the state pattern, one- and two-person households consistently dominate the category of labor force non-participation.

Occupation: The State

The occupational profile of the state's prospective Mount Laurel population is a function of not only the population itself but of changes in the work place. Generalizing on the 1980 data source providing characteristics of age cohort growth, we must assume that the work distribution will not change significantly over the intervening years. Given this assumption, we see from the exhibit that for those in the labor force, the occupational profile of the prospective Mount Laurel-eligible household head ranges from a high of 27.9 percent in the technical-sales category to a relative low of 13.5 percent in managerial occupations. These two categories combined, at 40 percent of future Mount Laurel labor force participants are one-third higher than equivalent categories of existing Mount Laurel households. Nearly 40 percent of present Mount Laurel households are in the occupational category of operatives/laborers.

Occupation: The Regions

In the East Central Region 4 (Monmouth and Ocean Counties), a slight swing toward the managerial professions is seen, indicating possibly the growth of small service-recreation-retirement activities within this region. Strength in the service occupations is seen in the South-Southwest Region 6, where only 25 percent of its prospective Mount Laurel-eligible labor force is assumed to be working.

Journey-to-Work: The State and the Region

For most (82.6 percent) prospective Mount Laurel-eligible households, the journey-to-work will be under thirty minutes. This pattern is remarkably consistent across income category, size of household, and region. Two compensating forces are at work here. The housing region is expanded to include multiple counties possibly lengthening the commuting time; yet, more housing will be built in the region, possibly improving access to jobs, thereby shortening the time.

Means of Journey-to-Work: The State

Statewide, the dominant conveyance to work will continue to be the private automobile (82.9 percent). This is so true that the residual transportation catgegory "other" (walking and biking, etc.) holds a 10 to 7 percent lead over public transportation use. The difference between this percentage and 64 percent automobile use of present Mount Laurel households reflects the more urban nature of the present Mount Laurel population and the suburbanizing composition of the prospective population. Further, younger black/Spanish families in the northern part of the state, use public transportation more frequently than older, white families in the southern part of the state.

Means of Journey-to-Work: The Regions

The major variable affecting the means used by the eligible prospective Mount Laurel population to commute to work is the availability of public transportation. The three relatively mature regions: the Northeast, Northwest and Southwest, all urban-based, have significant elements of a public transportation system available. This fact shows in the projected means to work in these regions vis-à-vis the remaining three regions. Against the statewide average of 7 percent usage of public transit for future Mount Laurel households, these three regions have public transit utilization rates of 19 percent, 15 percent and 7.9 percent respectively. In the remaining regions, the use of the automobile clearly dominates.

Automobiles Available: The State and the Region

The final category of socioeconomic characteristics to be considered in this analysis is the availability of automobiles within the prospective Mount Laurel eligible population. Statewide, while over one-quarter of this population has no auto available this is only one-half the rate found for the present Mount Laurel population.

The low income 1-to-2 person family is the most disadvantaged in this respect with 40 percent of this group being without auto access. To a certain degree, however, this project parallels the regional existence of public transit.

In the Northeast and Northwest regions, relatively rich in public transit facilities, 45 percent and 33 percent of the prospective Mount Laurel population are without an auto; while a region relatively poor in public transit such as the East Central Region is projected to have only 22 percent of this population without an automobile. Obviously a self-selection process is also at work here.

SUMMARY OF SIMILARITIES AND DIFFERENCES OF PRESENT AND PROSPECTIVE MOUNT LAUREL POPULATIONS

Let us review for a moment the distinction between the two basic subsets of Mount Laurel eligible population. Clearly, by definition, both fall below the income ceilings set up under the Mount Laurel II decision. The present Mount Laurel population represents income constrained households living in what is estimated to be deficient housing. It is assumed that the actions of municipalities through new construction as well as other mechanisms such as rehabilitation, can relieve this deficiency. The prospective Mount Laurel population is the projected purely income constrained increment to the state's population to be added through natural increase and migration and to be addressed primarily through new construction. In Chapter 2, we examined the aggregate housing demand differences between these two categories of present and future need. In the following chapters we will compare supply and demand for these two sectors.

Contrasts at the State Level

The present versus prospective Mount Laurel-eligible population is more racially and ethnically concentrated. At the state level, the currently ill-housed Mount Laurel population is 28 percent black and 25 percent Spanish origin. The prospective population, in contrast, is projected to be 15 percent black and 5 percent of Spanish origin.

The age structure across the two Mount Laurel subpopulations also shows significant differences. The present, ill-housed population is largely oriented toward younger families (42 percent), those with household

EXHIBIT 3-29

SOCIOECONOMIC CHARACTERISTICS (RACE, SEX, AGE, INCOME)
OF PROSPECTIVE MOUNT LAUREL-ELIGIBLE HOUSEHOLDS - STATEWIDE

	MODERATE INCOME (50-80% of Median)			LOW INCOME (Below 50% of Median)			
	1-2 Person	3-4 Person	5 or more Persons	1-2 Person	3-4 Person	5 or More Persons	TOTAL
Race							
White	30,417	12,416	4,791	48,286	10,871	3,268	110,049
	(89.7)	(82.5)	(77.5)	(84.5)	(68.5)	(56.1)	(82.1)
Black	3,105	2,012	1,080	7,721	3,930	1,961	19,809
	(9.2)	(13.4)	(17.5)	(13.5)	(24.8)	(33.7)	(14.8)
Other	387	629	309	1,123	1,071	594	4,113
	(1.1)	(4.2)	(5.0)	(2.0)	(6.7)	(10.2)	(3.1)
Total	33,909	15,057	6,180	57,130	15,873	5,823	133,971
	(25.3)	(11.2)	(4.6)	(42.6)	(11.8)	(4.3)	(100.0)
Spanish Origin							
Not Spanish	33,256	14,107	5,596	55,440	14,098	4,873	127,369
	(98.1)	(93.7)	(90.6)	(97.0)	(88 8)	(83.7)	(95.1)
Spanish Origin	652	949	584	1,688	1,774	950	6,598
	(1.9)	(6.3)	(9.4)	(3.0)	(11.2)	(16.3)	(4.9)
Total	33,908	15,056	6,180	57,128	15,872	5,823	133,966
	(25.3)	(11.2)	(4.6)	(42.6)	(11.8)	(4.3)	(100.0)
Sex of Chief Income Producer							
Male	18,897	11,620	5,151	21,232	6,966	3,164	67,018
	(55.7)	(77.2)	(83.4)	(37.2)	(43.9)	(54.3)	(50.0)
Female	15,019	3,439	1,028	35,905	8,909	2,660	66,960
	(44.3)	(22.8)	(16.6)	(62.8)	(56.1)	(45.7)	(50.0)
Total	33,916	15,059	6,179	57,137	15,875	5,824	133,978
	(25.3)	(11.2)	(4.6)	(42.6)	(11.9)	(4.4)	(100.0)
Age of Chief Income Producer							
Under 25	3,079	1,997	327	5,854	3,198	518	14,974
	(9.1)	(13.3)	(5.3)	(10.2)	(20.1)	(8.9)	(11.2)
25-44	6,961	8,854	4,359	7,200	9,062	4,316	40,753
	(20.5)	(51.2)	(70.6)	(12.6)	(57.1)	(74.1)	(30.4)
45-64	9,599	3,308	1,436	12,354	2,762	946	30,406
	(28.3)	(21.9)	(23.3)	(21.6)	(17.4)	(16.2)	(22.7)
65 and Over	14,276	899	58	31,726	851	43	47,853
	(42.1)	(6.0)	(0.9)	(55.5)	(5.4)	(0.8)	(35.7)
Total	33,914	15,059	6,180	57,135	15,874	5,823	133,986
	(25.3)	(11.2)	(4.6)	(42.6)	(11.8)	(4.3)	(100.0)
Household Income							
Under $10,000	11,933	388	19	56,606	13,645	4,113	86,703
	(35.2)	(2.6)	(0.3)	(99.1)	(86.0)	(70.6)	(64.7)
$10,000-14,999	21,028	9,161	1,854	492	2,037	1,574	36,146
	(62.0)	(60.8)	(30.0)	(0.9)	(12.8)	(27.0)	(27.0)
$15,000-19,999	946	5,209	3,665	21	131	80	10,053
	(2.8)	(34.6)	(59.3)	(0.0)	(0.8)	(1.4)	(7.5)
$20,000-24,999	0	298	636	1	34	48	1,017
	(0)	(2.0)	(10.3)	(0)	(0.2)	(0.8)	(0.8)
Total	33,909	15,057	6,180	57,127	15,872	5,823	133,969
	(25.3)	(11.2)	(4.6)	(42.6)	(11.8)	(4.3)	(100.0)

Source: Bureau of Census, U.S. Census of Population and Housing: New Jersey Public Use Sample, 1980.

EXHIBIT 3-30

SOCIOECONOMIC CHARACTERISTICS (LABOR FORCE PARTICIPATION, OCCUPATION, JOURNEY-TO-WORK) OF PROSPECTIVE MT LAUREL-ELIGIBLE HOUSEHOLDS - STATEWIDE

	MODERATE INCOME (50-80% of Median)			LOW INCOME (Below 50% of Median)			
	1-2 Person	3-4 Person	5 or more Persons	1-2 Person	3-4 Person	5 or More Persons	TOTAL
Labor Force Participation							
At Work	17,210	12,211	5,308	13,586	8,204	2,918	59,437
	(50.8)	(81.1)	(85.9)	(23.8)	(51.7)	(50.2)	(44.4)
With Job	614	258	114	825	411	194	2,417
Not at Work	(1.8)	(1.7)	(1.8)	(1.4)	(2.6)	(3.3)	(1.8)
Unemployed	1,217	793	303	2,499	1,460	519	6,791
	(3.6)	(5.3)	(4.9)	(4.4)	(9.2)	(8.9)	(5.1)
Not in Labor Force	14,707	1,476	342	40,059	5,521	2,085	64,191
	(43.4)	(9.8)	(5.5)	(70.2)	(34.8)	(35.9)	(47.9)
Total*	33,910	15,057	6,180	57,061	15,870	5,815	133,892
	(25.3)	(11.2)	(4.6)	(42.6)	(11.9)	(4.3)	(100.0)
*Includes Armed Forces	163	318	111	92	274	98	1056
	(0.5)	(0.1)	(1.8)	(0.2)	(1.7)	(1.7)	(0.8)
Occupation							
Manager	4,142	2,125	683	2,946	1,212	457	11,565
Professional	(17.3)	(15.2)	(11.6)	(11.6)	(9.8)	(10.5)	(13.5)
Technical, Sales,	7,815	3,422	1,117	7,566	3,221	826	23,968
Supervisor	(32.6)	(24.5)	(18.9)	(29.9)	(26.1)	(19.0)	(27.9)
Service	3,957	1,783	890	5,954	2,760	838	16,183
	(16.5)	(12.8)	(15.1)	(23.5)	(22.4)	(19.2)	(18.9)
Farming	314	217	110	453	223	83	1,401
	(1.3)	(1.6)	(1.9)	(1.8)	(1.8)	(1.9)	(1.6)
Precision	2,880	2,961	1,455	2,788	1,653	831	12,568
Craftsman	(12.0)	(21.2)	(24.6)	(11.0)	(13.4)	(19.1)	(14.6)
Operatives, Labor	4,881	3,441	1,652	5,587	3,265	1,319	20,145
	(20.3)	(24.7)	(28.0)	(22.1)	(26.5)	(30.3)	(23.5)
Total	23,990	13,950	5,907	25,294	12,333	4,356	85,829
	(28.0)	(16.3)	(6.9)	(29.5)	(14.4)	(5.1)	(100.0)
Journey-to-work							
Less than 30 min.	14,379	9,679	4,033	11,532	7,105	2,486	49,216
	(83.7)	(78.3)	(75.2)	(86.0)	(85.0)	(83.5)	(82.6)
30-60 min.	2,325	2,017	1,030	1,519	981	388	8,261
	(13.5)	(16.3)	(19.2)	(11.3)	(11.7)	(13.1)	(13.9)
60 min. and Over	454	671	300	352	276	105	2,160
	(2.6)	(5.4)	(5.7)	(2.6)	(3.3)	(3.5)	(3.6)
Total	17,160	12,367	5,363	13,403	8,363	2,980	59,636
	(28.8)	(20.7)	(9.0)	(22.5)	(14.0)	(5.0)	(100.0)
Means of Journey-to-work							
Automobile	14,392	10,391	4,775	10,636	6,973	2,465	50,171
	(82.8)	(87.2)	(88.1)	(77.8)	(82.2)	(81.7)	(82.9)
Public Transit	1,292	668	267	1,257	504	254	4,243
	(7.4)	(5.3)	(4.9)	(9.2)	(5.9)	(8.4)	(7.0)
Other (walk, bike)	1,689	930	377	1,785	1,002	298	6,081
	(9.7)	(7.4)	(7.0)	(13.0)	(11.8)	(9.9)	(10.1)
Total	17,374	12,530	5,420	13,678	8,478	3,016	60,496
	(28.7)	(20.7)	(9.0)	(22.6)	(14.0)	(5.0)	(100.0)
Automobile Available							
None	5,124	1,064	496	22,752	4,044	1,635	35,114
	(15.1)	(7.1)	(8.0)	(39.8)	(25.5)	(28.1)	(26.2)
1	22,865	7,821	2,940	28,662	7,953	2,842	73,083
	(67.4)	(51.9)	(47.6)	(50.2)	(50.1)	(48.8)	(54.5)
2 or More	5,922	6,172	2,745	5,718	3,876	1,346	25,779
	(17.5)	(41.0)	(44.4)	(10.0)	(24.4)	(23.1)	(19.2)
Total	33,910	15,057	6,180	57,132	15,873	5,823	133,976
	(25.3)	(11.2)	(4.6)	(42.6)	(11.8)	(4.3)	(100.0)

Source: Bureau of Census, U.S. Census of Population and Housing: New Jersey Public Use Sample, 1980.

EXHIBIT 3-31

SOCIOECONOMIC CHARACTERISTICS (RACE, SEX, AGE, INCOME) OF PROSPECTIVE MOUNT LAUREL-ELIGIBLE HOUSEHOLDS - NORTHEAST

	MODERATE INCOME (50-80% of Median)			LOW INCOME (Below 50% of Median)			
	1-2 Person	3-4 Person	5 or more Persons	1-2 Person	3-4 Person	5 or More Persons	TOTAL
Race							
White	1,037 (88.2)	446 (80.4)	155 (68.1)	2,768 (83.6)	588 (62.6)	173 (47.6)	5,167 (78.6)
Black	93 (7.9)	57 (10.3)	40 (17.4)	371 (11.2)	199 (21.2)	123 (33.8)	833 (13.4)
Other	46 (3.9)	52 (9.3)	33 (14.5)	172 (5.2)	152 (16.2)	68 (18.6)	522 (7.9)
Total	1,176 (17.9)	554 (8.4)	227 (3.5)	3,310 (50.4)	940 (14.3)	363 (5.5)	6,571 (100.0)
Spanish Origin							
Not Spanish	1,057 (89.9)	436 (78.7)	162 (71.1)	2,924 (88.3)	595 (63.3)	215 (59.1)	5,389 (82.0)
Spanish Origin	119 (10.1)	118 (21.3)	66 (28.9)	387 (11.7)	345 (36.7)	148 (40.9)	1,183 (18.0)
Total	1,176 (17.9)	554 (8.4)	227 (3.5)	3,310 (50.4)	940 (14.3)	363 (5.5)	6,571 (100.0)
Sex of Chief Income Producer							
Male	626 (53.2)	417 (75.3)	198 (87.2)	1,183 (35.7)	423 (45.0)	170 (46.6)	3,018 (45.9)
Female	550 (46.8)	137 (24.7)	29 (12.8)	2,127 (64.3)	516 (55.0)	194 (53.4)	3,554 (54.1)
Total	1,176 (17.9)	554 (8.4)	227 (3.5)	3,310 (50.4)	940 (14.3)	363 (5.5)	6,571 (100.0)
Age of Chief Income Producer							
Under 25	108 (9.2)	62 (11.2)	7 (3.3)	304 (9.2)	164 (17.5)	29 (7.9)	674 (10.3)
25-44	306 (26.0)	331 (59.6)	161 (70.7)	538 (16.2)	578 (61.5)	280 (77.1)	2,193 (33.4)
45-64	345 (29.3)	138 (24.8)	57 (25.0)	710 (21.4)	151 (16.0)	51 (14.0)	1,451 (22.1)
65 and Over	417 (35.5)	23 (4.3)	2 (1.0)	1,759 (53.1)	47 (5.0)	3 (0.9)	2,253 (34.3)
Total	1,177 (17.9)	554 (8.4)	227 (3.5)	3,311 (50.4)	940 (14.3)	363 (5.5)	6,572 (100.0)
Household Income							
Under $10,000	294 (25.0)	1 (0.3)	0 (0)	3,295 (99.5)	802 (85.4)	264 (72.6)	4,656 (70.9)
$10,000-14,999	882 (74.9)	310 (56.0)	49 (21.4)	13 (0.4)	129 (13.7)	96 (26.5)	1,479 (22.5)
$15,000-19,999	1 (0.1)	242 (43.6)	162 (71.1)	2 (0.1)	7 (0.7)	2 (0.6)	415 (6.3)
$20,000-24,999	0 (0)	0 (0)	17 (7.6)	0 (0)	2 (0.2)	1 (0.3)	21 (0.3)
Total	1,176 (17.9)	554 (8.4)	227 (3.5)	3,310 (50.4)	940 (14.3)	363 (5.5)	6,571 (100.0)

Source: Bureau of Census, U.S. Census of Population and Housing: New Jersey Public Use Sample, 1980.

EXHIBIT 3-32

SOCIOECONOMIC CHARACTERISTICS (LABOR FORCE PARTICIPATION, OCCUPATION, JOURNEY-TO-WORK) OF PROSPECTIVE MOUNT LAUREL-ELIGIBLE HOUSEHOLDS - NORTHEAST

	MODERATE INCOME (50-80% of Median)			LOW INCOME (Below 50% of Median)			
	1-2 Person	3-4 Person	5 or more Persons	1-2 Person	3-4 Person	5 or More Persons	TOTAL
Labor Force Participation							
At Work	700	471	198	851	482	191	2,893
	(59.5)	(85.0)	(87.2)	(25.7)	(51.4)	(52.4)	(44.1)
With Job	22	9	4	64	18	11	128
Not at Work	(1.9)	(1.6)	(1.6)	(1.9)	(1.9)	(3.0)	(2.0)
Unemployed	43	26	16	143	73	33	335
	(3.6)	(4.7)	(7.2)	(4.3)	(7.8)	(9.1)	(5.1)
Not in Labor Force	410	47	9	2,246	363	129	3,204
	(34.8)	(8.5)	(3.9)	(68.0)	(38.7)	(35.4)	(48.8)
Total*	1,176	554	227	3,305	938	363	6,565
	(17.9)	(8.4)	(3.5)	(50.3)	(14.3)	(5.5)	(100.0)
*Includes Armed Forces	1	1	0	1	2	0	6
	(0.1)	(0.1)	(0)	(0)	(0.2)	(0)	(0.1)
Occupation							
Manager	133	57	25	151	61	18	445
Professional	(14.3)	(10.7)	(11.3)	(10.0)	(8.5)	(6.6)	(10.6)
Technical, Sales,	349	135	41	442	182	55	1,204
Supervisor	(37.5)	(25.6)	(18.3)	(29.3)	(25.2)	(20.7)	(28.8)
Service	124	52	22	297	133	39	666
	(13.3)	(9.8)	(9.7)	(19.7)	(18.5)	(14.5)	(15.9)
Farming	4	2	0	10	4	1	22
	(0.5)	(0.4)	(0)	(0.7)	(0.6)	(0.4)	(0.5)
Precision	96	97	49	148	79	35	504
Craftsman	(10.3)	(18.4)	(21.7)	(9.9)	(10.9)	(13.2)	(12.1)
Operatives, Labor	224	186	88	459	261	120	1,337
	(24.1)	(35.1)	(39.0)	(30.9)	(36.3)	(44.6)	(32.0)
Total	930	529	224	1,507	720	268	4,179
	(22.3)	(12.7)	(5.4)	(36.1)	(17.2)	(6.4)	(100.0)
Journey-to-work							
Less than 30 min.	564	387	162	718	418	160	2,408
	(81.3)	(83.4)	(81.9)	(85.0)	(86.5)	(85.2)	(83.9)
30-60 min.	110	68	27	108	52	27	393
	(15.9)	(14.6)	(13.9)	(12.8)	(10.8)	(14.2)	(13.7)
60 min. and Over	20	8	8	19	13	1	69
	(2.9)	(1.9)	(4.1)	(2.2)	(2.8)	(0.6)	(2.4)
Total	694	464	198	844	483	187	2,871
	(24.2)	(16.2)	(6.9)	(29.4)	(16.8)	(6.5)	(100.0)
Means of Journey-to-work							
Automobile	483	370	162	481	324	126	1,946
	(68.9)	(78.4)	(81.5)	(56.4)	(66.8)	(66.3)	(67.1)
Public Transit	136	55	22	219	74	37	547
	(19.4)	(11.6)	(10.9)	(25.7)	(16.2)	(19.2)	(18.9)
Other (walk, bike)	82	47	15	152	82	28	406
	(11.7)	(10.0)	(7.5)	(17.8)	(16.9)	(14.5)	(14.0)
Total	702	472	198	852	484	191	2,899
	(24.2)	(16.3)	(6.8)	(29.2)	(16.7)	(6.6)	(100.0)
Automobile Available							
None	325	79	28	1,949	418	170	2,969
	(27.7)	(14.3)	(12.5)	(58.9)	(44.5)	(46.6)	(45.2)
1	704	321	121	1,166	391	142	2,844
	(59.8)	(57.9)	(53.2)	(35.2)	(41.6)	(39.0)	(43.3)
2 or More	147	154	78	196	131	52	758
	(12.5)	(27.8)	(34.2)	(5.9)	(13.9)	(14.3)	(11.5)
Total	1,176	554	227	3,310	940	363	6,572
	(17.9)	(8.4)	(3.5)	(50.4)	(14.3)	(5.5)	(100.0)

Source: Bureau of Census, U.S. Census of Population and Housing: New Jersey Public Use Sample, 1980.

EXHIBIT 3-33

SOCIOECONOMIC CHARACTERISTICS (RACE, SEX, AGE, INCOME) OF PROSPECTIVE MOUNT LAUREL-ELIGIBLE HOUSEHOLDS - NORTHWEST

	MODERATE INCOME (50-80% of Median)			LOW INCOME (Below 50% of Median)			
	1-2 Person	3-4 Person	5 or more Persons	1-2 Person	3-4 Person	5 or More Persons	TOTAL
Race							
White	2,213 (72.8)	914 (64.7)	353 (60.2)	1,517 (62.6)	353 (41.0)	100 (29.1)	5,451 (62.9)
Black	762 (25.1)	425 (30.1)	194 (33.0)	824 (34.0)	432 (50.1)	198 (57.5)	2,836 (32.7)
Other	64 (2.1)	74 (5.2)	40 (6.8)	82 (3.4)	77 (8.9)	64 (13.4)	383 (4.4)
Total	3,040 (35.1)	1,413 (16.3)	587 (6.8)	2,423 (28.0)	861 (9.9)	344 (4.0)	8,670 (100.0)
Spanish Origin							
Not Spanish	2,910 (95.7)	1,269 (89.8)	485 (82.7)	2,274 (93.8)	714 (82.8)	279 (81.1)	7,932 (91.5)
Spanish Origin	130 (4.3)	144 (10.2)	102 (17.3)	149 (6.2)	148 (17.2)	65 (18.9)	738 (8.5)
Total	3,040 (35.1)	1,413 (16.3)	587 (6.8)	2,423 (28.0)	862 (9.9)	344 (4.0)	8,670 (100.0)
Sex of Chief Income Producer							
Male	1,517 (49.9)	1,026 (72.6)	473 (80.6)	813 (33.5)	314 (36.4)	150 (43.6)	4,292 (49.5)
Female	1,523 (50.1)	387 (27.4)	114 (19.4)	1,611 (66.5)	549 (63.6)	194 (56.4)	4,377 (50.5)
Total	3,040 (35.1)	1,413 (16.3)	587 (6.8)	2,423 (28.0)	862 (9.9)	344 (4.0)	8,670 (100.0)
Age of Chief Income Producer							
Under 25	263 (8.7)	116 (8.2)	30 (5.1)	270 (11.2)	169 (19.6)	42 (12.3)	891 (10.3)
25-44	971 (31.9)	913 (64.7)	426 (72.4)	422 (17.4)	484 (56.1)	242 (70.3)	3,460 (39.9)
45-64	834 (27.5)	314 (22.2)	132 (22.5)	543 (22.3)	702 (18.4)	54 (15.8)	2,036 (23.5)
65 and Over	970 (31.9)	70 (5.0)	0 (0)	1,188 (49.1)	50 (5.9)	6 (1.5)	2,285 (26.3)
Total	3,040 (35.1)	1,413 (16.3)	587 (6.8)	2,423 (28.0)	862 (9.9)	344 (4.0)	8,670 (100.0)
Household Income							
Under $10,000	647 (21.3)	4 (0.3)	0 (0)	2,407 (99.3)	717 (83.1)	246 (71.4)	4,020 (46.4)
$10,000-14,999	2,281 (75.0)	730 (51.7)	130 (22.1)	14 (0.6)	134 (15.5)	93 (27.0)	3,382 (39.0)
$15,000-19,999	110 (3.6)	679 (48.0)	389 (66.3)	2 (0.1)	10 (1.2)	5 (1.3)	1,194 (13.8)
$20,000-24,999	0 (0)	0 (0)	68 (11.6)	1 (0.1)	1 (0.1)	1 (0.3)	71 (0.8)
Total	3,040 (35.1)	1,413 (16.3)	0 (0)	2,423 (28.0)	862 (9.9)	344 (4.0)	8,670 (100.0)

Source: Bureau of Census, U.S. Census of Population and Housing: New Jersey Public Use Sample, 1980.

EXHIBIT 3-34

SOCIOECONOMIC CHARACTERISTICS (LABOR FORCE PARTICIPATION, OCCUPATION, JOURNEY-TO-WORK) OF PROSPECTIVE MOUNT LAUREL-ELIGIBLE HOUSEHOLDS - NORTHWEST

	MODERATE INCOME (50-80% of Median)			LOW INCOME (Below 50% of Median)			
	1-2 Person	3-4 Person	5 or more Persons	1-2 Person	3-4 Person	5 or More Persons	TOTAL
Labor Force Participation							
At Work	1,942	1,166	521	616	410	172	4,826
	(63.9)	(82.5)	(88.8)	(25.4)	(47.7)	(49.9)	(55.7)
With Job	76	38	16	55	23	8	216
Not at Work	(2.5)	(2.7)	(2.7)	(2.3)	(2.6)	(2.4)	(2.5)
Unemployed	82	74	24	124	67	26	397
	(2.7)	(5.2)	(4.1)	(5.1)	(7.8)	(7.6)	(4.6)
Not in Labor Force	940	132	26	1,624	360	138	3,220
	(30.9)	(9.3)	(4.4)	(67.2)	(41.8)	(40.2)	(37.2)
Total*	3,040	1,413	587	2,419	861	344	8,663
	(35.1)	(16.3)	(6.8)	(27.9)	(9.9)	(4.0)	(100.0)
*Includes Armed Forces	0	4	0	0	1	0	5
	(0)	(0.3)	(0)	(0)	(0.1)	(0)	(0.1)
Occupation							
Manager	407	216	68	144	60	15	909
Professional	(16.9)	(15.9)	(11.7)	(13.0)	(9.6)	(6.3)	(14.4)
Technical, Sales,	848	355	132	330	187	43	1,896
Supervisor	(35.2)	(26.1)	(22.8)	(29.9)	(30.1)	(17.9)	(30.0)
Service	379	172	80	253	112	57	1,053
	(15.7)	(12.6)	(13.8)	(22.9)	(18.0)	(23.5)	(16.7)
Farming	24	16	2	4	5	4	55
	(1.0)	(1.2)	(0.3)	(0.3)	(0.9)	(1.5)	(0.9)
Precision	261	234	96	79	66	37	773
Craftsman	(10.8)	(17.2)	(16.6)	(7.1)	(10.6)	(15.3)	(12.2)
Operatives, Labor	491	367	202	296	191	86	1,632
	(20.4)	(27.0)	(34.8)	(26.8)	(30.7)	(35.4)	(25.8)
Total	2,411	1,359	579	1,105	621	242	6,317
	(38.2)	(21.5)	(9.2)	(17.5)	(9.8)	(3.8)	(100.0)
Journey-to-work							
Less than 30 min.	1,522	910	406	481	314	140	3,775
	(79.2)	(78.2)	(78.1)	(79.8)	(77.1)	(82.0)	(78.8)
30-60 min.	336	206	94	104	79	22	839
	(17.4)	(17.7)	(18.1)	(17.2)	(19.3)	(12.6)	(17.5)
60 min. and Over	64	48	20	19	15	10	174
	(3.3)	(4.1)	(3.9)	(2.9)	(3.6)	(5.3)	(3.6)
Total	1,922	1,164	519	604	408	171	4,787
	(40.2)	(24.3)	(10.8)	(12.6)	(8.5)	(3.6)	(100.0)
Means of Journey-to-work							
Automobile	1,483	958	435	373	286	118	3,653
	(76.4)	(81.9)	(83.5)	(60.6)	(69.5)	(68.4)	(75.6)
Public Transit	297	114	60	147	84	42	744
	(15.3)	(9.7)	(11.5)	(23.9)	(20.4)	(24.2)	(15.4)
Other (walk, bike)	162	98	26	95	42	13	435
	(8.3)	(8.4)	(5.0)	(15.4)	(10.1)	(7.4)	(9.0)
Total	1,942	1,170	521	616	411	172	4,831
	(40.2)	(24.2)	(10.8)	(12.7)	(8.5)	(3.6)	(100.0)
Automobile Available							
None	734	186	72	1,317	381	166	2,856
	(24.2)	(13.1)	(12.2)	(54.3)	(44.1)	(48.3)	(32.9)
1	1,858	719	295	922	360	122	4,276
	(61.1)	(50.8)	(50.3)	(38.0)	(41.7)	(35.4)	(49.3)
2 or More	447	509	220	184	122	56	1,538
	(14.7)	(36.0)	(37.4)	(7.6)	(14.2)	(16.3)	(17.7)
Total	3,040	4,113	587	2,423	862	344	8,670
	(35.1)	(16.3)	(6.8)	(28.0)	(9.9)	(4.0)	(100.0)

Source: Bureau of Census, U.S. Census of Population and Housing: New Jersey Public Use Sample, 1980.

EXHIBIT 3-35

SOCIOECONOMIC CHARACTERISTICS (RACE, SEX, AGE, INCOME) OF PROSPECTIVE MOUNT LAUREL-ELIGIBLE HOUSEHOLDS - WEST CENTRAL

	MODERATE INCOME (50-80% of Median)			LOW INCOME (Below 50% of Median)			
	1-2 Person	3-4 Person	5 or more Persons	1-2 Person	3-4 Person	5 or More Persons	TOTAL
Race							
White	4,549	2,475	1,069	8,892	2,240	589	19,814
	(94.0)	(89.3)	(92.2)	(92.2)	(82.1)	(68.9)	(90.0)
Black	246	162	65	564	299	158	1,493
	(5.1)	(5.8)	(5.6)	(5.8)	(10.9)	(18.4)	(6.8)
Other	45	136	26	191	191	108	697
	(0.9)	(4.9)	(2.2)	(2.0)	(7.0)	(12.6)	(3.2)
Total	4,840	2,773	1,160	9,648	2,729	854	22,004
	(22.0)	(12.6)	(5.3)	(43.8)	(12.4)	(3.9)	(100.0)
Spanish Origin							
Not Spanish	4,769	2,598	1,050	9,422	2,381	672	20,892
	(98.5)	(93.7)	(90.5)	(97.7)	(87.2)	(78.6)	(94.9)
Spanish Origin	71	175	110	224	348	183	111
	(1.5)	(6.3)	(9.5)	(2.3)	(12.8)	(21.4)	(5.1)
Total	4,840	2,773	1,160	9,646	2,729	854	22,004
	(22.0)	(12.6)	(5.3)	(43.8)	(12.4)	(3.9)	(100.0)
Sex of Chief Income Producer							
Male	2,767	2,145	1,050	3,849	1,452	581	11,843
	(57.2)	(77.3)	(90.5)	(39.9)	(53.2)	(68.0)	(53.8)
Female	2,074	629	110	5,798	1,278	274	10,162
	(42.8)	(22.7)	(9.5)	(60.1)	(46.8)	(32.0)	(46.2)
Total	4,841	2,773	1,160	9,648	2,729	854	22,005
	(22.0)	(12.6)	(5.3)	(43.8)	(12.4)	(3.9)	(100.0)
Age of Chief Income Producer							
Under 25	505	298	65	1,045	597	58	2,569
	(10.4)	(10.7)	(5.6)	(10.8)	(21.9)	(6.8)	(11.7)
25-44	1,179	1,672	875	1,411	1,477	639	7,252
	(24.4)	(60.3)	(75.4)	(14.5)	(54.1)	(74.7)	(32.9)
45-64	1,607	687	220	2,182	498	149	5,343
	(33.2)	(24.6)	(19.0)	(22.6)	(18.2)	(17.5)	(24.3)
65 and Over	1,549	117	0	5,011	157	8	6,842
	(32.0)	(4.2)	(0)	(51.9)	(5.8)	(1.0)	(31.1)
Total	4,841	2,773	1,160	9,648	2,729	854	22,006
	(22.0)	(12.6)	(5.3)	(43.8)	(12.4)	(3.9)	(100.0
Household Income							
Under $10,000	369	0	0	9,298	1,742	489	11,949
	(7.6)	(0)	(0)	(96.4)	(65.7)	(57.3)	(54.3)
$10,000-14,999	3,635	875	84	332	879	348	6,154
	(75.1)	(31.5)	(7.3)	(3.4)	(32.2)	(40.8)	(28.0)
$15,000-19,999	836	1,601	654	17	50	17	3,174
	(17.3)	(57.7)	(56.4)	(0.2)	(1.8)	(1.9)	(14.4)
$20,000-24,999	0	298	415	0	0	0	713
	(0)	(10.7)	(35.8)	(0)	(0)	(0)	(3.2)
Total	4,841	2,773	1,160	9,646	2,729	854	22,004
	(22.0)	(12.6)	(5.3)	(43.8)	(12.4)	(3.9)	(100.0

Source: Bureau of Census, U.S. Census of Population and Housing: New Jersey Public Use Sample, 1980.

EXHIBIT 3-36

SOCIOECONOMIC CHARACTERISTICS (LABOR FORCE PARTICIPATION, OCCUPATION, JOURNEY-TO-WORK) OF PROSPECTIVE MOUNT LAUREL-ELIGIBLE HOUSEHOLDS - WEST CENTRAL

	MODERATE INCOME (50-80% of Median)			LOW INCOME (Below 50% of Median)			
	1-2 Person	3-4 Person	5 or more Persons	1-2 Person	3-4 Person	5 or More Persons	TOTAL
Labor Force Participation							
At Work	3,007	2,495	1,089	2,928	1,659	614	11,792
	(62.1)	(90.0)	(93.9)	(30.4)	(60.8)	(72.5)	(53.6)
With Job	97	32	32	149	83	25	419
Not at Work	(2.0)	(1.2)	(2.8)	(1.6)	(3.0)	(2.9)	(1.9)
Unemployed	117	58	19	398	149	66	808
	(2.4)	(2.1)	(1.7)	(4.1)	(5.5)	(7.8)	(3.7)
Not in Labor Force	1,620	188	19	6,155	838	141	8,961
	(33.5)	(6.8)	(1.7)	(63.9)	(30.7)	(16.7)	(40.8)
Total*	4,841	2,773	1,160	9,631	2,729	846	21,980
	(22.0)	(12.6)	(5.3)	(43.8)	(12.4)	(3.8)	(100.0)
*Includes Armed Forces	0	0	0	0	0	0	0
	(0)	(0)	(0)	(0)	(0)	(0)	(0)
Occupation							
Manager	816	428	143	622	315	91	2,415
Professional	(21.0)	(16.0)	(12.5)	(12.6)	(13.8)	(12.0)	(15.4)
Technical, Sales,	1,192	706	181	1,560	589	133	4,361
Supervisor	(30.6)	(26.4)	(15.9)	(31.7)	(25.8)	(17.4)	(27.8)
Service	376	337	143	937	398	100	2,291
	(9.7)	(12.6)	(12.5)	(19.1)	(17.5)	(13.0)	(14.6)
Farming	58	39	19	158	100	8	382
	(1.5)	(1.5)	(1.7)	(3.2)	(4.4)	(1.1)	(2.4)
Precision	492	486	246	465	340	183	2,212
Craftsman	(12.6)	(18.2)	(21.6)	(9.4)	(14.9)	(23.9)	(14.1)
Operatives, Labor	959	680	408	1,178	539	249	4,014
	(24.6)	(25.4)	(35.8)	(23.9)	(23.6)	(32.6)	(25.6)
Total	3,894	2,676	1,140	4,919	2,281	763	15,675
	(24.8)	(17.1)	(7.3)	(31.4)	(14.6)	(4.9)	(100.0)
Journey-to-work							
Less than 30 min.	2,572	1,879	836	2,514	1,435	506	9,743
	(86.5)	(75.7)	(77.7)	(89.4)	(88.3)	(84.7)	(84.3)
30-60 min.	350	418	175	257	132	92	1,524
	(11.8)	(20.9)	(16.3)	(9.1)	(8.2)	(15.3)	(13.2)
60 min. and Over	51	83	64	41	58	0	301
	(1.8)	(3.4)	(6.0)	(1.5)	(3.5)	(0)	(2.6)
Total	2,974	2,482	1,076	2,812	1,626	597	11,567
	(25.7)	(21.5)	(9.3)	(24.3)	(14.1)	(5.2)	(100.0)
Means of Journey-to-work							
Automobile	2,676	2,255	953	2,356	1,369	514	10,123
	(89.0)	(90.4)	(87.5)	(80.5)	(82.5)	(83.8)	(85.8)
Public Transit	104	91	39	141	58	25	457
	(3.4)	(3.6)	(3.6)	(4.8)	(3.5)	(4.1)	(3.9)
Other (walk, bike)	227	149	97	431	232	75	1,211
	(7.5)	(6.0)	(8.9)	(14.7)	(14.0)	(12.2)	(10.3)
Total	3,007	2,495	1,089	2,928	1,659	614	11,792
	(25.5)	(21.2)	(9.2)	(24.8)	(14.1)	(5.2)	(100.0)
Automobile Available							
None	525	71	39	3,401	473	133	4,642
	(10.8)	(2.6)	(3.4)	(35.3)	(17.3)	(15.5)	(21.1)
1	3,084	1,225	499	4,853	1,319	448	11,428
	(63.7)	(44.2)	(43.0)	(50.3)	(48.3)	(52.4)	(51.9)
2 or More	1,231	1,477	622	1,394	937	274	5,936
	(25.4)	(53.3)	(53.6)	(14.4)	(34.3)	(32.0)	(27.0)
Total	4,841	2,773	1,160	9,648	2,729	854	22,006
	(22.0)	(12.6)	(5.3)	(43.8)	(12.4)	(3.9)	(100.0)

Source: Bureau of Census, U.S. Census of Population and Housing: New Jersey Public Use Sample, 1980.

EXHIBIT 3-37

SOCIOECONOMIC CHARACTERISTICS (RACE, SEX, AGE, INCOME) OF PROSPECTIVE MOUNT LAUREL-ELIGIBLE HOUSEHOLDS - EAST CENTRAL

	MODERATE INCOME (50-80% of Median)			LOW INCOME (Below 50% of Median)			
	1-2 Person	3-4 Person	5 or more Persons	1-2 Person	3-4 Person	5 or More Persons	TOTAL
Race							
White	11,141 (95.5)	4,073 (87.5)	1.297 (83.3)	17,266 (91.0)	3,726 (80.9)	1,144 (70.5)	38,648 (89.7)
Black	441 (3.8)	454 (9.7)	208 (13.3)	1,531 (8.1)	788 (17.1)	448 (27.6)	3,870 (9.0)
Other	78 (0.7)	130 (2.8)	52 (3.3)	186 (1.0)	93 (2.0)	31 (1.9)	569 (1.3)
Total	11,660 (27.1)	4,657 (10.8)	1,557 (3.6)	18,982 (44.1)	4,607 (10.7)	1,623 (3.8)	43,086 (100.0)
Spanish Origin							
Not Spanish	11,517 (98.8)	4,501 (96.7)	1,466 (94.2)	18,704 (98.5)	4,313 (93.6)	1,469 (90.5)	41,970 (97.4)
Spanish Origin	143 (1.2)	156 (3.3)	91 (5.8)	278 (1.5)	294 (6.4)	155 (9.5)	1,116 (2.6)
Total	11,660 (27.1)	4,657 (10.8)	1,557 (3.6)	18,982 (44.1)	4,607 (10.7)	1,623 (3.8)	43,086 (100.0)
Sex of Chief Income Producer							
Male	7,004 (60.1)	3,697 (79.4)	1,284 (82.5)	7,467 (39.3)	2,072 (45.0)	974 (60.0)	22,497 (52.2)
Female	4,657 (39.9)	960 (20.6)	272 (17.5)	11,516 (60.7)	2,535 (55.0)	649 (40.0)	20,590 (47.8)
Total	11,661 (27.1)	4,657 (10.8)	1,557 (3.6)	18,983 (44.1)	4,607 (10.7)	1,623 (3.8)	43,088 (100.0)
Age of Chief Income Producer							
Under 25	765 (6.6)	610 (13.1)	52 (3.3)	1,422 (7.5)	788 (17.1)	93 (5.7)	3,730 (8.7)
25-44	1,738 (14.9)	2,724 (58.5)	1,025 (65.9)	1,778 (9.4)	2,628 (57.0)	1,206 (74.3)	11,099 (25.7)
45-64	2,788 (23.9)	960 (20.9)	441 (28.3)	3,772 (19.9)	881 (19.1)	309 (19.0)	9,153 (21.2)
65 and Over	6,369 (54.6)	363 (7.8)	39 (2.5)	12,012 (63.3)	309 (6.7)	15 (1.0)	19,107 (44.4)
Total	11,662 (27.1)	4,657 (10.8)	1,557 (3.6)	18,984 (44.1)	4,607 (10.7)	1,623 (3.8)	43,090 (100.0)
Household Income							
Under $10,000	4,449 (38.2)	65 (1.4)	0 (0)	18,936 (99.8)	4,143 (89.9)	1,098 (67.6)	28,691 (66.6)
$10,000-14,999	7,212 (61.8)	3,178 (68.2)	506 (32.5)	46 (0.2)	402 (8.7)	464 (28.6)	11,808 (27.4)
$15,000-19,999	0 (0)	1,414 (30.4)	973 (62.5)	0 (0)	15 (0.3)	15 (1.0)	2,418 (5.6)
$20,000-24,999	0 (0)	0 (0)	78 (5.0)	0 (0)	31 (0.7)	46 (2.9)	155 (0.4)
Total	11,661 (27.1)	4,657 (10.8)	1,557 (3.6)	18,982 (44.1)	4,607 (10.7)	1,623 (3.8)	43,087 (100.0)

Source: Bureau of Census, U.S. Census of Population and Housing: New Jersey Public Use Sample, 1980.

EXHIBIT 3-38

SOCIOECONOMIC CHARACTERISTICS (LABOR FORCE PARTICIPATION, OCCUPATION, JOURNEY-TO-WORK) OF PROSPECTIVE MOUNT LAUREL-ELIGIBLE HOUSEHOLDS - EAST CENTRAL

	MODERATE INCOME (50-80% of Median)			LOW INCOME (Below 50% of Median)			
	1-2 Person	3-4 Person	5 or more Persons	1-2 Person	3-4 Person	5 or More Persons	TOTAL
Labor Force Participation							
At Work	4,423	3,645	1,310	3,571	2,350	881	16,181
	(37.9)	(78.3)	(84.2)	(18.8)	(51.0)	(54.3)	(37.6)
With Job Not at Work	117	78	26	232	108	46	607
	(1.0)	(1.7)	(1.7)	(1.2)	(2.3)	(2.9)	(1.4)
Unemployed	337	272	52	649	479	139	1,929
	(2.9)	(5.8)	(3.3)	(3.4)	(10.4)	(8.6)	(4.5)
Not in Labor Force	6,719	558	130	14,530	1,608	510	24,055
	(57.6)	(12.0)	(8.3)	(76.5)	(34.9)	(31.4)	(55.8)
Total*	11,661	4,657	1,557	18,983	4,607	1,623	43,088
	(27.1)	(10.8)	(3.6)	(44.1)	(10.7)	(3.8)	(100.0)
*Includes Armed Forces	65	104	39	0	62	46	316
	(0.6)	(2.2)	(2.5)	(0.0)	(1.3)	(2.9)	(0.7)
Occupation							
Manager Professional	1,297	739	182	989	325	232	3,764
	(18.9)	(17.6)	(12.4)	(13.4)	(9.2)	(18.8)	(15.2)
Technical, Sales, Supervisor	2,024	817	285	2,180	819	216	6,342
	(29.4)	(19.5)	(19.5)	(29.4)	(23.1)	(17.5)	(25.7)
Service	1,336	597	233	1,793	912	216	5,088
	(19.4)	(14.2)	(15.9)	(24.2)	(25.8)	(17.5)	(20.6)
Farming	91	91	65	108	31	31	417
	(1.3)	(2.2)	(4.4)	(1.5)	(0.9)	(2.5)	(1.7)
Precision Craftsman	843	1,116	428	943	572	247	4,149
	(12.3)	(26.6)	(29.2)	(12.7)	(16.2)	(20.0)	(16.8)
Operatives, Labor	1,284	830	272	1,391	881	294	4,953
	(18.7)	(19.8)	(18.6)	(18.8)	(24.9)	(23.8)	(20.0)
Total	6,875	4,190	1,466	7,405	3,540	1,237	24,713
	(27.8)	(17.0)	(5.9)	(30.0)	(14.3)	(5.0)	(100.0)
Journey-to-work							
Less than 30 min.	3,580	2,633	869	2,860	1,963	742	12,649
	(80.7)	(71.5)	(65.0)	(81.5)	(81.9)	(81.4)	(77.7)
30-60 min.	635	609	299	464	325	108	2,441
	(14.3)	(16.5)	(22.3)	(13.2)	(13.6)	(11.9)	(15.0)
60 min. and Over	221	441	169	185	108	61	1,185
	(5.0)	(11.9)	(12.6)	(5.3)	(4.5)	(6.8)	(7.3)
Total	4,436	3,684	1,336	3,509	2,396	912	16,274
	(27.3)	(22.6)	(8.2)	(21.6)	(14.7)	(5.6)	(100.0)
Means of Journey-to-work							
Automobile	3,853	3,269	1,258	1,307	2,056	788	14,332
	(85.8)	(87.2)	(93.3)	(87.0)	(85.3)	(85.0)	(86.9)
Public Transit	143	208	39	108	93	31	621
	(3.2)	(5.5)	(2.9)	(3.0)	(3.8)	(3.3)	(3.8)
Other (walk, bike)	493	272	52	356	263	108	1,544
	(11.0)	(7.3)	(3.8)	(10.0)	(10.9)	(11.7)	(9.4)
Total	4,488	3,749	1,349	3,571	2,412	928	16,497
	(27.2)	(22.7)	(8.2)	(21.6)	(14.6)	(5.6)	(100.0)
Automobile Available							
None	1,492	246	117	6,539	989	325	9,708
	(12.8)	(5.3)	(7.5)	(34.4)	(21.5)	(20.0)	(22.5)
1	8,197	2,426	765	10,821	2,458	897	25,564
	(70.3)	(52.1)	(49.2)	(57.0)	(53.4)	(55.2)	(59.3)
2 or More	1,972	1,985	675	1,623	1,159	402	7,816
	(16.9)	(42.6)	(43.3)	(8.6)	(25.2)	(24.8)	(18.1)
Total	11,661	4,657	1,551	18,983	4,607	1,623	43,088
	(27.1)	(10.8)	(3.6)	(44.1)	(10.7)	(3.8)	(100.0)

Source: Bureau of Census, U.S. Census of Population and Housing: New Jersey Public Use Sample, 1980.

EXHIBIT 3-39

SOCIOECONOMIC CHARACTERISTICS (RACE, SEX, AGE, INCOME) OF PROSPECTIVE MOUNT LAUREL-ELIGIBLE HOUSEHOLDS - SOUTHWEST

	MODERATE INCOME (50-80% of Median)			LOW INCOME (Below 50% of Median)			
	1-2 Person	3-4 Person	5 or more Persons	1-2 Person	3-4 Person	5 or More Persons	TOTAL
Race							
White	7,142	3,354	1,376	11,595	2,833	867	27,167
	(87.3)	(81.7)	(71.7)	(77.8)	(60.3)	(47.7)	(76.3)
Black	927	601	442	3,040	1,495	743	7,248
	(11.3)	(14.6)	(23.0)	(20.4)	(31.8)	(40.9)	(20.3)
Other	116	152	101	264	372	206	1,212
	(1.4)	(3.7)	(5.3)	(1.8)	(7.9)	(11.4)	(3.4)
Total	8,185	4,107	1,920	14,899	4,700	1,817	35,628
	(23.0)	(11.5)	(5.4)	(41.8)	(13.2)	(5.1)	(100.0)
Spanish Origin							
Not Spanish	8,062	3,912	1,818	14,559	4,279	1,594	34,224
	(98.5)	(95.2)	(94.7)	(97.7)	(91.0)	(87.7)	(96.1)
Spanish Origin	123	196	101	339	421	223	1,403
	(1.5)	(4.8)	(5.3)	(2.3)	(9.0)	(12.3)	(3.9)
Total	8,185	4,107	1,920	14,898	4,700	1,817	35,627
	(23.0)	(11.5)	(5.4)	(41.8)	(13.2)	(5.1)	(100.0)
Sex of Chief Income Producer							
Male	4,368	3,245	1,615	5,261	2,123	925	17,538
	(53.4)	(79.0)	(84.2)	(35.3)	(45.2)	(50.9)	(49.2)
Female	3,818	862	304	9,638	2.577	892	18,091
	(46.6)	(21.0)	(15.8)	(64.7)	(54.8)	(49.1)	(50.8)
Total	8,186	4,107	1,920	14,899	4,700	1,817	35,628
	(23.0)	(11.5)	(5.4)	(41.8)	(13.2)	(5.1)	(100.0)
Age of Chief Income Producer							
Under 25	1,058	608	116	1,982	991	223	4,979
	(12.9)	(14.8)	(6.0)	(13.3)	(21.1)	(12.3)	(14.0)
25-44	2,006	1,661	1,361	2,222	2,742	1,306	11,999
	(24.5)	(57.5)	(70.9)	(14.9)	(58.4)	(71.8)	(33.6)
45-64	2,500	964	435	3,362	752	289	8,299
	(30.5)	(23.5)	(22.7)	(22.5)	(16.0)	(15.9)	(23.3)
65 and Over	2,622	174	7	7,335	215	0	10,353
	(32.0)	(4.3)	(0.4)	(49.3)	(4.5)	(0)	(29.1)
Total	8,186	4,107	1,920	14,901	4,700	1,817	35,630
	(23.0)	(11.5)	(5.4)	(41.8)	(13.2)	(5.1)	(100.0)
Household Income							
Under $10,000	2,651	14	0	14,824	4,188	1,247	22,924
	(32.4)	(0.4)	(0)	(99.5)	(89.1)	(68.6)	(64.3)
$10,000-14,999	5,534	2,818	536	66	463	520	9,937
	(67.6)	(68.6)	(27.9)	(0.4)	(9.8)	(28.6)	(27.9)
$15,000-19,999	0	1,275	1,326	0	50	41	2,691
	(0)	(31.0)	(69.1)	(0)	(1.1)	(2.3)	(7.6)
$20,000-24,999	0	0	58	0	0	0	58
	(0)	(0)	(3.0)	(0)	(0)	(0)	(0.2)
Total	8,185	4,107	1,920	14,898	4,700	1,817	35,627
	(23.0)	(11.5)	95.4)	(41.8)	(13.2)	(5.1)	(100.0)

Source: Bureau of Census, U.S. Census of Population and Housing: New Jersey Public Use Sample, 1980.

EXHIBIT 3-40

SOCIOECONOMIC CHARACTERISTICS (LABOR FORCE PARTICIPATION, OCCUPATION, JOURNEY-TO-WORK) OF PROSPECTIVE MOUNT LAUREL-ELIGIBLE HOUSEHOLDS - SOUTHWEST

	MODERATE INCOME (50-80% of Median)			LOW INCOME (Below 50% of Median)			
	1-2 Person	3-4 Person	5 or more Persons	1-2 Person	3-4 Person	5 or More Persons	TOTAL
Labor Force Participation							
At Work	4,839	3,253	1,594	3,783	2,338	801	16,607
	(59.1)	(79.2)	(83.0)	(25.4)	(49.7)	(44.1)	(46.7)
With Job	188	72	36	273	149	83	801
Not at Work	(2.3)	(1.8)	(1.9)	(1.8)	(3.2)	(4.5)	(2.2)
Unemployed	297	239	116	884	463	182	2,180
	(3.6)	(5.8)	(6.0)	(5.9)	(9.8)	(10.0)	(6.1)
Not in Labor Force	2,774	362	101	9,836	1,553	710	15,337
	(33.9)	(8.8)	(5.3)	(66.2)	(33.0)	(39.1)	(43.1)
Total*	8,185	4,107	1,920	14,866	4,700	1,817	35,596
	(23.0)	(11.5)	(5.4)	(41.8)	(13.2)	(5.1)	(100.0)
*Includes Armed Forces	87	181	72	91	198	41	671
	(1.1)	(4.4)	(3.8)	(0.6)	(4.2)	(2.3)	(1.9)
Occupation							
Manager	1,137	543	246	801	306	91	3,125
Professional	(17.6)	(14.4)	(13.7)	(11.5)	(8.5)	(7.0)	(13.1)
Technical, Sales,	2,382	1,029	326	2,172	1,049	306	7,243
Supervisor	(36.5)	(27.3)	(18.1)	(31.2)	(29.1)	(23.4)	(30.3)
Service	927	427	261	1,677	768	281	4,341
	(14.3)	(11.3)	(14.5)	(24.1)	(21.3)	(21.5)	(18.2)
Farming	51	22	14	91	41	8	227
	(0.8)	(0.6)	(0.8)	(1.3)	(1.1)	(0.6)	(1.0)
Precision	790	782	456	727	430	215	3,399
Craftsman	(12.2)	(20.7)	(25.4)	(10.4)	(11.9)	(16.5)	(14.2)
Operatives, Labor	1,202	971	493	1,495	1,008	405	5,573
	(18.6)	(25.7)	(27.4)	(21.5)	(28.0)	(31.0)	(23.3)
Total	6,469	3,774	1,797	6,963	3,601	1,305	23,909
	(27.1)	(15.8)	(7.5)	(29.1)	(15.1)	(5.5)	(100.0)
Journey-to-work							
Less than 30 min.	4,057	2,847	1,267	3,287	2,123	710	14,291
	(83.5)	(84.0)	(77.4)	(86.1)	(85.1)	(84.3)	(83.8)
30-60 min.	724	464	341	471	330	99	2,429
	(14.9)	(13.7)	(20.8)	(12.3)	(13.2)	(11.8)	(14.3)
60 min. and Over	80	79	29	58	41	33	321
	(1.5)	(2.3)	(1.7)	(1.4)	(1.6)	(3.9)	(1.9)
Total	4,861	3,390	1,637	3,816	2,494	843	17,041
	(28.5)	(19.9)	(9.6)	(22.4)	(14.6)	(4.9)	(100.0)
Means of Journey-to-work							
Automobile	4,071	3,086	1,456	2,949	2,139	710	14,411
	(82.6)	(89.9)	(87.4)	(76.1)	(84.4)	(84.3)	(83.4)
Public Transit	442	145	80	454	149	99	1,369
	(9.0)	(4.2)	(4.8)	(11.7)	(5.9)	(11.8)	(7.9)
Other (walk, bike)	413	203	130	471	248	33	1,498
	(8.4)	(5.9)	(7.8)	(12.2)	(9.8)	(3.9)	(8.7)
Total	4,926	3,434	1,666	3,874	2,536	843	17,278
	(28.5)	(19.9)	(9.6)	(22.4)	(14.7)	(4.9)	(100.0)
Automobile Available							
None	1,166	283	145	6,037	1,222	603	9,457
	(14.2)	(6.9)	(7.5)	(40.5)	(26.0)	(33.2)	(26.5)
1	5,643	2,137	927	7,185	2.387	776	19,056
	(68.9)	(52.0)	(48.3)	(48.2)	(50.8)	(42.7)	(53.5)
2 or More	1,376	1,688	848	1,677	1.090	438	7,117
	(16.8)	(41.1)	(44.2)	(11.3)	(23.2)	(24.1)	(20.0)
Total	8,185	4,108	1,920	14,899	4,700	1,817	35,629
	(23.0)	(11.5)	(5.4)	(41.8)	(13.2)	(5.1)	(100.0)

Source: Bureau of Census, U.S. Census of Population and Housing: New Jersey Public Use Sample, 1980.

EXHIBIT 3-41

SOCIOECONOMIC CHARACTERISTICS (RACE, SEX, AGE, INCOME) OF PROSPECTIVE MOUNT LAUREL-ELIGIBLE HOUSEHOLDS - SOUTH-SOUTHWEST

	MODERATE INCOME (50-80% of Median)			LOW INCOME (Below 50% of Median)			
	1-2 Person	3-4 Person	5 or more Persons	1-2 Person	3-4 Person	5 or More Persons	TOTAL
Race							
White	4,340 (86.8)	1,156 (74.4)	540 (74.0)	6,253 (79.4)	1,132 (55.6)	395 (48.1)	13,816 (76.6)
Black	635 (12.7)	313 (20.1)	133 (18.2)	1,392 (17.7)	717 (35.2)	291 (35.4)	3,480 (19.3)
Other	38 (0.8)	85 (5.5)	57 (7.8)	229 (2.9)	187 (9.2)	135 (16.5)	731 (4.1)
Total	5,013 (27.8)	1,554 (8.6)	730 (4.0)	7,874 (43.7)	2,036 (11.3)	821 (4.6)	18,027 (100.0)
Spanish Origin							
Not Spanish	4,946 (98.7)	1,393 (89.6)	616 (84.4)	7,562 (96.0)	1,818 (89.3)	644 (78.5)	16,979 (94.2)
Spanish Origin	66 (1.3)	161 (10.4)	114 (15.6)	312 (4.0)	218 (10.7)	177 (21.5)	1,048 (5.8)
Total	5,012 (27.8)	1,554 (8.6)	730 (4.0)	7,874 (43.7)	2,036 (11.3)	821 (4.6)	18,026 (100.0)
Sex of Income Producer							
Male	2,615 (52.2)	1,090 (70.1)	531 (72.7)	2,659 (33.8)	582 (28.6)	364 (44.3)	7,840 (43.5)
Female	2,397 (47.8)	464 (29.9)	199 (27.3)	5,215 (66.2)	1,454 (71.4)	457 (55.7)	10,187 (56.5)
Total	5,013 (27.8)	1,554 (8.6)	730 (4.0)	7,874 (43.7)	2,036 (11.3)	821 (4.6)	18,027 (100.0)
Age of Chief Income Producer							
Under 25	379 (7.6)	303 (19.5)	57 (7.8)	831 (10.6)	488 (24.0)	73 (8.9)	2,131 (11.8)
25-44	757 (15.1)	852 (54.9)	512 (70.2)	832 (10.6)	1,154 (56.6)	644 (78.5)	4,750 (26.3)
45-64	1,526 (30.4)	247 (15.8)	152 (20.4)	1,787 (22.7)	322 (15.8)	93 (11.4)	4,125 (22.9)
65 and Over	2,350 (46.8)	152 (9.8)	9 (1.3)	4,425 (56.2)	72 (3.6)	10 (1.3)	7,019 (39.0)
Total	5,013 (27.8)	1,554 (8.6)	730 (4.0)	7,874 (43.7)	2,036 (11.3)	821 (4.6)	18,027 (100.0)
Household Income							
Under $10,000	3,525 (70.3)	303 (19.5)	19 (2.6)	7,853 (99.7)	2,005 (98.5)	769 (93.7)	14,474 (80.3)
$10,000-14,999	1,488 (29.7)	1,251 (80.5)	550 (75.3)	21 (0.3)	31 (1.5)	52 (6.3)	3,392 (18.8)
$15,000-19,999	0 (0)	0 (0)	161 (22.1)	0 (0)	0 (0)	0 (0)	161 (0.9)
$20,000-24,999	0 (0)	0 (0)	0 (0)	0 (0)	0 (0)	0 (0)	0 (0)
Total	5,013 (27.8)	1,554 (8.6)	730 (4.0)	7,874 (43.7)	2,036 (11.3)	821 94.6)	18,027 (100.0

Source: Bureau of Census, U.S. Census of Population and Housing: New Jersey Public Use Sample, 1980.

EXHIBIT 3-42

SOCIOECONOMIC CHARACTERISTICS (LABOR FORCE PARTICIPATION, OCCUPATION, JOURNEY-TO-WORK) OF PROSPECTIVE MOUNT LAUREL-ELIGIBLE HOUSEHOLDS - SOUTH-SOUTHWEST

	MODERATE INCOME (50-80% of Median)			LOW INCOME (Below 50% of Median)			
	1-2 Person	3-4 Person	5 or more Persons	1-2 Person	3-4 Person	5 or More Persons	TOTAL
Labor Force Participation							
At Work	2,303	1,184	597	1,839	966	260	7,149
	(45.9)	(76.2)	(81.8)	(23.4)	(47.4)	(31.6)	(39.7)
With Job	114	28	0	52	31	21	246
Not at Work	(2.3)	(1.8)	(0)	(0.7)	(1.5)	(2.5)	(1.4)
Unemployed	341	123	76	301	229	73	1,143
	(6.8)	(7.9)	(10.4)	(3.8)	(11.2)	(8.9)	(6.3)
Not in Labor Force	2,246	190	57	5,672	800	10	9,421
	(44.8)	(12.2)	(7.8)	(72.1)	(39.3)	(1.3)	(52.3)
Total*	5,013	1,554	730	7,863	2,036	457	18,017
	(27.8)	(8.6)	(4.0)	(43.6)	(11.3)	(55.7)	(100.0)
*Includes Armed Forces	9	28	0	0	10	10	59
	(0.2)	(1.8)	(0.0)	(0.0)	(0.5)	(1.3)	(0.3)
Occupation							
Manager	315	142	19	239	145	10	906
Professional	(10.3)	(10.0)	(2.7)	(7.0)	(9.3)	(1.9)	(8.2)
Technical, Sales,	1,042	379	152	883	395	73	2,923
Supervisor	(30.6)	(26.7)	(21.6)	(26.0)	(25.2)	(13.5)	(26.5)
Service	815	199	152	997	436	145	2,745
	(23.9)	(14.0)	(21.6)	(29.4)	(27.8)	(26.9)	(24.9)
Farming	85	47	9	83	42	31	298
	(2.5)	(3.3)	(1.4)	(2.4)	(2.6)	(5.8)	(2.7)
Precision	398	246	180	426	166	114	1,531
Craftsman	(11.7)	(17.3)	(25.7)	(12.5)	(10.6)	(21.2)	(13.9)
Operatives, Labor	720	407	190	769	384	166	2,636
	(21.1)	(28.7)	(27.0)	(22.6)	(24.5)	(30.8)	(23.9)
Total	3,411	1,421	701	3,397	1,569	540	11,040
	(30.9)	(12.9)	(6.4)	(30.8)	(14.2)	(4.9)	(100.0)
Journey-to-work							
Less than 30 min.	2,085	1,023	493	1,673	852	229	6,353
	(91.6)	(86.4)	(82.5)	(92.0)	(89.1)	(84.6)	(89.5)
30-60 min.	170	152	95	114	63	42	635
	(7.5)	(12.8)	(15.9)	(6.3)	(6.5)	(15.4)	(8.9)
60 min. and Over	18	9	9	31	42	0	111
	(0.8)	(0.8)	(1.6)	(1.7)	(4.4)	(0)	(1.6)
Total	2,274	1,184	597	1,818	956	270	7,099
	(32.0)	(16.7)	(8.4)	(25.6)	(13.5)	(3.8)	(100.0)
Means of Journey-to-work							
Automobile	1,829	995	512	1,371	800	208	5,714
	(79.1)	(82.0)	(85.7)	(74.6)	(81.9)	(76.9)	(79.3)
Public Transit	171	57	28	187	42	21	505
	(7.4)	(4.7)	(4.8)	(10.2)	(4.3)	(7.7)	(7.0)
Other (walk, bike)	313	161	57	280	135	42	988
	(13.5)	(13.3)	(9.5)	(15.3)	(13.8)	(15.4)	(13.7
Total	2,312	1,213	597	1,839	976	270	7,207
	(32.1)	(16.8)	(8.3)	(25.5)	(13.5)	(3.7)	(100.0)
Automobile Available							
None	881	199	95	3,511	561	239	5,486
	(17.6)	(12.8)	(13.0)	(44.6)	(27.6)	(29.1)	(30.4)
1	3,383	995	332	3,719	1,039	457	9,924
	(67.5)	(64.0)	(45.5)	(47.2)	(51.0)	(55.7)	(55.1)
2 or More	749	360	303	644	436	125	2,617
	(14.9)	(23.2)	(41.6)	(8.2)	(21.4)	(15.2)	(14.5)
Total	5,013	1,554	730	7,874	2,036	821	18,027
	(27.8)	(8.6)	(4.0)	(43.7)	(11.3)	(4.6)	(100.0)

Source: Bureau of Census, U.S. Census of Population and Housing: New Jersey Public Use Sample, 1980.

heads between 25 and 44 years of age. In contrast the prospective population has only 30 percent of the household heads within this age range. On the other hand, the present population has but 20 percent of its households in the over 65 age category compared to 36 percent of this elderly cohort in the prospective population.

The comparison of labor force participation will be limited to those not in the labor force. Here we find that the prospective population has twice the propensity to have left the labor force than the present population. This is consistent with the generally younger age structure and larger family orientation found within the currently ill-housed Mount Laurel population and growth in the elderly component of the future population.

While there is a greater degree of labor force participation in the currently ill-housed population, this group of urban households is more dependent on public transit and other means of conveyance than the suburbanizing prospective population where 83 percent of those employed will use a private auto for their journey-to-work. This finding is consistent with the data on autos available to the household where close to 50 percent of the ill-housed population have no auto; while, only one-half this percentage of the prospective population is without an auto.

Contrasts at the Region Level

It has been noted that the prospective Mount Laurel population will be for the most part, 1 and 2 person households. Barring other unanticipated changes, four of the six regions will find a shift out of low income households to moderate income households paralleling the slight shift from larger families in the present population to smaller, higher-income (relative to family size) families in the prospective population. These regions are the Northwest, East Central, Southwest and South-Southwest. Only in the Northeast is there projected to be a marked percentage increase in low income 1 and 2 person households in the prospective population over that in the currently ill-housed population.

We have seen that the ethnicity of the prospective population will be more often white. This racial distribution is reflected across all six regions; however, two regions gain more significantly than others in their relative concentration of white Mount Laurel households over black and Spanish groups; these regions are the Southwest and the South-Southwest. In the former, the white concentration in the present population was 49 percent; whereas, in the prospective population it will be 76 percent. A somewhat smaller growth in white household concentration occurs within the South-Southwest Region.

The relatively high proportion of older households noted in the statewide average is found to occur across all of the regions. Here, however, the percent difference in Mount Laurel households in the oldest age bracket is highest in the East Central Region 4, with the Northeast Region 1, being a close second.

Between these extreme age cohorts the young families in the age range 25 to 44 are dropping across all of the regions. However, two regions show extremely large percentage drops across all age categories of the two Mount Laurel income populations. The Northeast Region leads the projection decline of these households with a drop of 12 percentage points; the East Central Region follows close behind with a 10 point drop. Finally, the age cohort 45 to 64 shows a remarkable stability across all regions remaining practically consistent in percentage terms for both Mount Laurel populations. The latter reflects the last surge of the baby boom into the latter stages of middle age.

Recapitulation

The purpose of this chapter has been to examine the social and economic characteristics of the Mount Laurel eligible household. The Mount Laurel decision requires that municipalities consider the housing needs of two classes of households with income levels scaled by the size of the household. Each of these partitions has been found to produce distinctive subpopulations both currently and in the future. Perhaps the most significant difference in the time perspective is a relative difference of 10 percent in the number of households of low income in the present, ill-housed Mount Laurel category versus the prospective, purely income-constrained category. Crosscutting this change is the marked growth in older 1 and 2 person households in the prospective over the present Mount Laurel population. Finally, the spatial distribution of the two Mount Laurel categories: present and prospective, shows a remarkable disparity; one, however, that complements the social and economic differences noted above. The currently ill-housed or "existing" Mount Laurel population is for the most part residing in the Northeast and Northwest Regions 1 and 2. The prospective population is projected to reside for the most part in the East Central and the Southwest Regions 3 and 5 with the former composed primarily of retired white households while the latter exhibits a somewhat stronger minority concentration. The matching of these households with housing supply is the subject of the next two chapters.

NOTES

1. Connie O. Hughes, "New Jersey: The First Metropolitan State," New Jersey Economic Indicators (No. 229, August 5, 1983, New Jersey Department of Labor, Division of Planning and Research, Trenton, New Jersey), pp. 10-12.

2. Beth B. Hess, "New Faces of Poverty," American Demographics, Vol. 5, No. 5 (May 1983), pp. 26-31.

3. Cheryl Russell, "The News About Hispanics," American Demographics, Vol. 5, No. 3 (March 1983), p. 15-25.

4. Daphne Spain & Suzanne M. Bianchi, "How Women Have Changed," American Demographics, Vol.5, No. 5 (May 1983), pp. 18-25.

5. Jane Newitt, "A Nation of Elders Revisited," American Demographics, Vol. 5, No.4 (April 1983), pp. 32-36.

6. State of New Jersey, Department of Labor, Division of Planning and Research, Office of Demographic and Economic Analysis, New Jersey, 1980 Census of Population and Housing, Municipal Profiles, Vol. II: Characteristics of Households and Families (Trenton, NJ, January 1982).

7. Arthur F. Young and F. John Devaney, "What the 1980 Census Shows About Housing," American Demographics, Vol. 5, No. 1 (January 1983), pp. 16-25.

8. Courtenay Slater, "Favorable Demographics," American Demographics, Vol. 5, No. 1 (January 1983), pp. 38-41.

9. Connie O. Hughes, "New Jersey," American Demographics, Vol. 5, No. 6 (June 1983) pp. 42-45.

10. Scott Campbell Brown, "New Jersey Population Projections," New Jersey Economic Indicators (No. 229, August 5, 1983, New Jersey Department of Labor, Division of Planning and Research, Trenton, New Jersey), pp. 6-9.

11. Gregory Spencer and John F. Long. "The New Census Bureau Projections," American Demographics, Vol.5, No. 4 (April 1983), pp. 24-31.

12. Thomas M. Sheppard, Jr., "Occupational Outlook for New Jersey," New Jersey Economic Indicators (No. 229, August 5, 1983, New Jersey Department of Labor, Division of Planning and Research, Trenton, New Jersey), pp. 13-15.

13. Carol Boyd Leon, "Occupation Winners and Losers," American Demographics, Vol. 5, No. 3 (March 1983), pp. 28-35.

14. Graham B. Spanier, "Living Together in the Eighties," American Demographics, Vol. 4, No. 10 (November 1983), pp. 16-19.

CHAPTER 4—
PRESENT AND PROSPECTIVE MOUNT LAUREL HOUSING SUPPLY

INTRODUCTION

The preceding discussion of housing demand presents a measure of need represented by existing and prospective Mount Laurel-eligible households. How well is that need likely to be met given existing and projected dimensions of New Jersey housing supply? This chapter presents baseline data needed to begin to answer that question.

First, what are the characteristics of New Jersey's current (1980) housing stock? This discussion describes the existing supply in terms of gross magnitude, housing type, tenure (own versus rent), and value/rent levels.

Second, what have been recent trends in housing supply? Net change in the housing stock is a complex composite reflecting additions to the stock through new construction and conversion of units from single-family to multifamily or from non-residential to residential. Also reflected in net change, however, are losses from the housing inventory through demolition, condemnation, fire or other disaster, and conversion to non-residential. Data on these components of change in the housing stock are presented to provide a picture over time of recent housing supply trends in the state and to provide a basis for future supply projections.

Third, what are projections for New Jersey housing supply for the 1980-1990 and 1990-2000 decades? Information from the preceding two sections -- on the existing stock and recent trends in housing supply -- together with available data on national housing supply projections, are used to develop projections of net change in New Jersey housing supply over the next twenty years.

Fourth, what proportion of projected growth in housing supply will be affordable by Mount Laurel-eligible households? It is widely assumed that the existing delivery system is unable to provide affordable housing. How accurate is this assumption?

Analysis of housing supply trends is a critical component in responding to the challenge of Mount Laurel. A widespread assumption in public debate appears to be that the totality of Mount Laurel housing need requires new construction in a price range and housing type configuration not currently being provided in New Jersey. To what extent is the current housing delivery process providing housing for Mount Laurel-eligible households within normal market channels, i.e., in the absence of intervention? The answer to this question can only be obtained by looking at the numbers on the existing housing stock and recent construction trends.

Within this analysis, we focus on the key components of the housing inventory.[1] The tenure distinction presents a separate discussion for owner-occupied and renter-occupied housing units. Each of these components represents special considerations in meeting low-income housing needs. Down payment and financing requirements are likely to limit the ability of the owner-occupied sector to meet such needs, while various limitations on market return are likely to constrain construction within the rental sector. Secondly, housing type configuration (e.g., single-family versus multifamily) presents an additional significant distinction within the overall discussion of housing supply, encompassing important variations in costs, density, and amenability to intervention. Finally, the discussion throughout is disaggregated by region to capture the significant geographic variation in housing market dynamics in New Jersey.

In sum, these data provide a baseline view of existing and projected housing inventories from which housing for Mount Laurel-eligible households can potentially be drawn. It must be stressed that this discussion addresses housing supply and changes in the inventory in the absence of any Mount Laurel-mandated intervention. This represents the status quo: the ability of current and projected inventories to house the Mount Laurel-eligible population. Chapter 5 uses the information from this analysis to actually match existing and projected housing supply to existing and projected Mount Laurel need, and to estimate the resulting gap. Chapter 6 then addresses the range of possible bridge mechanisms that might be applied in the effort to close the gap between Mount Laurel need and pre-intervention supply.

THE NEW JERSEY EXISTING HOUSING STOCK

The existing housing stock in 1980 numbered some 2.7 million housing units, but within this total was a complex pattern of housing types and regional variations (Exhibit 4-1). Reflecting high population densities, the largest number of housing units in absolute terms are located in the Northeast Region (684,200 units) and Northwest Region (675,500 units). The smallest housing stock in absolute number of units is in the South-Southwest Region (191,600 units). This implies that just over half (51 percent) of New Jersey's 1980 housing inventory (in number of units) was located in the Northeast and Northwest Regions.

EXHIBIT 4-1

THE 1980 NEW JERSEY HOUSING STOCK, BY TENURE, TYPE, AND REGION
(Number of units in thousands)

Region	Single Family Detached #	%	Single Family Attached #	%	2-4 Family #	%	Multi-Family #	%	Total Units #	%
					TOTAL HOUSING UNITS					
1.Northeast	260.8	38.1	12.5	1.8	224.3	32.8	186.7	27.3	684.2	100.0
2.Northwest	330.7	49.0	9.9	1.5	165.6	24.5	169.2	25.1	675.5	100.0
3.West Central	215.4	64.9	12.0	3.6	50.7	15.3	53.7	16.2	331.8	100.0
4.East Central	225.3	71.3	16.7	5.3	29.3	9.3	44.5	14.1	315.7	100.0
5.Southwest	276.2	58.9	71.7	15.3	42.7	9.1	78.7	16.8	469.2	100.0
6.So.Southwest	122.7	64.1	11.5	6.0	27.9	14.6	29.4	15.4	191.6	100.0
State Total	1,431.1	53.6	134.3	5.0	540.5	20.3	562.2	21.1	2,668.0	100.0
					OWNER-OCCUPIED UNITS					
1.Northeast	243.1	71.8	9.0	2.6	77.1	22.8	9.5	2.8	338.7	100.0
2.Northwest	303.8	84.0	5.3	1.5	46.9	13.0	5.6	1.5	361.6	100.0
3.West Central	197.4	89.2	8.4	3.8	13.5	6.1	2.0	0.9	221.3	100.0
4.East Central	191.5	87.2	12.6	5.8	10.0	4.5	5.5	2.5	219.6	100.0
5.Southwest	251.5	80.9	45.8	14.7	9.0	2.9	4.7	1.5	310.9	100.0
6.So.Southwest	96.9	87.6	4.6	4.2	6.9	6.3	2.2	2.0	110.7	100.0
State Total	1,284.2	82.2	85.8	5.5	163.4	10.5	29.4	1.9	1,562.8	100.0
					RENTER-OCCUPIED UNITS					
1.Northeast	14.3	4.5	3.1	1.0	138.2	43.0	165.9	51.6	321.5	100.0
2.Northwest	18.8	6.6	4.0	1.4	110.2	38.7	151.7	53.3	284.7	100.0
3.West Central	13.4	13.6	2.7	2.7	34.6	35.2	47.8	48.5	98.4	100.0
4.East Central	19.3	26.3	3.1	4.2	16.3	22.2	34.7	47.3	73.4	100.0
5.Southwest	17.0	12.8	19.8	14.9	29.9	22.5	65.9	49.7	132.5	100.0
6.So.Southwest	12.9	23.6	5.5	10.1	16.0	29.2	20.3	37.1	54.7	100.0
State Total	95.7	9.9	38.1	3.9	345.1	35.8	486.2	50.4	965.1	100.0

Notes: Excludes mobile homes (0.83 percent of total units in 1980), but see text. Owner-occupied and renter-occupied units do not add to total units because of vacancies. Data are for year-round units and exclude seasonal or migratory units.

Source: U.S. Census, 1980 Census of Population and Housing, Advance Estimates of Social, Economic, and Housing Characteristics, PHC80-S2-32 (March 1983).

Housing Type

Just over half (53.6 percent) of the statewide extant inventory at the beginning of the 1980s consisted of single-family detached housing units, but this proportion varied widely among regions. Again reflecting population densities, single-family detached units account for only 38.1 percent of the inventory in the Northeast Region 1 and 49 percent in the Northwest Region 2. In contrast, such units comprise nearly three-fourths (71.3 percent) of total supply in the East Central Region, and intermediate proportions in the remaining regions.

Exactly the mirror image obtains in the pattern of 2-4 family and multifamily units. The former (2-4 family units) comprise nearly a third (32.8 percent) of all units in the Northeast and a fourth (24.5 percent) of units in the Northwest Region, but only 10 to 15 percent of units elsewhere. Similarly, housing units in multifamily structures (structures with five or more units) make up a fourth of all units in the Northeast and Northwest but only some 15 percent in the remaining regions.

Single-family attached, or townhouse, units comprise a significant share of the extant 1980 inventory in only the West Central Region 5, where the 71,700 units in this category account for 15.3 percent of the total inventory -- compared to only 5 percent statewide. Most of this townhouse stock is concentrated in Camden (33,871 units) and Mercer (22,645) Counties, although Burlington County accounts for an additional 12,518 townhouse units, and Ocean County (in the East Central Region) contains 11,450 such units; the remaining areas of the state contain relatively few townhouse units.

Not reflected in the data on housing type distributions in Exhibit 4-1 is information on mobile homes. U.S. Census data for 1980 show a total of 22,372 mobile homes in New Jersey, comprising less than one percent (0.83) of the total statewide housing inventory. As with the other housing types, the regional distribution of mobile homes reflects substantial disparity, ranging from a low of 1,116 mobile home units in Northwestern Region 2 to a high of 6,172 in South-Southwest Region 6. Mobile homes as a proportion of total regional housing inventories are as follows:

Northeast Region 1	- 0.24 percent
Northwest Region 2	- 0.17 percent
West Central Region 3	- 0.72 percent
East Central Region 4	- 1.81 percent
Southwest Region 5	- 1.10 percent
South-Southwest Region 6	- 3.12 percent

Housing Tenure

Nearly 62 percent of the 1980 occupied conventional housing stock (i.e., excluding mobile homes) in the state is owner-occupied, comprising

1.56 million units; the remaining 965,000 units (38 percent) are renter-occupied. The distribution of housing tenure closely mirrors the distribution of housing types in the state. The highest proportions of owner-occupancy are in the East Central Region (74.9 percent), Southwest Region (70.1 percent), and West Central Region (69.2 percent); renter-occupied units total 48.7 percent and 44.1 percent of occupied units in the Northeast and Northwest Regions, respectively.

As would be expected, 1.28 million of total owner-occupied units, or 82.2 percent, are single-family detached units. The remaining owner-occupied units, totalling some 278,000 units, are largely condominium units in either townhouse, 2-4 family, or multifamily configurations. Reflecting the data for total townhouse units, the largest share of owner-occupied townhouses is in Southwest Region 5, where such units comprise 14.7 percent of the owner-occupied stock.

The renter-occupied inventory encompasses a broader diversity of housing types. While the bulk of such units are in multifamily (five or more unit) structures, this structure configuration accounts for only 50.4 percent of rental units statewide. Units in 2-4 family structures comprise more than a third (35.8 percent) of total renter-occupied units, while single-family units (attached and detached) make up 13.8 percent, underlining the importance of relatively low-density rental housing in the state.

Rental units in the 2-4 family structure configuration comprise fully 43 percent of rental units in the Northeast Region 1 and 38.7 percent of rentals in the Northwest Region 2. Conversely, single-family detached homes accommodate 26.3 percent of renter households in the East Central Region 4 and 23.6 percent of renters in South-Southwest Region 6.

In sum, the existing housing inventory described in terms of housing type and tenure conforms to the broad outlines of population distributions and density within the state. Owner-occupied single-family units predominate, accounting for just under half (48.1 percent) of the state's 1980 total housing inventory. This predominance is particularly accentuated in the low density and developing southern portions of the state (Regions 4, 5, and 6), while it is tempered substantially in the urbanized, highly populated northern areas (Regions 1 and 2) where rental units and multifamily structures are far more in evidence.

Housing Value

The median value of single-family housing units varied widely by region in 1980 (Exhibit 4-2). This was true for both traditional single-family detached units as well as the attached townhouse configuration. For the former, median housing value ranged from a high of $72,759 in Northeast Region 1 (Bergen, Hudson, and Passaic Counties) to a low of $42,857 in South-Southwest Region 6 (Atlantic, Cape May, Cumberland, Salem), a spread of

EXHIBIT 4-2

HOUSING VALUE OF OWNER-OCCUPIED UNITS, BY HOUSING TYPE, 1980
(Percents)

	North-east Region (1)	North-west Region (2)	West Central Region (3)	East Central Region (4)	South-west Region (5)	South Southwest Region (6)	State Total
SINGLE-FAMILY DETACHED							
Less than $25,000	1.5	2.5	1.8	4.8	6.6	16.8	4.4
$25-34,999	2.8	4.7	4.8	9.3	13.3	18.2	7.7
$35-44,999	5.4	9.0	9.7	16.7	22.6	18.2	12.9
$45-59,999	17.8	18.7	24.2	25.0	26.1	17.8	21.7
$60-74,999	25.8	20.3	23.6	17.5	14.3	11.1	19.6
$75-99,999	25.7	23.0	20.5	15.3	10.7	9.5	18.6
$100,000+	20.8	21.8	15.4	11.4	6.4	8.4	15.1
Total	100.0	100.0	100.0	100.0	100.0	100.0	100.0
Number of Units	229,180	288,280	183,480	184,160	237,060	87,840	1,210,000
Median Value	$72,759	$71,772	$66,408	$56,525	$48,132	$42,857	
SINGLE-FAMILY ATTACHED							
Less than $25,000	23.5	21.4	11.3	11.8	54.2	50.7	38.7
$25-34,999	16.4	19.0	15.4	26.7	20.9	11.0	20.1
$35-44,999	19.0	18.5	15.6	27.1	12.3	12.4	15.8
$45-59,999	18.7	11.7	16.9	17.1	6.4	9.6	10.7
$60-74,999	8.8	7.3	22.6	10.8	4.5	7.2	7.9
$75-99,999	5.9	11.7	12.8	4.9	1.1	4.8	4.1
$100,000+	7.8	10.5	5.4	1.5	0.6	4.3	2.7
Total	100.0	100.0	100.0	100.0	100.0	100.0	100.0
Number of Units	8,440	4,960	7,800	11,820	44,500	4,180	81,700
Median Value	$41,648	$38,250	$52,361	$38,283	$23,154	$24,625	

Notes: Housing value data are available only for owner-occupied condominiums and one-family houses on less than 10 acres and with no business on the property. Value is the owner's estimate of the current (1980) dollar worth of the house and land, or the asking price of units vacant-for-sale.

Source: U.S. Census, 1980 Census Public Use File.

nearly 60 percent. Median housing values in the remaining regions reflect a relatively continuous north-south gradient, with values diminishing uniformly with travel from north to south.[2]

The data on housing value take on added meaning in light of regional differences in median family income. While both median house values and median incomes are higher in the north than in the southern part of the state, the value-income spread is greater in the north than in the south, i.e., higher housing value is not adequately compensated for by higher income in these areas. For instance, 1980 median family income in the Northeast Region (Bergen, Hudson, and Passaic Counties) was $23,078. A Northeast Region household with the median family income ($23,078) occupying a median value single-family detached house ($72,759) was supporting a 3.15 value/income ratio. In contrast, a household with the 1980 median family income for the Southwest Region 5 ($22,178) occupying a median-priced house ($48,132) supported a 2.17 value/income ratio. Corresponding value/income ratios taken at the 1980 median in the remaining regions were: Northwest, 3.03; West Central, 2.55; East Central, 2.56; and South-Southwest, 2.31.

The 1980 median value for single-family attached (townhouse or rowhouse) units was significantly below that of traditional detached units, yet still reflected a substantial regional variation. (Recall that once again, this does not take into account differences in unit condition, size, age, etc.) The median value for single-family attached units was highest ($52,361) in West Central Region 3, where this is a relatively newer form of housing, and ranged down to a low of $23,154 in Southwest Region 5, where the townhouse configuration has a relatively long history. (Note that the latter was the region with the highest frequency of such units.) Value-income ratios are far more manageable in this segment of the housing stock, more a reflection of lower median value levels than higher resident income levels. Once again, taken at the 1980 medians, value/income ratios for single-family attached units ranged from a high of 2.01 in the West Central Region to a low of 1.04 in the Southwest Region.

Given the above median value levels, the availability of affordable low-cost owner-occupied housing within the extant stock is extremely limited. As indicated in Chapter 3, some 70 percent of the existing Mount Laurel eligible population have household incomes below $10,000. Using this $10,000 income level as a highly liberal estimate of Mount Laurel household income, and applying a 2.5 value/income ratio, yields a generalized affordability threshold of $25,000.[3] (This is a liberal estimate since recall that approximately 70 percent of Mount Laurel existing households had 1980 incomes below $10,000; only 6.4 percent of Mount Laurel existing households resided in owner-occupied units valued above $25,000 in 1980.)

As indicated in Exhibit 4-2, only 4.4 percent of the existing single-family detached housing stock was valued at $25,000 or less in 1980 -- without considering size, age, or condition of the units. The proportion of units valued at $25,000 or less is less than 2 percent in the Northeast

Region and West Central Region and is just 2.5 percent in the Northwest Region. Only the South-Southwest Region exhibits a significant share of units (16.8 percent) valued at $25,000 or less, but note that this represents a share of the smallest regional stock of units in absolute numbers. Interestingly, the share of units valued at $100,000 or more is greater -- by a substantial margin -- than the proportion below $25,000 in all Northern and Central Regions (1 through 4), is about equal in the Southwest Region, and is exceeded only in the South-Southwest.

Applying this same affordability measure to the single-family attached rowhouse or townhouse inventory in the state yields a far better picture, though of course this represents a much smaller pool of units in absolute terms. Statewide, 38.7 percent of units in this configuration are valued below $25,000. This is nearly eight times the level of single-family detached housing and suggests the potential of this segment of the inventory to provide affordable housing for Mount Laurel-eligible households. Regional variation is also apparent, ranging from only 11-12 percent of single-family attached units valued at less than $25,000 in the East and West Central Regions to just over half in the Southwest and South-Southwest Regions.

The overall picture displayed by 1980 housing value data for the extant stock of owner-occupied units is one of quite limited potential for affordability by Mount Laurel-eligible households. Even if units valued up to $35,000 are included in calculations (a more generous extension of the income multiplier), it seems evident that only a small share of such households can find shelter in owner-occupied single-family units, whether detached or attached -- once again leaving aside questions of housing unit condition. The current inventory of owner-occupied units is priced largely beyond the reach of most Mount Laurel households. Indeed, as indicated previously in Chapter 3, only 23 percent of existing Mount Laurel households reside in owner-occupied units, and the majority of these are in the moderate income category or are 1-2 person elderly households.

Gross Rent Level

Gross rents in the 1980 renter-occupied inventory varied widely by type of housing, and by region within housing types (Exhibit 4-3).[4] Median gross rent is generally highest for rented single-family units, and for rental units in the high-cost regions of the state, specifically the Northeast and Northwest Regions. The disparity in median rents is also greatest across housing types in the high-cost regions, while rent levels are far more homogeneous in the lower-rent areas of the state. In the Northeast Region, for instance, median gross rent ranges from $423 in single-family detached units to $239 in multifamily units, nearly a $200 spread. In the South-Southwest Region, in contrast, median gross rent ranges from $285 in single-family detached units to $226 in townhouse/rowhouse units, a spread of only $59. The greater homogeneity of rent levels across housing types in the Southern Regions (4, 5, and 6) as com-

EXHIBIT 4-3

GROSS RENT OF RENTER-OCCUPIED UNITS,
BY HOUSING TYPE AND REGION, 1980
(Percents)

	North-east Region (1)	North-west Region (2)	West Central Region (3)	East Central Region (4)	South-west Region (5)	South-Southwest Region (6)	State Total
	SINGLE-FAMILY DETACHED						
Less than $100	0.2	0.6	0.7	0.8	1.5	2.3	1.0
$100-199	6.0	4.8	5.8	10.3	8.3	15.1	8.3
$200-299	18.4	18.7	20.2	21.8	30.5	38.8	24.3
$300-399	22.1	24.1	26.2	34.2	26.3	27.4	27.1
$400-499	16.1	20.8	22.7	21.0	15.3	10.3	18.0
$500+	37.3	31.0	24.4	11.9	18.0	6.2	21.3
Total	100.0	100.0	100.0	100.0	100.0	100.0	100.0
Number of Units	10,680	13,720	8,620	15,020	12,000	9,700	69,740
Median Rent	$423	$408	$384	$347	$325	$285	
	SINGLE-FAMILY ATTACHED						
Less than $100	4.4	1.8	8.8	5.9	5.5	15.4	6.7
$100-199	8.9	15.0	10.8	12.6	16.7	22.8	16.0
$200-299	31.9	24.0	20.6	25.2	39.4	35.1	34.0
$300-399	26.7	31.7	31.4	25.2	25.5	18.9	25.7
$400-499	17.8	15.0	14.7	17.6	8.6	6.1	10.9
$500+	10.4	12.6	13.7	13.4	4.2	1.8	6.7
Total	100.0	100.0	100.0	100.0	100.0	100.0	100.0
Number of Units	2,700	3,340	2,040	2,380	15,540	4,560	30,560
Median Rent	$312	$345	$323	$325	$265	$226	
	2-4 FAMILY UNITS						
Less than $100	0.8	0.7	0.9	0.8	1.5	2.6	0.9
$100-199	17.0	14.5	11.3	12.9	24.3	23.1	16.3
$200-299	45.1	47.9	39.5	52.5	51.2	40.2	46.1
$300-399	27.7	27.9	33.9	24.2	18.5	24.5	27.3
$400-499	7.0	6.8	11.0	7.3	3.4	6.1	7.0
$500+	2.4	2.2	3.4	2.3	1.1	3.6	2.4
Total	100.0	100.0	100.0	100.0	100.0	100.0	100.0
Number of Units	132,100	105,420	32,440	15,800	27,860	14,640	328,260
Median Rent	$270	$272	$296	$272	$238	$248	
	5+ FAMILY UNITS						
Less than $100	7.5	10.6	4.0	6.6	6.8	13.8	8.2
$100-199	23.7	17.9	7.0	11.0	11.4	21.0	17.6
$200-299	39.4	39.4	33.8	44.9	50.0	40.1	40.7
$300-399	18.9	24.3	43.3	29.9	26.7	18.7	24.8
$400-499	6.1	5.6	9.6	5.8	4.1	3.9	5.9
$500+	4.5	2.1	2.4	1.9	1.1	2.5	2.8
Total	100.0	100.0	100.0	100.0	100.0	100.0	100.0
Number of Units	161,420	147,660	46,200	33,260	63,980	20,340	472,860
Median Rent	$239	$254	$307	$277	$262	$236	

Note: Gross rent represents contract rent plus the estimated average monthly cost of utilities and fuel.

Source: U.S. Bureau of the Census, 1980 Census Public Use File.

pared to those of the North (Regions 1 and 2) reflects the narrower range of housing size and characteristics in the former areas and the relatively constrained rent-paying ability of residents in those areas.

By far the greatest numerical share of rental units are in multifamily structures (structures with five or more units). Median gross rents in such units in 1980 ranged from $236 in the South-Southwest to $307 in the West Central Region. (Recall once again that these medians are calculated for all rental units without regard to size or condition). If we once again apply a $10,000 median 1980 household income cutoff as indicative of Mount Laurel households, and assume 25 percent of gross income for rent as a desirable goal, this yields a $200 per month maximum rent-paying ability.[5]

On a statewide basis, some 25 percent of rental units in multifamily structures (5 or more units) had 1980 gross rents below $200. The proportion of multifamily rental units below $200 ranged from 34.8 percent in the South-Southwest Region to just 11 percent in the West Central Region. <u>These data suggest that the state's inventory of rental units with 1980 gross rents under $200 appears to be the primary source of affordable housing currently available to the existing Mount Laurel population.</u> While some 60 percent of Mount Laurel existing households in rental units actually paid more than $200 in rent in 1980, this was at a cost of rent/income ratios approaching the 50 percent level and higher. (Some of this may have been buffered by welfare support.)

RECENT CONSTRUCTION TRENDS

Having considered the basic outlines of the standing housing inventory in the state as of 1980, we turn next to a look at recent trends in housing construction in New Jersey. New construction represents the largest component of change in the housing inventory, and is clearly a crucial factor in meeting future housing needs. This section addresses recent trends in residential construction, in terms of both magnitude and housing type characteristics. The discussion in the subsequent section will incorporate data on demolitions and conversions to arrive at estimates of net change in the housing inventory.

Magnitude

Housing start trends historically reveal an abrupt pattern of fluctuation over time, both nationally and for the state and its regions. At the national level, the peak years for housing starts, when production hovered at the 2.0 million plus annual mark in the early 1970s, will probably not soon be repeated, and contrast sharply with the steep decline in starts recorded during the 1974-75 recession. Similarly, the recovery achieved by the end of the 1970s only preceded the drastic slump in new housing construction suffered in 1980-81, when starts reached the lowest level in decades. The impact of high inflation and high interest rates effectively cut the bottom out of the housing construction industry during this period, with national housing starts in 1980-81 barely reaching the 1.0 million annual level. According to the National Association of Home Builders, national housing starts are expected to be up slightly in 1983-84 over the 1980-81 level, to approximately 1.6 - 1.7 million units annually, but then should dip back again in 1985-86 to the 1.3 million annual level as a result of continuing large budget deficits, uncertain financial markets, and demographic tendencies slowing the rate of new household formation.

The data for residential construction in New Jersey since 1970 precisely mirror these national trendlines (Exhibit 4-4). The three-year period from 1971 to 1973 was a peak period for housing activity in the state, with total permits issued reaching 65,539 in 1972. (Though not coterminous, for the sake of simplicity, housing permits and starts are used here interchangeably.)[6] The 1974-75 national recession was clearly felt in New Jersey, as housing starts fell precipitously to the 25,000 annual level. A moderate recovery in 1977-79 pushed total housing starts in the state to the 35-40,000 annual mark, but the boom years of the beginning of the decade were clearly not to be repeated. The real crunch came with the 1980s, when annual starts reached the lowest mark since complete recordkeeping began in the state in 1960. The record low of 1980 was only to be broken in 1981 and again in 1982, when construction permits issued totalled only 21,404 annually -- one-third the peak level of 1972. Reflecting national trends, the early months of 1983 (not shown in Exhibit 4-4) reveal a slight upswing in permits issued, reflecting the recent drop in interest rates and relatively mild winter weather. Permits issued in the first four months of 1983 totalled 7,525, up noticeably from the total of 4,357 for the same period in 1982, but not yet at the pre-recession level of 8,215 recorded in 1979. And the summer months of 1983 have continued at a strong pace. These early data provide some support for the NAHB's projection of a strong upswing in starts nationally in 1983-84.

Despite these substantial fluctuations in the total magnitude of residential construction in the state, the distribution of housing starts across regions has remained fairly stable throughout the entire 1970-1982 period (Exhibit 4-4). The East Central and Southwest Regions together accounted for 40 to 50 percent of total statewide housing starts for every year from 1970 to 1980. Only in 1981 and 1982 did the share of total starts captured by these two regions fall to about 35 percent, as the West Central Region (Hunterdon, Middlesex, Somerset, and Warren Counties) increased its share to about 20 percent, thereby vindicating its claim to be "New Jersey's Sunbelt."

Characteristics of New Construction

Within these parameters of magnitude, the characteristics of new construction have shifted in subtle ways over the decade of the 1970s and into the 1980s. Statewide, the most notable shift over time has been a steady

EXHIBIT 4-4

RESIDENTIAL CONSTRUCTION AUTHORIZED BY BUILDING PERMITS, BY REGION, TOTAL HOUSING UNITS, 1970-1982

Region	1970	1971	1972	1973	1974	1975	1976	1977	1978	1979	1980	1981	1982
						NUMBER OF UNITS							
Northeast	5,720	5,631	8,079	7,028	4,866	2,977	4,079	3,713	4,326	3,534	3,159	2,802	2,700
Northwest	6,101	8,300	8,739	6,699	4,618	3,607	4,950	6,628	6,492	4,618	3,687	2,736	2,936
West Central	3,659	5,566	9,482	5,582	3,185	3,721	6,896	5,917	6,229	7,415	2,967	4,319	5,139
East Central	9,014	14,932	16,996	2,590	4,143	4,206	6,859	7,967	8,745	8,135	5,308	4,741	4,742
Southwest	10,054	15,923	14,887	13,664	5,805	5,971	6,559	7,697	9,481	8,005	3,889	2,615	3,536
South-Southwest	5,349	7,688	7,356	6,582	3,261	2,733	3,185	2,965	3,785	3,201	3,247	4,080	2,351
State Total	39,897	58,040	65,539	52,145	25,878	23,215	35,528	34,887	39,058	34,908	22,257	21,293	21,404
						PERCENT DISTRIBUTION							
Northeast	14.3	9.7	12.3	13.5	18.8	12.8	12.5	10.6	11.1	10.1	14.2	13.2	12.6
Northwest	15.3	14.3	13.3	12.8	17.8	15.5	15.2	19.0	16.6	13.2	16.6	12.8	13.7
West Central	9.2	9.6	14.5	10.7	12.3	16.0	21.2	17.0	15.9	21.2	13.3	20.3	24.0
East Central	22.6	25.7	25.9	24.1	16.0	18.1	21.1	22.8	22.4	23.3	23.8	22.3	22.2
Southwest	25.2	27.4	22.7	26.2	22.4	25.7	20.2	22.1	24.3	22.9	17.5	12.3	16.5
South-Southwest	13.4	13.2	11.2	12.6	12.6	11.8	9.8	8.5	9.7	9.2	14.6	19.2	11.0
State Total	100.0	100.0	100.0	100.0	100.0	100.0	100.0	100.0	100.0	100.0	100.0	100.0	100.0

Note: Includes permits for publicly-owned housing units.

Source: N.J. Department of Labor and Industry, New Jersey Residential Building Permits, annual summaries.

increase in single-family homes as a share of total starts, and a consequent decrease in the proportion of multifamily units (Exhibit 4-5). This reflects national trends and may be related to a lack of investor interest in rental housing, reflecting a perception that rent control, rent strikes, and eviction limitations restrict cash flow and owner control. At the beginning of the 1970s, single-family units accounted for just under half of total starts in the state. This proportion increased steadily until 1978, when single-family units comprised 70.8 percent of housing starts statewide, and subsequently fell slightly to the 60 percent level in the early 1980s. In converse fashion, 1970-72 witnessed a major spurt in multifamily unit construction, with such units accounting for 42-46 percent of total starts -- virtually equal to the proportion of single-family starts. Units in the 2-4 family configuration consistently maintained a 6-8 percent share of total starts throughout the period from 1970-1982.

Housing type composition of new construction also varies significantly within regions (Exhibit 4-5). Multifamily construction has clearly been far more prevalent in the Northeast (Bergen, Hudson, and Passaic Counties) and the Northwest (Essex, Morris, Sussex, and Union) than elsewhere in the state. During the peak multifamily construction years in the early 1970s, for instance, such units accounted for upwards of 60 percent of new construction in the Northeast Region, with 2-4 family units adding another 10-15 percent. Single-family units, in contrast, comprised less than 25 percent of starts in the Northeast.

In direct contrast, single-family units account for 60-75 percent of new construction in the West Central Region for almost the entire 1970-82 period, with multifamily units exceeding 40 percent in only four of the thirteen years. Single-family units also dominate new construction in the Southwest Region (Burlington, Camden, Gloucester, and Mercer Counties), comprising 80 percent or more of housing starts in that region in every year from 1975 to 1981. The share of starts in single-family units in the East Central Region (Monmouth and Ocean), was only slightly lower than that in the Southwest Region, and substantially in excess of that found in the high-density urbanized regions in the northern part of the state.

Finally, housing type characteristics of new construction not only vary across regions, but have varied over time <u>within</u> regions as well. Most notable is the fluctuation in multifamily construction indicated above for the state as a whole. In the Northeast Region, for instance, multifamily units were 65 percent of starts in 1972-74 but fell to 35-45 percent in the remainder of the 1970s and into the 1980s. In the East Central Region multifamily starts that comprised an already low 25-30 percent of new construction in 1970-73 fell to a statewide low of 6-8 percent in 1975-78 and reached only 14-17 percent during 1979-82. Similarly, while multifamily units were more than half of total starts in the Southwest (Burlington, Camden, Gloucester, and Mercer) during the first three years of the 1970s, they were only 5-10 percent of new construction in that region during 1979-81.

EXHIBIT 4-5

RESIDENTIAL CONSTRUCTION AUTHORIZED BY BUILDING PERMITS, BY HOUSING TYPE, 1970-1982
(percents)

Housing Type and Region	1970	1971	1972	1973	1974	1975	1976	1977	1978	1979	1980	1981	1982
State Total	100.0	100.0	100.0	100.0	100.0	100.0	100.0	100.0	100.0	100.0	100.0	100.0	100.0
Single Family	49.1	49.0	45.2	53.4	57.9	67.7	63.2	67.9	70.8	65.2	65.9	58.6	60.6
2-4 Family	7.1	6.9	7.7	6.6	6.5	7.4	7.7	6.5	7.1	7.2	8.6	8.3	6.0
Multifamiy	42.1	42.4	46.2	39.1	33.6	23.8	26.6	23.6	19.4	25.3	23.1	30.7	32.4
Public	1.8	1.8	0.9	0.9	2.0	1.1	2.6	2.0	2.7	2.2	2.5	2.5	1.0
Region 1	100.0	100.0	100.0	100.0	100.0	100.0	100.0	100.0	100.0	100.0	100.0	100.0	100.0
Northeast													
Single Family	24.7	32.8	22.1	24.6	20.1	33.8	38.3	36.1	42.0	38.9	42.2	35.3	26.6
2-4 Family	14.9	16.4	12.0	10.4	12.8	15.1	17.8	17.0	17.4	15.2	13.9	12.8	10.3
Multifamily	56.1	45.3	65.8	63.6	65.1	46.1	31.2	44.9	34.6	45.5	39.4	34.0	61.0
Public	4.4	5.5	0.2	1.4	2.1	5.0	12.7	2.1	6.0	0.4	4.5	17.8	2.0
Region 2	100.0	100.0	100.0	100.0	100.0	100.0	100.0	100.0	100.0	100.0	100.0	100.0	100.0
Northwest													
Single Family	50.0	45.2	46.2	54.9	48.7	61.3	59.9	44.8	52.4	55.3	56.4	60.6	60.1
2-4 Family	3.4	4.0	4.2	5.3	5.5	5.0	4.0	4.9	3.4	5.1	4.8	4.1	3.0
Multifamily	46.3	50.5	43.0	39.8	45.8	33.7	36.1	46.3	41.9	36.9	36.0	35.4	35.8
Public	0.3	0.3	6.6	0.0	0.0	0.0	0.0	3.9	2.3	2.8	2.7	0.0	1.1
Region 3	100.0	100.0	100.0	100.0	100.0	100.0	100.0	100.0	100.0	100.0	100.0	100.0	100.0
West Central													
Single Family	74.0	63.5	43.8	62.8	68.8	61.1	51.1	69.5	75.3	54.2	72.8	57.1	63.3
2-4 Family	6.4	8.6	3.7	1.7	3.1	4.6	1.6	2.0	2.1	3.0	4.6	2.2	3.3
Multifamily	19.5	28.0	52.5	30.3	28.1	31.6	43.4	28.5	17.7	42.8	15.7	40.6	30.8
Public	0.0	0.0	0.0	5.2	0.0	2.7	3.9	0.0	4.9	0.0	6.9	0.0	2.6
Region 4	100.0	100.0	100.0	100.0	100.0	100.0	100.0	100.0	100.0	100.0	100.0	100.0	100.0
East Central													
Single Family	61.4	62.5	54.5	61.6	75.2	79.8	73.0	81.7	85.6	75.4	76.8	76.3	80.6
2-4 Family	11.3	9.5	11.7	12.9	8.3	13.1	12.9	7.7	7.5	7.6	6.0	7.0	2.7
Multifamily	26.8	26.6	33.8	25.5	16.6	7.1	14.1	8.4	6.2	14.3	17.1	16.8	16.7
Public	0.5	1.4	0.0	0.0	0.0	0.0	0.0	2.1	0.7	2.8	0.0	0.0	0.0

EXHIBIT 4-5 (continued)

RESIDENTIAL CONSTRUCTION AUTHORIZED BY BUILDING PERMITS, BY HOUSING TYPE, 1970-1982
(percents)

Housing Type and Region	1970	1971	1972	1973	1974	1975	1976	1977	1978	1979	1980	1981	1982
Region 5	100.0	100.0	100.0	100.0	100.0	100.0	100.0	100.0	100.0	100.0	100.0	100.0	100.0
Southwest													
Single Family	47.5	42.3	45.2	58.9	73.6	79.8	79.2	84.2	80.4	82.1	87.0	84.3	70.3
2-4 Family	0.6	1.6	2.5	1.9	1.6	1.4	1.3	1.0	3.7	4.9	5.2	6.2	9.2
Multifamily	51.9	56.1	52.3	39.1	20.7	18.9	18.7	12.1	13.1	9.1	5.3	9.6	20.3
Public	0.0	0.0	0.0	0.0	4.1	0.0	0.8	2.7	2.8	8.9	2.6	0.0	0.2
Region 6	100.0	100.0	100.0	100.0	100.0	100.0	100.0	100.0	100.0	100.0	100.0	100.0	100.0
South-Southwest													
Single Family	39.2	41.9	49.5	47.6	67.3	77.2	72.2	76.6	70.1	65.8	50.2	37.8	44.3
2-4 Family	8.2	7.8	13.3	5.9	8.2	10.6	15.3	16.9	17.2	16.3	19.6	17.3	11.7
Multifamily	45.1	44.0	37.2	45.4	19.3	12.2	12.6	6.5	12.6	14.7	30.2	44.3	44.0
Public	7.6	6.2	0.0	1.1	5.2	0.0	0.0	0.0	0.0	3.2	0.0	0.6	0.0

Source: N.J. Department of Labor and Industry, New Jersey Residential Building Permits, annual summaries.

To summarize recent construction trends in a few words, the 1980s have seen a drastic decline in the magnitude of new housing construction in the state, while a growing share of what little housing has been built has been in single-family units. These trends have been deepened with the concentration of housing starts in the "growth hubs" of the East Central and Southwest Regions, where the lion's share of new construction has been in single-family units.

NET CHANGE IN HOUSING SUPPLY 1960-1980 AND 1980-2000

The new construction trends discussed above represent just one component of net change in the housing inventory. Other sources of additions to the inventory fall under the heading of non-new construction additions, including conversion of a single unit into two or more units and conversion of a non-residential structure into residential units. Offsetting these additions is an array of losses from the housing stock. Included in this category are demolitions, condemnations, units lost through fire, structural damage, or other disaster, and conversions from residential to non-residential use.[7] The importance of these additions and losses relative to new construction is likely to vary over time in response to fluctuating interest rates, changing household size, and similar factors affecting the pattern of housing demand. Indications are that the rate of non-new construction additions has increased in recent years while demolitions have slowed, both in response to rising construction costs and shrinking household size reducing demand for larger units.

While these components of change in the inventory are thus increasingly important in determining overall housing supply, data on losses and on non-new construction additions are extremely unreliable and difficult to come by. Using Annual Housing Survey data collected by the Bureau of the Census, it has been estimated that the "scrappage rate" for housing nationally approaches 1 percent of the extant stock annually.[8] Unfortunately, no such estimate is available for the State of New Jersey or its counties or regions. Permitted demolitions, which average approximately 5,000 units a year statewide, seriously under-estimate total losses through demolition and provide no estimates of units lost through fire, damage, or other disaster. Similarly, comprehensive data on conversions -- whether to or from residential use -- is virtually nonexistent for the state or any of its subdivisions.

To account for these data shortcomings, we have adopted a measure of net additions minus losses as a residual category of change left after accounting for new construction. The Census Bureau provides a count of the housing stock at ten-year intervals, and also yields data on actual new construction during the decade. The net change in total housing units over the decade, minus new construction during the decade, yields a measure of net change in existing units through losses and non-new construction additions. If the net change in existing units is a positive number, additions through conversions, etc., exceeded losses due to demolitions, fires, and the like. If demolitions exceed conversions, the net change in existing units will be negative.

This component of change analysis for the total New Jersey housing inventory, for 1960-1970 and 1970-1980, is summarized in Exhibit 4-6. Beginning with the period 1960-1970, net change in total housing units for the state as a whole equalled 419,542 (on a 1960 base of 1.89 million units). This net change figure represents the difference between total new construction of 505,436 units statewide minus a net loss of 85,894 existing units through an excess of demolitions over conversions.

Similarly, for 1970-1980, net change in total housing units equalled 385,084 (on a 1970 base of 2.31 million units). This net change represents the difference between total new construction of 434,160 units statewide minus a net loss of 49,076 existing units.[9] Comparison of the components of change data for the two decades reveals a significant slowing of both new construction as well as demolitions in 1970-80 as compared to 1960-70. New construction during the 1970s was some 70,000 units less than during the earlier decade. Likewise, the net loss in existing units was some 36,800 units lower during 1970-80 than during the 1960s. These data support our earlier contention regarding the declining importance of new construction and greater survival and reuse of the existing stock during periods of high interest rates and high construction costs.

Components of change in the housing inventory vary significantly across regions (Exhibit 4-6). As we have seen, new construction differs markedly from region to region in both decades. In addition, net change in existing units reflects differing regional dynamics of demolitions and conversions. The Northwest Region (Essex, Morris, Sussex, and Union), for instance, experienced a net loss of 32,365 existing units between 1960 and 1970 reflecting high demolition rates in Essex and Union Counties. In contrast, the central and most southern areas (Regions 3, 4, and 6) experienced relatively low net loss rates in existing units, most likely as losses were nearly completely offset by conversion of seasonal and migratory units as additions to the year-round housing stock. Patterns for the 1970-80 decade are quite similar although, as indicated, both new construction and net change in the existing stock were at a lower level than during the preceding decade. Indeed, the East Central Region (Monmouth and Ocean) experienced a net increase in the existing stock as additions exceeded losses within this component of the inventory.

Projected Net Growth, 1980-2000

The foregoing trends, plus our assessment of both state and national dynamics, provide a baseline for projecting future net change in statewide and regional housing inventories. Actual net change for 1960-1980 (from Exhibit 4-6), as well as projected net change in housing supply for 1980-2000, are summarized in Exhibit 4-7.

EXHIBIT 4-6

COMPONENTS OF CHANGE IN THE HOUSING STOCK, BY REGION, 1960-1970 AND 1970-1980

Region	Total Housing Units 1960	1970	1980	Net Change, 1960 - 1970: Net Loss Existing Units	New Construction	Net Change	Net Change, 1970 - 1980: Net Loss Existing Units	New Construction	Net Change
Northeast	571,685	649,333	685,899	-19,957	97,605	77,648	-23,850	60,416	36,566
Northwest	544,608	623,342	676,576	-32,365	111,099	78,734	-14,651	67,885	53,234
West Central	204,125	276,417	334,228	- 9,012	81,304	72,292	- 4,076	61,887	57,811
East Central	142,052	223,387	321,527	- 1,335	82,670	81,335	2,781	95,359	98,140
Southwest	296,788	378,384	474,437	-17,705	99,301	81,596	- 7,594	103,647	96,053
South-Southwest	126,493	154,430	197,710	- 5,520	33,457	27,937	- 1,686	44,966	43,280
State Total	1,885,751	2,305,293	2,690,377	-85,894	505,436	419,542	-49,076	434,160	385,084

Notes: a) Data for year-round housing units, excluding seasonal or migratory units but including mobile homes.
b) Net loss in existing units represents the difference between losses due to demolitions, fire, etc. and gains due to conversions.
c) New construction includes new mobile home placements.

Source: U.S. Bureau of the Census, U.S. Census of Housing, 1960, Final Report HC(1)-32; Census of Housing, 1970, Detailed Housing Characteristics, Final Report HC(1)-B32; 1980 Census of Population and Housing, Advance Estimates of Social, Economic, and Housing Characteristics, PHC80-S2-32.

EXHIBIT 4-7

NET GROWTH IN TOTAL HOUSING UNITS, 1960-1980, AND PROJECTED GROWTH, 1980-2000, BY REGION

	Actual Net Change				Projected Net Change			
	1960-1970		1970-1980		1980-1990		1990-2000	
Region	Number	Percent	Number	Percent	Number	Percent	Number	Percent
1. Northeast	77,648	13.6	36,566	5.6	46,330	6.7	39,203	5.3
2. Northwest	78,734	14.5	53,234	8.5	54,428	7.9	46,055	6.3
3. W. Central	72,292	35.4	57,811	20.9	48,309	14.4	40,877	10.7
4. E. Central	81,335	57.3	98,140	43.9	70,669	19.7	59,797	13.9
5. Southwest	81,596	27.5	96,053	25.4	72,417	15.2	61,277	11.2
6. South-Southwest	27,937	22.0	43,280	28.0	36,577	15.7	30,950	11.5
State Total	419,542	22.2	385,084	16.7	328,729	11.9	278,159	9.0

Source: Exhibit 4-6 and CUPR projections.

As we have indicated, the rate of growth in the housing supply slowed significantly between 1960-1970 and 1970-1980. Net growth of 419,542 during the 1960s, representing a net growth rate of 22.2 percent, was followed in the 1970s by a net increase of 385,084, for a growth rate of 16.7 percent. Available data for 1980-1990 and 1990-2000 suggest a continuation of this downward spiral in the rate of growth in net housing supply. Among the factors contributing to this assessment are: (1) the dismal record of new construction to date in the first three-and-a-half years of the 1980s; (2) the expectation of continued high interest rates and large budget deficits impacting negatively on housing starts throughout the foreseeable future; (3) continuing declines in the rate of new household formation as the "baby bust" generation enters the housing market.

As a consequence of these factors and our assessment of trends in the state over the preceding twenty years, we have projected a net growth in total housing units for 1980-1990 of approximately 325,000 units, for an 11.9 percent increase, and for 1990-2000 of approximately 275,000, for a 9 percent increase. These projections represent our consensus of a most probable mid-point estimate, recognizing that actual starts realized will be open to the vagaries of both national and international conditions as well as events within the state. Available econometric methods for statistically forecasting housing starts are recognized to be valid only over the extremely short term (i.e., generally up to six months).[10] As a result, our long-term projections should be viewed as estimates to be tested against actual data that become available as the decade progresses.

Projected net growth figures for the respective decades have been allocated to regions and across housing types according to the proportional distribution of new construction at mid-decade of the 1970s, i.e., 1975-1978. The resulting projected pattern of net growth in housing supply by region is summarized in Exhibit 4-8 for 1980-1990 and in Exhibit 4-9 for 1990-2000. Again, these projections do <u>not</u> factor in the impact of Mount Laurel II.

For the 1980-1990 decade, we project that the East Central (Monmouth and Ocean Counties) and Southwest (Burlington, Camden, Gloucester, and Mercer Counties) Regions will continue to account for the largest shares of net growth in the housing inventory, together producing 44 percent of statewide growth in total units. In contrast, the Northeast Region will account for only 14 percent of net growth during the 1980s, and the smallest share (11 percent) will be found in the South-Southwest Region.

The tenure composition of projected net growth during 1980-1990 will also vary substantially by region. Of the total net growth of 46,330 units in the Northeast Region, only 18,358 units (39.6 percent) will be in the owner-occupied inventory, while 25,075 units (54.1 percent) will be renter-occupied. (The remaining 2,897 units will be in the vacant pool.) In sharp contrast, fully 78.5 percent (55,440 units) of projected net growth in the East Central Region will be in owner-occupied units, with only 12.8 percent

EXHIBIT 4-8

PROJECTED NET GROWTH IN HOUSING UNITS, BY TENURE, TYPE, AND REGION
1980-1990

Region	Single Family Detached	Single Family Attached	2-4 Family	Multi-Family	Total Units
	TOTAL HOUSING UNITS				
1.Northeast	11,272	1,472	9,524	24,062	46,330
2.Northwest	28,065	1,702	5,751	18,909	54,428
3.West Central	27,053	5,107	2,945	13,204	48,309
4.East Central	48,676	8,328	3,497	10,168	70,669
5.Southwest	47,664	8,098	2,485	14,171	72,417
6.South/Southwest	23,556	1,610	5,015	6,395	36,577
State Total	186,287	26,317	29,216	86,910	328,729
	OWNER-OCCUPIED UNITS				
1.Northeast	10,628	874	4,417	2,439	18,358
2.Northwest	26,087	920	1,334	828	29,169
3.West Central	25,995	3,957	782	1,242	31,976
4.East Central	43,432	6,855	2,024	3,129	55,440
5.Southwest	45,042	6,441	552	1,518	53,554
6.South/Southwest	18,127	552	506	552	19,738
State Total	169,311	19,599	9,615	9,708	208,235
	RENTER-OCCUPIED UNITS				
1.Northeast	506	552	4,739	19,277	25,075
2.Northwest	736	736	3,911	17,253	22,636
3.West Central	644	828	2,024	11,272	14,769
4.East Central	1,334	1,012	736	5,981	9,064
5.Southwest	1,104	1,288	1,794	11,732	15,919
6.South/Southwest	1,150	506	1,748	3,589	6,993
State Total	5,474	4,922	14,952	69,104	94,456

Note: Projected regional totals are allocated to housing type and tenure categories in proportion to the characteristics of net growth in housing units in base years 1975-78. Owner and renter sub-totals do not add to total units because of vacancies.

Source: U.S. Census, 1980 Census Public Use File.

EXHIBIT 4-9

PROJECTED NET GROWTH IN HOUSING UNITS, BY TENURE, TYPE, AND REGION
1990-2000

Region	Single Family Detached	Single Family Attached	2-4 Family	Multi-Family	Total Units
	TOTAL HOUSING UNITS				
1.Northeast	9,538	1,246	8,059	20,361	39,203
2.Northwest	23,747	1,441	4,867	16,000	46,055
3.West Central	22,891	4,322	2,492	11,173	40,877
4.East Central	41,188	7,047	2,959	8,604	59,797
5.Southwest	40,331	6,852	2,102	11,991	61,277
6.South/Southwest	19,932	1,363	4,244	5,412	30,950
State Total	157,628	22,269	24,722	73,540	278,159
	OWNER-OCCUPIED UNITS				
1.Northeast	8,993	740	3,738	2,063	15,534
2.Northwest	22,073	779	1,129	701	24,682
3.West Central	21,996	3,348	662	1,051	27,057
4.East Central	36,750	5,801	1,713	2,647	46,911
5.Southwest	38,113	5,450	467	1,285	45,315
6.South/Southwest	15,339	467	428	467	16,701
State Total	143,264	16,585	8,137	8,214	176,200
	RENTER-OCCUPIED UNITS				
1.Northeast	428	467	4,010	16,312	21,217
2.Northwest	623	623	3,309	14,599	19,154
3.West Central	545	701	1,713	9,538	12,497
4.East Central	1,129	857	623	5,061	7,670
5.Southwest	934	1,090	1,518	9,927	13,470
6.South/Southwest	973	428	1,479	3,037	5,918
State Total	4,632	4,166	12,652	58,474	79,926

Note: Projected regional totals are allocated to housing type and tenure categories in proportion to the characteristics of net growth in housing units in base years 1975-78. Owner and renter sub-totals do not add to total units because of vacancies.

Source: U.S. Census, 1980 Census Public Use File.

in the rental inventory. To summarize, the largest share of units in the highest-growth areas will be owner-occupied units; statewide, fully 63 percent (208,235 units) of projected net growth during the 1980s will be in the owner-occupied stock.

The patterns of net growth by region, tenure and housing type during 1990-2000 (Exhibit 4-9) will closely parallel trends for 1980-1990 but at a lower level of absolute number of units reflecting the slower net growth rate projected for the 1990s.

A word is in order to clarify the relationship between our projected net growth in housing units and projected household growth discussed in Chapter 2. To back-cast to the decade of the 1970s, the 1970-80 net increase in housing units of 385,000 exceeded the 321,000 increase in households over the decade. The result of housing units increasing faster than households was a loosening of the housing market, and indeed, housing vacancy rates climbed in 1980 as compared to 1970. The percent of ownership units vacant and for sale grew from 0.73 percent in 1970 to 1.39 percent in 1980. Likewise, vacancy in the rental inventory increased from 3.46 percent to 4.86 percent from the beginning to the end of the decade. Our projections for 1980-1990 and 1990-2000 suggest that we can anticipate a reversal of this pattern. For the 1980-90 decade, for example, our projected net increase in housing units of 325,000 is some 15,000 units less than our household growth projection of 340,000. The consequence that we can expect will be a greater retention of and more intensive use of the existing housing stock, and a decrease in the vacancy rate by 1990. This is in line with our expectations regarding change in the components of the housing inventory, i.e., a decrease in demolitions and increased retention of the existing stock.

AFFORDABILITY OF NET GROWTH IN HOUSING SUPPLY

The remaining question in this chapter is to assess the share of projected net growth in the housing inventory that will be affordable by Mount Laurel-eligible households. Given the projected growth rates summarized above for 1980-2000, what proportion of this net growth will be within the rent-paying and home-buying ability of Mount Laurel households? Data responding to this question have been analyzed by tenure and region for the 1980-1990 and 1990-2000 decades.

Identification of affordable units was undertaken through a complex computerized matching of projected net growth in housing supply (from the preceding discussion) with projected net growth in Mount Laurel households (from Chapter 2). This matching routine sequentially assessed each projected housing unit against the characteristics of each projected Mount Laurel household to determine affordability. On the housing unit side, each unit was defined in terms of rent or value, tenure (own or rent), housing type, and unit size (number of rooms). Correspondingly, on the household side, each projected Mount Laurel household was defined in terms of income and family size (number of persons). Housing unit characteristics were projected from the characteristics of new construction during the 1975-1978 period. Household characteristics were projected from the 1980 Census. The computerized matching routine sequentially evaluated each projected unit (in terms of cost, tenure, type, and number of rooms) against the projected Mount Laurel demand (described in terms of income and family size). Housing units were identified through this matching routine as either affordable or not affordable, and affordable units were further disaggregated between low- and moderate-income households. (See Chapter 5 for a discussion of the matching routine.)

The results of this matching routine are summarized in Exhibit 4-10. First, for the 1980-1990 period, for the state as a whole, 1.3 percent of projected growth in owner-occupied units, and 25 percent of growth in renter-occupied units, will be affordable by Mount Laurel households. The proportion of affordable units within the owner inventory ranges from less than one percent in the West Central and Northwest Regions to a high of only 2.0 percent in the East Central Region. Throughout all regions, these numbers indicate that a relatively small share of net growth in owner-occupied units will be affordable by Mount Laurel households. The data show further that virtually all of the owner units defined as affordable can be afforded only by the moderate-income segment. Virtually none of the growth in the owner inventory will be within the range of the low-income population.

A somewhat larger share of the 1980-1990 projected increase in the rental stock will be affordable by the Mount Laurel population -- as we would expect from our earlier discussion of the characteristics of the <u>existing</u> housing stock. This share ranges from a low of 11.3 percent of new rental units in the West Central Region (where rent levels are high) to a high of 29.8 percent in the Northwest Region (where some rental housing is church or union subsidized). It must be noted, however, that in those Regions where the affordable <u>share</u> of rental units is quite high, the <u>absolute number</u> of such units is quite low. In the South-Southwest Region, for instance, although 24.6 percent of new rental units are identified as affordable, this is 24.6 percent of only 6,993 projected units, furnishing just 1,408 affordable units for the Region over the decade. Secondly, it is also apparent that a large majority of affordable rental units are affordable only by moderate-income households, and not by low-income households. Statewide, of the 24.6 percent of projected rental units defined as affordable, 21.1 percent are within the moderate-income category and only 3.5 percent are affordable by low-income Mount Laurel households.

The patterns of affordability for 1990-2000 are almost identical to those for the preceding decade, but at an even lower level of absolute numbers of units.

<u>In sum, the current housing delivery system is projected to supply some housing within the range of affordability of Mount Laurel households. Virtually all of this housing will be within the rental sector, and most will still be beyond the range of the low-income Mount Laurel population.</u>

EXHIBIT 4-10

PROJECTED GROWTH IN HOUSING UNITS AFFORDABLE BY MOUNT LAUREL-ELIGIBLE HOUSEHOLDS, 1980-1990 AND 1990-2000

Tenure and Region	NET GROWTH 1980-1990							NET GROWTH 1990-2000						
	Total Projected Units	Affordable Units						Total Projected Units	Affordable Units					
		Total		Moderate		Low-Income			Total		Moderate		Low-Income	
		Number	Percent	Number	Percent	Number	Percent		Number	Percent	Number	Percent	Number	Percent
Owner-Occupied Units														
Northeast	18,358	162	0.9	142	0.8	20	0.1	15,534	136	0.9	122	0.8	14	0.1
Northwest	29,169	161	0.6	141	0.5	20	0.1	24,682	92	0.4	76	0.3	16	0.1
West Central	31,976	235	0.7	235	0.7	0	0.0	27,057	152	0.6	152	0.6	0	0.0
East Central	55,440	1,089	2.0	1,060	1.9	29	0.1	46,911	856	1.8	831	1.8	25	0.1
Southwest	53,554	708	1.3	682	1.3	26	0.0	45,315	441	1.0	435	1.0	6	0.0
South-Southwest	19,738	346	1.8	346	1.8	0	0.0	16,701	255	1.5	255	1.5	0	0.0
STATE TOTAL	208,235	2,701	1.3	2,606	1.3	95	0.0	176,200	1,932	1.1	1,871	1.1	61	0.0
Renter-Occupied Units														
Northeast	25,075	7,428	29.6	5,745	22.9	1,683	6.7	21,217	5,926	27.9	4,576	21.6	1,350	6.3
Northwest	22,636	6,737	29.8	5,614	24.8	1,123	5.0	19,154	3,829	20.0	2,949	15.4	880	4.6
West Central	14,769	1,674	11.3	1,573	10.7	101	0.6	12,497	1,005	8.0	929	7.4	76	0.6
East Central	9,064	1,418	15.6	1,292	14.3	126	1.3	7,670	1,103	14.4	990	12.9	113	1.5
Southwest	15,919	4,568	28.7	4,283	26.9	285	1.8	13,470	2,689	35.1	2,567	33.5	122	1.6
South-Southwest	6,993	1,408	20.1	1,398	20.0	10	0.1	5,918	1,049	17.7	1,041	17.6	8	0.1
STATE TOTAL	94,456	23,233	24.6	19,905	21.1	3,328	3.5	79,926	15,601	19.5	13,052	16.3	2,549	3.2

Source: Exhibits 4-8 and 4-9 and CUPR projections.

SUMMARY

The preceding discussion has addressed recent and projected trends in housing supply absent any intervention introduced under the Mount Laurel decision. The analysis revealed conditions that to a large degree gave rise to the Mount Laurel suit and the Court's decision. In brief, the rate of growth in housing supply has slowed significantly and will continue to do so. Such housing as is being built is largely in the single-family configuration and most is beyond the reach of affordability of Mount Laurel-eligible households.

We project net housing additions for 1980 to 1990 at a level of approximately 325,000 units, down 15 percent from the previous decade. Net housing additions will fall by another 15 percent during 1990-2000, to a level of 275,000 units. These lowered growth rates will reflect and accentuate current patterns, in which new growth is concentrated in the single-family, owner-occupied portion of the housing inventory.

Within this projected net growth, some one percent of new owner-occupied units, and about 25 percent of new renter-occupied units, will be affordable by Mount Laurel-eligible households. Most of these affordable units, however, are still well beyond the range of the low-income segment of the Mount Laurel population.

These data serve to summarize current and projected characteristics of the New Jersey housing stock. The following chapter addresses the issue of explicitly matching the existing and projected Mount Laurel population to projected housing supply to define the proportion of Mount Laurel households that can be housed within present housing supply parameters. Chapter 6 then examines the range of interventionary mechanisms available in the attempt to bridge the gap.

NOTES

1. American Institute of Planners, Regional Housing Planning: A Technical Guide (Washington, D.C.: AIP), March 1972.

2. It should be noted that the comparison of housing value across regions does not account for differences in unit size, characteristics, age, condition, or land costs. The same caveat applies to the subsequent discussion of gross rent levels.

3. This calculation represents a crude rule-of-thumb estimate of affordability unadjusted for unit and household size, and assuming that household incomes under $10,000 and housing values under $25,000 are similarly distributed. The explicit case-by-case matching of household size and income to housing value and rent is undertaken in the following chapter.

4. Gross rent represents contract rent plus the estimated average monthly cost of utilities and fuel.

5. See footnote 3 above. In the case of rental units, a necessary assumption is that household incomes under $10,000 and gross rents under $200/month are similarly distributed. See Chapter 5 for the explicit matching of income to rent levels to determine the proportion of units actually affordable by Mount Laurel households.

6. It is recognized that building permit data are an imperfect measure of actual residential construction, since they are subject to varying levels of non-reporting and some portion of permitted units never reach construction. Nonetheless, the permit data provide the best available information on relative trendlines in new housing construction, since there are no consistent New Jersey data on starts per se.

7. For an excellent discussion of components of change in the national housing inventory, see William C. Apgar, Jr., The Changing Utilization of the Housing Inventory: Past Trends and Future Prospects, Working Paper No. W83-1, Joint Center for Urban Studies of MIT and Harvard University, July 1983.

8. George Sternlieb, The Maintenance of America's Housing Stock, prepared for the Office of the Secretary, U.S. Department of Housing and Urban Development, Washington, D.C., August 1980.

9. New construction recorded by the 1980 Census for the period 1970-1980 somewhat exceeds the estimate of new construction provided by building permits issued for the same period. This might result from some non-reporting of permit data and/or from incorrect information given to the Census regarding the year in which the householder's structure was built.

10. See, for instance, Barry Falk, "Forecasting Housing Starts Using Multivariate Time Series Methods," Housing Finance Review, Vol. 2 (April 1983), 109-126; Kenneth Rosen and James Kear, "A Model of Housing Starts, Mortgage Flows, and the Behavior of the Federal Home Loan Bank Board and the Federal National Mortgage Association," Paper No. 27, Joint Center for Urban Studies of MIT and Harvard University, 1974; John Weicher, Lorene Yap, and May S. Jones, Forecasting the National Need for New Construction, Working Paper No. 1345-1 (Washington, D.C.: The Urban Institute, 1979).

CHAPTER 5—
DEMAND VERSUS SUPPLY—
UNMET MOUNT LAUREL HOUSING NEED

INTRODUCTION

The purpose of the following chapter is to discuss the housing demand/supply relationships for the Mount Laurel-eligible population. It begins by summarizing the numbers of housing demand both statewide and by region. It further discusses housing demand related to present housing deficient/income-constrained need, as well as prospective or purely income-constrained need.

Supply will concentrate on net-new (new construction plus conversions minus demolitions) Mount Laurel-affordable additions to the housing stock, yet will be further augmented by specific tallies for within-stock change related to both filtering and rehabilitation.

Demand and supply suitability will be evaluated by characteristics of potential occupants viewed in the presence of characteristics of net new additions to the housing stock. A computer algorithm will be used to match Mount Laurel-eligible households by size, income, and geographic area with affordable, adequately-sized, and regionally-located housing units. A net figure will be derived which will represent unanswered Mount Laurel housing need, both statewide and by housing region. This figure will also be partitioned by size of unit needed and by the Mount Laurel income category to which the housing must be delivered.

PART I

MOUNT LAUREL HOUSING DEMAND

PRESENT HOUSING DEMAND - 1980 (HOUSING DEFICIENT-RELATED)

The present Mount Laurel housing demand defined by income limitations as well as by housing deficiency is approximately 11 percent of the purely income-constrained low- and moderate-income household population state-

EXHIBIT 5-1

PRESENT AND PROSPECTIVE MOUNT LAUREL HOUSING DEMAND
(UNREFINED BY CONVENTIONAL SOURCES OF SUPPLY)

	STATEWIDE	NORTHEAST REGION 1	NORTHWEST REGION 2	WEST CENTRAL REGION 3	EAST CENTRAL REGION 4	SOUTHWEST REGION 5	SOUTH-SOUTHWEST REGION 6
	(All Region Total)	Bergen Hudson Passaic	Essex Morris Sussex Union	Hunterdon Middlesex Somerset Warren	Monmouth Ocean	Burlington Camden Gloucester Mercer	Atlantic Cape May Cumberland Salem
Present Demand (Housing Deficient-Income-Constrained)							
1980 Demand	120,160	52,160	33,440	8,520	4,960	13,360	7,720
50-80%	(38,800)	(17,000)	(11,000)	(3,240)	(1,080)	(3,800)	(2,680)
<50%	(81,360)	(35,160)	(22,440)	(5,280)	(3,880)	(9,560)	(5,040)
Prospective Demand (Purely Income-Constrained)							
1980-1990 Demand	133,981	6,570	8,669	22,002	43,086	35,627	18,027
50-80%	(55,152)	(1,957)	(5,040)	(8,773)	(17,874)	(14,212)	(7,296)
<50%	(78,829)	(4,613)	(3,629)	(13,229)	(25,212)	(21,415)	(10,731)
1990-2000 Demand	79,952	-8,720	1,513	11,955	36,868	24,506	13,830
50-80%	(29,156)	(-4,498)	(566)	(3,802)	(15,008)	(8,938)	(5,340)
<50%	(50,796)	(-4,222)	(947)	(8,153)	(21,860)	(15,568)	(8,490)

Source: Rutgers University, Center for Urban Policy Research Projections, Winter 1983.

wide. Housing deficiency was determined by age of structure and one or more indications of negative housing quality as developed by the measures listed in Chapter 2. Of the 1.1 million low- and moderate-income households which meet the Mount Laurel-eligible income standards, approximately 120,000 live in deficient housing (see Exhibit 5-1, upper half). As indicated in Chapter 3, these households living in deficient housing and comprising this segment of Mount Laurel demand are poorer, more likely to be black or Spanish, and to have slightly larger households than prospective or future Mount Laurel-eligible households. Two-thirds of these deficient unit households are found primarily in the central cities and older close-in suburbs of the Northeast Region 1 (52,160) and Northwest Region 2 (33,440), with a smaller concentration in Southwest Region 5 (13,360). These are areas which are adjacent to New York City and Philadelphia and represent the lion's share of the state's oldest and least cared-for housing.

Two-thirds of the 120,160 unit present Mount Laurel housing demand is composed of demand generated by low-income households (81,360), the remaining one-third (38,800) is made up of demand generated by households of moderate income.

Slightly over one-half (55%) of the demand is composed of households whose size is two persons or less; the remaining 45 percent is split relatively evenly between three- to four-person households and those households of five persons or more. Exhibit 5-2 provides a summary of Mount Laurel housing demand by income category, location within the state, and household size.

EXHIBIT 5-2

1980 PRESENT MOUNT LAUREL HOUSING DEMAND SUMMARY
(120,000 Units-Statewide)

Income Category	Low Income	Moderate Income
	2/3	1/3
Location	Northeast and Northwest Regions	Rest of State
	2/3	1/3
Household Size	Small Size Households	Medium-Large Size Households
	1/2	1/2

Source: Exhibit 5-1

PROSPECTIVE HOUSING DEMAND - 1980-1990, 1990-2000 (PURELY INCOME-CONSTRAINED)

Over the period 1980 to 1990, the population in New Jersey is expected to grow by slightly over 200,000 (207,000).[1] Using projected age structure concentrations and future headship rates, the number of households statewide will grow by 340,000 from 1980 to 1990. The Mount Laurel-eligible share of this growth or prospective Mount Laurel need for this decade, based on similar percentages of 1980 income distribution, is just under 134,000 (133,981).

The next decade will experience a slight increase in statewide population growth from 207,000 to 221,000 yet due to movement of the baby boom generation into the 45-54 age group and the post World War II elderly into the 75-80 age group, and the lower household formation rates associated with these two age groups, the projected increase in households will drop to approximately 260,000. Prospective Mount Laurel need (1990-2000), reflecting, in part, absolute population decreases in one region of the state will be just under 80,000 households (79,952) (see Exhibit 5-1; lower half).

Of the combined Mount Laurel prospective demand (1980-2000) of 214,000 (134,000 + 80,000), two-thirds (140,000) is located in the East Central Region 4 (80,000) and Southwest Region 5 (60,000). This is a growth belt which extends from the middle of the state in Middlesex and Somerset counties southward to the northern borders of Salem and Atlantic Counties (see Exhibit 5-3).

EXHIBIT 5-3

1980-2000 PROSPECTIVE MOUNT LAUREL HOUSING DEMAND SUMMARY
(214,000 Units -- 134,000 1980-1990; 80,000 Units 1990-2000)

Income Category	Low Income	Moderate Income
	60%	40%
Location	East Central and Southwest Regions	Rest of State
	2/3	1/3
Household Size	Small Size Households	Medium-Large Size Households
	2/3	1/3

Source: Exhibit 5-1.

Sixty percent of prospective Mount Laurel housing demand is to answer need generated by low-income households, the remaining 40 percent to answer demand generated by households of moderate income. The distribution of Mount Laurel prospective housing demand among low- versus moderate-income families is 10 percent lower (60 versus 66 percent) than is the case for present housing demand. Future demand for small size households is significantly more than present demand. Two-thirds of future Mount Laurel household demand will be created by 1-2 person households.

In summary, statewide there is a gross demand for 334,000 additional Mount Laurel housing units for the period 1980 to 2000. Approximately 120,000 of the 334,000 is comprised of present housing-deficient Mount Laurel demand; the remainder of 214,000 is to provide for future income-constrained demand -- 134,000 projected for the period 1980 to 1990, and approximately 80,000 for the period 1990 to 2000. Of all units, about 124,000 are required for Mount Laurel moderate-income families and 210,000 for low-income families.

The majority (60%) of grouped present and prospective Mount Laurel housing demand is composed of small, 1-2 person families. The remaining portion is relatively evenly split between 3-4 person and 5 or more person families. In Appendix I to this chapter, several parallel exhibits are displayed showing in a comparable format the level of Mount Laurel households housed and not housed through conventional supply mechanisms.

PART II

MOUNT LAUREL HOUSING SUPPLY

PRESENT - PROSPECTIVE HOUSING SUPPLY

Over the period 1970 to 1980 in New Jersey, we delivered approximately 385,000 net new housing units to the housing inventory. Just under 435,000 units were newly built and demolitions exceeded conversions by close to 50,000.

Of the 435,000 units built, approximately 62 percent or 270,000 were single-family, 31 percent or 135,000 were multifamily units (5 or more units), and 7 percent or 30,000 were 2 - 4 family units. Of the multifamily housing, 6 percent of overall housing was subsidized -- slightly over one-third via the public housing program and the remainder from all other state, federal and local subsidized housing programs.

Since supply is usually driven by demand and the rate of household formation will decrease in the State of New Jersey over the next two decades, we project (Exhibit 5-4) approximately 328,000 net new units (new construction and conversions minus demolitions) to be added over the period 1980 to 1990, and 278,000 net new housing units over the period 1990 to

EXHIBIT 5-4

TOTAL MARKET HOUSING UNITS*PROJECTED IN NEW JERSEY
1980 TO 1990 AND 1990 TO 2000 - STATEWIDE AND BY REGION

Region	Actual 1970 to 1980	Projected 1980 to 1990	Projected 1990 to 2000
Northeast Region 1	36,566	46,330	39,203
Northwest Region 2	53,234	54,428	46,055
West Central Region 3	57,811	48,309	40,877
East Central Region 4	98,140	70,669	59,797
Southwest Region 5	96,053	72,417	61,277
South-Southwest Region 6	43,280	36,557	30,950
Total - Statewide	385,084	328,729	278,159

*Net new housing supply
Source: Exhibit 4-7

2000. In the first decade, this is down by 60,000 from the 385,000 net new units built 1970 to 1980; in the second decade, it is down by close to 110,000 from the 1970 to 1980 pace.

Ownership Housing

If we use two times Mount Laurel income as a standard for ownership housing affordability,* a rough approximation of the share of net new ownership housing available to Mount Laurel households is at hand (see Exhibit 5-5).

Not to belabor the obvious, across all regions, essentially no new ownership housing (attached or detached), will be delivered that is affordable by low-income households. For moderate-income households, except for a small percentage in the East Central Region 4 (specifically Ocean County) in the form of very small attached retirement units, essentially the same scenario is true. One percent of Mount Laurel housing demand, all within the moderate-income sector, can be answered by net new ownership housing in its current form. This estimate is without taking into account the efforts mandated by the Court. Thus, private ownership housing in its present (single-family detached) configuration is essentially unavailable to the Mount Laurel population. As noted before, this is by far the dominant form of housing construction in New Jersey today.

Rental Housing

New rental housing (at an annual cost of 25 percent of income)* is affordable only to Mount Laurel low-income households to the degree that it has some form of subsidy. Because the 1980 Census of Population and Housing[2] does not separately classify subsidized housing units, it is difficult to remove the portion which is publicly subsidized from the overall tally. Using the Annual Housing Survey[3] information to remove public subsidy, only three percent of net new rental units constructed are affordable by low-income households (see Exhibit 5-5). These are most probably conversions and privately subsidized units. Thus, very few private multifamily units are being added newly to the stock within the range of affordability of Mount Laurel low-income households.

For moderate-income households, the amount of private rental housing affordable by Mount Laurel households (in addition to what is affordable by low-income households) would be about 20 percent of the net new rental housing projected for the future.

---

*See Appendix I to Chapter 6 for derivation of this standard.

EXHIBIT 5-5

1980-2000 MOUNT LAUREL HOUSING SUPPLY FROM NET NEW SOURCES

Income Category	Low Income	Moderate Income
Housing type		
Ownership	None	1% (elderly - condo)
Rental	3%	20%
Location	N/A	East Central, Southwest Regions
Size	N/A	Small units (1-2 person)

Source: Exhibit 4-10.

Thus, using very crude estimates of affordability (neither adjusting income for family size nor pairing family and unit size), gross Mount Laurel housing demand of approximately 334,000 would be reduced by approximately 43,500 via the current (net new) housing delivery system of rental and ownership housing. Within this housing supply generated reduction of demand, a large share would be converted units, almost all would flow to the moderate-income sector, and much of this housing would be delivered in the southern versus northern part of the state. Almost all affordable net new units are of rental tenure; only those Mount Laurel households of moderate income can afford any segment of conventional housing. For the most part, these are Mount Laurel families at the top of the moderate-income scale whose family size characteristics require only very small housing units.

PART III

MOUNT LAUREL DEMAND VERSUS CONVENTIONAL SUPPLY

MATCHING CONVENTIONAL DEMAND AND SUPPLY: THE MOUNT LAUREL NUMBERS

The preceding sections have specified the magnitude of individual segments of the demand-supply equation. This has been done using raw demand and supply figures without a careful matching of the individual components on each side of the equation. In order to complete the analysis, the elements of demand must be combined with those of supply. The method used to do this will construct estimates both of the number of Mount Laurel eligible-households housed as well as those who will not be adequately housed. The results are expressed in three parts. First, the projected numbers of present and prospective Mount Laurel households successfully housed by the conventional, net new housing market will be shown. The term conventional, net new housing includes both new construction and conversion (minus losses due to demolition) both of which may be estimated by unit size and cost with some level of accuracy. There are other sources of supply which include public production and rehabilitation/filtering. The level and degree of persistence of government-related subsidy programs designed to meet low-income housing demand has been projected to be minimal. Rehabilitation/filtering, since it is difficult to estimate, will be addressed in another section.

The second part of the results will concern the number and type of Mount Laurel households not adequately housed according to Mount Laurel II criteria. This number represents households that conventional housing does not touch and, in the absence of successful bridge programs or mechanisms designed to bring them into decent housing, may be forced to live in poor quality or overcrowded housing.

The third part completes the joining of supply and demand by examining the rent-paying capacity of Mount Laurel households in search of adequate shelter through the year 2000 and expressed in 1983 dollars. This section should serve as a guide to both municipalities and developers alike as they jointly begin the complicated resolution of unmet lower income housing need.

The exhibits joining supply and demand are grouped according to the time period during which the demand will be impressed upon the market and by its source, present or prospective demand. An element of compromise has also entered in the construction of these estimates. The extremely large backlog of present Mount Laurel housing demand* would, if immediate efforts were made to completely satisfy it by conventional supply, exhaust the latter. Feeling that it is unrealistic to show the entire share of present Mount Laurel-eligible households both actively entering the market and competing for housing in a single decade that is already one-third past, present demand has been phased into the market in equal numbers over the period 1980 to 1990 and 1990 to 2000. Further, while both components of demand (present and prospective) will be in the market for both decades at the same time, their numbers will be presented in tabular form separately in order to: (1) keep distinct the unique socioeconomic characteristics brought by both groups to the housing market, and (2) lend recognition to

---

*All units deficient and occupied by Mount Laurel income-eligible households as of 1980.

the fact that each may have unique and nonequivalent supply sources, i.e., present demand -- more rehabilitation/filtering and prospective demand, more new construction/conversion.

THE MATCHING PROGRAM

The matching program that permits a comparison of supply and demand is a simple hunting mechanism that simultaneously searches two populations with stored matching characteristics of each. It permits combinations to take place when a match of characteristics is created. This routine is taken from a class of routines written in FORTRAN and used extensively in socioeconomic and planning analyses.[4]

In the specific case at hand the program has been adapted to link housing demand of certain types with various forms of housing supply. Housing demand is composed of present (1980) and prospective (1980-2000) Mount Laurel demand. Housing supply is all conventional net new supply for the period 1980-2000 consisting of new construction and conversions (minus demolitions).

Stored characteristics of demand are income, family size and location. Stored characteristics of supply are gross rent/value of unit, unit size, and location (See Exhibit 5-6). A match is created when certain predetermined linkages of supply and demand take place. These are: (1) location of unit and household only within the same region as determined in Chapter 1; (2) unit size of one more room than occupant size of household; and (3) a ratio of 25 percent of income or less to be spent for gross rent for rental units or income more than one-half the value of ownership units.[5] Present and prospective households search for housing in the same region simultaneously and their family size and incomes determine who is housed. Matches first take place on location, then size, and finally, affordability. If there are two identical incomes from the present and prospective population for a single specific housing unit, they are randomly assigned higher or lower priority. In the first instance of such dual qualification, the household will be drawn and successfully matched from the present demand while the equivalent prospective demand household must continue to search or be ultimately classified as not housed. In the second instance, the reverse will be true wherein the prospective household demand segment will be housed and the present demand household must continue to search.

All households queue for an appropriate housing unit by ability to pay. Those who are best able to afford the units supplied are matched. Two points should be mentioned here. If a rental unit's cost drops to below 15 percent of income for moderate-income families, the unit is passed down to a lower-income family of the same size. Further, since the number of persons and rooms are grouped for data presentation, yet in the algorithm were matched on an individual person to room basis, it is possible that a 4 person moderate income-family could not occupy a 4 room unit because of

EXHIBIT 5-6

OUTLINE OF COMPUTERIZED MATCHING ROUTINE
TO TEST AFFORDABILITY OF PROJECTED CONVENTIONAL HOUSING SUPPLY
FOR PRESENT AND PROSPECTIVE MOUNT LAUREL HOUSEHOLDS

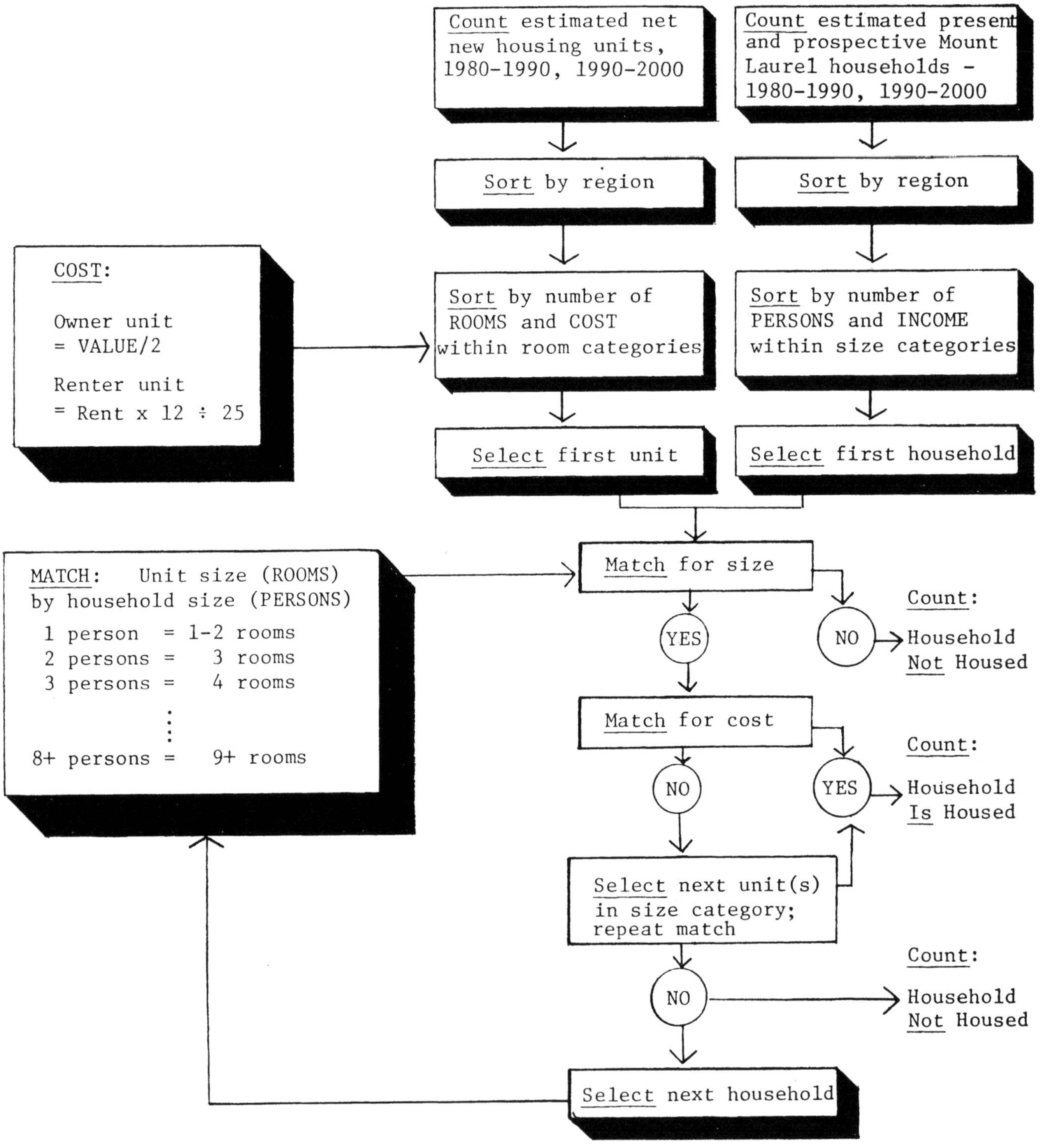

Source: Rutgers University, Center for Urban Policy Research,
Household-Housing Computer Matching Program

size and no 3 person, moderate-income families be left. This unit, if affordable, would be passed down to a 3 person, low-income family. In both instances, lower-income families would be shown as housed on the tabular presentations while moderate income families remained on the queuing line.

The presentation strategy also deserves comment. The share and distribution of the present and prospective Mount Laurel population who are housed are examined first, followed by their counterparts who are not so fortunate. The discussion moves sequentially -- from the 1980 to 1990 period to the 1990 to 2000 span for the present and prospective Mount Laurel categories, respectively. Much of the information is presented in tabular form, first for the state as a whole and then by the six Mount Laurel regions. Exhibits 5-7 through 5-10 indicate the statewide results, starting with the 1980 to 1990 Mount Laurel components of present demand (Exhibit 5-7), and prospective demand (Exhibit 5-8), and then for the 1990 to 2000 components of Mount Laurel present demand (Exhibit 5-9) and prospective demand (Exhibit 5-10). Exhibits 5-11 through 5-32 follow a parallel presentation for the six Mount Laurel regions. Exhibits 5-11 to 5-16 contain 1980 to 1990 present demand by region; Exhibits 5-17 to 5-22 contain 1980 to 1990 prospective demand for the same region. Exhibits 5-23 to 5-28 contain 1990-2000 present demand by region; Exhibits 5-29 to 5-34 contain 1990-2000 prospective demand by region. Exhibits 5A-2 and 5A-3 to this chapter present a statewide summary of "housed" and "not housed" (the Mount Laurel numbers) in the same format as Exhibit 5-1. It should be reiterated at this point that one-half of 1980 present demand is being phased in during the period 1980 to 1990; the remaining one-half is phased in during the period 1990 to 2000.

THE MOUNT LAUREL HOUSING MANDATE: WHO IS HOUSED?

1980-1990 Present/Prospective Demand "Housed": The State (Exhibits 5-7 and 5-8)

In the discussion of supply in this chapter, it was shown that it is reasonable to project total state housing supply levels over the decade 1980 to 1990 at 328,729. This number represents the net new production of housing units. That is, new construction is combined with projected conversions and the sum reduced for the anticipated demolition and permanent removal of units from the housing stock. Ten thousand, five hundred fourteen (10,514) present households and 15,420 prospective households will be successfully housed statewide during the decade 1980 to 1990. This represents 16.7 percent of present Mount Laurel housing demand for this decade* and 11.6 percent of prospective demand, also for this decade. The same exhibits also show that the majority of those successfully housed will come

*Present or housing-deficient, income constrained Mount Laurel demand is being phased in over two decades.

from the moderate-income category. For the present component of demand (housing deficient, income-constrained), 82 percent of the units successfully placed by the market will be absorbed by those of the moderate-income group. The disparity between income groups is even more marked in the prospective component of demand (purely income-constrained). Here, fully 93 percent of the successfully placed income-eligible households are projected to be from the moderate-income category. In both present and prospective components of demand, the great majority of successfully placed households are small one- and two-person, and to a lesser extent, three- and four-person households.

1980-1990 Present/Prospective Demand "Housed": The Regions (Exhibits 5-11 to 5-16; Exhibits 5-17 to 5-22)

Given that each region is projected to have unique demand functions (i.e., serving as either regions of present or prospective demand and rarely of a combination of the two), it is not surprising to find a marked difference in the absorption of new units when comparing the two temporal components of demand. The present component of demand is housed to the greatest degree in the Northeast and Northwest Regions 1 and 2; the exact location of heaviest present demand. Ninety-three percent of the present demand that was successfully housed came from these two regions. These are also two of three locations statewide, of the heaviest levels of housing conversions as sources of housing supply.

In contrast, the region that most successfully meets the Mount Laurel prospective demand is the Southwest Region 5. This is also the location of one of the most significant components of prospective demand. The Northwest Region 2 also meets a significant share of prospective demand. Some of this may come from conversions in the housing stock of Essex, Union and Morris County and cheaper new construction in Sussex County. Combining the housing ability of both of these regions, the distribution of housed households across the regions is less concentrated than was the case with the present demand scenario. Here, the two regions with the largest level of answered demand represent only 53 percent of the prospective demand successfully met during the decade.

1990-2000 Present/Prospective Demand "Housed": The State (Exhibits 5-9 and 5-10)

For the last decade of this century, in the housing supply summary of this chapter, we show a projected net new statewide housing supply of 278,159 units. Of this number, the conventional housing market will deliver 17,533 units to low- and moderate-income Mount Laurel present and prospective households. This represents roughly 16.7 percent of present demand and 8.0 percent of prospective demand.

The market allocation algorithm splits the numerical allocation of 17,533 units relatively in favor of the present population to be housed. These households are currently living in deficient housing, in neighborhoods where conversion is taking place and thus benefit from this. When it comes to the two income categories of Mount Laurel population, the allocation is also one-sided by continuing to favor those of moderate income. For the present demand population in the market during the decade 1990-2000, fully 82 percent of the units delivered will go to those households of moderate income; for the prospective population the comparable figure is 95 percent. As was the case in the previous decade, the largest number of units supplied will go to the one- and two-person households, with a negligible number available to large (5+) member households.

1990-2000 Present/Prospective Demand "Housed": The Regions (Exhibits 5-23 to 5-28; Exhibits 5-29 to 5-34)

The final decade of the century presents planners with a diverse pattern of housing need and supply. The Northeast Region 1 faces an absolute decline in households and thus has no new prospective Mount Laurel demand placed upon its housing market. What remains is the portion of present demand brought forward into this decade's housing market.

For the remaining five regions, Southwest Region 5 leads in delivering units to prospective Mount Laurel households with the delivery of 2,730 units; while the least productive region in this case is the Northwest Region 2, with only 484 units. Housing prices in this region are one of the highest in the state and difficult to meet even if incomes are higher there. Northeast Region 1 leads in the delivery to the present Mount Laurel market with 6,062 units completed, with Northwest Region 2 a distant second with only 3,437 delivered.

THE MOUNT LAUREL HOUSING MANDATE: WHO IS NOT HOUSED?

1980-1990 Present/Prospective Demand "Not Housed": The State (Exhibits 5-7 and 5-8)

While it is of value to recognize that some Mount Laurel households are successfully housed by the conventional housing market, of greatest concern, under the Mount Laurel II decision, is the number that probably will not be housed conventionally. In the section to follow, we examine what may be considered the "Mount Laurel numbers," absent filtering and rehabilitation as mitigation measures, for both income categories during the periods 1980 to 1990 and 1990 to 2000.

Summarizing the numbers presented in the above Exhibits, clearly the level of unmet or unanswered demand for 1980 to 1990 is quite high. For the present component of demand, 49,566 of 60,080 will not be housed; for the prospective component, 118,561 of 133,981 will not be housed. That is, 86.6

percent of the Mount Laurel-eligible housing demand for the period 1980 to 1990 will not be met by unassisted conventional new sources. Low-income households dominate both components of unmet demand with 38,389 units of present demand (78 percent) and 77,697 units of prospective demand (66 percent) left unanswered.

These are significant figures indeed. One hundred sixteen thousand low-income units alone make up the gap during the current decade; while, an additional 52,041 units of moderate-income housing are also unavailable. The bulk of the unanswered housing need is that coming from one- and two-person households; this is 109,682 units, or 65 percent of total need, most of which comes from prospective demand in the 1980 to 1990 period. At the other extreme, 21,697 large (5+-person) families, or 12.8 percent of the total, are in a similar condition. These are split approximately 50/50 from present/prospective demand. In sum, the statewide unanswered demand for Mount Laurel housing during the 1980 to 1990 decade is 168,127 dwelling units -- most of this demand is for small, low-income units.

1980-1990 Present/Prospective Demand "Not Housed":
The Regions (Exhibits 5-11 to 5-16; 5-17 to 5-22)

The regions taken individually present a wide range of housing needs and supply capabilities. We have seen that present demand dominates the Northeast and Northwest Regions 1 and 2 while migration spurred by economic activity and life cycle factors shift the vast majority of prospective demand southward. An examination of the unanswered housing need during the decade of the 1980s highlights the problems to be found by planners and policy makers regarding the solution to this problem.

The unanswered housing need of present housing deficient, income-constrained Mount Laurel households is dominated by the two northern regions. The combined existing unanswered demand is 33,454 units, of which 80 percent are in the low-income category.

The prospective or purely income-constrained Mount Laurel demand for the Northeast and Northwest Regions 1 and 2 is small in comparison to that of the remaining four regions. The East Central Region 4 dominates this measure with 40,679 units; while the Southwest Region 5 is secondmost of concern with 30,945 units of unanswered need. However, the income levels of these households differ significantly across the two regions. The East Central region has 38 percent of its unmet need coming from its moderate-income households; while only 31 percent of the Southwest's unanswered need is from this same income class of moderate-income households.

1990-2000 Present/Prospective Demand "Not Housed": The State (Exhibits 5-9 to 5-10)

The final decade of the century finds the second half of the present housing need in the market along with the new prospective demand for that period. The unanswered housing need for these groups is estimated to be 49,600 and 81,619 respectively, for a total of 131,219 units. As was the case for the decade of the 1980s, the 1990s will have a disproportionate concentration of underhoused from the low-income category (71 percent). Lastly, the distribution of unanswered housing need is also similarly concentrated among one- and two-person households (64 percent) with the largest household size category containing only 14 percent of the unmet housing need.

1990-2000 Present/Prospective Housing Demand "Not Housed": The Regions (Exhibits 5-23 to 5-28; 5-29 to 5-34)

The present housing demand impressed upon the market during the final decade of the century is by construction, the same as was the case for the 1980s.* The unanswered need remaining after the market successfully allocated available supply is practically identical by region to what it was in the 1980s. To recap, the Northeast and Northwest Regions 1 and 2 possess the greatest amount of unmet present housing demand, lacking 33,301 units among them. This amounts to 67 percent of the total unmet present housing need for this second decade.

Unanswered prospective housing demand also varies across regions in a manner similar to that found in the previous decade. Again, the Northeast Region 1 has no new prospective demand due to its declining population base. The region with the largest unmet prospective need remains the East Central Region 4, with a 34,988-unit shortfall; this is six thousand fewer units in shortage than in the previous decade. Following the East Central region in severity of unmet prospective need is the Southwest Region 5. The regional unmet demand in this case is 21,776. This is sharply down from the level of unmet need in the 1980s when the level at that time was 30,945. As in all of the previous cases, each region's unmet prospective housing need is dominated by small households.

RENT-PAYING CAPACITY OF MOUNT LAUREL HOUSEHOLDS IN SEARCH OF HOUSING

The preceding analysis has shown that the conventional housing market will successfully directly deliver units to only 13.4 percent of the 1980-1990 Mount Laurel demand and 11.9 percent of the 1990-2000 demand. While statewide production of housing is projected to run 328,729 units and

*Each decade was given one-half of total present demand.

278,159 in the last two decades of the century respectively, only 8.0 percent and 6.3 percent of this housing can be absorbed by the Mount Laurel populations.

Taking only the net new supply of housing units into consideration, a shortfall of 168,127 units for 1980-1990 and 131,219 units for 1990-2000 is projected to exist. In order for municipal planners and developers to better comprehend the type of development required to satisfy some portion of this unmet Mount Laurel need, not only are the numbers of units by size of household necessary, but also their expected rent- or shelter-paying capacity must be known.

As a component of the housing market algorithm that produced the income and household size-specific projections of housed and not-housed Mount Laurel populations, the rent-paying capacities of all Mount Laurel households including those not housed have been produced. The rent-paying capacities are expressed in terms of the regional medians as well as the 90th and 10th percentile values. (A percentile value is the percentage of cases in the distribution that will be found below the specified value. That is, if the 10th percentile is $280 per month of rent-paying capacity, 10 percent of the target population has a rent-paying capacity less than $280. The median is a special percentile value in that it is a measure of central tendency and is the 50th percentile or the exact middle of the distribution.)

The use of the percentile values alerts planners and developers to the fact that a wide range of income levels is contained within each income class of Mount Laurel household. Supplying housing at the upper threshold values of each income category would not meet the income constraints of a majority of the target population.

Finally, before proceeding to analyze the rent-paying capacity values we must make clear what the terms rent and income include. Rent is the gross monthly outlay which also includes shared costs for heat and maintenance. Income is gross household income not reduced for numbers of dependents. Gross rent and gross income produce essentially similar rent-to-income ratios as contract rent and adjusted income. Gross rent is used here in order to remain consistent with other definitions used elsewhere in the report (Chapter 4). In New Jersey median gross and contract rents in 1980 differed by only $30 per month. Rent paying capacity is 25 percent of household income in 1983 dollars. As explained in the Appendix to Chapter 6, the 25 percent-of-income factor is a rough rule of thumb to show shelter-paying capacity of lower income-families. The Appendix explains in detail the rent-to-income ratio and its use as a standard of affordability, both historically and currently.

The specific values of rent- or shelter-paying capacity are shown in the preceding series of exhibits. Separate values are reported for the state as a whole, and for each of the regions including both present and prospective components of Mount Laurel demand for the decades 1980-1990 and

1990-2000. We have assumed a constant dollar income capacity for all segments of demand through the twenty year projection by observing that the figures across each component of demand are identical for the two decades. We can further simplify the descriptive analysis by observing that the shelter payment levels across the two components of demand (present and prospective), while distinct from one another, do not sufficiently differ in value to require a separate analysis of each. The analysis to follow will be based on the data derived for the 1980-1990 unanswered Mount Laurel present housing demand.

1980-2000 Monthly Shelter Payment Capacity: The State (Constant 1983 Dollars) (Exhibits 5-7 and 5-8)

The statewide aggregate shelter-paying capacities are displayed in Exhibit 5-7 and 5-8. We have reported these figures in disaggregated form; their appropriate use in policy projection will require, according to the Mount Laurel II decision, consideration of both income class and size of household. In order to simplify the shift from household size to dwelling unit size, all of the relevant exhibits report unit size in terms of the number of rooms in the average dwelling unit needed to satisfy the needs of the households in the column directly above the room-size value. An assumption of one room greater than household size has been used to match unit size and household size.

It is important to recognize that shelter-paying capacity varies directly by the size of the household requiring the unit. Referring to the statewide aggregate distribution we see that moderate-income households of 3-4 persons in the central part of the state (West Central Region 3) can afford from a high of $540 to a median of $480. In contrast, the low-income households of the same size and in the same region can afford from a high of $315 to a median of $240. On average, low income households of the mid-range household size category, can pay slightly more than one-half of what moderate-income households can afford. Further, for moderate-income households, median rent varies by $100 per month for each room grouping; for low-income households the size difference is represented by an approximate $50 per month median rent difference across room sizes. Assuming that dedicated markets exist for low- and moderate-income households, if developers market units at median dollar values, only the upper 50 percent of each segment of housing demand would be capable of entering the market. Thus, for the total picture, it is important to look at the reported extremes in each market segment; for example, again in the West Central Region, two- and three-room units dedicated to the moderate-income market would be open to 90 percent of the demand if rent levels were at $275 per month. This may be more possible through the use of bridge mechanisms discussed in the next chapter.

Monthly Shelter Payment Capacity: The Regions
(Exhibits 5-11 to 5-16; 5-17 to 5-22)

Each region has been shown to present a unique demand and supply picture to the Mount Laurel decision. The above listed exhibits show the projected number of units needed for each decade by income class and unit size. In addition, directly below these figures, the range of anticipated shelter-payment capacities is reported.

Without repeating each of the Exhibits, certain generalizations can be noted. The West Central Region 3, illustrated above, possesses the highest rent-paying capacities for all moderate-income market segments and for all but the largest household sizes for the low-income segment. Households requiring six or more rooms have the highest paying capacities in the Northwest and East Central Regions 2 and 4, respectively.

The lowest shelter-paying capacities are found across all market segments of the South-Southwest Region 6. These patterns are, by and large, reproduced within the prospective component of the Mount Laurel population.

Summary

It is important now to summarize the general trends of these sections. The conventional housing supply system, that is, new construction and conversions minus demolitions, is projected to provide housing for approximately 10-12 percent of the Mount Laurel demand for each of the decades rounding out the century. The demand of the moderate-income component for each time period and market segment is better met than low-income demand, but conventional supply clearly falls far short of the total Mount Laurel obligation. Given the type/costs of units normally built, it is projected that the needs of one- and two-person households will be met to a greater proportion than that of larger households.

Clearly, the unmet demand for decent housing is significant: across the two decades, an unmet demand for 168,000 and 131,000 units respectively is projected -- absent rehabilitation, filtering or governmental cost reduction mechanisms.

Lastly, the shelter-paying capacities show the importance of targeting construction and non-new production to each market segment. Given that there is a range of payment capacities within each segment, the fraction of households capable of entering the market will vary depending upon how the proposed monthly carrying charges fit in a given market segment's range of shelter-paying capacities.

EXHIBIT 5-7

UNANSWERED MOUNT LAUREL PRESENT HOUSING DEMAND 1980-1990 STATEWIDE

	MODERATE INCOME (50-80% of Median)			LOW INCOME (Below 50% of Median)			
	1-2 Person	3-4 Person	5 or more Persons	1-2 Person	3-4 Person	5 or more Persons	Total
Housed	4,097	3,043	1,083	1,756	305	230	10,514
Not Housed	4,943	2,037	4,197	21,144	9,935	7,310	49,566
Total	9,040	5,080	5,280	22,900	10,240	7,540	60,080

REQUIRED HOUSING FOR THOSE NOT HOUSED

Unit Size	2-3 Room	4-5 Room	6 or more Rooms	2-3 Room	4-5 Room	6 or more Rooms	Total
Number of Units	4,943	2,037	4,197	21,144	9,935	7,310	49,566
Rent(1983 Dollars)							
90th Percentile	370	470	555	220	300	345	
Median	300	395	470	160	210	250	
10th Percentile	245	315	380	120	140	170	

Source: Rutgers University, Center for Urban Policy Research, Winter 1983.

EXHIBIT 5-8

UNANSWERED MOUNT LAUREL PROSPECTIVE HOUSING DEMAND 1980-1990 STATEWIDE

	MODERATE INCOME (50-80% of Median)			LOW INCOME (Below 50% of Median)			
	1-2 Person	3-4 Person	5 or more Persons	1-2 Person	3-4 Person	5 or more Persons	Total
Housed	6,611	5,949	1,728	840	207	85	15,420
Not Housed	27,302	9,109	4,453	56,293	15,667	5,737	118,561
Total	33,913	15,058	6,181	57,133	15,874	5,822	133,981

REQUIRED HOUSING FOR THOSE NOT HOUSED

Unit Size	2-3 Room	4-5 Room	6 or more Rooms	2-3 Room	4-5 Room	6 or more Rooms	Total
Number of Units	27,302	9,109	4,453	56,293	15,667	5,737	118,561
Rent (1983 Dollars)							
90th Percentile	370	475	540	230	295	340	
Median	300	395	470	175	240	265	
10th Percentile	240	315	375	125	155	175	

Source: Rutgers University, Center for Urban Policy Research, Winter 1983.

EXHIBIT 5-9

UNANSWERED MOUNT LAUREL PRESENT HOUSING DEMAND 1990-2000 STATEWIDE

	MODERATE INCOME (50-80% Median)			LOW INCOME (Below 50% of Median)			
	1-2 Person	3-4 Person	5 or more Persons	1-2 Person	3-4 Person	5 or more Persons	Total
Housed	4,088	3,096	1,054	1,857	307	78	10,480
Not Housed	4,952	1,984	4,226	21,043	9,933	7,462	49,600
Total	9,040	5,080	5,280	27,900	10,240	7,540	60,080

REQUIRED HOUSING FOR THOSE NOT HOUSED

Unit Size	2-3 Room	4-5 Room	6 or more Rooms	2-3 Room	4-5 Room	6 or more Rooms	Total
Number of Units	4,952	1,984	4,226	21,043	9,933	7,462	49,600
Rent (1983 Dollars)							
90th Percentile	370	470	555	270	300	345	
Median	300	395	470	160	210	250	
10th Percentile	245	315	380	120	140	170	

Source: Rutgers University, Center for Urban Policy Research, Winter 1983.

EXHIBIT 5-10

UNANSWERED MOUNT LAUREL PROSPECTIVE HOUSING DEMAND 1990-2000 STATEWIDE

	MODERATE INCOME (50-80% Median)			LOW INCOME (Below 50% of Median)			
	1-2 Person	3-4 Person	5 or more Persons	1-2 Person	3-4 Person	5 or more Persons	Total
Housed	2,788	2,971	926	171	134	63	7,053
Not Housed	18,258	6,020	2,691	39,925	10,794	3,931	81,619
Total	21,046	8,991	3,617	40,096	10,928	3,994	88,672

REQUIRED HOUSING FOR THOSE NOT HOUSED

Unit Size	2-3 Room	4-5 Room	6 or more Rooms	2-3 Room	4-5 Room	6 or more Rooms	Total
Number of Units	18,258	6,020	2,691	39,925	10,794	3,931	81,619
Rent (1983 Dollars)							
90th Percentile	370	475	540	230	295	340	
Median	300	395	470	175	240	265	
10th Percentile	240	315	375	125	155	175	

Source: Rutgers University, Center for Urban Policy Research, Winter 1983.

EXHIBIT 5-11

UNANSWERED MOUNT LAUREL PRESENT HOUSING DEMAND 1980-1990 NORTHEAST REGION

	MODERATE INCOME (50-80% of Median)			LOW INCOME (Below 50% of Median)			
	1-2 Person	3-4 Person	5 or more Persons	1-2 Person	3-4 Person	5 or more Persons	Total
Housed	2,746	1,413	497	1,140	98	0	5,894
Not Housed	1,394	807	1,643	8,840	4,242	3,260	20,186
Total	4,140	2,220	2,140	9,980	4,340	3,260	26,080

REQUIRED HOUSING FOR THOSE NOT HOUSED

Unit Size	2-3 Room	4-5 Room	6 or more Rooms	2-3 Room	4-5 Room	6 or more Rooms	Total
Number of Units	1,394	807	1,643	8,840	4,242	3,260	20,186
Rent (1983 Dollars)							
90th Percentile	375	470	560	215	285	330	
Median	305	405	475	140	185	240	
10th Percentile	240	320	370	120	135	180	

Source: Rutgers University, Center for Urban Policy Research, Winter 1983.

EXHIBIT 5-12

UNANSWERED MOUNT LAUREL PRESENT HOUSING DEMAND 1980-1990 NORTHWEST REGION

	MODERATE INCOME (50-80% of Median)			LOW INCOME (Below 50% of Median)			
	1-2 Person	3-4 Person	5 or more Persons	1-2 Person	3-4 Person	5 or more Persons	Total
Housed	1,174	1,240	255	616	147	20	3,452
Not Housed	1,286	140	1,405	5,544	2,913	1,980	13,268
Total	2,460	1,380	1,660	6,160	3,060	2,000	16,720

REQUIRED HOUSING FOR THOSE NOT HOUSED

Unit Size	2-3 Room	4-5 Room	6 or more Rooms	2-3 Room	4-5 Room	6 or more Rooms	Total
Number of Units	1,286	140	1,405	5,544	2,913	1,980	13,268
Rent (1983 Dollars)							
90th Percentile	390	505	555	230	315	370	
Median	310	415	465	175	230	270	
10th Percentile	250	330	390	120	140	160	

Source: Rutgers University, Center for Urban Policy Research, Winter 1983.

EXHIBIT 5-13

UNANSWERED MOUNT LAUREL PRESENT HOUSING DEMAND 1980-1990 WEST CENTRAL REGION

	MODERATE INCOME (50-80% of Median)			LOW INCOME (Below 50% of Median)			
	1-2 Person	3-4 Person	5 or more Persons	1-2 Person	3-4 Person	5 or more Persons	Total
Housed	20	90	40	0	20	20	190
Not Housed	700	370	400	1,560	640	400	4,070
Total	720	460	440	1,560	660	420	4,260

REQUIRED HOUSING FOR THOSE NOT HOUSED

Unit Size	2-3 Room	4-5 Room	6 or more Rooms	2-3 Room	4-5 Room	6 or more Rooms	Total
Number of Units	700	370	400	1,560	640	400	4,070
Rent (1983 Dollars)							
90th Percentile	420	540	580	250	315	380	
Median	340	470	520	190	240	260	
10th Percentile	275	350	425	120	150	170	

Source: Rutgers University, Center for Urban Policy Research, Winter 1983.

EXHIBIT 5-14

UNANSWERED MOUNT LAUREL PRESENT HOUSING DEMAND 1980-1990 EAST CENTRAL REGION

	MODERATE INCOME (50-80% of Median)			LOW INCOME (Below 50% of Median)			
	1-2 Person	3-4 Person	5 or more Persons	1-2 Person	3-4 Person	5 or more Persons	Total
Housed	40	20	0	0	20	20	100
Not Housed	240	160	80	1,040	420	440	2,380
Total	280	180	80	1,040	440	460	2,480

REQUIRED HOUSING FOR THOSE NOT HOUSED

Unit Size	2-3 Room	4-5 Room	6 or more Rooms	2-3 Room	4-5 Room	6 or more Rooms	Total
Number of Units	240	160	100	1,040	420	460	2,420
Rent (1983 Dollars)							
90th Percentile	375	475	490	205	280	360	
Median	280	340	415	165	220	270	
10th Percentile	240	300	405	125	145	170	

Source: Rutgers University, Center for Urban Policy Research, Winter 1983.

EXHIBIT 5-15

UNANSWERED MOUNT LAUREL PRESENT HOUSING DEMAND 1980-1990 SOUTHWEST REGION

	MODERATE INCOME (50-80% of Median)			LOW INCOME (Below 50% of Median)			
	1-2 Person	3-4 Person	5 or more Persons	1-2 Person	3-4 Person	5 or more Persons	Total
Housed	80	200	124	0	20	170	594
Not Housed	680	280	536	2,500	1,240	850	6,086
Total	760	480	660	2,500	1,260	1,020	6,680

REQUIRED HOUSING FOR THOSE NOT HOUSED

Unit Size	2-3 Room	4-5 Room	6 or more Rooms	2-3 Room	4-5 Room	6 or more Rooms	Total
Number of Units	680	280	536	2,500	1,240	850	6,086
Rent (1983 Dollars)							
90th Percentile	335	445	560	210	290	335	
Median	280	365	450	170	220	255	
10th Percentile	245	325	365	120	140	165	

Source: Rutgers University, Center for Urban Policy Research, Winter 1983.

EXHIBIT 5-16

UNANSWERED MOUNT LAUREL PRESENT HOUSING DEMAND 1980-1990 SOUTH-SOUTHWEST REGION

	MODERATE INCOME (50-80% of Median)			LOW INCOME (Below 50% of Median)			
	1-2 Person	3-4 Person	5 or more Persons	1-2 Person	3-4 Person	5 or more Persons	Total
Housed	37	80	167	0	0	0	284
Not Housed	643	280	133	1,660	480	380	3,576
Total	680	360	300	1,660	480	380	3,860

REQUIRED HOUSING FOR THOSE NOT HOUSED

Unit Size	2-3 Room	4-5 Room	6 or more Rooms	2-3 Room	4-5 Room	6 or more Rooms	Total
Number of Units	643	280	133	1,660	480	380	3,576
Rent (1983 Dollars)							
90th Percentile	305	385	430	190	260	280	
Median	240	315	390	155	175	210	
10th Percentile	200	235	320	115	130	150	

Source: Rutgers University, Center for Urban Policy Research, Winter 1983.

EXHIBIT 5-17

UNANSWERED MOUNT LAUREL PROSPECTIVE HOUSING DEMAND 1980-1990 NORTHEAST REGION

	MODERATE INCOME (50-80% Median)			LOW INCOME (Below 50% of Median)			
	1-2 Person	3-4 Person	5 or more Persons	1-2 Person	3-4 Person	5 or more Persons	Total
Housed	781	358	92	451	12	2	1,696
Not Housed	395	196	135	2,859	928	361	4,874
Total	1,176	554	227	3,310	940	363	6,570

REQUIRED HOUSING FOR THOSE NOT HOUSED

Unit Size	2-3 Room	4-5 Room	6 or more Rooms	2-3 Room	4-5 Room	6 or more Rooms	Total
Number of Units	395	196	135	2,859	928	361	4,874
Rent (1983 Dollars)							
90th Percentile	380	480	540	220	280	330	
Median	310	405	475	160	220	235	
10th Percentile	250	320	380	115	140	175	

Source: Rutgers University, Center for Urban Policy Research, Winter 1983.

EXHIBIT 5-18

UNANSWERED MOUNT LAUREL PROSPECTIVE HOUSING DEMAND 1980-1990 NORTHWEST REGION

	MODERATE INCOME (50-80% Median)			LOW INCOME (Below 50% of Median)			
	1-2 Person	3-4 Person	5 or more Persons	1-2 Person	3-4 Person	5 or more Persons	Total
Housed	1,727	1,177	182	333	25	2	3,446
Not Housed	1,313	236	405	2,090	837	342	5,223
Total	3,040	1,413	587	2,423	862	344	8,669

REQUIRED HOUSING FOR THOSE NOT HOUSED

Unit Size	2-3 Room	4-5 Room	6 or more Rooms	2-3 Room	4-5 Room	6 or more Rooms	Total
Number of Units	1,313	236	405	2,090	837	342	5,223
Rent (1983 Dollars)							
90th Percentile	395	495	560	235	300	355	
Median	320	420	480	165	250	270	
10th Percentile	260	335	390	125	150	170	

Source: Rutgers University, Center for Urban Policy Research, Winter 1983.

EXHIBIT 5-19

UNANSWERED MOUNT LAUREL PROSPECTIVE HOUSING DEMAND 1980-1990 WEST CENTRAL REGION

	MODERATE INCOME (50-80% Median)			LOW INCOME (Below 50% of Median)			
	1-2 Person	3-4 Person	5 or more Persons	1-2 Person	3-4 Person	5 or more Persons	Total
Housed	569	811	278	8	46	7	1,719
Not Housed	4,271	1,962	882	9,638	2.683	847	20,283
Total	4,840	2,773	1,160	9,646	2,729	854	22,002

REQUIRED HOUSING FOR THOSE NOT HOUSED

Unit Size	2-3 Room	4-5 Room	6 or more Rooms	2-3 Room	4-5 Room	6 or more Rooms	Total
Number of Units	4,271	1,962	882	9,638	2,683	847	20,283
Rent (1983 Dollars)							
90th Percentile	435	555	610	270	330	390	
Median	350	460	520	190	265	280	
10th Percentile	280	365	420	125	170	180	

Source: Rutgers University, Center for Urban Policy Research, Winter 1983.

EXHIBIT 5-20

UNANSWERED MOUNT LAUREL PROSPECTIVE HOUSING DEMAND 1980-1990 EAST CENTRAL REGION

	MODERATE INCOME (50-80% Median)			LOW INCOME (Below 50% of Median)			
	1-2 Person	3-4 Person	5 or more Persons	1-2 Person	3-4 Person	5 or more Persons	Total
Housed	984	1,093	215	15	58	42	2.407
Not Housed	10,676	3,564	1,342	18,967	4,549	1,581	40,679
Total	11,660	4,657	1,557	18,982	4,607	1,623	43,086

REQUIRED HOUSING FOR THOSE NOT HOUSED

Unit Size	2-3 Room	4-5 Room	6 or more Rooms	2-3 Room	4-5 Room	6 or more Rooms	Total
Number of Units	10,676	3,564	1,342	18,967	4,549	1,581	40,679
Rent (1983 Dollars)							
90th Percentile	370	465	520	220	300	350	
Median	295	380	470	180	260	270	
10th Percentile	240	305	365	120	150	170	

Source: Rutgers University, Center for Urban Policy Research, Winter 1983.

EXHIBIT 5-21

UNANSWERED MOUNT LAUREL PROSPECTIVE HOUSING DEMAND 1980-1990 SOUTHWEST REGION

	MODERATE INCOME (50-80% Median)			LOW INCOME (Below 50% of Median)			
	1-2 Person	3-4 Person	5 or more Persons	1-2 Person	3-4 Person	5 or more Persons	Total
Housed	2,145	1,857	559	33	56	32	4,682
Not Housed	6,040	2,250	1,361	14,865	4,644	1,785	30,945
Total	8,185	4,107	1,920	14,898	4,700	1,817	35,627

REQUIRED HOUSING FOR THOSE NOT HOUSED

Unit Size	2-3 Room	4-5 Room	6 or more Rooms	2-3 Room	4-5 Room	6 or more Rooms	Total
Number of Units	6,040	2,250	1,361	14,865	4,644	1,785	30,945
Rent (1983 Dollars)							
90th Percentile	365	455	520	220	290	330	
Median	300	385	450	170	230	265	
10th Percentile	240	305	365	130	150	180	

Source: Rutgers University, Center for Urban Policy Research, Winter 1983.

EXHIBIT 5-22

UNANSWERED MOUNT LAUREL PROSPECTIVE HOUSING DEMAND 1980-1990 SOUTH-SOUTHWEST REGION

	MODERATE INCOME (50-80% Median)			LOW INCOME (Below 50% of Median)			
	1-2 Person	3-4 Person	5 or more Persons	1-2 Person	3-4 Person	5 or more Persons	Total
Housed	405	653	402	0	10	0	1,470
Not Housed	4,607	901	328	7,874	2,026	821	16,557
Total	5,012	1,554	730	7,874	2,036	821	18,027

REQUIRED HOUSING FOR THOSE NOT HOUSED

Unit Size	2-3 Room	4-5 Room	6 or more Rooms	2-3 Room	4-5 Room	6 or more Rooms	Total
Number of Units	4,607	901	328	7,874	2,026	821	16,557
Rent (1983 Dollars)							
90th Percentile	305	375	430	195	245	280	
Median	250	315	380	165	190	225	
10th Percentile	200	255	310	120	140	170	

Source: Rutgers University, Center for Urban Policy Research, Winter 1983.

EXHIBIT 5-23

UNANSWERED MOUNT LAUREL PRESENT HOUSING DEMAND 1990-2000 NORTHEAST REGION

	MODERATE INCOME (50-80% Median)			LOW INCOME (Below 50% of Median)			
	1-2 Person	3-4 Person	5 or more Persons	1-2 Person	3-4 Person	5 or more Persons	Total
Housed	2,751	1,456	491	1,266	98	0	6,062
Not Housed	1,389	764	1,649	8,714	4,242	3,260	20,018
Total	4,140	2,220	2,140	9,980	4,340	3,260	26,080

REQUIRED HOUSING FOR THOSE NOT HOUSED

Unit Size	2-3 Room	4-5 Room	6 or more Rooms	2-3 Room	4-5 Room	6 or more Rooms	Total
Number of Units	1,389	764	1,649	8,714	4,242	3,260	20,018
Rent (1983 Dollars)							
90th Percentile	375	470	560	215	285	330	
Median	305	405	475	140	185	240	
10th Percentile	240	320	370	120	135	180	

Source: Rutgers University, Center for Urban Policy Research, Winter 1983.

EXHIBIT 5-24

UNANSWERED MOUNT LAUREL PRESENT HOUSING DEMAND 1990-2000 NORTHWEST REGION

	MODERATE INCOME (50-80% Median)			LOW INCOME (Below 50% of Median)			
	1-2 Person	3-4 Person	5 or more Persons	1-2 Person	3-4 Person	5 or more Persons	Total
Housed	1,190	1,240	247	591	149	20	3,437
Not Housed	1,270	140	1,413	5,569	2,911	1,980	13,283
Total	2,460	1,380	1,660	6,160	3,060	2,000	16,720

REQUIRED HOUSING FOR THOSE NOT HOUSED

Unit Size	2-3 Room	4-5 Room	6 or more Rooms	2-3 Room	4-5 Room	6 or more Rooms	Total
Number of Units	1,270	140	1,413	5,569	2,911	1,980	13,283
Rent (1983 Dollars)							
90th Percentile	390	505	555	230	315	370	
Median	310	415	465	175	230	270	
10th Percentile	250	330	390	120	140	160	

Source: Rutgers University, Center for Urban Policy Research, Winter 1983.

EXHIBIT 5-25

UNANSWERED MOUNT LAUREL PRESENT HOUSING DEMAND 1990-2000 WEST CENTRAL REGION

	MODERATE INCOME (50-80% Median)			LOW INCOME (Below 50% of Median)			
	1-2 Person	3-4 Person	5 or more Persons	1-2 Person	3-4 Person	5 or more Persons	Total
Housed	40	120	40	0	20	19	239
Not Housed	680	340	400	1,560	640	401	4,021
Total	720	460	440	1,560	660	420	4,260

REQUIRED HOUSING FOR THOSE NOT HOUSED

Unit Size	2-3 Room	4-5 Room	6 or more Rooms	2-3 Room	4-5 Room	6 or more Rooms	Total
Number of Units	680	340	400	1,560	640	401	4,021
Rent (1983 Dollars)							
90th Percentile	420	540	580	250	315	380	
Median	340	470	520	190	240	260	
10th Percentile	275	350	425	120	150	170	

Source: Rutgers University, Center for Urban Policy Research, Winter 1983.

EXHIBIT 5-26

UNANSWERED MOUNT LAUREL PRESENT HOUSING DEMAND 1990-2000 EAST CENTRAL REGION

	MODERATE INCOME (50-80% Median)			LOW INCOME (Below 50% of Median)			
	1-2 Person	3-4 Person	5 or more Persons	1-2 Person	3-4 Person	5 or more Persons	Total
Housed	20	20	0	0	20	19	79
Not Housed	260	160	80	1,040	420	441	2,401
Total	280	180	80	1,040	440	460	2,480

REQUIRED HOUSING FOR THOSE NOT HOUSED

Unit Size	2-3 Room	4-5 Room	6 or more Rooms	2-3 Room	4-5 Room	6 or more Rooms	Total
Number of Units	260	160	80	1,040	420	441	2,401
Rent (1983 Dollars)							
90th Percentile	375	475	490	205	280	360	
Median	280	340	415	165	220	270	
10th Percentile	240	300	405	125	145	170	

Source: Rutgers University, Center for Urban Policy Research, Winter 1983.

EXHIBIT 5-27

UNANSWERED MOUNT LAUREL PRESENT HOUSING DEMAND 1990-2000 SOUTHWEST REGION

	MODERATE INCOME (50-80% Median)			LOW INCOME (Below 50% of Median)			
	1-2 Person	3-4 Person	5 or more Persons	1-2 Person	3-4 Person	5 or more Persons	Total
Housed	60	180	120	0	20	20	400
Not Housed	700	300	540	2,500	1,240	1,000	6,280
Total	760	480	660	2,500	1,260	1,020	6,680

REQUIRED HOUSING FOR THOSE NOT HOUSED

Unit Size	2-3 Room	4-5 Room	6 or more Rooms	2-3 Room	4-5 Room	6 or more Rooms	Total
Number of Units	700	300	540	2,500	1,240	1,000	6,280
Rent (1983 Dollars)							
90th Percentile	335	445	560	210	290	335	
Median	280	365	450	170	220	255	
10th Percentile	245	325	365	120	140	165	

Source: Rutgers University, Center for Urban Policy Research, Winter 1983.

EXHIBIT 5-28

UNANSWERED MOUNT LAUREL PRESENT HOUSING DEMAND 1990-2000 SOUTH-SOUTHWEST REGION

	MODERATE INCOME (50-80% Median)			LOW INCOME (Below 50% of Median)			
	1-2 Person	3-4 Person	5 or more Persons	1-2 Person	3-4 Person	5 or more Persons	Total
Housed	27	80	156	0	0	0	263
Not Housed	653	280	144	1,660	480	380	3,597
Total	680	360	300	1,660	480	380	3,860

REQUIRED HOUSING FOR THOSE NOT HOUSED

Unit Size	2-3 Room	4-5 Room	6 or more Rooms	2-3 Room	4-5 Room	6 or more Rooms	Total
Number of Units	653	280	144	1,660	480	380	3,597
Rent (1983 Dollars)							
90th Percentile	305	385	430	190	260	280	
Median	240	315	390	155	175	210	
10th Percentile	200	235	320	115	130	150	

Source: Rutgers University, Center for Urban Policy Research, Winter 1983.

EXHIBIT 5-29

UNANSWERED MOUNT LAUREL PROSPECTIVE HOUSING DEMAND 1990-2000 NORTHEAST REGION

	MODERATE INCOME (50-80% Median)			LOW INCOME (Below 50% of Median)			
	1-2 Person	3-4 Person	5 or more Persons	1-2 Person	3-4 Person	5 or more Persons	Total
Housed	None	None	None	None	None	None	None
Not Housed	"	"	"	"	"	"	"
Total	"	"	"	"	"	"	"

REQUIRED HOUSING FOR THOSE NOT HOUSED

Unit Size	2-3 Room	4-5 Room	6 or more Rooms	2-3 Room	4-5 Room	6 or more Rooms	Total
Number of Units	None	None	None	None	None	None	None
Rent (1983 Dollars)							
90th Percentile	N/A	N/A	N/A	N/A	N/A	N/A	
Median	"	"	"	"	"	"	
10th Percentile	"	"	"	"	"	"	

NA = Not applicable

Source: Rutgers University, Center for Urban Policy Research, Winter 1983.

EXHIBIT 5-30

UNANSWERED MOUNT LAUREL PROSPECTIVE HOUSING DEMAND 1990-2000 NORTHWEST REGION

	MODERATE INCOME (50-80% Median)			LOW INCOME (Below 50% of Median)			
	1-2 Person	3-4 Person	5 or more Persons	1-2 Person	3-4 Person	5 or more Persons	Total
Housed	194	134	20	129	7	0	484
Not Housed	147	25	46	503	218	90	1,029
Total	341	159	66	632	225	90	1,513

REQUIRED HOUSING FOR THOSE NOT HOUSED

Unit Size	2-3 Room	4-5 Room	6 or more Rooms	2-3 Room	4-5 Room	6 or more Rooms	Total
Number of Units	147	25	46	503	218	90	1,029
Rent (1983 Dollars)							
90th Percentile	395	495	560	235	300	355	
Median	320	420	480	165	250	270	
10th Percentile	260	335	390	125	150	170	

Source: Rutgers University, Center for Urban Policy Research, Winter 1983.

EXHIBIT 5-31

UNANSWERED MOUNT LAUREL PROSPECTIVE HOUSING DEMAND 1990-2000 WEST CENTRAL REGION

	MODERATE INCCME (50-80% Median)			LOW INCOME (Below 50% of Median)			
	1-2 Person	3-4 Person	5 or more Persons	1-2 Person	3-4 Person	5 or more Persons	Total
Housed	292	430	159	5	28	4	918
Not Housed	1,805	772	344	5,939	1,654	523	11,037
Total	2,097	1,202	503	5,944	1,682	527	11,955

REQUIRED HOUSING FOR THOSE NOT HOUSED

Unit Size	2-3 Room	4-5 Room	6 or more Rooms	2-3 Room	4-5 Room	6 or more Rooms	Total
Number of Units	1,805	772	344	5,939	1,654	523	11,037
Rent (1983 Dollars)							
90th Percentile	435	555	610	270	330	390	
Median	350	460	520	190	265	280	
10th Percentile	280	365	420	125	170	180	

Source: Rutgers University, Center for Urban Policy Research, Winter 1983.

EXHIBIT 5-32

UNANSWERED MOUNT LAUREL PROSPECTIVE HOUSING DEMAND 1990-2000 EAST CENTRAL REGION

	MODERATE INCOME (50-80% Median)			LOW INCOME (Below 50% of Median)			
	1-2 Person	3-4 Person	5 or more Persons	1-2 Person	3-4 Person	5 or more Persons	Total
Housed	765	847	169	13	50	36	1,880
Not Housed	9,026	3,063	1,138	16,446	3,944	1,371	34,988
Total	9,791	3,910	1,307	16,459	3,994	1,407	36,868

REQUIRED HOUSING FOR THOSE NOT HOUSED

Unit Size	2-3 Room	4-5 Room	6 or more Rooms	2-3 Room	4-5 Room	6 or more Rooms	Total
Number of Units	9,026	3,063	1,138	16,446	3,944	1,371	34,988
Rent (1983 Dollars)							
90th Percentile	370	465	520	220	300	350	
Median	295	380	470	180	260	270	
10th Percentile	240	305	365	120	150	170	

Source: Rutgers University, Center for Urban Policy Research, Winter 1983.

EXHIBIT 5-33

UNANSWERED MOUNT LAUREL PROSPECTIVE HOUSING DEMAND 1990-2000 SOUTHWEST REGION

	MODERATE INCOME (50-80% Median)			LOW INCOME (Below 50% of Median)			
	1-2 Person	3-4 Person	5 or more Persons	1-2 Person	3-4 Person	5 or more Persons	Total
Housed	1,241	1,093	308	24	41	23	2,730
Not Housed	3,907	1,490	899	10,807	3,375	1,298	21,776
Total	5,148	2,583	1,207	10,831	3,416	1,321	24,506

REQUIRED HOUSING FOR THOSE NOT HOUSED

Unit Size	2-3 Room	4-5 Room	6 or more Rooms	2-3 Room	4-5 Room	6 or more Rooms	Total
Number of Units	3,907	1,490	899	10,807	3,375	1,298	21,776
Rent (1983 Dollars)							
90th Percentile	365	455	520	220	290	330	
Median	300	385	450	170	230	265	
10th Percentile	240	305	365	130	150	180	

Source: Rutgers University, Center for Urban Policy Research, Winter 1983.

EXHIBIT 5-34

UNANSWERED MOUNT LAUREL PROSPECTIVE HOUSING DEMAND 1990-2000 SOUTH-SOUTHWEST REGION

	MODERATE INCOME (50-80% Median)			LOW INCOME (Below 50% of Median)			
	1-2 Person	3-4 Person	5 or more Persons	1-2 Person	3-4 Person	5 or more Persons	Total
Housed	296	467	270	0	8	0	1,041
Not Housed	3,373	670	264	6,230	1,603	649	12,789
Total	3,669	1,137	534	6,230	1,611	649	13,830

REQUIRED HOUSING FOR THOSE NOT HOUSED

Unit Size	2-3 Room	4-5 Room	6 or more Rooms	2-3 Room	4-5 Room	6 or more Rooms	Total
Number of Units	3,373	670	264	6,230	1,603	649	12,789
Rent (1983 Dollars)							
90th Percentile	305	375	430	195	245	280	
Median	250	315	380	165	190	225	
10th Percentile	200	255	310	120	140	170	

Source: Rutgers University, Center for Urban Policy Research, Winter 1983.

PART IV

OTHER THAN NEW CONSTRUCTION ADDITIONS TO THE HOUSING STOCK

REUSING THE EXTANT HOUSING STOCK

Shelter can be provided in many ways. To date, the dominant choice has been through new construction. Over the last decade, there is in evidence a shift, however. Changes in affluence, consumer tastes and the like have made the reuse of the extant housing stock a much more palatable, and in many cases the only affordable, residential housing strategy. This section briefly considers non-new construction additions. It discusses three prominent examples -- conversion, rehabilitation, and filtering -- and then briefly explores the significance of each as providers of lower-income housing. It should be noted at this point that conversion produces a net new unit while rehabilitation and filtering only affect either the quality of the housing unit or who is using it.

HOUSING CONVERSIONS

There are two categories of housing conversion. The first consists of the reuse of nonresidential space for residential purposes. Examples include the reuse of older and/or surplus commercial, warehouse, manufacturing, educational and similar structures for apartments. While a detailed breakout of such activity is lacking, studies by the Urban Land Institute, Rutgers University Center for Urban Policy Research, and others[6] indicate that nonresidential-to-residential conversions are occurring in both large and small communities across the United States. This activity is being conducted both with and without public subsidy and is delivering a diversity of units by type (finished or unfinished, rental versus condominium, etc.) and price range.

A second category of conversion consists of the subdivision of larger residential units to additional smaller dwellings:[7]

> ...Residential conversions, wherein one large unit is converted to two or more units, usually result in permanent additions to the stock. The equipment additions and structural changes, which require substantial investment, are unlikely to be withdrawn to return the units to their former state of one larger unit. In the process, obsolete equipment and amenities can be replaced to achieve better quality and design. Declining household size and the often superior . . . locations of many large, older units make such conversions a potentially important source of additions to the housing stock.

Residential conversions historically have been prohibited by zoning, building, and other codes. Despite this obstacle, illegal conversions have often occurred. Cases of illegal "twos" -- a single family unit subdivided into two units -- abound. The incidence of conversions has, if anything, increased in recent years. Again, while a separate tally is lacking, studies by the Urban Land Institute and others[8] suggest a growing phenomenon. In recognition of this, there have been numerous efforts to change the law to allow, but regulate, conversions. The following two examples are illustrative. The Tri-State Regional Planning Commission has issued a model ordinance permitting conversions.[9] And in response to the Mount Laurel II decision, the Township of Mount Laurel has recently allowed conversion of single-family to two-family units provided certain conditions are met: (1) the added unit complies with the building code; and that (2) one of the two units is occupied by a low/moderate-income family which is (3) related by blood to the other dwellers.[10]

A recent analysis by the U.S. Department of Housing and Urban Development (HUD) points to the significance of the reuse of the extant housing stock.[11] HUD terms reuse as "additions to the housing supply by means other than new construction." It includes in this group, both the rehabilitation of previously uninhabitable housing (a very small percentage) as well as conversions of residential/nonresidential buildings to apartments. According to HUD, the magnitude of "non-new construction additions," primarily conversions, is inverse to the level of new housing production -- if the latter is vigorous there is less need to reuse the extant stock and vice versa.

In the 1950s to 1960s, new housing production in the United States was often insufficient to the need so conversion was frequently turned to -- about 10 percent of the units added to the housing stock in this period came from "non-new" sources. In contrast, in the early 1970s, new production was very vigorous and conversion fell to an almost negligible 3 percent. With the decline in new housing starts from 1973 onward, conversion again became a major housing segment -- contributing almost 30 percent of all the units added to in the housing stock over the last decade:[12]

> In the 1950s and 1960s, reuse supplied roughly 10 percent of the units added to the stock of housing. The importance of this source has increased greatly in the 1970s. Since 1973, reuse supplied almost 28 percent of all units added to the stock. The numbers supplied from this source varied each year from less than 200,000 to almost 850,000 during the 1973 to 1980 period. On average, 150,000 more units (both single and multifamily) were supplied each year by reuse than by new multifamily construction, i.e., 670,000 conversions compared with 520,000 new multifamily units. Moreover, reuse appears to be countercyclical to new production, that is, additions from sources other than new production increase when new production additions decline, and decrease when new additions increase...

The cyclical swing of these numbers is clearly significant, possibly masking a basic increase. If in New Jersey, we assume that conversions and rehabilitations (of such magnitude as to take a housing unit from out of the stock and bring it back in) are at one-half the highest rate (30%) projected by HUD, a rough estimate of the conversions (and demolitions) are at hand.* We are able to employ a three variable simultaneous equation to derive the conversion supply.

Relationship A — 435,000 New Units Were Built from 1970 to 1980

Relationship B — 385,000 Net New Units (New Construction + Conversion - Demolition) Were Added from 1970 to 1980

Relationship C — Conversions on Average Equal 15 percent of New Units

Let X = New Construction during a decade (435,000 Units)

Let Y = Conversion during a decade

Let Z = Demolitions during a decade

Equation A: $X = 435{,}000$

Equation B: $X + Y - Z = 385{,}000$

Equation C: $Y = 0.15\ X$

Then (EQ.B.):

$$435{,}000 + 0.15\ (435{,}000) - Z = 385{,}000$$

$$435{,}000 + 65{,}000 - Z = 385{,}000$$

$$-Z = -115{,}000$$

$$Z = 115{,}000$$

New Construction		Conversions		Demolitions		Net New Production
435,000	+	65,000	-	115,000	=	385,000

The decade of the 1970s could have produced as many as 65,000 conversions. These units are counted as part of the tally of net additional housing units. They represent a large share of the number that is affordable by moderate-income families.

---

*No accurate information on additional demolitions is at hand. Permitted demolitions far underestimate the actual field level and were reported as approximately 50,000 in New Jersey for the period 1970 to 1980.

HOUSING REHABILITATION

Housing rehabilitation is defined as the upgrading of a property through improvement.[13] This definition is intentionally broad to reflect this strategy's encompassing nature. Rehabilitation ranges from "cosmetic," entailing only facade and other minor repairs, to "gut," in which everything but the exterior walls is replaced.[14]

Housing rehabilitation offers numerous advantages compared to new construction. Besides preserving the historic built environment, the former approach capitalizes on the extant infrastructure (i.e., streets, roads, utilties, etc.) and usually can be effected more expeditiously. These attributes allow for cost savings. Several studies suggest that most gut rehabilitation is at least 20-40 percent less expensive than new construction at a similar amenity level.[15] In some cases even greater savings are possible. In New York City, for instance, the Community Preservation Corporation is presently rehabilitating multifamily dwellings for $10,000 per unit for "cosmetic" renovation and $30,000 for "gut."[16] The equivalent cost for new construction in this city is at least $60,000 per unit.

The economy and other attributes of rehabilitation have brought it to the forefront as a significant housing delivery strategy. The federal government's support is indicative.[17] Starting from the late 1960s, rehabilitation has constituted between 15 and 20 percent of the total federal housing assistance in the form of <u>direct</u> programmatic aid (i.e., Sections 202, 221(d)(3), 236, 8, etc.). From 1970 to 1980,[18] a total of over 300,000 units were renovated with direct, federal aid. The peak year was 1980 when almost 60,000 units were rehabilitated.

In recent years, directly subsidized federal housing assistance, and in turn aided rehabilitation production, has fallen dramatically. In fiscal year 1983, for example, a total of about 70,000 units were assisted by the federal government (new construction and rehabilitation). Of this total one-sixth or only 12,000 units were renovated.[19] These figures understate, however, the continued federal support for rehabilitation in the form of <u>indirect</u> assistance (i.e., Community Development Block Grants) monies given to local governments -- who in turn establish renovation programs themselves. In contrast to the decline of activity of the direct federal rehabilitation subsidies, indirect production has been growing vigorously. In fiscal year (FY) 1976 it was responsible for the rehabilitation of approximately 28,000 units; in FY 1977, 50,000 units; FY 1978, 75,000 units; FY 1979, 100,000 units; FY 1980, 150,000 units; FY 1981, 175,000 units and FY 1982, 225,000 units.[20] In sum, from 1970 to 1983, a total of about 1.3 million units were improved with direct (500,000 units) and indirect (800,000 units) federal assistance.

Rehabilitation is also effected in the <u>private, unaided sector</u>. While a separate breakout of such production is unavailable, indirect evidence suggests that unaided rehabilitation is also quite substantial. For example, a survey conducted by the Urban Land Institute of 250 central cities indicated that most were experiencing significant levels of non-subsidized housing renovation.[21] This typically occurred in neighborhoods of some historic or architectural importance and was done mainly for owner-occupancy rather than for investment.

The key to rehabilitation is that many deteriorated units may be rendered sound with its application. The installation of central heating, a partition in a room to create another room and thereby to provide privacy, adding a kitchen component, or providing a bathroom -- all may render a deteriorated unit sound.

There is, however, no information provided by any of the traditional information sources (U.S. Census, Annual Housing Survey) on the extent of rehabilitation. The Annual Housing Survey does list additions, alterations, replacements, and repairs (four separate categories) completed during a year at a cost of $100 or more.[22]

EXHIBIT 5-35

REHABILITATION AS A SOURCE OF HOUSING SUPPLY

	1974-1977* Percentage of All Mount Laurel-Income Occupied Units On Which More than $100 Was Spent For Additions, Alterations, Replacement and Repairs		
	Median	High	Low
Additions	.5	.8	.4
Alterations	3.5	5.6	3.2
Replacements	6.1	7.3	4.6
Repairs	7.0	13.0	6.6

	1974	1975	1976	1977	Median
Percent with three or more Expenditure Categories	0.9	1.1	1.0	2.8	0.95

Source: Annual Housing Survey, National Survey Computer Tapes, 1974, 1975, 1976, 1977.

*In 1977 the dollar increment was raised to $200 or more.

The above table shows alterations of $100 or more to occur at a frequency of 3.5 percent annually in low- and moderate-income housing units whereas repairs and replacements of the same dollar magnitude occur at about the 6.5 percent level. Additions affect 0.5 percent of the housing stock annually. If we use three of four of these categories to signal a unit which has undergone sufficient alteration, addition, replacement and/or repair to be brought to sound condition, a potential estimate of rehabilitation is at hand. The rationale behind the approach is that a particular unit in a given year underwent three separate categories of improvement. If the unit was deficient, this level of physical attention probably rendered it sound.

There are approximately 2.7 million housing units in New Jersey; 39.1 percent are occupied by low- and moderate-income families of which 12 percent or 120,000 units are deficient. Over the four years of the Annual Housing Survey, approximately 0.95 percent annually of the units occupied by low- and moderate-income families had three categories of improvement of $100 or more. Using this percentage as a gauge of potential impact on housing production, and applying it to those units deteriorated and occupied by low- and moderate-income families, yields approximately 11,500 units a decade that might be rendered habitable through this process. Over the two decade period, the number of units potentially rehabilitated would be close to 23,000.

FILTERING

As is indicated in Chapter 1, a housing market is a geographic area relative to the journey-to-work wherein like units are in mutual competition. For a single household a housing market is that portion of the housing stock in which its socioeconomic peers reside and from which members of all households can conveniently commute to work.

There obviously are a number of submarkets within an overall housing market which key to different sectors of housing value. Submarkets within a housing market are linked by filtering -- a process by which higher class housing that becomes older and less desirable is passed on to less affluent users at cheaper costs.[23] A critical dimension of filtering is supply. New, expensive housing must be provided at the top* of the market and it must be sought by those of more affluence; if used, lower cost housing is to be passed to those of less affluence. Another aspect of downward filtering is that the unit's value must fall more rapidly than its quality. In this way housing is available at reduced costs while it still retains some of its structural integrity and living quality.

The reverse process of upward filtering, although not to the same magnitude, also characterizes the market. In this case, more modest housing,

---

*Some economists say throughout the market.

in a very tight housing market or in areas experiencing redevelopment, is passed from lower income to more affluent households at higher costs.

Those who discuss filtering recognize its impact on the market. Most poor people live in old housing which, unless publicly or privately subsidized, was usually previously occupied by more affluent families (in constant dollars) relative to those who currently live there. There is, however, difficulty gauging its magnitude or its worth. Filtering must be separated, for instance, from the simple turnover of comparably priced units to households of similar income. It must also be expressed as a net figure separating out filtering down from filtering up. Another aspect is the quality of the filtered stock. If the housing is deficient because it has not been maintained, then the concept of sound housing delivery at reduced cost is not a viable one because <u>sound</u> housing has <u>not</u> filtered.

There are very few empirical analyses of filtering. Analysis of filtering requires continuous tracking of specific housing units. Prior to the <u>Annual Housing Survey</u> of the 1970s, most analyses of the standing stock of structures came indirectly from interviews of households. The decennial (1970, 1980) <u>Census of Population and Housing</u> is based on interviewing <u>people</u> wherever they are found, whereas the <u>Annual Housing Survey</u> returns to the same unit even if different people are found to be living there.[24]

Using the <u>Annual Housing Survey</u> for the years 1974 and 1980, and standardizing Mount Laurel incomes for the two time periods using the Consumer Price Index as well as HUD income eligibilities, some limited estimate of change in housing stock utilization by low- and moderate-income households versus those households which are more affluent, is available.

Exhibit 5-36 presents housing units in New Jersey occupied by Mount Laurel income-eligible households in 1974 and in 1980. This exhibit attempts to trace the share of a constant stock of housing (that was available in 1974) according to its occupancy by those of Mount Laurel incomes in 1974 and 1980. A significant share of housing was built over the period 1974 to 1980 (new-construction), most of which was occupied by more affluent households than those of Mount Laurel incomes. This new housing production is what releases older housing for filtering. A small share of this housing was lost due to demolition, some portion of which came from the stock occupied by Mount Laurel-type households. Summarizing these figures in tabular form below provides the following information.

What is clear from this exhibit is that over the six year period, 1974-1980, 13.7 percent of housing filtered into Mount Laurel income-eligible families and 7.2 percent filtered out -- a net of 6.5 percent. Moderate-income families had 6.4 percent of the stock filter in, yet lost 4.4 percent from that which filtered out -- lower-income families had 7.3 percent filter in and 2.8 percent filter out. This yielded six year nets of 2.0 percent to moderate-income families and 4.5 percent to lower-income families. In addition, 1.7 percent was passed down from moderate to lower-income families.

EXHIBIT 5-36

ESTIMATES OF FILTERING TO AND FROM THE LOW AND MODERATE INCOME POPULATION OF NEW JERSEY

Filter "Out" (1974-1980)	Filter "In" (1974-1980)		Net "In" 1974-1980	Net"In" 1970-1980*
7.2%	13.7%	Net Addition to Mount Laurel Income-Eligible Stock (From Non-Mount Laurel)	6.5%	10.8%
4.4	6.4	Net Addition to Moderate-Income Stock (From Non-Mount Laurel)	2.0	3.3
2.8	7.3	Net Addition to Lower-Income Stock (From Non-Mount Laurel)	4.5	7.5
2.3	3.3	Net Addition to Lower-Income Stock (From Moderate to Low)	1.0	1.7

*1970 to 1980 = 1974 to 1980 ÷ 0.6

Source: Annual Housing Survey, National Survey Computer Tapes, 1974-1980.

These percentages are deceptive in that they do not account for either: (1) a deficient unit being passed down, or (2) a family becoming poor (loss of employment, movement of household income contributor) in a unit over the two time periods. In the latter case the unit does not become part of an increase in the share of units for the lower-income households but rather reflects an income reclassification of the unit's occupant. Assume that the aggregate of these situations render the filtering figure 40 percent higher than it should. A 10.8 percent addition to the Mount Laurel stock from the non-Mount Laurel stock (middle-income housing) is therefore reduced to 7 percent taking into account this potential overcount. The following example serves to illustrate the potential decade impact of filtering.

EXHIBIT 5-37

FILTERING AS A SOURCE OF HOUSING SUPPLY

TOTAL NEW JERSEY HOUSING STOCK
2.7 MILLION UNITS

Mount Laurel Component - 39.1% = 1,085,700 Units

Non-Mount Laurel Component - 60.9% = 1,644,300 Units

1,644,300 x .065* = 106,880

*.065 = Decade net filtering to Mount Laurel households (.108 x .60)

Source: See Exhibit 5-36.

The potential impact of filtering can render significant levels of used housing units (200,000 over a two decade period) to low- and moderate-income families. Its pace is ultimately dependent, however, on the overall throughput of the housing industry.

SUMMARY

The preceding chapter has indicated that of a gross low- and moderate-income housing demand of close to 334,000, less than 10 percent is answerable though unaltered conventional housing supply. There remain approximately 300,000 units of combined present/prospective demand to be met over the next two decades; about one-third of this to answer present need; two-thirds for prospective need. The same percentages apply to those for which the housing must be directed, i.e., less than one-third to moderate income, more than two-thirds to lower income. New construction is not available to most moderate-income families and the portion of this income group that is served through net additions to the housing stock is housed through conversions of residential properties and to a lesser extent, conversions of nonresidential properties. These create "new" units by subdividing extant, larger, structures.

Rehabilitation is another source of housing supply in that it renders a deficient unit sound with improvement. Rehabilitation potentially serves both low- and moderate-income housing need through the upgrading of deficient units currently occupied by these two groups. Rehabilitation that is less than returning an abandoned, unoccupied unit to the housing stock yet more than cosmetic is estimated to impact approximately 9.5 percent of the deficient stock over a ten year period. This would render approximately 23,000 deficient units sound over the period 1980 to 2000.

Filtering is yet another source of supply to low- and moderate-income families. It is the largest source of housing delivery to this income sector. It has the capacity to deliver a significant amount of housing to low- and moderate-income households if there is significant supply throughout the market. Yet, some of this housing may be in locations or neighborhoods that are not desirable even though the specific units to be passed down are sound. Thus, only a share of it may be counted as potentially meeting Mount Laurel need. The market for affluent and middle income families must be active for housing to be released by these groups to lower-income households.

What is very clear from this chapter is that all forms of housing supply must be invoked to meet Mount Laurel housing demand. The next chapter will show the bridge mechanisms necessary to make generally unaffordable privately provided housing affordable by at least some sector of those of lower income. In addition to employing these types of cost saving strictures for Mount Laurel housing, we must continue to build substantial amounts of housing for the middle and upper demand sectors of the market. If this is done, many of the non-conventional sources of supply will be activated to assist in meeting low- and moderate-income housing demand.

NOTES

1. State of New Jersey, Department of Labor, New Jersey Revised Total and Age and Sex Population Projections July 1, 1985 to 2000 (Trenton, NJ: Department of Labor, July 1983).

2. U.S. Department of Commerce, Bureau of the Census, The 1980 Census of Population and Housing (Washington, D.C.: Government Printing Office, 1982).

3. U.S. Department of Commerce, Bureau of the Census and U.S. Department of Housing and Urban Development, Annual Housing Survey - Series (Washington, D.C.: Government Printing Office, series).

4. Donald J. Veldman, Fortran Programming for the Behavioral Sciences (New York: Holt, Rinehart and Winston, 1967).

5. See Appendix to Chapter 6 of this study.

6. Urban Land Institute, Adaptive Reuse Development Economics, Process, and Profiles (Washington, D.C: Urban Land Institute, 1978); Robert W. Burchell and David Listokin, The Adaptive Reuse Handbook (New Brunswick: Center for Urban Policy Research, 1981).

7. U.S. Department of Housing and Urban Development, "Additions to the Housing Supply by Means Other Than New Construction" (December 1982). Paper prepared by the Division of Housing and Demographic Analysis, Office of Policy Development and Research.

8. J. Thomas Black, "Private Market Housing Renovation in Central Cities: A ULI Survey," Urban Land (November 1975), pp. 3-9; J. Thomas Black, Allan Bouet, and Robert Bubinsky, Private-Market Housing Renovation in Older Urban Areas (Washington, D.C.: Urban Land Institute, 1977); Martin Gellen, "A House in Every Garage: The Economics of Secondary Units," Center for Real Estate and Urban Economics Working Papers Series, Working Paper 82-43.

9. "Draft Model Conversion Ordinance," Tri-State Regional Planning Commission, Housing and Community Division, January 1981.

10. Mount Laurel Township Ordinance 1983-15.

11. See footnote 7 in this chapter.

12. Ibid., p. I.

13. See David Listokin, The Dynamics of Housing Rehabilitation (New Brunswick: Center for Urban Policy Research, 1973).

14. See, for example, Frank Kristof, A Large Scale Rehabilitation Program for New York City (New York: City Housing and Redevelopment Administration, 1967).

15. D. Gordon Bagby, Housing Rehabilitation Costs (Lexington, MA: Lexington Books, 1973); A.H. Schaaf, Economic Aspects of Urban Renewal: Theory Policy and Area Analysis (Berkeley, CA: Real Estate Research Program, Institute of Business and Economic Research, University of California, 1960); A.H. Schaaf, "Economic Feasibility Analysis for Urban Renewal Housing Rehabilitation," Journal of the American Institute of Planners, Vol. 35, No. 6 (November 1969); George Sternlieb and David Listokin, "Rehabilitation Versus Redevelopment: Cost-Benefit Analysis," in Housing in the Seventies, Vol. II (Washington, D.C.: Government Printing Office, 1976).

16. Michael D. Lappin, "Community Preservation Corportion." Statement of Michael D. Lappin, President of the New York City Community Preservation Corporation before the President's Commission on Housing, December 2, 1981. See David Listokin (editor), Housing Rehabilitation: Economic, Social, and Policy Perspectives (New Brunswick: Center for Urban Policy Research, 1983).

17. David Listokin, "Housing Rehabilitation: A Strategy and Literature Come of Age," in Listokin, Housing Rehabilitation, p. 1.

18. Ibid., pp. 13-15.

19. Ibid.

20. *Ibid.*

21. J. Thomas Black, "Private Market Housing Renovation."

22. See footnote 3 in this chapter.

23. See, for example, E.M. Fisher and L. Winnick, "A Reformulation of the 'Filtering' Concept," *Journal of Social Issues*, Vol. 7, Nos. 1 and 2 (1951), p. 47; Wallace Smith, *Filtering and Neighborhood Change* (Berkeley: Center for Real Estate and Urban Economics, 1964); Ira Lowry, "Filtering and Housing Standards: A Conceptual Analysis," *Land Economics*, Vol. 36 (November 1960), p. 362; Richard Muth, *Cities and Housing* (Chicago: University of Chicago Press, 1969); J.B. Lansing, *New Homes and Poor People: A Study of Chains of Moves* (Ann Arbor, MI: Institute for Social Research, 1969); William Brueggeman, "An Analysis of the Filtering Process with Special Reference to Housing Subsidies" (Washington, D.C.: U.S. Department of Housing and Urban Development, 1973); James T. Little, "Household Preferences, Relocation and Welfare: An Evaluation of the Filtering Concept," Working Paper HMS 2, Institute for Urban and Regional Studies, Washington University (1974); J.C. Ohls, "Public Policy Toward Low-Income Housing and Filtering in Housing Markets," *Journal of Urban Economics*, Vol. 2 (April 1975), p. 144; and John C. Weicher, "A Decent Home: An Assessment of Progress Toward the National Housing Goal and Policies Adopted to Achieve It," in Donald Phares (editor), *A Decent Home and Environment: Housing Urban America* (Cambridge: Ballinger, 1977).

24. See footnote 3 in this chapter.

APPENDIX I

MOUNT LAUREL DEMAND - HOUSED, NOT HOUSED AGGREGATE TOTALS

The following two exhibits present a summary of the data reported in Exhibits 5-7 through 5-34. Where the detailed exhibits discussed throughout this chapter showed data disaggregated by household size, these Appendix exhibits present total counts of present and prospective Mount Laurel households to be either housed or not housed by projected conventional housing supply. Further, these Appendix exhibits tally the Mount Laurel population according to the time period when demand is generated (i.e., either present demand or projected demand); the earlier exhibits tallied demand according to when that demand will have to be confronted (i.e., present 1980 demand was distributed out over two decades on a 50/50 basis, assuming that half of present demand would have to be met during 1980-1990 and the remaining half during 1990-2000).

Exhibits 5A-2 and 5A-3 can be directly related to the summary data on Mount Laurel housing demand presented in Exhibit 5-1. Exhibits 5A-2 and 5A-3 sum to Exhibit 5-1. For instance, Exhibit 5-1 shows a total present (1980) demand for housing by 120,160 Mount Laurel households. Of this total present demand, Exhibit 5A-2 shows that 20,994 households (17.5 percent) can be expected to find affordable housing during 1980-2000; Exhibit 5A-3 shows that 99,166 households (82.5 percent) will not be housed by conventional housing supply absent Mount Laurel intervention. Thus, the sum of 20,994 and 99,166 add to 120,160. Similarly, the proportions of low- and moderate-income households from Exhibit 5-1 who will and will not be housed by conventional supply are tabulated in Exhibits 5A-2 ("housed") and 5A-3 ("not housed"). This information is presented in these exhibits for the state as a whole and for each of the six Mount Laurel regions. The same procedure applies to estimates of prospective demand for 1980-1990 and 1990-2000.

A note is in order to clarify data for the "housed" and "not housed" proportions of prospective demand for the 1990-2000 decade in the Northeast Region 1. As shown in Exhibit 5-1 (and discussed in detail in Chapter 2), prospective Mount Laurel households in the Northeast Region are projected to show a net loss during the period 1990-2000, largely due to the decrease in total population projected for the region during that period. As a consequence, statewide prospective demand for 1990-2000 is shown in Exhibit 5-1 as equal to an increase of 88,672 households (Regions 2 through 6) minus the decrease of 8,720 households in Northeast Region 1, for a statewide net growth of 79,952 prospective Mount Laurel households.

This total is at variance with the data on the "housed" and "not housed" prospective Mount Laurel households in Exhibits 5A-2 and 5A-3 to the extent that the latter exhibits do not reflect the loss of population projected for the Northeast Region for 1990-2000. The Appendix exhibits present the proportions of prospective households that will or will not obtain affordable housing; the actual decrease in Mount Laurel households is presented here as a zero tally of households that will be either housed or not housed. Consequently, since the actual loss of households is treated as a zero increase, the total of "housed" and "not housed" prospective households (88,672) in Exhibits 5A-2 and 5A-3 exceeds total prospective demand reported in Exhibit 5-1 (79,952) by the 8,720 net loss of prospective households projected for the Northeast Region. The alternative of expressing this loss in households as a potential surplus of available housing units is not possible for at least two reasons. First, there is no practicable method available for predicting what proportion of those potentially surplus units will be available to Mount Laurel households (i.e., affordable and in non-deteriorated condition). Secondly, the possibility of utilizing such housing units to meet prospective demand in other regions is not available given the independence of housing markets implied in the regional definition as well as the excessive commuting times incurred in pursuing the housing from other regions.

EXHIBIT 5A-2

PRESENT AND PROSPECTIVE MOUNT LAUREL HOUSING DEMAND
"HOUSED" BY CONVENTIONAL SOURCES OF SUPPLY - 1980 to 2000

	STATEWIDE	NORTHEAST REGION 1	NORTHWEST REGION 2	WEST CENTRAL REGION 3	EAST CENTRAL REGION 4	SOUTHWEST REGION 5	SOUTH-SOUTHWEST REGION 6
	(All Region Total)	Bergen Hudson Passaic	Essex Morris Sussex Union	Hunterdon Middlesex Somerset Warren	Monmouth Ocean	Burlington Camden Gloucester Mercer	Atlantic Cape May Cumberland Salem
Present Demand "Housed" (Housing Deficient-Income-Constrained)							
<u>1980 Demand "Housed"</u>	20,994	11,956	6,889	429	179	994	547
50-80%	16,461	9,354	5,346	350	100	764	547
<50%	4,533	2,602	1,543	79	79	230	0
Prospective Demand "Housed" (Purely Income-Constrained)							
<u>1980-1990 Demand "Housed"</u>	15,420	1,696	3,446	1,719	2,407	4,682	1,470
50 -80%	14,288	1,231	3,086	1,658	2,292	4,561	1,460
<50%	1,132	465	360	61	115	121	10
<u>1990-2000 Demand "Housed"</u>	7,053	NA	484	918	1,880	2,730	1,041
50-80%	6,685	NA	348	881	1,781	2,642	1,033
<50%	368	NA	136	37	99	88	8

* Net household loss in this region for this time period.

Source: Rutgers University, Center for Urban Policy Research Projections, Winter 1983.

EXHIBIT 5A-3

PRESENT AND PROSPECTIVE MOUNT LAUREL HOUSING DEMAND
"NOT HOUSED" BY CONVENTIONAL SOURCES OF SUPPLY - 1980 to 2000

	STATEWIDE (All Region Total)	NORTHEAST REGION 1 (Bergen, Hudson, Passaic)	NORTHWEST REGION 2 (Essex, Morris, Sussex, Union)	WEST CENTRAL REGION 3 (Hunterdon, Middlesex, Somerset, Warren)	EAST CENTRAL REGION 4 (Monmouth, Ocean)	SOUTHWEST REGION 5 (Burlington, Camden, Gloucester, Mercer)	SOUTH-SOUTHWEST REGION 6 (Atlantic, Cape May, Cumberland, Salem)
Present Demand "Not Housed" (Housing Deficient-Income-Constrained)							
1980 Demand "Not Housed"	99,166	40,204	26,551	8,091	4,781	12,366	7,173
50-80%	22,339	7,646	5,654	2,890	980	3,036	2,133
<50%	76,827	32,558	20,897	5,201	3,801	9,330	5,040
Prospective Demand "Not Housed" (Purely Income-Constrained)							
1980-1990 Demand "Not Housed"	118,561	4,874	5,223	20,283	40,679	30,945	16,557
50-80%	40,864	726	1,954	7,115	15,582	9,651	5,836
<50%	77,697	4,148	3,269	13,168	25,097	21,294	10,721
1990-2000 Demand "Not Housed"	81,619	NA*	1,029	11,037	34,988	21,776	12,789
50-80%	26,969	NA*	218	2,921	13,227	6,296	4,307
<50%	54,650	NA*	811	8,116	21,761	15,480	8,482

* Net household loss in this region for this time period.

Source: Rutgers University, Center for Urban Policy Research Projections, Winter 1983.

CHAPTER 6—
BRIDGE MECHANISMS TO MEET THE MOUNT LAUREL MANDATE

INTRODUCTION

Previous chapters of this report identified the spatial and numerical Mount Laurel parameters: housing regions were defined, their respective housing demand and supply totals were calculated, and the overage of Mount Laurel housing demand compared to "normal" market supply was projected. The last figure, aggregate Mount Laurel housing demand less steady state supply, adjusted by household, unit profile, and locational attributes, constitutes the target required to meet the Mount Laurel goal of housing production for low/moderate-income households. This chapter analyzes how the Court's mandate is to be met. It considers what are termed bridge mechanisms -- techniques to bridge the gap between what housing currently costs and the shelter budget affordable by low/moderate-income families. The basic partitions of the chapter are as follows:

I. Components of Housing Costs:
Development, Construction, Delivery, and Occupancy

II. Individual Bridge Mechanisms Affecting
Each Component of Cost: Impact on
Housing Affordability

III. Broader-Base Bridge Mechanisms Affecting
Multiple Components of Cost: Impact on
Housing Affordability

The analysis proceeds as follows. To better comprehend the challenge of and the response to the Mount Laurel mandate, the chapter initially discusses the components of housing costs -- development, construction, delivery and occupancy. Attention then turns to bridge mechanisms. The State Supreme Court's identification of these strategies is considered first, followed by a more encompassing listing and analysis of such techniques. This discussion is based on national (e.g. HUD, American Planning Association) and state (e.g., Connecticut, New Jersey) studies on affordable housing. The examination of the broad array of bridge approaches is keyed to the components of housing costs. For example, increasing density may lower land and other development expenses, reducing housing size can moderate housing construction outlays, and providing below-market mortgages would relieve the monthly occupancy charge. Each bridge mechanism is evaluated in terms of its applicability, availability, and effect on reducing housing costs so as to meet the Mount Laurel mandate.

THE MOUNT LAUREL CHALLENGE: THE COMPONENTS AND COST OF HOUSING

To better understand the need for and workings of bridge mechanisms it is important to first consider the components of housing and their respective costs. These have been differentiated in many ways. At one end of the spectrum are very general approaches. One example is the annual compilation of single-family cost components reported by the National Association of Home Builders (NAHB).[1] The NAHB considers only four components -- land, financing, labor and materials, and overhead and profit. Others follow a much more detailed breakdown. The Means Building Construction Cost Data[2] handbook, for instance, apportions housing costs among literally thousands of individual items, e.g., clamps, panels, siding, caulking, etc.

For our objective of considering housing costs and necessary Mount Laurel bridge mechanisms, neither of the above-described approaches is adequate. The NAHB format is too general; the Means, much too detailed. In addition, neither presents the sequential flow of the housing delivery process -- land is first acquired and developed, a unit and surrounding subdivision improvements are built, and the house is ultimately sold or rented with attendant costs borne by the purchaser or renter. Much more satisfactory for our purposes is the housing cost breakout initially utilized in the Kaiser and Douglas[3] Commissions of the late 1960s. It was then adopted by the Rutgers University Center for Urban Policy Research to first consider urban housing potential and then the issue of land use controls and affordable housing.[4] This methodology categorizes housing expenses into the stages of development, construction, delivery, and occupancy defined as follows:

1. Development Costs - The expenses incurred on a housing project not directly related to construction outlays. The most important development expense typically is the amount paid for land. To this must be added interim financing (points and interest on a construction loan), public fees (for sewer/water tap-in, inspection, bonding, etc.) and other soft expenses (attorney, architect, engineer and similar professional fees, advertising expenses, property taxes during development/construction, etc.).

2. Construction Costs - The expenses incurred on a project which are directly related to the physical improvement of the property. The two component items are outlays for the housing unit itself (building/preparation of the site and foundation, frame, interior systems, etc.), as well as improvements (on- and off-site roads, streets, sidewalks, utilities, re-

creation, and landscaping amenities). While the unit construction price is usually far more substantial than the improvement expense, in recent years the latter's cost has escalated.

3. Delivery Cost - Expenses related to contingency, overhead, and profit. These are often expressed as a percentage of development and construction charges with a combined 20 to 30 percent add-on not being uncommon.

4. Occupancy Cost - The final housing delivery expense is not paid for by a developer in lump sum but rather by the occupant, over time. The recurring housing carrying charge is termed the occupancy cost. It is usually expressed on a monthly basis -- either as the rent to be paid, or in fee situations, when a unit is sold, as the recurring owner's cost to be met. The most important constituent member of occupancy cost is the principal and interest -- the payback of the financed portion (delivery cost less down payment) of the housing unit. Principal and interest payments increase as the down payment is reduced, interest rates may rise, and the payback period (term) of the loan commonly is shortened. In addition to principal and interest expenses, other important occupancy costs include: (1) property taxes (a function of the property's value and local tax rate); (2) maintenance (a charge for recurring repair, replacement, and operations); (3) hazard insurance for fire and other major hazards; and (4) when it is used (e.g., where the downpayment is less than 20 to 25 percent), mortgage insurance paid to FHA, VA or private carriers. When a maintenance fee is paid to a homeowners/condo association, the latter usually provides casualty insurance. In that case, the homeowner would secure only mortgage insurance, and then only in cases of a small downpayment.

In the enumeration of occupancy expenses, maintenance has been included, while utility costs have not. This is done to reflect standardized charging practices for rental units as well as the underwriting of for-sale housing. In the former case, the increasingly prevailing practice is to "unbundle" all utility provision from the monthly contract rent. Maintenance, however, continues to be provided under and paid from the rental agreement. The exclusion of utilities and inclusion of maintenance in the enumeration of housing costs also reflects the underwriting practice where housing is purchased and an application is made for a mortgage. This calculation is applied in townhouse, garden condominium, and similar housing offerings where maintenace is provided by a central association for a mandatory fee imposed on each homeowner -- a likely Mount Laurel configuration. (See the Technical Appendix for details.)

In sum, occupancy costs encompass principal and interest payments, property taxes, maintenance, and insurance. The same expenses are counted whether a unit is sold or rented. The difference between renting or buying concerns only the federal income tax treatment of the occupancy cost. In a purchase situation, some of the occupancy outlay (interest and property taxes) is deductible from gross income for taxation purposes; with renting no such treatment is offered. Consequently, while a buyer versus renter of shelter may incur the same nominal occupancy expense, the net cost to the former may be less.

Housing Costs Illustrated: The Inexpensive Garden Condominium

The components of housing costs -- development, construction, delivery and occupancy -- and their interrelationships can be better visualized by examining the actual component expenses of housing currently being built in New Jersey. As the future Mount Laurel housing will often closely resemble the least-cost offering currently on the market, we will focus on this configuration. The figures presented here while reasonably representative of the low-end of the housing market, are for illustrative purposes only.

With the exception of mobile homes, the least expensive new housing unit is the garden apartment. While configurations vary, this unit is typically contained in 2.5 story structures with a total of from 8 to 15 apartments in each building. Amenities also differ, but increasingly the garden apartment complex has some type of common recreational facility ranging from tot lots to tennis courts and swimming pools. In years past, the garden apartment was almost exclusively rental; with the imposition of rent control and changes in financing terms, the unit is increasingly being sold as a "garden condominium." This chapter shall therefore refer to this type of housing as a garden condominium and calculate the monthly carrying cost for homeowners. The latter, however, is roughly the same as the monthly contract rent for an equivalent rental unit.

Information on 1983 delivery prices of garden condominiums in New Jersey is available from the Home Owners Warranty (HOW) Corporation.[5] HOW provides warranty coverage against major construction and mechanical defects in new housing -- a provision required by a 1978 New Jersey state law. While there are other carriers, HOW dominates with a 70 percent market share. For each unit that it insures, HOW collects information on the selling price, location, type (e.g. garden condominium), and other factors. The HOW files thus provide an invaluable record of the current New Jersey profile of for-sale housing.

According to HOW, the least expensive for-sale units in New Jersey, as of the Summer 1983 (June through September 1983), are garden condominums. In the northern part of the state (Northeast and Northwest Regions 1 and 2 respectively), the least costly garden condominiums are sold in the $70,000 to $80,000 range and prices escalate sharply from that point. Considerably lower prices are found in the rest of the state. In the West Central Region 3, East Central Region 4, Southwest Region 5, and South-Southwest Region 6, garden condominium prices start between $40,000 to $60,000. These prices are for either one or small two-bedroom units (roughly 700 $ft.^2$), built at densities of about eight units to the acre. Much of this construction is done by the state's largest builders who can capitalize on the economies of volume production. In sum, the least costly new, for-sale housing currently being delivered in New Jersey, albeit not in the North, is a one to small two-bedroom garden condominium produced by a volume builder and sold at a price from $40,000 to $60,000.

Development, construction, delivery, and occupancy costs for this inexpensive garden condominium are shown in Exhibit 6-1. These figures are presented to show rough order of magnitude as exact costs will differ between builders, and even for the same builder, between projects. While the garden apartment is presented here, clearly other types of housing will figure in the municipal answer to Mount Laurel. Our objective in presenting the garden unit is to illustrate in an ordered fashion one response to the decision.

Present day (1983) costs of the case study garden condominium are considered first.* The following development costs are indicated. Raw (unimproved) land, in the areas where these relatively inexpensive units are being built, is sold at roughly $40,000 per acre. Given a density of eight units to the acre, the land cost per unit is about $5,000. Interim financing, which includes points and interest paid on a construction loan, amounts to $2,500 (see Exhibit 6-1 for a detailed explanation of each item). Public fees, encompassing sewer/water connection charges, building permits, inspection and bonding outlays are another $2,500. Other soft expenses for professional services, property taxes and the like amount to $1,500. Total development expenses, are therefore, $11,500.

Construction outlays pertain to both the unit and improvements. At a $28 cost per square foot for the condominium's "bricks and mortar," the 700 ft.^{2} unit costs $19,500. Improvement outlays for streets, utilities, lighting, and recreational/landscaping amenities amount to another $6,000 per unit. Total construction costs are therefore $25,500.

Development and construction expenses combined amount to $37,000. Factoring a 5 percent contingency for cost-overruns, and a 20 percent mark-up for developer overhead and profit, brings the garden condominium's delivery price to $46,000 (see Exhibit 6-1).

Occupancy costs flow from this figure. With a 10 percent down payment the purchaser of the $46,000 unit will carry a mortgage of $41,400. At a 13 percent finance rate and 30-year maturity, the monthly principal and interest payments are $458. Further monthly charges consist of about $90 for property taxes, $50 for maintenance (usually paid to a central homeowners or condominium association), and $10 for mortgage premium insurance (fire insurance is provided by the homeowners association and paid for from the maintenance fees collected; see Exhibit 6-1 for details). Summing the principal and interest payment, property tax, maintenance, and insurance charges yields a monthly carrying cost for the homeowner of about $600.

If this unit were rented rather than purchased, the monthly contract rent would be roughly equivalent since similar charges would have to be met. The property owner would invest an amount equal to roughly 10 percent

---

*Much of the housing cost information described here was derived from large developers active in the central portion of the state (West Central Region).

EXHIBIT 6-1

IMPACT OF THE BRIDGE MECHANISMS: GARDEN CONDOMINIUM EXAMPLE (700 ft.^{2})

HOUSING COSTS

COST COMPONENT	At Today's Standards	With Regulatory Reform	With Regulatory Reform and Public Subsidy
DEVELOPMENT			
Land[1]	\$ 5,000[2]	\$ 4,000[3]	\$ 3,000[4]
Interim Financing[5]	2,500[6]	2,000[7]	1,000[8]
Public Fees	2,500[9]	2,000[10]	2,000[10]
Soft Costs	1,500[11]	1,000[12]	1,000[12]
Total Development	\$11,500	\$ 9,000	\$ 7,000
CONSTRUCTION			
Unit Construction	19,500[13]	18,000[14]	18,000[14]
Development Improvements	6,000[15]	5,000[16]	4,000[17]
Total Construction	\$25,500	\$23,000	\$22,000
DELIVERY			
Total Development	11,500	9,000	7,000
Total Construction	25,500	23,000	22,000
Contingency	1,500[18]	1,000[18]	1,000[18]
Overhead and Profit	7,500[19]	6,000[20]	5,500[20]
Total Delivery	\$46,000	\$39,000	\$35,500
MONTHLY OCCUPANCY			
Principal & Interest[21]	458[22]	388[23]	281[24]
Property Taxes[25]	86[26]	73[27]	67[28]
Maintenance[29]	50	50	50
Insurance[30]	10	10	10
Total Occupancy	\$ 604	\$ 521	\$ 408
AFFORDABILITY			
Minimum Household Income to Afford Occupancy Cost[31]	\$28,992	\$25,008	\$19,584
Minimum Household Income as Share of Median Household[32] Income	.95	.82	.64

Notes:

1. Assumes unimproved land cost of \$40,000 per acre.
2. At density of 8 units per acre (\$40,000 / 8 = \$5,000).
3. At density of 12 units per acre. Note: As land for unimproved development is often purchased on a per-unit basis rather than on gross acreage, the full costs savings of increased density (e.g., 12 as opposed to 8 units per acre) are usually not fully captured. Consequently a \$4,000 cost is assumed rather than \$3,333 (\$40,000 / 12).
4. Assumes 20 percent write-down of land cost from \$4,000 with regulatory reform to \$3,000 with public subsidy.
5. Assumes all costs are financed except overhead and profit.
6. Assumes financial terms of: 1-point placement fee and 16 percent annual interest rate. Assumes 10-month development period, during which half of the principal loan amount is outstanding. Consequently, construction loan interest is effectively equal to 6 percent (16% x .8 x .5) plus 1-point placement fee for a total of 7 percent. In this case, all costs except overhead and profit total \$36,000. Consequently, financing costs equal \$2,500 (\$36,000 x .07).
7. Assumes 8 month development period and construction loan/draw terms as in note 6. Consequently construction loan interest is effectively equal

to roughly 5 percent (16% x .67 x .5) plus 1 point for a total of 6 per cent. In this case, all costs except overhead and profit total $31,000. Consequently, financing costs equal roughly $2,000 ($31,000 x .06).

8. Assumes 8 month development period during which half the principal is outstanding. Assumes subsidized 10 percent construction loan interest rate and no points. Consequently construction loan interest is effectively equal to roughly 3 percent (10% x .67 x.5). In this case, all costs except overhead and profit total $29,000. Consequently, financing costs equal roughly $1000 ($29,000 x .03).
9. Includes $1,400 fee for sewer and water tap in, $300 building permit fee, inspection fee equal to 6 percent of $8,000 bondable improvement (130 percent of $6,000 subdivision cost) or roughly $500, and performance bond equal to 3 percent of bondable amount or $250 ($8,000 x .03). Total public fees therefore amount to roughly $2,500.
10. Assumes $500 savings from amount calculated in note 9 because of reduction in sewer-water tap in, and building permit fees and allowing a letter of credit rather than requiring a performance bond.
11. Assumes $1000 cost per unit for professional fees and $500 for advertising, property taxes during construction, etc.
12. Assumes $500 savings because of accelerated regulatory processing.
13. Assumes $28 cost per square foot for unit "bricks and mortar". Total unit construction costs are therefore $19,500 ($28 x 700).
14. Assumes 5 percent cost savings in construction. This would reduce costs to roughly $18,500 ($19,500 x .95). A further reduction is offered by not applying sales tax to building materials. As materials constitute about half of unit construction costs, not applying the 6 percent sales tax would lower cost by 3 percent to $18,000 ($18,500 x .97).
15. Estimated from interviews with developers and municipal engineers.
16. A conservative $1,000 savings is realized from the increased density of the units, changes in improvement standards, and not applying the state sales tax to building materials.
17. Assumes a 20 percent writedown of improvement cost from $5,000 with regulatory reform to $4,000 with public subsidy.
18. Equals 5 percent of "variable" (e.g. more difficult to predict cost items) -- soft expenses, unit construction, and subdivision improvements.
19. Equals 20 percent of total development, construction, and contingency.
20. Equals 18 percent of total development, construction, and contingency.
21. Assumes 10 percent down payment.
22. Assumes loan amount of $41,400 ($46,000 x .9) at 13 percent interest rate, 30 year maturity.
23. Assumes loan amount of $35,100 ($39,000 x .9) at 13 percent interest rate, 30 year maturity.
24. Assumes loan amount of $32,000 ($35,500 x .9) at 10 percent interest rate, 30 year maturity.
25. Assumes $2.25 per hundred equalized (full value) property tax rate.
26. Equals ($46,000 x .0225)/12.
27. Equals ($39,000 x .0225)/12.
28. Equals ($35,500 x .0225)/12.
29. Paid to homeowners or condo association; includes fire insurance.
30. For mortgage insurance premium.
31. Assumes 25 percent housing expense to income ratio. Derived by dividing monthly occupancy cost by .25 to obtain minimum monthly income, and then multiplying by 12 to obtain minimum annual income.
32. Median household income for West Central Region 3 for 1983 is estimated at $30,500. Income data for this area is utilized because much of the housing cost information was derived from builders active in the central portion of the state.

Note: Wherever possible, figures have been rounded to nearest $500.

Source: Center for Urban Policy Research, Interviews with New Jersey developers, June-September 1983.

of the unit's delivery price and finance the remainder at an amortization schedule equivalent to that of a loan with a 13 percent interest rate and thirty-year maturity. (While in practice, a balloon rather than a fixed mortgage would likely be granted, the former's payout would be roughly equivalent to the latter's payback.) The investor would also have to remit property taxes, provide maintenance, and pay for hazard and mortgage premium insurance at amounts equivalent to that described in the paragraph above. An investor in rental housing would also expect a small profit. (In recent years, rental projects have typically yielded only a minimal cash flow; their investment attraction is mainly tax syndication.) All of these charges -- principal and interest, maintenance, insurance, and a small profit -- would encompass the gross monthly rent. In the 700 $ft.^2$ garden unit example, the monthly contract rent would be about $600.

What is the minimum household income necessary to afford the $600 charge? The answer depends on what is the tolerable share of earnings which can be applied to housing costs. The Technical Appendix indicates that as a benchmark, one appropriate housing expense-to-income ratio is 25 percent. Given a 25 percent housing-expense-to-income share, we can work backwards to calculate that to reside in our case example garden condominium, a home-buyer would have to earn at least $29,000 annually. In 1983, the median New Jersey household income* is estimated at roughly $30,500.[6] Consequently, the $29,000 entry household income to purchase the garden unit is 95 percent of the 1983 median or above the upper threshold point (80 percent) of moderate-income Mount Laurel families. The objective of the bridge mechanisms is to lower housing costs so that increasing segments of the moderate-income Mount Laurel group, and hopefully even their lower income counterparts, will be provided with affordable shelter. Our measure of progress in this regard will be the extent to which successive applications of bridge strategies result in housing being made affordable to increasingly less affluent households as measured by their declining ratios of income compared to the areawide median.

The following section introduces the means of bringing about this change -- the bridge mechanisms. This is followed by a detailed presentation and analysis of each bridge strategy.

BRIDGE MECHANISMS: INTRODUCTION

In the Mount Laurel decision, the State Supreme Court discussed four major bridge techniques.[7] The first consisted of "removing excessive restrictions and exactions." In the words of the Court:[8]

---

*Income is for the West Central Region 3. As most of the housing cost data in this chapter was derived from builders active in central New Jersey, the income profile for the West Central area (adjusted to 1983) is utilized. The reader should realize, however, that income for the other Mount Laurel regions is below that of the West Central Region 3.

> ...In order to meet their Mount Laurel obligations, municipalities, at the very least, must remove...zoning and subdivision restrictions and exactions that are not necessary to protect health and safety....Particularly helpful...as to what the minimum standards should be in a particular community, are the Department of Housing and Urban Development's Minimum Property Standards and the suggestions as to minimum zoning and subdivision standards made by the Rutgers Center for Urban Policy Research in Housing Costs and Government Regulations.

The Court presented three other approaches. One it termed "subsidies" -- the use of whatever public housing (Section 8, Community Development Block Grant, etc.) assistance is available to write-down shelter costs.[9] The second was inclusionary zoning, either encouraging or forcing builders to provide affordable housing.[10] The last was to allow mobile homes and other cost-efficient manufactured housing.[11]

In presenting these four strategies, the State Supreme Court itself recognized it was not giving an exhaustive set of remedies but rather that it was pointing the way to avenues of cost reduction which would be elaborated by others. As stated by the Court in its consideration of inclusionary devices:[12]

> Although we will discuss some of them here, we in no way intend our list to be exhaustive; municipalities and trial courts are encouraged to create other devices and methods for meeting fair share obligations...

This chapter presents a range of "other devices and methods" to meet the Mount Laurel mandate of low- and moderate-income housing production. These consist of a score of various actions (see Exhibit 6-2), encompassing two general approaches -- regulatory reforms (e.g., zoning, development and building code changes), and public subsidies (e.g., Section 8, and CDBG). Before examining this roster in detail, it is important to clarify our focus, format, and methodology.

The focus of the bridge strategies is to reduce the cost of housing for Mount Laurel families only. The various techniques are not intended to be applied to non-Mount Laurel units, although they could be at the discretion of the local community. Stated otherwise, once a community has met its Mount Laurel obligation, it may or may not decide to apply the bridge mechanisms. As stated by the State Supreme Court:[13]

> Once a municipality has revised its land use regulations and taken other steps affirmatively to provide a realistic opportunity for the construction of its fair share of lower income housing, the Mount Laurel doctrine requires it to do no more....Mount Laurel is

EXHIBIT 6-2

BRIDGE STRATEGIES TO LOWER THE COST OF MOUNT LAUREL HOUSING

HOUSING COST COMPONENT	BRIDGE STRATEGY
I. DEVELOPMENT COST	
1. Land	1. Increase density (through upzoning and other means) 2. Provide landbanking and/or land write-down
2. Interim Financing	3. Lower principal (through other bridge approaches) 4. Shorten term (by reducing delays in development-regulatory process) 5. Reduce interest rate (through tax-exempt financing or CDBG "float" -- Section 108 advances)
3. Public Fees	6. Schedule fees according to true costs 7. Consider alternatives to traditional bonding approaches 8. Provide public subsidy
4. Other Soft Costs	9. Reduce professional costs (as a result of accelerated development processing) 10. Provide public subsidy
II. CONSTRUCTION COST	
1. Unit Cost	11. Allow smaller homes 12. Improve the building code and its administration 13. Utilize cost-efficient materials/techniques 14. Provide tax changes (eliminate state sales tax on building materials)
2. Improvement Costs	15. Increase development density 16. Eliminate overly stringent improvement standards 17. Provide public subsidy and tax changes (see 14).
III. DELIVERY COST	18. Lower builder mark-up
IV. OCCUPANCY COST	
1. Principal and Interest	19. Use tax-exempt financing to lower interest rates
2. Property Taxes	20. Apply redevelopment property tax abatement where applicable

Source: See text.

not an indiscriminate broom designed to sweep away all distinctions in the use of land. Municipalities may continue to reserve areas for upper income housing, may continue to require certain community amenities in certain areas, may continue to zone with some regard to their fiscal obligations: they may do all of this, provided that they have otherwise complied with their Mount Laurel obligations.

The format of the bridge strategies also deserves comment. A range of options, is presented. It is not necessary to apply all of the individual approaches. In some cases, in fact, the recommendations may work at cross purposes. For example, utilizing tax-exempt mortgages from the New Jersey Housing Finance Agency (NJHFA) would reduce the loan constant but would increase construction costs as NJHFA projects must be built at prevailing (union) wages. In another case, increasing density lowers land costs per unit, yet at the same time demands more stringent improvement standards capable of accommodating the more intense development. Finally, treating mobile homes as personal rather than real property reduces their tax obligations but also means that the more favorable loan terms available on real estate purchases cannot be secured. Such cross-purposes must be recognized and their consequences evaluated. The purpose of presenting a roster of bridge mechanisms is to provide a listing of many possible approaches from which some may be chosen.

Another characteristic of the bridge approaches is that they are directed at the many participants in the housing delivery process, both public (municipality, county, and state) and private (builders and non-profit groups). The intent is not to lay the burden of affordable housing cost delivery on a single door step -- public or private.

A final comment concerns the basis of the proposed bridge mechanisms. Inherent in many of these items is an attempt to remove excessive restrictions or procedures which unnecessarily increase the cost of housing. This begs the question of what is absolutely necessary; there are few benchmarks identifying basic housing requirements that are indisputably required by health, structural, or other compelling considerations as opposed to the more stringent standards that are normally imposed by communities. To illustrate, one significant requirement affecting housing cost is minimum house size. It is extremely difficult to determine what is the basic minimum square footage mandated by physical and/or mental health needs versus "frills." Housing as shelter can be seen at its barest minimum in Hong Kong's public housing units with 45 square feet per capita. But in order for housing in the United States to be satisfactory, much more space is necessary for the residents to consider themselves full members of society. In addition to these cross-national variations, there are often both inter-regional and intra-state differences in housing size and amenity values. California, for example, "tolerates" much higher density than New Jersey and within the latter state there are distinct north-to-south variations with respect to density preferences. In the absence of firm scientific grounding, who is to judge what are "basic housing standards?"

There is no definitive answer to the last question. Fortunately, for the past decade various national and state groups have grappled with the issue of making housing affordable. To this end they have published studies and guidelines on methods to reduce housing costs. Examples include: Affordable Housing: How Local Regulatory Improvements Can Help (HUD),[14] Changing Development Standards for Affordable Housing (APA),[15] Building Affordable Homes (NAHB),[16] Streamlining Local Regulations (ICMA),[17] Community Options for Lowering Housing Costs (State of Connecticut),[18] and Manual for Reducing Housing Costs (California Building Industry Association).[19] New Jersey has also been active in this regard, publishing The Affordable Housing Handbook,[20] Housing Handbook for New Jersey Municipalities,[21] and the Princeton Housing Proposal.[22] New Jersey legislative documents, such as The Final Report of the New Jersey Assembly Housing Emergency Action Team[23] and the Report and Recommendations of the Mobile Home Study Commission,[24] are also useful resource materials. These many national and state publications form the basis of the following bridge strategies to meet the Mount Laurel mandate.

Each of the bridge mechanisms listed in Exhibit 6-2 will be discussed according to its impact on the stages and components of housing costs previously described. After they all have been introduced, their effects will be illustrated by considering specific impact on the garden condominium example. While the focus is on the garden condo, similar changes would be realized for the garden unit in its rental configuration.

INDIVIDUAL BRIDGE MECHANISMS AFFECTING EACH COMPONENT OF HOUSING COST: IMPACT ON HOUSING AFFORDABILITY

BRIDGE MECHANISMS TO REDUCE DEVELOPMENT COSTS

Reducing Development Costs: Land Expenses

This goal can be accomplished by increasing density and providing for landbanking and/or land write-down.

There are many ways for increasing permitted density.[25] The most important is upzoning -- upping the maximum units allowed per acre. This raises the question of limits. A first concern is the presence of special environmental or other physical constraints which restrict development. In the absence of these, the density recommendations of the national and state literature on affordable housing should be considered as a starting point for determining Mount Laurel standards. (See the Bibliography in this study.) For single-family detached units, this literature commonly recommends densities of four to seven units per acre; for townhouses, densities of six to twelve units; and for garden apartments, twelve to twenty units. These standards are analogous to those mentioned in New Jersey's The

Affordable Housing Handbook.[26] While indicating that there is "no ideal density," and that development intensity should reflect community values, and site and surrounding area physical constraints, this publication states:[27]

> As a means of providing some indication of what constitutes appropriate densities for various housing types we offer the following table: . . .

Type of Unit	Optimum Density Range (Per Gross Acre)
Single-family detached	1-10 units
Two-family duplex, zero lot line	6-20 units
Townhouse, Quadruplex, etc.	10-20 units
Garden apartments	15-25 units

In addition to upzoning, there are other means to increase density.[28] Required setbacks from the right-of-way, rear lot line, etc., can be shortened.[29] Relatedly, zero lot line unit siting could be permitted. Minimum lot frontage can be reduced. Finally, reducing or eliminating minimum housing size requirements would permit additional, more compact units to be placed on the same acreage.

Public Landbanking/Write-down

The difficulty and expense of acquiring land for Mount Laurel housing would be ameliorated by having a municipal agency, other public authority, or non-profit group, assemble and hold land (landbanking)[30] and then offer these lots at a reduced cost (write-down). Landbanking does not necessarily require the use of eminent domain taking, or purchase from private property owners -- two expensive and in other ways problematical approaches. Instead, landbanking for Mount Laurel purposes could consist of assembling and making available surplus municipal or other public lands. For instance, a school closed due to enrollment decline often offers a multiacre site that is most suitable for development. This type of property resource is currently available in most New Jersey communities.

The write-down of site costs is a further important assist. Write-down is expensive, typically available only to public authorities with access to outside funding for such activity. Fortunately, the Community Development Block Grant (CDBG), a federal intergovernmental transfer available to many communities and counties, and in turn often used to support non-profit groups, can be drawn upon to defray the costs of both landbanking and write-down for low and moderate-income housing such as Mount Laurel units. According to the revised (1983) CDBG regulations,[31] block grant funds can be used for:[32]

§570:201(a) Acquisition. Acquisition in whole or in part by a public agency or private nonprofit entity, by purchase, lease, donation, or otherwise, of real property....

It is interesting to note that there is usually some restriction on the use of CDBG funds for new housing construction as opposed to rehabilitation.* An exception is expressly made, however, for the provision of low- and moderate-income housing[33] -- a class under which Mount Laurel units, by definition, qualify:[34]

§570:207(b)(3) New housing construction. Assistance may not be used for the construction of new permanent residential structures or for any program to subsidize or finance such new construction... For the purpose of this paragraph, activities in support of the development of low or moderate income housing including clearance, site assemblage, provision of site improvements and provision of public improvements and certain housing pre-construction costs... are not considered as activities to subsidize or finance new residential construction. [emphasis added]

An example of CDBG-funded landbanking and write-down to facilitate the provision of lower cost housing is found in Bergen County. Since the late 1970s, this county's Housing Authority has operated an Affordable Ownership Housing Program (AOHP).[35] AOHP acquires land suitable for development, preferring physically suitable sites which are publicly owned (e.g., belonging to municipalities or the county), or privately-owned parcels zoned for two-family or other multiple dwellings. Drawing on the county's CDBG allotment, the Housing Authority then writes-down a portion (usually 50 percent) of the land acquisition cost. This subsidy, coupled with the savings garnered from a cost-efficient building design (e.g., attached construction, smaller units, etc.), permits the Housing Authority to deliver a new unit for much less than what is conventionally offered in the Bergen County market.[36] The AOHP unit is sold to households earning less than the county median income. (To ensure that the AOHP housing remains "affordable," a cap on the resale price linked to the Consumer Price Index, is set.) What the AOHP is doing in Bergen County, one of the costliest areas in New Jersey in which to build, can be replicated in other parts of the state.

Reducing Development Costs: Interim Financing

Construction-period financing charges can be reduced by (a) lowering the principal borrowed, (b) shortening the term -- the time period over which the loan is outstanding, and/or (c) lowering the interest rate.

---

*Rehabilitation is also part of the Mount Laurel mandate and is a prime source of housing supply to meet present, housing-deficient Mount Laurel need.

Reduction of the loan principal will result if the overall cost of housing is lowered. This is precisely the intent of the bridge strategies presented in this chapter.

The term of the interim financing can be shortened if developers adopt faster, more efficient building technologies such as using component prefabrication. Examples include the use of preassembled wall panels, plumbing trees, and stair assemblies. These are discussed later under innovative approaches to reduce construction costs.

Public authorities must also do their part. Delays in the administration and regulation of the zoning, environmental-transportation clearance, subdivision, and building inspection process make for a longer than necessary development period, which adds to financing costs. New Jersey has made considerable strides in providing some order and structure to the development system. Its Municipal Land Use Law delimits areas of responsibility of local zoning, planning, and other municipal land use agencies and establishes time limits for the consideration of development plans. While considerable progress has been made, time delays still remain. Two examples considered by the (New Jersey) Governor's Housing Task Force are illustrative. The first entailed delays at state agencies such as unspecified review procedures, and inconsistent and/or overly stringent demands by the Departments of Environmental Protection and Transportation.[37] The second problem area was at the local level and was particularly pronounced with large projects. Difficulties included delays arising from the interpretation of the Municipal Land Use Law on such matters as the definition of a "complete" development application, the jurisdiction of zoning versus planning boards in certain variance situations, and the limits of the appeals process once an application was approved.[38]

Interim financing costs will be reduced if delays and uncertainties in the development regulatory process can be addressed. Such change is possible. The League of Municipalities' Drafting Committee has proposed a package of amendments to the Municipal Land Use Law (already adopted by the State Assembly) which, among other things, requires municipalities to prepare a checklist so confusion over required submissions (and therefore "completion") are eliminated, clarifies when a proposal should be heard by a zoning versus planning board, and amends the variance definition to enable large-scale projects to have a "one-stop review" at the local planning board.[39]

Further changes should be examined. State and local officials should consider the strategies detailed in a 1983 report by the International City Management Association, Streamlining Local Regulations: A Handbook for Reducing Housing and Development Costs,[40] and an earlier report by the American Planning Association and the Urban Land Institute, Streamlining Land Use Regulations: A Guidebook for Local Governments.[41]

A final means of reducing interim financing costs is to lower the interest charge.* This could be accomplished by financing via tax-exempt securities which would carry a below-market interest rate.[42] The developer and the ultimate consumer of low/moderate-income housing, would still have the financial responsibility to pay interest costs on these obligations, but the remittance would be considerably less expensive than the conventional construction loan charge.

Such Mount Laurel construction bonds could possibly be issued by the State, or the municipality. Another source is the New Jersey Housing Finance Agency. The NJHFA has indicated it would consider providing tax-exempt and therefore below market-cost, construction loans for Mount Laurel developers <u>provided</u> a permanent take-out loan would be secured.[43] At today's rates, the NJHFA construction loan would have a 10 percent interest coupon compared to the prevailing 16 percent for short-term financing given by private lenders. (With NJHFA assistance, however, prevailing wages would have to be paid on the residential construction, thereby increasing construction costs by about 20 to 30 percent according to some sources.)[44]

Another source of tax-exempt financing is to have a specially created local improvement district issue bonds. Such an approach was discussed in the New Jersey Department of Community Affairs' <u>The Affordable Housing Handbook</u>:[45]

> IMPROVEMENT BONDS
>
> To this end a community might create an improvement district in conjunction with a specific development, in which some affordable housing will be incorporated.
>
> This improvement district would have the ability to float bonds to finance off-site (and in some instances on-site) improvements. If these "utility" bonds are offered tax-free, their retirement is less costly to the homeowner and they offer an attractive inducement to investors....

As discussed later in this chapter, the tax-exempt market is fraught with its own special risks, namely possible restrictions by the federal government. Other sources of low-cost construction financing should therefore be considered. The Community Development Block Grant is a leading candidate.

As indicated previously, CDBG funds can be used to subsidize new housing provided the units are for low/moderate-income families -- a class that certainly includes Mount Laurel households. Given this authoriza-

---

*Another possible source is to utilize the HUD Title X program. The latter offers a HUD guarantee on financing for land purchase and improvement costs. Because of this guarantee a slightly lower interim financing rate can sometimes be secured.

tion, CDBG monies could be drawn upon by municipalities, counties, and other grant recipients to provide a reduced or zero-interest construction loan for Mount Laurel development. According to CDBG officials at the regional HUD Newark office, as well as their counterparts at various New Jersey county planning boards,[46] this advance could be structured in at least two ways. The first is for CDBG recipients to draw from what is referred to as their "CDBG float"* -- the difference between CDBG monies authorized and actually spent. For instance, if a community were entitled to $500,000 in block grants for, say, sewer improvements and had drawn only $250,000 for this long-term project, then it could request a $250,000 advance. This amount could then be loaned at a zero or reduced interest rate as interim financing to a Mount Laurel developer. The latter would construct and then sell the Mount Laurel units, and with these proceeds repay the community, who in turn would return its advance to HUD.**

A second means of obtaining CDBG monies for a Mount Laurel construction loan is via what is referred to as the Section 108 program.* This provision allows CDBG recipients to obtain an advance from HUD of up to three years of their future entitlements. Unlike a "CDBG float," with the Section 108 advance, the CDBG recipient must <u>pay</u> interest to the federal government. This charge, however, is at the federal funds borrowing rate -- considerably below market rates, especially for short-term advances such as construction loans. In short, a CDBG recipient could apply for a Section 108 advance, then use the proceeds to provide a construction loan to a Mount Laurel developer. The builder would be charged the favorable federal borrowing rate, thus realizing a considerable savings; the CDBG recipient would transfer these interest payments to the federal government thus incurring no out-of-pocket expenses (besides administration). Both the Section 108 and "CDBG float" mechanisms would have to be carefully structured, however, with a <u>guarantee</u> that there is a permanent take-out mortgage so that the construction advances remain just the -- a short-term loan.

<u>Reducing Development Costs: Public Fees</u>

These expenses consist of sewer/water connection charge, inspection and permit fees, and bonding. Connection charges, inspection and permit costs

---

*These techniques have only recently been utilized. See Michael Calvert, "A New Tool for Development," <u>Urban Land,</u> Vol. 42, No. 9, September 1983, p. 22.

**The implementation of the program would proceed as follows. The CDBG recipient could build the Mount Laurel housing itself (if it encompassed a housing agency); or it could finance a non-profit, housing corporation which would construct the Mount Laurel units; or it could contract with a private builder to construct and possibly market the Mount Laurel units as well. Note: construction aided by CDBG funds would usually have to be done at prevailing (union) wages.

are supposed to reflect the actual outlays incurred as a result of incoming residents (e.g., the expense of extending a sewer or water line, the staffing of a building department, etc.). In some cases, however, they go beyond cost recovery and serve as a special tax or exclusionary mechanism.[47] Such imposition adds to the costs of new housing. Municipalities should therefore examine their local fee, permit, and similar practices to determine that they cover only the actual cost of extending needed services to the new residents rather than subsidizing the existing population by overcharging newcomers.[48]

In addition to this general reevaluation, specific cost savings approaches should be considered. Bonding is illustrative. Most municipalities require a construction performance bond, which in turn costs three points of the face value. At minimum, communities should allow a reduction in the bond face value commensurate with the satisfaction of the bonded improvements. Failure to do so means that the developer is paying for protection which is not needed. Alternatives to the posting of a bond should also be considered. If instead of securing a bond, builders were allowed to obtain a letter of credit (LC), then savings would be realized since the LC would cost only a point or two.[49] (The LC would have to be structured so as to offer adequate protection to the community that improvements would be finished.) An alternative is a developer Trust Account. Montville, New Jersey[50] has successfully used this approach. It requires builders to establish a Trust Account in the amount necessary to finish improvements. This account is tapped only if needed and in the interim pays interest to the developer. Such an approach dramatically reduces bonding charges.

Reducing Development Costs: Other Soft Expenses

This category includes compensation for the developer's engineer, architect and other professional staff plus miscellaneous expenses for such items as advertising, realtor fees, property taxes during construction and so on. Costs for some of these items will be reduced as a result of recommendations described already. For instance, refining the land-use development process to reduce uncertainties, allowing "one-step processing," etc., should moderate professional expenses. Further changes should be considered. The following recommendations of the New Jersey Assembly Housing Emergency Action Team concerning property taxation during construction are illustrative:[51]

> Unsold housing units should not be taxed as real property. These housing units place no burden on the municipality yet they are taxed as real property. This unfair taxation leads to increased housing prices with no commensurate increase in the value of the home.
>
> HEAT (Housing Emergency Action Team) recommends that only the land upon which unsold and unoccupied housing units are located be taxed....(note added)

It should be noted that HEAT's recommendations have recently been adopted in Chapter 220 of the Laws of 1982 (December 29, 1982) and Chapter 155 of the Laws of 1983 (April 14, 1983). This action points to how legislative action can reduce the tax and other costs of development.

CDBG funds can also be drawn upon to reduce soft costs. To help provide low- and moderate-income housing such as Mount Laurel units, block grants can be applied to cover:[52]

> §570.206(g)(1983) preconstruction surveys, market analyses, site and utility plans, preliminary cost estimates and "sketch drawings."

BRIDGE MECHANISMS TO REDUCE CONSTRUCTION COSTS

The "bricks and mortar" cost of the housing unit can be moderated by at least four strategies: (1) amending zoning code regulations affecting building size; (2) improving the building code and its administration; (3) utilizing cost-efficient materials and techniques; and (4) providing tax changes.

Reducing Unit Construction Costs: Allow Smaller Homes

The costs of building a housing unit increase with its size. Historically, many New Jersey municipalities imposed square footage minimums which were greater than those dictated by health or safety considerations. More recently numerous jurisdictions have moderated these requirements or have even deregulated this factor and leave size to the dictates of the market. Not all communities, however, have so acted. This is probably necessary, however, to foster the construction of lower cost Mount Laurel units. Deregulation of housing size should be considered or alternatively, if minimums are imposed in zoning or other codes, these should reflect "basic health and safety criteria." The recommendations in this regard in the affordable housing literature and by state and federal housing agencies deserve consideration. (See the Bibliography in this study.) The NJHFA, for example, recommends that for elderly occupants, studio apartments have a minimum of 437, and one-bedroom units, 598 square feet.[53] It has further schedules for family units, garden apartments, and so on.[54] (NJHFA requirements are higher than those contained in HUD's Minimum Property Standards [MPS].)[55] Interestingly, Cherry Hill's inclusionary program, described later in this chapter, specified both minimum and maximum floor areas for the affordable housing to be provided. The minimums for one, two, and three bedroom units are 600, 750, and 900 square feet respectively; the maximums are 750, 900, and 1000 square feet respectively.[56] The demographics of prospective Mount Laurel need outlined in Chapter 5 is particularly relevant in this regard.

Reducing Unit Construction Costs: Improving The Building Code and Its Administration

A decade ago New Jersey personified the proverbial development problem of builders having to satisfy different building codes in each community. Since 1975, however, the state has a uniform construction code described as one of the "strongest, more inclusive building codes" in the country.[57] While much progress has been made, further improvements are needed. Code administration can be bolstered. For instance, all code inspectors should have been licensed before January 1, 1981, but at least according to some reports this has not been universally adhered to.[58] Even if licensed, local code officials are not always given sufficient municipal support in terms of their training and staff -- an essential prerequisite if these officials are to keep track of the many updates and amendments to the Uniform Code.[59]

Substantive changes to the Uniform Code should also be considered. Modifications concerning rehabilitation, an important low-cost housing delivery policy considered in Chapter 5, are illustrative. Currently the code encompasses a "25 to 50 percent rule" whereby extensive rehabilitation must conform to new building standards[60] -- an expensive and often unnecessary mandate.[61] While this requirement is commonplace,[62] some jurisdictions, most notably Massachusetts, have adopted more appropriate rehabilitation provisions recommended by HUD and the National Bureau of Standards.[63] These would allow such things as retaining extant stairway width and room sizes and thus contribute to lower renovation and therefore housing costs. New Jersey should consider following suit and should also be sensitive to possible needed code changes governing new construction.

Reducing Unit Construction Costs: Utilize Cost-Efficient Building Materials/Technology

Building codes govern the materials and techniques which can be used. They do not require, however, that builders take advantage of permitted products or approaches which can reduce costs.[64] This may be necessary to deliver Mount Laurel housing. This objective will be facilitated by drawing on the considerable technical work in this area done by HUD, the National Association of Home Builders (NAHB), and others to show how affordable housing can be delivered. HUD and NAHB have developed "Optimum Value Engineering" (OVE) -- "a procedure of comparing alternative materials and methods to determine the least costly combination that will result in an acceptable product."[65] Examples include using: single-layer plywood siding (eliminating sheathing and corner bracing), in-line-off-center spliced joists (allowing use of smaller floor joists and reduced labor costs), and "Sturdi-floor" systems (reducing material and labor costs and contributing to a stiffer floor).[66] HUD-NAHB demonstrations suggest that OVE realizes savings of about 10 percent compared to conventional construction approaches.[67] Developers of Mount Laurel housing should consider OVE techniques, especially since HUD's OVE manual incorporates materials/techniques permitted by BOCA -- the basis of New Jersey's Uniform Code.[68]

OVE is just one of a series of recent efforts to demonstrate construction cost savings for affordable housing. Others include the "Cost-Buster Demonstration," "Building Value Into Housing," "Approach 80," "Housing Cost Reduction Demonstration" and the techniques considered by the Joint Venture for Affordable Housing. An example of the recommendations culled from these initiatives is shown in the "Affordable Housing Checklist" prepared by NAHB and shown in Exhibit 6-3. (Many of these have been adopted already by New Jersey's volume builders.) This list divides the construction process into the components of foundations, floors, exterior walls, roof, interior partitions, plumbing, etc. and under each of these headings indicates cost-saving approaches. More detailed findings and recommendations of the recent affordable housing demonstrations can be found in: Building Affordable Homes, Affordable Housing: Twenty Examples From the Private Sector, An Approach for the 80s: Affordable Housing Demonstration, Approach 80, Housing Cost Reduction Demonstration, Affordable Housing Demonstration Case Study -- Lincoln Nebraska, Reducing Housing Development Costs: Strategies for Affordable Housing, and Home Building Cost Cuts.[69]

Reducing Unit Construction Costs: Provide Tax Changes

Suggestions by the New Jersey Assembly Housing Emergency Action Team (HEAT) regarding the taxation of building materials could lower unit construction costs.[70] HEAT recommended that building materials should not be subject to the state sales tax but instead should be exempt, as are food and clothing purchases. It contended that shelter was as basic a consumption as food and clothing and therefore should be treated similarly. Adoption of the HEAT recommendation would lift the 6 percent sales tax currently paid on the housing unit's building materials -- a levy currently passed along to the housing consumer. As building materials amount to about 50 percent of the total unit expense (the remainder is labor), removing the 6 percent sales tax would result in a 3 percent savings in the unit's construction cost. Similar savings would be realized with respect to subdivision construction outlays. Further bridge strategies for subdivision expenses follow.

Reducing Improvement Construction Costs

Improvement expenses can be moderated by (1) increasing development density; (2) eliminating overly stringent requirements; and (3) providing public subsidies.

Density increases were discussed already as a means to lower land costs.[71] Added density also moderates per unit improvement costs as total improvement outlays are amortized over additional units.

Improvement standards themselves also bear scrutiny. Improvements required by municipalities should reflect local physical conditions (e.g., soil type, drainage), and the intensity of development -- more stringent

EXHIBIT 6-3

CHECKLIST OF STRATEGIES FOR REDUCING HOUSING UNIT CONSTRUCTION COSTS
(WHERE WARRANTED BY LOCAL CONDITIONS -- SELECTED EXAMPLES)

A. FOUNDATIONS

1. Allow slab-on-grade construction.
   (Slabs are usually less costly than other foundation types.)
2. Eliminate welded wire mesh (wwm) in concrete slabs.
   (Under normal conditions, wwm provides no significant function.)
3. For crawl space or basement construction, use pressure-treated wood foundations.
   (Wood foundations are often less costly than concrete or concrete block.)

B. WOOD FLOORS

1. Eliminate or reduce the size of sill plates.
   (If foundations are level, sill plates may be eliminated. Otherwise, 2x4 is adequate.)
2. Use 24-inch o.c. floor joists.
   (Often joist spacing can be increased if plywood is glue-nailed.)
3. Eliminate double joists under non-bearing partitions.
   (Weight of partitions does not need extra support if 5/8" or 3/4" sub-floor is used.)

C. EXTERIOR WALLS

1. Use tilt-up construction.
   (End-nailing is less time-consuming than toe-nailing.)
2. Use 2-stud corners.
   (A 3-stud corner post is not structurally necessary. Drywall back-up can be provided by metal clips or wood cleats.)
3. Eliminate partition posts.
   (Partition posts are not necessary where interior partitions intersect exterior walls.)

D. ROOF

1. Use engineered roof trusses.
2. Use prefabricated gable ends.
3. Use gable end vents (for detached units only).
   (These are less costly than ridge/eave vents.)

E. INTERIOR PARTITIONS AND FINISH

1. Use 2x3 non-loadbearing interior studs spaced 24" o.c.
   (where utility placement permits.)
2. Eliminate bulkhead (furr-down) over kitchen cabinets.
3. Design for straight-run stairs.

F. PLUMBING

1. Cluster plumbing, preferably back-to-back.
2. Use one-piece molded fiberglass tub and shower modules.
3. Use PVC or ABS drain, waste and vent pipe.

G. ELECTRICAL

1. Wire most circuits with #14 copper wire.
2. Locate heavy loads near to service entry panel.
3. Use plastic utility boxes.

H. HEATING, VENTILATION, AIR CONDITIONING

1. Engineer the duct system for least cost.
2. Use dropped hall ceiling plenum.

Note: Exhibit contains selected examples. For a full listing of over 100 recommendations, see source below. It should also be noted that many New Jersey developers already follow many of these suggested economies.

Source: National Association of Home Builders Research Foundation, Building Affordable Homes - A Cost Savings Guide for Builders/Developers (Washington, D.C.: NAHB, 1983). Report prepared for the U.S. Department of Housing and Urban Development, Office of Policy Development and Research.

requirements must accompany more intense settlement and therefore use of and wear on streets, sidewalks, etc. Street width is illustrative. It is not very instructive to recommend that "narrower streets should be allowed" without further clarification. Proper street width is a product of many factors,[72] including traffic volume[73] and parking, sidewalk and other characteristics (see Exhibit 6-4 for details).

Improvement standards for Mount Laurel housing should be formulated by balancing the need to economize so as to make these units affordable with the imperative of adequate design so as to protect the new residents and the community at large. Recommendations for cost savings abound. The New Jersey Affordable Housing Handbook discusses four such measures: shortening the required length and width of roadways, eliminating curbs and gutters in residential streets, reducing the amount of sidewalk paving, and avoiding excessive landscaping where possible.[74] The national affordable housing literature[75] suggests a broader array of possible changes. These approaches merit adoption to the extent permitted by engineering design criteria. A summary of the latter considerations, prepared with the assistance of members of the New Jersey Society of Municipal Engineers, is shown in Exhibit 6-4.

Another area of consideration is the issue of off-site improvements. Here the question is not so much the standard to be met as the division of responsibility. While in years past, off-site improvements were typically the obligation of the community at large, increasingly the burden has shifted to the developer and ultimately the housing consumer. Mount Laurel households should not be asked to bear, and they cannot afford, an unfair loading of off-site expenses.

A final means of reducing improvement expenses is via public subsidy. It has already been determined that CDBG monies can be drawn upon to assist Mount Laurel housing. To this end, Community Development Block Grants can clearly be applied for infrastructure purposes. As indicated by the 1983 CDBG regulations, block grants for low/moderate-income housing can be used for "provision of site improvements and provision of public improvements."[76] Communities have already drawn on this resource. East Brunswick has utilized CDBG monies to provide sewer and other improvements for housing built under its inclusionary zoning option -- a program described later in this Chapter.[77]

BRIDGE STRATEGIES FOR REDUCING HOUSING DELIVERY COSTS

Delivery costs start with development and construction expenses to which are added factors for contingency, overhead, and profit. Some savings are possible here. Given the adoption of OVE and similar building systems described earlier, which incorporate "simple" design, prefabrication, and the like, cost overruns and therefore contingency may be reduced slightly. Overhead is another matter. While building Mount Laurel units may increase a developer's volume and therefore moderate the overhead charge per unit,

EXHIBIT 6-4

AFFORDABLE HOUSING CHECKLIST - CONSIDERATIONS FOR DESIGNING IMPROVEMENTS

I. STREET DESIGN

1. Are streets properly designed? Design should reflect such factors as demand (as measured by Average Daily Traffic, Peak Hour Traffic and access for emergency service vehicles); physical conditions (e.g., soil type); parking (is on-street parking allowed, is it permitted on one or two sides, and what is the configuration -- diagonal, perpendicular, or parallel? The greater the parking use, the wider the street that is needed.); sidewalks (are they present, and if so, on one or two sides of the street? The greater the sidewalk presence, the wider the street right of way that is needed.); and other characteristics (e.g., is there curbing? If so, what type -- vertical, rolled or monolithic? Will the street be dedicated to the municipality or remain private, etc.? A wider street is suggested if it has vertical curbs and is publicly dedicated.)

2. Are curb and gutter requirements properly designed? The decision whether or not to require curbs and gutters should factor such considerations as density of development (there is a greater need as density increases); physical considerations (e.g. drainage and slope) and the application (e.g. street versus parking lot). If curbs are required, the most economical configuration should be considered, such as rolled versus vertical or monolithic.

3. Are public sidewalks required? Sidewalk requirements and their specification (one or two sides, and width) should consider such factors as density of development, street type, proximity to schools, etc. There is greater need for sidewalks with higher density development, and for walking areas alongside major thoroughfares, and/or schools.

4. Are street light requirements properly designed? This should factor need (e.g., additional lighting is needed in higher density developments); and design (e.g., lighting requirements should reflect footcandle-per-square-foot standards recommended by national engineering organizations).

II. UTILITY DESIGN

5. Is the water supply system properly designed? This should reflect such factors as demand (Average Daily Demand and Peak Usage based on realistic projections of resident household size, fire protection needs, etc.); materials (the economies of plastic pipe should be considered, weighed against possible disadvantages concerning installation and settlement problems); and design (economical designs should be considered, such as using a single lateral off the street, placing fire hydrants at the maximum allowable spacing, etc.)

6. Is the sanitary sewer system properly designed? (Similar recommendations as for water supply, e.g., use economical designs such as maximum manhole spacing and prefabricated manholes.)

7. Is the storm water management properly designed? This should consider demand (area watershed management soil and runoff factors - the greater the density of development, the more sophisticated the storm drainage system should be); and design (where possible, use economical approaches such as where applicable, natural drainage and unpaved swales for storm water management, and retention/detention approaches to reduce peak runoff).

8. Are economies in utility placement considered? (Above-ground utilities are less expensive than underground; and for underground utilities the use of a common utility trench for compatible lines, such as electric, telephone and cable, should be considered.)

III. PARKING DESIGN

Are parking requirements properly designed? This should factor demand (based on household type and size, use of mass transit, etc.); available parking resources (e.g., on-street parking, parking at adjacent non-residential uses); and other factors (downsizing of automobiles).

Source: Interviews with the members of the New Jersey Society of Municipal Engineers, September-October 1983.

the special design and marketing of this housing could increase overhead expenses. Such inflation is especially likely if builders are required to monitor the resale of Mount Laurel housing so as to ensure their continued low/moderate-income status.

Impact on the profit margin is also difficult to predict. Non- or limited-profit sponsors of Mount Laurel housing have this factor defined by statute. Such sponsorship is required in certain cases (e.g. when NJHFA financing is utilized). In other instances, profits are not restricted (e.g. when loans are obtained from the New Jersey Mortgage Finance Agency, see discussion later in the chapter). Even when profits are not limited, private builders on their own volition could shave their profit margin on Mount Laurel units so as to make them affordable. It should be pointed out, however, that the state's volume builders, who can deliver shelter for the most competitive prices, already are operating at relatively low profit margins. Their willingness or ability to reduce returns on Mount Laurel housing is difficult to predict.

In sum, while there may be some moderation on contingency, overhead, and profit in Mount Laurel situations, significant savings are unlikely. The major cost reduction in the Mount Laurel units must come from the development and construction stages described already and at the occupancy stage considered below.

BRIDGE MECHANISMS TO REDUCE OCCUPANCY COSTS

Housing Mount Laurel families would be simpler if federal subsidies could be secured. Presently there are only a few sources of such aid. One is the Urban Development Action Grant (UDAG) which can be used for both residential and non-residential purposes. UDAG is a flexible subsidy vehicle with an already impressive list of accomplishments. It has only limited potential for Mount Laurel purposes, however. To apply for UDAG funds, a community must be "distressed" as defined by very stringent socioeconomic characteristics. Many communities with Mount Laurel obligations will not pass muster on this test.

Other sources of federal housing aid are not so narrowly targeted and so are available in a larger number of areas. Two prominent examples are the Section 8 and 202 rental assistance programs. The former offers a deep operating subsidy equal to the difference between the market occupancy cost ("Fair Market Rent"), and what lower-income beneficiaries can pay for housing (30 percent of adjusted gross income). The latter provides a subsidized long-term mortgage and is available to elderly households only. In practice, Section 202 projects are also typically provided with Section 8 rental assistance, and regular Section 8 housing often has a large elderly contingent. In short, the occupancy and financing distinctions between Sections 8 and 202 are somewhat blurred.

Both Section 8 and 202 are available to low- and moderate-income Mount Laurel households. While there are differences in terminology, the Mount Laurel low/moderate-income definitions are substantively the same as the "very low" and "lower income" thresholds used in Sections 8 and 202. Given their significant subsidy, these two programs could be significant bridge mechanisms for the Mount Laurel population.

The potential of housing Mount Laurel families with the assistance of the Section 8 and 202 subsidies is constrained by their very limited availability. For Fiscal Year 1983 (October 1, 1982 to September 30, 1983), Congress authorized a national total of 14,600 Section 8-202 commitments for new construction. There were considerably more Section 8-202 commitments for existing housing -- approximately 91,000.[78] (The latter figure is somewhat misleading because it reflects a one-time "recapture" of prior housing subsidy monies left unspent, such as Section 23, Rent Supplement, and Public Housing.) New Jersey secured a very small fraction of the national allocation. For Fiscal Year 1983, it received commitments for 347 new Section 8-202 units, and 1,630 for existing units.[79] New Jersey's allocation for Fiscal Year 1984 will likely be less -- there will be a small cut in new housing assistance, and aid for existing units will drop as recapture has spent itself. These figures speak for themselves -- for all practical purposes, there are only limited housing funds to assist Mount Laurel families. There is thus need to further chip away at the components of housing costs.

Reducing Occupancy Costs: Principal and Interest Expenses

The permanent financing terms of the Mount Laurel housing is the single most important factor affecting its affordability. Unlike the strategies discussed thus far which by and large affected only one cost factor, the loan constant acts on the composite of all the individual cost items. It thus has considerable leverage in either increasing or decreasing costs. The garden condominium example is illustrative. This unit, which sells today for $46,000, typically is purchased with a 10 percent down payment -- implying a mortgage of roughly $41,000. Conventional, fixed rate financing terms for this loan are currently 13 percent with a 30-year maturity. With this mortgage, every $1,000 reduction in the cost of housing, and subsequently the amount to be financed, reduces monthly principal and interest costs by $11. In contrast, every 1 percent drop in the interest rate has nearly three times the effect, lowering payment expenses by about $30. As the principal and interest charges dominate the monthly occupancy cost, which in turn is the determining factor of affordability, financing terms are a critical consideration. To make Mount Laurel housing affordable, it is imperative to secure favorable financing.

One way of accomplishing this is to utilize one of the skewed rate mortgages which recently have become available on the market. A Graduated Payment Mortgage (GPM) is a likely candidate. With a GPM, repayment is scheduled so that it is lower at the loan's inception than with a straight-line payback, and rises with time so as to compensate for the initial shortfall. Currently, GPMs issued in New Jersey have an initial effective rate of 9.75-10.0 percent -- about three points less than the straight-line charge. A Mount Laurel unit purchased with a GPM would thus realize this three-point savings.

Financing Mount Laurel housing with GPM or equivalent instruments would pose difficulties. Inherent in the GPM approach is the assumption that both borrower income and hence repayment capacity will rise over time, and/or that the value of the financed housing will increase so as to protect the lender. Are these assumptions valid in Mount Laurel situations? Given the fact that many of the Mount Laurel households are elderly or have marginal job skills (see Chapter 3), is it reasonable to assume that their incomes will keep pace with the increasing demands of the GPM? There are similar uncertainties concerning the future value of the Mount Laurel units -- will they appreciate sufficiently to protect the GPM lender, especially in instances where a deed or other restriction has been placed so as to cap the future sales price? The goal of so maintaining Mount Laurel affordability conflicts with the lender's fiduciary need to expect rising property values, especially in GPM situations. In short, while it is tempting to capitalize from the initial rate advantages of GPM and similar mortgages, the underlying assumptions of these loans may not be applicable in Mount Laurel cases.

A more fruitful source of below market-rate mortgages for Mount Laurel housing is provided by the tax-exempt market. Mortgage-backed tax-exempt securities can be sold by state or local governments and the proceeds then used to make available attractive rate loans. New Jersey is fortunate in having two public agencies experienced in such offerings. The NJHFA, described earlier, issues tax-exempt multifamily mortgages.[80] A sister authority, the New Jersey Mortgage Finance Agency (NJMFA), deals in single-family loans.[81] (The NJHFA and NJMFA may shortly be merged.) Both the NJHFA and NJMFA have indicated to the Center for Urban Policy Research that they would be receptive to providing financing to assist Mount Laurel households, to the extent allowed by federal law.[82] The last proviso is an important qualification because federal law regulates, and currently threatens, the future of tax-exempt mortgage-backed securities (TEMBS).

In the late 1970s, as interest rates rose, many state and local governments entered the TEMBS market. Perceived abuses in this practice (e.g., tax-exempt financing was often used by higher-income families to purchase expensive homes), coupled with lost revenues to the federal government,[83] led to the enactment of the Mortgage Subsidy Bond Act of 1980.[84] This legislation, often referred to as the Ullman Act after its sponsor, Congressman Al Ullman, removed the public TEMBS from the general rule excluding the interest income of publicly issued securities to a restricted tax exemption linked to strictly specified provisions.[85] For <u>single-family homes</u> (defined as "detached, condominiums, and cooperatives"), revenue bond mortgages were limited to first-time homebuyers purchasing units with prices not exceeding 90 percent of the average for the surrounding SMSA.[86] At least 20 percent of the proceeds of the bond issue had to be made available for targeted areas (defined as census tracts where at least 20 percent of the families have incomes 80 percent or less of the statewide median).[87] In targeted areas, the first-time homebuyer rule was waived and a higher unit price ceiling (110 percent of SMSA prices) was permitted. For multifamily rental housing aided by the TEMBS, there was the added requirement that at least 20 percent (15 percent in targeted areas) of the units in each project be occupied by persons of low- or moderate-income (defined as a maximum of 80 percent of area median income).[88] The 1982 Tax Bill amended these requirements slightly (e.g., it modified the first-time homebuyer rule and increased the housing purchase price limits).[89]

These restrictions pose some limits on the ability to use tax-exempt mortgage financing for Mount Laurel units. The 10 percent of the Mount Laurel households already owning homes will largely be precluded (except for the 1982 exceptions) from these favorable-rate loans since they are not "first-time homebuyers." Target area restrictions may also have some restraining effect on the availability of TEMBS loans in the more affluent New Jersey communities with Mount Laurel obligations. Most other Ullman Act provisions should not affect tax-exempt financing in Mount Laurel situations. Mount Laurel units, by definition, will not exceed area price ceilings; and the Mount Laurel households similarly satisfy the low/moderate-income Ullman Act requirement in multifamily rental cases.

The main threat of the Ullman Act to tax-exempt Mount Laurel financing is a sunset clause in the law disallowing TEMBS issues for single-family housing after December 31, 1983. Unless amended, the Ullman Act would eliminate the main source of low-cost financing for single-family housing, albeit assistance for multifamily rental units would continue. NJMFA officials believe, however, that the Ullman Act sunset clause will either be lifted, the date extended, or an exception be made for lower cost housing.[90] If this occurs,* TEMBS financing will continue to be available to Mount Laurel units, at least temporarily. This would allow a discount of two to three percent from the prevailing rate, currently 13 percent.

A final source of mortgage discount is provided by the Community Development Block Grant. CDBG recipients could use their grant monies to subsidize mortgage payments by Mount Laurel families. The subsidy could be in the form of a recurring monthly or annual payment equal to the difference between the nominal principal and interest obligation and the lower amount decided upon as appropriate for the Mount Laurel household. More likely, it is a one-time payment of CDBG monies equal to the discounted value of a loan at a market interest rate versus a lower charge made available to the Mount Laurel homebuyer. The latter approach is simi-

---

*As of November 1983, it appears that Congress will enact a 1983 Tax Bill continuing housing bond programs and providing for a new option -- tax credit certificates -- originally proposed by Senator Robert Dole.

lar to builder "buy-down" of loans in periods of high interest rates. However structured, the CDBG write-downs could be applied as a replacement to tax exempt financing in the event the Ullman sunset provision remains intact. Alternatively, if tax-exempt funds remain available, the CDBG assistance could piggy-back the tax-exempt discount to further lower interest rates.

Reducing Occupancy Costs: Property Taxes

Property taxes on Mount Laurel housing could be reduced provided preferred property tax treatment, such as a total exemption or partial abatement, could be secured.

At the present time, the only New Jersey program offering property tax concessions on new construction is the Fox Lance Program (N.J.S.A. 40: 55C-40 et seq.).[91] Under specified conditions -- where a "blighted area" is being "redeveloped" according to a "redevelopment plan" by a "redevelopment agency" -- then the "project" may be granted preferred property taxation for a period up to thirty-five years as follows. Instead of full property taxes, an annual in-lieu payment is required equal to either 15 percent of the property's annual revenue, or an escalating share (from 20 to 80 percent) of the nominal property tax obligation over the term of the abatement, whichever is greater.[92]

Fox Lance is presently applicable only in the legally defined situation of a "blighted area" being "redeveloped" by an authorized "redevelopment agency," and so on. This would seem to exclude the likely pattern of most new construction Mount Laurel projects serving prospective needs -- where non-urban renewal entities would be building in non-blighted areas, not following an urban renewal redevelopment plan, etc. Since express statutory authority is needed to allow the granting of preferred property taxation, and the one such provision, Fox Lance, does not seem to apply in Mount Laurel situations, then Mount Laurel units will have to pay full taxes. This assumption will be made in considering the effectiveness of the different bridge mechanisms, an analysis undertaken momentarily.

Two caveats to the exclusion of Fox Lance to Mount Laurel cases should be mentioned, however. First, the Fox Lance statute itself could be amended to apply to Mount Laurel housing. Second, a "liberal" reading of the current Fox Lance provision might qualify some Mount Laurel properties. Such a "broad" interpretation of the law is called for by the program itself. As stated in its "Declaration of Policy," the Act warrants "liberal" judicial construction in order to effectuate the beneficient legislative design.[93] Will "liberal construction" of Fox Lance encompass Mount Laurel development?

Reducing Occupancy Cost: Maintenance and Insurance

The two remaining occupancy cost components are maintenance and insurance. It is assumed that these expenses are fixed. While they could be reduced with a broad-based subsidy (e.g., Section 8-202), the likelihood of such write-down is slim. Another possibility is to exempt the Mount Laurel units from the obligation of meeting the monthly homeowners/condo charge. While this change can dramatically extend affordability, it raises serious question of equity to the other condo members who will be forced to make up the shortfall.

This concludes the analysis of the principal bridge mechanisms. Their respective effects on reducing Mount Laurel housing costs and affordability will now be illustrated by referring to the garden condominium example.

CALCULATING THE IMPACT OF THE BRIDGE MECHANISMS: THE GARDEN CONDOMINIUM EXAMPLE

Detailed calculations on the impact of the bridge mechanisms are found in Exhibit 6-1. The findings are highlighted here following the sequential housing cost components of development, construction, delivery, and occupancy. Costs for the garden condominium are discussed at today's standards, which allow for a $46,000 delivery price, and then as they might be reduced given the various bridge techniques. While the focus is on the garden unit in its for sale configuration, similiar strategies could be applied for rental garden apartments.

Development Costs

At current standards, the garden condominium has a $11,000 total development cost. This can be reduced in many ways.

Land. At today's density of 8 units to the acre, the land cost per unit, given a $40,000 value for an acre of unimproved land, is $5,000. One way of reducing this is by increasing density to say 12 units to the acre. Given that land acquired by volume builders is typically purchased on a per-unit basis from intermediaries (as opposed to buying acreage and then going through a rezoning process), the density increase from 8 to 12 units will likely not decrease the land cost per unit directly proportional to the upzoning. Nonetheless, at the higher density, the land cost per apartment should drop, to say $4,000. Additional density provision may permit some measure of land cost reduction. This may become marginal in the light both of marketability and additional infrastructure requirements.

The land charge could be reduced further with a CDBG write-down. (If past trends hold, the CDBG subsidy will most likely be applied to reduce land and infrastructure costs -- a focus incorporated in our calculations.) Communities have many existing demands on their CDBG funds. Realistically they will be able to apportion only a small share of their block grants for Mount Laurel purposes. For the sake of calculation, we will therefore assume a 20 percent land write-down by CDBG. This would reduce the land cost per unit from $4,000 to $3,000.

Interim financing. At today's standards, interim financing for the garden condominium at a sixteen percent rate (plus one point) for a ten-month period costs $2,500 (see Exhibit 6-1 for details). This can be reduced by lowering the principal borrowed, the loan term, and the interest rate. The many regulatory bridge mechanisms allow for a reduction in the loan principal from $41,000 to $35,000 (see Exhibit 6-1). Assuming accelerated processing and faster building technologies, a loan period of eight rather than ten months is possible. Reduction in the loan amount and time factors combined reduce interim financing expenses from $2,500 to $2,000 per unit. A further savings is secured by using tax-exempt or CDBG monies which would permit a construction interest rate of say 10 percent (with no points) rather than the currently prevailing 16 percent with one point. Given this discount, interim financing would drop to $1,000 per unit.

Public Fee and Other Soft Costs. At today's standards, these amount to $2,500. Assuming reduction in sewer-water connection and permit fees, and the use of a letter of credit rather than a performance bond, public fees can be reduced to $2,000. Soft expenses experience a similar $500 savings from $1,500 to $1,000 per unit -- an economy based on a slight reduction in professional costs (e.g., allowed by faster public processing), and taxing only land and not improvements during construction.

In sum, at today's standards, development expenses for the garden condominium amount to $11,500. With a series of regulatory changes -- higher density, faster processing, and lower fees -- development outlays can be lowered to $9,000. With an added overlay of public subsidy for land write-down and financing, the final development tally is $7,000.

Construction Costs

Unit Construction. At today's standards, construction costs are $25,500 for both the unit ($19,500) and subdivision improvements ($6,000). While unit construction costs can be moderated in many ways such as building smaller homes, according to an improved code, and using improved technology, etc., many of these avenues are not available for the garden condominium example because this unit is already small, and is built quite efficiently by volume builders. Nonetheless, a small savings of say 5 percent can be factored. This would reduce construction costs from $19,500 to $18,500. Further regulatory change in the form of not applying the sales tax to building materials could reduce the $18,500 by another 3 percent (6 percent sales tax multiplied by the 50 percent materials component of the total unit construction figure) to roughly $18,000.

Improvements. Improvement expenses can be moderated by increasing development density and eliminating overly stringent requirements as well as the sales tax change mentioned above. These factors combined should conservatively shave subdivision costs from $6,000 to $5,000 per unit. Public subsidy in the form of say a 20 percent CDBG write-down would further drop costs to $4,000 per unit.

In summary, at today's standards, construction costs for the garden condominium are $25,500. With regulatory change affecting building code requirements/administration, density, subdivision standards, and the sales tax, the outlay can be brought down to $23,000. With public subsidy, the figure is $22,000.

Delivery Cost

Contingency. The contingency factor is a percentage, typically 5 percent, applied against the foregoing expenses. At today's standards, contingency amounts to a rounded sum of $1,500 per unit. As housing costs decline as a result of regulatory and public subsidy changes described earlier, so will contingency to roughly $1,000.

Overhead and Profit. The original calculation of garden condominium costs assumed a 20 percent add-on for these two items or $7,500 per unit. Overhead may drop on Mount Laurel units because of increased building volume. (Overhead may also rise however; see prior discussion in the text.) Additionally, builders may lower profit margins slightly on these units to make them affordable. These changes may permit a small drop in the overhead and profit percentage from say 20 to 18 percent. At the latter rate, overhead and profit on the unit with the regulatory changes described in this section would drop to $6,000; for the unit with public subsidy to $5,500. It is important to remember, however, that considerable variation exists with respect to both existing overhead and profit costs, and the ability/willingness of builders to adjust these charges in Mount Laurel situations.

In sum, at today's standards and practices, the garden condominium case example has a total delivery price of $46,000. With regulatory changes, the final figure is $39,000, with public subsidy, $35,500. Savings of a similar order of magnitude can be realized with the garden unit in its rental configuration.

Occupancy Costs

Principal and Interest. This item is a function of how much is borrowed and at what rate. A downpayment of 10 percent is considered realistic for Mount Laurel families. Given that constant, and the variations in housing delivery prices just cited, a larger loan is required to finance the garden condominium at today's standards and higher costs ($41,400 loan), than under the scenarios of regulatory reform ($35,100 loan), or public subsidy ($32,000 loan, see Exhibit 6-1 for details). A second factor is the interest rate. With both the garden condominium as delivered today, and the unit with regulatory reform, a market rate of 13 percent (30-year maturity) is applied. With the garden condominium benefitting from public subsidy, a 10 percent, 30-year mortgage from NJMFA is assumed. These two factors of loan amount and amortization schedule produce dramatic differences in principal and interest payments. These are $458 monthly for the garden unit at today's standards, $388 for the housing produced with regulatory reform, and $281 given public subsidy.

Property Taxes. Because of the uncertainty of utilizing Fox Lance in Mount Laurel situations, we assume that full property taxes are paid on all the garden unit examples. Property taxes are a function of property value and the local property tax rate. Assuming an equalized (full-value) tax rate of $2.25, the different garden apartments cases would be paying varying property taxes because of their gradations in value. At today's standards, the garden unit would remit $86 monthly, with regulatory reform, $73, and with public subsidy $67.

Maintenance and Insurance. The former is estimated at $50 monthly paid to a homeowners association; the latter $10 for the mortgage insurance premiums. Identical obligations are assumed for all three garden unit scenarios.

In sum, the total occupancy cost for the garden condominium at today's standards is about $600 monthly (see Exhibit 6-1). At a 25 percent housing expense to income ratio, a household must earn about $29,000 yearly to occupy this unit -- an income 95 percent of the 1983 household median of $30,500.* With regulatory reform, the monthly charge drops to $520, and the qualifying household income to $25,000 -- 82 percent of the regional median.* With public subsidy, the monthly charge is about $410, and the requisite household income, roughly $19,500 -- 64 percent of the areawide median.*

These changes have significant Mount Laurel implications. At today's standards, the garden condominium case example is above the range of affordability of the most affluent of the moderate-income Mount Laurel population (those closest to the 80 percent of median income cut-off). With the regulatory bridge mechanisms, the garden unit can house the upper range of the moderate-income Mount Laurel families. With public subsidy, the garden apartment is opened to the middle range of the moderate incomed. Similar changes would occur with respect to garden housing in a rental rather than for-sale configuration. The bridge mechanisms are thus serving their goal of spanning the gap between housing costs and the Mount Laurel population's ability to absorb these expenses.

Additional economies are offered by the following encompassing bridge mechanisms.

---

*Income for the West Central Region 3 -- the area from which much of the housing cost data were derived.

BROADER-BASE BRIDGE MECHANISMS AFFECTING MULTIPLE COMPONENTS OF HOUSING COST: IMPACT ON HOUSING AFFORDABILITY

The bridge approaches discussed thus far were by and large directed to individual housing cost components, e.g., increased density would lower land costs, tax-exempt construction loans would reduce interim financing expenses, etc. There is a further class of bridge strategies which are broader in both their effect -- they influence many housing cost components -- and intent -- they sometimes require, rather than more passively encourage, the production of lower cost housing. Two such encompassing mechanisms are examined here -- adopting inclusionary zoning and allowing manufactured housing, most notably mobile homes. Both were cited by the Mount Laurel decision as important techniques to meet its mandate of delivering affordable housing.

INCLUSIONARY REQUIREMENTS

An inclusionary program is a "process intended to set aside a portion of the total number of units in a development at below-market prices in order to expand housing available to low- and moderate-income persons."[94] While it has been applied in other contexts, inclusionary provisions typically have the objective of expanding housing* opportunity. They usually have a triggering specification (e.g., development of a particular size, type, or location). The inclusionary mandate may be either mandatory or optional on the developer; in the former case, the builder must comply, in the latter he is encouraged to do so. In either case, the inclusionary requirement is usually stated as a share of the total new housing production, usually 10 to 25 percent. To allow or encourage the developer to comply, many inclusionary programs offer a density bonus or other inducements (e.g., reducing subdivision/parking/set-back requirements, or offering lower-cost financing). To ensure that units produced under an inclusionary program remain a low/moderate-income housing resource, as opposed to providing a windfall profit to the initial occupant, most inclusionary strategies retain some type of affordability control. These commonly consist of a deed restriction capping subsequent resale or rental prices and/or monitoring of future occupancy by a local housing authority or other entity.

We can obtain a better sense of the inclusionary approach by briefly surveying its history, both nationally and in New Jersey. This is done in detail in the Technical Appendix. In brief, inclusionary programs in the United States date to the early 1970s.[96] In 1971, Fairfax County, Virginia required builders of fifty or more units to commit at least 15 per-

*In some cases, its purview has been broader. For instance, the California Coastal Commission required a hotel developer in Marina del Rey to provide a youth hostel, moderate-cost coffee shop, and special weekend discount rates for low/moderate income families.[95]

cent of their production for low/moderate-income families.[97] Within a short period, a number of its neighbors followed suit, most notably Arlington County, Virginia, and Montgomery County, Maryland.[98]

The inclusionary spirit soon leaped the continent, especially in California. In the early 1970s, Palo Alto and Los Angeles imposed inclusionary requirements.[99] A few years later, Orange County followed suit with an encompassing program.[100] It mandated that 25 percent of all newly constructed units in developments of five or more houses be made affordable to families earning below 120 percent of the county's median income. Developers could satisfy this requirement by: (1) building the one-quarter share in each project, (2) "overbuilding" (going above a 25 percent share) affordable units in one of their developments and then transferring the excess as a "credit" to another of their projects which is under quota, (3) buying "credits" from <u>other</u> builders who have an excess to sell, and (4) through other means, such as land donation or in-lieu cash payments to the county. To help foster compliance, the Orange County program offered developers density bonuses and other inducements (e.g., accelerated processing and tax-exempt financing).

New Jersey has a fledgling inclusionary record. A handful of municipalities -- Bridgewater, Cherry Hill, East Brunswick, East Windsor, Franklin Township (Somerset), Mount Laurel, Raritan Township, and South Brunswick -- have either voluntary or mandatory programs. Special area authorities -- for the Coastal Zone, Meadowlands, and Pinelands -- also have nominal inclusionary provisions. The Technical Appendix considers the components of both the municipal and area-wide approaches in detail. In brief, most of the New Jersey inclusionary programs are mandatory. They require that from 5 to 40 percent of new housing production be set aside for low/moderate-income families, with the latter as defined by HUD and NJHFA guidelines. Many impose the inclusionary set-aside <u>without</u> offering a density bonus or other inducement for compliance. This factor, plus others ranging from legal uncertainties before the <u>Mount Laurel</u>, <u>Uxbridge Associates</u>, and <u>Egg Harbor</u> decisions,[101] to very stringent inclusionary requirements (e.g., 40 percent in Bridgewater), have inhibited the throughput of New Jersey's existing inclusionary program. There are some encouraging exceptions, however, most notably in Cherry Hill, East Brunswick, and South Brunswick. The experience in these communities points to the potential of the inclusionary mechanism to produce affordable housing.

<u>The Inclusionary Mechanism as a Mount Laurel Bridge Strategy</u>

The inclusionary approach can help satisfy the Mount Laurel decision in two ways. First, it <u>forces</u> production of lower-cost housing and second, if properly structured, it provides a <u>financial means</u> for affordable housing delivery. Our review of the national and New Jersey state-of-the-art revealed that the major financial prop offered by many inclusionary programs is a density bonus -- the permission to construct additional units. This differs from the density increase discussed earlier in this chapter because the latter applied to Mount Laurel units only, while the density increase offered by the inclusionary approach applies to market -- (non-Mount Laurel) housing as well. By so increasing the number of market units which can be built, value is being created, both in the form of added buildable lots, and/or from the ultimate profit to be made by constructing additional units on these added lots and then selling them. By creating value, the inclusionary program in concept provides the financial wherewithal for builders to internally subsidize housing delivery prices so as to write-down the cost of Mount Laurel units to make them affordable.

The operation of the density bonus can be illustrated by again referring to the garden condominium example. Previously, this chapter determined that this unit currently sold for about $46,000. With regulatory reform, the price could be brought down to $39,000, and with public subsidy to $35,500. An inclusionary mechanism allows us to go further.

Assume a developer currently owns a twenty-five acre tract zoned for garden condominiums and townhouses at a blended density of eight units to the acre. The builder can thus now construct a total of 200 units. If these units would sell for a blended average of $80,000, then assuming a 5 percent profit, the buildout of the full development would return $800,000 ($80,000 x 200 x .05). An inclusionary mechanism would alter these figures. Assume that the inclusionary requirement is 20 percent Mount Laurel units and that a bonus density of 50 percent is given for its satisfaction. This program would now allow the owner of the twenty-five acre tract to build 300 instead of 200 units. Of the 300 homes, 20 percent, or sixty, would be Mount Laurel units, say garden condominiums, with the remainder -- 240 units -- a mixture of market townhouses and garden condominiums. The economics of the development are now as follows. For the market component of the project, units may sell for slightly less than previously (e.g., say $75,000 versus $80,000 per unit), because of the increase in density. Despite this, the builder would reap a higher over-all project profit since more units are available for sale. At a 5 percent profit margin, the market portion of the project would return $900,000 ($75,000 x 240 x .05) -- $100,000 more compared to the lower-density case.

The $100,000 figure represents value created by the inclusionary density bonus. It now in theory can be applied to the sixty Mount Laurel units, thereby allowing an internal subsidy write-down of $1,500 per unit. The inclusionary program has another effect. By increasing density, it has in effect created free land on which to build the Mount Laurel garden condominiums. This land addition means a further savings of $3,000 to $4,000 per unit (see Exhibit 6-1). In sum, the inclusionary mechanism in this example creates a minimum $4,000 financial pool per unit which can be used to lower the price of Mount Laurel housing. This would allow the following savings. The Mount Laurel garden condominium, which with regulatory relief would cost $39,000, could now be delivered for $35,000; its counterpart with a public subsidy add-on would experience a price reduction from roughly $35,500 to $31,500. The former unit is affordable by a family earning roughly $23,000, the latter roughly $17,500. These incomes are 75 and 58 percent respectively of the 1983 median household income.* Similar economies could be realized with rented garden apartments. The inclusionary mechanisms in this example thus permit the production of housing affordable by the lesser affluent moderate-income Mount Laurel families and begin to approach the most affluent of the low-income Mount Laurel families as well. The inclusionary approach is thus an important overlay to the individual bridge mechanisms discussed earlier in the chapter.

Greater value and therefore internal subsidy would be made available if the inclusionary strategy and attendant density bonus would be applied to more expensive and therefore more profitable housing, and/or a greater proportional increase in density were tendered than in the above example. For instance, say on our twenty-five acre tract, a developer was selling $150,000 townhouses built at five units to the acre. This upper-level priced housing traditionally has a higher mark-up, say 10 percent, compared to the 5 percent ratio used previously. Consequently, the 125-unit townhouse project currently returns a $1,875,000 profit ($150,000 x 125 x .10). If an inclusionary program were adopted with a 20 percent affordable housing requirement and a density increase of 100 percent, then the owner of the twenty-five acre tract could build at ten units to the acre, or 250 homes (see Exhibit 6-5). Of this total, 200 would be market and fifty Mount Laurel. If the former sold for $130,000 apiece, then the project would now show a $2,600,000 profit ($130,000 x 200 x .10). This figure, $725,000 higher than at the five-unit density, permits an internal subsidy of $14,500 for each of the fifty Mount Laurel units (see Exhibit 6-5). The $14,500 value, combined with the minimum $3,000 land savings offered by the inclusionary program (e.g., with this strategy's density increase, the land cost for the Mount Laurel units is in effect free) means that the Mount Laurel garden condominium could be delivered for roughly $17,500 less than just with the regulatory changes ($39,000) and/or public subsidies ($35,500) discussed earlier. In other words, the Mount Laurel garden condominiums could be offered at roughly $21,500 ($39,000 - $17,500) with regulatory changes to $18,000 ($35,500 - $17,500) with public subsidies -- an amount affordable by households earning from roughly $13,000 (with regulatory reform) to about $11,000 (with public subsidies) annually or 43 and 37 percent respectively of the 1983 median household income* (see Exhibit 6-5). These figures come well into the low income Mount Laurel range. Again, the inclusionary mechanism serves as a significant bridge strategy.

Admittedly, the above calculations are a numbers exercise. They do not touch upon many issues. How marketable are and what is the price discount of the market units when combined with Mount Laurel housing? Specifically,

---

*Income for the West Central Region 3 -- the area from which much of the housing cost data were derived.

EXHIBIT 6-5

MOUNT LAUREL INCLUSIONARY BRIDGE MECHANISM: ILLUSTRATION

LAND/PROJECT COMPONENT	PROJECT TYPE: TOWNHOUSE PROJECT	
	Without Mount Laurel Garden Units/Density Bonus	With Mount Laurel Garden Units/Density Bonus
Overall Project Profile		
Land Parcel (size)	25 acres	25 acres
Density	5 per acre	10 per acre
Number of housing units		
Conventional[1]	125	200
Mount Laurel[1]	0	50
Total[1]	125	250
Market Unit Component (Townhouse)		
Unit price	$ 150,000	$ 130,000[5]
Unit profit[2]	$15,000	13,000
Total profit[3]	$1,875,000	$2,600,000
Added profit from density[4] increase	NA	$ 725,000
Mount Laurel Unit Component (Garden)		
Unit price without density subsidy[6]	NA	$ 32,500
Density subsidy per unit[7]	NA	$ 14,500
Unit price with density[8] subsidy	NA	$ 18,000
Monthly carrying cost with density subsidy[9]	NA	$ 236
Minimum household income/ share of areawide median household income[10]	NA	$ 11,328/.37
Total Project Profit[11]	$1,875,000	$1,875,000

Notes:

NA = not applicable

1. Total units equals allowable density multiplied by land parcel size; Mount Laurel units constitute one-fifth of total units where such housing/density bonus is provided.
2. Equals ten percent of market unit price.
3. Equals unit profit multiplied by number of market units.
4. Equals difference in total market unit profit with as opposed to without Mount Laurel density bonus (applies only in cases with Mount Laurel units/bonus).
5. Assumes 10 to 15 percent discount in conventional units' selling price with inclusion of Mount Laurel units.
6. Equals garden unit price (with public subsidy) calculated in Exhibit 6-1 less land cost item. This calculation assumes that with Mount Laurel density bonus, land costs for the Mount Laurel units are absent or minimal.
7. Equals added total market unit profit from Mount Laurel density bonus divided by the number of Mount Laurel units.
8. Equals base Mount Laurel unit price (item 6) minus density subsidy per unit or $32,500-$14,500.
9. Follows calculations as discussed in Exhibit 6-1.
10. Assumes 25 percent housing expense-to-income ratio. For an $18,000 unit, the monthly principal and interest charge would be $142 (assumes 10 percent downpayment and 10 percent, 30-year mortgage), the monthly property tax $34, and $60 for maintenance and insurance for a total of $236. Qualifying income is matched to the West Central Region 3 areawide income.
11. Equals total market unit profit minus added profit from density increase.

how are the Mount Laurel and conventional units to be mixed -- cheek-by-jowl or in separate areas/quads of the development? The former approach, incidentally, required by the Cherry Hill and encouraged by the East Brunswick inclusionary ordinances, promotes a closer integration of the units and their occupants; the latter offers possible project-marketing advantages but at the risk of inculcating social divisiveness. What improvement requirements should govern the project -- the prevailing community standards or the less stringent but still serviceable Mount Laurel criteria discussed in this chapter? The former strategy could negate some of the economies of producing the Mount Laurel units; the latter might adversely affect the conventional units' marketability, price, developer profit, and therefore internal subsidy. Who will monitor the continued moderate price and affordability of the Mount Laurel units? If the burden is placed on the builder, costs will be incurred, thereby reducing the resources available for the internal subsidy.

Another important issue concerns the practicality of the strategy as far as builder capacity, market demand, and other factors are concerned. In the previous examples, it was assumed that: a builder capable of multi-family construction was present, development scale was such that it was sensible to add inclusionary units, an increase in density was allowed by physical site conditions, and that the added units produced as a result of the density bonus could be absorbed by the market. Clearly, these and other necessary conditions will not always be satisfied. Nonetheless, such constraints do not invalidate the inclusionary strategy but point to the need for flexibility in its design. The experience of other programs can serve as a guide. For example, Orange County, California allows considerable leeway in the exact satisfaction of its inclusionary mandate -- builders can physically construct affordable units themselves or buy sufficient credits from those who do, and they are not necessarily within the same development.

In sum, inclusionary requirements are a potent Mount Laurel bridge mechanism. They must be carefully designed, however. Important programmatic issues include:

1. Inclusionary requirement. Inclusionary strategies are currently being discussed in New Jersey as if the 20 or 25 percent affordable housing share is fixed. This is not the case, as the prior national and state review of inclusionary approaches indicated a range from 5 to 40 percent. The specific local inclusionary mandate -- both the total share of affordable housing to be produced and the allocation of that share between low- and moderate-income components -- should be custom-tailored by each municipality, taking into account such local factors as the fair-share obligation and prevailing housing production constraints. The role of small scale developments requires review -- and they are far more important in our state than in Orange County.

2. Inducement provision. A similar need for local design applies to the inducements which should be offered to allow compliance with the in-

clusionary requirement. The absence of this provision has hindered the implementation of many of New Jersey's existing inclusionary programs. What should be offered? Typically, the benefit will involve a density bonus. Municipalities can also be more creative in the "give-backs" they offer to create the value which permits the developer write-down. In Orange County, California, these have ranged from lowered off-site parking requirements to reduced landscaping designs, to "one-stop" permit processing.[102] Just such an encompassing package of inducements should be considered. Their specific composition and magnitude should be formulated by each community considering such variables as existing local land-use requirements, the share of affordable housing called for in the inclusionary program, and the necessary builder write-down to meet this goal given local land and other costs.

Assistance in the specification of inducement provisions is provided by an economic analysis routine formulated by Stanford University to model the effects of inclusionary scenarios in Palo Alto.[103] Work in this regard by the Real Estate Research Corporation, reported in The Princeton Housing Proposal, also deserves scrutiny.[104]

The inducement provision can also be applied as a creative means to foster social policy. In East Brunswick, for example, a higher density bonus is offered if the affordable units are dispersed in, rather than separated from, the market housing.

3. Affordability Control/Monitoring. An important aspect of the inclusionary approach is to ensure that the low/moderate-income units remain affordable. A good discussion on this issue is found in The Princeton Housing Proposal. This study recommended a two-tier approach -- first a disposition covenant limiting the use of the unit to low/moderate-income families, and second, monitoring of this restriction by a Public Trust.[105]

Affordability monitoring entails possible conflict with lender interests. Lenders desire unfettered appreciation of mortgaged properties so as to better protect their security. An inclusionary program cap on the future sales/rental price does not allow this. Important mortgage institutions such as FNMA and FHLMC have indicated their unease with affordability controls which cloud their interest. Both have issued regulations indicating they would not deal in mortgages that carry deed restrictions subordinated (upon foreclosure) to other designees, such as a housing authority[106] -- a not uncommon inclusionary program combination. This hurdle is not insurmountable as indicated by the fact that both FNMA and FHLMC have purchased mortgages issued on homes in Orange County and other jurisdictions with inclusionary programs and affordability controls. A careful structuring of these measures is needed so as to abide with the fiduciary needs of mortgage institutions.

In addition to the mechanics, there is also the question of who will administer and pay for enforcement of the affordability controls. Possible candidates include the developer, a local housing authority, municipal planning department, or a homeowner's association. Such assumption would ultimately entail hundreds of separate entities doing the monitoring. Besides the diseconomies involved in this approach, there is the further question of permanence (e.g., what happens when a builder goes bankrupt or a housing authority disbands?). Monitoring by one or a limited number of players is called for. The State Department of Community Affairs is a leading candidate. Its involvement in this matter would provide a needed central authority. It would also enable the state to monitor the progress of meeting the Mount Laurel mandate and to see first-hand which bridge strategies are most promising.

4. Inclusionary Compliance. As discussed earlier, a wide range of means should be allowed for satisfying the inclusionary mandate. If the Orange County program would be used as a model, the low/moderate-income housing requirement could be met by production on-site, overproduction above quota at another site, purchase or sale of housing credits from one builder to another builder, and other means, such as in-lieu cash payments, or land donations. With such a flexible approach, developers could choose compliance strategies best suited for them. A small builder might find it best to purchase credits, a volume builder might specialize in Mount Laurel production and sell credits to others.

Once an inclusionary program goes beyond the concept of physical production of affordable units by housing developers on each site to a transfer-of-credits system, a number of interesting possibilities are raised. What is the tax status of these credits? Is a credit a capital asset and if so, is the purchaser entitled to an investment tax credit? Is the purchase a business expense, deductible only against profits? Or is it akin to a charitable donation and therefore directly deductible from taxes? The answers to these questions make a financial world of difference.

Another issue of interest concerns the responsibility of purchasing the Mount Laurel housing credits. Should the obligation be limited to residential builders only as opposed to their nonresidential counterparts? The latter's activities tend to increase the municipal fair-share obligation of Mount Laurel housing. Should the nonresidential builders not then have some measure of responsibility to meet the ensuing housing commitment by purchasing Mount Laurel credits? Such cross-sector responsibility is already a reality in San Francisco, as office developers there must purchase Section 8 commitments or in other ways foster housing production.[107] New York City is evaluating a similar mechanism for Manhattan.[108] Should New Jersey follow suit?

Inclusionary requirements can be a powerful bridge mechanism. Allowing manufactured housing also deserves consideration. The latter strategy is analyzed in the following and final section of the chapter.

ENCOURAGING MANUFACTURED HOUSING

Manufactured housing is a generic term that refers to housing built in a factory rather than on-site.[109] While there is no standard nomenclature, we can discuss different categories of manufactured units depending on their degree of off-site assembly. "Panelized" or "component" homes refer to buildings where individual components or sections (e.g., roof and floor trusses, or utility cores) are factory-manufactured, with the remainder constructed conventionally.[110] With modular housing, the entire unit is built off-site, typically in two or more sections which are delivered to and then assembled and placed on a permanent foundation.[111] A mobile home* is also manufactured entirely off-site. It differs from modular in that the mobile home: (1) has a chassis construction; (2) is governed by HUD building standards, and is inspected off-site; (3) may or may not be considered as real property for taxation purposes; and (4) may or may not have a permanent foundation, although in most cases it does.

New Jersey is experiencing growing utilization of selected types of manufactured housing. Volume builders are turning increasingly to the economies of panelized, or component construction, and modular units are also sometimes used in such applications as stacked, multifamily configurations. There are no significant regulatory restrictions to either panelized/component or modular construction as both are allowed by the State's Uniform Building Code.

An entirely less favorable situation exists with respect to mobile homes. Only one percent of New Jersey's total housing stock consists of mobile units.[113] From 1970 to 1980, while 430,000 conventional units were constructed in the state, only about 10,000 mobile units were delivered.[114] Their availability remains restricted. According to the Final Report of the 1983 (New Jersey) Mobile Home Taxation Commission, only 400 mobiles were sold statewide in 1982.[115]

The main reason for the scanty representation of mobile homes in New Jersey is that most communities discourage or prohibit them. The findings of the 1980 Mobile Home Study Commission, that municipalities often categorically excluded mobile homes or else severely restricted their entry, (e.g. by limiting mobile homes to parks and then placing restrictions on such parks), remain nearly as true today as they were three years ago.[116]

---

*In 1980 the U.S. Congress technically legislated the term "mobile home" out of existence.[112] The 1980 Omnibus Housing Act defined any mobile home larger than 320 square feet as a "manufactured home", while a mobile home smaller than 320 square feet was called a "company trailer," "recreational vehicle," or "park model." Despite the Congressional action, this chapter continues to use the term "mobile home" because that is how the Mount Laurel decision referred to it and it still remains the popular reference.

A review of local restrictions comes at a particularly opportune time. In years past, some mobile units may have had inferior standards, especially relative to stick-built construction. This is no longer true. The 1974 Federal Mobile Home Construction and Safety Act provided that uniform national standards be developed.[117] Two years later, HUD promulgated a National Manufactured Home Contruction and Safety Code which has become the industry standard.[118]

Significant financing changes have also occurred. In the 1950s and 1960s, mobile homes were financed at less-than-attractive consumer terms.[119] Matters improved considerably in the 1970s. The 1969 Housing Act allowed Title I FHA insurance on mobile home loans. Lenders, in turn, offered better mortgage terms -- smaller down payments, longer maturities (up to twelve years), and more attractive rates. The 1969 legislation reflected the growing reality of mobiles being turned to as permanent shelter by increasing numbers of families. This shift has fostered further amendments to bring mobile home financing in line with that available to conventional housing. In 1972, GNMA included mobile home loans in its secondary mortgage market operations.[120] It was ultimately followed by FNMA and FHLMC. HUD also encouraged the mobile home market. Throughout the 1970s, Title I ceilings were revised upward. As of 1983, these consist of a maximum $22,500 loan with a 20-year term for a single-wide unit (14-foot width), while for a double-wide (or multi-section), the figures are $35,000 and twenty-three years, respectively.[121] The transition of mobile home financing to conventional terms is most dramatically evidenced by HUD's action in 1983, permitting FHA to apply its Title <u>II</u> coverage to mobile homes in instances where the mobile unit <u>and</u> land are owned rather than rented, and this "unit-land combination" is treated as real property for taxation purposes.[122] With Title II backing, a mobile home purchaser will now be able to secure an FHA-insured loan for up to $90,000 with a maximum thirty-year repayment. No better terms are available for residential housing.

The Cost Advantage of the Mobile Home: An Important Mount Laurel Bridge Strategy

New Jersey municipal restrictions on mobile homes result in the state's citizens not being afforded the opportunity to take advantage of shelter that today may be on a par in safety and financing with conventional construction. It also means that a significant, low-cost housing opportunity is lost. The price attractiveness of the mobile home is shown in Exhibit 6-6. For purposes of <u>illustration</u>, it refers to a single-wide, 14' x 55' unit, since this configuration is roughly comparable in usable space to the 700 square foot condominium which has been examined thus far as the least costly housing available. At <u>today's</u> land-use standards (see Exhibit 6-6 for details), the 14' x 55' mobile has a delivery cost without public subsidy of $39,000, compared to $46,000 for the garden condominium (see Exhibits 6-1 and 6-6). The specific areas of the mobile home's price

EXHIBIT 6-6

IMPACT OF THE BRIDGE MECHANISMS: MOBILE HOME EXAMPLE (14' x 55' SINGLE-WIDE)

Housing Cost Component	HOUSING COSTS At Today's Standards	With Regulatory Reform	With Regulatory Reform and Public Subsidy
DEVELOPMENT			
Land[1]	$ 6,000[2]	$ 4,500[3]	$ 3,500[4]
Interim Financing[5]	1,000[6]	500[7]	200[8]
Public Fees	2,000[9]	1,500[10]	1,500[10]
Soft Costs	500[11]	500[12]	500[12]
Total Development	$ 9,500	$ 7,000	$ 5,700
CONSTRUCTION			
Unit Construction	16,000[13]	16,000[13]	16,000[13]
Development Improvements	6,500[14]	5,500[15]	4,500[16]
Total Construction	$22,500	$21,500	$20,500
DELIVERY			
Total Development	9,500	7,000	5,700
Total Construction	22,500	21,500	20,500
Contingency[17]	500	500	500
Overhead and Profit	6,500[18]	5,000[19]	5,000[19]
Total Delivery	$39,000	$34,000	$31,700
MONTHLY OCCUPANCY			
Principal & Interest[20]	411[21]	360[22]	275[23]
Municipal Service Fee/ Property Taxes	40[24]	40[24]	40[24]
Maintenance[25]	50	50	50
Insurance[26]	10	10	10
Total Occupancy	$ 511	$ 460	$ 375
AFFORDABILITY			
Minimum Household Income to Afford Occupancy Cost[27]	$24,528	$22,080	$18,000
Minimum Household Income as Share of Median Household Income[28]	.80	.72	.59

Notes:

1. Assumes unimproved land cost of $30,000 per acre. In this case, the land is purchased and financed by the mobile home park owner. Note the $30,000 cost is less than the $40,000 utilized in the condo case study.) This was done to reflect the common practice of placing mobile home parks on relatively less expensive land.
2. At density of 5 units per acre ($30,000 / 5 = $6,000).
3. At density of 8 units per acre (Full savings of density increase is not passed along. See note 3 in Exhibit 6-1).
4. Assumes 20 percent write-down of land cost from $4,500 with regulatory reform to $3,500 with public subsidy.
5. Assumes all costs are financed in construction loan except overhead, profit, and unit cost. (The last item would be financed for only a short period.)
6. Assumes financial terms of 1 point placement fee and 16 percent annual interest rate. Assumes 6 month development period during which half the principal loan amount is outstanding. Consequently, construction loan interest is effectively equal to 4 percent (16% x .5 x .5) plus 1 point fee or 5 percent. An amount of $15,500 is financed (see note 5); therefore interim financing costs about $1,000 (15,500 x .05).

Notes (continued)

7. While there might be some savings here because of accelerated processing, etc., it is doubtful that the development period would be shorter than the 6 month span assumed in note 6. Consequently, the same 5 percent effective interest rate is used. This is applied, however, against a smaller sum $12,500 (see note 5), suggesting interim financing costs of roughly $500 ($12,500 x .05).
8. Assumes same financial terms (except length of loan) as in note 8, Exhibit 6-1, yielding an effective interest rate of about 2 percent. This rate is applied to $10,500 amount (see note 5 in this exhibit), suggesting interim financing costs of $200.
9. Assumes similar costs as in note 9, Exhibit 6-1 except that building permit fee is not applied.
10. See note 10, Exhibit 6-1.
11. Assumes $300 cost per unit for professional fees, and $200 for advertising and other cost items.
12. Assumes no significant savings from those indicated in footnote 11.
13. Equals $500 for shipping charge, plus $11,000 for the 14' x 55' unit, plus $4,500 for set-up costs (e.g. skirting, blocking, concrete pad, etc.).
14. Derived from interviews with developers and municipal engineers.
15. The savings is realized from the increased density of the units, changes in improvement standards, and not applying sales tax to building materials.
16. Assumes a 20 percent write-down of improvement costs from $5,500 with regulatory reform to $4,500 with public subsidy.
17. Equals 5 percent of "variable" (e.g. more difficult to predict cost items)--soft expenses, the set-up of the mobile unit, and subdivision improvements.
18. Equals 20 percent of total development, construction, and contingency.
19. Equals 18 percent of total development, construction and contingency.
20. Assumes 10 percent down payment. The calculation shows the full financing charge for the total final delivery price. In reality, the mobile home park owner would be financing some items (e.g. land and improvements) with the remainder financed by the mobile homeowner. (The former recoups his costs through rent charged to the latter.) In that case, the homeowner's principal and interest payments would be less than the figure indicated here, but this would be "washed" by a higher maintenance fee charged.
21. Assumes loan amount of $35,100 ($39,000 x .9) at 13 percent interest rate, 20 year term. In this and other calculations, assumes loan amount above FHA Title I limits can be secured.
22. Assumes loan amount of $30,600 ($34,000 x .9) at 13 percent interest rate, 20 year term.
23. Assumes loan amount of $28,500 ($31,700 x .9) at 10 percent interest rate, 20 year term.
24. Assumes mobile home is taxed as personal rather than real property and pays only municipal service fee (MSF). The amount shown includes the MSF plus property taxes paid on land value/improvements. In reality, the latter would usually be paid by the park owner with this cost passed along in the monthly rental and/or maintenance fee.
25. Paid to mobile home park owner.
26. For mortgage insurance premium.
27. See Exhibit 6-1, note 31.
28. See Exhibit 6-1, note 32.

Note: Wherever possible, figures have been rounded to nearest $500.

Source: Interviews with New Jersey developers, June-September 1983.

advantage,* are gleaned by examining the components of housing costs -- development, construction, delivery, and occupancy.

In the development stage, land costs for the mobile home are slightly higher than with the garden condominium because the former is typically sited at a lower density (the example assumes a current mobile home density of five units to the acre versus eight for the garden condominium case study). For the remaining development items, the mobile home maintains a distinct cost advantage relative to the garden unit. Interim financing is not as costly since a construction loan for building the mobile unit is unnecessary and there is less down time in ordering a unit from the factory and then selling it as opposed to building it from scratch. Public fees are lower for the mobile home since building and other permit/inspection costs related to the housing unit are avoided. Other soft costs are less for the mobile unit since professional expenses for the architecture and engineering of the building unit are not necessary. Summing these individual items indicates a total development expense of $9,500 for the mobile home compared to $11,500 for the garden condominium.

Savings in construction costs are also realized. While improvement expenses per unit are higher with the mobile home as compared to the garden unit, a consequence of the former's lower relative density and therefore a lesser ability to amortize total site improvement costs, unit construction costs are lower with the mobile home (see Exhibit 6-6). Consequently, total construction costs are $22,500 for the mobile home compared to $25,500 for the garden condominium.

Economies in delivery cost add to the mobile unit's overall savings. Since less is being constructed, a smaller amount can be set aside as a reserve for contingencies. This, coupled with the other savings described above, allows the 14' x 55' mobile unit at today's standards to be sold for $39,000 compared to $46,000 for the comparable garden unit.

These savings translate into occupancy expense advantages (see Exhibit 6-6). Components of the mobile's monthly charge, and their relationship to recently enacted New Jersey legislation, deserve comment. A series of bills (A-3355 and A3600-3603), passed by both the New Jersey Assembly and Senate would, amongst other things, classify mobile homes sited in parks as personal rather than real property. Given this definition, the mobile unit in our example could not be financed at FHA Title II terms (allowing a 30-year repayment), but rather at the less-generous FHA Title I basis (allowing a maximum 20-year term for a single-wide). Consequently, the mobile has a shorter mortgage maturity and hence a less advantageous financing constant

---

*In comparing prices of mobile units versus conventional housing, product differences should be remembered. The former typically come equipped with major appliances, furniture, draperies, lamps, and carpeting included in the purchase price, while the latter has only major appliances.

compared to the garden condominium (see Exhibits 6-1 and 6-6). This is somewhat offset, however, by the fact that since the mobile unit has a lower delivery price, a smaller amount has to be borrowed. Another consideration is that the mobile home has a clear advantage with respect to property taxes. As a result of the passage of A-3355 and A-3600-3603, the mobile unit would not pay property taxes, albeit the land and site improvements could be taxed, and the municipality could impose a reasonable service fee. Despite these two add-ons, the mobile units would reap the savings of a moderate local tax obligation ($40 monthly compared to $90 for the garden unit; see Exhibits 6-1 and 6-6). Summing all the occupancy cost charges indicates that at today's standards the mobile home has a total monthly cost of about $500 compared to $600 for the garden unit.

In comparing the monthly occupancy cost of mobile home versus garden units, it is important to remember that more than half of the savings results from differential tax treatment -- personal versus property. The calculation assumes that this economy is not offset by the Municipal Service Fee (MSF) which can be imposed on mobile homes in lieu of property taxes. It must be noted, however, that the MSF will not necessarily be less than property taxes as the governing legislation on this matter is quite open-ended (Assembly Bill No. 3600-1983):

> "Municipal service fee" means a fee imposed on manufactured homes installed in a mobile home park for the purpose of reasonable payment for services rendered the owners of the manufactured homes by the municipality or any other local taxing authority established pursuant to an ordinance of the municipal governing body and for the reimbursement of the municipality for payments made thereby to the school district in which the mobile home park is located for educational costs occasioned by pupils residing in that park. (emphasis added)

In the case study example of the 14' x 55' mobile home, we have incorporated an MSF suggested by the New Jersey Manufactured Housing Association. The Association's figure is based on the actual municipal fees which some communities have imposed even prior to the passage of A-3355 and A-3600-3603. Given this MSF, the 14' x 55' mobile home would have a monthly occupancy cost of about $500.

At a monthly occupancy cost of $500, the mobile unit can be afforded by households earning roughly $24,500 -- an income 80 percent of the 1983 areawide median* and thus at the top range of the moderate-income range of Mount Laurel households. The comparable figures for the garden condominium at today's standards were $29,000 and 95 percent of the regional median.*

In the same manner that the regulatory and public subsidy bridge mechanisms discussed earlier could reduce the cost of the garden condo-

*Income for the West Central Region 3 -- the area from which much of the housing cost data were derived.

minium from $46,000 to $39,000 and $35,500 respectively, application of similar bridge approaches would lower the mobile home's delivery price. These calculations are detailed in Exhibit 6-6. With regulatory changes, such as allowing increased density, faster processing, more reasonable public fees, and the like, the final cost of the mobile home could be brought to $34,000 with a monthly occupancy cost of about $450 (see Exhibit 6-6 for details). A family with yearly earnings of $22,000 could afford this unit -- an income 72 percent of the regional median.* Public subsidy would further drop the mobile home's delivery price. With CDBG land and infrastucture write-downs, and below market-rate mortgage, the mobile unit would have a delivery cost of roughly $32,000, a monthly occupancy expense of $375, and could thus house families earning as little as $18,000. This figure is 59 percent of the areawide median* or approaching the low-income Mount Laurel threshold. Thus, mobile homes, albeit with public assistance, can come close to beginning to meet the needs of low-income Mount Laurel households.

Clearly, mobile homes are an important bridge approach. To facilitate its practical assistance, the following actions should be considered:[123]

1. Municipalities should reevaluate restrictions against mobiles. These include exclusion of mobile home parks, or the siting of such facilities in undesirable locations. Restrictions against the mobile units in single-family zones should also be reconsidered, provided these units are compatible. The mobile home legislative package (A-3355 and A-3600-3603) enacted by the New Jersey Assembly and Senate, called for this latter action in the case of double-wide units. To further ease the entry of mobiles into single-family areas, municipalities should consider requirements or recommendations for the siding and roofing of these units to make them more compatible with surrounding site-built homes. These standards must be cost-sensitive, however, for if too stringent, they would add significantly to costs, thereby defeating the mobile home's attractiveness as a Mount Laurel resource. Examples of how communities have dealt with the compatibility issue nationally are contained in Streamlining Local Regulations by the International City Management Association.[124]

2. With the passage of A-3355 and A-3600-3603, mobile units located in parks will not be taxed as real property. Municipalities will, however, be able to impose Municipal Service Fees (MSF). These Municipal Service Fees must be reasonable and should not serve as special taxing or exclusionary mechanisms. Guidelines for determining the MSF, contained in the recently enacted mobile home legislative package, should be carefully adhered to.

3. Residents in mobile home parks also must be protected from unreasonable rental charges for their park sites and for maintenance. In years past, there were some abuses in this regard, mainly as a result of

*Income for the West Central Region 3 -- the area from which much of the housing cost data were derived.

some park owners taking advantage of the tight availability of mobile home pads. With the opening of the mobile home market in New Jersey in response to Mount Laurel, hopefully mobile home locations will more closely equal demand -- a market balance which should curb rent-gouging. To guarantee against abuses, this situation deserves future scrutiny by municipal governments.

4. The State of New Jersey should encourage in-state manufacture of mobile homes. Presently there is only one such factory, producing fifteen units annually. Mobile homes must therefore be delivered from other states. According to the National Manufactured Housing Federation, the cost of delivery to a site amounts to $1.75 per mile, plus $0.70 per mile if an escort is needed, plus a $50 highway movement permit if required by law. Delivery expense for New Jersey mobile homes would be much lower with an in-state manufacturer. Such production would also allow the state to reap the benefit of the new jobs created to fill New Jersey's expanded mobile home consumption in response to Mount Laurel.

CONCLUSION

The Mount Laurel decision set the ambitious goal that housing be produced for low and moderate-income families. To meet this mandate, cost reductions must be realized at all the stages of the housing process -- development, production, delivery, and occupancy. The means of achieving these savings are termed bridge mechanisms and their responsibility falls on all the participants in the housing cycle.

This chapter has examined the applicability, availability, and effect of bridge strategies. For illustration purposes, a garden condominium and then a mobile home were used as case study examples. Successive applications of bridge mechanisms resulted in these case study units being made available to increasingly less affluent households. These changes are summarized in Exhibit 6-7.

While hopefully the mechanisms illustrated here can be implemented with even greater effect, housing for the truly low-incomed will require subsidies outside of the framework of shelter development as such. One possibility is subsidy in the form of purchasers of market units paying more so as to allow for a reduction in the price of Mount Laurel housing. The benefits of this strategy must be viewed together with the issues that it raises. For instance, market realities must be recognized -- New Jersey's housing market, with few exceptions, does not have the vigor of those areas which can "pass along" the costs of deep subsidies to avid market homebuyers. The low-income Mount Laurel population can also be housed with deep public subsidy. This could take numerous possible forms: 1) special taxation of nonresidential facilities (as in San Francisco); 2) forgiveness of local property taxes on Mount Laurel units (assuming state statutory changes are made to allow this); 3) forgiveness of local building permit and other fees on Mount Laurel housing (again assuming legally this

EXHIBIT 6-7

CASE STUDY ILLUSTRATIONS OF MOUNT LAUREL BRIDGE MECHANISMS: SUMMARY

HOUSING UNIT/TYPE	PRICE/AFFORDABILITY PARAMETERS		
	Delivery Price (1983)	Minimum Household Income To Purchase Unit (1983)[3]	Minimum Income As Percent of Regional Median[2] Household Income[3]
Garden Condominium (700 ft.[2])			
•At today's standards :	$46,000	$28,992	95%
•With regulatory reform :	$39,000	$25,008	82%
•With regulatory reform and public subsidy :	$35,500	$19,584	64%
Garden Condominium (700 ft.[2]) Produced Under Inclusionary Program[1]			
•With regulatory reform :	$21,500	$13,000	43%
•With regulatory reform and public subsidy :	$18,000	$11,000	37%
Mobile Home (14' x 55' single-wide)			
•At today's standards :	$39,000	$24,528	80%
•With regulatory reform :	$34,000	$22,080	72%
•With regulatory reform and public subsidy :	$31,700	$18,000	59%

[1]With significant density bonus and inclusion with higher-price units. These figures are approximate; see chapter for details.
[2]Income data for West Central Region 3 -- the area from which much of the cost data were derived.
[3]At 25 percent housing expense-to-income ratio. Note: At a higher ratio, say 30 percent, both the qualifying incomes and the regional median percentages would be lower.

Source: See chapter for details.

can be done); or, 4) the extension of other assistance financed from general revenues (e.g. a municipal public works department possibly could provide street and other improvements for Mount Laurel projects). These strategies all offer significant housing cost-reduction possibilities. They each penalize the individual host community and its taxpayers. Nonetheless the gap between housing costs, even when the latter are optimized, and the truly low-incomed household's capacity to pay is evident and requires statewide consideration.*

The chapter's listing of some score bridge mechanisms, and its reference to the garden unit and mobile homes examples, surely do not exhaust the richness of responses to Mount Laurel. Some communities will work to make the traditional, single-family, detached home more affordable. Still others may utilize the bridge techniques discussed here but combine them in ways not touched in our analysis. No one document can describe all of the permutations of Mount Laurel responses. The objective of this chapter has been to present the framework of common housing cost elements which must be reduced to achieve the Mount Laurel mandate, and then to discuss and illustrate the most promising techniques of achieving this goal.

---

*New York City, for example, is considering the following wide net of resources to house lower-income families. A total of $200 million yearly could be raised from a number of sources including: $30-$60 million a year in developer contributions -- based on 6 million square feet at a modest $5.00 per square foot contribution per year; $20 million in inclusionary zoning payments made in lieu of on-site units; $22 million in New York City's share of State Mortgage Recording fees (New York City's pro rata share); $17.5 million in repayments of PLP and other CD/UDAG funded loans and sale of non-residential city-owned property; $5 million in Building Department fees -- based on a revised schedule of filing fees; $17.5 million to be derived from registration fees for limited partnership syndications and interest earned on real estate-related escrow accounts; $7.5 million from the filing fees for cooperatives and condominiums; $15 million to be derived from a tax on large-scale real estate transfers; $7 million to be derived from filing fees for incorporation based on the capital structure of the incorporating organization; $20 million in Capital Budget appropriations from the city of New York; $20 million in Budget appropriations from the State of New York; and $11 million plus in annual repayment of loans previously made by the Housing Trust Fund. See Citizens Housing and Planning Council, "Memorandum."

NOTES

1. See, for example, Urban Land Institute, Land Use Digest, Vol. 16, No. 8, August 15, 1983.

2. Robert Snow Means Company, Building Construction Cost Data (Annual Series) (Duxbury, Massachusetts: Robert Snow Means, annual).

3. See U.S. Commission of Urban Problems, Building the American City (Washington, D.C.: U.S. Government Printing Office, 1968).

4. Robert W. Burchell, et al. Housing Costs and Housing Restraints: Newark, New Jersey (New Brunswick, New Jersey: Center for Urban Social Science Research, 1970); Stephen R. Seidel, Housing Costs and Government Regulation (New Brunswick, New Jersey: Center for Urban Policy Research, 1978); Robert W. Burchell and David Listokin, "Improving Design Standards in Fringe Communities: Local and State Initiatives," in U.S. Department of Housing and Urban Development, Reducing the Development Costs of Housing: Actions for State and Local Government (Washington, D.C.: U.S. Government Printing Office, 1979), p. 15; Robert W. Burchell and David Listokin, "The Impact of Local Government Regulations on Housing Costs and Potential Avenues of State Meliorative Measures," in George Sternlieb and James W. Hughes, America's Housing (New Brunswick, New Jersey: Center for Urban Policy Research, 1980), p. 313.

5. The 1980 U.S. Census is the last comprehensive roster of the numbers and prices/rentals of New Jersey housing being built. There is no comparable source of more current conditions. The best proxy, albeit for fee units only, is provided by the files of the HOW (Home Owners Warranty) Corporation headquartered in Woodbridge, New Jersey. Before describing its files, the coverage and services of this organization deserve mention.

A 1978 New Jersey statute (P.L. 1977, Chapter 467, approved March 3, 1978) required that all newly built, for-sale units in the state must have a 10-year insurance policy covering major mechanical and construction defects. Insurance for each unit is paid for by the builder and the costs passed along to the beneficiary, the homebuyer. HOW has captured about 70 percent of the New Jersey market (in terms of housing production). The remainder is met by builder self-insurance as well as a pool handled by the State of New Jersey. According to HOW officials, these other insurance sources are not capturing a segment of the market which appreciably differs from their company's.

While HOW has offered coverage for half a decade, it has only recently computerized its files so as to allow a statewide analysis. Computerized data is available starting from June 1983 to the present -- a space of four months. For each unit insured by HOW, computerized data are available on the location (municipality, county, zip code), selling price, size estimates (square footage), and type (garden condominium or not). Given HOW's capture of the market, its computerized file should be providing a profile of roughly three-quarters of the for-sale housing offered for sale in New Jersey.

6. This was derived by taking the 1979 median income for the West Central Region 3 and adjusting it for inflation.

7. *Southern Burlington County NAACP v. The Township of Mount Laurel*, 67 N.J. 151, 336 A. 2nd 713, *Appeal Dismissed and Cert. Denied*, 423 U.S. 808 (1975) (Mount Laurel I); 92 N.J. 158, 456 A.2nd 390 (1983) (hereinafter referred to as Mount Laurel II Decision). See also Middlesex, Somerset, Mercer Regional Study Council, "Mount Laurel II Points to a Better Way," Newsletter, May 1983; Jerome G. Rose, "The Mount Laurel II Decision: Is It Based on Wishful Thinking?", *Real Estate Law Journal*, Vol. 12, No. 2 (Fall 1983), p. 115; Jerold S. Kayden and Leonard A. Zax, "Mount Laurel II: Landmark Decision in Zoning and Low Income Housing Holds Lessons for Nation," *Zoning and Planning Law Report*, Vol. 6, No. 8, September 1983.

8. *Mount Laurel II Decision*, pp. 97-98.

9. *Ibid.*, pp. 104-106.

10. *Ibid.*, pp. 108-109.

11. *Ibid.*, pp. 121-122.

12. *Ibid.*, p. 108.

13. *Ibid.*, pp. 98-99.

14. U.S. Department of Housing and Urban Development, *Affordable Housing: How Local Regulatory Improvements Can Help* (Washington, D.C.: U.S. Government Printing Office, 1982).

15. Wilford Sanders and David Mosena, *Changing Development Standards for Affordable Housing* (Chicago, Illinois: American Planning Association, 1982), report prepared for the Joint Venture for Affordable Housing.

16. National Homebuilders Association Research Foundation, Inc., *Building Affordable Homes: A Cost Savings Guide for Builder/Developers* (Washington, D.C.: NAHB, 1982), Report prepared for the U.S. Department of Housing and Urban Development, Office of Policy Development and Research.

17. International City Management Association, *Streamlining Local Regulations: A Handbook for Reducing Housing and Development Costs* (Washington, D.C.: ICMA, 1983), Management Information Services Special Report, May 1983, No. 11. Report prepared by Stuart S. Hershey and Carolyn Garmise.

18. State of Connecticut, Department of Housing, *Housing and Land Use: Community Options for Lowering Housing Costs* (Hartford, Connecticut: Connecticut Department of Housing, 1981).

19. California Building Industry Association, *Manual for Reducing Housing Costs* (Sacramento, California: California Building Industry Association, 1979). Report prepared by the Affordable Housing Task Force, Orange County Chapter, California Building Association.

20. New Jersey Department of Community Affairs, Division of Housing and Planning, and the Tri-State Regional Planning Commission, *The Affordable Housing Handbook* (Trenton, New Jersey: New Jersey Department of Community Affairs, 1972).

21. New Jersey Department of Community Affairs, *Housing Handbook for New Jersey Municipalities* (Trenton, New Jersey: Department of Community Affairs, December 1976).

22. New Jersey Department of Community Affairs, *Princeton Housing Proposal: A Strategy to Achieve Balanced Housing Without Government Subsidy* (Trenton, New Jersey: Department of Community Affairs, 1977).

23. New Jersey Assembly Housing Emergency Action Team, *Final Report* (Trenton, New Jersey: New Jersey Assembly, 1981).

24. State of New Jersey, Legislative Study Commission, *Report and Recommendations of the Mobile Home Study Commission* (Trenton, New Jersey: Legislative Study Commission, October 1980).

25. U.S. Department of Housing and Urban Development, *Affordable Housing: How Local Regulatory Improvements Can Help*, p. 4.

26. New Jersey Department of Community Affairs, *The Affordable Housing Handbook*, p. 27.

27. *Ibid.*

28. U.S. Department of Housing and Urban Development, *Affordable Housing: How Local Regulatory Improvements Can Help*, p. 4.

29. *Ibid.* See also National Association of Homebuilders, *Cost-Effective Site Planning*, p. 24.

30. Suburban Action Institute, *Housing Choice* (New York: Suburban Action Institute, no date), p. 37. See also, American Planning Association, *Low- and Moderate-Income Housing - Part I, Increasing the Supply and Accessibility*, by Denise Roudebush and Leslie J. Wells (Chicago, Illinois: American Planning Association, 1980), Planning Advisory Service Report No. 350.

31. 24 C.F.R. §570 (1983).

32. 24 C.F.R. §570.201(a) (1983).

33. See California Building Industry Association, Manual for Reducing Housing Costs, p. 42.

34. 24 C.F.R. §570.207(b)(3) (1983).

35. Housing Authority of Bergen County, "New Concepts for Affordable Housing in Bergen County" (no date); Letter from the Housing Development Corporation of Bergen County, to the Center for Urban Policy Research, August 10, 1983.

36. Housing Authority of Bergen County, "New Concepts for Affordable Housing in Bergen County," p. 6.

37. Memorandum from Henry A. Hill, Esq., to the New Jersey Governor's Task Force on Housing, "Recommendation for State Government Action to Further Development," August 5, 1982.

38. Memorandum from Harry S. Pozycki, Jr., to the New Jersey Governor's Task Force on Housing, "Explanation of Land Use Reform Legislation Prepared for Immediate Introduction."

39. Ibid.

40. International City Management Association, Streamlining Local Regulations.

41. John Vranicar, Wilford Sanders, and David Mosena, Streamlining Land Use Regulation -- A Guidebook for Local Governments (Washington, D.C.: U.S. Government Printing Office, November 1980). Report prepared by the American Planning Association, with the assistance of the Urban Land Institute, for the U.S. Department of Housing and Urban Development.

42. Urban Land Institute, Reducing the Development Costs of Housing: Actions for State and Local Governments -- Proceedings of the HUD National Conference on Housing Costs (Washington, D.C.: U.S. Government Printing Office, October 1979).

43. Telephone interview with Joseph Chieppa, Assistant Executive Director, New Jersey Housing Finance Agency, September 1983.

44. Ibid.

45. New Jersey Department of Community Affairs, The Affordable Housing Handbook, p. 37.

46. Based on interviews with Anthony Marchetta, Director, Middlesex County Department of Housing and Community Development; Michele Dushkin, Assistant Director, Middlesex County Department of Housing and Community Development; Nancy Milman, Community Development Block Grant Office, HUD Regional Office, Newark, New Jersey. See also, Suburban Action Institute, Housing Choice.

47. See Bernard J. Frieden, The Environmental Protection Hustle (Cambridge, Massachusetts: MIT Press, 1979); National Association of Homebuilders, "Infrastructure Financing Trends and Alternatives" (1983).

48. National Association of Homebuilders, Building Affordable Homes, p. 5.

49. California Building Industry Association, Manual for Reducing Housing Costs.

50. Interview with John Vitale, municipal engineer, Montville, New Jersey, September 1983.

51. New Jersey Assembly Housing Emergency Action Team (1981), Final Report, p. 19.

52. 24 C.F.R. §570.206(g) (1983).

53. See New Jersey Housing Finance Agency, "Guidelines for Project Development," "Minimum Design Standards," "Recommended Dwelling Unit Layout," and "Standard Outline Specifications."

54. Ibid.

55. Letter to the Center for Urban Policy Research from Robert H. Lee, Director of Technical Services, New Jersey Housing Finance Agency, July 26, 1983.

56. "An Ordinance Amending Ordinance 76-71." As Amended, known as the Zoning Ordinance of the Township of Cherry Hill (Ordinance 83-2).

57. Council of State Community Affairs Agencies, State Actions for Affordable Housing (Washington, D.C.: Council of State Community Affairs Agencies, July 1982). Report prepared by Marvin Tick and John Sidor of the Council of State Community Affairs Agencies for the U.S. Department of Housing and Urban Development.

58. Interview with Mr. Cy Rubin, September 1983. Mr. Rubin was formerly the Chief Building Code Official in the New Jersey Department of Community Affairs.

59. See "Applying Building Technology to Lower Housing Costs," Urban Land, June 1982, p. 25.

60. Telephone interview with Mr. Dask, Code Official at the New Jersey Department of Community Affairs, September 1983.

61. See Eugene F. Metz et al., "Housing Conservation Technology Assessment Shows Need for Progress in Accomplishments, Attitudes," Journal

of Housing, Vol. 35, January 1978, pp. 21-22; see National Institute of Building Sciences, The Rehabilitation Guidelines (Washington, D.C.: U.S. Department of Housing and Urban Development, 1980).

62. James H. Pielert, Removing Regulatory Restraints to Building Rehabilitation: The Massachusetts Experience (Washington, D.C.: National Bureau of Standards, 1981).

63. See footnotes 61 and 62.

64. Comptroller General of the United States, Why Are New Housing Prices So High...? (Washington, D.C.: Government Printing Office, 1978), p. 37.

65. See New Jersey Department of Community Affairs, The Affordable Housing Handbook, p. 46.

66. See, for example, National Association of Homebuilders and the U.S. Department of Housing and Urban Development, An Approach for the '80s -- Affordable Housing Demonstration (no date).

67. See New Jersey Department of Community Affairs, The Affordable Housing Handbook, p. 46.

68. U.S. Department of Housing and Urban Development, Reducing Homebuilding Costs With OVE Design and Construction, Guideline 5 (Washington, D.C.: U.S. Government Printing Office, 1981).

69. National Association of Homebuilders, Building Affordable Homes; Douglas R. Porter and Susan Cole, Affordable Housing: Twenty Examples From the Private Sector (Washington, D.C.: The Urban Land Institute, 1982); National Association of Homebuilders and the U.S. Department of Housing and Urban Development, An Approach for the '80s: Affordable Housing Demonstration (Washington, D.C.: NAHB and HUD, no date); U.S. Department of Housing and Urban Development, Approach 80 (Washington, D.C.: U.S. Government Printing Office, December 1980); U.S. Department of Housing and Urban Development, Housing Cost Reduction Demonstration (Washington, D.C.: U.S. Government Printing Office, no date); National Association of Homebuilders Research Foundation, Inc., The Affordable Housing Demonstration Case Study -- Lincoln, Nebraska (Washington, D.C.: U.S. Government Printing Office, October 1982); Center for Community Development and Preservation, Reducing Housing Development Costs: Strategies for Affordable Housing (White Plains, New York: Center for Community Development and Preservation, 1980); U.S. Department of Housing and Urban Development, Homebuilding Cost Cuts (Washington, D.C.: U.S. Government Printing Office, 1983). See also U.S. Department of Housing and Urban Development and the National Homebuilders Association, Energy-Efficient Residence; National Association of Homebuilders, Productivity Improvement Manual; U.S. Department of Housing and Urban Development, Building Value into Housing: 1980 Awards; U.S. Department of Housing and Urban Development, Design for Affordable Housing: Cost-

Effective/Energy-Conserving Homes. See also, Chapter 14 in the National Association of Homebuilders, Building Affordable Homes, on "Cost-Effective Construction Publications."

70. New Jersey Assembly Housing Emergency Action Team, Final Report, p. 18.

71. National Association of Homebuilders, Cost-Effective Site Planning, p. 98.

72. Ibid.

73. See National Association of Homebuilders, Building Affordable Homes, p. 10.

74. New Jersey Department of Community Affairs, The Affordable Housing Handbook, pp. 35-36; see also Robert Freilich, Model Subdivision Regulations (Chicago, Illinois: American Society of Planning Officials, 1975), p. 97.

75. See California Building Industry Association, Manual for Reducing Housing Costs, pp. 10+; U.S. Department of Housing and Urban Development and The Urban Land Institute, Reducing the Development Costs of Housing: Actions for State and Local Government, p. 249; Sanders and Mosena, Changing Development Standards for Affordable Housing, p. 65; International City Management Association, Streamlining Local Regulations, p. 27; State of Connecticut, Department of Housing, Housing and Land Use: Community Options for Lowering Housing Costs, p. 51+.

76. 24 C.F.R. §570.207(b)(3) (1983).

77. Telephone interview with Carl Hintz, Director of the East Brunswick Department of Planning and Community Development, September 1983.

78. Telephone conversation with John Riley, U.S. Department of Housing and Urban Development, Washington, D.C., September 1983.

79. Telephone conversation with John Kemp, HUD economist, HUD Newark Office, September 1983.

80. See New Jersey Housing Finance Agency, 1982 Annual Report (Trenton, New Jersey: N.J.H.F.A., 1982).

81. New Jersey Mortgage Finance Agency, Annual Reports.

82. Telephone interview with Connie Gibson, of the New Jersey Mortgage Finance Agency, August 1983; see also footnote 43.

83. John Fernsler, "Tax-Exempt Financing for Housing and Community Development: A Year of Activity," The Urban Lawyer, Fall 1981, Vol. 13, No. 4, p. 706.

84. Pub. L. No. 96-499, Section 1102, 94 Common Statutes 2660 (1980).

85. Fernsler, "Tax-Exempt Financing," p. 707.

86. Connerly and Associates, Inc., Using Tax-Exempt Revenue Bonds in California (Sacramento, California: California Building Industry Association, Mortgage Finance Task Force, 1982), Chapter 3.

87. Ibid.

88. Ibid.

89. California Building Industry Association, "Using Tax-Exempt Mortgage Revenue Bonds in California," Update No. 1, April 1983.

90. See Note 82.

91. N.J.S.A. 40:55C-40 et seq.

92. N.J.S.A. 40:55C-65.

93. N.J.S.A. 40:55-C-2.

94. State of Connecticut, Department of Housing, Housing and Land Use: Community Options for Lowering Housing Costs, p. 9.

95. Robert C. Ellickson, "The Irony of Inclusionary Zoning," Southern California Law Review, Vol. 54, No. 6, September 1981, p. 1172. See also "Density Bonus Zoning to Provide Low- and Moderate-Cost Housing," Hastings Constitutional Law Journal, Vol. 3, No. 4, Fall 1976, p. 1015+; and Herbert M. Franklin et al., In-Zoning -- A Guide for Policymakers on Inclusionary Land Use Programs (Washington, D.C.: The Potomac Institute, 1974).

96. See the Technical Appendix.

97. Fairfax County, Va. Code Ch. 30 (1961) as amended by Amendment 156 (1971), cited in Hastings Constitutional Law Journal, p. 1053.

98. Arlington County, Va. Resolution on Developer Provision of Moderate-Income Housing (February 22, 1972); Montgomery County Council Bill 372, Montgomery County, Md. Code 25A (1974). See Seymour I. Schwartz and Robert A. Johnston, "Inclusionary Housing Programs," Journal of the American Planning Association, Winter 1983, Vol. 49, No. 1, p. 3; Barbara Taylor, "Inclusionary Zoning: A Workable Option for Affordable Housing?" Urban Land, Vol. 40, No. 3, March 1981, p. 3; Ellickson, "The Irony of Inclusionary Zoning," p. 1173; Linda J. Bozung, "A Positive Response to Growth Control Plans: The Orange County Inclusionary Housing Program," Pepperdine Law Review, Vol. 9, No. 4 (1982), p. 824; California Building

Industry Association, *The Implications of Inclusionary Housing Programs* (April 1979); California Building Industry Association, *Inclusionary Housing in Orange County: A Look at Preliminary Results* (April 1981).

99. See historical discussion in *Hastings Constitutional Law Journal*; see also Linda J. Bozung, "Inclusionary Housing Experience Under a Model Program," *Zoning and Planning Law Report*, Vol. 6, No. 1, January 1983.

100. *Ibid.*

101. *Uxbridge Associates v. Township of Cherry Hill*, No. L-47451-77 (N.J. Super. Ct., Jan. 11, 1980) and *In the Matter of Egg Harbor Associates*, 185 N.J. Super. 507, 449 A.2d 1324 (App.Div. 1982).

102. Schwartz and Johnston, "Inclusionary Housing Programs," p. 8; Bozung, "A Positive Response to Growth Control Plans: The Orange County Inclusionary Housing Program," p. 843; California Building Industry Association, *A Look at Preliminary Results*, pp. 20-23.

103. "Density Bonus Zoning to Provide Low-and Moderate Cost Housing," p. 1070.

104. New Jersey Department of Community Affairs, *The Princeton Housing Proposal*.

105. *Ibid.*

106. Federal National Mortgage Association, *Lending Handbook*, Section 421, March 31, 1983, p. 12; See Federal Home Loan Mortgage Corporation, "Bulletin," 11-15-82, Section 3.201a(8), p. 122.

107. *The New York Times*, July 11, 1982.

108. *Ibid.*

109. International City Management Association, *Streamlining Local Regulations*, p. 21; see also, Thomas E. Nutt-Powell, *Manufactured Homes -- Making Sense of a Housing Opportunity* (Boston: Auburn House, 1982); Manufactured Housing Institute, "Quick Facts About the Manufactured Housing Industry" (July 1982).

110. New Jersey Department of Community Affairs, *The Affordable Housing Handbook*, p. 43-45.

111. *Ibid.*

112. International City Management Association, *Streamliniing Local Regulations*, p. 21.

113. 1980 U.S. Census of Housing (see Chapter 4).

114. Data obtained from the New Jersey Manufactured Housing Association, October 1983.

115. Mobile Home Study Commission, Final Report of the Mobile Home Taxation Commission, p. 25.

116. State of New Jersey Legislative Study Commission, Report and Recommendations of the Mobile Home Study Commission, p. 10. See also, "Public Hearing Before Mobile Home Study Commission on Local Land Use Regulations on Mobile Homes." Hearings held March 14, 1979, New Jersey Assembly Chamber.

117. International City Management Association, Streamlining Local Regulations, p. 22.

118. See Nutt-Powell, Manufactured Homes, p. 21.

119. Richard I. Peyster and Harvey E. Weiner, "Manufactured Housing Finance on the Move," Mortgage Banking (August 1983), p. 31.

120. Ibid.

121. Ibid.

122. Manufactured Housing Institute, Manufacturing Housing Quarterly (Spring 1983), p. 1. See also "Manufactured Homes Help Buyer Beat Affordability Woes," Savings Institutions (September 1983), p. 30.

123. Telephone conversation with A. E. Petrick, Executive Director, New Jersey Manufactured Housing Association, September 1983.

124. International City Management Association, Streamlining Local Regulations.

APPENDIX I

BRIDGE MECHANISMS TO MEET THE MOUNT LAUREL MANDATE: TECHNICAL CONSIDERATIONS

INTRODUCTION

This appendix considers two technical matters referred to in Chapter 6 of the study. The first concerns the housing expense-to-income ratio; the second, inclusionary programs, designed to force or encourage the production of affordable housing.

HOUSING EXPENSE-TO-INCOME RATIO

To determine the household income necessary to dwell in a housing unit of a given price, either as a renter or buyer, an important consideration is the tolerable share of household earnings which can be allocated to shelter expense. This share is technically referred to as the housing-expense-to-income ratio. Chapter 6 assumed that for Mount Laurel households, one possible ratio is 25 percent of gross income. This is a conservative approach as is explained below.

The housing expense-to-income ratio encompasses three considerations: what is included in the housing expense, what is meant by income, and finally what is the proper relationship between the former two variables.

Housing expense. This includes the shelter outlays which must be paid in the sense that default will result in a dispossess in rental situations, or a lien claim and ultimately a foreclosure in fee (for-sale) cases. A renter is dispossessed for financial reasons if the monthly contract rent is not satisfied. Historically the latter was set to meet the property owner's payments for PITI (principal, interest, taxes, and insurance) plus maintenance and heating utility costs. (While rent typically would include a profit factor, this amount was usually negligible as much rental housing was built for tax write-off rather than cash flow.) In recent years, the heating utility component has frequently been "unbundled" from the monthly contract rent. Instead of utility consumption being measured by a master meter, and being paid for collectively by all tenants in their rental payments, prevailing practice is to delete utilities from the rental charge and have tenants pay for their own consumption directly as measured by separate meters for each unit. In sum, in rental situations, the housing expense to be met is the monthly contract rent. This in turn encompasses PITI and maintenance outlays.

To determine the components of housing costs in fee situations, we again must consider the shelter outlays which must be remitted. Historically, as evaluated by mortgage underwriters, these included only PITI.[1] Underwriters recognized that maintenance and heat would have to be paid for. They felt, however, that these items were not as compelling, since if delinquent they would not constitute a lien, threatening the lender's interest. In contrast, delinquency on PITI items would.

Change in housing configurations and delivery have altered underwriting practice. For reasons of economy, life-style preferences, and the like, maintenance in townhouses, garden condominiums and similar complexes is often provided for by a central condo or homeowners' association. In these cases, maintenance must be remitted and if delinquent constitutes a lien which can be foreclosed. In such instances, the following change has been made in the underwriting determination of the housing costs to be met by would-be purchasers. Instead of just counting the traditional PITI items, underwriters add maintenance as well since the latter now has the same compelling claim and recourse as the former.

In sum, the definition of the housing expense is the shelter outlays which must be met -- whether in the form of monthly contract rent or the most pressing of homeowner charges. In rental cases, these encompass PITI and maintenance; in fee situations, PITI is again counted and maintenance is included if it assumes a lien status.

Some underwriters seemingly follow a different approach than that enumerated above. For instance, the Federal Housing Administration (FHA) includes maintenance even in cases where this is provided for individually by the homeowner. The FHA also adds a utility charge. In other words, FHA underwriting of the housing expense includes PITI, and maintenance, and utilities.[2] This practice is not so radical a departure, however, for while FHA has an extensive tally of housing costs, it also allows a very generous ratio of these costs to income -- 35 to 38 percent -- as compared to the 25 percent "rule of thumb." FHA counts income differently as well, as is explained below.

Income. The earnings commonly considered in determining housing affordability is the gross income as derived from primary employment and other stable, recognizable sources (e.g., dividends or interest). There are variations, however. The FHA starts with gross earnings and then deducts state and federal taxes in order to determine the net effective income. The latter is the basis for all FHA underwriting -- the 35 to 38 percent ratio is applied against the net effective income.

Another exception is the income determination in the Section 8 program. The basis here is the adjusted gross income. The latter is equal to gross income less three items: (1) a $300 deduction for each child; (2) child-care expenses for working mothers; and (3) non-reimbursed medical costs above 4 percent of gross income. How significant are these deductions? Interviews with major Section 8 developers in the metropolitan area indicate that the deductions are generally not considerable, with the exception of a female-headed household where the mother works full-time.[3] In such a case, child-care expenses can be significant, especially as measured against the "very low" and "lower" incomes of Section 8 tenants.

It is important to understand the Section 8 basis of "adjusted gross" rather than "full gross" income to comprehend the significance of the 30 percent ratio the program then applies to determine the rental payment to be paid by tenants. The issue of the expense ratio is explained below.

Expense Ratio.* It is commonly stated that the traditional rule of thumb is that a borrower's housing expense should not exceed 25 percent of gross income.[4] Even traditionally, this oversimplified the underwriting practice. We have already indicated that FHA allowed a higher share, albeit against a smaller income basis (net effective rather than gross income). The Veterans Administration (VA) never applied a set housing expense-to-income ratio.[5] Instead, it has and continues to follow what is referred to as a "residual approach" or a "balance for family support."[6] The VA first sums housing expenses (including maintenance and utilities) and other fixed outlays (e.g. automobile and long-term debts) and then deducts these debits from total gross income. If a mortgage is affordable, a "sufficient amount" should then remain. A "sufficient reserve" is defined as a VA-specified monthly dollar stipend per adult, teenager, and child.

Most other underwriters have followed the traditional analysis of allocating a set percentage of gross income for housing expenses. What has changed, however, is the percentage. While in the years past, the one-quarter ratio was frequently applied, rising housing prices, and the view that housing is as much an investment as a needed consumption, have bumped this percentage upward. For instance, private mortgage insurers (PMI), as well as major secondary market mortgage purchasers, such as the Federal National Mortgage Association (FNMA) and the Federal Home Loan Mortgage Corporation (FHLMC) currently accept up to a 28 percent expense ratio.[7] The New Jersey Mortgage Finance Agency similarly allows a 28 percent ratio. Some tolerate even higher shares. The Mortgage Guarantee Insurance Corporation (MGIC), a major PMI, will sometimes accept 30 to 32 percent ratios. And at the current time in New Jersey, the Residential Funding Corporation (RFC), a private mortgage underwriter, permits up to a 33 percent share (RFC, however, limits its market to larger than-average-loans, and charges higher than average fees in the form of points).[8]

The Federal government has also pushed upward from the 25 percent housing expense-to-income ratio in its Section 8 program -- the major rental housing subsidy available today. At Section 8's inception in 1974, very low- and lower-income tenants (equivalent to the Mount Laurel low- and moderate-income thresholds) were asked to pay a quarter of their adjusted gross income. This has now changed to a two-tier system. New Section 8 tenants pay 30 percent of their adjusted gross income; existing tenants are

---

*Actually there are two ratios considered by underwriters. The first is the housing expense-to-income ratio. The second is the long-term debt-(housing outlays plus other financial obligations such as alimony and child support) to-income ratio. This appendix focuses on the former ratio since it is most directly concerned with housing.

being moved up to the 30 percent figure at a rate of one percent per year.*

In considering the HUD Section 8 housing expense-to-income ratio, it is important to remember its different income basis -- adjusted rather than full gross. Since the former is less than the latter, the HUD Section 8 housing expense-to-income ratio is actually lower than 30 percent as this share is commonly referred to in industry terms.* How much less depends on the level of family, children, and health expense deductions described earlier. If these are significant, the ratio can be considerably below 30 percent; if minor the effective share will be close to 30 percent as it is typically understood in industry terms.

In sum, the 25 percent housing expense-to-income ratio is no longer a universally governing "rule of thumb," if it ever was. Underwriters are beginning to recognize that many households must pay a larger share of their earnings for shelter. The burden for all New Jersey households as reported by the 1980 Public Use Sample is illustrative. For New Jersey households renting their units, more than half exceed the 25 percent housing expense-to-income ratio. For their homeowner counterparts,[9] one-third exceed the 25 percent threshold. Clearly, for the state as a whole, the 25 percent "rule of thumb" is more wishful thinking than fact. The situation is even more burdensome when Mount Laurel households are examined separately. This was done in Chapter 3. It indicated that about half of the moderate-income Mount Laurel families had a housing expense-to-income ratio exceeding 25 percent; for their low-income counterparts, more than 70 percent exceeded the one-quarter threshold.

Despite the fact that underwriters have moved upward from the 25 percent "rule of thumb," and the reality of many New Jersey households and especially Mount Laurel families paying considerably more than this ratio for shelter, Chapter 6 applied the one-quarter figure. This was done to correspond to footnote 8 in the Mount Laurel decision in which the Court expressed its leaning towards a 25 percent housing expense-to-income approach.[10]

> ...When we refer in this opinion to housing being "affordable" by lower income families ("lower" meaning "low and moderate") we mean that the family pays no more than 25 percent of its income for such housing, the 25 percent figure being widely accepted in the relevant literature...

In sum, Chapter 6 applied a 25 percent housing expense-to-income ratio. The housing expense includes the items described earlier (in rental situations, the monthly contract rent; in fee situations, PITI expenses

---

*Another consideration is that HUD allows a utility stipend which is deducted against the nominal rent obligation. For instance, if 30 percent of adjusted gross monthly income is $300, and tenant utility expenses are $30 monthly, then the final rent payment would be $270.

plus a maintenance fee if paid to a homeowners/condo association). And following most underwriting practice, the 25 percent ratio was applied to gross income. It should be noted, however, that the 25 percent ratio is conservative. It is less than the share allowed by many major mortgage underwriters and insurers. It is also less than the ratio used in related efforts to provide for lower-income housing. For example, the fair share guidelines promulgated by the New Jersey Office of Coastal Zone Management incorporate a two-tier housing expense-to-income ratio of 25 percent for rental, and 30 percent for fee situations (see N.J.A.C. 7:7E-72(e)).

The Income-to-Housing-Price Ratio

In addition to the housing expense-to-income-ratio, another commonly referred to "rule of thumb underwriting" is the relationship between income and the price of housing. A multiple of 2.0 to 2.5 is commonly applied.[11] This means that a family with an income of say $20,000 can afford housing priced at $40,000 to $50,000. It is important to realize that the income-to-housing-price guideline is a much less accurate gauge of housing affordability than the housing expense-to-income ratio. The latter is carefully defined; housing expenses are calculated and then matched to household earnings. In contrast, the income-to-housing price multiple, of say 2.0 to 2.5, itself depends on numerous non-specified variables such as the size of the down payment, mortgage interest rate, items included in the housing cost package (see prior discussion), local property tax rate, as well as the acceptable housing-expense-to-income ratio.

While recognizing these drawbacks, the income-to-housing-price ratio is useful precisely in those cases where the items specified above are unknown (e.g. down payment or interest rate) and the only information available is income and housing price. Where the income-to-housing price ratio is utilized, it is advisable to apply it at its lower threshold, at say a multiple of 2.0 rather than 2.5, to reflect today's higher interest rate and lower down payments (in Mount Laurel cases). The 2.0 ratio, for example, roughly corresponds to the affordability calculations of the garden apartment unit with regulatory reform and public subsidy (see Exhibit 6-1). It is also a rough approximation for the other units if the maintenance fee is not included in housing costs.

The Appendix now turns to a second matter referred to in Chapter 6 -- inclusionary housing programs. The national experience is considered first, followed by an overview of the New Jersey state-of-the-art.

INCLUSIONARY PROGRAMS: NATIONAL OVERVIEW

Inclusionary programs in the United States date to the early 1970s. In 1971, Fairfax County, Virginia required builders of fifty or more units to commit at least 15 percent of their production for low/moderate-income families.[12] In 1973, Arlington County, Virginia enacted a 10 percent inclusionary goal which if realized would result in a 10 percent density bonus.[13] In the same year, Montgomery County, Maryland, adopted a mandatory inclusionary requirement for builders of 50 or more units that they set aside 15 percent of their production for moderate-income families.[14] To facilitate compliance, up to a 20 percent density bonus was authorized. And in response to the DeGroff[15] decision, which declared Fairfax County's 1971 inclusionary requirement an unconstitutional taking, Fairfax amended its requirement in 1973 to provide for a density bonus.[16]

The inclusionary spirit soon leaped the continent. In 1973, Lakewood, Colorado required that 10 to 15 percent of the units in housing projects of fifty or more homes be offered at below-market prices.[17] Shortly thereafter, Boulder, Colorado added a similar provision.[18] It was in California, however, that inclusionary mechanisms became most commonplace. As a result of a series of state statutory requirements relating to expanded housing opportunities, (e.g., mandating that local governments "make adequate provision for the housing needs of all economic segments of the community,"[19] requiring municipalities to provide "regulatory concessions and incentives" to foster such housing,[20] and preparing model local inclusionary ordinances),[21] scores of California municipalities adopted inclusionary approaches. In 1973, Palo Alto required that developers of twenty or more units provide that one-in-five be low- or moderate-cost units.[22] A year later, Los Angeles imposed a 15 percent low/moderate inclusionary share in developments of five or more units.[23]

The most extensive California inclusionary program, in terms of the housing production affected, is found in Orange County.[24] It requires that 25 percent of all units in developments of five or more houses located in most areas of the county (only locations already fulfilling their inclusionary mandate are exempt) be affordable to families earning below 120 percent of the county's median income. Of the 25 percent inclusionary units: 10 percent must be affordable by low/moderate-income families (those earning below 80 percent of the median), another 10 percent for "medium I" households (those earning between 80 and 100 percent of the median), and a final 5 percent for "medium II" households (those earning between 100 and 120 percent of the median). Developers can satisfy their inclusionary requirement by: (1) building the one-quarter share in each project, (2) "overbuilding" (going above a 25 percent share) affordable units in one of their developments and then transferring the excess as a "credit" to a project which is under quota, (3) buying "credits" from other builders who have an excess to sell, and (4) through other means, such as land donation or in-lieu cash payments to the county. However it is satisfied, the inclusionary requirement is costly to builders. To compensate, developers are offered density bonuses, modifications to subdivision requirements, accelerated processing, and tax-exempt financing. To ensure that the units built under the program remain affordable, there are resale controls, such as a twenty-year deed restriction. The latter gives the county the right of first refusal to buy the unit at a price that allows appreciation limited to the percentage increase in county median income plus substantial improvements made by the original housebuyer.

Orange County's inclusionary program has resulted in a considerable amount of affordable housing being planned and/or produced. As of 1982, there were commitments to build over 5,000 such units; 800 of this total were already built and occupied.[25] The bulk of this was in exclusively low cost development. More affluent developments subsidized them by buying their fair share obligation off site. By contrast, New Jersey's inclusionary programs have been far less successful.

INCLUSIONARY PROGRAMS: NEW JERSEY EXPERIENCE

While as a result of the Mount Laurel decision, inclusionary zoning will likely become commonplace in New Jersey, as of 1983 there are only about a dozen such examples (see Exhibit 6A-1).[26] Most of these have been enacted by individual municipalities. There are examples, however, of inclusionary mandates required by the state's special area authorities -- Hackensack Meadowlands Commission, Office of Coastal Resources, and the Pinelands Commission. There is little substantive difference, however, between the provisions of the municipal versus special authority programs, as is indicated by the following overview.

Most of New Jersey's inclusionary mechanisms are mandatory; only Raritan Township and East Brunswick have voluntary approaches whereby developers do not have to provide a set share of affordable housing but are given special inducements if they do so. Almost universally, the New Jersey inclusionary programs are imposed in local PUD, multifamily, or similar zones. In other words, the inclusionary device is typically limited to relatively large-scale development occurring in relatively higher-density locations where there is a frequent bargaining process with the municipality. The programs also share the intent to expand housing opportunity for low- and moderate-income families, with these groups defined by HUD and NJHFA guidelines (e.g. 50 percent of area median income for low, and 80 percent of the area median for moderate income). There are exceptions, however. The Office of Coastal Resources uses an 80 percent of median income cut-off for low income, and a 95 percent threshold for moderate-income (the latter definition was utilized in the formerly available HUD Section 235 program). The Pinelands Commission approach is even more distinctive. In a strategy analogous to that utilized in Orange County, California, the Commission attempts to foster housing for three income groups: low (less than 80 percent of median), moderate (80-100 percent of median), and middle (100 to 120 percent of median).

The New Jersey inclusionary programs have the greatest variation with respect to the share of affordable housing to be provided. At the low end is Cherry Hill, with a 5 percent low- and moderate-income requirement; at the high end is Bridgewater Township, with a 40 percent mandatory share. More common is a 10-20 percent inclusionary ratio. In many cases there is a further stipulation of a certain share of low- versus moderate-housing production. In the Pinelands, there is a three-tier breakdown of separate low-, moderate-, and middle-income housing requirements which themselves

EXHIBIT 6A-1

NEW JERSEY INCLUSIONARY PROGRAMS

	INCLUSIONARY PROGRAM						
AREA	PLAN TYPE	APPLICATION	INCLUSIONARY PROVISION	LOW/MODERATE INCOME DEFINITION	AFFORDABILITY CONTROL	COMPLIANCE BONUS	PROGRESS-TO-DATE/ CHANGES
MUNICIPALITIES							
Bedminster Township (proposed)	Mandatory	PUD zone	20% for low/moderate-income families (this 20% must include specified percentages of senior citizen, rental, for-sale units, etc.)	50%-80% of median	To be proposed by developer	None	Proposed Plan
Bridgewater Township	Mandatory	In Township's multifamily zones	40% low/moderate (15% low, 25% moderate).	50%-80% of median	Yes, but not defined nor effected	15% density bonus over 8-unit per acre ceiling	No units built under provision. Township considering reduction to 25% low/moderate.
Cherry Hill	Mandatory	In specific township zones	5% "modest" priced housing (25% of these units must be 1-bedroom, 25% 2-bedroom, 25% 3-bedroom, & remainder mixed. Modest-priced housing must be "dispersed" and not have different facade treatment. For-sale units have specified minimum/maximum sizes and prices based on these sizes. Rental units are linked to Section 8 "Fair Market Rents."	Not to exceed SMSA median income adjusted by family size	Deed restriction. Sale price cannot exceed original price adjusted by CPI.	None	4 projects proposed or under construction.
East Brunswick Township	Optional	Planned Unit Residential Development and other zones	Optional inclusion of low/moderate income units	50%-80% of median	Deed restrictions. Town has first right of buy-back at set future price equal to original selling price as inflated by CPI plus improvements.	Up to 2 bonus units for every low/moderate income unit provided. A maximum density of from 8-20 units/acre permitted.	Three projects: (1) senior citizen (Section 236) (2) single family (Section 235) (3) single family
East Windsor Township	Mandatory	In Township's Planned Development District	15%-25% low and moderate	50%-80% of median	Not in ordinance, but "to be worked out with developer."	Development District's higher densities (e.g., up to 24 units per acre).	No units built under provision

EXHIBIT 6A-1

NEW JERSEY INCLUSIONARY PROGRAMS (continued)

AREA	INCLUSIONARY PROGRAM						
	PLAN TYPE	APPLICATION	INCLUSIONARY PROVISION	LOW-MODERATE INCOME DEFINITION	AFFORD-ABILITY CONTROL	COMPLIANCE BONUS	PROGRESS-TO-DATE/ CHANGES
MUNICIPALITIES							
Franklin Township (Somerset)	Mandatory	In PUD and R-40 zones	5% low income, 10% moderate	50%-80% of median	None yet, but would be provided when units built	None, except that inherent in zone's higher densities	No units built under provision; however, commitment from developer of Township's first PUD.
Mount Laurel	Mandatory	In all of the Township's land use zones (only projects approved before adoption of program are exempt)	10 percent for low- and another 10 percent for moderate-income	50%-80% of median	Yes, deed restriction limiting resale to original price as adjusted by CPI	5% density bonus to projects exempt from program (see Application)	Plan recently adopted in wake of <u>Mount Laurel</u> decision. Numerous applications currently being considered.
Raritan Township	Voluntary	Planned Residential Development zone	Density increase if low- and moderate-income housing provided	50%-80% of median	Not specified	10% increase in number of bedrooms from zone base of 8 per acre	No units built under provision. Some developer interest with internal developer subsidy.
South Brunswick Township	Mandatory	In Township's two PRD's	20% of PRD units for low- and moderate-income	None currently. Awaiting judicial interpretation.	Yes, in deed.	Only that inherent in PRD's higher densities (e.g., up to 7 units per acre).	2 projects (64 rental and 108 condo) have been constructed. 736 moderate-income apartments plus town center development (600 units) under consideration.
Princeton Plan (Proposal)	Plan Proposed in 1973	Floating PRD zones	14% low, 20% moderate	Defined by local income distribution	Yes, deed restrictions and public trust monitoring	Yes, density bonus	Plan never adopted

EXHIBIT 6A-1

NEW JERSEY INCLUSIONARY PROGRAMS (continued)

AREA	INCLUSIONARY PROGRAM						
	PLAN TYPE	APPLICATION	INCLUSIONARY PROVISION	LOW-MODERATE INCOME DEFINITION	AFFORD-ABILITY CONTROL	COMPLIANCE BONUS	PROGRESS-TO-DATE/ CHANGES
SPECIAL DISTRICTS							
Coastal Zone	Mandatory	Any project of 200 units or more. Threshold has since been lowered to 25 units.)	If housing subsidies available, 10% low and 10% moderate; if subsidies not available, low income waived, but 20% moderate.	80% and 95% of median	Deed restriction for 10 years	None	Inclusionary requirement applied to 20 projects since 1978; however, negotiations still continuing. Initial focus on Atlantic County now expanding to entire Coastal Zone.
Hackensack Meadowlands District	Mandatory	Within three Development Districts	10% low, moderate, or elderly	Not defined	None	None	No units built under provision
Pinelands	Mandatory	Communities within Pinelands have an obligation in revising their Master Plans to provide that 25% of their housing stock be available to low/moderate/middle-income families	For projects 100+ units: 10% low, 10% moderate, and 5% middle income; For projects 25-100 units: a total of 25% for all three categories	<u>Low</u>: less than 80% of median; <u>Moderate</u>: 80%-100% of median; <u>Middle</u>: 100% to 120% of median; families can spend 30% of income for housing	None	None	Communities in process of revising Master Plans. Some claim they already meet goal; <u>Mount Laurel II</u> decision has raised questions concerning Pinelands housing obligation.

Source:

Bedminster Township	: "An Ordinance to Amend and Supplement an Ordinance Entitled 'The Land Development Ordinance of Township of Bedminster'," 1983
Bridgewater Township	: John Madden, Township Planner
Cherry Hill Township	: Marty Keoughn, Community Developer Planner
East Brunswick Township	: Carl Hintz, Director, Housing & Community Development Department
East Windsor Township	: Michael Muller, Township Planner
Franklin Township (Somerset)	: Frank Colpini, Township Planner
Mount Laurel Township	: Louis Glass, Mount Laurel Planning Consultant
Raritan Township	: Douglas Kimball, Township Planner
South Brunswick Township	: David Engel, Township Planner
Princeton Township	: "The Princeton Housing Proposal - A Strategy to Achieve Balanced Housing Without Government Subsidy," May 1977
Coastal Zone	: Joe Weingarten, Office of the Coastal Zone
Hackensack Meadowlands	: Department of Residential Planning
Pinelands	: John Stolees, Pinelands Commission

further vary depending on project size (e.g. 25 to 99 units, 100 units or more, etc.) Finally, in all cases, except one, these ratios apply to new housing production. The exception is the Pinelands, where the ratio applies to the municipality's total housing stock. To illustrate, a community with a total of 1,000 existing units and a projected growth which will double its size has to plan for the provision of 500 affordable units -- one-quarter of the municipality's future 2,000 unit housing base. The implications of the Pinelands approach is that localities with a large share of affordable housing present already are practically exempt from the inclusionary requirement, while the opposite is true for jurisdictions with few existing lower cost units.

Unlike their counterparts in other areas of the country, New Jersey's inclusionary programs are less generous in providing special density or other bonuses to facilitate compliance. In most cases, the only concession offered is that which is inherent already in the higher density of the PUD or multifamily zone where the inclusionary mandate is set. There are exceptions, however. East Brunswick, Bridgewater, and Raritan Townships all offer varying levels of density bonuses (see Exhibit 6A-1).

Many of the New Jersey inclusionary programs nominally have some provision to guarantee that the units produced will remain affordable. To illustrate, in East Brunswick there is a deed restriction giving the Township the right of first refusal to purchase the inclusionary units when they are offered for sale at an amount equal to their original selling price (inflated by the Consumer Price Index), plus improvements. In many instances, however, this aspect of the program has not been specified because most of the inclusionary approaches have had insignificant throughput. The only production of any note is found in Cherry Hill, East Brunswick, and South Brunswick (see Exhibit 6A-1). In East Brunswick, for example, a total of roughly seventy affordable housing units were provided in three developments (see Exhibit 6A-1).

There are several reasons for the slow start of New Jersey's inclusionary program. Questions concerning the legality of the mechanisms, resolved only recently, stalled progress. The frequent absence of density or other bonuses was another problem. Very stringent inclusionary requirements, such as Bridgewater's 40 percent ratio, were still another deterrent. Problems incidental to the inclusionary requirement also arose. For instance in Franklin Township, controversy concerning the community's two PUD's -- the areas slated for the 25 percent inclusionary requirement -- has stalled any production in these developments, market as well as inclusionary, for almost a decade.

NOTES

1. See U.S. Federal Housing Administration, Underwriting Training Handbook (Washington, D.C.: U.S. Government Printing Office, series).

2. See Tom Morton, Texas Real Estate (Glenview, Illinois: Scott, Foresman & Co., 1982), p. 176.

3. Center for Urban Policy Research interviews with Section 8 developers in the New York Metropolitan area.

4. See Federal National Mortgage Association, Underwriting Guidelines Home Mortgages (Washington, D.C.: FNMA, 1979).

5. Morton, Texas Real Estate, p. 177.

6. Ibid., p. 178.

7. See, for example, Federal Home Loan Mortgage Corporation, Guidelines (Washington, D.C.: FHLMC, 1982). Telephone conversation by CUPR with Linda Talloway, underwriter, Northeast Regional Office, Federal Home Loan Mortgage Corporation. See also "Figuring the Mortgage Costs A Family's Income Can Carry." The New York Times, Sunday, October 23, 1983, Section 8, p. 1.

8. Center for Urban Policy Research interviews with major New Jersey Mortgage Bankers.

9. Center for Urban Policy Research computer analysis of 1980, New Jersey Public Use Sample.

10. Mount Laurel II Decision, p. 37.

11. See U.S. Department of Housing and Urban Development, Selecting and Financing a Home (Washington, D.C.: Government Printing Office, 1978) HUD Publication 267, H-8.

12. Fairfax County, Va. code ch. 30 (1961) as amended by Amendment 156 (1971), cited in Hastings Constitutional Law Journal, Vol. 3, No. 4, Fall 1976, p. 1053.

13. Arlington County, Va. Resolution on Developer Provision of Moderate-Income Housing (February 22, 1972).

14. Montgomery County Council Bill 372. Montgomery County, Md. Code 25A (1974).

15. Board of Supervisors v. DeGroff Enterprises, 214, Va 235, 198, S.E. 2d 600 (1973).

16. Fairfax County, Va. code ch. 30 (1961), as amended by Amendment 249 (1975).

17. Lakewood, Colorado Planning Commission Policy, No. 15 (1973).

18. Boulder, Colorado City Council Resolution 115 (1977).

19. California Government Code, Section 65302(c). Cited in Seymour I. Schwartz and Robert A. Johnston, "Inclusionary Housing Programs," Journal of the American Planning Association, Winter 1983, Vol. 49, No. 1, p. 20.

20. Assembly Bill 2853 (Roos, 1980), Chapter 1143 of the Statutes of 1980. Cited in Schwartz and Johnston, "Inclusionary Zoning," p. 20.

21. California Department of Housing and Community Development, Model Inclusionary Zoning Ordinance" (1978).

22. See Schwartz and Johnston, "Inclusionary Zoning."

23. Los Angeles, CA. Municipal Code §§12.03, 12.39, 13.04 as amended by Ordinance No. 145. 927 (1974).

24. See Barbara Taylor, "Inclusionary Zoning: A Workable Option for Affordable Housing?" Urban Land, Vol. 40, No. 3, March 1981, p. 3; Linda J. Bozung, "A Positive Response to Growth Control Plans: The Orange County Inclusionary Housing Program," Pepperdine Law Review, Vol. 9, No. 4 (1982), p. 824; Linda J. Bozung, "Inclusionary Housing Experience Under a Model Program," Zoning and Planning Law Report, Vol. 6, No. 1, January 1983; see also California Building Industry Association, Inclusionary Housing in Orange County: A Look at Preliminary Results (April 1981).

25. Schwartz and Johnston, "Inclusionary Housing Programs," p. 13.

26. This discussion is based on interviews with municipal officials and special area authorities in New Jersey having inclusionary programs; see Exhibit 6A-1.

CHAPTER 7 — AN INTRODUCTION TO THE FAIR SHARE CONCEPT

Originating in the early 1970s, fair share housing allocation is a relatively new concept. While its implementation has remained limited, important refinements in technique and method have occurred. With the recent reaffirmation of the landmark Mount Laurel decision, fair share allocation has become an issue of critical importance in New Jersey.

This chapter has three objectives: to examine the fair share methodology, to review its historical legacy, and to establish a framework for developing alternative fair share formulas. The chapter proceeds as follows. The first section defines fair share and fair share allocation. The second details its encompassing measures and variables. The third section presents an historical overview of the evolution of fair share plans in a national context. This is followed by a parallel New Jersey review. The analysis concludes with a point-by-point presentation of some of the possible fair share components.

FAIR SHARE: DEFINITION

Fair share has been defined in a number of related ways. In an early monograph on the subject, David Listokin of Rutgers University considers fair share as "a plan which typically determines where housing, especially low- and moderate-income units, should be built within a region according to such criteria as placing housing where it will expand housing opportunity, where it is most needed, and where it is most suitable."[1] Mary Brooks, formerly with the American Society of Planning Officials and more recently with Suburban Action Institute, explains fair share as a means for obtaining "dispersal policies for the future development of lower-income units."[2]

Leonard Rubinowitz, another student of housing choice, defines fair share as a strategy "to provide for distribution of lower-income housing within an entire metropolitan region in a way that it is equitable to recipient communities, while providing potential occupants with wide geographical choice, as well as access to the full range of community services and facilities."[3]

Implicit in fair share allocation is dissatisfaction with prevailing housing placement, namely the concentration of lower-cost units in the urban and older suburban core as opposed to being dispersed throughout the metropolitan area. Fair share attempts to enhance housing opportunity by formulating a plan or policy for distributing housing, typically the lower-cost or subsidized sector, throughout the region according to defined allocation factors.

Fair share plans address three basic considerations: defining housing regions, determining regional housing need, and allocating the unmet regional need to specific communities or subareas. The bulk of this report to this point has been concerned with the first two steps. Chapter 1 defined Mount Laurel regions, while Chapters 2 through 6 calculated Mount Laurel housing demand, the steady state housing supply, and the consequent unmet Mount Laurel housing shortfall. This chapter focuses on the third fair share component -- allocation. It examines alternative methods which might be used to allocate the unmet Mount Laurel housing need within the six respective Mount Laurel housing regions.

ALLOCATION METHODOLOGY

In devising fair share allocation strategies, three fundamental methodological steps are usually taken into account. These involve the initial determination of criteria by which to allocate housing, the transformation of these benchmarks into operational indicators, and the integration of a range of indicators into an actual allocation formula.

This fair share process can be explained as follows. Allocation criteria are the basic standards or principles by which housing is to be distributed. An example of this would be placing housing in areas of local advantage or need such as municipalities benefiting from rapid employment growth. Such locations typically have both the public service infrastructure to serve a new population as well as the added responsibility to provide housing for the new work force. Other criteria include placing housing where it is economically and/or physically suitable (e.g., where there are sufficient financial and land resources to accommodate growth). A final important objective is to foster dispersal -- to steer lower cost housing placement away from locations with prior concentrations of affordable and/or subsidized housing units.

Allocation indicators provide a way to operationalize these fundamental criteria. Essentially, they link policy guidelines to concrete strategies to implement the policy. In doing so, they specify variables and data that carry out the policy objectives and can be used as components of allocation formulas. For example, the distribution of housing in a region according to local advantage/need, economic/physical suitability, and to foster dispersal might refer to such data as local share of: regional employment growth, regional property wealth, regional land resources, and prior subsidized housing production. The types of indicators and variables that are chosen pose clearcut impacts for regional distribution. A plan emphasizing existing local share of low- and moderate-income households may bias the distribution toward older core areas which already possess high concentrations of disadvantaged populations. Fair share strategies which emphasize employment growth as a basic indicator result in a distributional bias toward those communities which have received jobs; those that emphasize property valuation per capita or land availability bias allocations towards wealthier, land-rich communities; those that factor prior subsidized housing production bias distribution away from older, core areas. Ultimately, allocation formulas themselves determine which indicators are used and how they are weighted and manipulated in the determination of actual distributional targets.

ALLOCATION CRITERIA AND INDICATORS

While there are many possible choices of allocation criteria and indicators, the extant fair share plans have many commonalities in their approach and operationalization. This characteristic is evident from Exhibits 7-1 and 7-2 which present the types of criteria and indicators utilized in the extant fair share strategies.

One simple allocation criteria is equal share -- distributing the burden of unmet regional housing need to sub-areas on a proportional basis. Some variants of this strategy set strict numerical quotas for meeting targets. Others locate priority areas for development. Still others establish minimum floors for low- and moderate-income production which developers must provide when constructing new housing. Equal share offers the advantage of simplicity of calculation. It also has the appeal of ensuring that all communities equally share the mandate of accepting/fostering lower-cost housing. Equal share has drawbacks, however. Communities differ in scores of ways -- size, employment base, environmental sensitivity, etc. -- that influence the need for and suitability of added growth. Equal share does not factor these considerations. Consequently, equal share is not a prominent fair share factor. If used, it typically is combined with more central considerations which allocate housing according to the measure of local: advantage/need, economic capacity, development potential, and subsidized housing production. These categories attempt to allocate housing to suitable areas where suitability is defined as locations benefiting from employment growth, are financially most capable of providing services to new housing development, and which have been remiss in meeting their affordable housing responsibility. Each of these categories is relatively independent although there is often some overlap (e.g., between local advantage/need and economic capacity). These major allocation criteria, summarized in Exhibits 7-1 and 7-2, are described in detail below.

EXHIBIT 7-1

TYPES OF MEASURES AND INDICATORS EMPLOYED IN FAIR SHARE FORMULAE

	ALLOCATION CRITERIA			
MEASURE OF LOCAL ADVANTAGE/NEED	MEASURE OF LOCAL ECONOMIC CAPACITY		MEASURE OF LOCAL DEVELOPMENT POTENTIAL	MEASURE OF LOCAL SUBSIDIZED HOUSING PRODUCTION
	Fiscal Capacity	Financial Capacity		
	ALLOCATION INDICATORS: LOCAL SHARE OF REGIONAL TOTALS AS INDICATED BELOW			
Employment-Related (Advantage)				
.Share of regional total employment	.Share of regional total equalized valuation	.Share of regional total personal income	.Share of regional vacant land	.Inverse of local share of existing regional subsidized units
.Share of change in regional total employment	.Share of regional per capita equalized valuation	.Share of regional percent of high-income households	.Share of regional vacant, developable land (taking account infrastructure, and environmental suitability)	.Inverse of change in local share of existing regional subsidized units
.Share of change in regional lower-income employment	.Share of regional school district equalized valuation per pupil			
.Share of regional non-residential ratables	.Inverse of local tax rate expressed as proportion of summed average ratios relative to region			
.Share of change in regional residential ratables				
Population-Related (Need)				
.Share of regional low-moderate income households				
.Share of change in regional minority households				

Source: Rutgers University, Center for Urban Policy Research, Fall 1983

EXHIBIT 7-2

TYPES OF MEASURES EMPLOYED IN FAIR SHARE ALLOCATION FORMULAE, NATIONALLY

	ALLOCATION CRITERIA				
AGENCY/LOCATION	LOCAL ADVANTAGE/NEED	LOCAL ECONOMIC CAPACITY Fiscal Capacity	Financial Capacity	LOCAL DEVELOPMENT POTENTIAL	LOCAL SUBSIDIZED HOUSING PRODUCTION
1. Dade County Planning Department, Florida	.proportion non-mod/low-income households .proportion non-black households .proportion non-Cuban households	---	---	.vacant developable land .infrastructure	---
2. Denver Regional Council of Governments, Colorado	.Change in employment (1960-1970)	.assessed valuation per capita	.households earning over $15,000 in income	.vacant developable land	---
3. Jacksonville Department of Housing and Urban Development, Jacksonville, Florida	.share low-income households .low-income jobs	---	---	.vacant developable land .land costs .access to retail, school, health, facilities .infrastructure	.existing subsidized housing
4. Metropolitan Washington Council of Governments, Washington, D.C. Original, <u>1972</u>	.low-mod. income households .commuting patterns .affordability .overcrowded and deficient housing	.total real property value + total personal income divided by total population	---	.vacant developable land .vacant units	---

continued

EXHIBIT 7-2 (Continued)

AGENCY/LOCATION	LOCAL ADVANTAGE/NEED	ALLOCATION CRITERIA LOCAL ECONOMIC CAPACITY Fiscal Capacity	Financial Capacity	LOCAL DEVELOPMENT POTENTIAL	LOCAL SUBSIDIZED HOUSING PRODUCTION
5. Metropolitan Washington Council of Governments Washington, D.C. Revised 1978	.low-mod. income households .change in low-income employment .share low-income employment .overcrowded and deficient housing	---	---	---	.existing subsidized housing .concentration of low-mod income housing
6. Miami Valley Regional Planning Commission, Dayton, Ohio Original 1970	.low-and mod-income households	.assesed valuation per pupil .pupils in excess of normal capacity	---		---
7. Miami Valley Regional Planning Commission, Dayton, Ohio Revised 1973	.low-mod. income households .rent-income ratio .overcrowded and deficient housing	.assessed valuation per pupil .pupils in excess of normal capacity	---	.vacant developable land	---
8. Miami Valley Regional Planning Commission, Dayton, Ohio Revised 1978					
9. Twin Cities Metropolitan Council, Minneapolis, St. Paul, Minnesota, 1973	.share of population .population change .share of employment .change in employment	---	---	---	---

continued

EXHIBIT 7-2 (Continued)

	ALLOCATION CRITERIA				
	LOCAL	LOCAL ECONOMIC CAPACITY		LOCAL	LOCAL SUBSIDIZED
AGENCY/LOCATION	ADVANTAGE/NEED	Fiscal Capacity	Financial Capacity	DEVELOPMENT POTENTIAL	HOUSING PRODUCTION
10. Twin Cities Metropolitan Council, Minneapolis, St. Paul Minnesota, 1976	.share of population .population change .share of employment .employment change	---	---	.access to jobs, transit, retail .level of urbanization	.existing subsidized housing
11. Pueblo Area Council of Governments, Pueblo, Colorado	.share of ethnic families	---	.households with incomes exceeding 3 x's the poverty level	.vacant developable land	.existing subsidized housing
12. Puget Sound Governmental Conference, 1974	.low/mod income households .change in employment (1970-80) .substandard housing affordability	.total assessed valuation .total revenue sharing funds	.households over $10,000 in income	.vacant developable land	---
13. Sacramento Regional Planning, San Bernardino, California	.low- and mod-income households	.school district assessed valuation per pupil	---	.vacant developable land	.existing subsidized housing
14. San Bernardino County Planning, San Bernardino, California	.low-mod. income households .change in jobs .substandard housing	.pupils in excess of normal capacity	---	.vacant developable land	.existing subsidized housing

Source: David Listokin, Fair Share Housing Allocation (New Brunswick, NJ: Center for Urban Policy Research, 1976); Miami Valley Regional Planning Commission, Housing in the Miami Valley Region: A Regional Program and Areawide Housing Opportunity Plan (Dayton, Ohio, 1976); Metropolitan Washington Council of Governments, Fair Share Housing Plan: Procedures for Allocation of Housing Assistance Funds (Washington, D.C.: 1983); Metropolitan Council, Estimated Housing Assistance Needs and Program Mix Goals for Metropolitan Area Communities (St. Paul, Minnesota, 1977).

Measure of Local Advantage/Need

As is evident from Exhibit 7-1, a common indicator of the local advantage/need criteria is job-related. Examples include the local share of total regional employment or the municipal share of the region's aggregate job growth. The Metropolitan Washington COG, Twin Cities, and the Denver COG fair share plans, amongst others, all incorporate some sensitivity to the job dynamic (See Exhibit 7-2). There are significant reasons for selecting an employment-based variable. In tax-dependent municipalities, non-residential ratables usually provide much more in the way of revenues than they impose in costs. As such, locations that attract jobs enhance their fiscal advantage. In addition, communities with a pronounced non-residential sector typically have both public services and a capital facilities infrastructure in place which can accommodate new residents. Moreover, the fact that jobs have been created adds to the responsibility that residences be built to house workers. Communities garnering significant shares of regional job growth thus have a commensurately significant obligation to satisfy regional housing need.

A subset of the local advantage/need category, often found in the older allocation strategies, is local share of the total regional low-income population and/or deficient housing stock (see Exhibit 7-2). This factor should be considered when the aggregate housing need to be allocated is first being determined. Housing/income deficiency was thus factored in Chapters 2 and 3 of the study, which defined the Mount Laurel housing need. Housing/income deficiency is much less appropriate as an allocation indicator, however, because its use would have the effect of concentrating low-cost housing in core areas rather than dispersing it. The very concept of dispersal has been questioned by big city mayors, however, as negatively impacting their communities.

Measure of Local Economic Capacity

A second set of indicators examines the economic capacity of municipalities to absorb the service demands generated by the development of new housing. If direct subsidy, tax abatement, or other fiscal assistance measures are associated with housing, new low-income households, or these households require more or specialized public services, a more affluent community will be better able to absorb such supportive expenses. Indicators of local economic capacity typically fall into two categories: fiscal and financial. The former measures the resources available to the public sector, usually the property value which can be taxed. Common indicators include valuation per capita or per student. Financial capacity indicates the ability of community residents to absorb the potential costs of new development. The measures employed here include total personal income, per capita income, median income, and percentage of households with incomes exceeding a specified cutoff. Fiscal and financial indicators are found in the Dayton Plan, Metropolitan Washington COG, Denver Region COG and other fair share plans (see Exhibit 7-2).

Measure of Local Development Potential

If measures of fiscal and financial capacity focus upon local economic ability to absorb new housing, indicators of development potential look at the amount of land that is available for new construction. These types of measures include the local share of the region's vacant land, as well as this land's ability to support development. The latter concerns any possible environmental or infrastructure restrictions. The Dade County, Dayton Plan, Metropolitan Washington COG, and numerous other fair share plans incorporate such development potential factors (See Exhibit 7-2).

Measure of Local Subsidized Housing Production

Finally, measures of prior subsidized housing production gauge past performance in this area. These indicators attempt to direct allocation away from areas of high concentrations of low- and moderate-income and/or subsidized housing. The rationale behind this criterion, applied in inverse proportion, is that (1) the poor should be dispersed rather than concentrated in any particular geographical location, and/or (2) locations which have existing relatively high levels of housing for the poor are already doing a part of or their full "fair share." The basic measures utilized here are existing low- and moderate-income housing and existing subsidized housing. This factor is found in the Metropolitan Washington COG, Twin Cities, and other fair share strategies (See Exhibit 7-2).

ALLOCATION FORMULAS

Allocation criteria and indicators comprise the basic fair share components. Allocation formulas combine and manipulate these components in order to yield concrete numerical allocation quotas. There are a number of ways that this can be accomplished. At the simplest level, individual indices are calculated for each variable on the basis of proportional shares and are averaged to create multipliers. To illustrate, the Pueblo, Colorado fair share plan applied a simple averaging approach. It divided its defined allocation region into four quadrants. One such subarea, for instance, contained 25 percent of the region's total population, 24 percent of its year-round dwelling units, 28.1 percent of its low- and moderate-income families, 13.6 percent of its current subsidized housing, 24.3 percent of its higher income families, and 30.4 percent of the region's total minority population. Adding these averages and dividing by six yielded a simple average of 24.23 percent. This area was therefore allocated 451 low- and moderate-income units: 24.23 percent of the total 1,860 units in the allocation pool.[4]

While some fair share formulas consider all factors equally, others establish differential weights for factors in light of their perceived relative importance. To illustrate, the Jacksonville, Florida fair share plan discussed assigning equal weights to all five of its allocation factors and then examined the operation of an alternative approach assigning one factor

-- avoidance of lower-income households -- as heavily as the first four factors combined.[5] The Monroe County (New York) fair share plan gave its employment allocation factor a heavier weight because, in its words, "it was considered a more important variable and it was a major objective to better locate housing with respect to job locations."[6]

A few fair share plans eschew a simple averaging approach and instead favor more sophisticated statistical techniques. In these cases, Z-scores (which reflect the standard deviation from the mean) are typically used to show the precise magnitude of dispersion between local and regional trends. Z-scores express the range of all indices to a common base. In this way, movement in a narrow scale cannot outweigh movement in a wide scale. A few fair share strategies have used a Z-score approach, the most prominent being the 1973 Dayton Plan.[7]

Further insight into fair share criteria, indicators, and formulas can be gleaned from the following national historical overview.

FAIR SHARE ALLOCATION NATIONALLY

This section overviews fair share as it has evolved since the early 1970s. It looks specifically at the types of allocation plans that were initially developed and the refinements that have been made in those strategies since their inception. Three plans are looked at in detail -- Dayton, Washington, D.C., and Minneapolis-St. Paul -- and a wide variety of other plans are summarized. In order to frame the details which follow, Exhibit 7-2 outlines the various fair share plans and their inclusive criteria and indicators. Taken together, Exhibit 7-2 and the following narrative provide the necessary background from which to consider fair share in New Jersey.

The Dayton Plan

The nation's first fair share plan, the Dayton Plan, was developed in Ohio by the Miami Valley Regional Planning Commission (MVRPC).[8] The plan specified guidelines for addressing the housing shortage faced by low- and moderate-income residents in and around Dayton, Ohio. It emphasized that efforts to meet this outstanding housing need should be shared by all municipalities comprising the Miami Valley Region and should not be limited to the central city.

The original allocation formula that was developed used five variables to distribute housing to municipalities within the region. The first three of these were indicators of local need. These included: proportionate share of future households, proportionate share or future low- and moderate-income households, and the inverse share of low- and moderate-income households currently housed. This formula also used two indicators of economic capacity for the suitability to absorb new housing. These included assessed school district valuation per pupil, and the inverse of pupils in excess of normal capacity. These five variables were weighted to emphasize the share of low- and moderate-income housing and pupils in excess of capacity, and indexed to comprise the basic allocation formula.

In 1973, the original plan and allocation strategy were updated. The new allocation formula added indicators of local need (based on municipal housing quality and affordability). It further added measures of development potential -- vacant developable land -- and past production -- the inverse of new subsidized units built. All told, the 1973 formula employed 11 variables as a basis for allocating housing.

In 1978, the Dayton Plan was revised once again. This time, however, the formula was drastically simplified. Indicators of economic capacity were dropped. Only very basic measures of local need and past production were retained.[9] The issue became -- "You do your share, regardless of fiscal or financial capacity. Only to the degree that you have already done something (subsidized units built) is your share lessened." A shift to indicator consolidation and greater clarity of focus characterizes the current thinking and application of fair share.

Metropolitan Washington Council of Governments

The Council of Governments (COG) for Washington, D.C., adopted its fair share plan in 1972. The Washington Plan was somewhat more sophisticated than the original Dayton Plan.[10] It employed as an indicator of local need, share of low-income households. It also used commuting patterns, and housing affordability to determine where housing should be built. It used a compound measure of economic capacity: the sum of total real property value, and total personal income per capita. Development potential was expressed in terms of vacant developable land and vacant housing units.

The Washington plan was also revised in the late 1970s. The formula was altered to reflect low- and moderate-income employment patterns as affecting local advantage/need. The indicator of economic capacity was dropped because it was evident that all municipalities had the ability to absorb some new housing. A measure of past production was added -- one that included both the prevalence of existing low- and moderate-income housing as well as the presence of subsidized units.[11]

Twin Cities Metropolitan Council

The Twin Cities Metropolitan Council, a regional entity overseeing housing development in the Minneapolis-St. Paul area, made initial strides toward a fair share approach in 1971. In the comprehensive development plan for that year, it linked the distribution of discretionary federal and state funding to the local provision of affordable low- and moderate-income housing. By 1973, a formal fair share allocation strategy had been developed. The 1973 allocation formula emphasized local advantage/need (e.g., local share of population and employment growth) as the primary means to distribute housing. The fair share plan specified exact housing goals that municipalities would have to meet and established a formal mechanism for monitoring progress toward fair share objectives.[12]

In 1976, the original plan was refined. Major changes were made in the allocation formula. The basic distributional criteria -- local advantage/need -- was retained. Areas were also ranked, however, in terms of five additional factors pertaining to degree of development potential/suitability. These included: (1) level of urbanization, (2) proximity to metropolitan centers, and availability of: (3) transit service, (4) jobs, and, (5) shopping centers. The allocation formula combined this composite index with basic trends in employment and population to determine municipal allocations.[13] It specified numerical targets for all communities within the Twin Cities region.

Other Fair Share Plans

A wide variety of other governmental bodies and agencies have adopted or at least considered fair share plans.[14] While all of these are similar in scope and coverage to the three outlined above, a summary evaluation of their basic components is useful. Most of fair share strategies factor local advantage/need, economic capacity, development potential, and past production. Exhibit 7-2 outlines their specific encompassing criteria and indicators.

In Dade County, Florida, for example, housing allocation is determined by inverse need. Allocation is based on the municipal share of non-low- and moderate-income households, non-black households, and non-Cuban households. Each municipality's housing obligation is thus based on the concentration of relatively advantaged groups. This plan also uses vacant land as a measure of development potential.

The Denver Regional Council of Government emphasizes local advantage/need, namely change in employment, to distribute allocation targets. It also employs a measure of local economic capacity -- households earning over $15,000 and assessed valuation per capita. Its formula further includes vacant land as an indicator of local development potential.

The Jacksonville, Florida fair share approach similarly emphasizes local advantage/need (e.g., local share of lower income jobs) as its basic allocation criteria. It adds vacant land as a measure of local development potential, and existing subsidized housing as an indicator of past performance.

The Pueblo Area (Colorado) Council of Governments utilizes share of households with income three times the poverty level as its measure of local advantage. It also includes vacant developable land and the inverse of existing subsidized housing to reflect development potential and past production respectively. Similarly, the Puget Sound Governmental Conference employs measures of local advantage, economic capacity, and development potential. Local advantage is taken into account using change in employment. Economic capacity is evaluated via four indicators -- total assessed valuation, per capita assessed valuation, total revenue sharing funds, and households earning over $10,000 annually. Vacant land is incorporated to provide a measure of development potential.

Finally, the Sacramento Area Planning Council, and the San Bernardino County Planning Board have developed very similar fair share formulas. Both use the concentration of low- and moderate-income households as the basic indicator of need. Economic capacity is measured in terms of school district valuation. Both employ vacant land as an indicator of local development potential. Finally, both use existing subsidized housing as a measure of prior affordable housing production.

Summary

The ten programs discussed above are the major fair share housing plans that have been developed nationally since the mid-1970s. Their common characteristics are evident. Almost all of the formulas contain criteria of local advantage or need. These include the indicators of employment growth, and impacted population/housing distributions. Most of the fair share plans factor local economic capacity -- usually in the form of fiscal vigor, (e.g., assessed valuation) though financial strength (e.g., total personal income or incomes in excess of a specified cutoff) is sometimes referred to. Many incorporate local development potential, usually vacant land. Some include indicators of past housing production, typically existing subsidized units. These basic indicators are combined to create composite averages or scores which are then used to determine actual housing obligations.

THE NEW JERSEY EXPERIENCE

With the national picture presented, it is now opportune to concentrate on the New Jersey experience. Since the early 1970s, fair share housing has been an issue in New Jersey. Efforts have been made by the courts, the legislature, and various governors to require suburban municipalities to provide increased housing opportunities for low- and moderate-income families. In the courts, the Mount Laurel decisions have confronted the issue of exclusionary zoning. The State Legislature has reviewed a series of fair share housing bills. The executive branch has, in times past, expressed its own guidelines for fair share housing allocation and has tied state funding to compliance with these objectives.

Early Progress

The impetus for fair share housing in New Jersey dates back at least to 1970.[15] Then Governor William Cahill led the zoning reform effort, stressing that change was long-overdue in New Jersey, and that in the absence of legislative action, the courts were certain to step in. In a special message to the New Jersey legislature in 1970, Governor Cahill discussed the growing number of lawsuits against exclusionary zoning and warned that New Jersey could not "afford the luxury of continuing the status quo." The emphasis of Cahill's address was to alert both the public and the legislature to the need for zoning changes. Two years later, in his second housing message, Governor Cahill again reviewed the need for land use reform and introduced a balanced housing plan which would include "low, moderate, and expensive, single and multi-family" housing.

In November 1972, Assemblyman Albert Merck introduced a bill establishing a voluntary fair share plan. This bill, which never became law, laid responsibility with the Department of Community Affairs (DCA) to establish a statewide goal for low- and moderate-income housing. DCA would allocate some share of the total figure to each county. The counties, in turn, would allocate housing objectives to each municipality. Specifically, this bill called for DCA to conduct a biennial survey of the state's unmet low- and moderate-income housing needs. This determination would be based upon a variety of factors, including employment and population trends, existing concentrations of low- and moderate-income jobs, area wage levels, projected housing trends and costs, available mortgage financing, and the infrastructure needs required for housing development.[16]

This legislation also provided allocation guidelines for the county planning boards that were responsible for distributing the total housing goal to municipalities. Allocation would be based on a variety of fair share criteria. These included basic indicators of local advantage/need, such as municipal share of low- and moderate-income households, proximity to low- and moderate-income employment, and substandard housing. Local economic capacity was measured in terms of the relative tax burden faced by each community. Development potential was evaluated by the vacant land suitable for construction of low- and moderate-income housing and the available infrastructure for such development.

In 1975, State Senator Martin Greenberg introduced Bill S-3100 in the State Senate.[17] This comprehensive proposal called upon DCA to formulate fifteen-year overall housing goals for each county and to break those down into concrete five-year targets. The allocation of the total county housing goals was left to the county planning boards, but was to be determined in light of specific allocation criteria. These included the following:

1. Local Advantage/Need

   (a) Employment opportunity - The location of major employment centers, particularly in areas where an imbalance or net deficit exists between existing and prospective employment opportunities and the availability of sufficient and adequate dwelling units to satisfy housing need.

(b) Housing condition - The nature, quality and distribution of the existing housing supply and the need to broaden housing opportunity for all segments of the population.

2. Economic Capacity/Other Suitability Measures

(c) Fiscal capacity - The relative fiscal capacity of each county or municipality to absorb new housing development.

(d) Accessibility - The proximity of prospective housing sites to public transportation, and other services.

3. Development Potential

(e) Development potential - The availability of vacant and readily developable land and the capacity of existing or planned infrastructure to absorb new development.

On the basis of the state housing survey and the Commissioner's specific allocation guidelines, the county planning boards would set allocation targets for each municipality. DCA would continue oversight of each allocation system and allocation objectives. Failure to comply with DCA's guidelines could lead the agency to impose the changes necessary to ensure compliance. This bill has been revised several times since then, surfacing most recently as Senate Bill No. 5057.

Mount Laurel and the State Housing Allocation Report

In March 1975, the New Jersey Supreme Court handed down its landmark decision in the first Mount Laurel case. This decision focused widespread public attention on the issues of exclusionary zoning and fair share. The Court emphasized the responsibility of municipalities to provide reasonable opportunities in their land-use regulations to accommodate a mix of housing. Not only were communities directed to provide for low- and moderate-income families residing within their own boundaries, but they had to meet their fair share of the regional need as well.

In the wake of the first Mount Laurel decision, in April 1976, then-Governor Brendon Byrne issued Executive Order No. 35 directing the Division of State and Regional Planning to prepare statewide housing goals, especially for the construction of low- and moderate-income housing.[18] Specific municipal allocations were to be established along with criteria for determining which communities were meeting their goals. The order also mandated that discretionary state intergovernmental aid would be prioritized on the basis of successful local satisfaction of fair share goals. Thus, municipalities which failed to meet fair share requirements would be financially penalized.

By late 1976, the Division submitted a preliminary report to the Governor's office entitled "A Statewide Housing Plan for New Jersey." It did three things. First, it established a statewide housing goal based on present and projected need for low- and moderate-income housing. Second, it delineated basic allocation regions. Third, and most importantly, it formulated a fair share allocation formula aimed at distributing the overall statewide housing goal to municipalities in the various regions. The specific formula projected municipal allocations on the basis of local advantage/need (e.g., employment) and local economic capacity. However, the Governor returned this report and issued another Executive Order -- No. 36 -- which directed the Division to consider the issues of central city redevelopment and statewide planning within its overall report. The Governor also extended the completion date for the report to December 1977 under Executive Order No. 46.

The new report was completed in September 1977 and issued as the "Statewide Housing Allocation Plan for New Jersey" in May, 1978.[19] The revised plan retained much of the earlier report: its basic projections, regional delineation, and allocation formula. It did make several modifications, though. It emphasized the distinction between indigenous (housing-deficient) need and prospective (employment/population-related) need. It recognized the realities of limited acreage to house needy families in some locations and thus redistributed allocation from municipalities with insufficient land to other land-rich municipalities in the same region. Revisions also included a procedure for deferring allocations in locations where growth was being discouraged by state policy to protect farmlands and open space. Many of these same types of determinations were incorporated into the growth designations of the State Development Guideplan.

The allocation formula established by this report was a simple one. It distinguished between the allocation of present (1970) housing need and the distribution of prospective (1970-1990) housing need. Present need was distributed on an equal proportional basis. This meant that municipalities were required to provide an equivalent share of total present need. In other words, if the unmet housing need for the region comprised 10 percent of the total housing stock, each municipality received an allocation target equivalent to 10 percent of its housing stock.

The formula utilized to distribute prospective housing need was similar to the allocation formula employed in the original plan. It included three criteria and four encompassing indicators to determine the local share of overall prospective need. These are outlined in Exhibit 7-3 and include the following:

1. Local Advantage/Need

    (a) Employment - This factor is a measure of the relative responsibilities of municipalities to provide housing in relation to where new jobs were being located. The indicator was increase in covered employment (1969-1975).

EXHIBIT 7-3

FAIR SHARE ALLOCATION APPROACHES IN NEW JERSEY: SELECTED EXAMPLES

AGENCY LOCATION/ DATE	ALLOCATION CRITERIA				
	LOCAL ADVANTAGE/ NEED	ECONOMIC CAPACITY: FISCAL CAPACITY	ECONOMIC CAPACITY: FINANCIAL CAPACITY	DEVELOPMENT POTENTIAL	LOCAL SUBSIDIZED HOUSING PRODUCTION
	ALLOCATION INDICATORS				
N.J. Division of State and Regional Planning, 1978	.change in employment (1969-1975)	.change in non-residential ratables (1968-1974)	.personal income (families + unrelated individuals)	.vacant developable land	---
Mahwah Township, 1983	.change in employment (1972-1981)	.share of commercial and industrial ratables	---	.vacant developable land	---
Burlington, Camden, Gloucester Counties, 1983	.total employment 1983 .change in employment (1972-1981)	---	---	.vacant developable land	---
Morris Township, 1983	---	---	---	.local share of regional growth area as defined by the State Development Guide Plan	---

Source: 1. New Jersey Division of State and Regional Planning, A Revised Statewide Housing Allocation Report for New Jersey, May 1978.

2. Clarke and Caton, Inc. Mahwah Township: Fair Share Housing Report (Consultant Report prepared for Honorable Harvey Smith, Superior Court of New Jersey), July 1983.

3. Alan Mallach, Fair Share Housing Allocation Study for the Tricounty Region, August 1983.

4. Harvey S. Moskowitz, Housing Allocation Analysis for Morris Township, October 11, 1983.

2. Economic Capacity

(b) Local fiscal capacity - This was employed to measure municipal capability to accommodate growth. The basic indicator was growth in non-residential ratables (1968-1974).

(c) Local financial capacity - This was also used as a measure of local capability to absorb low- and moderate-income housing. The indicator was a local/regional comparison of 1970 per-capita income.

3. Local Development Potential

(d) Developable land - This was included as a measure of municipal capability to assume additional housing construction. The basic indicator utilized here was local/regional share of vacant developable land.

The construction of the formula from these basic indicators was quite straightforward. On the basis of local/regional comparisons, municipal quotas were developed for each measure. The results from the four separate indices were then averaged to obtain a single prospective allocation index, which in turn was used to determine the prospective allocation target. Finally, present and prospective need were summed to arrive at the total allocation.

Mount Laurel II -- Recent Fair-Share Strategies

The Mount Laurel II[20] decision of January 20, 1983 provided important new directions for fair share allocation in New Jersey.[21] It reaffirmed and extended the fair share mandate handed down in Mount Laurel I.[22]

> The existence of a municipal obligation to provide a realistic opportunity for a fair share of the region's present and prospective low and moderate income housing will no longer be determined by whether or not a municipality is "developing." The obligation extends, instead, to every municipality, every portion of which is designated by the state, through the SDGP as a "growth area." (emphasis added)

In the wake of Mount Laurel II, a few fair-share plans have been completed for various regions and municipalities. Selected examples are presented here for illustration purposes. The consulting firm of Clarke and Caton prepared a fair share plan for Mahwah, New Jersey.[23] Alan Mallach completed a fair share report for the Southern Tri-County region which includes Camden, Gloucester, and Burlington counties.[24] Harvey Moskowitz prepared a housing allocation analysis for Morris Township and other communities.[25] These fair share plans and the allocation formulas that they employed have been developed in light of the specific guidelines set down in Mount Laurel II. The basic indicators utilized are outlined in Exhibit 7-3.

The fair share plan for Mahwah is quite straightforward. An eight county greater Mahwah housing region was determined first. Regional housing need was then projected. This consisted of both present need (based on physical housing deficiencies and other characteristics) and prospective need (based on projected future regional population and households).

This analysis set the stage for allocating the regional housing need. According to the Clarke and Caton plan, allocation encompassed three variables: change in employment, municipal fiscal capacity, and vacant land. Employment growth between 1972 and 1981 was measured as local share of total regional employment growth. Municipal fiscal capacity was operationalized as the local share of total regional commercial and industrial ratables. Development potential was measured as the local share of total vacant developable land in the region. The three individual ratios were averaged to create a composite municipal allocation ratio. This measure was then used to derive the local allocation of present and prospective housing need from regional totals. Both present and prospective housing need were allocated using the same compound ratio.

The Mahwah Plan encompassed three commonly utilized allocation criteria. By referencing gain in employment, local advantage/need was incorporated. Economic capacity was factored by the ratable data. Finally, development potential was indicated by the degree of vacant land. The expression of each variable as a local percentage of the regional sum, and the averaging of the three percentages, were also approaches common to the national and New Jersey fair share state-of-the-art.

The fair share allocation methodology prepared by Alan Mallach for Camden, Burlington, and Gloucester counties also reflects extant practice. It separated the derivation of present housing need from that of prospective need. Present housing need was shown for all municipalities on the basis of two components of 1980 Census data on deficient housing (e.g., units lacking plumbing and overcrowding). This present need was then adjusted so that responsibility for meeting it would be spread throughout the region by the proportion of existing housing units. For example, a municipality with a large indigenous need was required to address only part of it to the degree that housing deficiency represented the regional average. The remainder of indigenous need was transferred to other communities in the region which had less than the regional average. Consequently, no municipality would be excessively burdened by historic levels of deficient housing.*

---

*See discussion later in this chapter.

Once present need was calculated, the Mallach plan then addressed prospective housing need. This was done on the basis of a simple allocation formula which utilized three variables: total employment, employment growth and vacant developable land. These three indices were expressed as the local share of total regional employment, employment growth, and vacant land respectively. All three factors were weighted equally and simply averaged. The resulting multiplier was used to determine the local shares of total regional prospective housing need.

The Mallach plan emphasized local advantage/need as indicated by local employment vigor. It added an overlay of sensitivity to development potential, namely vacant developable land. This selection of allocation criteria reflects common, albeit a reduced list, of fair share factors. The Mallach plan's expression of each variable as the local share of the respective regional totals, and the simple averaging of these percentages, also represents common fair share practice, both nationally and in New Jersey.

The Harvey Moskowitz fair share plan for Morris Township focused on defining the housing region, projecting the region's housing need and then allocating the aggregate need to the region's municipalities. The region was defined as those municipalities within a 30-minute "commutershed" of Morris Township; regional housing need was determined by projecting the number of new jobs expected in the region by 1990 and converting those jobs into housing demand; and local allocation was accomplished by calculating Morris Township's proportional share of the region's growth area as shown by the State Development Guide Plan. Since Morris Township had 1.7 percent of the total regional growth area, it was allocated 1.7 percent of the region's total housing need.

The Moskowitz allocation is based on the State Development Guide Plan (SDGP).[26] The latter, in turn, emphasizes local development potential primarily as influenced by the siting of the built infrastructure and environmental sensitivity. In choosing development potential as an allocation criteria, Moskowitz conforms to national and state practice. What is unusual however is that other allocation factors are not added. This is perhaps due to the importance of the SDGP imbued by the Mount Laurel decision. Much more reflective of the state-of-the-art is Moskowitz's methodology in that the local profile is compared to that of the region, that this relationship is expressed as a percentage, and that the percentage defines the local fair share.

In sum, the Clarke and Caton, Mallach, and Moskowitz plans are examples of the allocation formulas currently being devised in the wake of the Mount Laurel decision. Building from our national and New Jersey state-of-the-art analysis, the following and final section presents a procedural framework for examining alternative fair share approaches.

PROCEDURAL FRAMEWORK FOR FAIR SHARE HOUSING ALLOCATION

Fair share is a key Mount Laurel consideration. It was recognized by the State Supreme Court as a challenging issue:[27]

> The most troublesome issue in Mount Laurel litigation is the determination of fair share. It takes the most time, produces the greatest variety of opinions, and engenders doubt as to the meaning and wisdom of Mount Laurel. Determination of fair share has required resolution of three separate issues: identifying the relevant region, determining its present and prospective housing needs, and allocating those needs to the municipality or municipalities involved (emphasis added).

This report can provide guidance on the three fair share considerations of region, housing need and allocation.

Region and Housing Need

Chapter 1 of the study defined six housing regions for the state of New Jersey. These regions were determined on the basis of journey- to-work and other common areal characteristics. The six Mount Laurel regions are in conformance with the most current research in this area, namely the metropolitan aggregations delineated by the U.S. Bureau of the Census and Office of Management and Budget. The six Mount Laurel areas also somewhat parallel the state's service regions for transportation, water supply, solid waste, and other services.

Chapters 2 through 5 of this study can help define the second fair share issue of housing need. Following the Court's declination in the Mount Laurel decision, housing need was disaggregated into present and then prospective components. Present need consists of the unanswered housing demand of extant households with Mount Laurel-defined incomes living in deficient housing. Prospective housing need is the unanswered demand of future households with Mount Laurel-defined earnings.

Both the Mount Laurel decision and many fair share plans differentiate the responsibility of addressing present versus prospective need. The former, encompassing the local factor of housing deficiency, is therefore primarily a local responsibility. The only exception to this would be a community so burdened with a substandard housing stock that it would be very taxing for it to provide a full replacement. Such a situation is characteristic of many central cities with older, marginal housing. This sentiment of local responsibility to meet present need with the exception of the overburdened municipality is expressed by the Mount Laurel decision:[28]

> Every municipality's land use regulations should provide a realistic opportunity for decent housing for at least some part of its resident poor who now occupy dilapidated housing...In other words, each municipality must provide a realistic opportunity for decent housing for its indigenous poor except where they represent a disproportionately large segment of the population as compared with the rest of the region. This is the case in many of our urban areas. (emphasis added)

In short, present housing need is primarily a local responsibility with the exception of the overly burdened community which can realistically meet only a portion of this housing component. Who then must accommodate the latter's shortfall? The fair share plans offer some guidance. For instance, the 1978 "A Revised Statewide Allocation Report for New Jersey" used a sharing approach as follows:[29]

> The existing housing need in each region was allocated to component municipalities based on an equal proportion method. This method utilizes the ratio of 1970 housing needs (based on housing deficiency) to the total housing stock in the particular region. This method is shown in the following illustrative example:

Municipality	1970 Housing Needs (Based on Housing Deficiency)	1970 Housing Stock	Allocation of 1970 Housing Need	Difference
		Housing Units		
A	10	200	20	+10
B	20	50	5	-15
C	40	150	15	-25
D	50	800	80	+30
Region Total	120	1,200	120	0

> This region's total of 120 units of needed housing (based on housing deficiency) is 10 percent of the regional housing stock of 1,200 units. As such, each municipality receives an allocation equal to 10 percent of its housing stock. The "difference" column shows whether a municipality receives more or less than the 1970 housing need originating within its own municipality. (notes added)

The Alan Mallach fair share plan for Burlington, Camden, and Gloucester counties used a roughly similar approach for distributing existing need to the tri-county area:[30]

> A calculation has determined that, in the region as a whole, present lower-income housing need represents 3.3 percent of the total housing stock in the region. The adjustment, therefore, is that the indigenous present housing need that any municipality must take responsibility for shall not exceed 3.3 percent of its housing stock...This adjustment resulted in a total of 2,766 units being removed from indigenous need totals, to be reallocated. A second allocation percentage was calculated, which represented the same percentage, but adjusted to reflect the smaller number of municipalities in the pool, and that amount allocated among the remaining municipalities in the pool. The

municipalities in the pool were those who (a) had an indigenous housing need of less than 3.3 percent of their housing stock; and (b) were not affected by the (State Development Guide Plan) development limit. (note added)

In contrast to present housing need where the responsibility is primarily on those communities with the existing housing deficiencies (albeit some adjustment is made for extreme, e.g. central city cases), prospective housing need is a regional responsibility. Fractional shares of the regional tally are then allocated to individual communities slated to receive growth. As initially defined by the Mount Laurel II decision, these are primarily municipalities in the "growth" areas as opposed to those in "limited development" or "conservation" areas as defined by the State Development Guide Plan. These growth-suitable municipalities are assigned a housing responsibility according to their "fair share."

Housing Allocation

Allocation stands at the heart of fair share. In the Mount Laurel decision, the State Supreme Court recognized allocation's importance.[31]

> In short we foresee that within several years the fair share question will be confined to the allocation issue. Our use of the SDGP should end practically all disputes over the existence of the Mount Laurel obligation and, in relatively short time, adjudication by the three judges should end most disputes over region and regional need. In practically all cases the only issue (other than the adequacy of the housing opportunity provided by the ordinance) that may require serious litigation is a particular municipality's fair share of that need. (emphasis added)

What is a municipality's fair share? It is important to recognize that there is no definitive single allocation methodology -- fair share is a planning technique characterized by a range of approaches. While recognizing this characteristic, the national and state allocation state-of-the-art presented in this chapter can guide the fair share distribution. Fair share plans typically allocate on the basis of the following four criteria: (1) local advantage/need, (2) economic capacity, (3) development potential, and (4) past production. The following discussion links these allocation criteria to possible statistical indicators and variables. It locates those variables which are promising candidates to reflect the spirit of the various criteria -- ones for which consistent and reliable data are available. After enumerating the basic indicators and data, the construction of alternative formulas is briefly considered.

Local Advantage/Need

There are numerous possible indicators of advantage/need ranging from local share of regional population or local share of low- and moderate-income households to differentials in employment trends. Here, employment-based factors are clearly preferred. The Mount Laurel decision is explicit in its insistence that allocation be based on local advantage/need based on employment indicators as opposed to population or household income/housing quality deficiency.[32]

> Formulas that accord substantial weight to employment opportunities in the municipality, especially new employment accompanied by substantial ratables, shall be favored; formulas that have the effect of tying prospective lower-income housing needs to the present proportion of lower-income residents to the total population of a municipality shall be disfavored; formulas that have the effect of unreasonably diminishing the share because of a municipality's successful exclusion of lower-income housing in the past shall be disfavored. (emphasis added)

In utilizing a jobs-based indicator of local advantage/need, it is preferable to factor the dynamic gain in employment rather than the static total employment figure. The former pinpoints areas of current or shortly ensuing need for and responsibility to provide new housing for the entering workforce -- a key consideration in determining where housing is to be allocated. In contrast, total employment data largely reflects the aggregate historical record rather than current employment patterns and may misdirect housing production to areas of low current need. For example, despite recent losses, central cities still typically contain a large share of total regional jobs. If total employment is used as a fair share indicator, then central cities would receive a large housing allocation -- an outcome flying in the face of the housing dispersal goal prompting the fair share process.

The local job gain may be expressed in terms of the comparison of local-to-regional trends over a specified time period, say five to ten years.* Consequently, if employment growth in a given municipality comprised 10 percent of total regional job expansion, that community would receive a 10 percent allocation of the regional housing obligation. Conversely, if a municipality did not experience growth or experienced a loss of employment, it would receive a zero share of the regional burden.

---

*Employment data are readily available in the form of covered employment -- jobs subject to the New Jersey Employment Compensation Law. Covered employment for each municipality can be obtained from the State of New Jersey, Department of Labor and Industry, Division of Planning and Research.

Economic Capacity*

Economic capacity can be measured in both fiscal and financial terms. The former indicates the municipality's capability to absorb new development. In other words, can the community provide the infrastructure and service that become necessary when growth occurs? Expansion and/or the value of non-residential ratables (commercial and industrial only) has often been utilized as the primary indicator of fiscal capacity. However, there are a number of problems with this strategy. Non-residential ratables may reflect only a very small part of local fiscal capability. For instance, there are numerous cases of municipalities that possess little industry, but derive considerable revenue from highly valued, residential sources. Further, the value and/or growth of non-residential ratables is less a measure of fiscal capacity and more an indicator of employment vigor -- a criteria encompassed already under local advantage/need.

A preferred measure of fiscal advantage is share of total regional property valuation.** This should be expressed on a per capita/equalized basis.*** The per capita form should be included, as opposed to total valuation, because the former, unlike the latter, indicates the draw or demand on the property tax base for public purposes. Property wealth should be indicated on an equalized or full value basis because this standardizes for variation in local assessment practices. A dollar of equalized property value is the same for all communities; the same can not be said for its assessed counterpart.

Another consideration is the expression of the per capita equalized valuation data. It is not advisable to utilize the growth in per capita equalized value as opposed to the total per capita equalized figure because in measuring fiscal capacity we are interested in determining the municipality's ability to support public services. Growth in the per capita ratable base does not give this indication. While it does show which communities have been gaining most in ratables, this is more an indicator of local advantage -- a criteria encompassed already by the local gain in job growth. In contrast, the total per capita equalized value, the form sug-

---

*As with the case of the Metropolitan Washington COG, attention should be paid to the need for this variable (e.g. what is the fiscal impact of the low- and moderate-income units, how affluent are the communities within the allocation region, etc.).

**Equalized property value for each municipality is available on an annual basis in the Abstract of Ratables published by each county. For a statewide compilation of property value, see the following annual publication - State of New Jersey, Department of the Treasury, Division of Taxation, Annual Report.

***In addition, or as an alternative the equalized valuation per pupil can be utilized. This measure, available from the State Department of Education, indicates the level of property resources backing each student.

gested here, does convey the measure we are searching for -- the community's resources to accommodate new housing.

The equalized per capita real property valuation can be calculated for each municipality in the region and expressed as a ratio of the regional average. The ratios are summed and a local share is taken of the sum of the region. This provides a reasonable gauge of the potential fiscal resources of a community by indicating the revenue-raising potential backing each resident as compared to that backing other residents in the region.

Municipal economic vigor may also be measured in terms of local financial capacity. This index is usually complementary to the fiscal gauge. Financial capacity evaluates the ability of a municipality's resident population to absorb the costs of new development. Simply put, can residents withstand the property-tax hikes that are likely to be an offshoot of principally subsidized new construction? This subsidy may be in the form of tax forgiveness, extra public services and the like, unique to the specially housed population.

There is a choice among possible financial indicators, the primary ones being per capita income and household income. These differ in meaning. Household income -- which specifies the aggregate income of all family and non-family members of a household -- does not provide an indication of the members being supported by the given earnings. As such it minimizes the differences between large and small families drawing from the same income. Per capita income, on the other hand, provides a broader gauge of municipal resident wealth as it specifies the dollars backing <u>each</u> resident in terms of earnings.* The measure of affluence of the indicated local per capita income is given meaning by comparing it to the regional average. As with the per capita property valuation figure, per capita income is specified for each municipality expressed as a ratio of the regional average, and the ratios then summed. Each local ratio is then taken as a share of the regional tally.

Development Potential

This is a measure of land available for the construction of low- and moderate-income housing -- essentially total developable acreage. In 1978, the Division of State and Regional Planning in the Department of Community Affairs (DCA) defined such land as any vacant acreage except: (1) that with a slope greater than 12 percent; (2) under farmland assessment; or (3)

---

*Information on per capita income is available from <u>Income and Poverty in New Jersey; 1980 Census of Population and Housing</u>, State Data Center, Office of Demographic and Economic Analysis, Division of Planning and Research, Department of Labor and Industry, State of New Jersey, October, 1982. The data contained in this report, based on the 1980 Census, can be updated using CPI or other inflationary indices.

protected by critical area designation (wetland, flood plain, etc.). With the assistance of the Department of Environmental Protection, vacant developable land was calculated for each community in the state. While dated and in need of refinement (e.g. especially concerning the slope threshold and the exclusion of all land under farmland assessment), these data are still the first pass best source of information on developable land in each New Jersey municipality.* As with the other indicators, the developable land measure can be expressed relative to the regional sum -- the local share of total regional developable land.

It is important to realize that the developable land information is more than just one allocation criteria but is a fundamental threshold concern. That is after a fair share allocation is projected, it is important to examine whether the allocated units can in fact be built given each community's developable acreage. If not, then the shortfall must be absorbed by sister, more land-rich communities, within the allocation pool.

Past Production

There are a variety of measures encompassing this criteria -- a factor which attempts to channel allocation away from current concentrations of low- and moderate-income households or give credit to those locations that have already built or are building subsidized housing. Basic indicators used here can include: local share of existing regional subsidized units, or local share of newly constructed (say over the past ten years) subsidized housing units. These figures are more meaningful if expressed in a form that indicates the level of penetration or significance of past production (e.g., subsidized units per 100 units of the existing stock) as opposed to simply total past production. In addition, these ratios are usually expressed in their inverse form such that those locations with a high level of subsidized housing participation are allocated fewer new units.** As with the other measures, the local value, here the inverse of past production, can be expressed relative to the regional sum of these values.

---

*These data are available from the New Jersey Department of Community Affairs. See also New Jersey Department of Community Affairs, Division of State and Regional Planning, A Revised Statewide Housing Allocation Report for New Jersey (Trenton, 1978).

**Information on past subsidized production is available from a number of sources. Housing permit data for each municipality includes a separate category for "public housing" (see Chapter 4 in this study). In addition, the annual report of the New Jersey Housing Finance Agency lists where NJHFA-assisted units have been built. It is important to realize, however, that data on past production is not as comprehensive, nor is it available from a single source, as is the case for the other criteria/indicators included in this section.

Formula Allocation

Each of the above-detailed indicators represents examples of ways to operationalize the four basic measures. The means of combining these measures is the concern of the fair share formula.

One formula approach is to simply aggregate the individual indicators to derive an average composite index. Alternatively, one or a number of the measures may be weighted more heavily to reflect perceived heightened significance. A leading candidate for such treatment is local advantage/need as indicated by the local success in securing employment growth -- a factor emphasized by the New Jersey Supreme Court.

As a further approach, each of the indicators could be expressed not as a percentage of the regional profile, but rather as a Z-score. A composite Z-score could then be derived. This method, adopted by the 1973 Dayton Plan, offers the advantage of incorporating a more accurate measure of dispersion. Z-scores show the deviation of individual values from the central value. In doing so, they provide a precise gauge of municipal variance from regional totals. Z-scores also standardize for indicators of different magnitudes, eliminating the possibility that indicators expressed in higher values will overwhelm their lower score counterparts. For further details in this approach, the technical appendix to the 1973 Dayton Plan should be consulted.[33]

NOTES

1. David Listokin, Fair Share Housing Allocation (New Brunswick, NJ: Center for Urban Policy Research, 1976), p. 1.

2. Mary Brooks, Lower Income Housing: The Planner's Response (Chicago: American Society of Planning Officials, 1972), p. 11.

3. Leonard Rubinowitz, Low Income Housing: Suburban Strategies (Cambridge, MA: Ballinger, 1974), p. 66.

4. Listokin, Fair Share Housing Allocation, p. 59.

5. Ibid., p. 66.

6. Ibid.

7. Ibid., Appendix B.

8. On the early history of the Dayton Plan, see Listokin, Fair Share Housing Allocation, pp. 118-126.

9. Revisions included in the 1978 Formula are discussed in Miami Valley Regional Planning Commission, Housing in the Miami Valley Region: A Regional Program and Areawide Housing Opportunity Plan (Dayton, Ohio, 1976), pp. 51-57.

10. See Listokin, Fair Share Housing Allocation, pp. 66, 112-118.

11. See Metropolitan Washington Council of Governments, Fair Share Housing Plan: Procedures for Allocation of Housing Assistance Funds (Washington, D.C.: 1983).

12. See Listokin, Fair Share Housing Allocation, pp. 110-112, 187-192.

13. See Metropolitan Council, Estimated Housing Assistance Needs and Programs: Goals for Metropolitan Area Communities (St. Paul, Minnesota, 1979).

14. Much of the information presented in this section is adapted from Listokin, Fair Share Housing Allocation, pp. 173-203, Appendix A.

15. On the origins of these early proposals for fair share in New Jersey, see Robert Mulcahy, "Executive Strategy," in Fair Share Housing: A Conference on New Jersey Issues (New Brunswick: Rutgers University, Bureau of Government Research, 1979), pp. 57-66.

16. Ibid.

17. On early legislative proposals see, State Senator Martin Greenberg, "Legislative Strategy," in Bureau of Government Research, Fair Share Housing: A Conference on New Jersey Issues.

18. See Bureau of Government Research, Fair Share Housing: A Conference on New Jersey Issues.

19. New Jersey Department of Community Affairs, Division of State and Regional Planning, A Revised Statewide Housing Allocation Report for New Jersey (Trenton, NJ: 1978), pp. 15-20.

20. Southern Burlington County N.A.A.C.P. v. Mount Laurel Township, 92 NJ 158, 456 A.2d 390 (1983). Hereinafter cited as Mount Laurel II decision.

21. An excellent summary of Mount Laurel II and the major participants in it is contained in Ernest Erber, "Mount Laurel II: Planners Against Exclusionary Zoning" (unpublished, 1983).

22. Mount Laurel II Decision, p. 26 (slip opinion).

23. Clarke and Caton, Mahwah Township: Fair Housing Report (prepared for Justice Harvey Smith, Superior Court of New Jersey, 1983), pp. 24-29.

24. Alan Mallach, Fair Share Housing Allocation Study for the Tri-County Burlington, Camden, and Gloucester Regions (1983).

25. Harvey S. Moskowitz, Housing Allocation Analysis for Morris Township, October 11, 1983.

26. New Jersey Department of Community Affairs, State Development Guide Plan (Trenton: Division of State and Regional Planning, 1980).

27. Mount Laurel II Decision, p. 80 (slip opinion).

28. Ibid., p. 26.

29. New Jersey Department of Community Affairs, A Revised Statewide Housing Allocation, p. 15.

30. Mallach, Fair Share Housing Allocation Study, p. 12.

31. Mount Laurel II Decision, p. 90-91 (slip opinion).

32. Ibid., p. 93.

33. See Listokin, Fair Share Housing Allocation, Appendix B.

BIBLIOGRAPHY

I. GENERAL OVERVIEW -- HOUSING THE LOW- AND MODERATE-INCOME SECTOR

Babcock, Richard F. and Fred P. Bosselman. Exclusionary Zoning: Land Use Regulations and Housing in the 1970s. New York: Praeger Publishers, 1973.

Danielson, Michael N. "The Politics of Exclusionary Zoning in Suburbia." Political Science Quarterly, Spring 1976, pp. 1-18.

Falk, David and H.M. Franklin. Local Growth Management Policy: A Legal Primer. Washington, D.C.: The Potomac Institute, 1975.

Fishman, Richard P. Housing for All Under Law -- New Directions in Housing, Land Use, and Planning Law. Cambridge, MA: Ballinger, 1978.

Gruen, Nina Jaffe and Claude Gruen. Low- and Moderate-Income Housing in the Suburbs. New York: Praeger, 1972.

Haar, Charles M. and Demetrius S. Iatridis. Housing the Poor in Suburbia: Public Policy at the Grass Roots. Cambridge, MA: Ballinger, 1974.

Kain, John F. and John M. Quigley. "Housing Market Discrimination, Home Ownership and Savings Behavior." American Economic Review, Vol. 62, 1972, pp. 263-277.

King, Paul. "Exclusionary Zoning and Open Housing: A Brief Judicial History." Geography Review, October 1978, pp. 459-469.

Listokin, David. Land Use Controls: Present Problems and Future Reform. New Brunswick, NJ: Rutgers University, Center for Urban Policy Research, 1974.

Mann, Mary Sullivan. The Right to Housing: Constitutional Issues and Remedies in Exclusionary Zoning. New York: Praeger, 1976.

"Mount Laurel 2: A Case of National Significance." Land Use Law and Zoning Digest, Vol. 35, No. 3, March 1983, pp. 3-12.

Potomac Institute. Fundamental Fairness in Zoning: Mount Laurel Reaffirmed. Washington, DC: Potomac Institute, 1983.

Rose, Jerome G. and Robert E. Rothman. After Mount Laurel: The New Suburban Zoning. New Brunswick, NJ: Rutgers University, Center for Urban Policy Research, 1977.

Rubinowitz, Leonard S. Low Income Housing: Suburban Strategies. Cambridge, MA: Ballinger, 1974.

Sagalyn, Lynn B. and George Sternlieb. Zoning and Housing Costs. New Brunswick, NJ: Rutgers University, Center for Urban Policy Research, 1972.

Schneider, Mark and John R. Logan. "Fiscal Implications of Class Segregation: Inequalities in the Distribution of Public Goods and Services in Suburban Municipalities." Urban Affairs Quarterly, September 1981, pp. 23-37.

Scott, Randall, ed. Management and Control of Growth. Washington, DC: Urban Land Institute, 1975.

Shlay, Anne B. and Peter H. Ross. "Keeping Up the Neighborhood: Estimating Net Effects of Zoning." American Sociological Review, Vol. 46, December 1981, pp. 703-719.

Stutz, Frederick P. and Arthur E. Kartman, ed. "Housing Affordability and Spatial Price Variations in the United States." Economic Geography, Vol. 58, July 1982, pp. 221-235.

Wilson, Franklin D. Residential Consumption, Economic Opportunity and Race. New York: Academic Press, 1979.

Windsor, Duane. Fiscal Zoning in Suburban Communities. Lexington, MA: Lexington Books, 1979.

II. DEFINITION OF A HOUSING MARKET/REGION

Bergman, Edward M. Eliminating Exclusionary Zoning: Reconciling Workplace and Residence in Suburban Areas. Cambridge, MA: Ballinger, 1974.

Bertsh, Dale F. and Shafor, Ann M. A Regional Housing Plan. Chicago, IL: American Institute of Planners, 1971.

Burchell, Robert W., David Listokin, and James W. Hughes. "Exclusionary Zoning: Pitfalls of the Regional Remedy." Urban Lawyer, Spring 1975, pp. 262-291.

Cronin, Francis J. Search and Residential Mobility: Part 1 - Economic Models of the Decision to Search and Move Among Low Income Households. Washington, DC: The Urban Institute, 1980.

Floyd, C.F. et al. Effects of Journey-to-Work Commuting on the Development of Low-Income Areas. Springfield, VA: NTIS, 1974.

Gera, S. and P. Kuhn. Residential and Job Location and the Journey-to-Work: A Review and Theoretical Perspective. Ottawa, Ontario: Economic Council of Canada, 1977.

Goodman, J.L., Jr. and M. Berkman. "Radical Differences in Commuting Behavior: New Evidence from the Panel Study of Income Dynamics." Review of Public Data Use, Vol. 5, No. 4, June 1977, pp. 29-36.

Halvorson, P.L. "Income Factor in the Journey-to-Work Attitudes and Behavior." Professional Geographer, Vol. 25, No. 4, November 1973, pp. 357-362.

Hammer, Greene, Siler Associates. Regional Housing Planning: A Technical Guide. Chicago, Il: American Institute of Planners, 1972.

Housing Advocates, Inc. Regional Housing Mobility Programs: A Guidebook for the Promotion of Housing Opportunities. Washington, DC: U.S. Government Printing Office, 1980.

Lerman, S.R. "Location, Housing, Automobile Ownership, and Mode to Work: A Joint Choice Model." Transportation Research Record, No. 610, 1976, pp. 6-11.

Mouchahoir, G.E. "Work Trip and Trip Maker Characteristics." Traffic Engineering, Vol. 43, No. 5, 1973, pp. 26-30.

Rhode Island Public Transit Authority. Arriving Late in Suburbia: The Buttonwoods-Providence Express and Local Shoppers' Shuttle. Providence, RI: Rhode Island Public Transit Authority, 1968.

Richardson, David H. and Richard Thalheimer. "On the Use of Grouping Methods in the Analysis of Residential Housing Market." Regional Science and Urban Economics, May 1982, pp. 211-233.

Rohe, W.M. Travel to Work Patterns: A Preliminary Analysis of Selected Data from the Annual Housing Survey. Springfield, VA: NTIS, 1981.

Sirmans, C.F. "Determinants of Journey-to-Work Flows: Some Empirical Evidence." Annals of Regional Science, Vol. 11, No. 1, March 1977, pp. 98-108.

Stid, Larry O. "Regional Housing Allocation Techniques." Rochester, NY: Genesee/Finger Lakes Regional Planning Board, 1971.

Strazheim, M.R. "Household Interview Data." Review of Economics and Statistics, Vol. 55, No. 1, February 1973, pp. 1-8.

United States Bureau of the Census, Population Division. The Journey-to-Work in the United States, 1979. (Current Population Reports, P-23, No. 122.) Washington, DC: U.S. Government Printing Office, 1982.

United States Bureau of the Census, Population Division. Selected Characteristics of Travel to Work in 20 Metropolitan Areas 1977. (Current Population Reports, P-23, No. 105.) Washington, DC: U.S. Government Printing Office, 1981.

U.S. Department of Housing and Urban Development, Office of Planning and Program Coordination. A Guide to Assist in Preparing an Areawide Housing Opportunity Plan. Washington, DC: U.S. Department of Housing and Urban Development, 1979.

Voorhees, A.M. et al. "Factors in Work Trip Lengths and Discussion." Highway Research Record, No. 141, pp. 24-46 (n.d.).

III. SOCIOECONOMIC CHARACTERISTICS OF LOW- AND MODERATE-INCOME FAMILIES

Feins, Judith D. and Terry Saunders Lane. How Much for Housing? New Perspectives on Affordability and Risk. Cambridge, MA: Abt Books, 1981.

Fischel, William A. Zoning and Suburban Housing Costs: The Effects of Legal Rights and Governmental Structure. Springfield, VA: NTIS, 1981.

Harris, Britton. "The Uses of Theory in the Simulation of Urban Phenomena." The Journal of the American Institute of Planners, Vol. 37, No. 5, September 1966.

Johnson, Robert E. Assessing Housing Preferences of Low-Cost Single-Family Home Buyers. Ann Arbor: University of Michigan, Architectural Research Laboratory, 1980.

Karn, Valerie A. Position of Lower Income Households in the Owner-Occupied Housing Market of the U.S.A. and Great Britain. Springfield, VA: NTIS, 1981.

Neiman, Max. "Zoning Policy Income Clustering and Suburban Change." Social Science Quarterly, December 1980, pp. 666-675.

Rubinowitz, Leonard S. "A Question of Choice: Access of the Poor and Black to Suburban Housing." In The Urbanization of the Suburbs. Lewis H. Massoti and Jeffrey K. Hadden, eds. Beverly Hills: Sage, 1973, pp. 329-366.

IV. FORECASTING LOW- AND MODERATE-INCOME HOUSING DEMAND

American Public Health Association, Inc., Committee on Hygiene of Housing. Basic Principles of Healthful Housing, 2nd ed. New York: American Public Health Association, 1961.

Brooks, Mary E. Lower Income Housing: The Planner's Response. Chicago, IL: American Society of Planning Officials, 1972.

Chapin, F. Stuart Jr. Urban Land Use Planning. Urbana, IL: University of Illinois Press, 1965.

Clark, W.A.V. Modelling Housing Market Search. New York: St. Martin's Press, 1982.

Ellis, Neil R. "Zoning for the Regional Welfare." The Yale Law Journal, Vol. 89, No. 4, March 1980, pp. 748-768.

Goedert, Jeanne E. and John L. Goodman, Jr. Indicators of Housing Quality: An Exploration of the Annual Housing Survey. Washington, DC: The Urban Institute, 1976.

Horowitz, Grace. Housing Quality Data Needs of Users. Needs for Data on Housing Quality. Washington, DC: U.S. Department of Health, Education & Welfare, Office of Technical Support and Statistics, 1977.

Housing Needs and Housing Supply: The Effectiveness of Estimates and Responses. Springfield, VA: NTIS, 1979.

Inman, Robert P. and Daniel L. Rubenfeld. "The Judicial Pursuit of Local Fiscal Equity." Harvard Law Review, Vol. 92, No. 2, June 1979, pp. 1662-1750.

Masnick, George. The Demographic Factor in Household Growth. Cambridge, MA: The Joint Center for Urban Studies of MIT and Harvard, 1983.

New Jersey, Department of Community Affairs, Division of State and Local Planning. State Development Guide Plan. Trenton, NJ: Department of Community Affairs, 1980.

Perin, Constance. Everything in Its Place: Social Order and Land Use in America. Princeton, NJ: Princeton University Press, 1978.

Schnidman, Frank. Housing Supply and Affordability. Washington, DC: Urban Land Institute, 1963.

Smith, Phyllis Woodham. "Demand for Housing in the 1980s." Business and Economic Review (University of South Carolina), Vol. 28, November 1981, pp. 4-10.

Sternlieb, George et al. Demographic Trends and Economic Reality: Planning and Markets in the 80s. New Brunswick, NJ: Rutgers University, Center for Urban Policy Research, 1982.

U.S. Bureau of the Census. Measuring the Quality of Housing: An Appraisal of Census Statistics and Methods. (Working Paper No. 25.) Washington, DC: U.S. Department of Commerce, Bureau of the Census, 1967.

U.S. Bureau of the Census. Housing Division. A Preliminary Look at the Results of the Five-City Survey. Washington, DC: U.S. Government Printing Office, 1975.

V. FORECASTING LOW- AND MODERATE-INCOME HOUSING SUPPLY

American Institute of Planners. Regional Housing Planning: A Technical Guide. Chicago, IL: American Institute of Planners, 1972.

Apgar, William C., Jr. The Changing Utilization of the Housing Inventory: Past Trends and Future Prospects. Cambridge, MA: Joint Center for Urban Studies of MIT and Harvard, 1983.

Falk, Barry. "Forecasting Housing Starts Using Multivariate Time Series Methods." Housing Finance Review, Vol. 2, April 1983, pp. 109-126.

Malpezzi, Stephen, Larry Ozanne, and Thomas Thibodeau. The Characteristic Prices of Housing in Fifty-Nine Metropolitan Areas. Springfield, VA: NTIS, 1980.

Mills, Edwin S. and Wallace E. Oates, eds. Fiscal Zoning and Land Use Controls. Lexington, MA: Lexington, 1975.

Rosen, Kenneth and James Kearl. A Model of Housing Starts, Mortgage Flows, the Behavior of the Federal Home Loan Bank Board and the National Mortgage Association. Cambridge, MA: Joint Center for Urban Studies of MIT and Harvard, 1974.

Schafer, Robert. Exclusionary Land Use Controls: Conceptual and Empirical Problems in Measuring the Invisible Wall. Cambridge, MA: Harvard University, Department of City and Regional Planning, 1975.

Scott, Randall W. Exclusionary Land Use Practices or, the Rise and Fall of Exclusionary Zoning. Washington, DC: National Association of Homebuilders, 1972.

Sternlieb, George. The Maintenance of America's Housing Stock. Washington, DC: U.S. Department of Housing and Urban Development, 1980.

Weicher, John et al. Forecasting the National Need for New Construction. Washington, DC: The Urban Institute, 1979.

White, Michelle J. "Self Interest in the Suburbs: The Trend Toward No-Growth Zoning." Policy Analysis, April 1978, pp. 185-203.

VI. MAKING HOUSING AVAILABLE TO LOW- AND MODERATE-INCOME FAMILIES

California, Office of Appropriate Technology. The Affordable Housing Book: Strategies for the Eighties from the California Affordable Housing Competition. Sacramento, CA: Office of Appropriate Technology, 1982.

Clapp, John M. "The Impact of Inclusionary Zoning on the Location and Type of Construction Activity." American Real Estate and Urban Economics Association Journal, Vol. 9, No. 4, Winter 1981, pp. 436-456.

Council of State Community Affairs Agencies. State Actions to Promote Affordable Housing: Final Report. Springfield, VA: NTIS, 1982.

Franklin, Herbert M. et al. In-Zoning: A Guide for Policy Makers on Inclusionary Land Use Programs. Washington, DC: The Potomac Institute, 1974.

Grieson, Ronald E. "The Effects of Zoning on Structure and Land Markets." Journal of Urban Economics, November 1981, pp. 271-285.

Hershey, Stuart. Streamlining Local Regulations: A Handbook for Reducing Housing and Development Costs. Washington, DC: International City Management Association, 1983.

National Association of Home Builders Research Foundation. Building Affordable Housing: A Cost Savings Guide for Builder/Developers. Rockville, MD: NAHB Research Foundation, 1982.

New Jersey, Department of Community Affairs. Affordable Housing Handbook. Springfield, VA: NTIS, 1982.

Porter, Douglas R. and Susan Cole. Affordable Housing: Twenty Examples from the Private Sector. Washington, DC: The Urban Land Institute, 1982.

Rutgers University, Bureau of Governmental Research et al. Fair Share Housing: A Conference on New Jersey Issues. New Brunswick, NJ: Rutgers University, The Bureau of Governmental Research, 1980.

Sanders, Welford and David Mosena. Changing Development Standards for Affordable Housing. Chicago, IL: American Planning Association, 1982.

Taylor, Barbara. "Inclusionary Zoning: A Workable Option for Affordable Housing." Urban Land, March 1981, pp. 6-12.

Weitz, Stevenson. Affordable Housing: How Local Regulatory Improvements Can Help. Washington, DC: Department of Housing and Urban Development, Office of Policy Development and Research, 1982.

Yannacone, U.J.et al. "Impact Zoning: Alternative to Exclusion in the Suburbs." Urban Lawyer, Summer 1976, pp. 417-488.

VII. FAIR SHARE HOUSING - PLANS AND ALLOCATION

Brooks, Mary. Housing Choice: A Handbook for Suburban Officials, Non-Profit Organizations, Community Groups and Consumers. New York: The Suburban Action Institute, 1980.

Downs, Anthony. Opening Up the Suburbs: An Urban Strategy for America. New Haven, CT: Yale University Press, 1973.

Economic Consultants Organization, Inc. Housing Allocation: Criteria and Strategies. (s.l.) New York: Southern Tier Central Regional Planning and Development Board, 1974.

Erber, Ernest. Housing Allocation Plans: A National Overview. Washington, DC: National Committee Against Discrimination in Housing, 1974.

Listokin, David. Fair Share Housing Allocation. New Brunswick, NJ: Rutgers University, Center for Urban Policy Research, 1976.

Marando, Vincent L. "HUD's Metropolitan Lower-Income Housing Policy: Fair-Share Planning." In Management and Policy Science in American Government. Michael White, Michael Radnor and David Tansik, eds. Lexington, MA: Lexington Books, 1973, pp. 101-127.

Moskowitz, David H. "Regional Housing Allocation Plans: A Case History of the Delaware Valley Regional Plan." Urban Lawyer, Vol. 7, Spring 1975, pp. 292-309.

Rose, Jerome G. "Fair Share Housing Allocation Plans: Which Formula Will Pacify the Contentious Suburbs?" Real Estate Law Journal, Fall 1977, pp. 91-103.

Southern California Association of Governments. Technical Study of Selected Housing Allocation Models. Los Angeles: Southern California Association of Governments, 1973.

VIII. LEGAL ISSUES IN EXCLUSIONARY ZONING

Ackerman, B.L. "Mount Laurel Decision: Expanding the Boundaries of Zoning Reform." University of Illinois Law Forum, 1976, pp. 1-73.

Anderson, Robert M. "'Introduction' to Exclusionary Zoning Symposium." Syracuse Law Review, Vol. 22, 1971, pp. 465-473.

Blumstein, James F. "A Prolegomenon to Growth Management and Exclusionary Zoning Issues." Law and Contemporary Problems, Spring 1979, pp. 5-10.

Burke, Paul. Housing Affordability Problems and Housing Need in Canada and the United States. Washington, DC: U.S. Department of Housing and Urban Development, 1981.

"Constitutional Law -- Equal Protection -- Zoning -- Snob Zoning: Must a Man's Home be a Castle?" Michigan Law Review, Vol. 69, December 1970, pp. 339-359.

Diamond, Douglas B., Jr. "Income and Residential Location: Muth Revisited." Urban Studies, February 1980, pp. 1-12.

Hagman, Donald. "Taking Care of One's Own Through Inclusionary Zoning: Bootstrapping Low- and Moderate-Income Housing by Local Government." Urban Law and Policy, June 1982, pp. 169-187.

Kelly, E.D. "Will the Housing Market Evaluation be the Solution to Exclusionary Zoning?" Real Estate Law Journal, Spring 1975, pp. 373-394.

Lamb, Charles M. and Mitchell S. Lustig. "The Burger Court, Exclusionary Zoning, and the Activist-Restraint Debate." University of Pittsburgh Law Review, Vol. 40, Winter 1979, pp. 169-226.

Mallach, Alan. "Exclusionary Zoning Litigation: Setting the Record Straight." Real Estate Law Journal, Spring 1981, pp. 275-310.

Margolis, Emanuel. "Exclusionary Zoning: For Whom Does Belle Terre Toll?" California Western Law Review, Vol. 11, Fall 1974, pp. 85-116.

McDougall, Harold A. "The Judicial Struggle Against Exclusionary Zoning: The New Jersey Paradigm." Harvard Civil Rights-Civil Liberties Law Review, Vol. 14, Fall 1979, pp. 625-654.

National Committee Against Discrimination in Housing. Office of General Counsel. Fair Housing and Exclusionary Land Use. Washington, DC: Urban Land Institute, 1974.

Rose, Jerome G. "The Mount Laurel II Decision: Is it Based on Wishful Thinking?" Real Estate Law Journal, Vol. 2, No. 2, Fall 1983, pp. 115-137.

Sies, Dennis E. "Exclusionary Zoning: Its Development, Effects and an Analysis of Challenges in Selective Forums." Northern Kentucky Law Journal, Vol. 8, No. 2, 1981, pp. 349-376.

Stemmler, Hal. "Inclusionary Zoning -- New Wave or Washout?" Western City, August 1980, pp. 13-15+.

Williams, Norman, Jr. and Thomas Norman. "Exclusionary Land Use Controls: The Case of North-Eastern New Jersey." Syracuse Law Review, Vol. 22, 1971, pp. 475-507.

Williams, Norman, Jr. and Tatyana Doughty. "Studies in Legal Realism: Mount Laurel, Belle Terre, and Berman." Rutgers Law Review, Vol. 29, Fall 1975, pp. 73-109.

Kolibri 360 GmbH
Ferdinand-Jühlke-Straße 7
99095 Erfurt, Deutschland
produktsicherheit@kolibri360.de